# Lecture Notes in Computer Science          9603

*Commenced Publication in 1973*
Founding and Former Series Editors:
Gerhard Goos, Juris Hartmanis, and Jan van Leeuwen

More information about this series at http://www.springer.com/series/7410

Jens Grossklags · Bart Preneel (Eds.)

# Financial Cryptography and Data Security

20th International Conference, FC 2016
Christ Church, Barbados, February 22–26, 2016
Revised Selected Papers

 Springer

*Editors*
Jens Grossklags
Department of Informatics
Technical University Munich
Garching
Germany

Bart Preneel
Department of Electrical Engineering-ESAT
KU Leuven
Leuven
Belgium

ISSN 0302-9743                  ISSN 1611-3349  (electronic)
Lecture Notes in Computer Science
ISBN 978-3-662-54969-8          ISBN 978-3-662-54970-4  (eBook)
DOI 10.1007/978-3-662-54970-4

Library of Congress Control Number: 2017940629

LNCS Sublibrary: SL4 – Security and Cryptology

Printed on acid-free paper

This Springer imprint is published by Springer Nature
The registered company is Springer-Verlag GmbH Germany
The registered company address is: Heidelberger Platz 3, 14197 Berlin, Germany

# Preface

FC 2016, the 20th International Conference on Financial Cryptography and Data Security, was held during February 22–26, 2016, at the Accra Beach Hotel and Spa Barbados. This edition was a special 20th anniversary edition featuring some extra items in the program.

We received 137 paper submissions, out of which 36 were accepted, nine as short papers and 27 as full papers, resulting in an acceptance rate of 26%. These proceedings contain revised versions of all the papers. The 20th anniversary keynotes were delivered by privacy pioneer David Chaum, who spoke on "Privategrity" and Turing award winner Adi Shamir who shared with the audience his perspective on "The Past, Present and Future of Financial Cryptography." The program was complemented by a special anniversary panel entitled "The Promises and Pitfalls of Distributed Consensus Systems: From Contract Signing to Cryptocurrencies."

The Program Committee consisted of 49 members with diverse backgrounds and broad research interests. The review process was double-blind. Each paper received at least three reviews; for submissions by Program Committee members this was increased to four. During the discussion phase, additional reviews were solicited when necessary. An intensive discussion was held to clarify issues and to converge towards decisions. The selection of the program was challenging; in the end some high-quality papers had to be rejected due to lack of space.

We would like to sincerely thank the authors of all submissions for contributing high-quality submissions and giving us the opportunity to compile a strong and diverse program.

Special thanks go to the Program Committee members; we value their hard work and dedication to write careful and detailed reviews and to engage in interesting discussions. A few Program Committee members, whom we asked to serve as shepherds, spent additional time in order to help the authors improve their works. More than 60 external reviewers contributed to the review process; we would like to thank them for their efforts.

We are greatly indebted to Rafael Hirschfeld, the conference general chair, for his tireless efforts to make the conference a success. We also would like to thank the anniversary chairs, Sven Dietrich and Ahmad Sadeghi. Special thanks go the board of directors of the International Financial Cryptography Association for their support and advice.

Finally, we would like to thank the Office of Naval Research Global (ONR Global), bitt, the CROSSING project at TU Darmstadt, Rohde & Schwartz, AtenCoin, Gemini, Google, the *Journal of Cybersecurity*, KOBIL, SAP, KPMG, Worldpay, and the NSF for their generous support of the conference.

We hope that the papers in this volume prove valuable for your research and professional activities and that Financial Cryptography and Data Security will continue to play its unique role in bringing together researchers and practitioners in the area of secure digital commerce.

February 2017                                                            Jens Grossklags
                                                                        Bart Preneel

# FC 2016

## Financial Cryptography and Data Security 2016
## Accra Beach Hotel and Spa, Barbados
## February 22–26, 2016

Organized by the
*International Financial Cryptography Association*

In cooperation with the
*International Association for Cryptologic Research*

## General Chair

Rafael Hirschfeld        Unipay, The Netherlands

## Anniversary Chairs

Sven Dietrich        City University of New York, USA
Ahmad Sadeghi        TU Darmstadt, Germany

## Program Chairs

Jens Grossklags        TU Munich, Germany
Bart Preneel        KU Leuven, Belgium

## Program Committee

Masayuki Abe        NTT Laboratories, Japan
Alessandro Acquisti        Carnegie Mellon University, USA
Ross Anderson        Cambridge University, UK
Elli Androulaki        IBM Research Zurich, Switzerland
N. Asokan        Aalto University, Finland
Paulo Barreto        University of Sao Paulo, Brazil
Steven Bellovin        Columbia University, USA
Daniel Bernstein        University of Illinois at Chicago, USA
Rainer Böhme        University of Innsbruck, Austria
Alvaro Cardenas        University of Texas at Dallas, USA
Jeremy Clark        Concordia University, USA
Nicolas Courtois        University College London, UK
George Danezis        University College London, UK
Serge Egelman        UC Berkeley, USA

| | |
|---|---|
| Seda Gürses | NYU, USA |
| Feng Hao | Newcastle University, UK |
| Thorsten Holz | Ruhr University Bochum, Germany |
| Trent Jaeger | The Pennsylvania State University, USA |
| Markus Jakobsson | Qualcomm, USA |
| Benjamin Johnson | Carnegie Mellon University, USA |
| Aniket Kate | Purdue University, USA |
| Florian Kerschbaum | SAP, Germany |
| Aggelos Kiayias | National and Kapodistrian University of Athens, Greece |
| Bart Knijnenburg | Clemson University, USA |
| Markulf Kohlweiss | Microsoft Research, UK |
| Aron Laszka | UC Berkeley, USA |
| Anja Lehmann | IBM Research Zurich, Switzerland |
| Arjen Lenstra | EPFL, Switzerland |
| Patrick Loiseau | EURECOM, France |
| Travis Mayberry | US Naval Academy, USA |
| Catherine Meadows | Naval Research Laboratory, USA |
| Sarah Meiklejohn | University College London, UK |
| Tyler Moore | University of Tulsa, USA |
| Steven Murdoch | University College London, UK |
| Tatsuaki Okamoto | NTT Laboratories, Japan |
| Kenneth Paterson | Royal Holloway, University of London, UK |
| Roberto Perdisci | University of Georgia, USA |
| Avi Rubin | Johns Hopkins University, USA |
| Ahmad Sadeghi | TU Darmstadt, Germany |
| Rei Safavi-Naini | University of Calgary, Canada |
| Nigel Smart | University of Bristol, UK |
| Jessica Staddon | Google, USA |
| Carmela Troncoso | Gradiant, Spain |
| Damien Vergnaud | École Normale Supérieure, France |
| Nicholas Weaver | International Computer Science Institute, USA |
| Xinyu Xing | The Pennsylvania State University, USA |
| Moti Yung | Google and Columbia University, USA |

## Additional Reviewers

| | | |
|---|---|---|
| Svetlana Abramova | Zekeriya Erkin | Vijay Kamble |
| Enrique Argones | Sadegh Farhang | Gabe Kaptchuk |
| Ero Balsa | Ben Fisch | Carmen Kempka |
| Erik-Oliver Blass | Oana Goga | Sheharbano Khattak |
| Matthias Carnein | Steven Goldfeder | Ryo Kikuchi |
| Joseph Carrigan | Marian Harbach | Markus Krause |
| Alex Davidson | Heqing Huang | Junichiro Kume |
| Angelo De Caro | Brittany Johnson | Stefan Laube |

# Contents

## Mobile Malware

## Social Interaction and Policy

## Cryptanalysis

**Payment Use and Abuse**

# Fraud and Deception

# Understanding Craigslist Rental Scams

Youngsam Park[1(✉)], Damon McCoy[2], and Elaine Shi[3]

[1] University of Maryland, College Park, USA
yspark@cs.umd.edu
[2] New York University, New York, USA
[3] Cornell University, Ithaca, USA

**Abstract.** Fraudulently posted online rental listings, rental scams, have been frequently reported by users. However, our understanding of the structure of rental scams is limited. In this paper, we conduct the first systematic empirical study of online rental scams on Craigslist. This study is enabled by a suite of techniques that allowed us to identify scam campaigns and our automated system that is able to collect additional information by conversing with scammers. Our measurement study sheds new light on the broad range of strategies different scam campaigns employ and the infrastructure they depend on to profit. We find that many of these strategies, such as credit report scams, are structurally different from the traditional advanced fee fraud found in previous studies. In addition, we find that Craigslist remove less than half of the suspicious listings we detected. Finally, we find that many of the larger-scale campaigns we detected depend on credit card payments, suggesting that a payment level intervention might effectively demonetize them.

## 1 Introduction

Today, many people use the Internet for at least part of their housing search [6]. This inevitably has led to profit-driven scammers posting fake rental listings, commonly known as *"rental scams"*. Despite the ubiquitous presence of online rental scams, we currently lack a solid understanding of the online rental scam ecosystem and the different techniques rental scammers use to deceive and profit off their victims. While most efforts to mitigate this problem focus on filtering the posts, this is only the visible part of a well-honed set of scams and infrastructure established to extract money from their marks. An end-to-end understanding of a scam and its structural dependencies (message posting, email accounts, location of scammers, support companies, automated tools and payment methods) is often a crucial first step towards identifying potential weaknesses along the chain that can serve as effective choke-points for the defender [8,27]. In particular, this "understand, and then deter" trajectory has resulted in suggesting weak points for disrupting other domain-specific threats, such as payment processing in the counterfeit software and pharmacy spam domain [8,18,19].

In this paper, we conduct the first systematic empirical study of the online rental scams ecosystem as viewed through the lens of the Craigslist rental section.

© International Financial Cryptography Association 2017
J. Gros!klags and B. Preneel (Eds.): FC 2016, LNCS 9603, pp. 3–21, 2017.
DOI: 10.1007/978-3-662-54970-4_1

Our in-depth analysis of these rental scam campaigns allows us to address questions geared at improving our understanding of the supporting infrastructure with the goal of exploring alternate points to undermine this ecosystem, such as: "What are the common underlying scams?", "Where are these scammers located and what tools do they use?", "How effective are current defences?", "What payment methods do they use?". We summarize our contributions and findings below.

By developing several effective detection techniques, we are able to identify several major rental scam campaigns on Craigslist. In addition, we extend Scambaiter automated conversation engine [21] to automatically contact suspected rental scammers, which enabled us to understand what support infrastructure they used and how they were monetizing their postings. In total we detected about 29 K scam listings over the 20 cities we monitored, within a period of 141 days.

We find a diverse set of methods utilized for monetizing the rental scam campaigns we identified. These include attempts to trick people into paying for credit reports and "bait-and-switch" rental listings. When we explored the payment method used, five of the seven major scam campaigns identified used credit cards. Many campaigns also depended on businesses registered in the USA to collect payments. We also find that Craigslist's filtering methods are currently removing less than half of the rental scam ads we detected.

Our results highlight the fact that scammers are highly customizing their monetization methods to the United States rental market. They also expose new scams and infrastructure that were not encountered in previous studies [7,15,21]. This difference highlights the need to understand a wider range of scam domain and suggests potential bottlenecks for many rental scam monetizing strategies at the regulatory and payment layers. For instance, United States regulatory agencies, such as the Federal Trade Commission (FTC) could investigate these companies and levy fines for their deceptive advertising practices. Another potential method of demonetizing these companies might be to alert credit card holder associations, such as Visa or MasterCard, to these merchants' deceptive billing and refund policies.

## 2   Data Sets

This paper focuses solely on *scams* and we consider spam, such as off-topic and aggressive repostings, as outside the scope of this paper. In this paper, we define a rental listing as a scam if (i) it is fraudulently advertising a property that is not available or not lawfully owned by the advertiser and (ii) it attempts to extract money from replies using either advanced fee fraud or "bait-and-switch" tactics.

The basis of our study relies upon repeated crawls of the rental section on Craigslist in different geographic locations to collect all listings posted in these regions and detect listings that are subsequently flagged. We then use a combination of manual searching for reported rental scams and human-generated regular expressions to map fraudulent listings into scam campaigns. For a small subset of listings that are difficult to identify as scams or legitimate, we build an automated conversation engine that contacts the poster to determine the validity of the listing. Finally, we crawl five other popular rental listing sites to detect cloned listings that have been re-posted to Craigslist potentially by scammers.

## 2.1 Rental Listing Crawling

Our primary data set is based on listings collected from daily crawls of rental sections on Craigslist across 20 different cities and areas in the United States with the largest population [5]: New York, Los Angeles, Chicago, Houston, Philadelphia, San Antonio, San Diego, Dallas, San Francisco (Bay area), Austin, Jacksonville, Indianapolis, Columbus, Charlotte, Detroit, El Paso, Memphis, Boston and Seattle. Our crawler revisited each crawled ad three days after the first visit to detect if they have been flagged by Craigslist. The crawler performed a final recrawl of any unflagged listings 7 days after the first visit to determine if they have been flagged or expired. We also collected rental ads from five additional major rental listing websites, *Zillow, Trulia, Realtor.com, Yahoo! Homes* and *Homes.com.*

Our crawler tracked all rental section ads on 20 cities/areas on Craigslist, for a total duration of 141 days, from 2/24/2014 to 7/15/2014. Table 1 shows the overall summary of this dataset. In whole, we collected over two million ads, among which 126, 898 have been flagged by Craigslist.

**Table 1.** Dataset summary. About 6% of rental ads are flagged for removal by Craigslist. Rental ads are considered to be expired 7 days after being posted.

| Overview | Duration | 141 days (2/24/14-7/15/14) |
|---|---|---|
| | Cities/areas | 20 |
| Rental ads | Total posted | 2, 085, 663 |
| | Flagged for removal | 126, 898 (6.1%) |
| | Deleted (by user) | 338, 362 (16.2%) |
| | Expired* | 1, 620, 403 (77.7%) |

## 2.2 Campaign Identification

Our crawling of Craigslist produced a large set of flagged and non-flagged ads that are potentially scam listings. We know that some of these ads are scams and that many of these are linked to a smaller number of distinct scam campaigns.

Due to the large number of ads in our data set a brute-force approach of manually analyzing a large set of ads would not be effective and would require a domain specific understanding of how scam ads differ from legitimate ads. In order to overcome these challenges, we bootstrap our knowledge of scam postings by finding a small number of suspicious ads in a semi-automated manner.

To this end, we manually surveyed a broad range of user submitted scam reports online [1,3,4] to gain some initial insights about rental scams. Based on these insights, we constructed the following heuristics to identify an initial set of suspicious rental listings:

- Detect suspicious cloned listings by correlating listings posted to Craigslist with other rental listing websites, in particular, cloned ads from other sites that exhibit a substantial price difference.
- Detect posts with similar contents across multiple cities, e.g., posts with the same phone number or email addresses.
- Focus on ads flagged by Craigslist, and manually identify suspicious scam listings. As we will report in detail later, not all flagged posts are scam listings; and conversely, not all scam posts were flagged by Craigslist
- Identify ads that are similar to user-reported scams.

## 2.3   Campaign Expansion Phase: Latitudinal

For some of the campaigns we identified and hand labelled a small number of initial scam posts. Based on these we would like to identify other similar listings that are part of the same campaigns using automated and semi-automated methods. To this end, we used an approach that uses human-generated scam signatures.

**Human-Generated Scam Signatures.** Our first approach is to manually inspect the handful of ads that we identified to be in the same campaign, and summarize a unique signature to identify this campaign. For example, one of the credit report scam campaigns have the following unique signatures: email accounts corresponding to the regular expression "[a–z]+[ ]@[ ]yahoo[ ](dot)[ ] com" and no other contact information is included.

We then applied our signatures to all of our crawled ads, to identify additional ads that belong to the same campaign. As detailed in later sections, we will rely on a combination of human and automated verification techniques to confirm that scam ads identified by these signatures are indeed scams.

## 2.4   Campaign Expansion Phase: Longitudinal

For the initial scam postings we identified above, and the suspicious listings we identified in the latitudinal campaign expansion phase (Sect. 2.3), we wanted to confirm whether these are indeed scam messages. To this end, we built an automated conversation engine to converse with the suspected scammer, to see if the conversation would lead to a phase where the scammer requested payment from us.

**Automated Conversation Engine.** We manually inspected the suspicious ads and found that some of them were clearly scams, e.g., the ads with a specific phone numbers that were reported as scams by many users. For others, while the ads appear highly suspicious, we were not sure whether they were scams as opposed to the more harmless spam posting from aggressive realtors or other service providers advertising their service/rentals.

We therefore relied on an automated conversation engine to (i) verify whether a suspicious ad is a scam and (ii) collect additional data. More specifically, we first selected a few suspicious ads and performed the email conversations manually. Then it was fairly straightforward to distinguish between legitimate users and malicious scammers during the email conversation. For example, clone ads scammers usually wanted to proceed with the rental process online since they were not in town for good purposes (e.g., serving in mission trip to Africa). From the preliminary conversations, we were able to generate a set of linguistic features (e.g., keywords such as "serving in mission" or rent application templates) and other types of features (e.g., embedded links to certain redirection servers) that distinguish rental scammers from other legitimate users.

We ran the automated conversation engine only for the emails selected based on a predefined set of features. During the email conversations, we were able to collect additional data such as email accounts, IP addresses, phone numbers, links and payment information from the scammers. As in [21], the automated conversation engine embedded an external image link into the emails. Once a scammer clicks or loads the link in any way, the link leads the scammer to our private web server that logs the visitor's IP address. In this way, we were able to collect the IP addresses of the scammers from two sources: email headers and access logs to the web server.

**Ethics.** The longitudinal automation phase is the only part of the data collection that involved human subjects. We took care to design our experiments to respect common ethical guidelines and received approval from our institution's IRB for this study. As mentioned above, sometimes we rely on automated conversations to confirm (or disconfirm) whether scams we identify are truly scams. To minimize the inconvenience brought on legitimate users, we abided by the following guidelines. First, we only sent automated emails to ads that we suspected to be scams. Detailed methods are explained in Sects. 3.1 and 3.2. Second, we kept the automated conversations to a low volume. In the entire data collection, we sent out 2,855 emails, from which we received 204 responses that were confirmed to be from scammers out of a total of 367 responses. From these initial results, we were able to improve our methods for detecting suspicious ads, which would further reduce the number of legitimate posters contacted. Finally, in some cases we called the phone number provided by the poster in order to collect additional information. These phone calls where all manually placed, restricted to low volumes and we only contacted suspected scam posters.

## 2.5   Campaign Summaries

We present a high-level summary of the major scam categories and campaigns we identified in Table 2. For each campaign we assign it a name based on either the name of the company that is monetizing the scam when known or a feature used to identify the listings in the campaign. Applying our campaign identification methods from Sect. 3, we find seven distinct scam campaigns that account for 32 K individual ads. For each campaign the table lists the monetization category of the scam, the raw number of listings associated with that campaign, the percentage of ads that were flagged, the number of cities we found listings in out of the 20 total cities we monitored and the payment method used.

**Table 2.** Major rental scam campaigns. Rental scam campaigns of relatively large size in various rental scam types.

| Scam category | Campaign | # Ads | % Flagged | City | Payment |
|---|---|---|---|---|---|
| Credit report | CreditReport_Yahoo | 15,184 | 33.0% | 20 | Credit card |
| | CreditReport_Gmail | 5,472 | 59.3% | 9 | Credit card |
| Rent | Clone scam campaigns | 85 | 87.1% | 17 | Wire transfer |
| Realtor service | American Standard Online | 3,240 | 62.4% | 19 | Credit card |
| | New Line Equity | 3,230 | 43.3% | 12 | Credit card |
| | Search Rent To Own | 1,664 | 77.5% | 17 | Credit card |
| Total | | 28,875 | 45.2% | | |

# 3   Analysis of Scam Campaigns

In this section, we will present our detailed findings for each campaign, including our insights on how the scams are organized, where they are geographically located and the degree of automation used by each campaign.

## 3.1   Credit Report Scams

In a typical credit report scam, a scammer posts a false rental ad for a property not owned by the scammer. When a victim user replies to the rental ad, the scammer asks the victim to obtain their credit score by clicking on a link included in the email. When the victim clicks the link, a scammer-operated redirection server redirects the victim to a credit score company and includes a referral ID. If the victim pays for the credit score service which accepts credit card payments, the scammer will be paid a commission by the credit score company through its affiliate program.[1]

---

[1] According to the affiliate program of *Rental Verified*, which is used by one of the credit report campaigns we found, it pays up to $18 per customer. https://rentalverified.com/affiliates.

**Data Collection.** We identified initial postings for each campaign by manually examining the Craigslist-flagged ads, and correlating contact information and unique substrings included in the postings with user reports found on scam report sites [1, 3, 4]. In this manner, we identified two major campaigns, henceforth referred to as *CreditReport_Yahoo* and *CreditReport_Gmail* respectively, due to their usage of signature Yahoo and Gmail email addresses.

From the few examples that we found manually, we latitudinally expanded the campaign dataset through human-generated signatures. Using the human generated signatures, we were able to identify additional scam ads from the same campaigns. Craigslist had failed to flag many of the scam ads we identified. Specifically, for CreditReport_Yahoo campaign, we found 15,184 scam ads of which 33.01% were flagged for removal by Craigslist. We also found 5,471 scam ads posted by CreditReport_Gmail of which 59.27% were flagged. More details are provided in Table 2.

**Dataset Sanity Check.** We verified the suspicious ads identified by the signatures are indeed scams in two ways. First, we performed a sanity check by manually investigating 400 randomly selected suspicious ads, 200 from each campaign. We considered a suspicious ad as a scam if (1) an ad contained no additional contact information such as name, phone number, street address or URL and (2) there existed same or similar ads with different email addresses in the same campaign. Through the manual inspection, we found only one false positive ad in CreditReport_Yahoo campaign and two in CreditReport_Gmail. The email addresses used in the false positive ads were also found in other suspicious ads, and we could also find out actual realtors who used those email addresses. Second, among a total number of 20,256 credit report scam ads we identified, we randomly selected 227 and 89 credit report scam ads from the CreditReport_Yahoo and CreditReport_Gmail campaigns respectively, and sent emails in response to the selected ads. Among the emails sent, we received 41 and 78 email responses and all of them were verified to be credit report scams.

**In-depth Analysis.** We present further analysis results of the two credit report scam campaigns. Both credit report scam campaigns appear to be located in the United States. In particular, the CreditReport_Gmail campaign appears to be located in New York city; while evidence described later (e.g., diverse IP addresses and short inter-arrival times within bursts) suggests that the CreditReport_Yahoo campaign appears to rely on a botnet for their operation. We now provide an in-depth analysis of the IP addresses and email accounts of both campaigns. Table 3 lists the overview of two credit report scam campaigns we found during the experimental period.

**IP address analysis.** For both campaigns, all the IP addresses observed are located in USA. However, two campaigns show completely different IP address usage patterns as shown in Table 3.

**Table 3.** Credit report scam campaigns.

|  | CreditReport_Yahoo | CreditReport_Gmail |
|---|---|---|
| Email account found | 14,545 from 15,187 ads | 1,133 from 5,472 ads |
| Affiliated websites | rentalverified.com, matchverification.com | freecreditnation.com, efreescore.com |
| IP addresses | 69 | 30 |
| IP addresses used once | 65 (94.2%) | 10 (33.3%) |
| Country | USA (100%) | USA (100%) |
| State | 28 states | New York (100%) |
| ISP | Various | Verizon (100%) |

For CreditReport_Yahoo, 69 IP addresses were found from 41 email conversations. The number of observed IP addresses are much larger than the number of corresponding email conversations since CreditReport_Yahoo uses mostly different IP addresses for each round of conversations. In addition, they rarely reuse any IP addresses across different email conversations. 94.64% are used only in a single email conversation, and every IP address is used in at most two email conversations. The IP addresses are distributed over 24 states in USA and mapped back to residential ISPs. These observations, combined with others described later (e.g., level of automation), suggest that this campaign is potentially using a botnet for operation.

In the case of the CreditReport_Gmail campaign, 30 IP addresses were found from 78 email conversations. Of the 30 IP addresses, about 66.7% were reused in more than one email conversations and the maximum number of email threads that share the same IP address is 7. All the observed IP addresses of the CreditReport_Gmail campaign are located in New York City, and map back to a single ISP, *Verizon Online LLC*.

**Level of automation.** We observed many signs of scam process automation, including extremely short inter-arrival time in a burst of emails and duplicate or templated email messages. Table 4 lists example email bursts received from CreditReport_Yahoo campaign. Many email bursts consisting of up to 7 emails were observed and an average inter-arrival time between two emails ranges between 4.5 s and 24.7 s. Within each burst, emails were always sent from different IP addresses and therefore, usually sent from different cities. This observation also supports the use of the widely-deployed botnet. We also observed many duplicate or templated emails from both campaigns, which are also strong signs of automation. Example email message frequently observed during the whole experiment is shown in Fig. 4 in Appendix B.

On the other hand, we also observed signs of manual labor. One example is a distribution of time of day that we received email messages from scammers. In the case of CreditReport_Yahoo, we never received any email response between 7 PM

**Table 4.** Example inter-arrival time for burst email responses of CreditReport_Yahoo. Emails in the same burst have different content, although they contain a similar embedded link to a direction server.

| # Emails in burst | Burst duration (sec) | Mean inter-arrival time (sec) | # Cities | # IP locations |
|---|---|---|---|---|
| 7 | 62 | 10.3 | 5 | 7 |
| 4 | 67 | 22.3 | 3 | 4 |
| 4 | 74 | 24.7 | 3 | 4 |
| 3 | 9 | 4.5 | 3 | 3 |
| 3 | 11 | 5.5 | 3 | 3 |

and 9 AM EST (Eastern Standard Time) and in case of CreditReport_Gmail, there was no response between 8 PM and 7 AM EST.

## 3.2   Clone Scam

In clone scams, typically a scammer copies another legitimate rental ad from a different rental website, e.g., *realtor.com*. The cloned ad typically has the same street address and sometimes has the same description as the original ad. However, often the scammer lowers the rental price. This scam is typically monetized by the scammer requesting a money wire transfer or bank transfer for first months rent and a deposit.

**Data Collection.** To detect clone scams, our crawler tracked rental posts on Craigslist and 5 other major rental websites. We compared these ads and identified Craigslist rental ads cloned from other websites.

Overall, we identified 22,852 cloned ads spanning all 20 cities on Craigslist – however, not all of these are necessarily scam ads. The majority of these appear to be legitimate users advertising their rentals on multiple websites. We then focused on the subset of 2,675 cloned ads with a price difference of at least $300. These ads are deemed to be suspicious, but we still cannot be sure whether they are truly scam ads. To verify whether the identified suspicious ads are truly scams, we sent 2,517 emails to suspicious ads using our automated conversation engines. From the emails we sent, we received 237 responses among which 85 are verified to be scams.

**In-depth Analysis of Confirmed Scams.** We now report statistics on the 85 confirmed clone scams. Our major insight is that most of these scams originate from Nigeria, and are likely operated by a small number of scam factories. To reach this conclusion, we performed a detailed analysis of the IP addresses, email addresses, wire transfer requests and bank account information contained in the scam attempts. We then performed a clustering algorithm based on identifying information.

**IP address analysis.** Excluding IPs from well-known web mail provider, such as Gmail and Microsoft, we observed a total of 89 unique IP addresses located in 7 countries. We used DB-IP database [2] to geolocate each IP address offline in order to prevent the leakage of the scammer's IP address information that would result from using an online service. 66.29% of the collected IP addresses are from Nigeria and 15.73% were from the U.S. The result shows fairly similar trend compared to the result of the previous study by Park et al. [21] which shows 50.3% and 37.6% of IP addresses of Nigerian sales scammers were from Nigeria and the U.S. Even though we consider the possibility of proxies or anonymous networks, the consistent results from two studies strongly imply that the major number of the scammers were actually located in Nigeria.

**Payment Request Analysis.** From our conversations with clone ad posters, we collected a total of 12 unique payment requests and 8 duplicated requests for the same name or bank account. Interestingly, the proportion of payment request geolocation is significantly different from that of IP geolocation. 41.67% of requests are located in the US while 25% are located in Nigeria. For a money transfer via Western Union or MoneyGram, a sender needs to specify the receiver's location information including street address, city and country. However, due to the small sample size of payment requests it is unclear if there is any bias in the subset of conversations that resulted in a payment request versus those for which we were able to collect an IP address.

**Phone number analysis.** We collected a total of 22 distinct phone numbers from 24 email threads. 64% of the phone numbers are registered in the USA, but half of these are identified as VoIP numbers. The rest (36%) were registered in Nigeria.

**Clustering.** In order to better understand how scammers are organized, we clustered the emails messages into groups based on similarities of their attributes. We used a conservative clustering strategy. Any two email threads are classified into a same group only if they shared one of the following: exactly the same email accounts, phone numbers, bank accounts, IP addresses or rent application templates. Since those attributes provide us with fairly explicit clues for clustering, we are highly confident of our clustering result. The result suggests that these clone scammers are likely to originate from *a small number of scam factories*.

**Table 5.** Top 3 clone scam groups.

| Group | Ads (%) | Email accounts | Bank accounts | Phone numbers |
|-------|---------|----------------|---------------|---------------|
| 1 | 31 (36%) | 21 | 4 | 9 |
| 2 | 16 (19%) | 16 | 2 | 3 |
| 3 | 6 (7%) | 6 | 0 | 2 |
| Others | 32 (38%) | 29 | 5 | 8 |
| Total | 85 | 70 | 11 | 22 |

Through the clustering, we found a total of 15 scammer groups. Among them the top 3 groups account for 72% of all observed email threads. More detailed information of the top 3 groups are illustrated in Table 5. While IP addresses of the second and third groups are largely located in Nigeria, those of the first group are spread over Nigeria, the US, Malaysia and Egypt.

## 3.3   Realtor Service Scam

Realtor service scams involve a special type of realtor service, such as *pre-foreclosure rental* or *rent-to-own rental*. This type of rental is attractive to renters, since they may be able to own the property while paying monthly rent similar to the usual monthly rent of the same area. Realtor service scam campaigns usually request a victim to sign up for a private realtor service to get a list of rent-to-own rentals or pre-foreclosure rentals. To sign up for the service, the victim needs to pay up to $200 initial fee and/or $40 monthly fee.

While these businesses actually provide their customers with a list of homes, their rental ads are still considered scams since the ads are typically fake with unreasonably low rent prices, and/or for properties they do not own. Moreover, many user scam reports claim that in most cases, the properties in the provided list are not even for rent or sale at all. In addition, the refund process is extremely difficult but this is not explained clearly before the customer signs up for their services.

**Data Collection.** As listed in Table 2, we found a total of 8,134 realtor service scam ads over all 20 cities of Craigslist, and about 57% of the ads were flagged by Craigslist. Through the manual inspection on the crawled Craigslist rental ads, we found several phone numbers and URLs observed frequently across multiple cities on Craigslist. We then extended the initial sets of phone numbers and URLs by correlating them with various user scam reports [1,3,4]. Based on the human generated signatures of phone numbers and URLs, we identified three large realtor services with advance fee campaigns: *American Standard Online, New Line Equity* and *Search Rent To Own*.

Among the three campaigns we found, two were identified by sets of phone numbers and the other campaign was identified by a set of URLs. For the soundness of the collected phone numbers, we manually called each number and confirmed a set of numbers actually belong to a same campaign. We confirmed that all phone numbers of a single campaign leaded us to the same automatic response system. Then we conversed with a representative over the phone and confirmed the business name of each campaign. Table 6 lists three large realtor services scam campaigns.

**American Standard Online.** American Standard Online (ASO) was identified based on a total of 20 phone numbers. We gathered the set of phone numbers from our suspicious phone number detection method and many other sources such as *800notes.com*. Using the set of phone numbers, we found 3,240 rental ads posted by ASO over 19 cities on Craigslist. Among them, 62.34% were flagged

**Table 6.** Realtor service with advance fee campaigns.*: BBB rating of the sibling websites.

|  | American Standard Online | New Line Equity | Search Rent To Own |
|---|---|---|---|
| Scam signatures | 20 phone numbers | 22 phone numbers | 5 URLs |
| Payment | Initial fee ($199) | Initial fee ($9.95), Monthly fee ($40.95) | Initial fee ($109.95), Monthly fee ($39.95) |
| BBB rating | F | Not found | Not found (C/F*) |

for removal. Their ads offer rentals with much lower rent prices than other ads in the same area. However, a user is not able to get the information of the property from ASO representatives on the phone.

Because ASO is a registered company in the USA, we could find their record from *Better Business Bureau (BBB)*. BBB website shows that the company ASO has a total of 302 customer complaints and its rating is at the lowest 'F'. The record obviously tells us that doing business with ASO could be highly risky. This also means that the Federal Trade Commission (FTC) could potentially investigate this company and enforce fines or criminal penalties that would demonetize this campaign.

According to many user scam reports, the scam process of ASO is as follows. If a victim calls the number to ask about the rental ad, ASO never answers the questions about the rental ads. Instead, ASO requests a payment of $199 for an initial fee to get an access to their pre-foreclosure (or rent-to-own) property database. Once the victim signs up for the service, ASO provides the victim with a property list. Due to the nature of the term "pre-foreclosure", it is usually uncertain that the properties in the list are actually in the status of pre-foreclosure, and most of them turns out to be not for rent or sale.

At the time of contract, ASO lures victims by guaranteeing 100% refund after 90 days from the contract in case ASO does not satisfy their customers. However, their actual refund policy requires a wait of at least 90 days from the contract and at least 3 denial letters from the owners of the properties in the provided list. It is obvious that getting the multiple denial letters is extremely difficult.

**New Line Equity.** New Line Equity (NLE) is another campaign which provides a special type of realtor service. We identified NLE based on 22 phone numbers observed over 12 cities. Based on the set of phone numbers, a total of 3,230 NLE rental scam ads were identified, and 43.34% of them were flagged.

Many user reports claim that the scam process of NLE is quite similar to that of ASO. A victim calls the number found in a Craigslist rental ads, and NLE requests an initial fee $9.95 and monthly fee $40.95. Once the victim makes a payment, NLE provides him with a list of pre-foreclosure properties. In many cases, however, it turns out that most of the listed properties are not for rent or sale. We could not find a record of NLE from BBB, but there exists a record with a similar business name, *New Line of Equity* which has a BBB rating of 'D'. Many user reports complain about the difficulties in terminating the monthly fee payment.

**Search Rent To Own.** We identified Search Rent To Own (SRO) based on five URLs frequently observed over 17 cities on Craigslist. Among the five URLs, one was used as the main URL and the rest were redirection links to the main URL. Based on the set of URLs, we identified 1,664 SRO rental scam ads of which 77.46% of them were flagged. Similarly to the other two campaigns, SRO posts false rental ads on Craigslist and ask the victims to sign up their services with initial and monthly fees. The BBB record of this campaign did not exist but we found the records of two sibling websites listed in SRO website. BBB rating of those two sibling websites were 'F' and 'C', which are poor ratings for legitimate businesses.

According to the user reports, SRO first lures a customer by offering 3-day free trial service. However, SRO does not fully explain that a $39.95 monthly fee will be charged automatically after the free trial. We found many customer complains indicating that they were not notified upfront about the fact that monthly fee would be charged automatically after the free trial.

# 4  Flagged Ads Analysis

Currently, Craigslist relies on a flagging mechanism to filter out scam and spam ads. Our measurement study reveals that Craigslist currently flags only about 47% of all the scam ads that we identified. Further, for a subset of the scams (specifically, clone scams) that we closely monitored, the median time till flagging (for the ads that do get flagged) is about 13 h – see Fig. 1. The figure also shows that roughly 60% of clone scam ads remain active for more than 10 h and 40% remain active for more than 20 h.

For other scam categories, our data collection method did not allow us to obtain the time of flagging due to limitations of our measurement study: First, monitoring all ads on a per-hour basis would generate too much traffic, and our experiments were designed to keep our crawler's traffic volume low. Second, detecting these unknown scams required some manual effort. Hence, for some scam categories, we did not identify the scam ads soon enough to allow us to monitor them on a per-hour basis.

Even though revisiting all ads on a per-hour basis is too aggressive, we were able to revisit all ads we crawled twice after three and seven days to determine whether they have been flagged. Table 7 presents a summary of the composition of the Craigslist-flagged ads. Of 126,898 Craigslist-flagged ads, we found about 10.2% are *Scams* where we found concrete proof of scams via automated email conversation. On the other hand, about 70.3% are classified as *Spams* which consists of local ads that are found usually within a single cities and a few renown

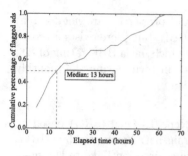

**Fig. 1.** Time taken to flag scam clone ads. Our system monitored 85 clone scam ads and found that among the flagged ads, only 40% were flagged within 10 h from ad posting time. In addition, about 60% were flagged within a day.

**Table 7.** Flagged ads categorization. 10.17% of flagged ads are identified as scams while 70.30% are identified as spams.

| Category | Campaigns | # Ads (%) |
|---|---|---|
| Scams | Credit report scam | 8, 255 (6.51%) |
| | Clone scam | 74 (0.06%) |
| | Realtor service scam | 4, 572 (3.60%) |
| Spams | Local ads | 76, 752 (60.48%) |
| | Credit repair ads | 2, 234 (1.76%) |
| | Legitimate rental ads | 10, 224 (8.06%) |
| Unidentified | | 24, 787 (19.53%) |
| **Total** | | 126, 898 (−%) |

legitimate real estate companies. This leaves 24,787 (19.5%) ads as *Unidentified* where we were not able to ascertain if the ads were benign or malicious. Some of these could be clone ads or other lower volume Rent scams, but they are unlikely to be part of a higher volume template-based campaign based on the diversity of their content.

## 5  Discussion

This section will serve to provide a higher level view of our analysis to put into context the value of this study and potential limitations.

**Potential Detection and Conversation Limitations.** The heuristics we used to detect and validate scam posting were highly accurate based on our analysis. However, it still leaves the question of how many scam listings we did not detect. Without ground truth we cannot provide an estimate for this question. A fair set of assumptions is that our heuristics performed well at detecting the majority of listings associated with larger templated campaigns and worse on the cloned and manually generated rent scam listings, due to the fact that it is difficult to detect these based on the contents of the listing. In spite of this, we do detect some cloned ads and are able to gain an understanding of the structure of their scams from our conversations with these scammers.

**Similarities and Differences with Other Study.** Park et al. [21] focused on understanding the structure of scammers posing as buyers on Craigslist. The study found that 70% of scammers provided physical shipping addresses located in Nigeria. Furthermore, the study found evidence of a largely manual work force that would respond to scams within 1–2 days during peak work hours in Nigeria.

In this study, we find a diversity of scams that depend on different sets of infrastructure as well as rent scammers that are structured similarly to those that were encountered in their study. The credit report scams depend on credit report companies in the United States that operate affiliate programs and payout commissions for generating sales. The "bait-and-switch" campaigns depend on rental service businesses that are often incorporated in the United States and accept credit card payments with deceptive refund and re-billing policies.

# 6    Related Works

**Advanced Fee Fraud.** There have been a number of previous studies that have looked at the structure by Smith [23], Buchanan and Grant [7] and estimated losses from advance fee fraud by Dyrud [9]. Whitty and Buchaman [29] and Rege [22] have investigated the dynamics of online dating scams. More closely related to our domain, Johnson [15] explored the offline methods of real estate scammers. More broadly, Stajano and Wilson [24] created a taxonomy of the different types of psychology motivations used by scammers. Garg and Nilizadeh [11] investigated whether economic, structural and cultural characteristics of a community affects the scams on Craigslist. Tive [28] introduced in his study various techniques of advance fee fraud. Herley [12] has argued that Nigerian scammers deliberately craft their messages to be unbelievable as a method of reducing the number of replies from people that are unlikely to fall victim to these scams. In contrast, our study aimed to be more focused on collecting empirical data to enable a data-driven analysis of rental scams that does not rely on self reported statistics.

Goa et al. [10] investigates the use of ontology-based knowledge engineering for Nigerian scam email text mining. Isacenkova et al. [14] analyzed public scam email datasets mostly aggregated from numerous user reports. They identified over 1,000 different scam campaigns largely based on phone numbers. Huang et al. [13] measured romance scammer techniques on dating websites. Most recently, Park et al. [21] created Scambaiter, a measurement infrastructure that can automatically converse with scammers that reply to sales listings and performed an analysis of the methods and structure of these groups of scammers. Our work builds on this, but focuses on scammers that are posting fraudulent rental lists targeting people seeking housing on Craigslist. Unlike previous studies, our investigation we have focused on (1) understanding in-depth the modi operandi and infrastructure leveraged by rental scammers operating on Craigslist, and (2) identifying methods to detect larger-scale scam campaigns and scammers that are engaged in posting fraudulent rental lists.

**Underground Studies.** Another large body of recent work has set about conducting empirical measurements to understand the dynamics and economic underpinnings of different types of cybercrime. Much of this work has been focused on spam email [16,25], illicit online pharmacies [20], and mapping out scam hosting infrastructure [17,26]. Our work builds on this, but focuses deeply on fraudulent rental lists in particular. We have conducted, to our knowledge, the first large scale empirical measurement study of fraudulent rental lists. It provides us with insights into how these scams are monetized and how they might be better detected in the future.

# 7  Conclusion and Future Work

Rental scams on Craigslist are a real threat encountered by many people searching for housing online; we found about 29 K rental scam postings on Craigslist across 20 major cities in 141 days. These fraudulent postings are designed to attract people interested in locating housing and target them with scams tailored to the rental domain. Based on our analysis of these scams we have identified a few potential chokepoints in rental scams that merit further investigation. We also note that analysis of online rental markets in other countries would be beneficial to improving our understanding of rental scams in other locations.

**Craigslist's Detection Methods.** Based on our analysis Craigslist removed 87% of the cloned ad postings we detected, after an average delay of around 10 h. Their flagging rate for the larger templated campaign postings was far lower at 50%. As future work, we plan to investigate automated detection approaches to improve filtering.

**Regulatory and Payment Follow Up.** As future work, we plan to contact the Federal Trade Commission (FTC) and card holder associations, such as Visa and MasterCard to inform them of our findings. We also, plan to perform test purchases from merchants to understand which banks they are contracting with to process credit card transactions.

**Expanding to Other Countries.** Many of these scams were specific to the United States. We plan to expand our studies to other countries in order to understand how scammers adapt their methods to other regions.

**Conclusion.** In this paper, we presented a systematic empirical measurement study of rental scams observed on Craigslist. As part of this study we present techniques that are effective at identifying rental scam postings and classifying them into larger scam campaigns. In parallel, we contacted a subset of these scammers to gain detailed information about the infrastructure required for them to profit. In total we identify seven major rental scam campaigns of which five depend on credit card payments for deceptively advertised services and businesses that are often registered in the United States. Finally, we find that filtering efforts by Craigslist remove less than half of the listings we detected. We believe that our techniques for identifying scam campaigns and understanding of their infrastructure could provide more effective methods for disrupting rental scams.

**Acknowledgements.** We thank Markus Jakobsson and the anonymous reviewers for their valuable feedback. This work was supported by the National Science Foundation grant CNS-1619620. This work was funded in part by NSF grants CNS-1314857, CNS-1453634, CNS-1518765, CNS-1514261, a Packard Fellowship, a Sloan Fellowship, two Google Faculty Research Awards, a VMWare Research Award, and an NSA Lablet grant.

## A    Example Scam Ads

(See Figs. 2 and 3)

```
*Come See this stunning 2 bedroom 2.5 bathroom home*
*Come See this quiet 3 bedroom 2 bathroom rental property* 2014 Deal
*Come See this lovely 1 bed / 1.5 bath rental* Discount for 2014
*Come Lay your eyes upon this wonderful 2 bedroom 1.5 bathroom property*
*Come Lay your eyes upon this gorgeous 1 bed 1 bath place*
*Come Lay your eyes upon this gorgeous 1 bed / 1.5 bath rental*
```

**Fig. 2.** Example ad titles with sophisticated templates used by CreditReport_Yahoo campaign.

## B    Example Scam Emails

```
Thanks for emailing me regarding the house is still available, but
presently I'm on business trip to Kuala Lumpur,Malaysia.
...
PLEASE TELL US ABOUT YOURSELF
Full Name_____
Home Phone ( )_____
Cell Phone ( ) _____
Date of Birth_____
Current Address_____
City_____State_____ Zip_____
Reasons for Leaving_____Rent $_____
Are you married_____
How many people will be living in the house_____
Do you smoke_____
Do you have a pet_____
Do you have a car_____
Move In Date_____
```

**Fig. 3.** Example rent application template. Clone scam campaigns usually request a victim to fill out their rent application form.

```
Hello,
I hope you are having a wonderful day. Here's some good news: the
apartment's still available!
...
When you're ready for a personal appointment, then please go to the link
below and grab your free credit score. We recommend this site because
all of our tenants used it and never had any problems. Just fill out the
form and indicate that you want the score. What is in the report isn't
important to us, it's more of a formality to have it on file, to make
sure there are no previous property related issues. You can get your
free credit score at CLICK HERE
Remember, we only need to see the page about the rental history. That's
all we need to see at the showing. We typically waive the security
deposit with a score of 560+.
...
```

**Fig. 4.** Credit report scam email.

# References

1. 800notes. http://800notes.com/
2. DB-IP. http://db-ip.com/
3. Report craigslist Scams. http://reportcraigslistscams.com/
4. Ripoff Report. http://www.ripoffreport.com/
5. United States Census Bureau. http://www.census.gov/
6. National association of realtors - field guide to quick real estate statistics. http://www.realtor.org/field-guides/field-guide-to-quick-real-estate-statistics (2013)
7. Buchanan, J., Grant, A.J.: Investigating and prosecuting Nigerian fraud. U. S. Attorneys' Bull. **49**(6), 39–47 (2001)
8. Clayton, R., Moore, T., Christin, N.: Concentrating correctly on cybercrime concentration. In: Proceedings of the Fourteenth Workshop on the Economics of Information Security (WEIS), Delft, Netherlands, June 2015
9. Dyrud, M.A.: I brought you a good news: an analysis of Nigerian 419 letters. In: Proceedings of the 2005 Association for Business Communication Annual Convention (2005)
10. Gao, Y., Zhao, G.: Knowledge-based information extraction: a case study of recognizing emails of Nigerian frauds. In: Montoyo, A., Muñoz, R., Métais, E. (eds.) NLDB 2005. LNCS, vol. 3513, pp. 161–172. Springer, Heidelberg (2005). doi:10.1007/11428817_15
11. Garg, V., Nilizadeh, S.: Craigslist scams and community composition: investigating online fraud victimization. In: International Workshop on Cyber Crime, IEEE (2013)
12. Herley, C.: Why do Nigerian Scammers say they are from Nigeria? In: WEIS (2012)
13. Huang, J.M., Stringhini, G., Yong, P.: Quit playing games with my heart: understanding online dating scams. In: Almgren, M., Gulisano, V., Maggi, F. (eds.) DIMVA 2015. LNCS, vol. 9148, pp. 216–236. Springer, Cham (2015). doi:10.1007/978-3-319-20550-2_12

14. Isacenkova, J., Thonnard, O., Costin, A., Balzarotti, D., Francillon, A.: Inside the scam jungle: a closer look at 419 scam email operations. In: Security and Privacy Workshops (SPW), 2013 IEEE, pp. 143–150. IEEE (2013)

15. Johnson, C.: Fakers, breachers, slackers, and deceivers: Opportunistic actors during the foreclosure crisis deserve criminal sanctions. Cap. Univ. Law Rev. **40**(4), 853 (2012)

16. Kanich, C., Kreibich, C., Levchenko, K., Enright, B., Voelker, G.M., Paxson, V., Savage, S.: Spamalytics: an empirical analysis of spam marketing conversion. In: Proceedings of the 15th ACM Conference on CCS. ACM (2008)

17. Konte, M., Feamster, N., Jung, J.: Dynamics of online scam hosting infrastructure. In: Moon, S.B., Teixeira, R., Uhlig, S. (eds.) PAM 2009. LNCS, vol. 5448, pp. 219–228. Springer, Heidelberg (2009). doi:10.1007/978-3-642-00975-4_22

18. Levchenko, K., Pitsillidis, A., Chachra, N., Enright, B., Félegyházi, M., Grier, C., Halvorson, T., Kanich, C., Kreibich, C., Liu, H., McCoy, D., Weaver, N., Paxson, V., Voelker, G.M., Savage, S.: Click trajectories: end-to-end analysis of the spam value chain. In: IEEE Symposium on Security and Privacy (2011)

19. McCoy, D., Dharmdasani, H., Kreibich, C., Voelker, G.M., Savage, S.: Priceless: the role of payments in abuse-advertised goods. In: Proceedings of the 2012 ACM Conference on CCS, CCS 2012 (2012)

20. McCoy, D., Pitsillidis, A., Jordan, G., Weaver, N., Kreibich, C., Krebs, B., Voelker, G.M., Savage, S., Levchenko, K.: Pharmaleaks: Understanding the business of online pharmaceutical affiliate programs. In: USENIX Security Symposium (2012)

21. Park, Y., Jones, J., McCoy, D., Shi, E., Jakobsson, M.: Scambaiter: understanding targeted nigerian scams on craigslist. In: NDSS (2014)

22. Rege, A.: What's love got to do with it? Exploring online dating scams and identity fraud. Int. J. Cyber Criminol. **3**(2), 494–512 (2009)

23. Smith, A.: Nigerian scam e-mails and the charms of capital. Cult. Stud. **23**(1), 27–47 (2009)

24. Stajano, F., Wilson, P.: Understanding scam victims: seven principles for systems security. Commun. ACM **54**, 70–75 (2011)

25. Stone-Gross, B., Holz, T., Stringhini, G., Vigna, G.: The underground economy of spam: a botmaster's perspective of coordinating large-scale spam campaigns. In: Proceedings of the 4th USENIX Conference on Large-Scale Exploits and Emergent Threats, LEET 2011, p. 4. USENIX Association, Berkeley (2011)

26. Stone-Gross, B., Moser, A., Kruegel, C., Kirda, E., Almeroth, K.: FIRE: FInding Rogue nEtworks. In: Proceedings of the Annual Computer Security Applications Conference (ACSAC), Honolulu, HI, December 2009

27. Thomas, K., Huang, D., Wang, D., Bursztein, E., Grier, C., Holt, T., Kruegel, C., McCoy, D., Savage, S., Vigna, G.: Framing dependencies introduced by underground commoditization. In: Proceedings of the Fourteenth Workshop on the Economics of Information Security (WEIS), Delft, Netherlands, June 2015

28. Tive, C.: 419 scam: Exploits of the Nigerian con man. iUniverse (2006)

29. Whitty, M.T., Buchanan, T.: The online romance scam: a serious cybercrime. CyberPsychol. Behav. Soc. Netw. **15**(3), 181–183 (2012)

# Graph Analytics for Real-Time Scoring of Cross-Channel Transactional Fraud

Ian Molloy[1(✉)], Suresh Chari[1], Ulrich Finkler[1], Mark Wiggerman[2],
Coen Jonker[2], Ted Habeck[1], Youngja Park[1], Frank Jordens[2],
and Ron van Schaik[2]

[1] IBM Thomas J. Watson Research Center, Yorktown Heights, USA
{molloyim,schari,ufinkler,habeck,young_park}@us.ibm.com
[2] ABN AMRO Bank N.V., Amsterdam, The Netherlands
{mark.wiggerman,frank.jordens,ron.van.schaik}@nl.abnamro.com

**Abstract.** We present a new approach to cross channel fraud detection: build graphs representing transactions from all channels and use analytics on features extracted from these graphs. Our underlying hypothesis is *community based fraud detection*: an account (holder) performs normal or trusted transactions within a community that is "local" to the account. We explore several notions of community based on graph properties. Our results show that properties such as *shortest distance* between transaction endpoints, whether they are in the same *strongly connected component*, whether the destination has high *page rank*, etc., provide excellent discriminators of fraudulent and normal transactions whereas traditional social network analysis yields poor results. Evaluation on a large dataset from a European bank shows that such methods can substantially reduce *false positives* in traditional fraud scoring. We show that classifiers built purely out of graph properties are very promising, with high AUC, and can complement existing fraud detection approaches.

## 1 Introduction

Fraud in payment transactions is a large problem for consumers: card fraud alone is estimated to result in losses of €1.33B in the EU in 2013 [7]. The reasons for the continued prevalence of transactional fraud are varied: reliance on outdated technologies (e.g., magnetic stripes), new banking models (e.g., online banking, P2P payments), man-in-the-browser malware, phishing, etc. Banks have turned to preventive technologies, such as EMV (chip-and-pin/signature) for card-present transactions. Mitigations for card-not-present transactions (e.g., online) include: CVV2 numbers, multifactor transactional authentication numbers (TANs), etc. Despite their partial success, fraud is still a big problem: Criminals devise malware specifically crafted to a particular bank's web pages and mobile apps that modify transactions prior to any additional user authorizations. Preventive measures introduce friction by requiring additional equipment or steps that customers need to perform. Thus, fraud detection algorithms and analytics based on transactional information is a fundamental technique all banks rely on. Most

© International Financial Cryptography Association 2017
J. Grossklags and B. Preneel (Eds.): FC 2016, LNCS 9603, pp. 22–40, 2017.
DOI: 10.1007/978-3-662-54970-4_2

fraud detection solutions work on specific channels and use two key methods: rule based systems and statistical analytics. Rule based systems flag known fraudulent patterns, e.g., multiple transactions at petrol stations in quick succession. Channel specific rules e.g., blacklisting malicious IPs or Tor exit nodes or incorrect billing/shipping addresses are common. Statistical methods attempt to build profiles of customers based on frequency and amount of normal transactions, changes in geography, or merchant types. Real-world constraints require fraud detection to finish in a few milliseconds, limiting the scope and sophistication of analytics, resulting in higher error rates, and even small false positive rates can be extremely costly e.g., irate customers, investigation costs.

This paper describes a completely new approach to cross-channel fraud detection based on graph analytics. Our primary objective is reducing false positives of current methods. Our hypothesis is that payment patterns define communities, and fraud manifests as deviations from these communities. We discover communities by building transaction graphs irrespective of the channel, and analyzing the structure of such graphs. These notions of community become stronger as financial institutions open up new means for person-to-person payments, such as popmoney and QuickPay. Our work is closely related to social network analysis (SNA) that attempts to identify communities and relationships, like friendship and followers. Our analysis shows that semantic differences between social and financial anomalies limit applicability of existing SNA work to this domain.

This work represents the first step in evaluating graph-based anomaly detection for fraud detection: we seek to determine which graph features, if any, provide measurable benefit in identifying fraudulent transactions. Our experiments with cross-channel transaction data from a European bank (ABN AMRO) show that several graph features provide discrimination between fraudulent and benign transactions. In a graph model where a node represents an account and an edge is a completed transaction we show that the following features can be used to substantially reduce false positives (upwards of 30%):

- the shortest distance between the endpoints of the target transaction
- if the endpoints are in the same strongly connected component
- the page rank of the destination and the reverse page rank of the source
- which clusters (defined by different methods) do the endpoints belong to and the likelihood of a transaction between these clusters.

These features, their variants and other path-based features provide excellent discrimination. We find that SNA features, such as node properties and features derived from the egonet of an account, do not perform well. Our solution is orthogonal and complementary to existing techniques, and is not intended to replace existing customer and channel profiling, but rather to improve accuracy by reducing false positives. Scalability of graph algorithms are a major hurdle in their adoption for real-time scorin g (a cache miss takes around 100 ns [24], limiting processing to around 1000 vertices in 100 ms): our features can be precomputed, accelerated using time-storage tradeoffs, approximations, and heuristics to meet performance targets. Finally, we illustrate how to build classifiers, based solely on graph features and independent of traditional statistical features for fraud detection, and evaluate their performance on a small subset of the transactional data showing excellent promise.

There are clear benefits to graph based methods: they are channel independent and applicable to new channels, are more adaptive than rule based systems and more expressive than statistical methods. They define fraud based *directly* on the accounts involved in a transaction, not on *indirect* indicators *e.g.* statistical measures (how much the account has spent in a day) or channel-specific measures (indications of malware on the endpoint). Note that a transaction where the destination account has been modified, just prior to user authorization, cannot be detected by statistical source-account profiling. Our work is, to our knowledge, the first to show a completely new scientific approach to fraud detection in transaction networks that is channel independent. Our results are highly promising with great false positive reduction, and through clever pre-processing and algorithmic selection we can perform scoring in real-time on a commodity x86 machine without specialized hardware.

## 2   Related Work

Fraud detection is a mature area with almost every bank and card issuer deploying some solution using rules, analytics, and predictive models. They use existing products (e.g., [10,11,22]), proprietary risk engines, or combinations of these components. Both SAS and FICO Falcon rely on neural networks for their scoring engine for speed and efficiency. Existing solutions focus on statistical anomalies (min, max, average, etc.) on hand-picked features of accounts to build customer profiles, such as recency, frequency, and monetary value of transactions (RMF) [9] etc., and must be tuned for specific companies. Typically, "cross channel" means combining such properties from multiple channels into one.

There are many works describing applications of machine learning to fraud detection. Most work focuses on feature selection and building supervised classifiers. Many products [10] and published works [3,5,18,26,27] use neural networks to score transactions from statistical features. Other techniques include Bayesian learning [18], decision trees [26], association rules [25], and genetic algorithms [8].

There is a large body of work on social network analysis [2,13,19], often focused on identifying anomalous nodes [2], fake accounts [12], or spam [14,17]. As discussed in Sect. 5.5 while these methods identify anomalous nodes they are somewhat unconnected with fraud. One can view SNA as focused on identifying anomalous/special nodes while fraud detection finds anomalous edges.

APATE [29] combines traditional features (RMF) with graph-based features connecting credit cards and merchants through transactions. They use influence propagation [17] to measure the propagation of fraud labels through the network. Such analysis identifies "hot spots" where merchants have been compromised and cards used in subsequent fraudulent transactions, such as CNP transactions without a second factor for authorization, which ABN AMRO currently uses.

# 3 Problem Definition: Data Sets and Real-Time Constraints

This section briefly introduces the types of transactions used in the evaluation, the types of fraud addressed, and domain specific constraints that need to be considered. We provide some details on the private dataset used to evaluate our methodology and the possible public datasources. Our test data comes from a European bank that fully deployed EMV in both card-present and card-not-present transactions using chipTANs (Chip Authentication Program). This is very different from the fraud problem in the USA where cards mostly rely on magnetic stripe for card-present transactions and CVV2 for card-not-present transactions. While EMV has some security issues [4,20] both EMV and TANs substantially reduce vectors for committing fraud and necessitates increasingly sophisticated attacks. Known since 2005 is man-in-the-browser malware which replaces destination account numbers with account numbers the adversary controls, called a mule account. When the customer verifies the transaction, using chipTAN or mTAN, they authorize illegitimate transactions. Mobile malware can intercept mTANs, and customers may still fall victim to phishing attacks, e.g. the Boleto scams in Brazil [23].

This work complements existing fraud monitoring solutions by analyzing the utility in graph-based features that are orthogonal to traditional approaches. There are several key requirements: First, it is desirable to be able to score all transactions, and not simply subsample. Second, it is preferable to score transactions in real-time and block fraudulent transactions. Some transactions are non-reversible, such as wire transfers, saving both the customer and the bank time and money if the transaction can be blocked rather than discovered through forensics. Thus we expect our analytics to run in the order of milliseconds to support the real-time blocking of suspected transactions.

## 3.1 Data Sets

The data set that we use is proprietary to ABN AMRO and combines incoming and outgoing transactions from different channels: online banking, point of sale, ATM, mobile banking, and person-to-person payments during the period June 1, 2012 through Aug. 30, 2012. For this period we also had labels: false positive (transactions flagged as fraudulent by the current system, later determined to be benign), transactions correctly flagged as fraudulent, and fraudulent transactions not flagged. There were hundreds of millions of transactions in this period. Other details of the data set including specific properties are described with the results.

The only large public data set is the Bitcoin [21] blockchain, currently having 420 million transactions and about 85 million Bitcoin addresses which can be seen as accounts. Unlike traditional banks, Bitcoin allows (and encourages) a distinct account number for each transaction. We expect that account profiling mechanisms to be unsuccessful on this data and use it only to test scalability of our feature evaluation.

# 4   Graph Analytic Approach

This section outlines the graph analytic approach, the underlying motivation and how we use transaction graphs to score fraud. We view financial transactions transferring money from one account to another as (temporal) edges connecting accounts. Using this we can build powerful analytics leveraging recent advances in scalable analytics and anomaly detection in graphs. A successful payment can be seen as establishing a trust relationship relying only on the entities in the transaction and not on the channel or any other parameters. An account trusts the accounts/entities that it pays directly the most. The "web of trust" model can be used to transitively infer trust relationship—we then trust accounts that are paid by the accounts we pay and so on—and these relationships naturally define *communities* of normal transactions. If we can find graph features which are indicative of fraud then this approach achieves two big goals:

- Establishes a channel independent mechanism of detecting fraud.
- Graph feature based fraud detection uses a completely new set of features and would complement the accuracy of the traditional fraud detection.

## 4.1   Formal Definition

While banking systems record numerous attributes about transactions, we restrict ourselves to four attributes: source account, destination account, timestamp, and amount (in a common currency). From the many timestamps associated with a transaction (time initiated, processed, cleared, etc.), we assume there is one authoritative timestamp which we use. Using this data, there are several graph models one can define. First, we can model transactions as a quiver.

**Definition 1.** *A quiver (or multidigraph) $\Gamma = (V, E, s, t)$ where $V$ is a set of vertices of $\Gamma$, $E$ is a set of edges, and $s$ and $t$ are mappings $s : E \to V$ and $t : E \to V$ that returns the source and destination vertices for an edge, respectively.*

Each edge has two properties: the timestamp and the value of the transaction. Alternatively, we can define a vertex type to represent transactions as follows:

**Definition 2.** *A heterogeneous information network (HIN) is a digraph $G = (V, E, \gamma, \tau)$ where $\gamma$ and $\tau$ are functions mapping vertices and edges to types: $\gamma : V \to \mathcal{A}$, and $\tau : E \to \mathcal{R}$ for vertex types $\mathcal{A}$ and edge types $\mathcal{R}$.*

We assume two vertex types: accounts and transactions. Only one edge type, pays is necessary, however more expressive HINs are possible. Transaction vertices can be annotated with the timestamp and amount. Collapsing multiple transactions between the same endpoints into one *representative* transaction yields a digraph.

**Definition 3.** *A digraph is a graph $G = (V, E)$ where $V$ is a set of vertices (accounts), and $E \subseteq V^2$ is a set of edges (transactions). The edges may be weighted (by the total value or the number of transactions etc.).*

These representations can be enhanced by additional information such as account owners, types (savings, chequing, credit card) etc. leading to enhanced insights. We use the quiver representation but process digraphs for scalability (Fig. 1).

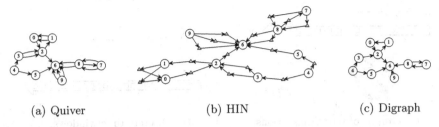

(a) Quiver                      (b) HIN                      (c) Digraph

**Fig. 1.** Transaction data with three different graph representations. In the HIN, shaded triangles represent transaction vertices.

### 4.2 Graph Construction and Scoring

Figure 2(a) depicts the overall process of graph construction for fraud scoring. Only transactions that occur strictly prior to the one being evaluated are used to construct the graph (1). Given a transaction $T = X \xrightarrow{v} Y$ (from account $X$ to $Y$ for amount $v$) to be scored, the accounts are identified in the graph (2). Features from the graph are then extracted (3), and scored using a trained classifier (4).

The strategy to select past transactions to construct graphs has tradeoffs in accuracy, speed of construction and maintenance, and scalability of graph algorithms. We can score a transaction against many different graphs taken from (possibly overlapping) time windows as shown in Fig. 2(b). Some choices for defining such a prior window for a transaction occurring at time $t$ are: a fixed number of recent transactions (e.g., one million); *real-time* scoring with a time window of size $\delta$, i.e., $[t - \delta, t)$; or rounding time to a unit of granularity $n$, such as one day, i.e., $\left[n * \left(\lfloor \frac{t}{n} \rfloor - i\right), n * \left(\lfloor \frac{t}{n} \rfloor - j\right)\right]$, where $i > j \geq 1$, which we call *discrete time*. This work uses discrete time with a granularity of one week, and score transactions against one, two, four, and ten week windows.

Given a graph $G$, we extract two basic types of features: features about the vertices, $F_G(X)$, such as the page rank or size of the egonet; and features about the pair of vertices, $F_G(X, Y)$, such as the shortest distance from $X$ to $Y$. We assume any feature extractor $F$ returns a special value $\perp$ when the input account, or either account for the pair, is not in the graph $G$, and we can assign a prior fraudulent probability derived from all transactions not seen in a graph.

We can define ensemble scoring variants with this framework using multiple features from the same graph or features from multiple graphs. The classifier we construct for evaluation uses three different features from the same graph for scoring. Standard machine learning techniques on feature selection and training can be used given features from multiple graphs and labelled transactions.

### 4.3 Community Based Fraud Detection

Our notion of fraud detection is based on notions of community: any transactions done outside a *normal* community are considered suspicious. We explore various notions of community in Sect. 5 such as: trusted accounts within a small degree

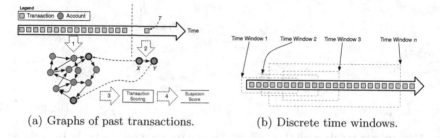

(a) Graphs of past transactions.          (b) Discrete time windows.

**Fig. 2.** How individual transactions relate to graphs to be scored.

of separation (shortest-path metric in Sect. 5.1), accounts which have a bidirectional flow of money (strongly connected components in Sect. 5.2), accounts which are "reputed" (PageRank in Sect. 5.3), and accounts belonging to the same cluster (Sect. 5.4). Some natural notions of community such as accounts to which there is a sufficient flow of money (maximum-flow) are not feasible to compute in real-time. A longer version of the paper will discuss related notions *e.g.* connectivity, centrality, clustering, link prediction, etc.

## 5    Binary Features for Fraud Detection

This section provides results of the experiments on the transaction data. We discuss the analytics evaluated, details of the evaluation, observations and finally, if the feature can distinguish between classes of transactions: random benign, false positives (generated by the current system), and fraud. The transaction data and labels used were extracted from 2 June 2012 to September 2012. From this we construct graph models over different windows of time and use these to score subsequent transactions. We experimented with different window sizes to determine the appropriate size: choosing a small window can cause instability in the graph features while choosing a large windows results in graphs computationally expensive graphs without recency. We constructed graphs from the transaction data of lengths 1–4 weeks. Before we discuss the specific features and how we will evaluate their utility, we must consider how the features may be used in practice. There are several ways in which graph features can be integrated into existing fraud detection and management system depending on the particular use case or type of fraud. For example, if false positive reduction is the primary goal then only transactions the existing fraud detection system flags need to be scored. Specifically, when the existing fraud detection system flags a transaction as potentially fraudulent, graph features are extracted and scored. If the graph-based analytics indicate the transaction is not fraud, then it may be dropped without further processing. The reduction in false positives can either yield significant savings for the bank (e.g., fewer incidents to investigate). Alternatively, the savings can be spent in other ways. For example, investigating the same number of transactions, decreasing the false negatives and catching more fraud, or by decreasing customer friction by increasing the allowed risks. In other use cases, transactions can also be scored using graph-based features (see Sect. 7). This can be performed independently (as we demonstrate), or in combination with existing analytics and channel-specific features, such as geolocation, transaction amount, and other channel specific features.

Our experiments are designed to evaluate two of these use cases. First, we evaluate how well they reduce false positives produced by existing analytics. We also indicate how well the individual features perform at identifying fraudulent transactions if they were to be used alone (note that typical fraud detection systems score using tens-to-hundreds of features). Finally, we will build a classifier using several features and score held-out transactions.

## 5.1 Shortest Path

This analytic is easiest to understand: Viewing a transaction as a trust relationship, a path between two accounts is a series of trust relationships. The central hypothesis we investigate is: trust in financial networks is transitive *i.e. if account x pays y and y pays z then can we view this a trust relationship between x and z*. This model is especially relevant for person-to-person payments. We test whether this transitive notion of trust can be used to identify fraudulent transactions. Specifically, we measure the length of the shortest chain of transactions between the source and destination accounts and evaluate its ability to discriminate between normal and fraudulent transaction. In effect the analytic is *the existence of a short path is indicative of a non-fraudulent transaction.*

For directed transaction graphs, where each edge has a weight (value), there are two possible notions of closeness: shortest path and shortest distance. Shortest path treats all edges equally, and counts the length of the path that connect two accounts. Shortest distance could weight this path with the transaction value or any other metric. For any pair of transactions, we compute *three* shortest paths: the direct shortest path from the source account to the destination; the reverse directed shortest path, i.e., the path from the destination account to the source and the undirected shortest path. An undirected shortest path may exist even if there are no paths from the source to the destination or vice-versa.

**Experimental Results.** We evaluate shortest path metrics using a graph built from four weeks of transactions and scoring transactions in the subsequent week with it. The *null hypothesis* is: *the shortest path feature does not statistically distinguish normal from fraudulent transactions*. Over all periods, the null hypothesis is rejected: the distribution of shortest paths for fraudulent transactions compared to that of a sample of normal transactions differs significantly ($\chi^2$ for $p \ll 0.05$). For each shortest path variant, we evaluate the intrinsic value of a one-dimensional binary classifier at distinguishing between normal and fraudulent transactions, producing a receiver operating characteristic (ROC) curve illustrating the false positive and false negative tradeoffs. Figure 3 shows the distribution of the shortest path (in the graph constructed from the prior 4 weeks)

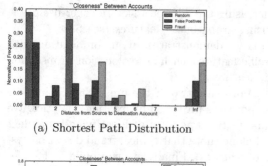

(a) Shortest Path Distribution

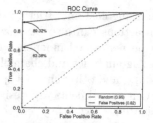

(b) Shortest Path ROC Curve

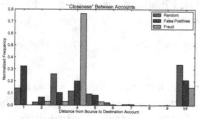

(c) Reverse Shortest Path Distribution

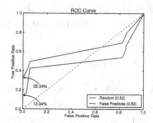

(d) Reverse Path ROC Curve

**Fig. 3.** Distribution of shortest path for transactions during 2012-06-29 through 2012-07-05 in graph constructed from the previous four weeks of transactions.

for transactions in the period of 2012-06-29 through 2012-07-05. The histograms are scaled for the different populations. Normal and false positive transactions show a clearly distinct statistical distribution compared to fraudulent transactions. In this case, the shortest path binary feature is able to reduce false positive rates by 63%!

The results for the reverse shortest path, a closeness measure for "repayment", is shown in Fig. 3. Reverse shortest path is the poorest performing of the three illustrative measures, but still yields an almost 14% reduction in false positives. Other time periods yielded equally impressive, or better, reductions for shortest path.

Similar results are obtained for other time periods validating shortest path as a good feature for fraud detection. In these periods, with the exception of a fraudulent transaction where a prior relationship existed, a minimum of 39% false positive reduction was obtained; the smallest improvement was 13.9% false positive reduction using the reverse shortest path (and an AUC of only 0.52). We have explored many variants such as building graph models from transactions over a larger time period. In the 4-week graph models in Fig. 3 there is a small percentage (about 5%) of normal transactions whose endpoints don't appear in the 4 week graph *i.e.* the accounts were inactive for the previous four weeks. This impacts the accuracy of classifiers we can build with this feature. Building models with larger windows of transactions will reduce the number of inactive accounts: building a graph model from 10 weeks of transactions from June 1, 2012 through Aug 16, 2012 reduces the number of inactive accounts to

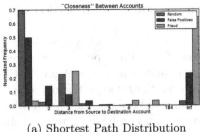

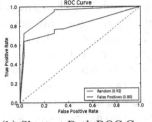

(a) Shortest Path Distribution                    (b) Shortest Path ROC Curve

**Fig. 4.** Distribution of shortest path for transaction in the period 2012-08-17 through 2012-08-23 using a ten-week graph model

about 1.8%. As Fig. 4 shows, scoring two weeks of subsequent transactions with this graph model displays the same statistical discrimination. Note however that there is a fraudulent transaction where the endpoints conducted a valid transaction before. A longer version of this paper will report on discrimination using shortest *distance* weighting by the value of the edge. These results show that shortest path and distance and their variants provide excellent discrimination between normal and fraudulent transactions.

## 5.2   Strongly Connected Components

A strongly connected component (SCC) is a subgraph such that all pairs of vertices are connected. We use SCC as a notion of bi-directional transitive trust: when account $x$ pays account $y$, if $x$ and $y$ are in the same strongly connected component, then, in theory, money already flows from $x$ to $y$, and money flows from $y$ back to $x$. When there exists a path from $x$ to $y$, yet there is no return path, we can view $y$ as a sink account. Paying money into sink accounts could be risky and we suspect such sink account (or entire subgraphs) to be suspicious. However, these may be external accounts for which we do not have visibility.

We evaluate the following aspects of strongly connected components: size and distribution of SCCs, impact of window size on SCCs, whether the two accounts involved in a transaction are members of the same SCC.

The sizes of strongly connected components naturally follow a powerlaw and the size of the largest components increases with the length of the time window. Unlike other clustering methods, adding a new transaction can only merge two SCCs into one, making it easily adapted to real-time applications and SCC numbers can be stored and later looked up. This is important because the smaller the component, the less likely the two randomly selected accounts will be members of the same SCC.

**Transactions and Strongly Connected Components.** We use strongly connected component for identifying fraudulent transactions and reducing false positives based on the hypothesis that transactions *within* an SCC are less likely to be fraudulent than transactions than span two strongly connected components. Such edges (transactions) in graph theory are known as bridges.

To evaluate, we build graphs for one- two- and four-week windows that advance one week at a time. Next, transactions for a target period are scored against the strongly connected components and placed into one of four categories: the source and destination accounts are in the same SCC; source end destination accounts are in different strongly connected components, but a prior transaction exists; source and destination accounts are in different strongly connected components and a prior transactions does not exist; either the source or destination accounts was inactive and is not a member of any strongly connected component.

The results from our ten week experiment are shown in Fig. 5, clearly illustrating that two accounts are more likely to be in the same SCC, or have a prior transaction, for the benign transactions than the fraudulent transactions (the null hypothesis is rejected). We also measure the increase in conditional probability given which of the four classes the transaction falls into. We summarize these results using the conditional probability gain by grouping all graphs (one, two, four, and ten week windows) based on their duration in Table 1. We can clearly see that the majority of fraudulent transactions occur where one of the endpoints was previously inactive or the accounts are members of different strongly connected components.

**Fig. 5.** SCC results for transactions 2012-08-17 through 2012-08-30 on graph from prior ten weeks.

**Table 1.** Conditional probability gain from SCCs.

| Window size | Gain |
| --- | --- |
| 1 | 0.58 |
| 2 | 1.02 |
| 3 | 2.68 |
| 4 | 2.13 |
| 10 | 4.88 |

## 5.3   Page Rank

PageRank [6] is an algorithm for measuring the importance and trust in accounts, originally developed to model the importance of web pages. In our graphs PageRank measures the reputation of an account in terms of the payments made to it. Our hypothesis is that accounts with a high PageRank are less likely to be fraudulent. In the PageRank algorithm, an account evenly distributes its own PageRank to the accounts it pays, and the algorithm iterates until convergence: $PR(u) = \frac{1-d}{N} + d\sum_{v \in P(u)} \frac{PR(v)}{|P(v)|}$, where $P(u)$ is the set of accounts $u$ pays and $d$ is a damping factor. Originally, the damping factor modeled the probability a random web surfer stops on a page. In financial transactions, the damping factor can be used to model an account saving. We use a default constant damping factor of 0.85; future work will explore using a per-account damping factor based on past spending behavior.

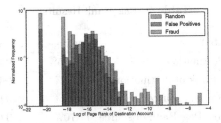

**Fig. 6.** Distribution of PageRank for transactions during 2012-06-29 through 2012-07-05 in graph constructed from the previous four weeks of transactions.

PageRank can be used either unweighted or weighted. In the weighted form, the distribution of an account's PageRank to its neighbors can be made proportional to the transaction amount. Alternatively, we could weight edges based on the number or frequency of the transactions. This may not be accurate as it is possible to send messages and hence use mobile payments as a chat service with €0.01 transactions. However, since frequent payments can indicate a level of trust, future work will investigate this method of weighting edges. We experiment with four different versions of PageRank: Forward unweighted, Forward weighted, Reverse unweighted, Reverse weighted. In the reverse forms, we reverse the directions of the transactions with the intuition that accounts performing many transactions are less likely to be in fraudulent transactions. We evaluate all four forms of PageRank against the same sample graphs used to evaluate shortest path: compute PageRank on a four-week graph and use that to score transactions from the subsequent week. In each case, we use PageRank of the source and destination accounts and evaluate the following question: *does the PageRank for victims or destination account of fraud follow a different distribution than randomly selected accounts?*

Figure 6 shows an example of how PageRank of the destination discriminates between normal and fraudulent transactions which is also seen in other periods evaluated. Table 2 shows the average performance of using the variants of the PageRank algorithm The unweighted PageRank of the destination produces a respectably average 39.3% reduction in false positives (ranging from 22–48%). Using the weighted version improves the reduction to 44.54% on average. The reverse PageRank of the source produces less impressive but useful reduction of 16.98% on average and 17.70% for the weighted version.

## 5.4  Clustering

We use clustering techniques to discover accounts which have similar profiles *e.g.* connectedness and transactional patterns, and score transactions based on whether they are consistent with the cluster. In particular, we use prior models of inter-cluster transaction likelihoods to score the transaction risk. We explore different features for clustering, each providing a different perspective on the data: *basic features* of vertices such as the number of outgoing edges, distinct

**Table 2.** PageRank Results

| Feature evaluated | Average ZER | Average AUC |
|---|---|---|
| PageRank of destination | 39.575% | 0.760 |
| Weighted PageRank of destination | 44.54% | 0.788 |
| Reverse PageRank of source | 16.98% | 0.625 |
| Weighted reverse PageRank of source | 17.70% | 0.652 |

destinations, incoming edges and accounts, types of edges (external, foreign, etc.); *egonet features* are extracted from the egonet of a vertex including weight and number of all transactions, number of distinct transactions of each type, number of nodes of each type etc.; *connectivity features* represent transactional information. We build an undirected graph where vertices denote accounts, and edges represent transactions. The edges are weighted by a function of the number of transactions and the total transaction amount between the two accounts.

*Clustering algorithms:* We use the BIRCH (Balanced Iterative Reducing and Clustering using Hierarchies) [30] algorithm to cluster basic and egonet features since they represent accounts as vectors in a multi-dimensional space. BIRCH is an algorithm which performs hierarchical clustering over a very large data-set, and is known to handle well very large and noisy data sets. We use the Markov Cluster (MCL) algorithm [28] to cluster nodes connected to endpoints similarly based on the connectivity features. MCL is a fast and scalable cluster algorithm for graphs based on simulation of random flow in graphs.

*Cluster evaluation:* Since known class membership labels are not available, we measure the results by cluster quality: how homogenous the clusters are and how well clusters are separated. Another measure is cluster stability across different time periods. We evaluated these strategies against the 1-week and 4-week transaction graphs. The produced clusters have excellent homogeneity, separation and stability for both egonet and basic features. We defer the detailed cluster evaluation figures to a longer version of the paper.

*Using Clusters for Scoring:* We hypothesize that accounts in the same cluster will have similar spending habits, i.e., pay similar accounts. We test this by investigating the inter-cluster transitions *i.e.* for all transactions from source accounts in the same cluster, we measure the distribution of the destination account clusters. We evaluate whether cluster-to-cluster distribution for fraudulent transactions deviates from that obtained by the false positives and random transactions. We show a single result leaving the rest to a longer version of the paper. We observed such spikes across multiple time periods for the clusters produced using the basic features. However, almost all fraudulent transactions are inter-cluster with egonet features, limiting its ability to score transactons (Fig. 7).

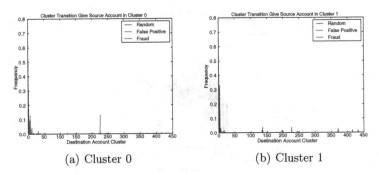

(a) Cluster 0                                     (b) Cluster 1

**Fig. 7.** Outgoing cluster transitions illustrating anomalous spikes for fraudulent transactions.

## 5.5   Egonet Features

Egonets, or subgraphs of radius two centered around a single account (the ego node) yield features similar to those obtained from the basic analysis. The egonet includes any transaction between the neighbors of the ego node, making concepts such as "incoming" and "outgoing" transactions and accounts, as used in the basic features, less meaningful. However transactions may be classified as those including the ego node, and those strictly between the neighbors of the ego node. Egonets have been studied extensively for anomaly detection in social network graphs and corporate graphs. For example, egonets have been used to analyze the Enron email corpus [16], political donations, and blogs. We investigate the use of a suite of egonet based anomaly detection features called OddBall [2]. OddBall explores powerlaws that exist between properties of an egonet: For example, in an undirected graph, the number of edges in an egonet of $n$ vertices, is bound between $n-1$ and $n*(n-1)$, giving a powerlaw between 1 and 2 approximately. OddBall analyzes such relationships for common properties of an egonet, computes powerlaws, and identifies anomalies that deviate significantly (are far from a regression line) or are in areas of low density (are not near other accounts when plotted by egonet properties). Several properties of egonets are of interest, mainly the number of nodes, the number of edges (total and distinct), the total weight of the edges, and the principal eigenvalue.

We evaluated how well OddBall performs at identifying accounts involved in fraudulent transactions, either the victim or the fraudster. The results indicate egonets are a poor indicator of malicious activity in financial networks, however they were successful in identifying several anomalous accounts. Figure 8 presents a scatter plot of two properties of an egonet, egonode was involved in fraud (green squares and red triangles), and the anomalies (yellow triangles). These anomalous accounts are actually *vostro accounts*, accounts for other banks held for accounting purposes, and should not be considered malicious.

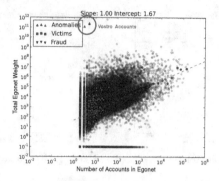

**Fig. 8.** OddBall anomalies identifying vostro accounts. (Color figure online)

## 6   Scalability

This section briefly discusses the scalability of the graph analytics discussed. To be effective in practice, a fraud detection algorithm must be able to score all transactions, in real-time (under 100 ms). Any property that depends on a single account, such as which SCC the account belong to, or the PageRank, can be precomputed. Properties that require the pair of accounts, such as the shortest path, are prohibitive to precompute and store, and must be computed in real-time. For large graphs, however, a single shortest path query can be costly; in some of our experiments exceeding 30 s. To handle throughput, we seek solutions which don't require massive parallelism or special hardware.

Architectural differences, such as faster processors and memory, typically yield a 2–8x performance increase, falling short of our goals. By bounding the maximum length of the paths, we can ensure that *most* queries are returned in sufficient time, however graphs and accounts with high branching factors still yield queries that are exhaustive and search the entire graph. Instead, we use approximation algorithms that store minimum spanning trees for a select subset of vertices, in an approach similar to other approximate algorithms [1,15]. Unlike [1], we store a small number (100) of spanning trees, reducing precomputation time from hours to minutes, and drastically reducing storage costs. To improve approximations that aren't the result of intersections between two spanning trees, we perform a breadth first search that caps the number of edges evaluated to ensure termination in a few ms. Our experiments used Neo4J, a graph database for storing and processing some of the data, but the performance was inadequate. We store computed features in MongoDB, and use graph-tool, a Python Boost graph library package, for some algorithms, such as PageRank. Our shortest path approximation was implemented in C++. All tests were performed on an AMD Opteron 8439 with 256 GB RAM.

# 7   Classifiers

While our primary objective was to reduce the number of false positives, we experimented with building classifiers, using only graph features evaluated and computable in real-time. We restricted our classifiers to features derived from SCC, PageRank, and shortest path (forward, reverse, and undirected). We divide transactions into one month graphs and train a support vector machine (SVM) classifier with a radial bias function (RBF) kernel on the first month and test on the remaining data. All features are extracted from the graph pertaining to the prior month and zero-mean unit-variance normalization is performed (relative to the first month's features). The results are shown in Fig. 9, which also indicates how currently deployed analytics perform. Because the deployed analytics make use of rules and blacklists, they cannot be parameterized and we can only represent them as a point on the ROC curve. These rules may reject transactions due to failed PIN or TAN, known mule accounts, or phishing campaigns. Note that the task here is different than previous sections, where the task was false positive reduction (the positive class is benign) while here it is fraud detection (positive class is fraudulent).

The results are clearly encouraging for the use graph features for fraud scoring. Our highest performing classifier reached an AUC score of 0.93; higher than the optimistic binary evaluations shown in the previous section. Importantly, this implies the features some of the features are independent, and combining them may yield better results. It is only built on three types of features: shortest path, SCC, and PageRank, but identifies many fraudulent transactions missed by the deployed analytics. The classifiers here built on graph feature alone currently yield too many false positives to be deployed in practice. However, graph models contribute a new set of features and we expect that ensemble classifiers built from these and traditional features to be substantially more accurate.

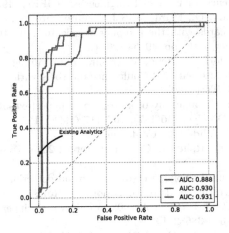

**Fig. 9.** Classifier performance using only graph features: Shortest path and SCC (blue), adding BFS query properties (green), and adding PageRank (red). (Color figure online)

Further work is needed on selecting the optimal time window, or windows, for producing graphs. The same one-month graph is used to score a month's worth of transactions, and not one week as we used previously. Here we observed a drop in AUC scores for the shortest path features, from 0.95 to 0.67 for example, but by combining all shortest path computations we were able to improve to an AUC of 0.888. Of course, best results are expected with ensembles of graph features and current fraud scoring mechanisms.

## 8   Conclusion

We have described a new approach to cross channel fraud detection based on graph analytics. Our results show that graph features can provide excellent discrimination between fraudulent and normal transactions. This strengthens our belief that graphs of financial transactions form accurate representations of actual social communities and relations. We expect that improvements in the scalability of graph analytics, this new approach can be a feasible solution to enhance the accuracy of fraud detection. Further, they offer a default fraud model for all new transaction channels. We expect that graph models will also be beneficial to applications such as commercial banking and anti-money laundering.

## References

1. Agarwal, R., Caesar, M., Godfrey, B., Zhao, B.Y.: Shortest paths in microseconds. CoRR, abs/1309.0874 (2013)
2. Akoglu, L., McGlohon, M., Faloutsos, C.: Anomaly Detection in Large Graphs. Technical Report CMU-CS-09-173, Carnegie Mellon University, November 2009
3. Aleskerov, E., Freisleben, B., Rao, B.: CARDWATCH: a neural network based database mining system for credit card fraud detection. In: IEEE/IAFE 1997 Computational Intelligence for Financial Engineering (CIFEr) (1997)
4. Bond, M., Choudary, O., Murdoch, S.J., Skorobogatov, S., Anderson, R., Chip, S.: Cloning EMV cards with the pre-play attack. In: 2014 IEEE Symposium on Security and Privacy (SP), pp. 49–64 (2014)
5. Brause, R., Langsdorf, T., Hepp, M.: Neural data mining for credit card fraud detection. In: 11th International Conference on Tools with Artificial Intelligence, TAI 1999, pp. 103–106 (1999)
6. Brin, S., Page, L.: The anatomy of a large-scale hypertextual web search engine. Comput. Netw. ISDN Syst. **30**(1–7), 107–117 (1998). Proceedings of the Seventh International World Wide Web Conference
7. Brown, A., Divitt, D., Rolfe, A.: Card fraud report 2015. Technical report, Alaric, March 2015
8. Duman, E., Elikucuk, I.: Solving credit card fraud detection problem by the new metaheuristics migrating birds optimization. In: Rojas, I., Joya, G., Cabestany, J. (eds.) IWANN 2013. LNCS, vol. 7903, pp. 62–71. Springer, Heidelberg (2013). doi:10.1007/978-3-642-38682-4_8
9. Fader, P.S., Hardie, B., Lee, K.L.: RFM and CLV: using iso-value curves for customer base analysis. J. Mark. Res. **42**(4), 415–430 (2005)

10. FICO: FICO Falcon Fraud Manager for Debit and Credit Card. Technical report, FICO (2012)
11. fiserv: fiserv: Compliance & fraud management (2015). https://www.fiserv.com/risk-compliance/financial-crime-risk-management.aspx
12. Gong, N.Z., Frank, M., Mittal, P.: SybilBelief: a semi-supervised learning approach for structure-based sybil detection. IEEE Trans. Inf. Forensics Secur. **9**, 976–987 (2014)
13. Gong, N.Z., Xu, W., Huang, L., Mittal, P., Stefanov, E., Sekar, V., Song, D.: Evolution of social-attribute networks: measurements, modeling, and implications using Google+. In: The 2012 ACM Conference, pp. 131–144. ACM, New York, November 2012
14. Grier, C., Thomas, K., Paxson, V., Zhang, M.: @spam: the Underground on 140 Characters or Less. In: Proceedings of the 17th ACM Conference on Computer and Communications Security, pp. 27–37 (2010)
15. Gubichev, A., Bedathur, S., Seufert, S., Weikum, G.: Fast and accurate estimation of shortest paths in large graphs. In: CIKM 2010: Proceedings of the 19th ACM International Conference on Information and Knowledge Management, pp. 499–508 (2010)
16. Klimt, B., Yang, Y.: The enron corpus. In: ECML, pp. 217–226 (2004)
17. Chandy, R., Faloutsos, C., Akoglu, L.: Opinion fraud detection in online reviews by network effects. In: International AAAI Conference on Weblogs and Social Media, pp. 1–10, April 2013
18. Maes, S., Tuyls, K., Vanschoenwinkel, B.: Credit card fraud detection using Bayesian and neural networks. In: Proceedings of the 1st International NAISO Congress on Neuro Fuzzy Technologies (2002)
19. Mislove, A., Marcon, M., Gummadi, P.K., Druschel, P., Bhattacharjee, B.: Measurement and analysis of online social networks. In: Internet Measurement Comference, pp. 29–42 (2007)
20. Murdoch, S.J., Drimer, S., Anderson, R., Bond, M.: Chip and PIN is broken. In: 2010 IEEE Symposium on Security and Privacy, pp. 433–446. IEEE (2010)
21. Nakamoto, S.: Bitcoin: a peer-to-peer electronic cash system (2009). https://bitcoin.org/bitcoin.pdf
22. NICE: Nice actimize: Fraud detection & prevention (2015). http://www.niceactimize.com/fraud-detection-and-prevention
23. RSA: RSA Discovers Massive Boleto Fraud Ring in Brazil. Technical report, EMC, July 2014
24. Saini, S., Chang, J., Jin, H.: Performance evaluation of the intel sandy bridge based NASA pleiades using scientific and engineering applications. In: Jarvis, S.A., Wright, S.A., Hammond, S.D. (eds.) PMBS 2013. LNCS, vol. 8551, pp. 25–51. Springer, Cham (2014). doi:10.1007/978-3-319-10214-6_2
25. Sánchez, D., Vila, M.A., Cerda, L., Serrano, J.M.: Association rules applied to credit card fraud detection. Expert Syst. Appl. Int. J. **36**(2), 3630–3640 (2009)
26. Shen, A., Tong, R., Deng, Y.: Application of classification models on credit card fraud detection. In: 2007 International Conference on Service Systems and Service Management, pp. 1–4. IEEE (2007)
27. Syeda, M., Zhang, Y.-Q., Pan, Y.: Parallel granular neural networks for fast credit card fraud detection. In: 2002 IEEE World Congress on Computational Intelligence, 2002 IEEE International Conference on Fuzzy Systems, FUZZ-IEEE 2002, pp. 572–577. IEEE (2002)
28. van Dongen, S.: Graph Clustering by Flow Simulation. Ph.D. thesis, University of Utrecht (2000)

29. Van Vlasselaer, V., Bravo, C., Caelen, O., Eliassi-Rad, T., Akoglu, L., Snoeck, M., Baesens, B.: APATE: a novel approach for automated credit card transaction fraud detection using network-based extensions. Decis. Support Syst. **75**, 38–48 (2015)
30. Zhang, T., Ramakrishnan, R., Livny, M.: BIRCH: an efficient data clustering method for very large databases. ACM SIGMOD **25**(2), 103–111 (1996)

# Android UI Deception Revisited: Attacks and Defenses

Earlence Fernandes[✉], Qi Alfred Chen, Justin Paupore,
Georg Essl, J. Alex Halderman, Z. Morley Mao, and Atul Prakash

University of Michigan, Ann Arbor, USA
{earlence,alfchen,jpaupore,gessl,jhalderm,zmao,aprakash}@umich.edu

**Abstract.** App-based deception attacks are increasingly a problem on
mobile devices and they are used to steal passwords, credit card numbers, text messages, etc. Current versions of Android are susceptible to
these attacks. Recently, Bianchi *et al.* proposed a novel solution *"What
the App is That"* that included a host-based system to identify apps to
users via a security indicator and help assure them that their input goes
to the identified apps [7]. Unfortunately, we found that the solution has
a significant side channel vulnerability as well as susceptibility to clickjacking that allow non-privileged malware to completely compromise the
defenses, and successfully steal passwords or other keyboard input. We
discuss the vulnerabilities found, propose possible defenses, and then
evaluate the defenses against different types of UI deception attacks.

## 1 Introduction

App-based user-interface (UI) attacks pose an increasing threat to smartphone
users [9,29,30]. In such attacks, a malicious app tricks the user into entering
sensitive input into a window the malware controls or providing *incorrect* input
into a window the malware does not control. UI attacks are particularly serious
since they collect or control information at the end point closest to the user.
Once a malicious app gets a foothold on a mobile device, it is possible for it
to steal credentials and cause the user to grant additional privileges, totally
compromising the device.

One class of such attacks is app-based phishing. For example, *svpeng* is a
malicious mobile app that deceives the user into providing sensitive information, including bank credentials and credit card numbers, to a window that the
attacker controls (see Fig. 1). This deception can be stealthy and convincing due
to the rich ways in which modern mobile apps share the screen. We discuss other
types of attacks in Sect. 2.

UI deception attacks are possible due to two primary reasons: (a) The smartphone GUI environment is complex and allows for intricate interactions between
GUIs to support a multitude of use cases, and (b) Users cannot verify the provenance of an app (or window) they are interacting with. A few approaches have
been attempted to defend against these attacks, for example DECAF [23] uses

© International Financial Cryptography Association 2017
J. Grossklags and B. Preneel (Eds.): FC 2016, LNCS 9603, pp. 41–59, 2017.
DOI: 10.1007/978-3-662-54970-4_3

dynamic app exploration to detect ad UI fraud, and Liu *et al.* [24] use OCR techniques to automatically detect spoofed keyboards. However, these techniques are limited to specific types of UI attacks, and are usually based on heuristics and not foolproof.

A more general defense approach against UI deception was recently proposed by Bianchi *et al.* and involves a two-layered defense consisting of a static analysis and a runtime security indicator modeled after the well-known HTTPS lock icon and EV infrastructure [7]. Bianchi *et al.* conducted a user study that established that the security indicator helped 76% of users correctly identify UI deception under a particular attack setting.

Since Bianchi *et al.* strike directly at the root cause of the problem—lack of attribution, we believe this is the right approach to tackling UI deception. Therefore, our aim is to investigate the security properties of this defense in further detail.

The first part of our work finds that the state-of-the-art defense is still vulnerable to a subtle form of clickjacking attack that we built. Our clickjacking attack exploits a race condition and uses a newly discovered IPC side-channel to precisely time the display of attack windows to steal user input without causing any change in the visualization of the security indicator.

The second part of our work discusses challenges in achieving a secure defense against UI deception. The primary challenge is ensuring temporal integrity of the security indicator in a seamless and correct way. To that end, we introduce the concept of an *Overlay Mutex*, whose purpose is to give the user a guarantee that no other windows may interfere with the current GUI the user is interacting with. The following are our contributions:

1. *New Attacks:* We analyze the security of a state-of-the-art defense against UI deception and discover a subtle class of clickjacking attacks. Furthermore, we introduce a new IPC-based side-channel on Android and use it to elude security checks proposed in prior defenses. To the best of our knowledge, this is the first known exploitation of Android Binder IPC statistics to enhance UI deception (Sects. 3 and 4). We have uploaded demo videos [13], and proof-of-concept code [1] of our work.
2. *New Defenses:* We introduce the Overlay Mutex as a UI stack modification and discuss how it achieves temporal integrity for the security indicator, even in the presence of sophisticated, side-channel based clickjacking attacks. Our design is intended as an addition to the work of Bianchi *et al.*, thereby extending the state of the art in UI deception defense (Sect. 5).
3. *Evaluation:* We evaluate our defense against known UI deception and against our new side-channel based clickjacking attack and find that the overlay mutex successfully ensures temporal integrity of the security indicator, helping to block clickjacking attacks.

## 2   Threat Model and Example UI Attacks

Our threat model assumes that the Android OS is not compromised via root exploits. Malicious apps are assumed to be unprivileged, which is the norm

**Fig. 1.** The svpeng malware overlays Google Play with a phishing window soliciting credit card details.

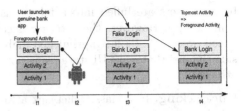

**Fig. 2.** An attack scenario to steal banking passwords. Alice launches the genuine bank app at t1. Mallory, the attacker, detects a change in the activity stack at time t2 and immediately injects the fake login activity at t3. After Alice provides the password, Mallory's fake login activity removes itself simulating a failed login attempt and reveals the real login activity. Ideally, Mallory wants (t2–t1) and (t3–t2) to be small. Real attacks achieve this in approximately 45 ms.

on Android. Prior work showed that even unprivileged apps on Android can spoof other apps to steal input, overlay windows of other apps, and perform activity hijacking attacks to inject overlay windows when passwords are entered [7,11,17]. We also note that Trojan apps have been successfully distributed on the Play Store [22,33]. We assume that soft-keyboards are not compromised or malicious. Recent research has made strides in achieving this goal [10]. We now discuss examples of powerful attacks that are possible under our threat model.

**Direct Phishing.** This type of attack pops up a window soliciting sensitive information, such as passwords, by presenting a malicious window (only associated with a background service) that looks exactly like a trusted app window. A sophisticated example of this attack is mentioned by Felt *et al.* [8], where a malicious app embeds a Facebook Like button. When the user clicks on this button, the attacker presents a malicious Facebook login window copy and steals login information. Other variants involve displaying attack windows out of context to the user and mimicking trustworthy screens.

**Activity hijacking.** A recently discovered malware strain—Trojan-Banker. AndroidOS.Svpeng.A [21], a member of the well-known svpeng family performs context-sensitive phishing. Figure 1 is a screenshot of the attack in action. Once on the device, it waits until the screen displays the `AssetBrowserActivity` of the genuine Play Store and then pre-empts the UI to display its fake version of the authentic credit card dialog.

The general structure of such attacks is shown in Fig. 2. The crucial parts involve detecting a state-change in the UI and precisely timing the launch of a spoofed activity soliciting credentials. This kind of attack is context-sensitive because users are lulled into a false sense of security since they are within a genuine app. However, the attacker deceives users through a quick and well-timed overlay [3,4,12]. Unprivileged malware can also use a recently discovered side-channel that leaks UI state transitions to build precisely timed UI deception attacks [11].

**Clickjacking.** In a classic clickjack attack, an attack UI element is displayed just in time to steal a portion of user input without alerting the user [5,20]. On Android, different kinds of clickjacking is possible. Attackers can use Toast windows (transient windows) to steal input and let that input passthrough to the underlying window. Attackers can also randomly display transparent windows that grab input and do not let it go to the underlying window, thus stealing portion of the input and simulating a random failure that explains why an input did not appear on the underlying window. This attack is interesting because even in the presence of security indicator-like defenses, users might miss changes because the attack relies on quickness of UI transitions and the inability of the human motor system to easily cancel actions once issued [5].

## 3   What the App Is That?

Recently, Bianchi *et al.* introduced a defense against UI deception [7] (What the App is That—*WhatTheApp* for short in this paper). This system consists of two portions: (1) a static analysis portion that is used to flag apps that may perform UI deception attacks for execution at an App Store and (2) a security-indicator based Android system in which apps are EV-certified and the security indicator provides a visual indicator of any UI deception attempts by background apps. Bianchi *et al.* note that while the static analysis may catch some instances of UI deception, the analysis is intended as a market-level tool and not as a complete defense against UI deception. In fact, the XCodeGhost attack on the Apple vetting process is clear evidence that on-device solutions are necessary [2].

Bianchi *et al.* address that need by including an on-device defense mechanism, partly based on the security indicator design of the HTTPS lock icon and EV bar in browsers. They propose a clever security bar for mobile devices that uses a reserved portion of the screen to identify the top activity to users as well as indicate via a lock icon whether the display is tampered with (Fig. 3). They conducted a human subjects study where 76% of participants correctly determined when UI deception attacks took place under an attack setting. Based on a security indicator design in [17], the security bar consists of a security image only known to the OS to further prove the authenticity of the indicator. Based on the HTTPS lock icon, they included a lock icon which could be green (no tampering of display contents), yellow (display possibly tampered with), or red (non-certified app executing).

Listing 1.1 shows the core logic for managing the contents of the bar, based on the code that they have publicly released for their system. This core logic executes once per second and determines the color of the lock icon and the identity of the app the user is interacting with. The logic works as follows:

[Green] Locked,
System Apps

[Green] Locked,
Verified App

[Yellow] Unlocked,
Unverified Content Present

[Red] Unlocked,
Verification Failure

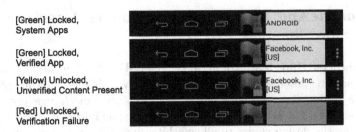

**Fig. 3.** *WhatTheApp* visualization for various screen states. The first image is for system apps, the second for a verified app, the third is shown when a window is overlayed on a verified app and the last visualization is when an unverified app is opened. (Color figure online)

```
1  //execute every second
2  LockStatus getVerificationStatus() {
3    if (topActivity identity is SYSTEM)
4      return GREEN_LOCK_ICON
5    else
6    {
7      if(topActivity identity is not VERIFIED)
8        return RED_LOCK_ICON
9      else if(topActivity identity is VERIFIED)
10     {
11       if(current WindowStack only contains windows of topActivity and SYSTEM)
12         return GREEN_LOCK_ICON
13       else
14         return YELLOW_LOCK_ICON
15     }
16   }
17 }
```

**Listing 1.1.** Logic of UI defense proposed in [7].

**Table 1.** Effect of a transient window when the user is in a verified app.

| Condition | Visualization |
|---|---|
| Verified app | Green Lock Icon, Verified App Identity |
| Malware window appears | Yellow Lock Icon, Verified App Identity |
| Malware window hidden | Green Lock Icon, Verified App Identity |

(a) if the top activity is owned by SYSTEM, it displays a green lock and an indicator displaying "ANDROID." Thus, the user should be able to trust that the input provided will go to a system application. (b) Otherwise, it verifies whether the app for top-level activity is EV-certified. If not, a red lock icon is displayed (i.e., an unverified app is the top activity). Otherwise, the name of the app from the EV certificate is displayed. An additional check is made to ensure that all the windows in window stack are owned by the verified app. If not, a yellow lock is displayed. Otherwise, a green lock is displayed. Green lock is meant to convey to the user that the entered input will go to the app identified in the security indicator. We found the prototype code to be consistent with the paper.

## 4   *WhatTheApp* Vulnerabilities—Timing Attacks and Side Channels

**Design choices that lead to attacks.** The *WhatTheApp* design choice to verify the screen contents at a particular frequency embodies the time-of-check-time-of-use design flaw, because the screen contents can change just after a check is complete, forcing the indicator to display stale information for the user. Furthermore, the design choice to allow arbitrary window pre-emptions requires the user to *always* be cognizant of indicator contents—prior research discusses that users do not constantly pay attention to security indicators [15]. Ideally, a user should only check an indicator once before commencing a security sensitive operation.

**Clickjack attacks.** We found that a malware app can bypass the periodic check in *WhatTheApp* by quickly rendering a rogue window on top of an app's UI and then hiding that window. Often, one tap on the soft keyboard is successfully stolen. To the end user, this appears as a random fluctuation in input and the user may not even notice the absence of a single character—missing input can be auto-corrected or, for passwords, the user may simply retype the password on an error. For passwords, as a result of malware stealing some characters, bruteforce attacks become easier due to entropy reduction.

We tested all our attacks on an Android emulator running Android 4.4 with *WhatTheApp* modifications, the same version as published by Bianchi *et al.* To make the malware inject the rogue window only when password windows were displayed, we used a previously known side channel on Android that is described in [11] that allows monitoring the window transitions of other apps by unprivileged malware.

In practice, we found the attack to be only partly effective since, at times, the lock icon would turn yellow if the check logic of Listing 1.1 happens to trigger while the rogue window is displayed (hand caught in the cookie jar, so to speak). Our attack used the `WindowManager.addView` API to quickly create attack windows whenever an app we wished to attack became a foreground app and displayed the password window[1]. The detailed effect of showing and hiding a malware deception window while a user is interacting with a verified app is shown in Table 1.

**Leveraging new side-channels.** We discovered a new side-channel that makes the previous attack very effective—in most cases, it was missed entirely by *WhatTheApp* defenses. The side channel enables a background malware app to discover whenever a security check occurs, enabling it to predict the approximate time of the next check and thus precisely time the display of a phishing window to occur during an interval prior to the next check. The end effect was that malware could steal user's input without causing any changes in their security bar (the lock icon stayed green during our tests).

---

[1] We chose to attack Facebook in our examples, though it could equally well have been a banking app.

Our side channel exploits the publicly available information on the timing of the binder IPC calls. Binder is the *de facto* Android IPC mechanism. The security bar in *WhatTheApp* runs as its own process and makes a binder IPC call to verify screen contents every second using a timer. A test malware app monitored the timing of the binder IPC calls and inferred the ones that came from the *WhatTheApp* security indicator. To the best of our knowledge, this is' the first exploitation of binder calls on Android for a side channel.

In particular, binder IPC calls are referred to as binder transactions. In a single call-return IPC, there is one transaction for the outgoing call and one transaction for the incoming reply. The binder kernel driver publishes debugging statistics to /sys/kernel/debug/binder. There are several publicly accessible logging files under this directory. These files are present on factory images of real devices. Of particular interest is the transaction_log[2] file that lists a history of transactions occurring between processes on the system. Sample transaction logs are shown in Listing 1.2. For every transaction, there is a line containing a debug identifier, transaction type (call, reply, async), source process and thread id, destination process and thread id, and other bookkeeping information. Therefore, our test malware app can determine that a transaction occurred between two processes, but it does not know the name of the called remote method. The system server on Android hosts multiple important services, including the window manager. Any process hosting UI makes several calls a second to the window manager portion of the system server. Thus the attack app has to disambiguate and locate the security check call by *WhatTheApp* from other events in the log.

```
1 587398: call   from 1323:1455 to 1141:0 node 585 handle 34 size 72:0
2 587399: reply  from 1141:1389 to 1323:1455 node 0 handle -1 size 212:4
3 587400: async  from 1323:1323 to 928:0 node 1341 handle 22 size 80:0
4 587401: call   from 1323:1323 to 928:0 node 2428 handle 38 size 100:0
```

**Listing 1.2.** Sample binder transaction logs. Each line corresponds to a single transaction. Each line is of the form (debug id), (txn type), (source Pid/Tid), (dest. Pid/Tid), (bookkeeping data). The first 2 lines contain relevant transaction logs from the security bar to the security check service.

To do that, our test malware measured the sizes of the transaction data and discovered that the call-reply transaction pair corresponding to the security check had unique values for the sizes at approximately one second intervals. This allowed the test malware to determine the transactions of the security indicator (nav bar) display process and the security check service. The test malware then measured the time intervals between transactions for these two processes by sampling the log file at an interval of 50 ms. We determined that the interval between consecutive events was approximately 1 s ± 600 ms. In some cases, the error was upto 3 s. This error is due to scheduling policies, context switches, and memory pressure. Thus, the side channel we discovered was relatively noisy.

---

[2] At the time of writing, this file was publicly accessible to any app. Recently, the current version of Android (Marshmallow) tightened its SELinux policy to prevent arbitrary apps from accessing the file.

```
1  void sideChannelAttack() {
2    while(shouldAttack()) {
3      TempTxnLog = getTxnLog("/sys/kernel/debug/binder/transaction_log")
4      (srcPid, destPid) = getPids("EVBar", "VerifierService")
5      TxnLog = filterLogs(srcPid, destPid)
6      if(TxnLog contains new transaction from srcPid to destPid)
7      {
8        delta = NOW - prev_txn_timestamp
9        if(delta >= 800 AND delta <= 1200)
10         show_attack_window(400)
11
12         prev_txn_timestamp = NOW
13       }
14
15     sleep(50)
16   }
17 }
18
19 boolean shouldAttack() {
20   TopOfStackActivity = readTopOfStack()
21   if(TopOfStackActivity == "com.facebook")
22     return true
23   else
24     return false
25 }
```

**Listing 1.3.** Control algorithm exploiting Binder side channel.

**Table 2.** Effect of using a side channel to predict attack times. Tests were run for 6 hours.

| Condition | Successful attacks/total attacks | %Success |
|---|---|---|
| No side channel (random) | 5475/11199 | 48.8% |
| Side channel | 9923/10783 | 92% |

Experimentally, we found that the malware could overcome the noise in the side channel by only performing attacks when the channel indicated relatively stable time intervals between the checks (Listing 1.3). Our test malware computed the time interval between the previously observed security check and the latest observed security check. Ideally, we expect this delta to be close to 1 s (based on public code for *WhatTheApp*). If the delta value was between 800 ms and 1200 ms, then the malware assumed that side channel information was relatively stable and it launched an attack window; otherwise, it waited for the next stable interval. Thus, this algorithm is conservative and does not utilize all possible intervals, only those that it deemed stable for attack. Experimentally, we found this algorithm to be effective, as detailed below.

**Quantifying the efficacy of the side channel.** We conducted an experiment to quantify how much the side channel helps improve the stealthiness of the click-jack attack. On an Android device running *WhatTheApp* defenses, we deployed a Facebook App and a background malware app (unprivileged). We launched Facebook automatically and brought it to the login screen for 20 s, then exited Facebook, slept a random amount of time (3 to 5 s) and repeated the process (this was done automatically). The background app launched its attack when Facebook's login screen was up. It then overlayed an attack window fashioned like a keyboard for 400 ms ten times during the 20 s interval. The aim was to realistically simulate user login and a malware's attempt to capture parts of the password during the login without getting detected by *WhatTheApp*'s defenses, which were executing all the time. This process was repeated for 6 h to give us substantial amount of data for statistically valid results.

We compared two attack strategies (Table 2): (1) with no side channel information on the security checks; and (2) with exploiting the new side channel to predict the time till the next security check. The first strategy waited for Facebook to start and then began an attack sequence where a clickjacking window is shown for 400 ms followed by a pause of 600 ms where no window a shown, ten times with each 20-s duration when the Facebook's login window was up. Since the security check of *WhatTheApp* is 1 s apart, our random strategy aimed to randomly synchronize with the security checks so that it could elude the check for 10 consecutive clickjack events per login window display. We found that out of a total of 11199 attack events, 5724 attack events were caught and marked as yellow. This was generally consistent with our intuition in that if the first clickjacking event evaded the check (60% odds, since the attack window was 400 ms in each second), others were likely to evade as well in that attack window.

The side-channel strategy used the binder transaction statistics as an additional signal to help time the 400 ms long attacks. The process was same as the above in other respects, except that the 400 ms attack was only launched when dictated by the side channel. We again ran the experiment over 6 h with Facebook configured identically. There were a total of 10783 attacks out of which, only 860 were caught (i.e., security indicator's lock turned yellow)[3].

In summary, the random strategy, without side channel information, was found to be successful approximately 48.8% of the time compared to 92% of the time for the strategy using the binder log side-channel. Statistically, this is a significant increase in stealthiness. Our attack demonstrations are available here [13][4].

**Overlay attacks on a system window.** Based on the code of the *WhatTheApp* prototype (Listing 1.1, lines 3–4), we noticed that if the top activity was SYSTEM, the green lock icon stays on all the time. This was the case even if a malware window was layered on top of the system window. This enabled our test malware to freely display attack windows over sensitive system apps such as the default EMail client and WiFi password boxes and capture the input. We also tried this attack using random show/hide durations and the lock icon visualization always remained green. We believe this attack is possible due to an implementation flaw in *WhatTheApp*—the defense does not inspect the identities of all windows on the stack when the foreground window is of type SYSTEM.

---

[3] There are slightly fewer attacks than the random strategy since the channel strategy is conservative and chooses to let some intervals go without attack attempts rather than to risk detection.

[4] Our attack demonstrations in the video use a window type that captures input without passing the input to the underlying window. We subsequently verified that our attacks are feasible using toast windows, that allow input to be both captured and passed to the underlying window; in this case the user will not notice missing characters.

# 5   Proposed Design

Addressing the problem we illustrated with the *WhatTheApp* UI defense turns out to be tricky with some tradeoffs. We thus describe two solutions to the problem, with the first solution a variant of Bianchi's solution to make it harder to evade check logic and the second solution introducing an additional mechanism to render window overlay attempts by background apps harmless. The second solution is more robust from a security perspective, and thus more appropriate for high-assurance environments, but it also limits some aspects of the way Android apps are allowed to interact with users.

Before we describe the two designs, we note that this paper is not about the design of security indicators. We assume that both designs that we are presenting use security indicators in the style of *WhatTheApp* since end-users found them to be effective according to a systematic user study conducted by Bianchi *et al.* Instead, the goal of this paper is to provide systematic defenses against the newly discovered vulnerabilities that are discussed in Sects. 3 and 4.

## 5.1   Design 1: Improving Attack Detection with Existing UI Defenses

An obvious first step towards defense is to plug the newly discovered side channel by preventing access to information in `/sys/kernel/debug/binder` to apps. However, other side channels cannot be ruled out. There are other shared resources (e.g., lock on the window manager) that could potentially leak timing data. A more robust strategy could be to randomize the security check time intervals in *WhatTheApp*. Unfortunately, even that would not rule out successful attacks. Some characters could still be stolen via clickjacking as intervals where no checks take place would still exist.

Furthermore, transient windows like Toasts or Chat heads or Now-on-Tap-style widgets occur in Android normally. Those would turn the lock yellow, perhaps desensitizing a user to occasional occurrences of a yellow lock.

*WhatTheApp* has a potential implementation error where SYSTEM-owned windows can be pre-empted without a change in indicator visualization because the code assumes the system is safe if the top level activity is system-owned. A simple fix is to use the same logic for system windows that is used for other apps, namely, checking that all activites in the stack are from the SYSTEM when the top-level activity is SYSTEM. We confirmed that this fix helps, however, clickjack attacks remain feasible.

Thus, overall, interceptions of user input by malware via clickjacking becomes harder, but remains feasible, despite the additional defenses. The fundamental problem is that short-duration clickjacking attacks can go undetected if they fall between security checks.

## 5.2   Design 2: Secure Entry Mode Using an Overlay Mutex

Design 2 blocks clickjacking attacks while the soft keyboard is being used. In the current proof-of-concept prototype, we focused on deploying the defenses of design

2 whenever the soft keyboard is used since that is a typical method for entering passwords and sensitive input, leaving generalizations to other inputs as future work. Note that our overlay mutex algorithms, however, are independent of the specific mechanism used for activation. As in *WhatTheApp*, design 2 requires the user to verify the green lock and app name in the security bar once, after a soft keyboard comes up, but before entering any sensitive text input (e.g., a password). Unlike *WhatTheApp*, Design 2 guarantees that any keyboard input entered goes to the identified app only, even if background malware attempts to perform clickjack attacks to intercept input secretly by exploiting the binder side channel.

**Overlay Mutex.** To provide the guarantee, design 2 uses a novel security mechanism that we term *overlay mutex* designed as an addition to Android's UI stack. Overlay mutex utilizes an inter-process synchronization lock, as opposed to the visual green/yellow lock in Bianchi *et al.* The overlay mutex is acquired and released on behalf the foreground app, whenever the soft keyboard is shown and hidden respectively. It provides the following invariant during the period that an overlay mutex is held:

*A background non-system app cannot overlay a window on top of the foreground app's window(s). Instead, an attempt to do so is converted to a safe user notification.*

On Android, the invariant has a significant implication with respect to the ability of a background app to surreptitiously become the foreground app and hijack input (see the Activity Hijacking attack discussion in Sect. 2). The net result of the above is that a background app cannot tamper with the screen in arbitrary ways, cannot become the foreground app unless the user explicitly chooses to switch, and it cannot therefore intercept the input intended for the foreground app. We elaborate on that below.

Background apps have three options to pre-empt foreground apps. Toasts are customizable transient windows and Activities are full screen windows that can be created by malicious apps. Also, arbitrary sized windows can be created and added to the window hierarchy by directly invoking `WindowManager.addView`.

The overlay mutex mechanism prevents all pre-emption attack vectors. When the overlay mutex is active, a background app's request to display a window is blocked. The active overlay mutex converts the pre-emption window into a system-generated, fixed-size textual notification with the interrupting app's identity. Our system displays the notification on the Android status bar at the top of the screen. Since malware has no control over the size and placement of these notifications, the ability of the background app to involuntarily cause a switch or overlay a window in unexpected ways is taken away. Furthermore, the precise timing of the switch is no longer under the control of the attacker. Upon seeing a notification, users can voluntarily resume the pre-empting window by tapping on the notification, after they have inspected the identity information—interrupts are not lost, merely delayed. We do not think this is particularly limiting for practical use in high assurance apps since other cues exist. Audio and haptic alerts can serve to draw the user's attention to the notification.

**Overlay Mutex Algorithm.** We discuss the logic of the Overlay Mutex in the case of the Android operating system. The Overlay Mutex is two functions

in the ActivityManager—EnterSecureMode and ExitSecureMode. Whenever
policy dictates that secure input should be available (such as when a keyboard is displayed), the EnterSecureMode function executes (Listing 1.6). First,
EnterSecureMode attempts to gain a synchronization lock maintained centrally
by the activity management service. The second step is to verify the identity of
the foreground app and update the visualization of the security indicator appropriately. The third step is to store a state variable CurrentVerifApp that is used
for checks during pre-emption attempts and finally release the activity manager
lock. ExitSecureMode simply resets the value of CurrentVerifApp.

If secure mode is disabled (CurrentVerifApp is null), windows can show up
at any point in time and the security indicator updates itself once a second to
reflect the current state of the display—no change from *WhatTheApp*.

Consider the case where secure mode is enabled (CurrentVerifApp is set
to an app's package name) and a background process tries to display an activity, pre-empting the user's current secure mode. If the background process is
the system, as a matter of policy, we let this pre-emption attempt succeed and
update our CurrentVerifApp state variable appropriately. The security indicator updates itself in the usual way.

However, if the background service does not have the same package name
as the current verified app, then we hold that pre-emption attempt and instead
show a safe notification to the user (Lines 9–10, Listing 1.4). This provides the
Overlay Mutex security guarantee that windows of unrelated provenance will
not appear on the display.

**Listing 1.4.** StartActivity

```
1  void ActivityMgr.startActivity() {
2    ActivityMgr.lock()
3    if(CurrentVerifApp == NULL or
4    callerUID == SYSTEM or
5    callerUID == CurrentVerifApp.UID) {
6      newAct = showActivity()
7      updateTopStackActivity(newAct)
8    } else {
9      ConvertActivityToNotification()
10     ShowSafeNotification()
11   }
12   ActivityMgr.unlock()
13 }
```

**Listing 1.5.** Adding a window to the display

```
1  status_code WindowMgr.AddView() {
2    retval = ERROR
3    ActivityMgr.lock() //IPC
4    if(CurrentVerifApp == NULL or
5    callerUID == SYSTEM or
6    callerUID == CurrentVerifApp.UID) {
7      showWindow()
8      retval = SUCCESS
9    }
10   ActivityMgr.unlock() //IPC
11   return retval
12 }
```

**Listing 1.6.** Entering and exiting secure mode

```
1  void ActivityMgr.lock() {
2    lock(ActivityLock)
3  }
4
5  void ActivityMgr.unlock() {
6    unlock(ActivityLock)
7  }
8
9  void ActivityMgr.EnterSecureMode() {
10   ActivityMgr.lock()
11   CurrentVerifApp = getTopActivityId('EV')
12   updateSecurityBar(CurrentVerifApp)
13   ActivityMgr.unlock()
14 }
15
16 void ActivityMgr.ExitSecureMode() {
17   ActivityMgr.lock()
18   CurrentVerifApp = NULL
19   ActivityMgr.unlock()
20 }
```

**Implementation Details.** We prototyped the Overlay Mutex algorithms on top of the released source code of *WhatTheApp*. We modified the `ActivityManagerService` to create a synchronization lock and modified functions related to creating windows on the screen—`startActivity`, `Toast.show`, and `addView`. A noteworthy point with `addView` is that it directly adds windows to the screen without an associated activity. If an `addView` call fails with error (like in Listing 1.5), Android will not try again. We modified the Android in-process helper library to retry adding a window upon receipt of an error from the `WindowManager`. This ensures that `addView` will succeed at a later point once the user exits secure mode.

# 6   Defense Evaluation

We analyzed existing UI attacks found in the wild. These attacks are representative of the general set of techniques attackers use to launch UI attacks and cover all classes discussed in Sect. 2. We tested and compared Design 2 with *WhatTheApp* against these attacks. Design 1 has similar limitations as *WhatTheApp*, since it does not eliminate clickjacking attacks; it only makes them less likely. We summarize the findings in Table 3 and discuss below.

**Direct Phishing.** Neither defense can prevent direct phishing where the top activity itself engages in phishing. However, both will provide a security indicator to alert users to the EV-certified identity of the app (if available) or indicate a red lock. The behavior of the two solutions is identical. The user is expected to verify the identity of the app and the lock status before entering input. We tested this with the following attack on the Google Wallet SDK (AliPay SDK). Alipay allows apps to fire an unrestricted intent to the Play Store to request its use. Unfortunately, any app can intercept this intent with a high priority receiver and instead become the foreground activity, as opposed to the Google PlayStore, and solicit sensitive banking information. This is similar to Felt's intent hijacking example of direct phishing [8]. For defense, the users will need to verify the security indicator in the security bar and realize that the activity soliciting the information is not Google Play Store.

**Activity Hijacking.** The behavior of the Overlay Mutex with this attack depends on the policy in use. In the most popular keyboard policy that we discussed, if the hijacking is attempted while the user is performing input, then the hijacking attempt is converted to a safe notification. We verified this with Trojan-Banker.AndroidOS.Svpeng.A [21]. However, if the hijacking attempt occurs during a time where the user does not have the keyboard up then, just like *WhatTheApp*, the security indicator turns yellow and the attack becomes user-detectable provided the user checks the indicator before a subsequent input attempt. At this point, the user must not enter any input and should try again, as is the case with *WhatTheApp*.

**Clickjacking.** Whenever the user is performing input using the soft keyboard, the overlay mutex is active and catches pre-emption attempts converting them to

safe notifications thus preventing clickjacking. In contrast, *WhatTheApp* allows
the pre-emption and updates the security bar visualization to a yellow unlocked
icon. Since the transition of the attack window is very fast, chances are high
that a user misses the change in the security indicator. Therefore, we mark
*WhatTheApp* in Table 3 as unreliably detected. In the case of the clickjacking
attack using our newly discovered side channel, as shown earlier (Sect. 4), the
security indicator does not change to yellow 92% of the time.

**Table 3.** Summary of findings from UI deception attacks tested on Android v4.4 using
our Overlay Mutex and *WhatTheApp*.

| Malware behavior | Overlay Mutex | Bianchi *et al.* (verified on prototype) |
|---|---|---|
| Direct phishing of another app's data | User-detectable | User-detectable |
| Activity hijacking(e.g., Trojan-Banker.AndroidOS.Svpeng.A) | User-detectable | User-detectable |
| Clickjacking without side channel | Prevented | Unreliably detected |
| Clickjacking with side channel info | Prevented | Not detected or only rarely detected |
| Malware overlaying active system app while user performing input | Prevented | Not detected |

**Malware overlaying system app during user input.** In a similar vein, if an
overlay mutex is active during user input into a system app, the pre-emption is
converted to a safe notification. However, *WhatTheApp* does not recognize any
overlays on top of system apps and the security indicator is green. Therefore,
*WhatTheApp* does not detect such attacks. A fix that we made to *WhatTheApp*
in this special case is to check the window stack just like it does for non-system
apps. If this attack were applied to the patched-*WhatTheApp*, then the security
indicator would display yellow and the attack will be user-detectable.

**Microbenchmark Performance.** Our overlay mutex solution changes window
creation to make two IPC calls and one lock/unlock sequence. We quantified the
overhead of these extra operations to determine the impact on interactivity using
a UI bench that created and removed a $200 \times 200$ pixel window, 300 times. We
ran our benchmark on a Nexus 4 running stock Android 4.4 and Android 4.4 with
the overlay mutex's secure mode active. We observed that, on average, it took
17.7 *upmus* for a window to display on stock Android compared to 35.3 *upmus*
on Android with our defense—a modest increase in window display time. For
comparison, launching an Android activity takes several hundred milliseconds.

**App Compatibility.** We manually tested popular apps by exercising common
functionality associated with each app on our overlay mutex prototype, and
observed whether any functionality failed. We used the following set and did not

observe any issues: standard (Messaging, Browser, Email, Search, Contacts), social networking (Facebook, Twitter), communication and business (Skype, TaxACT), banking (Chase, Bank of America), and top 2 free games (Angry Birds, Trivia Crack). For instance, we brought up the keyboard in Facebook (thereby gaining the Overlay Mutex), and initiated a Skype call from another device. The overlay mutex caught the Skype-initiated pre-emption for an incoming call, and later, when we clicked on the notification, the incoming call window pre-empted Facebook. The caller side experienced a delayed call answer.

## 7   Discussion

The attacks in this paper concerned stealing key input, such as passwords, credit card numbers, etc. However, clickjacking has a broader meaning—an attacker could display malicious windows strategically placed over UI elements to confuse the user. For example, a window placed over a permission listing screen can serve misinformation to the user about the permissions a particular app requests, or windows placed over "OK" and "Cancel" buttons can reverse their meaning. Such attacks are possible in limited situations on *WhatTheApp*. In the case of overlaying a system window, such attacks will go unnoticed. In the general case of overlaying any window, a flickering effect will occur since the attacker has to add and remove the attack window so that the security check does not turn yellow. In the case of our overlay mutex, such attacks will be blocked, and converted to notifications.

The iOS platform too has been a victim of recent UI deception attacks [6,34]. These attacks exploit the lack of UI provenance. For instance, the common iCloud popup password boxes are indistinguishable from fake ones. The recent Android Marshmallow update does not offer any UI provenance or overlay mutex mechanisms—UI deception attacks are still possible.

A limitation of our work is the lack of a usability study to assess effectiveness of the defenses in practice and to determine whether users require training to make effective use of the defenses. Another limitation is that the overlay mutex mechanism could cause side-effects on functionality of existing apps or certain use cases. While we did test a small set of apps manually, as future work, we plan systematic testing of the mechanism with a larger set of apps [19].

## 8   Related Work

UI deception, or phishing, has a long history of attacks and defenses, initially occurring in the context of browsers [14,15,26,31,32]. The fundamental issue that attackers exploit is lack of provenance. Even when provenance exists, practice has shown that users' lack of understanding of security indicators, visually similar UIs, and lack of user attention conspire to make phishing attacks very successful [15]. UI deception attacks also use other attack vectors as enhancements, e.g., phishing emails are a common way to get users to visit phishing pages [18].

A large body of previous work has focused on various forms of UI attacks on smartphone operating systems. Niemietz *et al.* introduced UI redressing attacks [25], Felt *et al.* discuss phishing on mobile devices [16] and Chen *et al.* [11] introduce a memory-statistics side channel that is used to enhance classic activity hijacking attacks [3,4,12]. svpeng demonstrates that UI deception occurs in the wild and uses the activity hijacking technique [21]. All these serve to motivate the necessity for a technical solution to UI deception.

Tong and Evans introduced GuarDroid, a trusted path for password entry that uses a trusted keyboard to encrypt sensitive information before delivering to apps and then automatically decrypts the data upon network communication [28]. However, endpoints of this system are still vulnerable to overlay attacks. Therefore, Bianchi *et al.* propose a two-layered defense comprising a market-level static analysis tool to catch particularly malicious patterns of UI deception. This tool is augmented with a runtime defense modeled after the well-known HTTPS lock icon and EV infrastructure [7]. We regard this work as the state-of-the-art and presented its detailed analysis in Sect. 3, along with a click-jacking vulnerability and a newly discovered side channel that makes clickjacking very effective.

Recently, Android 5.0 introduced the screen-pinning feature that locks the user into a single app and prevents navigation away from that app unless the owner explicitly exits screen-pinning using an unlock code [27]. However, screen-pinning is fundamentally different from overlay mutexes as they are not intended as a UI deception defense mechanism. We verified that direct phishing attacks and clickjacking attacks are possible on screen-pinned apps.

Huang *et al.* proposed InContext, a suite of defenses targetting visual and temporal integrity of browser UI elements [20]. Their solution requires introducing a delay of 250 ms or higher between the time the user issues an input command and the time the command is delivered to the browser UI element. Besides the potential impact on interactivity, subsequent work has demonstrated that defenses relying on time delays are still vulnerable to clickjacking [5]. Our work does not rely on delays and instead locks out window transitions while the user is performing secure input, converting attempted overlays to notifications.

## 9  Conclusion

Android is vulnerable to a wide range of UI attacks. The standard solution to handling UI attacks is to use security indicators to assist users in identifying the attacks and recent solutions have proposed security indicators inspired by HTTPS lock icons for Android [7]. We studied the security properties of a recent system by Bianchi *et al.* and determined that it remains vulnerable to side-channel-enhanced clickjacking attacks. Our work introduced the Binder statistics channel and demonstrated how to leverage it to elude security checks. We proposed the overlay mutex mechanism that guarantees temporal integrity of security indicators by converting window pre-emption attempts to safe notifications. We evaluated our defense against known UI deception as well as the new side channel attack introduced in this paper and found that the defense is effective against these attacks.

**Acknowledgements.** We thank the reviewers for their insightful feedback. This material is based upon work supported by the National Science Foundation under Grant No. 1318722. Any opinions, findings, and conclusions or recommendations expressed in this material are those of the author(s) and do not necessarily reflect the views of the National Science Foundation.

# References

1. Android UI Deception PoC Code. https://github.com/earlence/AndroidUI DeceptionRevisitedFC16. Accessed Oct 2015
2. Apple XCodeGhost Attack. http://www.apple.com/cn/xcodeghost/#english. Accessed Oct 2015
3. Activity hijacking pattern for Android. http://capec.mitre.org/data/definitions/501.html. Accessed Oct 2015
4. Android Touch-Event Hijacking. https://blog.lookout.com/blog/2010/12/09/android-touch-event-hijacking/. Accessed Oct 2015
5. Akhawe, D., He, W., Li, Z., Moazzezi, R., Song, D.: Clickjacking revisited: a perceptual view of UI security. In: Proceedings of the 8th USENIX Conference on Offensive Technologies, WOOT 2014, pp. 1–1. USENIX Association, Berkeley, CA, USA (2014). http://dl.acm.org/citation.cfm?id=2671293.2671294
6. Lovejoy, B.: Beware authentication popups in iOS Mail: bug allows convincing-looking phishing attacks. http://9to5mac.com/2015/06/10/ios-mail-phishing-popup/. Accessed Dec 2015
7. Bianchi, A., Corbetta, J., Invernizzi, L., Fratantonio, Y., Kruegel, C., Vigna, G.: What the app. is that? deception and countermeasures in the android user interface. In: Proceedings of the IEEE Symposium on Security and Privacy (SP), San Jose, CA, May 2015
8. Castillo, C.: McAfee Labs. Phishing attack replaces banking app. with malware. Published. http://blogs.mcafee.com/mcafee-labs/phishing-attack-replaces-android-banking-apps-with-malware. Accessed Oct 2015
9. Chebyshev, V., Unuchek, R.: Mobile malware evolution in 2013. http://secure list.com/analysis/kaspersky-security-bulletin/58335/mobile-malware-evolution-2013/. Accessed Oct 2015
10. Chen, J., Chen, H., Bauman, E., Lin, Z., Zang, B., Guan, H.: You shouldn't collect my secrets: thwarting sensitive keystroke leakage in mobile ime apps. In: 24th USENIX Security Symposium (USENIX Security 15), pp. 657–690. USENIX Association, Washington, D.C. https://www.usenix.org/conference/usenixsecurity15/technical-sessions/presentation/chen-jin
11. Chen, Q.A., Qian, Z., Mao, Z.M.: Peeking into your app. without actually seeing it: ui state inference and novel android attacks. In: Proceedings of the 23rd USENIX Security Symposium (2014)
12. Chin, E., Felt, A.P., Greenwood, K., Wagner, D.: Analyzing inter-application communication in android. In: Proceedings of the 9th International Conference on Mobile Systems, Applications, and Services, MobiSys 2011, pp. 239–252, NY, USA (2011). http://doi.acm.org/10.1145/1999995.2000018

13. Clickjacking SideChannel Demonstration videos. https://sites.google.com/site/clickjackingsidechannels/. Accessed Oct 2015

14. Dhamija, R., Tygar, J.D.: The battle against phishing: dynamic security skins. In: Proceedings of the 2005 Symposium on Usable Privacy and Security, SOUPS 2005, pp. 77–88, NY, USA (2005). http://doi.acm.org/10.1145/1073001.1073009

15. Dhamija, R., Tygar, J.D., Hearst, M.: Why phishing works. In: Proceedings of the SIGCHI Conference on Human Factors in Computing Systems, CHI 2006, pp. 581–590, NY, USA (2006). http://doi.acm.org/10.1145/1124772.1124861

16. Felt, A.P., Wagner, D.: Phishing on mobile devices. In: W2SP (2011)

17. Fernandes, E., Chen, Q., Essl, G., Halderman, J.A., Mao, Z.M., Prakash, A.: TIVOs: trusted visual I/O paths for android. Technical report CSE-TR-586-14, CSE Department, University of Michigan, Ann Arbor (2014)

18. Fette, I., Sadeh, N., Tomasic, A.: Learning to detect phishing emails. In: Proceedings of the 16th International Conference on World Wide Web, WWW 2007, pp. 649–656, NY, USA (2007). http://doi.acm.org/10.1145/1242572.1242660

19. Hao, S., Liu, B., Nath, S., Halfond, W.G., Govindan, R.: PUMA: programmable UI-automation for large-scale dynamic analysis of mobile apps. In: Proceedings of the 12th Annual International Conference on Mobile Systems, Applications, and Services, MobiSys 2014, pp. 204–217, NY, USA (2014). http://doi.acm.org/10.1145/2594368.2594390

20. Huang, L.S., Moshchuk, A., Wang, H.J., Schechter, S., Jackson, C.: Clickjacking: attacks and defenses. In: Proceedings of the 21st USENIX Conference on Security Symposium, Security 2012, pp. 22–22. USENIX Association, Berkeley, CA, USA (2012). http://dl.acm.org/citation.cfm?id=2362793.2362815

21. Kaspersky: svpeng android malware targets banking apps. http://www.kaspersky.com/about/news/virus/2014/Kaspersky-Lab-detects-mobile-Trojan-Svpeng-Financial-malware-with-ransomware-capabilities-now-targeting-US-users. Accessed Oct 2015

22. Kelly, M.: Badlepricon: bitcoin gets the mobile malware treatment in Google Play. https://blog.lookout.com/blog/2014/04/24/badlepricon-bitcoin/. Accessed Oct 2015

23. Liu, B., Nath, S., Govindan, R., Liu, J.: DECAF: detecting and characterizing ad fraud in mobile apps. In: NSDI (2014)

24. Liu, D., Cuervo, E., Pistol, V., Scudellari, R., Cox, L.P.: ScreenPass: secure password entry on touchscreen devices. In: Proceeding of the 11th Annual International Conference on Mobile Systems, Applications, and Services, MobiSys 2013, pp. 291–304, NY, USA (2013). http://doi.acm.org/10.1145/2462456.2465425

25. Niemietz, M., Schwenk, J.: UI redressing attacks on android devices. In: Proceedings of BlackHat Abu Dhabi (2012)

26. Schechter, S.E., Dhamija, R., Ozment, A., Fischer, I.: The emperor's new security indicators. In: Proceedings of the 2007 IEEE Symposium on Security and Privacy, SP 2007, pp. 51–65 (2007). http://dx.doi.org/10.1109/SP.2007.35

27. Android 5.0 Screen Pinning. https://support.google.com/nexus/answer/6118421?hl=en. Accessed Oct 2015

28. Tong, T., Evans, D.: GuarDroid: a trusted path for password entry. In: Proceedings of Mobile Security Technologies (MoST) (2013)

29. TrendMicro: mobile phishing attacks ask for government ids. http://blog.trendmicro.com/trendlabs-security-intelligence/mobile-phishing-attack-asks-for-users-government-ids/. Accessed Oct 2015

30. Unuchek, R.: Svpeng android malware targets Google Play with fake credit card window. http://securelist.com/blog/incidents/63746/latest-version-of-svpeng-targets-users-in-us/. Accessed Oct 2015

31. Whittaker, C., Ryner, B., Nazif, M.: Large-scale automatic classification of phishing pages. In: NDSS (2010)

32. Wu, M., Miller, R.C., Garfinkel, S.L.: Do security toolbars actually prevent phishing attacks? In: Proceedings of the SIGCHI Conference on Human Factors in Computing Systems, CHI 2006, pp. 601–610, NY, USA (2006). http://doi.acm.org/10.1145/1124772.1124863

33. Zhang, Y., Xue, H., Wei, T.: Occupy your icons silently on android. http://www.fireeye.com/blog/technical/2014/04/occupy_your_icons_silently_on_android.html. Accessed Oct 2015

34. Chen, Z., Wei, T., Xue, H., Zhang, Y.: Three new masque attacks against iOS: demolishing, breaking and hijacking. https://www.fireeye.com/blog/threat-research/2015/06/three_new_masqueatt.html. Accessed Dec 2015

# Introducing Reputation Systems to the Economics of Outsourcing Computations to Rational Workers

Jassim Aljuraidan[1](✉), Lujo Bauer[1], Michael K. Reiter[2], and Matthias Beckerle[1]

[1] Carnegie Mellon University, Pittsburgh, PA, USA
jaljurai@andrew.cmu.edu
[2] University of North Carolina at Chapel Hill, Chapel Hill, NC, USA

**Abstract.** Outsourcing computation to remote parties ("workers") is an increasingly common practice, owing in part to the growth of cloud computing. However, outsourcing raises concerns that outsourced tasks may be completed incorrectly, whether by accident or because workers cheat to minimize their cost and optimize their gain. The goal of this paper is to explore, using game theory, the conditions under which the incentives for all parties can be configured to efficiently disincentivize worker misbehavior, either inadvertent or deliberate. By formalizing multiple scenarios with game theory, we establish conditions to discourage worker cheating that take into account the dynamics of multiple workers, workers with limited capacity, and changing levels of trust. A key novelty of our work is modeling the use of a reputation system to decide how computation tasks are allocated to workers based on their reliability, and we provide insights on strategies for using a reputation system to increase the expected quality of results. Overall, our results contribute to make outsourcing computation more reliable, consistent, and predictable.

## 1 Introduction

A powerful recent trend in computing has been the outsourcing of computation tasks to other parties. This trend has spanned the government and commercial sectors, with examples of outsourcing ranging from scientific computation (e.g., CERN's grid computing[1], and the Folding@home distributed computing project for disease research[2]) to commercial web and content delivery services (e.g., Netflix's use of Amazon's EC2[3]) and sensitive government computing tasks (e.g., the U.S. Central Intelligence Agency's use of Amazon's cloud[4] and the U.S.

---

[1] http://home.web.cern.ch/about/computing/worldwide-lhc-computing-grid.

[2] https://folding.stanford.edu/.

[3] http://www.theatlantic.com/technology/archive/2014/07/the-details-about-the-cias-deal-with-amazon/374632/.

[4] https://aws.amazon.com/cloudfront/.

© International Financial Cryptography Association 2017
J. Grossklags and B. Preneel (Eds.): FC 2016, LNCS 9603, pp. 60–77, 2017.
DOI: 10.1007/978-3-662-54970-4_4

Department of State's use of Datamaxx[5]). The use of cloud infrastructure brings many advantages, including a high degree of flexibility and cost savings.

At the same time, outsourcing computation carries inherent risks for the party doing the outsourcing (which we call the *outsourcer*). Since the compute infrastructure is not under control of the outsourcing party, the correctness of these computations cannot necessarily be trusted. In particular, the parties to whom tasks have been outsourced (*workers*) may have an economic incentive to perform sub-standard work (e.g., to guess at answers, saving computational effort; or to use sub-standard hardware, increasing chance of data loss). To reassure customers, service level agreements (SLAs) and increasingly precise and complex certification requirements for cloud providers (e.g., the FBI's CJIS security policy requirements[6]) are often devised.

In parallel with such steps, crucial to increasing the trustworthiness of outsourcing is to understand how to leverage technical mechanisms for verifying that outsourced tasks are being performed correctly and to appropriately reward correct and penalize incorrect behavior. To that end, researchers have used game-theoretic models of outsourcing to determine the optimal strategies and parameters to be used by the party interested in outsourcing (e.g., [4,18]). More specifically, recent work in the context of single-round games has shown how to wield incentives such as fines, budgets, and auditing rates to design optimal outsourcing contracts with one or two workers [18].

In this paper we extend this line of work on game-theoretic analysis of economic incentives to encompass richer, more realistic scenarios. In particular, our models consider two additional important factors. First, we use infinite-round (rather than single- or limited-round) games to model the realistic long-term interaction between the outsourcer and the workers. Second, we explore the use of two forms of simple reputation systems as a mechanism for outsourcers to choose how to direct future outsourcing tasks based on past performance and to model the realistic incentive of the outsourcing of future tasks depending on the successful completion of earlier ones. Using these models, we show which values of the game parameters (e.g., job cost, how much workers value future transactions as opposed to current ones) ensure that the workers have no incentive to cheat, i.e., that an equilibrium exists only when all workers play honestly. We calculate these values for five games representing different scenarios. In addition, we demonstrate the practical implications of our results.

This paper proceeds as follows. We describe related work in Sect. 2 and provide a more detailed problem description in Sect. 3. Section 4 presents our main results. Section 5 summarizes our findings and concludes the paper.

## 2   Background and Related Work

The problem of outsourcing computations to untrusted workers is an active area of research, with multiple general approaches being advanced simultaneously.

---

[5] https://www.datamaxx.com/.

[6] https://www.fbi.gov/about-us/cjis/cjis-security-policy-resource-center.

One direction, surveyed by Walfish and Blumberg [24], uses advances in probabilistically checkable proofs (e.g., [10]) and/or interactive proofs (e.g., [8]) to enable an outsourcer to determine that a worker probably performed an outsourced task correctly, at a cost less than that of performing the task itself. This approach to verification is largely complementary to the incentive frameworks that we propose here, in the sense that an outsourcer could use this approach to verify a worker's computation when it chooses to do so in the context of our framework. However, since this approach requires changes to the worker software that can increase the worker's computational cost by orders of magnitude (e.g., see [24, Fig. 5]), we do not consider its use here.

An alternative approach is to leverage trusted computing technologies to improve the trustworthiness of workers. For example, Trusted Platform Modules [23] permit a worker machine to attest to the software it runs; provided that the outsourcer trusts the worker's hardware, it can have confidence that the worker will execute the attested software to perform the outsourcer's task. The emergence of Intel's SGX [2,9,14] should make this approach more practical (e.g., [20]). Again, however, these approaches are complementary to ours; rather than leverage trusted hardware primitives to gain confidence in workers, we apply incentives, instead.

Use of game theory to reason about allocation of jobs to distributed entities has been considered previously, such as in the context of grid computing (e.g., [3,17,26]). The work that is most related to ours, however, is on incentive-based approaches that utilize rewards and fines to ensure the honesty of workers when outsourcing computations. Belenkiy et al. first analyzed the idea of using rewards, fines, and bounties (given to workers who catch other workers cheating) to incentivize (rational) workers to behave honestly [4]. In their work on computation-outsourcing contracts, Pham et al. explore the best options when making such contracts to ensure workers' honesty while minimizing the cost to the outsourcer [18]. While these works [4,18] do cover scenarios with more than two workers, neither models multi-round interactions or the use of reputation systems as a mechanism to incentivize workers to be honest.

More recent work by Nojoumian et al. [16] uses a specific reputation system [15] to incentivize players in a secret-sharing scheme to cooperate. However, the mechanics of the secret-sharing game are different than the computation outsourcing game we are considering here. For example, the concept of testing or verifying results at a certain frequency and its effect on detecting cheaters in computation outsourcing does not have an equivalent in the secret-sharing game. In addition, the reputation system used in that work would be a poor fit in our scenario. That reputation system gives significant leeway to cheaters, which does not interfere with assuring honesty in the secret-sharing game but would make it significantly harder to guarantee honesty in our setting.

The implementation of a reputation system as used in our game of outsourcing has similarities to, but also important differences from, those of *game triggers* [7,13]. Game triggers are strategies that make non-optimal choices for a fixed period after a trigger event (e.g., prices falling below some threshold or another player choosing to not cooperate) as a punishment, and are used by the players themselves to influence the behavior of other players in repeated noncooperative games. For example, they are often used in games that model cartels [5,19], where cartel members use these strategies, e.g., by selling goods at lower prices for a period of time to maintain higher prices overall. In our setting, reputation systems are (and are modeled as) an integral part of an infinite-round game and are imposed by the outsourcer, not the players (i.e., workers). With game triggers, punishments usually affect all players, while in our setting punishment affects only the offending player. Another difference between game triggers and our work is that with game trigger strategies each player in the game can choose whether to use them, while in our setting the outsourcer enforces the reputation system on all players. Finally, while game triggers are used in repeated games, the games in our setting are single games with multiple rounds with explicit state (i.e., player reputations) that influence the game at each round.

## 3    Problem Description and Notation

In this section we describe the aspects of our models and the assumptions we make, common to all the games that we explore. We also provide a brief explanation of our formal notation, which is summarized in Table 1.

All the games described in the paper share two main concepts. First, we include a simple *reputation* system, which assigns (dynamic) ratings to the workers and analyze how such systems can deter workers from cheating. Second, all

**Table 1.** Summary of notation. We assume that cost $(C)$, markup $(m)$, the discount factor $(\alpha)$, and detection probability $(p)$ are the same for all workers.

| | |
|---|---|
| $W_i$ | The worker $i$ |
| $IR_i$ | The initial reputation of $W_i$ |
| $N_i$ | The capacity of $W_i$, i.e., how many jobs $W_i$ can handle per round |
| $C$ | The cost for a worker to calculate the results for one job correctly $(C > 0)$ |
| $m$ | The markup or profit for each worker $(m > 0)$ |
| $\alpha$ | The discount factor that reduces the utility of each round; the effective utility of round $i$, assuming the first round is round 0, is the round's utility multiplied by $\alpha^i$ $(0 < \alpha < 1$, except in Game 2.2, where $\alpha = 1)$ |
| $q_i$ | The probability, per job, that $W_i$ will cheat $(0 < q_i \leq 1)$ |
| $t_i$ | The probability that the outsourcer will verify a job done by $W_i$ |
| $p$ | The probability that a worker who cheated on a job will be detected, given that the outsourcer verify the job |
| $n$ | Number of workers in group one (when there are two groups of workers) |
| $G$ | Total number of workers |
| $N$ | Number of jobs available in each round |

the games in this paper have an infinite number of rounds; considering multiple rounds is an essential requirement for a reputation system to be beneficial.

## 3.1   Basic Game Structure

We have two classes of entities in our games. The first is the outsourcer. The outsourcer provides *jobs* in the form of computations. The second class of entities are the workers that perform the computations and send the results back to the outsourcer. All our games have at least two workers. Moreover, in all these games the outsourcer is not an active player; that is, all the outsourcer's moves are based on a pre-specified algorithm, which we describe below, that decides how to distribute jobs to workers in each round of the game based on the game state (worker ratings).

The goal of all workers in the described games is to optimize their utility (i.e., benefits or gain). All parties are considered perfectly rational and all the games are noncooperative. That is, the workers are only interested in maximizing their own expected utility and are not cooperating with other players. Moreover, they are capable of performing any complex reasoning in order to achieve the maximum utility. The players only act maliciously (i.e., cheat) if it improves their expected utility. In addition, we don't take into account the risk-awareness of the workers, and we assume that all workers are risk neutral. This implies that they only care about the *expected* utility, and won't prefer one outcome over the other if both result in the same utility.

In order to make the total expected utility for each player finite, we employ a discount factor $\alpha$ ($0 < \alpha < 1$; except for Game 2.2 where $\alpha = 1$) per round, as is common. That is, the effective utility at round $i$ is the round's utility multiplied by $\alpha^i$. This discount factor is applied not only to calculate the utility but also to model the fact that in real life, people tend to value immediate gains more than gains in the future.

In each game we analyze, the goal will be to find the sufficient conditions to ensure that the only equilibrium that is possible is the one where all workers are honest. More specifically, the equilibrium we are considering is the Nash equilibrium, which requires that no single player be able to increase her utility by only changing her strategy, with strategies of all other players being the same.

We next provide a general description how the games in this paper are played out. The concrete games in Sects. 4.1 and 4.2 provide additional details like the number and grouping of workers, the initial setup, and the specific strategies of the players.

- At the beginning of each round the outsourcer offers $N$ jobs to all or some of the $G$ available workers and expects correct results in return. Performing the computation for a single job costs each worker $C$ ($C > 0$). For each job offered, a worker can either play honest or decide to cheat. If a worker cheats on a job, e.g., by guessing at the result instead of computing it, the cost of that job to the worker is considered to be 0. On returning a job's result, except as discussed below, each worker is paid $C + m$ by the outsourcer; we call $m$ the markup or profit ($m > 0$).

All strategies are mixed strategies; i.e., each choice is assigned a probability. For example, the probability of a worker to cheat on any given job might be 0.6. Each worker decides on a probability to cheat $q_i$ ($0 \leq q_i \leq 1$).

- The outsourcer will (randomly) verify some of the results returned by workers; the probability that the outsourcer will verify a particular job's result from worker $W_i$ is $t_i$. If a worker cheats and the outsourcer verifies the result, then the outsourcer detects the cheating with probability $p$. If the outsourcer detects that a returned result is wrong, i.e., the worker cheated, the worker gets penalized through a loss of reputation (see Sect. 3.2). If the outsourcer does not detect that a worker cheated in a round, either because it did not verify any of that worker's responses or because its verification attempts for that worker failed to detect misbehavior, then (and only then) does the outsourcer pay the worker for all the jobs it completed in that round. That is, a worker is given only *post-payments* and, in particular, does not receive any payment in a round where its cheating is detected.

The decisions to verify a result or to cheat are made randomly (Bernoulli distributions with parameters $t_i$ and $q_i$, respectively) and each decision is independent from the others. Also, in the remainder of this paper, when we refer to a worker being honest, we mean that $q_i = 0$ for the entire game, as opposed to deciding not to cheat on a single job. Similarly, when refering to a worker cheating or being dishonest, we specifically mean that $0 < q_i \leq 1$ for an entire game. Moreover, we don't distinguish between a worker being honest because cheating will decrease her utility and her being honest because other external (e.g., moral) incentives. In both cases, we will refer to her as an honest worker.

A key aspect that we examine in this paper is penalizing workers through the loss of future work. For this approach a reputation system is needed.

## 3.2 Reputation Systems

Reputations systems, especially those for on-line markets, are usually designed with one goal in mind: to share and compare results of former interactions with different entities. That gives customers or buyers a way to compare the quality of, e.g., products, service providers, or sellers [6,11].

Reputation systems differ in the assumptions made about service providers (or workers), with some assuming that all workers are inherently good or inherently bad [22], or that workers have a certain quality to be estimated [21,25]. Kerr et al. showed that many reputation systems will fail in the presence of cheaters who may offer good service on some occasions but cheat on others [12]. In our work we only assume that all workers are (infinitely) rational players, and as such will cheat if that increases their utility, but not otherwise. We believe that this threat model is more suitable for our setting of outsourcing potentially security sensitive computations to external workers whose incentives are not usually aligned a priori with the outsourcer.

One potential weakness of some reputation systems, particularly in the presence of opportunistic cheaters, is that they are not very reactive regarding recent rating changes, since they often only calculate a mean score over all interactions. In such systems, a long-time seller with excellent reputation might not care about a single bad rating since it might have negligible impact on his total score. Hence, even if sellers try to maintain a good overall reputation they might still cheat from time to time.

In this work, we employ a reputation system with variants that we call Zero-Reset and Knock-Out. If the Zero-Reset penalty is applied, the reputation of the cheating worker is reset to zero. The reputation then increases by 1, as for workers who had not been penalized, each time the worker completes a round without being caught cheating. Jobs are assigned to the worker $W_i$ with the highest reputation first, up to its capacity $N_i$. If more jobs are available than the workers with the highest reputation have capacity to handle, the workers with the next highest reputation will be assigned jobs, until all jobs are assigned. In case of a tie in reputation, the jobs are allocated randomly among the workers with the same reputation. If the Knock-Out penalty is applied, the cheating worker will no longer get jobs assigned by the outsourcer in any future round.

Both variants of the reputation system we study here are too strict for actual implementations. In reality, reputation systems should incorporate some leeway for accidental failures, such as user errors or network failures. Otherwise, workers will be discouraged from participating in the system. However, care must be taken to not give too much leeway as this will render systems susceptible to abuse by determined cheaters [12]. It is outside the scope of this paper to specify how much leeway should be given or what is the best reputation system to choose for actual implementations (which, we suspect, is application-dependent). For the purpose of this paper, we will assume that the actual implementation will be strict enough such that the conditions we derive for the various games we propose can serve as guidelines to narrow the space within which the incentives to all parties are aligned.

## 4     Improving Outsourcing with Reputation Systems

In this section, we show how a reputation system can be used to induce workers to maintain a high level of quality. All calculations are based on rational acting players that make optimal decisions regarding their own expected utility.

Table 2 shows the main differences between the games we explore. In general, we try to vary only one factor at a time between games, so as to make it possible to attribute different outcomes to specific variations in factors or assumptions.

In Sect. 4.1 we introduce the first set of games, which focuses on two workers that have, potentially different, initial reputations and play for an infinite number of rounds. The first game uses the Zero-Reset reputation system. The second game assumes that one worker has higher initial reputation, while the third game explores the effect of changing the reputation system to Knock-Out instead. After that, we investigate games with more than two workers in Sect. 4.2. We analyse

**Table 2.** Summary of games examined in this paper and their main assumptions.

| Game | Num. workers | Unlim. capacity | Rep. system | $\alpha$ | Notable assumptions |
|------|------|------|------|------|------|
| G1.1 | 2 | Yes | Zero-Reset | $< 1$ | $IR_1 = IR_2$; $N_1 \geq N$; $N_2 \geq N$ |
| G1.2 | | Worker 2 | Zero-Reset | $< 1$ | Same as G1.1 but: $IR_1 > IR_2$; $N \geq N_1$; $q_2 = 0$ |
| G1.3 | | Yes | Knock-Out | $< 1$ | Same as G1.2 but with Knock-Out |
| G2.1 | any | No | Zero-Reset | $< 1$ | 2 groups of workers; workers in the same group have the same $q$; $N = 1$ |
| G2.2 | | | Zero-Reset | n/a | Same as G2.1 but each worker has individual $q_i$; $N = 1$ |

two games, one with the workers split into two groups with a common choice for the cheating probability, and another game where workers are not grouped but no discount factor is considered (i.e., $\alpha = 1$).

Proofs for all the propositions can be found in our technical report [1].

### 4.1 First Set of Games: Two-Worker Games

We start our analysis with three games in which we consider scenarios with exactly two workers. We vary the capacity of the workers (we consider the case when both workers have more capacity than there is work available, as well as when one worker has insufficient capacity to perform all available work) and the reputation system we try.

**Game 1.1: Symmetric Initial Reputation.** In this first game we test our reputation system by using a simple scenario with only two workers. Both workers have the capacity to handle all the available jobs in each round ($N_1 \geq N$; $N_2 \geq N$), both workers start with the same initial reputation ($IR_1 = IR_2$), and both have the option to cheat ($q_1 \geq 0$; $q_2 \geq 0$).

**Proposition 1.** *For Game 1.1, with parameters $N$, $m$, $C$, $\alpha$, $p$, $t_1$, and $t_2$, if one worker ($W_2$) is always honest and one of the following conditions holds, then the only possible Nash equilibrium in the game will be the one where both workers are honest.*

– *$N = 1$, and*

$$\frac{m}{C} > (1 - \alpha)\frac{1 - p \cdot t_1}{p \cdot t_1} \tag{1}$$

– *Or, $N = 2k$, for some positive integer $k$, and*

$$\frac{m}{C} > (1 - \alpha)(1 - p \cdot t_1)\frac{(1 - p \cdot t_1)^{N/2 - 1}}{1 - (1 - p \cdot t_1)^{N/2}} \tag{2}$$

– *Or, $N = 2k + 1$, for some positive integer $k$, and*

$$\frac{m}{C} > (1 - \alpha)(1 - p \cdot t_1)\frac{(1 - p \cdot t_1)^{k-1}(1 - \frac{1}{2}p \cdot t_1)}{1 - (1 - p \cdot t_1)^{k}(1 - \frac{1}{2}p \cdot t_1)} \tag{3}$$

*Discussion.* The introduction of a reputation system leads to a clear benefit: as long as one worker ($W_2$) is honest and one of the conditions in Proposition 1 holds, the other worker ($W_1$) is forced to be honest too. Only the case where both workers decide to cheat stays unresolved for this game. In this case a repeating cycle of two stages takes place. Each cycle begins with both workers having equal reputations, and thus the jobs will be distributed equally (50%/50%). The first stage ends when one of the workers is detected cheating. In the second stage of a cycle the other worker will get all the jobs (100%/0% or 0%/100%); this stage lasts until this worker is detected cheating, which leads to an equal reputation of zero for both workers. The cycle repeats. This case results in a *noncentral hypergeometric distribution* for the job assignments, for which we have not yet found a closed-form solution. However, we will discuss the solution for the special case when $N = 1$ within the discussion of Game 1.3.

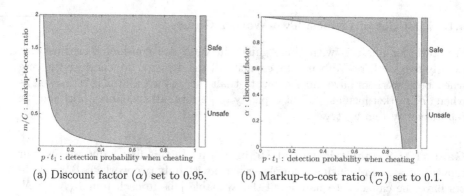

(a) Discount factor ($\alpha$) set to 0.95.     (b) Markup-to-cost ratio ($\frac{m}{C}$) set to 0.1.

**Fig. 1.** The safe region for the case of $N = 1$ in Game 1.1.

In Fig. 1a we plot the *safe* region, i.e., where not cheating is the only equilibrium, in terms of detection probability when cheating ($p \cdot t_1$) and the markup-to-cost ratio ($m/C$), with the discount factor set to 0.95. We do the same in Fig. 1b, but this time we fix the value of the markup-to-cost ratio to $m/C = 0.1$.

From the figures we can see that if the detection probability, i.e., the product of $p \cdot t_1$, is very small, then condition in Proposition 1 will be invalid for reasonable values of the markup-to-cost ratio and the discount factor. For example, if $p \cdot t_1 = 0.005$, then even the slightly extreme values of 0.99 and 1 for the discount factor and the markup, respectively, will not result in a safe outsourcing. In addition, it seems that discount factor $\alpha$ should be high enough, i.e., well above 0.90, for the valid range of $p \cdot t_1$ to be reasonable.

Let's imagine a company (outsourcer) wants to outsource scanning of incoming email attachments to a third party (worker). The results of this game show that, unless there is a large penalty or a high markup-to-cost ratio, a worker will have no incentive to be honest, because the probability of detection is very low in this case; an arbitrary email attachment has a very low chance of being malicious[7]. However, actively increasing $p$, for example by sending known malicious files to the third party, can significantly improve the chances that a worker will have no incentive to cheat.

In the next game we investigate asymmetric initial reputation combined with limited capacity of a worker.

**Game 1.2: One Worker with Higher Initial Reputation but Limited Capacity.** The assumption in game 1.1 that workers have equal initial reputation and unlimited capacity is a limitation that we remove in this game. We already considered the case when the initial reputations are equal, so we will assume that they are strictly different here.

Without loss of generality, we give $W_1$ a higher initial reputation compared to $W_2$. In addition, $W_1$'s capacity is limited, i.e., $W_1$'s capacity can always be saturated ($N > N_1$). We also tested the setup where both workers have limited capacity but since the interesting parts of the results were similar to Game 1.1, we only describe the former case here. As in game 1.1, both workers have the option to cheat ($q_1 \geq 0$; $q_2 \geq 0$).

**Proposition 2.** *For Game 1.2, with parameters $m$, $C$, $\alpha$, $p$, $t_1$, and $N_1$, if worker 2 is always honest and one of the following conditions holds, then the only possible Nash equilibrium in the game will be the one where worker 1 is also honest.*

– $N_1 = 1$, and

$$\frac{m}{C} > (1 - \alpha)\frac{1 - p \cdot t_1}{p \cdot t_1} \qquad (4)$$

– $N_1 > 1$, and

$$\frac{m}{C} > (1 - \alpha)(1 - p \cdot t_1)\frac{(1 - p \cdot t_1)^{N_1 - 1}}{1 - (1 - p \cdot t_1)^{N_1}} \qquad (5)$$

*Discussion.* This game shows that even with initially asymmetric ratings, the workers can still deter each other from cheating, if one of them is honest. Again the case where both workers decide to cheat was not resolved for the same reason as in Game 1.1. In fact, after both workers are detected cheating for the first time, they both will have a reputation of zero, which is almost exactly the situation in game 1.1. The only difference will be that $W_2$ will always have a number of jobs assigned to her ($N - N_1$), regardless of what happens in game because

---

[7] 2.3% and 3.9% in the second and third quarters of 2013, respectively, according to a Kaspersky Lab study (http://www.kaspersky.ca/internet-security-center/threats/spam-statistics-report-q2-2013).

of the limited capacity of $W_1$. However, these job assignments won't affect the equilibrium, because they are fixed and won't change during the entire game, and won't affect the rest of the assignments.

In the next game we investigate how changing our reputation system to the second variant (Knock-Out) influences the results.

**Game 1.3: A Knock-Out Reputation System.** In the third game we want to test the Knock-Out variant of our reputation system (see Sect. 3 for more details). The intuition is that the Knock-Out variant is more effective in deterring workers from cheating in comparison to the Zero-Reset variant tested in former games. This game is exactly like Game 1.1, except for the reputation system. In Game 1.1, we showed the result for both even and odd number of jobs. In this game we will only show the result for an even number of jobs, in adition to the case where there is only one job. As we saw in Game 1.1, the result for an odd number of jobs will be only slightly different.

**Proposition 3.** *For Game 1.3, with parameters $m$, $C$, $p$, $t_1$, $t_2$ and $N$, if the following condition holds, then the only possible Nash equilibrium in the game will be the one where both workers are honest.*

*Either $N = 1$ or $N = 2k$, for some positive integer $k$, and for both workers, and for all possible values of $q_1$ and $q_2$, the following holds $(i = 1, 2)$*[8]

$$\frac{\mathrm{d}f_i}{\mathrm{d}q_i} \cdot h_i < \frac{\mathrm{d}h_i}{\mathrm{d}q_i} \cdot f_i \tag{6}$$

*where*

$$f_i = u_i(1 - \beta_i)\left[\beta_i(1 - \beta_j)[1 - \alpha(1 - \hat{\beta}_i)] + \beta_j[1 + \alpha - \alpha(2B + \hat{\beta}_i - 2\hat{\beta}_i \cdot B)]\right]$$

$$h_i = (1 - B)(1 - \alpha \cdot B)[1 - \alpha(1 - \hat{\beta}_i)]$$

$$B = (1 - \beta_1)(1 - \beta_2)$$

$$\beta_i = \begin{cases} q_i \cdot p \cdot t_i & N = 1 \\ 1 - (1 - q \cdot p \cdot t_i)^{N/2} & N \text{ is even} \end{cases}$$

$$\hat{\beta}_i = \begin{cases} \beta_i & N = 1 \\ 1 - (1 - q_i \cdot p \cdot t_i)^{N} & N \text{ is even} \end{cases}$$

$$u_i = N(m + C \cdot \hat{q}_i)$$

$$j = 3 - i$$

*Discussion.* The switch to the second variant of the reputation system did not change the general results from Game 1.1 for the case where at least one of the workers is honest. In essence, the fact that one worker is honest makes the effect of both reputations systems the same from the point of view of the other worker.

---

[8] $\frac{\mathrm{d}y}{\mathrm{d}q_i}$ is the derivative of $y$ with respect to $q_i$.

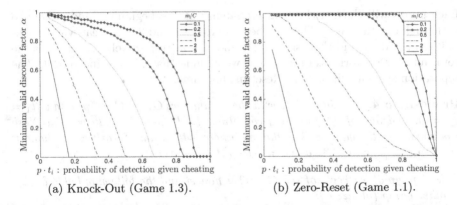

(a) Knock-Out (Game 1.3).          (b) Zero-Reset (Game 1.1).

**Fig. 2.** The minimum discount factor vs $p \cdot t_i$ (when $N = 1$ and $t_1 = t_2$). For example, at a markup-to-cost ratio of 0.2 and a detection probability (given cheating) of 0.8, the minimum discount factor needed in order to deter cheaters is 0.2 with the Knock-Out strategy and 0.7 with Zero-Reset.

Unfortunately, since we were not able to get a result for the case where both workers are dishonest and $N > 1$ in Game 1.1 (and 1.2), we cannot compare it with the result of this game. However, we can compare the results for the case when $N = 1$.

Regarding the condition for the case of two dishonest workers, in Fig. 2a we plot the minimum required discount factor ($\alpha$) versus the probability of detection given a cheating worker for several values of the markup-to-cost ratio. We obtained the minimum values for $\alpha$ using numerical minimization. Notice that the required values for a discount factor are still quite high. Although we did not have a general solution for the same case in the Zero-Reset setting, we did find the solution for the special case of $N = 1$. Figure 2b shows the results for that case. Comparing the two figures confirms the intuition that smaller values of $\alpha$ are needed with the stricter Knock-Out system than with Zero-Reset.

## 4.2   Second Set of Games: Many-Worker Games

The previous games considered only two workers. In this section, we investigate games with more workers. To derive a closed form expression for the expected utility for each worker, we had to limit the number of available jobs per round to one, i.e., $N = 1$. In the first game, we consider a special case, where the workers are split into two groups with a common cheating probability. In the second game, we relax this condition and allow every worker to chose her own cheating probability, but to retain our ability to calculate the expected utility, we will assume that the discount factor is not applied, i.e., $\alpha = 1$.

**Game 2.1.** This is the first game where we test the reputation system where we allow more than two workers. The workers are divided into two groups.

Each group will chose a cheating probability at the beginning, and adhere to it through out the game. The members of groups 1 and 2 will cheat with probabilities $q_1$ and $q_2$, and their sizes are $n$ and $G - n$, respectively. Where $G$ is the total number of workers. In addition, we assume that $N = 1$ and $\alpha < 1$. The reputation system will be Zero-Reset in this game.

**Proposition 4.** *In Game 2.1, with the parameters $G$, $m$, $C$, $\alpha$, $p$, and $t$ ($t_1 = t_2 = t$), and one of the following conditions hold, then the only possible Nash equilibrium in the game will be the one where both group of workers are honest. Also let $e = \frac{m}{C}$, $\gamma = \frac{1-\alpha}{\alpha}$, and $\omega = -e \cdot p \cdot t + 1 - p \cdot t$.*

- *One group of workers (of size $G - n$) is honest and the following holds for the other group (of size $n$):*

$$\frac{n}{G} < 1 - \frac{\gamma}{e}(1 - p \cdot t) + p \cdot t \tag{7}$$

- *Either $\omega \leq 0$ or the following holds:*

$$\frac{\omega \cdot p \cdot t + \omega \cdot \gamma}{e \cdot p \cdot t + \omega \cdot p \cdot t} < \frac{n}{G} < \frac{e \cdot p \cdot t - \omega \cdot \gamma}{e \cdot p \cdot t + \omega \cdot p \cdot t} \tag{8}$$

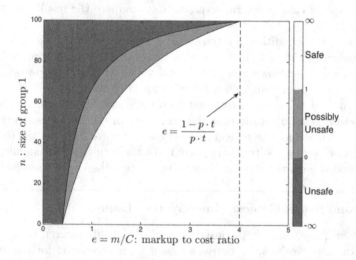

**Fig. 3.** The safe, unsafe, and possibly unsafe regions, w.r.t. group 1 size and the markup-to-cost ratio, when group 2 is always honest. ($G = 100$ and $\alpha = 0.95$)

*Discussion.* The following equations are the precursor for condition (8) (refer to the proof in [1] for details).

$$q_2 < F(n) = \frac{e}{\omega} \cdot \left(\frac{G - n}{n}\right) - \frac{\gamma}{p \cdot t} \cdot \frac{G}{n} \tag{9}$$

$$q_1 < F(G - n) = \frac{e}{\omega} \cdot \left( \frac{n}{G - n} \right) - \frac{\gamma}{p \cdot t} \cdot \frac{G}{G - n} \tag{10}$$

To understand the behavior of $F(n)$ we will use the plot in Fig. 3. The value of the discount factor $(\alpha)$ is chosen to be 0.9, because, as we saw earlier, values below 0.9 for $\alpha$ will render the game too biased toward cheating in games with many (or infinite) number of rounds. In addition, we will choose the detection probability to be 0.2, i.e., $p \cdot q = 0.2$, which will result in $\omega = 0$ at $e = 4$.

There are three regions in this plot (Fig. 3). The first region, colored in dark grey, covers the range of values of $n$ and $e$ where $F(n) < 0$. This is the unsafe region; since $F(n) < 0$, then there is no valid nonzero value for $q_2$ ($0 < q_2 \leq 1$) that will cause (9) to be always true, i.e., $\frac{dE[u_1]}{dq_1} > 0$. In other words, group 1 workers will have the incentive to always cheat, since more cheating will result in an increased utility. In this case, equilibrium is only possible when group 1 always cheats.

The second region, colored in white, represent the range of values where $F(n) > 1$. This is the safe region where, regardless of the value of $q_2$, the utility of group 1 workers will *decrease* when $q_1$ is increased, which will incentivize them not to cheat. In the safe region, equilibrium is only possible when group 1 is honest. In the grey region ($0 \leq F(n) \leq 1$) whether group 1's incentive is to cheat or not depends on $q_2$, which makes it possibly unsafe.

Ideally we want to control the parameters of the game to be always in the safe region to guarantee that the (untrusted) workers in group 1 have no incentive to cheat. However, this does not say anything about group 2 workers. This is fine if we either think that group 1 is trustworthy enough, or somehow can ensure their honesty. It can be seen in Fig. 3 that even at the relatively high markup-to-cost ratio of 1, we need the untrusted group size to be less than 50%.

An interesting scenario to consider is when we do not have any guarantees of honesty about both groups. Can we still achieve similar results that guarantee that they have no incentive to cheat? For such guarantees we need both (9) and (10) to hold, i.e., we need to be in the safe region of both $F(n)$ and $F(G - n)$. Figure 4 shows the intersection of both regions. Note that the conditions in Proposition 4 correspond to this intersection. It can be seen from the plot that a very high markup-to-cost ratio is needed to have reasonable guarantees that there is no incentive to cheat for both groups (at $\alpha = 0.95$ and $p \cdot t = 1$ nonetheless). Intuitively, this means that the outsourcer needs to promise to pay the workers enough to ensure that they value their future transactions more than the potential gains of cheating. Moreover, in order to have these guarantees, the relative sizes of the two groups need to be balanced. In this case, if the size of one of the groups is less than one fourth the size of the other group ($< 20\%$ of the total), then the guarantees cannot hold. In addition, the lower the markup-to-cost ratio, the more balanced these groups need to be. The same applies to $\alpha$: with lower values for $\alpha$, more balanced groups are required in order for them to deter each other from cheating.

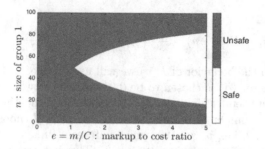

**Fig. 4.** The safe region, w.r.t. group size and markup-to-cost ratio, when both groups are not assumed to be honest. ($G = 100$ and $\alpha = 0.95$)

**Game 2.2.** In the previous games we divided the workers into two groups, where each group shares a common cheating probability. In this game, each worker is allowed to chose her own cheating probability. In addition, we consider the case were there is no discount factor (i.e., $\alpha = 1$). Since in this case it is not possible to find a Nash equilibrium considering the total utility, due to the infinite number of rounds, we analyze the expected utility per round. In addition to having no discount factor, we also restrict the number of jobs per round to one, otherwise finding an equilibrium will be too complex of a problem, probably without a closed form solution for the expected utility.

**Proposition 5.** *In Game 2.2, with parameters $G$, $m$, $C$, $p$, and $t_i$, for $i = 1, .., G$, if the condition below holds for at least one worker then the only equilibrium (as defined above) will be the one where every player is honest.*

$$\frac{C}{m} \cdot \frac{1 - p \cdot t_i}{p \cdot t_i} - 1 < \frac{1}{p} \cdot \sum_{j \in [1,G], j \neq i} \frac{1}{t_j} \tag{11}$$

*Discussion.* Due to the lack of discounting ($\alpha = 1$) we cannot directly compare the result here with the conditions in previous games. However, the same basic observations are true here. That is, we need a high enough markup-to-cost ratio and a reasonably high detection probability, i.e., $p \cdot t_i$. Of note here is that the sum $\sum_{j \in [1,G], j \neq i} \frac{1}{t_j}$ has a minimum value of $G - 1$, which means that the more workers we have available, the easier it is to incentivize the workers to be honest. Another observation, which might not be obvious, is that because we only need to incentivize one worker to be honest to force the others to also be honest, it actually makes sense to test those other workers less frequently. This is true because the more frequently we test the other workers, the more utility they will gain (from cheating) at the expense of the cheating utility of this one worker we are trying to incentivize.

# 5   Conclusion

In this paper we explored several games that model the outsourcing of computation and the long-term interaction between the outsourcer and the workers using models with infinite number of rounds. Instead of using penalties to deter workers from cheating, we used a reputation system and the potential loss of future work as way to incentivize workers to not cheat. Such a reputation system could not have been modeled with a one- or two-round game, or even (stateless) repeated games. While we have not utilized penalties in our games, a natural direction of future work is to formulate and analyze games where penalties are used in conjuction with reputations to ensure worker honesty.

We demonstrated that if specified conditions are met, then workers are compelled to behave honestly in our models. Moreover, these conditions enable us to calculate parameter settings that suffice to compel worker honesty. For example, these conditions enable us to calculate the outsourcer's detection probability $(p \cdot t_i)$ that suffices to compel workers, from which we can then adjust $p$ and/or $t_i$ to ensure that this detection probability is met. Doing so is important for scenarios where the *a priori* probability $p$ of detecting the worker cheating (when checked) is low, e.g., because the distribution over honest worker responses is so biased that a cheating worker can guess the correct response with high probability without performing the computation (e.g., guessing that an email attachment is benign, without actually checking it). In such cases, our conditions provide guidelines for increasing the testing rate $t_i$ or the detection probability $p$ when response are checked (e.g., by sending a larger fraction of malicious attachments for checking) to ensure worker honesty.

**Acknowledgments.** This work was supported in part by NSF grant 1330599 and by the Army Research Laboratory under Cooperative Agreement Number W911NF-13-2-0045 (ARL Cyber Security CRA). The views and conclusions contained in this document are those of the authors and should not be interpreted as representing the official policies, either expressed or implied, of the Army Research Laboratory or the U.S. Government. The U.S. Government is authorized to reproduce and distribute reprints for Government purposes notwithstanding any copyright notation here on.

# References

1. Aljuraidan, J., Bauer, L., Reiter, M.K., Beckerle, M.: Introducing reputation systems to the economics of outsourcing computations to rational workers. Technical report CMU-CyLab-16-001, Carnegie Mellon University, January 2016
2. Anati, I., Gueron, S., Johnson, S., Scarlat, V.: Innovative technology for CPU based attestation and sealing. In: Workshop on Hardware and Architectural Support for Security and Privacy (2013)
3. Awerbuch, B., Kutten, S., Peleg, D.: Competitive distributed job scheduling (extended abstract). In: 24th ACM Symposium on Theory of Computing, pp. 571–580 (1992)
4. Belenkiy, M., Chase, M., Erway, C.C., Jannotti, J., Küpçü, A., Lysyanskaya, A.: Incentivizing outsourced computation. In: Proceedings of the 3rd International Workshop on Economics of Networked Systems, NetEcon 2008 (2008)

5. Briggs, H.: Optimal cartel trigger strategies and the number of firms. Rev. Ind. Organ. **11**(4), 551–561 (1996)
6. Commerce, B.E., Jsang, A., Ismail, R.: The beta reputation system. In: 15th Bled Electronic Commerce Conference (2002)
7. Friedman, J.W.: A non-cooperative equilibrium for supergames. Rev. Econ. Stud. **38**(1), 1–12 (1971)
8. Goldwasser, S., Kalai, Y.T., Rothblum, G.N.: Delegating computation: interactive proofs for muggles. In: 40th ACM Symposium on Theory of Computing, May 2008
9. Hoekstra, M., Lal, R., Pappachan, P., Rozas, C., Phegade, V., del Cuvillo, J.: Using innovative instructions to create trustworthy software solutions. In: Workshop on Hardware and Architectural Support for Security and Privacy (2013)
10. Ishai, Y., Kushilevitz, E., Ostrovsky, R.: Efficient arguments without short PCPs. In: 22nd IEEE Conference on Computational Complexity, June 2007
11. Jøsang, A., Ismail, R., Boyd, C.: A survey of trust and reputation systems for online service provision. Decis. Support Syst. **43**(2), 618–644 (2007)
12. Kerr, R., Cohen, R.: Smart cheaters do prosper: defeating trust and reputation systems. In: AAMAS 2009, pp. 993–1000 (2009)
13. Krugman, P.R.: Trigger strategies and price dynamics in equity and foreign exchange markets. Technical report 2459, National Bureau of Economic Research (1987)
14. Mckeen, F., Alexandrovich, I., Berenzon, A., Rozas, C., Shafi, H., Shanbhogue, V., Savagaonkar, U.: Innovative instructions and software model for isolated execution. In: Workshop on Hardware and Architectural Support for Security and Privacy (2013)
15. Nojoumian, M., Lethbridge, T.C.: A new approach for the trust calculation in social networks. In: Filipe, J., Obaidat, M.S. (eds.) ICETE 2006. CCIS, vol. 9, pp. 64–77. Springer, Heidelberg (2008). doi:10.1007/978-3-540-70760-8_6
16. Nojoumian, M., Stinson, D.R.: Socio-rational secret sharing as a new direction in rational cryptography. In: Grossklags, J., Walrand, J. (eds.) GameSec 2012. LNCS, vol. 7638, pp. 18–37. Springer, Heidelberg (2012). doi:10.1007/978-3-642-34266-0_2
17. Penmatsa, S.: Game theory based job allocation/load balancing in distributed systems with applications to grid computing. Ph.D. thesis, The University of Texas at San Antonio (2007)
18. Pham, V., Khouzani, M.H.R., Cid, C.: Optimal contracts for outsourced computation. In: Poovendran, R., Saad, W. (eds.) GameSec 2014. LNCS, vol. 8840, pp. 79–98. Springer, Cham (2014). doi:10.1007/978-3-319-12601-2_5
19. Porter, R.H.: Optimal cartel trigger price strategies. J. Econ. Theor. **29**(2), 313–338 (1983)
20. Schuster, F., Costa, M., Fournet, C., Gkantsidis, C., Peinado, M., Mainar-Ruiz, G., Russinovich, M.: VC3: trustworthy data analytics in the cloud using SGX. In: 36th IEEE Symposium on Security and Privacy, May 2015
21. Teacy, W., Patel, J., Jennings, N., Luck, M.: Travos: trust and reputation in the context of inaccurate information sources. Auton. Agent. Multi-Agent Syst. **12**(2), 183–198 (2006)
22. Tran, T., Cohen, R.: Improving user satisfaction in agent-based electronic marketplaces by reputation modelling and adjustable product quality. In: AAMAS 2004, pp. 828–835 (2004)
23. Trusted Computing Group: Trusted platform module main specification, version 1.2, revision 103 (2007)
24. Walfish, M., Blumberg, A.J.: Verifying computations without reexecuting them. Commun. ACM **58**(2), 74–84 (2015)

25. Whitby, A., Jøsang, A., Indulska, J.: Filtering out unfair ratings in Bayesian reputation systems. In: Proceedings of 7th International Workshop on Trust in Agent Societies, vol. 6, pp. 106–117 (2004)
26. Yagoubi, B., Medebber, M.: A load balancing model for grid environment. In: 22nd International Symposium on Computer and Information Sciences, pp. 1–7 (2007)

# Payments, Auctions, and e-Voting

# Accountable Privacy for Decentralized Anonymous Payments

Christina Garman[✉], Matthew Green, and Ian Miers

Johns Hopkins University, Baltimore, USA
{cgarman,mgreen,imiers}@cs.jhu.edu

**Abstract.** Decentralized ledger-based currencies such as Bitcoin provide a means to construct payment systems without requiring a trusted bank. Removing this trust assumption comes at the significant cost of transaction privacy. A number of academic works have sought to improve the privacy offered by ledger-based currencies using anonymous electronic cash (e-cash) techniques. Unfortunately, this strong degree of privacy creates new regulatory concerns, since the new private transactions cannot be subject to the same controls used to prevent individuals from conducting illegal transactions such as money laundering. We propose an initial approach to addressing this issue by adding *privacy preserving* policy-enforcement mechanisms that guarantee regulatory compliance, allow selective user tracing, and admit tracing of tainted coins (e.g., ransom payments). To accomplish this new functionality we also provide improved definitions for Zerocash and, of independent interest, an efficient construction for simulation sound zk-SNARKs.

## 1 Introduction

The success of decentralized currencies like Bitcoin has led to renewed interest in anonymous electronic cash both in academia [2,9,20] and in practice (including Coinjoin, CryptoNote, and DarkWallet). It has also highlighted new problems related to trust, privacy and regulatory compliance. In modern electronic payment systems, users must trust that their bank is not tampering with the system (e.g., by "forging" extra currency), that no party is abusing the privacy of users' transactions, and simultaneously, that other users are not using the system to engage in money laundering or extortion. Unfortunately, these goals seem fundamentally at odds.

Decentralized payment systems such as Bitcoin address the first issue by replacing the central bank with a distributed ledger and consensus system. Unfortunately, this benefit comes at a significant cost to privacy [1,5,22], since any user can now view the transaction graph and potentially trace payments made by another user. Proposals such as Zerocoin and Zerocash [2,20] attempt to resolve the privacy problem by employing sophisticated zero knowledge proofs of transaction correctness. While such constructions address privacy concerns, they do not offer any additional protections against money laundering and other activity. From an investigative standpoint, Zerocash is no different than cash.

© International Financial Cryptography Association 2017
J. Grossklags and B. Preneel (Eds.): FC 2016, LNCS 9603, pp. 81–98, 2017.
DOI: 10.1007/978-3-662-54970-4_5

The problem of preventing money laundering in decentralized currencies is not theoretical. In May 2015 the decentralized payment network Ripple was ordered to pay a \$700,000 fine by the U.S. Financial Crimes Enforcement Network (FINCEN) due to inadequate monitoring of transactions on their network. This raises questions for the deployment of privacy-preserving payment networks, where individual network operators and currency exchanges may be held criminally liable for facilitating laundering. In general, the difficulty of preventing abuse may prove a barrier to the deployment of private currency systems. In particular, it seems likely that the application of existing reporting requirements will force exchanges/online wallets, even when dealing with anonymous currencies, to hold vast amounts of information about their users, their transactions, and the amounts. If, as in Bitcoin, most consumers use online wallets, then they gain little privacy.

In this paper we aim for a middle ground. Specifically, we design new Decentralized Anonymous Payment (DAP) systems [2] that are capable of enforcing compliance with specific transaction policies, while protecting the privacy of network participants. Our approach builds on the techniques of Ben-Sasson et al.'s Zerocash system [2], using efficient zero knowledge Arguments of Knowledge (zk-SNARKs) [3,4,6,11,13,18,19,21] to both prove the validity of transactions and to enforce transaction *policies*. These policies allow network participants to verifiably prove compliance with global transaction policies, such as tax payments, deposit limits, and verifiable coin tracing, all while protecting the privacy of each transaction. Interestingly, a side effect of our mechanisms is that even centralized banks or exchanges participating in our scheme are prevented from evading anti-money laundering controls, as these controls are enforced by cryptographically sound proofs.

*Improving security definitions for DAP schemes.* A necessary starting point for our exploration is to find a formal security definition for DAP schemes that can be readily extended to incorporate our policies. Previous security definitions for DAP schemes involve a series of distinct games, each of which addresses one aspect of the security requirements for the DAP scheme. Not only are these games complex, they fail to simultaneously ensure both *correctness* and privacy of the DAP scheme. In particular, we note that the Zerocash scheme [2] admits a practical attack due to a limitation of the correctness definition. In this paper we explore a more promising route: we define an ideal-world functionality to describe the security properties of a DAP scheme, which captures both the correctness and privacy of the scheme in a single intuitive definition. Moreover, as we show in later sections, this simulation-based definition can easily be augmented to incorporate policies.

*Augmenting existing constructions with simulation-sound zkSNARKs.* Given an improved simulation-based definition for DAP schemes, we encounter a technical problem that prevents us from proving security of the scheme: we require zero-knowledge proofs which are sound and extractable in the presence of simulated proofs, i.e., we need simulation sound proofs. However, the zk-SNARK used in

Zerocash provides no such guarantees. To address this we build the first instantiation of simulation sound zk-SNARKs.

While this seems like a small step and uses folklore techniques, it is necessary and must be done carefully to ensure security and efficiency. Our approach preserves succinctness and through clever choice of primitives, has almost no effect on Zerocash performance. For space reasons, we defer further description to the full paper [10].

*Anti-money laundering policies for DAP schemes.* Given a stronger formal foundation, we can now explore and reason about a wide range of anti-money laundering policies that still preserve user privacy. In fact we are able to go substantially beyond this and provide policies that simultaneously allow the authorities to both trace coins as they go from individual to individual and retrieve all of a particular user's transactions and provide an accountable record of when and why those powers were used. We provide examples of several concrete compliance policies that leverage our new techniques. These include policies to enforce regulatory closure, enforced tax payments, spending limits, coin tracing, and user tracing. We also provide the first schemes in the decentralized e-cash setting that allow for coin and user tracing while maintaining an accountable record to limit abuse of those powers.

**Paper outline.** The remainder of this paper proceeds as follows. In Sect. 2 we provide definitions for secure DAP schemes and propose our modified security definition. In Sect. 3 we introduce the Zerocash construction and propose modifications to achieve our new definitions. In Sect. 4 we show how to modify a DAP scheme to enforce various policies. In Sects. 5 and 6 we detail specific policies for coin tracing and accountable user tracing.

## 2    Decentralized Anonymous Payments

Decentralized Anonymous Payment (DAP) systems were introduced by Ben-Sasson et al. [2]. A complete formal definition can be found in [2]. A DAP system consists of an append-only ledger and a tuple of polynomial time algorithms (Setup, CreateAddress, Mint, Pour, VerifyTransaction, Receive) with the following (informal) semantics:

Setup($1^\lambda$) $\rightarrow$ *params* generates global parameters for the system.

CreateAddress(*params*) $\rightarrow$ (addr$_{pk}$, addr$_{sk}$) outputs an individual address (key pair) for each user.

Mint(*params*, addr$_{pk}$, $v$) $\rightarrow$ (cm, $\pi$, trap) creates a new transaction embedding a coin of value $v$, a proof $\pi$, and outputs a trapdoor trap for spending the coin.

Pour(*params*, cm$_1$, cm$_2$, trap$_1$, trap$_2$, addr$_{pk,1}$, addr$_{pk,2}$, $v_1$, $v_2$, $v_{pub}$) $\rightarrow$ (cm$_1$, cm$_2$, $\pi$) takes as input two coin commitments and the corresponding trapdoors, as well as a public value output and two new coin values and destination addresses, and outputs a new transaction embedding the new coins.

VerifyTransaction validates any of the above transactions.

Receive scans the transactions on the ledger, using the user's corresponding secret key to identify transactions addressed to the user.

Informally, a DAP scheme uses these transactions along with a trusted append-only ledger to transact funds between different users. By issuing "coins" in exchange for work, or for non-anonymous currencies, users can split, merge and combine coins of arbitrary value. Additionally, senders can transmit funds to another user without revealing the contents of the transfer to any third party.

## 2.1  Existing Definitions and Limitations

The DAP security definitions provided by Ben-Sasson et al. [2] are game based. As a result, these definitions are complex, spanning three games: one for anonymity, one for non-malleability (needed to ensure correct integration into Bitcoin), and one for balance. While non-malleability is simple, both the game for anonymity ("ledger indistinguishability") and the one preventing coin forgery ("balance") are quite complex. More importantly, these definitions are also incomplete: they do not fully enforce correctness. Unfortunately, malicious users can exploit these weaknesses to break other properties in cryptographic systems.

Specifically, in Zerocash, each Pour transaction contains one or more serial numbers related to the coins spent. These are designed to prevent double spending, and are formed as a combination of the coin recipient's private key and randomness chosen by the sender. Since the private key is fixed, if the sender uses the same randomness in two different transactions, then the serial numbers will be identical. As a result, the recipient will be unable to spend both transactions, since the duplicate serial numbers will appear to indicate a double spend. This would allow an attacker to send two payments of e.g. $500 and $1,000, and then ask for a refund on the "accidental" $1,000 dollar payment. While this attack costs the attacker $500, since both payments go through and she only gets one back, it also costs the victim $500, since the "accidental" payment can never be spent. This attack is easily fixed by having the recipient check for duplicate serial number randomness over all previous transactions they received.

Nonetheless, this attack shows that the "balance" definition does not fully capture what we assume about a currency system. Clearly, some part of the security definitions in a DAP scheme should prevent this, yet the definitions for Zerocash do not.

## 2.2  Simulation-Based Definition for DAP Schemes

An alternative to using game-based definitions like those of [2] is to use a simulation-based definition. In this approach, we define our system in terms of an ideal functionality implemented by a trusted party $T_P$ that plays the role that our cryptographic constructions play in the real system [12]. In the ideal-world experiment, a collection of parties interact with the trusted party according to a specific interface. In the real-world experiment, the parties interact with each other using cryptography. We now define the experiments:

**Ideal-world execution** $\text{IDEAL}_{T_P, \mathcal{S}, \Sigma}$. The ideal world attacker, $\mathcal{S}$, selects some subset of the $P_1, \ldots, P_n$ parties to corrupt and informs the $T_P$. The attacker controlled parties behave arbitrarily, the honest ones follow a set of strategies $\Sigma$. All parties then interact via messages passed to and from the $T_P$ implementing an ideal functionality outlined in Fig. 1.

---

We initialize two tables, one for addresses, and one for coins.

- RegisterID($\text{addr}_{\text{pk}}$). When called by party $U$, registers a new address $\text{addr}_{\text{pk}}$
  - The input is an address $\text{addr}_{\text{pk}}$.
  - If $\text{addr}_{\text{pk}}$ is not already in the address table, the trusted party $T_P$ stores $(U, \text{addr}_{\text{pk}})$ in the address table. Else, reject.
- $c \leftarrow \text{Mint}(v, \text{addr}_{\text{pk}})$. Creates a coin for party U
  - The input is a value $v$ and a destination address $\text{addr}_{\text{pk}}$.
  - The trusted party $T_P$ checks to make sure that $\text{addr}_{\text{pk}}$ has been registered to user $U$. If not, reject.
  - Else, $T_P$ generates a unique random transaction id $c$, stores $(c, v, \text{addr}_{\text{pk}})$ in the coin table, and notifies all parties of $Mint(v)$.
  - $T_P$ returns $c$ to the user.
- $[c_1^{new}, \ldots, c_n^{new}] \leftarrow \text{Pour}([c_1, \ldots, c_m], [(\text{addr}_{\text{pk},1}, v_1), \ldots, (\text{addr}_{\text{pk},n}, v_n)], v_{\text{pub}})$. Generates $n$ new coins. Party $U$ pours coins to new addresses
  - The input is a list of previous transaction id's $c_i$, tuples of (destination address $\text{addr}_{\text{pk},i}$, transaction value $v_i$), and a public value $v_{\text{pub}}$.
  - For each input $c_i$, $T_P$ retrieves each transaction, its associated value $v_i^{old}$, and address from the coin table and checks the address belongs to $U$ in the address table. If not, reject.
  - $T_P$ checks $\sum_{i=1}^{m} v_i^{old} = \sum_{i=1}^{n} v_i + v_{\text{pub}}$. If not, reject.
  - The trusted party then creates $n$ new random transaction id's $c_i^{new}$ each with value $v_i$ and for each stores $(c_i^{new}, v_i, \text{addr}_{\text{pk},i})$ in the coin table.
  - $T_P$ deletes the input transaction(s) from the coin table.
  - For each $\text{addr}_{\text{pk},i}$ that is not in the address table, $T_P$ notifies the corrupted parties of $Pour(c_i^{new}, v_i, \text{addr}_{\text{pk},i})$.
  - For all $\text{addr}_{\text{pk},i}$ in address table, $T_P$ notifies the party associated with $\text{addr}_{\text{pk},i}$ of $Pour(c_i^{new}, v_i, \text{addr}_{\text{pk},i})$.
  - The trusted party $T_P$ notifies all parties of $Pour(v_{\text{pub}})$.
  - $T_P$ returns $[c_1^{new}, \ldots, c_n^{new}]$ to the user.

---

**Fig. 1.** Ideal functionality. Security of a basic DAP scheme.

**Real world functionality** $\text{REAL}_{DAP, \mathcal{A}, \Sigma}$. The real world attacker $\mathcal{A}$ controls a subset of the parties $P_1, \ldots, P_n$ interacting with the real DAP scheme. The honest parties execute the commands output by the strategy $\Sigma$ using the DAP scheme while the attacker controlled parties can behave arbitrarily. We assume that all parties can interact with a trusted append only ledger.

For generality we present our ideal functionality definitions, as well as subsequent transaction policies, as operations on $n$ coins in and $n$ coins out. As we do not wish to re-present all of Zerocash, however, for brevity we deal concretely with the existing Zerocash construction which was defined for the 2-in-2-out case.

**Definition 1.** *We say that DAP securely emulates the ideal functionality provided by $T_P$ if for all probabilistic polynomial-time real-world adversaries $\mathcal{A}$ and all honest party strategies $\Sigma$, there exists a simulator $\mathcal{S}$ such that for any ppt distinguishers d:*

$$P[d(\text{IDEAL}_{T_P,\mathcal{S},\Sigma}(\lambda)) = 1] - P[d(\text{REAL}_{DAP,\mathcal{A},\Sigma})(\lambda) = 1] \leq negl(\lambda)$$

**Theorem 1.** *The basic DAP scheme described in [2] and the full version of this paper satisfies Definition 2.1 given the existence of simulation-sound zkSNARKs, collision resistant hash functions, PRFs, statistically hiding and computationally binding commitments, one-time strongly-unforgeable digital signatures, and key-private public key encryption.*

See the full version for a proof of Theorem 1 [10].

## 3    Modifying and Extending Zerocash

We use the same notation for addresses, Merkle tree, ledger, and other components as Zerocash [2]. However, to meet the new definitions we must lightly modify the existing construction. In particular, we need a mechanism to allow us to extract who a Mint transaction was authored by, and we need to extend the definitions to allow for policies to be applied that validate transactions.

We modify the Zerocash construction in two ways. First, by adding a proof to the Mint algorithm that $cm := \text{COMM}_s(v\|\text{COMM}_r(a_{\mathsf{pk}}\|\rho))$ and a verification of this proof to VerifyTransaction. This is to support our new definition. Second, we modify Receive to fix the attack described in Sect. 2 and check if the serial number randomness is distinct from any previously received coins, not just the ones already spent on the ledger. We refer the curious reader to the full version of the paper [2,10] for the complete details.

## 4    Policies

Given an extensible security model for Zerocash-like systems we can now consider more complex policies governing the transfer of funds than those originally embedded in Zerocash. Zerocash only enforced one restriction on funds transfer: the sum of the values in the list of output commitments must not exceed the sum of the input ones. Although that is the most basic policy governing any monetary system, far more complex ones govern our modern banking system. These include policies limiting money laundering, enforcing tax payments, and facilitating international funds transfers, among other examples. In this section, we explore several analogous policies for decentralized e-cash that still mostly preserve user privacy.

Formally, we define a policy as an algorithm that is executed each time a coin is spent ("poured"). The algorithm is parameterized by some constants (e.g., all transaction tax policies are the same except for the tax rate parameter) and takes public inputs, private inputs, and returns true or false. Policies are realized by a zero-knowledge proof, so we are essentially giving a procedural description of the standard efficiently decidable binary relation used in zero-knowledge proofs. We note that no fresh computation takes place in a policy, only validation of precomputed data.

## 4.1   Building Blocks

To construct our policies, we use a few basic techniques detailed here.

**Adding Information to Coins.** In order to accomplish various policies, we need to store more than a numeric value inside a coin (indeed, as shown later, we will need to use coins for other things).

We do this by replacing the 192 bit zero padding in the commitment with a special *tag* used to mark what kind of counter it is. To do this we can alter the creation of a coin from

$$\mathsf{cm} := \mathsf{COMM}_s(v\|k) \quad \text{as} \quad \mathcal{H}(k\|0^{192}\|v)$$

to

$$\mathsf{cm} := \mathsf{COMM}_s(v\|type\|data\|k) \quad \text{as} \quad \mathcal{H}(k\|type\|data\|v).$$

Policies will use the type information to ensure that an adversary cannot cause them to operate over the wrong data. Careful care must be taken so that one policy does not output data of a type used by a different policy for a different purpose. This also means that each new type requires a special Mint.

**Counters.** A recurring problem we will encounter in these policies is the problem of how to count, e.g., how do you count how much money a user has sent, how much they need to pay taxes on, etc? Many policies depend on counting funds or transactions and as such, we treat it as a basic building block.

The approach we take is to replace the content of a coin with a counter. Upon each transaction the *policy* governing it requires the user to input their current counter state and output the new counter with the appropriate increment. Counters are a new type of "coin" and we define MintCTR analogously to Mint but have it reveal the *tag* in addition to $v$ which is now called *ctr*. In order to maintain anonymity, these counters need to be input via the same mechanism that coin commitments are (i.e., by proving they are in a Merkle tree). In the policies below, we denote them as special inputs solely for clarity.

The particular mechanism for restricted mint depends on deployment. For certain scenarios, it may be enough to ensure that there is only one counter per address. For most scenarios where counters are tightly coupled with real world identity, we assume such mints must tied to some trusted party, probably via signature. There is thus an implicit policy on which MintCTRs will be accepted.

We also define a utility function for verifying a counter in Algorithm 1.

---

**input** : CTROld, CTRNew, delta, tag
**output:** True if counter is valid

**if** *not* tag = CTROld.*tag* = CTRNew.*tag* **then**
  | **return** False;
**end**
**return** CTRNew = CTROld.*value* + delta;

---

**Algorithm 1.** VerifyCounter

**Identity.** An important aspect of any regulatory system is user *identity*. Legal concepts of identity are decidedly centralized. Since most policies are a result of legal and regulatory requirements, most of them require some notion of legal identity. In the case of counters bound to an identity, a trusted third party can issue the counters. More practically, given any trusted party who issues identity certificates, we can require a signature under its certificate chain.

Another possibility is to simply bind counters or other objects to Bitcoin/Zerocash addresses and enforce real world identity enforcement at exchanges and online wallets. In this case then, a user would be associated with a set of addresses and would later have to tie these addresses to a real-world identity. This is analogous to the current approach used in Bitcoin, where exchanges and online wallets track user identities. We believe this is the most promising avenue for real deployment.

**Signatures and Encryption.** The final building block some of our policies use are public key encryption and signature schemes. Because Zerocash uses zk-SNARKs which are proofs over arithmetic circuits, the naive approach to instantiating these schemes would be extremely costly: first build a circuit for modular exponentiation operations in some group and then build the encryption scheme on top of that. However, it is possible instead to directly calculate the signature verification operations in an extension field [9] of the arithmetic circuit, vastly increasing efficiency.

### 4.2 Regulatory Closure

This policy allows multiple regulatory environments to coexist in the same system but the units of currency under each scheme do not mix. In practice, this policy ensures that transactions do not bridge between regulatory schemes, except through an outside mechanism such as an exchange (where legal requirements can be enforced). To implement this policy, coins, instead of just including a numeric value $v$, now include a regulatory type. These are created on Mint. The policy ensures that either:

1. the regulatory type of all input coins and all output coins is the same
2. or the type of all output coins is marked as ⊥.

The point of this policy is to ensure continuity of some other regulatory scheme which may or may not be enforced by zero-knowledge. For example, such a policy could ensure that coins only came from exchanges or hosted wallets in a particular jurisdiction. In the algorithm described in Algorithm 2, we allow coins to have an arbitrary regulator marking if the output coins are signed by a valid authority. This could be a bank, an exchange, or the government itself. This allows the transfer of coins from one scheme to the other.

---

**PrivateInput:** CoinsIn, CoinsOut, CA, sig
**Constants**    : inRegType, CA
**output**        : True if transaction is valid

if sig ≠ ⊥ then        // if tx signed by authorized party, skip policy
  | return *VerifySig*(CA, CoinsOut, sig);
end
outRegType ← inRegType;
for e ∈ CoinsIn do
  if e.*regType* ≠ inRegType then
    | outRegType ← ⊥; // if any regType is wrong, outRegType is ⊥
  end
end
for e ∈ CoinsOut do        // check each new coin has the correct regtype
  if e.*regType* ≠ outRegType then
    | return False;
  end
end
return True;

**Algorithm 2.** Regulatory closure

---

## 4.3 Spending Limits

In the US one common form of anti-money laundering control is a Suspicious Activity Report. This report is generated by a bank when any single transaction over $10,000 USD is reported. This can be easily implemented.

The mechanism is simple: no transaction over the limit is valid unless signed by an authority. This allows the authority to force reporting for transactions over the limit. Note, we explicitly require the signature to be public. The reason is to prevent fraud on the part of the authority. Were the signature private, a bank enforcing this could undetectably allow anyone to circumvent the reporting mechanism by issuing more signatures. On the other hand, when signatures are public, we can require that the authority log (privately) all transaction details along with the transaction itself (and perhaps a proof the details are valid). See Algorithm 3. Since the signature is used once and only known to the authority, revealing it does not impact privacy.

```
PrivateInput: CoinsIn,CoinsOut
PublicInput : sig
Constants    : limit
output       : True if transaction is valid

sent ← 0;
if sig ≠ ⊥ then       // if tx signed by authorized party, skip policy
 |  return VerifySig(CA, CoinsOut, sig);
end
for e ∈ CoinsOut do
 |  // if we are paying to an input address, it is ''change'' back
 |       to the user and not counted against the limit
 |  if e.addr ∉ {c.addr|c ∈ CoinsIn} then
 |   |  sent ← sent + e.value;
 |  end
end
return sent ≤ limit;
```

**Algorithm 3.** Transaction limit

A more sophisticated policy would place spending limit over all transactions instead of a limit on a single transaction. For this we require counters. See Algorithm 4.

MODIFIED IDEAL FUNCTIONALITY AND PROOF SKETCH. We now detail, informally, the modifications to the ideal functionality necessary to capture counter based spending limits and the changes necessary to the proof. The ideal functionality changes are small: we add a per user counter maintained by the ideal functionality and modify *pour* to increment the counter as appropriate and reject the transaction if the counter is over a given limit. The resulting proof change is similarly tiny: the simulator aborts if the attacker submits a real world transaction violating their counting limit or if they try and issue a new counter. The probability of the former event is negligible if the proof system is simulation sound and the second event is not allowed in either the real or ideal protocol since the attacker cannot make new counters.

## 4.4  Tax

Our policies also allow us to enforce taxes, such as income taxes, sales taxes, and Value Added Tax (VAT). We accomplish this by requiring a percentage payment to a tax account with each Zerocash transaction. Because Zerocash is payment based, in practice we charge taxes on the sending side of the transaction. Obviously, this cost can be passed on to the recipient.

---

PrivateInput: CoinsIn, CoinsOut, $CTRcm^{old}$, $CTRcm^{new}$
PublicInput : epoch, sig
Constants  : limit
output     : True if transaction is valid

spent $\leftarrow$ 0;
if sig $\neq \bot$ then      // if tx signed by authorized party, skip policy
  | return $VerifySig$(CA, CoinsOut, sig);
end
if $CTRcm^{new}.value \geq$ limit then      // if counter over limit, reject
  | return False;
end
for e $\in$ CoinsOut do
  | // if we are paying to an input address, it is ``change'' back
  |   to the user and not counted against the limit
  | if $e.addr \notin \{c.addr | c \in$ CoinsIn$\}$ then
  |  | spent $\leftarrow$ spent $+ e.value$;
  | end
end
return VerifyCounter($CTRcm^{old}$, $CTRcm^{new}$,
        spent, "limit");

**Algorithm 4.** Spending limit

---

PrivateInput: CoinsIn, CoinsOut, $CTRcm^{old}$, $CTRcm^{new}$
Constants  : taxrate, tag
output     : True if transaction is valid

spent $\leftarrow$ 0;
for e $\in$ CoinsOut do
  | if $e.addr \notin$ CoinsIn then
  |  | spent $\leftarrow$ spent $+ e.value$;
  | end
end
return VerifyCounter($CTRcm^{old}$, $CTRcm^{new}$,
        $\lfloor$spent $\cdot$ taxrate$\rfloor$, tag);

**Algorithm 5.** Tax

---

The tax algorithm is straight forward. All outputs being sent to other parties
are summed and a percentage of that amount is added to a user's tax counter.
We reveal the tag to support multiple tax authorities.[1]

Actually forcing users pay taxes is a problem left to the authority. Since they
know who they issued tax counters to, they can force those people to report their

---

[1] We note that this tax policy is ill defined if users collude to generate a transaction
using MPC where the input identities are different. This can be fixed by ensuring
that there is only one identity used for all input coins. However, the same MPC
mechanism could be used to share one identity and never pay taxes.

income. An alternate policy would be to directly pay taxes off each transaction. This would, however, leak transaction amounts to the authority, rather than just total income.

### 4.5 Identity Escrow

The identity escrow policy allows governments to selectively revoke the anonymity of individual transactions, using a master key held securely by some tracing authority. The implementation of this function is simple: a copy of the transaction details is encrypted under the public key of some authority. The policy validates that the encryption is correct. We note it may be possible to forgo public key encryption if every user has a pre-shared key with the tracing authority (since it is likely this would be a bank or government which users already had to register with, this is possible) and we can authenticate the key with a signature scheme if this proves more efficient.

| |
|---|
| **PrivateInput:** CoinsIn.CoinsOut, r |
| **PublicInput** : escrowct |
| **Constants** : CA |
| **output** : True if transaction is valid |
| **return** escrowct $= Pkenc(\mathsf{CA}, \mathsf{CoinsIn} \| \mathsf{CoinsOut}; r)$; |

**Algorithm 6.** Identity escrow

## 5 Coin Tracing

We now detail how to trace individual coins.

### 5.1 Construction

In a coin tracing scheme, individual coins can be marked for tracing. All subsequent coins resulting from transactions on those initial coins will themselves be traceable. To implement this in Algorithm 7, each coin commitment contains a fresh key for a public key encryption scheme. The idea is that all of the information needed to trace the output coins (including the new private keys) is encrypted under the existing key for the input coin commitments. Thus, if the inputs are traced, then the outputs are traceable. If we did only this, however, the sender would be able to trace the coins because he generated the fresh keys for the outputs. Thus, we encrypt all of this output under the authority's public key. For space efficiency, instead of encrypting everything under each input key, we encrypt the same symmetric key under each public key and encrypt everything under that key.

Our tracing scheme has two major limitations: first unless someone removes the tracing key for a coin and replaces it with a dummy key, eventually all coins in the network will be traced. This is an inherent limitation of a tracing mechanism that marks all coins involved in a transaction as tainted. Of course,

**PrivateInput:** CoinsIn, CoinsOut, r, pkCTs, rEnc, k, ct, rKeyGen, pk, sk
**PublicInput** : escrowct
**Constants**   : $\mathcal{G}$
**Constants**   : CA
**output**      : True if transaction is valid

**if** sig $\neq \bot$ **then**                  // tx is from e.g. a bank, skip tracing
| **return** $VerifySig$(CA, CoinsOut, sig)
**end**
$i, j \leftarrow 0$;
**for** e $\in$ CoinsOut **do**          // check new coins' tracing keys are correct
| **if** (pk[$i$], sk[$i$]) $\neq PKgen(\mathcal{G}; \text{rKeyGen}[i])$ *or* e.*key* $\neq$ pk[$i$] **then**
| | **return** False;                          // key was not generated honestly
| **end**
| $i \leftarrow i + 1$;
**end**
**for** e $\in$ CoinsIn **do**          // ensure k is encrypted under each tracing key
| **if** pkCTs[$j$] $\neq PKEnc$(e.*key*, k; rEnc[$j$]) **then**
| | **return** False ;    // symmetric key k is not encrypted under input
| | coin j's tracing key
| **end**
| $j \leftarrow j + 1$;
**end**
**if** ct $\neq enc$(k, CoinsIn$\|$CoinsOut$\|$sk; rEnc) **then**
| **return** False;    // new tracing private keys not encrypted under k
**end**
// ensure ct is encrypted under authority key
**return** escrowct $= PkEnc$(CA, ct$\|$pkCTs);

**Algorithm 7.** Coin tracing

we could have more limited versions where we map the taint bits from input coins to output coins directly (e.g., the largest input's taint bit maps to the largest output) but these lead to circumvention issues.

The second issue is that the user and the authority can collude to trace coins even if the input coins were not marked as traced. This is not an inherent limitation but rather arises from the fact that the authority always knows the decryption keys for the outer layer of encryption and the user always knows the inner layer keys.

Because of these limitations we anticipate that in a real system, coins will frequently return to exchanges and online wallets and at these locations tracing can be removed or added. To facilitate this we allow exchanges who have an authorized signing key to either add or remove tracing by changing the key associated with a coin. We note that when an exchange removes tracing this can be done in a verifiable manner by using a known dummy key as the coin key. Looking forward, we can use similar techniques to accountable user tracing in the next section to allow the exchange to accountably add or remove tracing by providing a randomized tracing key that is either the authority's key or a dummy key.

Given the above policy, the algorithm to actually do tracing is detailed in Algorithm 8.

---

**input** : The list of trace ciphertexts TraceCTs, the authority's decryption key sk, the initial coin tracing private key ck for the coin we want to trace
**output**: The trace for a particular coin Trace

**for** e ∈ TraceCTs **do**        // decrypt the outer layer of all transactions
  │ TraceRecords.append(PKDec(sk,TraceCTs));
**end**
KeysToTrace.append(ck);
**for** ck ∈ KeysToTrace **do**
  │ // For every public key ciphertext in every pour, we attempt to
  │    decrypt with the target key. On success, we get back the
  │    symmetric ciphertext associated with the pour, and the
  │    decrypted symmetric key.
  │ encrec, k ← $FindTxByTrialDecryption$(TraceRecords, ck);
  │ **if** encrec ≠ ⊥ **then**
  │   │ rec ← $SymDec$(k, encrec);                // now decrypt the record
  │   │ Trace.append(rec);        // add the decrypted record to the trace
  │   │ **for** $i ∈ \{0, 1, \ldots, \text{rec}.CoinsIn.Size() - 1\}$ **do**
  │   │   │ KeysToTrace.append(rec.sk[$i$]); // enqueue the new tracing keys
  │   │ **end**
  │ **end**
**end**
**return** Trace;

---

**Algorithm 8.** TraceCoin

The algorithm to trace coins takes an initial target coin commitment, the initial public key for that coin commitment, and the key to decrypt all tracing records. It simply searches for all coin commitments output by that transaction, maps the new keys to those coin, decrypts the record with the existing keys, and adds those coin commitments to the list of ones to search for.

## 5.2   Security

**Modified Ideal Functionality.** To allow tracing, we need to modify the Ideal Functionality to (1) have a special party designated the tracing authority, (2) allow coins to be marked as traced by that authority, (3) mark all output coins as traced if any of the inputs are traced and (4) allow a report on all traced coins to be made to that authority. Of course, since we allow static corruption, the tracing authority may be the adversary. We detail the modifications in Fig. 2.

- $[c_1^{new}, \ldots, c_n^{new}] \leftarrow \mathsf{Pour}([c_1, \ldots, c_m], [(\mathsf{addr}_{\mathsf{pk},1}, v_1), \ldots, (\mathsf{addr}_{\mathsf{pk},n}, v_n)], v_{\mathsf{pub}}, aux)$.
  - Perform steps one through eight of $\mathsf{Pour}$ in Fig. 1, adding an additional stored field (initially set to false) to denote whether a coin is being traced or not.
  - If any coin $c_i$ is marked as traced, mark all output coins as traced.
  - $T_P$ returns $[c_1^{new}, \ldots, c_n^{new}]$ to the user.
- $\mathsf{Trace}(c, U)$
  - The input is a coin $c$ and a requesting party $U$.
  - If the requesting party $U$ is the tracing authority, update the stored value for $c$ and mark it as traced. Else, reject.
- $[c_0, \ldots, c_m] \leftarrow \mathsf{Report}(U)$
  - The $T_P$ returns all entries $[c_0, \ldots, c_m]$ for coins marked as traced if the requesting party $U$ is the tracing authority, otherwise return $\perp$.

**Fig. 2.** Modified ideal functionality for coin tracing.

**Proof Sketch.** If the tracing authority is not corrupted, then the simulator can always use random values for the escrow ciphertext and the probability of abort is bounded by the security of the outer encryption scheme.

We now deal with the more complex case: a corrupted tracing authority who the simulator must generate notifications for. There are two subcases: traced coins and non-traced coins. For traced coins, the probability that the simulator fails in decrypting both layers of the tracing ciphertext (and hence cannot mark the coins appropriately in the ideal functionality) is bounded by the soundness of the proof system. For non-traced coins in the ideal model, the simulator can use a random ciphertext for the inner symmetric ciphertext $ct$ and the associated encryptions of its key. For untraced coins, since the real world tracing authority does not have the keys for non-traced coins, the probability of abort is bounded by the security of the public key encryption scheme.

## 6  Accountable User Tracing

The problem with the original escrow above is that it provides no privacy from the tracing authority: all users' data is encrypted under a single key the authority holds. The only privacy guarantees users have are based on trust. And even those are limited: in order to find the coins used by a specified user, the authority needs to decrypt all coins. Ideally, we would have a system that not only allows the authority to only open coins of traced users, it creates an accountable record that they did so.

To do so, we borrow an idea from Accountable Tracing Signatures [14]: each user encrypts their data under a unique key they are given by the authority. If they are being traced, this key is a randomized version of the authority's public key. If, as is the common case, users are not being traced, the key is a randomized version of a null key (e.g. a random group element). Crucially, without knowledge of the randomness, users cannot distinguish which key they are getting at the

---

**PrivateInput:** CoinsIn, CoinsOut, pk, sig, r
**PublicInput** : usertracect
**Constants**   : CA
**output**      : True if transaction is valid

if $VerifySig(\mathsf{CA}, \mathsf{pk}, \mathsf{sig})$ then
   |   return usertracect $= Pkenc(\mathsf{pk}, \mathsf{CoinsIn} \| \mathsf{CoinsOut}; r)$;
else
   |   return False;
end

**Algorithm 9.** Accountable user tracing

---

time, but if the authority later reveals the randomness they can provably tell they were or were not traced. Thus we term this system accountable user tracing.

This requires one small change to the standard identity escrow policy: we have to allow an arbitrary key and ensure that it is signed by the authority and for the current epoch.

The larger question is key management. If we simply require the authority to reveal who they were monitoring at some later point, this policy becomes simple to implement: each user receives a key at each time period (e.g. daily) and by the disclosure deadline for searches, the authority reveals the random coins used to make the key. Unfortunately, this approach is unlikely to be compatible with real-world requirements. Given the existence of National Security Letters and similar warrants containing "gag orders", it is likely there are cases where the authority will prefer not to reveal which users were monitored. The standard solution in practice is to produce a transparency report that details which fraction of users were searched, and/or offers a loose bound on the number of searches.

However, building a cryptographically binding transparency report over millions of users efficiently is challenging given that this would involve processing millions of records. There are various ways this might be accomplished (e.g. techniques for batched proofs). In this work we propose a simple one: use a separate instance of Zerocash to create tokens that allow search. Each user gets their key along with a proof that their key is either randomized from the null key or randomized from the authority's key and a zerocoin is spent. At the end of each time period, the authority can spend all unused coins, thus revealing what fraction of people they searched.

# 7 Related Work

## 7.1 Anti-money Laundering for Centralized e-cash

Many, if not all of the policies in this paper have been implemented in centralized e-cash schemes, be it spending limits [7] or user and coin tracing. Somewhat surprisingly accountable user and coin tracing exists for centralized schemes [16,17]. However none of these have been done in the decentralized setting. Moreover, the known techniques for coin and user tracing [16,17] require coins to be withdrawn from the authority and then deposited back and have only one transfer, whereas our techniques allow continual transactions with the need to interact with the authority only dictated by the allowable delay in starting a trace.

## 7.2  Hawk

In concurrent work Kosba et al. [15] present Hawk, a system for privacy preserving smart contracts with an ideal functionality based definition. Hawk's security is set in the UC model [8], which is a stronger setting than we explore here. Achieving UC security requires all proofs to include an encrypted copy of their witness and a proof of its validity. This entails two costs: first, the increase in proving cost due to circuits handling encryption and second, the loss of succinctness. In the case of Zerocash, this results in a dramatic increase in the size of the proof due to the need to encrypt all witnesses.[2] This trade off between security and performance does not appear to affect our actual constructions here: if built using a UC security proof scheme, they can achieve UC security.

**Acknowledgements.** This work was supported by: The National Science Foundation under awards EFRI-1441209 and CNS-1414023; Google ATAP; The Mozilla Foundation; and the Office of Naval Research under contract N00014-14-1-0333.

# References

1. Barber, S., Boyen, X., Shi, E., Uzun, E.: Bitter to better — how to make bitcoin a better currency. In: Keromytis, A.D. (ed.) FC 2012. LNCS, vol. 7397, pp. 399–414. Springer, Heidelberg (2012). doi:10.1007/978-3-642-32946-3_29
2. Ben-Sasson, E., Chiesa, A., Garman, C., Green, M., Miers, I., Tromer, E., Virza, M.: Zerocash: decentralized anonymous payments from Bitcoin. In: 2014 IEEE Symposium on Security and Privacy (SP), pp. 459–474. IEEE (2014)
3. Ben-Sasson, E., Chiesa, A., Genkin, D., Tromer, E., Virza, M.: SNARKs for C: verifying program executions succinctly and in zero knowledge. In: Canetti, R., Garay, J.A. (eds.) CRYPTO 2013. LNCS, vol. 8043, pp. 90–108. Springer, Heidelberg (2013). doi:10.1007/978-3-642-40084-1_6
4. Ben-Sasson, E., Chiesa, A., Tromer, E., Virza, M.: Succinct non-interactive zero knowledge for a von Neumann architecture. In: Proceedings of the 23rd USENIX Security Symposium, Security 2014 (2014). http://eprint.iacr.org/2013/879
5. Biryukov, A., Khovratovich, D., Pustogarov, I.: Deanonymisation of clients in Bitcoin P2P network. In: Proceedings of the 2014 ACM SIGSAC Conference on Computer and Communications Security, pp. 15–29. ACM (2014)
6. Bitansky, N., Chiesa, A., Ishai, Y., Paneth, O., Ostrovsky, R.: Succinct non-interactive arguments via linear interactive proofs. In: Sahai, A. (ed.) TCC 2013. LNCS, vol. 7785, pp. 315–33. Springer, Heidelberg (2013). doi:10.1007/978-3-642-36594-2_18

---

[2] It may be possible to reduce the cost of these proofs by introducing zero-knowledge proofs that are only partially extractable, although this technique is not described by the Hawk authors. For example, the exact Merkle tree path need not be extracted from the zkSNARK proof.

7. Camenisch, J., Hohenberger, S., Lysyanskaya, A.: Balancing accountability and privacy using e-cash (extended abstract). In: Prisco, R., Yung, M. (eds.) SCN 2006. LNCS, vol. 4116, pp. 141–55. Springer, Heidelberg (2006). doi:10.1007/11832072_10

8. Canetti, R.: Universally composable security: a new paradigm for cryptographic protocols. In: FOCS 2001, p. 136. IEEE Computer Society (2001). http://eprint.iacr.org/2000/067

9. Danezis, G., Fournet, C., Kohlweiss, M., Parno, B.: Pinocchio coin: building Zerocoin from a succinct pairing-based proof system. In: Proceedings of the First ACM Workshop on Language Support for Privacy-enhancing Technologies, pp. 27–30. ACM (2013)

10. Garman, C., Green, M., Miers, I.: Accountable privacy for decentralized anonymous payments. Cryptology ePrint Archive, Report 2016/061 (2016). http://eprint.iacr.org

11. Gennaro, R., Gentry, C., Parno, B., Raykova, M.: Quadratic span programs and succinct NIZKs without PCPs. In: Johansson, T., Nguyen, P.Q. (eds.) EUROCRYPT 2013. LNCS, vol. 7881, pp. 626–45. Springer, Heidelberg (2013). doi:10.1007/978-3-642-38348-9_37

12. Goldreich, O.: Foundations of Cryptography: Volume 2, Basic Applications. Cambridge University Press, Cambridge (2004)

13. Groth, J.: Short pairing-based non-interactive zero-knowledge arguments. In: Abe, M. (ed.) ASIACRYPT 2010. LNCS, vol. 6477, pp. 321–40. Springer, Heidelberg (2010). doi:10.1007/978-3-642-17373-8_19

14. Kohlweiss, M., Miers, I.: Accountable tracing signatures. Cryptology ePrint Archive, Report 2014/824 (2014). http://eprint.iacr.org/

15. Kosba, A., Miller, A., Shi, E., Wen, Z., Papamanthou, C.: Hawk: the blockchain model of cryptography and privacy-preserving smart contracts (2015)

16. Kügler, D., Vogt, H.: Auditable tracing with unconditional anonymity. In: International Workshop on Information Security Application - WISA 2001, pp. 151–163 (2001)

17. Kügler, D., Vogt, H.: Offline payments with auditable tracing. In: Blaze, M. (ed.) FC 2002. LNCS, vol. 2357, pp. 269–81. Springer, Heidelberg (2003). doi:10.1007/3-540-36504-4_19

18. Lipmaa, H.: Progression-free sets and sublinear pairing-based non-interactive zero-knowledge arguments. In: Cramer, R. (ed.) TCC 2012. LNCS, vol. 7194, pp. 169–189. Springer, Heidelberg (2012). doi:10.1007/978-3-642-28914-9_10

19. Lipmaa, H.: Succinct non-interactive zero knowledge arguments from span programs and linear error-correcting codes. In: Sako, K., Sarkar, P. (eds.) ASIACRYPT 2013. LNCS, vol. 8269, pp. 41–60. Springer, Heidelberg (2013). doi:10.1007/978-3-642-42033-7_3

20. Miers, I., Garman, C., Green, M., Rubin, A.D.: Zerocoin: anonymous distributed e-cash from Bitcoin. In: 2013 IEEE Symposium on Security and Privacy (SP), pp. 397–411. IEEE (2013)

21. Parno, B., Gentry, C., Howell, J., Raykova, M.: Pinocchio: nearly practical verifiable computation. In: Proceedings of the 34th IEEE Symposium on Security and Privacy, Oakland, pp. 238–252 (2013)

22. Reid, F., Martin, H.: An analysis of anonymity in the Bitcoin system. In: Proceedings of the 3rd IEEE International Conference on Privacy, Security, Risk and Trust and on Social Computing, SocialCom/PASSAT 2011, pp. 1318–1326 (2011)

# Private eCash in Practice (Short Paper)

Amira Barki[1,2], Solenn Brunet[1,3], Nicolas Desmoulins[1], Sébastien Gambs[4], Saïd Gharout[1], and Jacques Traoré[1(✉)]

[1] Orange Labs, Caen, France
{amira.barki,jacques.traore}@orange.com
[2] Sorbonne universités, Université de technologie de Compiègne (UTC), CNRS, UMR 7253 Heudiasyc, Compiègne, France
[3] Université de Rennes 1, Rennes, France
[4] Université du Québec à Montréal (UQAM), Montréal, Canada

**Abstract.** Most electronic payment systems for applications, such as eTicketing and eToll, involve a single entity acting as both merchant and bank. In this paper, we propose an efficient privacy-preserving post-payment eCash system suitable for this particular use case that we refer to, afterwards, as private eCash. To this end, we introduce a new partially blind signature scheme based on a recent Algebraic MAC scheme due to Chase et al. Unlike previous constructions, it allows multiple presentations of the same signature in an unlinkable way. Using it, our system is the first versatile private eCash system where users must only hold a sole reusable token (*i.e.* a reusable coin spendable to a unique merchant). It also enables identity and token revocations as well as flexible payments. Indeed, our payment tokens are updated in a partially blinded way to collect refunds without invading user's privacy. By implementing it on a Global Platform compliant SIM card, we show its efficiency and suitability for real-world use cases, even for delay-sensitive applications and on constrained devices as a transaction can be performed in only 205 ms.

**Keywords:** eCash · Post-payment · Refunds · Partially blind signature · Anonymity · eToll · eTicketing · EVC

## 1 Introduction

Electronic Cash (eCash), introduced by Chaum [6], is the digital analogue of hard currency in which users withdraw electronic coins from a bank and spend them to merchants. Later, each merchant deposits the collected coins to the bank.

Using eCash, user's anonymity is protected both from the bank and merchants. To ensure this, it should be impossible to link the following pair of events: either a withdrawal and a spending or two spendings. However, owing to its digital nature, eCash has to be protected from duplication. Thus, eCash protocols must enable the detection of double-spending and the identification of defrauders.

© International Financial Cryptography Association 2017
J. Grossklags and B. Preneel (Eds.): FC 2016, LNCS 9603, pp. 99–109, 2017.
DOI: 10.1007/978-3-662-54970-4_6

To be as attractive as possible, the user's side of an eCash system is sometimes implemented on a mobile device or even a smart card. Therefore, protocols have to comply with both the limited resources of such environments as well as the stringent delay constraint arising from transactions requirements.

Public transport [2], electronic Toll (eToll) [7] and Electric Vehicle Charging (EVC) [3] are the main emerging uses cases of private eCash (*i.e.* involving a single merchant managed by the same entity acting as the bank) that significantly invade user's privacy. Indeed, transactions records may disclose user's location at a given time and reveal personal information such as work, home or habits.

*Related work.* Recently, several proposals have addressed this issue. However, finding a good tradeoff between necessary security properties and performance has not always been completely successful. In the sequel, we only focus on schemes related to eCash although other approaches exist in the literature [4,10,13].

Public transport users' privacy was tackled in [2,11,14]. In the first two proposals, users pay for their trips through the use of payment tokens that are worth the highest possible fare. As fares have different values, a refund process is set up to guarantee the accurate charging of users. However, to ensure user's anonymity with respect to the transport company, the scheme of Rupp et al. [14] entails heavy verifications that constrained devices cannot handle [2]. The proposal of Milutinovic et al. [11] is also computationally expensive and less efficient than [14] as refunds are separately collected on distinct refund tokens. Arfaoui et al. [2] protocol meets the stringent delay requirement and is efficient even when implemented in constrained environment. It is also the only one allowing anonymity revocation under exceptional circumstances. Nevertheless, this scheme does not enable flexible prices. As regards to EVC user's privacy, it was addressed by Au et al. [3]. However, their scheme requires costly zero-knowledge proofs of knowledge and is not suitable for time-sensitive applications.

Finally, Day et al. [7] proposed two privacy-preserving payment systems for eToll. However, the first one is only partially private as it relies on spot checks that record some of the user's spatio-temporal information to detect and identify defrauders. Furthermore, through an exhaustive search on tokens, it is possible to trace all user's trips. In contrast, the second proposal provides full anonymity and enables double spending detection. Unfortunately, to be efficient, users have to hold a large number of tokens where each one can only be used at a specific time. Besides, similarly to eCoupons, both proposals do not allow flexible prices, which we believe to be an important issue.

*Contributions.* In this paper, we propose an efficient post-payment private eCash system designed for scenarios in which the same entity acts as both merchant and bank like public transport, eToll and EVC. Indeed, we leverage this feature to strike a balance between efficiency and privacy. Our system relies on a new partially blind signature scheme built based on the recent Chase et al. Algebraic MAC scheme [5]. Unlike ordinary eCash systems, users must only hold a single token that can be reused a specified number of times without allowing anyone to trace users or link their transactions. Through a refund process[1], our eCash system supports both post-payments (*i.e.* users are charged after the use of the service) and flexible prices while removing the need to withdraw several tokens of different values. Our proposal is proven secure in the random oracle model (ROM) and its implementation on a SIM card shows that it complies with the limited computational power of constrained devices and stringent time constraints.

The paper is organized as follows. Section 2 introduces our main notation and building blocks and details our partially blind signature scheme. Based on this first contribution, Sect. 3 explains our eCash system through the eToll use case. As an electronic payment system dedicated to toll roads, it illustrates the challenging requirements we have to face both in terms of privacy and performance. Finally, implementation results in Sect. 4 show that our system is truly efficient.

## 2 Preliminaries

### 2.1 Notation

To state that $x$ is chosen uniformly at random from the set $X$, we use one of the two following notations $x \xleftarrow{R} X$ or $x \in_R X$. In addition, $\overrightarrow{x}$ and $\{g_i\}_{i=1}^l$ respectively denote the vector $(x_0, x_1, \ldots, x_n)$ and the set $\{g_1, g_2, \ldots, g_l\}$.

Zero-Knowledge Proofs of Knowledge (ZKPK) allow a prover $\mathcal{P}$ to convince a verifier $\mathcal{V}$ that he knows some secrets verifying a given statement without revealing anything else about them. They are denoted by the usual notation in which Greek letters correspond to $\mathcal{P}$'s knowledge: $\pi := \mathrm{PoK}\{\alpha, \beta : statements\ about\ \alpha, \beta\}$.

### 2.2 Computational Hardness Assumptions

The security of our proposals relies on the following computational hardness assumptions. Let $\mathbb{G}$ be a cyclic group of prime order $q$.

*Discrete Logarithm* (DL) *Assumption.* The Discrete Logarithm assumption states that, given a generator $g \in_R \mathbb{G}$ and an element $y \in_R \mathbb{G}$, it is hard to find the integer $x \in \mathbb{Z}_q$ such that $g^x = y$.

*Decisional Diffie-Hellman* (DDH) *Assumption.* The Decisional Diffie-Hellman assumption states that, given a generator $g \in_R \mathbb{G}$, two elements $g^a, g^b \in \mathbb{G}$ and a candidate $X \in \mathbb{G}$, it is hard to decide whether $X = g^{ab}$ or not.

*Decisional Composite Residuosity* (DCR) *Assumption.* The Decisional Composite Residuosity assumption states that it is hard to distinguish $\mathbb{Z}_{n^2}^n$ from $\mathbb{Z}_{n^2}^*$ where $\mathbb{Z}_{n^2}^n = \{z \in \mathbb{Z}_{n^2}^* : \exists y \in \mathbb{Z}_{n^2}^*$ such that $z = y^n \mod n^2\}$ is the set of $n$th residues.

---

[1] As shown in [14], an aggregate refund amount should not enable to deduce the different toll fares and hence, the details of the individual trips the user has taken.

LRSW *Assumption.* For a generator $g \in_R \mathbb{G}$, $X_0 = g^{x_0}$ and $X_1 = g^{x_1}$, let $\mathcal{O}$ be an oracle that takes on input $m \in \mathbb{Z}_q$ and outputs $A = (a, a^{x_1}, a^{x_0 + mx_0 x_1})$ where $a \in_R \mathbb{G}$. The LRSW assumption states that, given $(X_0, X_1)$ and unlimited access to $\mathcal{O}$, it is hard to generate a triplet for a new $m'$ that has not been queried to $\mathcal{O}$.

Pointcheval and Sanders [12] introduced the following variant of the LRSW assumption in type-3 bilinear groups in order to prove the security of their signatures schemes.

*Assumption 1.* Let $(\mathbb{G}_1, \mathbb{G}_2, \mathbb{G}_T, q, e)$ be a bilinear group setting of type 3 and $h, \tilde{h}$ be two generators of $\mathbb{G}_1$ and $\mathbb{G}_2$ respectively. For $X_1 = h^{x_1}$, $\tilde{X}_0 = \tilde{h}^{x_0}$ and $\tilde{X}_1 = \tilde{h}^{x_1}$ such that $x_0, x_1 \in_R \mathbb{Z}_q^*$, let $\mathcal{O}_1$ be an oracle that takes on input $m \in \mathbb{Z}_q$ and outputs the pair $P = (u, u^{x_0 + mx_1})$ for $u \in_R \mathbb{G}_1$. The Assumption 1 states that, given $(h, X_1, \tilde{h}, \tilde{X}_0, \tilde{X}_1)$ and unlimited access to $\mathcal{O}_1$, it is hard to efficiently generate a valid pair for a new $m'$ that has not been queried to $\mathcal{O}_1$, with $u \neq 1_{\mathbb{G}_1}$.

## 2.3   Building Blocks

*Algebraic MAC in Prime-Order Group.* Chase et al. introduce in [5] two MAC schemes constructed using a cyclic group of prime order. An interesting feature of their schemes is that the issuer and the verifier are actually the same entity and consequently share a set of keys. To build our private eCash scheme, we focus on their $\text{MAC}_{\text{GGM}}$ construction, that can be seen as a digital signature scheme, proven unforgeable under chosen message and verification attack (UF-CMVA) in the generic group model. In the following, we briefly review their construction by explaining how to sign $n$ distinct messages $(m_1, \ldots, m_n)$:

1. $\text{Setup}(1^k)$ creates the system public parameters denoted $pp := (\mathbb{G}, q, g, h)$ where $\mathbb{G}$ is a cyclic group of prime order $q$, a $k$-bit prime, and $g, h$ are two random generators such that $\log_g h$ is unknown.
2. $\text{KeyGen}(pp)$ generates a secret key $sk := \vec{x} \in_R \mathbb{F}_q^{n+1}$ and a value $\tilde{x}_0 \in_R \mathbb{F}_q$ to build a commitment $C_{x_0} := g^{x_0} h^{\tilde{x}_0}$ to the secret value $x_0$. Denoted by $iparams$, $(C_{x_0}, X_1 := h^{x_1}, \ldots, X_n := h^{x_n})$ corresponds to the issuer's public parameters.
3. $\text{MAC}(sk, \vec{m})$ produces an authenticated token $(u, u')$ on $\vec{m} := (m_1, \ldots, m_n)$ where $u \in_R \mathbb{G} \backslash \{1\}$ and $u' := u^{x_0 + x_1 m_1 + \cdots + x_n m_n}$.
4. $\text{Verify}(sk, \vec{m}, (u, u'))$ checks the validity of the token with respect to the message $\vec{m}$. The token is accepted only if $u \neq 1$ and $u' = u^{x_0 + x_1 m_1 + \cdots + x_n m_n}$.

Based on $\text{MAC}_{\text{GGM}}$, Chase et al. proposed a keyed-verification anonymous credentials scheme allowing the blind issuance of credentials. However, it requires ZKPK for each hidden attribute and does not provide *perfect unlinkability* as the credential attributes are sent to the issuer encrypted, using ElGamal encryption scheme, before being signed. Thus, it is not suitable for eCash systems.

*Partially blind signatures.* A variation of basic digital signatures, called *blind signature*, allows a receiver $\mathcal{R}$ to get a signature on a message without revealing any information about it to the signer $\mathcal{S}$. However, in use cases like eCash, $\mathcal{S}$ may want to add some information to the blind signature such as a date, a validity period or an amount. To address this issue, Abe et al. [1] proposed an extension known as *partially blind signature*. It allows $\mathcal{R}$ and $\mathcal{S}$ to agree on a common information info to be added in the blind signature of a message $\vec{m}$. A partially blind signature scheme should be (1) *one-more unforgeable* (*i.e.* it should be impossible to obtain $L+1$ signatures with at most $L$ signing requests) and (2) *unlinkable* (*i.e.* it should be impossible to link two signatures or identify for whom the signature was issued).

Through the interactive protocol $\texttt{BlindIssue}(\mathcal{R}(\vec{m}), \mathcal{S}(sk))$ described below, we detail our partially blind signature scheme based on $\mathsf{MAC_{GGM}}$ and which is executed between $\mathcal{R}$ holding $\vec{m}$ and $\mathcal{S}$ who acts as the issuer holding $sk$:

1. $\mathcal{R}$ sends the common value info, a commitment $C_{\vec{m}} := h^r X_1^{m_1} \ldots X_n^{m_n}$ to the message $\vec{m}$ where $r \in_R \mathbb{Z}_q^*$ as well as the ZKPK $\pi_1$ defined as follows: $\pi_1 := PoK\{\alpha_1, \alpha_2, \ldots, \alpha_n, \beta : C_{\vec{m}} = h^\beta X_1^{\alpha_1} \ldots X_n^{\alpha_n}\}$.
2. If $\pi_1$ is valid, $\mathcal{S}$ computes $u'' := u^{x_0}(C_{\vec{m}}(X_n)^{\texttt{info}})^b$ s.t. $b \in_R \mathbb{Z}_q^*$ and $u := h^b$. Then, he provides $\mathcal{R}$ with the partially blind signature $((u, u''), \texttt{info})$ as well as a ZKPK $\pi_2$ proving that $u'' := u^{x_0 + x_1 m_1 + \ldots + x_{n-1} m_{n-1} + x_n(m_n + \texttt{info})} h^{br}$ and $\pi_2 := PoK\{\alpha, \beta, \gamma : u'' = u^\alpha(C_{\vec{m}}(X_n)^{\texttt{info}})^\beta \wedge C_{x_0} = g^\alpha h^\gamma \wedge u = h^\beta\}$.
3. If $\pi_2$ is valid, $\mathcal{R}$ unblinds $(u, u'')$ to obtain the signature $(u, u' := \frac{u''}{u^r})$.

To show the obtained signature in an anonymous way, the receiver has just to randomize it by computing $(u^l, (u')^l)$ where $l \in_R \mathbb{Z}_q^*$.

In our eCash system, info will correspond to the refund amount and will be used with $m_n$ to aggregate refunds. Usually, $m_n$ may be set to zero and info would be the validity period, thus enabling a convenient update of signatures.

**Theorem 1.** *Our partially blind signature scheme is* perfectly unlinkable, *and* one-more unforgeable *under the Assumption 1 in the ROM.*[2]

## 3   Our Private eCash System: The eToll Use Case

### 3.1   System Framework

*Stakeholders.* Our private eToll system involves three main entities: a user $\mathcal{U}$, a toll company $\mathcal{TC}$ and a set of revocation authorities $\mathcal{RA}$s that must collaborate to revoke user's anonymity or tokens.

*Overview.* To benefit from the eToll service, a user must first register to obtain a badge that will perform all computations on his behalf. At the beginning of each billing period, registered users receive a unique reusable token generated using our partially blind signature scheme detailed in Sect. 2.3. This token is worth the highest possible fare and can be reused at most $N_{\max}$ times. To be granted

---

[2] Owing to the lack of space, we defer the proofs of Theorem 1 and Theorem 2 to an extended version.

access while preserving his anonymity, the user shows a randomized version of his token. Concurrently, as toll fares are generally different, the user's token is updated in a blinded way, using our partially blind signature scheme, to add the refund amount associated to the transaction. At the end of the billing period, users are charged according to their token value. Such a post-payment approach prevent them from refilling a prepaid account with a large amount of money. However, if a user does not return his token, he will pay the maximal allowed amount corresponding to $N_{\max}$ trips with the highest fare.

*Security and performance requirements.* None of the entities can be fully trusted since all of them have some incentives to cheat. Only the user's badge is subject to the limited trust assumption that all the computations it performs are correct. Nevertheless, any attempt to cheat by tampering it must be detected. To this end, in addition to the usual *correctness* property, some security properties must be satisfied. Our private eCash system should provide (1) *unlinkability* (*i.e.* it should be impossible to link together two events such as two transactions or a transaction and a given token) which implies the regular *anonymity* property, (2) *revocability* (*i.e.* $\mathcal{RA}$s can always revoke user's anonymity and tokens), (3) *non-frameability* (*i.e.* nobody should be able to falsely accuse another user of performing a given transaction) and, (4) *unforgeability* (*i.e.* it should be impossible for users to cheat by paying less charges than what they have to). To be effective and suitable for most use cases, a transaction must be performed in at most 300 ms [2].

## 3.2  Description of the Protocols

Our private eCash system consists of six phases. (1) The public parameters and required keys are initialized during *setup*. (2) The *Registration* phase enables a user to register to the system and to obtain his badge. (3) The *Token Issuance* phase provides legitimate users with a unique reusable token. (4) During *Access Control*, a user uses his token to be granted access at tollbooths. (5) The *Toll Computation* phase allows the computation of the user's bill based on his token value. Finally, (6) the *Revocation* phase enables user's anonymity and token revocations. Below, we explain these phases and detail the main protocols in Fig. 1. Owing to space limitations, the ZKPKs are not detailed. Except otherwise specified, they are quite standard and many values in these proofs can be *precomputed*.

**Setup.** Let $pp = (\mathbb{G}, g, h, q, g_R, N_{\max}, \{g_i\}_{i=1}^{N_{\max}})$ denote the public parameters where $\mathbb{G}$ is a cyclic group of prime order $q$ and $(g, h, g_R, \{g_i\}_{i=1}^{N_{\max}})$ a set of random generators. $N_{\max}$ indicates the allowed number of reuses of a token and could be set according to user's needs. Each user $\mathcal{U}$ is also provided with a pair of keys $(sk_u, pk_u)$ that identifies him.

The toll company shares the secret key $\overrightarrow{x} := (x_0, x_1, x_2)$ with tollbooths that are denoted by $\mathcal{TC}$ as well. The associated public parameters are $C_{x_0} := g^{x_0} h^{\tilde{x}_0}$, a commitment to $x_0$ where $\tilde{x}_0 \in_R \mathbb{Z}_q^*$, and $X_1 := h^{x_1}$, $X_2 := h^{x_2}$. They are also provided with a pair of keys $(sk_{tc}, pk_{tc})$ used to sign transaction data.

The revocation authorities jointly generate two pairs of keys: $(sk_{ra}, pk_{ra})$ of the threshold ElGamal and $(sk_{rp}, pk_{rp})$ of the threshold Paillier cryptosystems. Paillier encryption scheme is used as an *extractable commitment* (see [9]) to satisfy the unforgeability requirement, even in a concurrent setting, where an adversary is allowed to interact with $\mathcal{TC}$ in an arbitrarily interleaving (concurrent) manner. Let $g_E$ and $g_P$ be two generators of $\mathbb{G}$. ElGamal keys are defined as $sk_{ra} := x_T \in \mathbb{Z}_q^*$ and $pk_{ra} := (g_E, X_T := g_E^{x_T})$. Paillier pair of keys consists of $sk_{rp} := (a, b)$ and $pk_{rp} := (g_P, n := ab)$ where $a$ and $b$ are two different random primes such that $|a| = |b|$ and $gcd(ab, (a-1)(b-1)) = 1$. The private keys are shared among $\mathcal{RAs}$ [8] and at least $t$ of them should cooperate to identify the user or revoke a token.

**Registration.** To use the service, $\mathcal{U}$ must provide $\mathcal{TC}$ with his public key $pk_u$ and a ZKPK proving the knowledge of the secret key $sk_u$. If the proof is valid, $\mathcal{U}$ receives a personal badge $\mathcal{B}_u$ including a SIM card. It allows $\mathcal{U}$ to anonymously use the service. Moreover, $pk_u$ is saved in a dedicated database denoted by $\text{DB}_{\text{REG}}$.

**Token Issuance.** The *token issuance* phase occurs at the beginning of each billing period upon a signed request of a registered user. During this phase, $\mathcal{TC}$ provides $\mathcal{U}$ with a permission token $T := (u, u' := u^{x_0 + x_1 s_u + x_2 m})$. It is a partially blind signature on the unknown message $s_u = s + s'$ and the common information $m$ corresponding to the refund amount, initially set to 0. In fact, $s_u$ is a secret value only known by $\mathcal{U}$: it involves a secret $s \in_R \mathbb{Z}_q^*$ chosen by $\mathcal{U}$ and hidden from $\mathcal{TC}$ and $s' \in_R \mathbb{Z}_q^*$ chosen by $\mathcal{TC}$ and provided to $\mathcal{U}$. The token is worth the highest possible toll fare and can be reused $N_{\max}$ times. Two ZKPKs $\pi_1$ and $\pi_2$ ensure that exchanged values are well-formed (see Fig. 1). Besides, $(g^s, s', D)$ is saved in $\text{DB}_{\text{REG}}$ where $D$ is a Paillier encryption of $s$ necessary for token revocation.

**Access Control.** To be granted access at tollbooths, $\mathcal{U}$ provides a randomized version of his token $T$ and an ElGamal encryption $E$ of $g^{s_u}$ along with a ZKPK $\pi_3$ proving that these values are well-formed. Upon receipt, $\mathcal{TC}$ checks the token both for the allowed number of uses and validity. Indeed, whenever reaching a tollbooth, $\mathcal{B}_u$ randomly chooses a $g_i$ among the set $F$ of unused ones. The selected $g_i$ is then removed from $F$ to prevent over-spending of a token. If checks succeed, $\mathcal{U}$ receives an updated $T$ with a new $m$ aggregating all the refunds collected so far. This new token is computed using our partially blind signature scheme with a common value equal to the current refund amount. Due to delay constraint, the associated ZKPK $\pi_4$ cannot be instantly verified. Thus, $\mathcal{U}$ is also provided with $S$, an RSA signature with a short public verification exponent, of all the received values. $S$ can be quickly verified upon receipt while $\pi_4$ is rather checked during the idle time of the SIM card. Concurrently, $(E, T_i := g_i^{s_u})$ is saved in the

| User $\mathcal{U}$ | Toll Company $\mathcal{TC}$ |
|---|---|
| **Public Input:** $pp$, $X_1$, $X_2$, $C_{x_0}$, $pk_{tc}$, $pk_{ra}$, $pk_{rp}$ and $pk_u$ | |
| **(1) Token Issuance Protocol** | |
| **Private Input:** $sk_u$ | **Private Input:** $(x_0, x_1, x_2)$, DB$_{\text{REG}}$ |
| Choose $r, r_1, s \xleftarrow{R} \mathbb{Z}_q^*$ | |
| Compute $C \leftarrow h^r X_1^s$, $W = g^s$, $D = g_P^s r_1^n$ | |
| Build $\pi_1 = \text{PoK}[\alpha, \beta, \gamma : C = h^\alpha X_1^\beta$ $\xrightarrow{C, \pi_1, W, D}$ | Check $\pi_1$ and Choose $s', b \xleftarrow{R} \mathbb{Z}_q^*$ |
| $\wedge W = g^\beta \wedge D = g_P^\beta \gamma^n]$ $\xleftarrow{Sign(C, \pi_1, W, D)}$ | Compute $u \leftarrow h^b$ |
| | $u'' \leftarrow u^{x_0}(CX_1^{s'})^b$ |
| Check $\pi_2$ $\xleftarrow{s', (u, u''), \pi_2}$ | Build $\pi_2 = \text{PoK}[\alpha, \beta, \gamma : u = h^\alpha$ |
| Compute $s_u \leftarrow s + s'$ and $u' \leftarrow \frac{u''}{u^r}$ | $\wedge u'' = u^\beta (CX_1^{s'})^\alpha \wedge C_{x_0} = g^\beta h^\gamma]$ |
| $T \leftarrow (u, u')$, $m \leftarrow 0$, $F \leftarrow \{g_i\}_{i=1}^{N_{\max}}$ | Save $(W, D, s')$ in DB$_{\text{REG}}$ |
| **(2) Access Control Protocol** | |
| **Public Input:** $m'$ | |
| **Private Input:** $T := (u, u')$, $m$, $s_u$, $F$ | **Private Input:** $(x_0, x_1, x_2)$, DB$_{\text{AC}}$ |
| Choose $l, r, z_1, z_2, t$ and $b \xleftarrow{R} \mathbb{Z}_q^*$, $g_i \xleftarrow{R} F$ | |
| Compute $w \leftarrow u^l$; $w' \leftarrow (u')^l$; $c' \leftarrow w' g^r$ | |
| $c_1 \leftarrow w^{s_u} h^{z_1}$; $c_2 \leftarrow w^m h^{z_2}$; $F \leftarrow F \backslash \{g_i\}$ | |
| $V \leftarrow g^{-r} X_1^{z_1} X_2^{z_2}$; $A \leftarrow h^t X_1^{s_u} X_2^m$ | |
| $E \leftarrow (e_1 = g_E^b, e_2 = g^{s_u} X_T^b)$; $T_i \leftarrow g_i^{s_u}$ | |
| Build $\pi_3 = \text{PoK}[\alpha, \beta, \gamma, \delta, \sigma, \mu, \eta : T_i = g_i^\sigma$ $\xrightarrow{w, c', c_1, c_2, V}$ | Check if $V \stackrel{?}{=} \frac{w^{x_0} c_1^{x_1} c_2^{x_2}}{c'}$ |
| $\wedge c_2 = w^\mu h^\gamma \wedge V = g^{-\alpha} X_1^\beta X_2^\gamma \wedge e_1 = g^\eta$ $\xrightarrow{T_i, A, g_i, \pi_3, E}$ | Check $\pi_3$ and $T_i \notin$ DB$_{\text{AC}}$ |
| $c_1 = w^\sigma h^\beta \wedge A = h^\delta X_1^\sigma X_2^\mu \wedge e_2 = g^\sigma X_T^\eta]$ | Choose $d \xleftarrow{R} \mathbb{Z}_q^*$; Compute $y \leftarrow h^d$ |
| | Compute $y'' \leftarrow y^{x_0}(AX_2^{m'})^d$ |
| | $S = Sign_{RSA}(m', y, y'', \pi_4)$ |
| Check $\pi_4$ and $S$ $\xleftarrow{m', y, y'', \pi_4, S}$ | Build $\pi_4 = \text{PoK}[\alpha, \beta, \gamma : y = h^\alpha$ |
| Compute $y' \leftarrow \frac{y''}{y^r}$, $m \leftarrow m + m'$ | $\wedge y'' = y^\beta (AX_2^{m'})^\alpha \wedge C_{x_0} = g^\beta h^\gamma]$ |
| and $T \leftarrow (y, y')$ | Save $(E, T_i)$ in DB$_{\text{AC}}$ |
| **(3) Toll Computation Protocol** | |
| **Private Input:** $T := (u, u')$, $m$, $s_u$ | **Private Input:** $(x_0, x_1, x_2)$, DB$_{\text{REG}}$ |
| Choose $l, r, z_1 \xleftarrow{R} \mathbb{Z}_q^*$ | |
| Compute $R \leftarrow u^l$; $R' \leftarrow (u')^l$; $c' \leftarrow R' g^r$ | |
| $c_1 \leftarrow R^{s_u} h^{z_1}$; $V \leftarrow g^{-r} X_1^{z_1}$; $T_g \leftarrow g_R^{s_u}$ | |
| Build $\pi_5 = \text{PoK}[\alpha, \beta, \gamma : T_g = g_R^\alpha$ $\xrightarrow{m, R, c', c_1}$ | Check if $V \stackrel{?}{=} \frac{R^{x_0 + m x_2} c_1^{x_1}}{c'}$ |
| $\wedge c_1 = R^\alpha h^\beta \wedge V = g^{-\gamma} X_1^\beta]$ $\xrightarrow{V, T_g, \pi_5}$ | Check $\pi_5$ and $T_g \notin$ DB$_{\text{REG}}$ |
| | Save $T_g$ in DB$_{\text{REG}}$ |

**Fig. 1.** Our private eCash system: the eToll use case

database of transactions DB$_{\text{AC}}$. Note that, to provide *full unlinkability*, one may add randomness in $T_i$ using a pseudo-random function as in [2].

**Toll Computation.** At the end of the billing period, $\mathcal{U}$ shows his randomized token $T$ and a tag $T_g := g_R^{s_u}$ to be charged for all his trips. The tag ensures that $\mathcal{U}$ has not already asked for a refund during that period. Based on the refund amount $m$, $\mathcal{TC}$ computes the user's charges and saves $T_g$ in DB$_{\text{REG}}$. If a user's token has been used less than $N_{\max}$ times, a specific process emulates their use with no associated charges to ensure that $\mathcal{U}$ will only pay for the trips he took.

**Revocation.** Two different revocations may be triggered in exceptional circumstances: the revocation of user's anonymity or tokens. In the former, the goal is to identify the user who performed a given access control (*e.g.* for national security reasons). To do so, $\mathcal{TC}$ sends to $\mathcal{RA}$s the ElGamal encryption $E$ of $g^{s_u}$. At least $t$ of them should collaborate to recover $g^{s_u}$. Using the information stored in DB$_{\text{REG}}$, $\mathcal{TC}$ identifies the corresponding user. In the latter, the aim is to revoke a token following, for example, the loss or theft of the badge. To this end, $\mathcal{RA}$s are provided with the Paillier encryption $D$ of the secret $s$ that they jointly decrypt. Thereby, $\mathcal{TC}$ can compute $s_u = s + s'$ and thus blacklists all the $\{T_i := g_i^{s_u}\}_{i=1}^{N_{\max}}$.

**Theorem 2.** *Our private eCash system is* unlinkable *under the Decisional Composite Residuosity* (DCR) *and the Decisional Diffie-Hellman* (DDH) *assumptions,* unforgeable *and* revocable *under the assumption that* MAC$_{\text{GGM}}$ *is UF-CMVA secure and* non-frameable *under the Discrete Logarithm* (DL) *assumption, in the ROM.*

## 4   Performance Assessment

Table 1 gives timing results of the implementation of the *Access Control* protocol on a Javacard 2.2.2 SIM card, Global Platform 2.2 compliant, embedded in a Samsung galaxy S3 NFC smartphone. The only particularity of our card, compared to the javacard specifications, is some additional API provided by the card manufacturer enabling modular and elliptic curve operations. Although the used SIM card is more powerful than most cards, as it requires a cryptoprocessor to be able to handle asymmetric cryptography, it is worth emphasizing that such powerful SIM cards with cryptoprocessors are already widely deployed by some mobile phone carriers, such as Orange in France, to provide NFC-based services.

**Table 1.** Timings ((min-max) average in ms) of the *Access Control* Protocol. The off-line computations (steps 1 and 5) are launched from the smartphone (battery-on). On-line computations concern steps 2, 3 and 4, and can be done battery-off.

| | Card Precomputation (1) | Get Data from card (2) | $\mathcal{TC}$ computation (3) | Send Data to card (4) | Card Verification (5) | Total On-line part |
|---|---|---|---|---|---|---|
| Battery-On: | (1672-1688) 1678 | (66-68) 67 | (9-34) 22 | (96-115) 102 | (501-522) 511 | (186-224) **205** |
| Battery-Off: | | 85 | | (175-184) 182 | | (298-322) **315** |

The implementation uses a 256-bit prime elliptic curve. To have the fastest possible verification on card, $\mathcal{TC}$ uses an RSA signature scheme with a short public verification exponent. Since our private eCash system is not only intended for eToll but also for public transport, communications between the SIM card in the smartphone and the PC (Intel Xeon CPU 3.70 GHz) acting as $\mathcal{TC}$ was done in NFC using a standard PC/SC reader (an Omnikey 5321). "Battery-Off" denotes a powered-off mobile phone either by the user or because its battery is flat. In this case, as stated by NFC standards, NFC-access to the SIM card is still possible, but with degraded performances. On average, the on-line part of the *Access Control* protocol is very fast even with a powered-off phone. In fact, data exchange is the most time-consuming task.

## 5 Conclusion

In this paper, our contribution is twofold. First, we proposed a perfectly unlinkable partially blind signature scheme that relies on Chase et al. Algebraic MAC scheme. Then, based on it, we designed a private eCash system that only requires users to hold a unique reusable token while preserving their privacy. Through a refund process, it also enables flexible prices as well as post-payments. Finally, implementation results show its efficiency even when implemented on a SIM card.

## References

1. Abe, M., Fujisaki, E.: How to date blind signatures. In: Kim, K., Matsumoto, T. (eds.) ASIACRYPT 1996. LNCS, vol. 1163, pp. 244–251. Springer, Heidelberg (1996). doi:10.1007/BFb0034851
2. Arfaoui, G., Lalande, J., Traoré, J., Desmoulins, N., Berthomé, P., Gharout, S.: A practical set-membership proof for privacy-preserving NFC mobile ticketing. In: Proceedings on Privacy Enhancing Technologies abs/1505.03048 (2015)
3. Au, M.H., Liu, J., Fang, J., Jiang, Z., Susilo, W., Zhou, J.: A new payment system for enhancing location privacy of electric vehicles. IEEE Trans. Veh. Technol. **63**(1), 3–18 (2014)
4. Balasch, J., Rial, A., Troncoso, C., Preneel, B., Verbauwhede, I., Geuens, C.: PrETP: privacy-preserving electronic toll pricing. In: Proceedings of the 19th USENIX Conference on Security, USENIX Security 2010, p. 5 (2010)
5. Chase, M., Meiklejohn, S., Zaverucha, G.: Algebraic MACs and keyed-verification anonymous credentials. In: Proceedings of the 2014 ACM SIGSAC CCS, CCS 2014, pp. 1205–1216. ACM, New York (2014)
6. Chaum, D.: Blind signatures for untraceable payments. In: Chaum, D., Rivest, R., Sherman, A. (eds.) Advances in Cryptology, pp. 199–203. Springer, New York (1983)
7. Day, J., Huang, Y., Knapp, E., Goldberg, I.: SPEcTRe: spot-checked private ecash tolling at roadside. In: WPES, pp. 61–68. ACM (2011)
8. Fouque, P.-A., Poupard, G., Stern, J.: Sharing decryption in the context of voting or lotteries. In: Frankel, Y. (ed.) FC 2000. LNCS, vol. 1962, pp. 90–104. Springer, Heidelberg (2001). doi:10.1007/3-540-45472-1_7
9. Hufschmitt, E., Traoré, J.: Fair blind signatures revisited. In: Takagi, T., Okamoto, E., Okamoto, T., Okamoto, T. (eds.) Pairing 2007. LNCS, vol. 4575, pp. 268–292. Springer, Heidelberg (2007). doi:10.1007/978-3-540-73489-5_14
10. Meiklejohn, S., Mowery, K., Checkoway, S., Shacham, H.: The phantom tollbooth: privacy-preserving electronic toll collection in the presence of driver collusion. In: Proceedings of the 20th USENIX Conference on Security, SEC 2011, p. 32 (2011)

11. Milutinovic, M., Decroix, K., Naessens, V., De Decker, B.: Privacy-preserving public transport ticketing system. In: Samarati, P. (ed.) DBSec 2015. LNCS, vol. 9149, pp. 135–150. Springer, Cham (2015). doi:10.1007/978-3-319-20810-7_9

12. Pointcheval, D., Sanders, O.: Short randomizable signatures. In: Sako, K. (ed.) CT-RSA 2016. LNCS, vol. 9610, pp. 111–126. Springer, Cham (2016). doi:10.1007/978-3-319-29485-8_7

13. Popa, R.A., Balakrishnan, H., Blumberg, A.J.: VPriv: protecting privacy in location-based vehicular services. In: Proceedings of the 18th Conference on USENIX Security Symposium, SSYM 2009, pp. 335–350 (2009)

14. Rupp, A., Hinterwälder, G., Baldimtsi, F., Paar, C.: P4R: privacy-preserving prepayments with refunds for transportation systems. In: Sadeghi, A.-R. (ed.) FC 2013. LNCS, vol. 7859, pp. 205–212. Springer, Heidelberg (2013). doi:10.1007/978-3-642-39884-1_17

# Practically Efficient Secure Single-Commodity Multi-market Auctions

Abdelrahaman Aly[1,2]([✉]) and Mathieu Van Vyve[1]

[1] CORE, Université catholique de Louvain,
Voie du Roman Pays 34, 1348 Louvain-la-Neuve, Belgium
mathieu.vanvyve@uclouvain.be
[2] imec-COSIC KU Leuven, Kasteelpark Arenberg 10,
3001 Leuven-Heverlee, Belgium
abdelrahaman.aly@esat.kuleuven.be

**Abstract.** We study the problem of securely building single-commodity multi-markets auction mechanisms. We introduce a novel greedy algorithm and its corresponding privacy preserving implementation using secure multi-party computation. More specifically, we determine the quantity of supply and demand bids maximizing welfare. Each bid is attached to a specific market, but exchanges between different markets are allowed up to some upper limit. The general goal is for the players to bid their intended valuations without concerns about what the other players can learn. This problem is inspired by day-ahead electricity markets where there are substantial transmission capacity between the different markets, but applies to other commodity markets like gas. Furthermore, we provide computational results with a specific C++ implementation of our algorithm and the necessary MPC primitives. We can solve problems of 1945 bids and 4 markets in 1280 s when online/offline phases are considered. Finally, we report on possible set-ups, workload distributions and possible trade-offs for real-life applications of our results based on this experimentation and prototyping.

## 1 Introduction

Auctions have been proved to be economically efficient under many settings [1]. In recent years, with the advent of larger scale markets e.g. online commerce and commodities, factors like secrecy, integrity and fairness have become more important. Parties need adequate incentives to bid truthfully, without the risk of loosing competitive advantages in future interactions. Our aim is to solve the problem where a commodity is to be transported between the different markets up to a given capacity limit. In our setting, buyers, sellers, markets and control agencies may have to interact in a competitive environment where information about prices and volume can reveal much more than what any party is willing to disclose. In the day-ahead electricity markets in Europe, this reluctance delayed by several years the integration of the national markets, until it was actually imposed by the European authorities (Directives 2005/89 and 2003/54 and Regulation 1228/2003).

© International Financial Cryptography Association 2017
J. Grossklags and B. Preneel (Eds.): FC 2016, LNCS 9603, pp. 110–129, 2017.
DOI: 10.1007/978-3-662-54970-4_7

Traditional solutions include a neutral third party in charge of all computations and responsible to exert secrecy, integrity an fairness in his own processes. However, such a third party is in general hard to find, and would concentrate all attacks making it a single vulnerable failure point.

We report on a mechanism where this third party can be replaced. Indeed, our *virtual third party* uses Secure Multi-Party Computation (MPC) and can be composed of any subset of players. MPC is a secure mechanism that allows several players to compute a function in a distributed environment. From Yao's original result in 1982 [2], to the current state of the art, secure multi-party computation has evolved from a theoretical object of study, to a field that is used in real life applications. MPC offers a variety of techniques, primitives and applications that provide security under diverse models, and in a distributed environment.

## 1.1   Our Contribution

We introduce a novel greedy algorithm and its secure formulation, for auctions with several geographical markets where exchange between them is possible. We analyze and introduce variations and trade-offs of these building blocks to obtain efficient running times, addressing the privacy-preserving protocol implementation and its security and performance constraints. Additionally, we report on computational experimentation using historical data from electricity markets. To the best of our knowledge, this is the first time the problem of secure single commodities multi-market auctions with transmission constraints has been addressed in detail. We focus our attention on the following aspects:

*Algorithm Design.* Although this is a standard problem, we describe a novel greedy algorithm to compute its solution. This algorithm is better suited for its adaptation to secure multi-party computation. We give proofs of its correctness and that its MPC version is secure. Also since in practice the number of markets is limited (e.g. a few) but the number of bids can be large (e.g. a few thousands) we have aimed at keeping the complexity of the algorithm (close to) linear in the number of bids.

*Complexity and Efficiency.* As similar works in the field, we use communication rounds (exchange of messages between parties involved in the computation) as the complexity measurement unit in our secure protocol. This is in line with our interest in practical use. Moreover, our general aim of minimizing the use of comparisons because of the constants associated to their computation. To facilitate reading, we abstract from our complexity analysis the cost associated to message exchange. Indeed, as in related works, this allow us to decouple our algorithm analysis from the sharing mechanism and the different implications linked to changes in the number of computational players.

*Implementation.* We have implemented our algorithm in C++, building from scratch our own modular MPC framework. Indeed, we could not find an open and efficient implementation suited to our need. We use NTL (Number

Theory Library) [3] and GMP (GNU Multiple Precision Library) as external libraries. This implementation enables us to show that the algorithm we propose is capable of treating close to 2000 bids from 4 markets in a time that is practically relevant for our motivating application (20 min).

## 1.2   Related Work

Secure Auctions have been studied from different perspectives, both in terms of security, computational and economic efficiency. In all cases questions on topics like performance, fairness and integrity have been raised. In this section we cover some of the works with similar characteristics and explore their differences with our contributions.

*Auctions with Secure Multi-party Computation.* Bogetoft et al. [4] consider the problem of a real-life auction with secure multi-party computation. In their setting, Danisco, the only sugar beet processor of the danish market, and several thousand farmers settled clearance market prices in a secret and distributed fashion using MPC. They provide a secure MPC protocol for this single market application. In this paper, we explore a different setting, where there are several markets and each pair can exchange the commodity up to a given capacity. This setting is realistic for other types of commodities e.g. power and gas markets. Additionally, they built their protocols using VIFF [5], which proved to be reliable for the size of their problem. However, previous results for similar problems [6] suggest that this does not scale up very well. We describe the behavior of a dedicated implementation, using the flexibility of C++ and OOP, that uses a compact set of secure MPC primitives to provide security and efficiency.

*Secure Auction Mechanisms with Secret Sharing.* Several authors have studied the properties of secure auctions with secret sharing e.g. [7–10]. These works explore several different auction mechanisms in various environments. Recently, Nojoumian and Stinson [11] introduced algorithms for second-price and combinatorial auctions. Their protocols offer security against active and passive adversaries, using amongst others, Shamir secret sharing [12] and a verifiable secret sharing schemes (VSS). They model their auction problems as graph problems, and devise theoretically efficient algorithms, but no computational experimentation is reported.

*Second Price Auctions.* Some authors have considered cryptographic alternatives to guarantee security in second price auctions. Catane and Herzerg [13] propose trusting a supervising entity to perform the computations and using randomization. Their goal is to keep the bids secret from other players. Our privacy-preserving protocol provides security and fairness without relying on any third party. Also, their approach does not take into account the transmission exchanges that are essential for our model. Similar to [4], this solution would work for one market but needs to be adapted for a multi-market scenario.

## 1.3   Overview of the Paper

The paper is organized as follows: Sect. 2 introduces the problem and some necessary concepts. Section 3 provides its network flow formulation and describes a novel polynomial-time algorithm for it that can be easily adapted to provide properties like data obliviousness. In Sect. 4, we describe the security model, building blocks and technical tools for later use in our secure protocol in the context of our secure algorithm. Section 5 describes our main protocol to solve the problem. We analyze complexity, security and correctness. Experimentation and prototyping are described in Sect. 6.

## 2   Problem Overview

### 2.1   Auction Mechanism

The process we consider here is a reverse auction with several sellers or bidders. Markets or auctioneers adjudicate orders to supply and demand bids that maximize social welfare, while respecting the capacities of the transmission network. A control agency may be part of the process, to supervise and guarantee the integrity of the result. The security follows from the use of secure multi-party computation. Individual interests and involvement level are the following:

**Markets and Transmission Network:** The set of markets and the capacity of the transmission network are assumed to be public. The transmission network is represented by a capacitated network flow, i.e. pairs of markets are binded by bidirectional transmission lines. Each transmission line has an upper limit (i.e. capacity). Notice that in this case, markets are geographically separated.

**Sellers/Buyers or Bidders:** The set of players interested in acquiring or selling the commodity submit bids. Each bid is attached to a specific market. Each bidder can submit more than one bid, and to different markets. Bids are composed by a certain quantity $Q$ (positive for buying and negative for selling) and a limit price $P$. All bids are enclosed and final i.e. no re-bidding is allowed. The bid placed by the player can be partially or totally adjudicated to the bidder depending on what maximizes social welfare. One of their interests is the secrecy of the information contained on each bid towards any other player e.g. other bidders and markets, for as long as the auction takes place. Their concerns are also correctness (the result of the auction is correct) and fairness (all players receive the same information at the same time, and are treated equally).

**Automated Auctioneer:** Is the proxy entity in charge of managing the auction. Our work proposes that the role of the auctioneer is to be taken by the computational parties representing markets, bidders and control agencies, in a distributed and secure fashion. This creates a virtual ideal functionality capable of determining the set of accepted supply and demand bids, guaranteeing correctness, without disclosing sensitive data.

**Control Agency:** Is a regulatory entity or any institution trusted by the Markets operators and Bidders. By the parties choosing, or environmental enforcement, it participates to add confidence to the process. Because of the nature of MPC, our secure protocol allows active participation of the Control Agency as a computational party, so that their presence would be necessary for the correct and secure operation of the protocols in conjunction with the model. The presence of a Control Agency remains optional.

*On Computational parties.* It is possible to have as many computational parties as considered necessary by the algorithm designer to guaranty security and bring confidence to the process. Although many of the building blocks require a minimum of three parties, the algorithm itself can be adapted to be used with two-party computation. As stated many auctions require the presence of an external supervisor. A basic configuration would include a computational party representing the bidders, another the markets, and a third one for the supervisor or control agency. Another logical set-up would is to have one party for each geographical market. A larger number of computational parties can increase security and trust, but will negatively influence the performance.

## 2.2  Problem Definition

Formally, participants in the auction submit bids of the form $(p_i, q_i, m_i)$ where $p_i$ is the limit price, $q_i$ is the quantity (positive for demand bid, negative for supply bid) and $m_i$ is the market where the bid is submitted. Bids can be adjudicated partially, completely or not at all. The network operator also provides a capacity matrix $C$, where entry $C_{i,j}$ is the maximum amount that can be shipped from market $i$ to market $j$. Note that this is similar to [14,15]. The goal is to adjudicate bids so that **(i)** social welfare is maximized, **(ii)** the exchanges implied can be executed on the network, **(iii)** the information contained in all bids is to be kept secret from other players until the end of the auction process. The network (its topology and the capacities) is assumed to be public. Another practical requirement is that the computations should not take more than, for instance, 30 min. Note that we do not associate costs to the transmission network.

*Input Data.* Data is provided as integer values over a finite field $\mathbb{Z}_q$ where input values are much smaller than $q$ such that no overflow occurs. Its size is tied to the application in hand. Note that when they are secretly shared we can not differentiate between a demand bid and a supply bid.

## 2.3  Problem Formulation

Let us denote by $N = \{1, \ldots, n\}$ the set of all bids, and $K \cup D = B$ the partition into supply and demand bids respectively, $M = \{1, \ldots, m\}$ the set of markets, $K_j \in K$ and $D_j \in D$ the set of supply and demand bids respectively at market $j$. We define the nonnegative decision variable $\bar{x}_i \ \forall i \in N$ as the accepted quantity of bid $i$ and variables $f_{i,j}$ as the flow on the line $(i,j) \in L = M \times M$

with capacity $C_{i,j}$. The problem can then be formulated as the following linear optimization problem:

$$\max \sum_{i \in D} p_i \bar{x}_i - \sum_{i \in K} p_i \bar{x}_i \tag{1}$$

$$\text{s.t.} \sum_{i \in K_j} \bar{x}_i + \sum_{i:(i,j) \in L} f_{i,j} = \sum_{i \in D_m} \bar{x}_i + \sum_{i:(j,i) \in L} f_{j,i} \quad \forall j \in M \tag{2}$$

$$0 \le f_{i,j} \le C_{i,j} \quad \forall (i,j) \in L \tag{3}$$

$$0 \le \bar{x}_i \le |q_i| \quad \forall i \in B. \tag{4}$$

Note that by complementing demand bids ($x_i = q_i - \bar{x}_i$ for $i \in D$) and keeping supply bids as is ($x_i = \bar{x}_i$ for $i \in K$), one obtains an equivalent formulation involving supply bids only (dropping the constant in the objective):

$$\min \sum_{i \in N} p_i x_i \tag{5}$$

$$\text{s.t.} \sum_{i \in K_j \cup D_j} x_i + \sum_{i:(i,j) \in L} f_{i,j} - \sum_{i:(j,i) \in L} f_{j,i} = \sum_{i \in D_j} q_i \quad \forall j \in M \tag{6}$$

$$0 \le f_{i,j} \le C_{i,j} \quad \forall (i,j) \in L \tag{7}$$

$$0 \le x_i \le |q_i| \quad \forall i \in B. \tag{8}$$

Note that in this version, there is an external demand of $T_j = \sum_{i \in D_j} q_i$ to be met at each market $j$. The goal is to find the cheapest set of supply bids to satisfy these demands. Having supply bids only makes the description of the algorithm simpler. The is therefore the form that we will use in the rest of the text.

## 3    Network Flow Formulation

The problem (5)–(8) can actually be seen as a minimum cost capacitated network flow problem (MCF) on the graph $G = (V, A)$ as shown at Fig. 1.

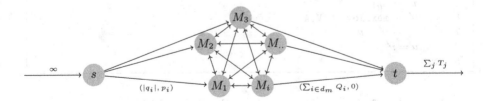

**Fig. 1.** The auction problem as a Minimum Cost Network Flow problem

Formally, the set of vertices is $V = M \cup \{s, t\}$ where $s$ and $t$ are artificial source and sink vertices. For each bid (supply and demand) $i \in K \cup D$, there is an arc $(s, m_i)$ where $m_i$ is the market of the bid $i$, with capacity $|q_i|$ and cost $p_i$.

For simplicity, let $S$ be the set of all arcs originated in $s$. For each pair of markets $(i, j) \in L$ there is an edge between the respective vertices with capacity $C_{i,j}$ and no cost. For each market $j$, there is an edge $(j, t)$ with capacity $T_j = \sum_{i \in d_j} q_i$ and zero cost. Finally there is (given) external flow arriving at vertex $s$ and a given external flow leaving vertex $t$, both of magnitude $\sum_j T_j$. The associated minimum cost flow problem is obviously equivalent to the linear program (5)–(8).

Secure protocols to solve the MCF problem have been described by Aly and Van Vyve [6]. They provide secure polynomial-time algorithms. Although the protocol is theoretically efficient, in practice, its applicability seems to be limited by the high degree ($|V|^{10}$) of the polynomial in the complexity bound. Their computational experiments, using an implementation over VIFF [5], indicates that it would take around a year to solve the problem with perfect security in a 10 vertex complete graph. But to recast our problem in their context, we would need to introduce one vertex for every bid, and with $\approx$2000 bids in the instances we aim at solving, making that approach grossly impractical.

### 3.1 Greedy Algorithm

We describe now a more efficient greedy algorithm than just solving the problem as a general minimum cost flow problem. This greedy algorithm makes use of the special structure of the MCF we want to solve and can be easily generalized into an MPC environment. Intuitively the algorithm proceeds as follows. It considers each order in turn, starting with the cheapest (i.e. best from the objective function point of view) one. At each iteration, a max-flow problem is solved to try to use as much as possible of the quantity offered by the bid. The incremental value obtained is the quantity adjudicated to that bid. The following is a formal description of this greedy procedure:

```
1.  ν ← 0
2.  B ← sort-price:B
3.  x_i ← 0   ∀i ∈ S
4.  for all:   i ∈ B :
5.      x_i ← |q_i|
6.      ν' ← maxflow: G(V,A)
7.      x_i ← ν' − ν
8.      ν = ν'
9.  End
```

**Algorithm 1.** Iterative Greedy Algorithm for Multi-Market Auctions

First, we sort the set of all bids $B$ in function of their price and set the capacities of edges in $S$ to 0. Second, we restore the capacity of the edge associated to bid $i$ to its original value $|q_i|$ and calculate then max-flow on $G$. We then set the capacity of such edge to the flow variation with respect to the max-flow calculated in the previous iteration. We repeat this process for all bids in the order of prices. Once this process is completed, the volume provided by demand bids is then automatically rejected and accepted for the supply bids.

## 3.2  Correctness

We now prove that the greedy algorithm described above is correct. To do this let us disaggregate each bid as a collection of bids of capacity 1, each with the same price as the original bid. This obviously does not modify the problem. So from now on in this section, we can safely assume that all bids have quantity 1, and that all bids will be completely accepted or rejected. For a given set of bids $I$, let $r(I)$ be the maximum amount of demand that can be satisfied using the bids of $I$ only. This can be seen as a max-flow problem on the graph $G$.

**Proposition 1.** *The set function* $r : 2^S \to \mathbb{R}^+$ *is the rank function of a matroid.*

**Proof.** We use a characterization of Whitney [16] for a function to be the rank function of a matroid:

(a) $r(\emptyset) = 0$.
(b) $r(I) \le r(I + i) \le r(I) + 1$ for $I \in S$ and $i \in S \setminus I$,
(c) for all $I \subseteq S$, $i, j \in S \setminus I$, if $r(I+i) = r(I+j) = r(I)$, then $r(I+i+j) = r(I)$.

The set of arcs associated to the bids themselves is a cut separating the source from the sink in the associated max-flow problem so $r(J) \le |J|$ for any $J$, proving (a). Moreover (b) comes from the fact that adding one bid $i$ to $I$ amounts to increase the capacity of one arc by one unit in the associated max-flow problem. Therefore the capacity of any cut increases by at most 1, and the size of the minimum cut will certainly increase, but by one unit at most.

We now prove (c). Let $S^I$ denote the set of vertices containing the source $s$ defining a minimum cut associated with the max-flow problem of computing $r(I)$. In other words, $r(I) = c(\delta^+(I))$.

Note first that since $r(I+i) = r(I)$, there exists $S^{I+i}$ such that the associated cut does not contain $(s, i)$ the arc associated to the bid $i$. Similarly there exists $S^{I+j}$ such that the associated cut does not contain $(s, j)$ the arc associated to the bid $j$. This implies also that $\delta^+(S^{I+i} \cup S^{I+j})$ does not contain the arcs $(s, i)$ and $(s, j)$.

By submodularity of cut functions in directed graphs, we obtain that $r(I+i)+r(I+j) = c(\delta^+(S^{I+i}))+c(\delta^+(S^{I+j})) \ge c(\delta^+(S^{I+i} \cup S^{I+j}))+c(\delta^+(S^{I+i} \cap S^{I+j}))$.

Since $\delta^+(S^{I+i} \cup S^{I+j})$ is an $s - t$ cut that does not contain $(s, i)$ and $(s, j)$, if $c(\delta^+(S^{I+i} \cup S^{I+j})) \le r(I)$, statement $(c)$ holds (the strict inequality case is ruled out by (b)). If $c(\delta^+(S^{I+i} \cup S^{I+j})) > r(I)$ then $c(\delta^+(S^{I+i} \cap S^{I+j})) < r(I)$. But this would contradict the minimality of $S^I$ since $\delta^+(S^{I+i} \cap S^{I+j})$ is an $s - t$ cut.                                                                                    □

By classical properties of matroid structures, the last proposition directly implies that we can solve the auction problem greedily: it suffices to use the cheapest supply bids first, as long as the transmission network allows the use the bid to satisfy some demand. This is exactly what Algorithm 1 does.

# 4 Cryptographic Preliminaries

## 4.1 Security Model

Ben-Or et al. [17] showed, amongst other things, how (with Shamir's secrete sharing for passive adversaries or Verifiable Secret Sharing (VSS) [18] for active adversaries) every functionality can be computed under the *information theoretic* model. However, that does not necessarily imply efficiency in terms of performance. In our secure algorithms, variations can be included, to accelerate some functionality, at the price of providing statistical security and/or some leakage. Moreover, changes in the communication or adversarial models would yield different security levels as well. Our protocols follow the same line of thought. Our privacy-preserving protocols can achieve the same level of security, than the underlying primitives (our algorithms have no leakage). A careful sub-routine selection can yield statistical security, with a significantly improvement in terms of performance. We study both aspects of the implementation of our secure protocols.

## 4.2 Basic Building Blocks

**On Secret Sharing and other Primitives.** Our algorithm is compatible with secret sharing methods and homomorphic encryption mechanisms that support MPC (e.g. Shamir Secret Sharing, Paillier Encryption). Our secure prototype uses secret-sharing to allow $n$ parties to share information amongst each other, to later be reconstructed by a subset of the players. This is also true for more elaborated primitives like multiplications, that in the case of [17, 19] can be executed with a single communication round guaranteeing perfect security. For an extended review on sharing mechanism we refer the reader to [20].

**Comparisons.** Which are an essential part of our algorithms. There have been several methods for secure comparisons proposed during the last decade that provide perfect security (e.g. [21, 22]). Here we use the constant rounds method of Catrina and Hoogh [23]. It is built upon a secure modulo operation. As for the equality test, we use the protocol of Limpaa and Toft [24] based on the hamming distance, that provides sub-linear complexity for the online phase. Although, these methods achieve constant complexity bounds, in practice, due to the high constants, they are typically much slower than multiplications.

## 4.3 Complex Building Blocks

Our privacy-preserving protocol requires to solve a series of more complex problems, combinatorial in nature. The methods used to solve these problems have to guarantee correctness and security while at the same time minimize their impact over the performance. This includes a practically efficient vector shuffling protocol, sorting and max-flow mechanisms. We succinctly review them in the context of the needs of the application at hand.

- **Vector Permutation Mechanism.** Our protocols require to securely permute a vector. This implies that for any vector of size $n$, the resulting configuration is uniformly distributed in the space of all permutations $n!$. Indeed, the state of the art describes several mechanisms for vector permutation that are compatible with our algorithms. We could mention, for instance, the work of Leur et al. [25] or Keller and Scholl [26] who introduced several permutation mechanisms that work with secret sharing (e.g. permutation matrix multiplication with $\mathcal{O}(n^2)$ and perfect security). They also offer other alternatives (e.g. sorting methods) to improve complexity with $\mathcal{O}(n \times log(n))$ and further. Additionally, Czumaj et al. [27] have shown how to build a permutation network using exchange gates with $\frac{1}{2}$ probability. The result is a permutation with (almost) uniform probability in the space of all possible permutations. Note that we could also build such networks using AKS or the randomized shell sort network introduced by [28] among others sorting networks to achieve better complexity times e.g. $\mathcal{O}(n \times log(n))$. This is also compatible with our protocols. A more realistic approach, uses sorting networks and being subject to the distribution it provides for its solutions e.g. Batcher's odd-even merge. Note that, in the same spirit, we could uniformly choose a random permutation amongst a sub-set of all possible permutations using the network generated by the Merge step of such algorithms. Indeed, these last 2 are later used for experimentation.

- **Sorting Mechanisms.** Our scheme needs to sort the bids in ascending order or price. Since the Sorting protocols are necessary building blocks of various complex solutions. Efficient secure sorting algorithms have been studied for several years, yielding interesting results (e.g. [28–30]). More interestingly for us, is the approach proposed by Hamada et al. [31]. Their idea is to first randomly and securely shuffle the vector to be sorted. Once this is done, any traditional sorting algorithm can be executed, revealing the results of the comparison, while keeping secret the values to be sorted.

- **Max Flow Mechanisms.** Max-Flow problems with perfect security have been recently studied by [32,33] amongst others. For the max-flow problem, Blanton et al. [33] introduced a mechanism to solve the problem using as building block the Bread First-Search algorithm with a complexity of $\mathcal{O}(n^5 log(n))$. The work by Aly et al. [32] provides 2 different data-oblivious protocols with perfect security as well. The most efficient method is $\mathcal{O}(n^4)$ and is based on the push-relabel algorithm. It also suggests the use of stopping conditions (with some leakage) to accelerate performance. This is what we have implemented here.

## 5 Secure Auction Mechanism

We extend the results of Sect. 3 and introduce a secure variant of Algorithm 1. We assume the configuration of the transmission network to be public, and all inputs to be integer.

## 5.1   Notation

Our protocol uses the traditional square brackets notation employed by several secure applications in distributed environments e.g. [21,32]. For instance, a secure assignment and secure addition are denoted by the use of the infix notation and the corresponding square brackets e.g. $[z] \leftarrow [x] + [y]$. The same treatment is extended to any other operation. Vectors are denoted by capital letters e.g. $E$ where $|E|$ denotes the number of elements in $E$ and $E_i$ is the $i$-th element. To represent negative numbers we use the typical approach of using the lower half of the field for positive values and the upper half of the field for negative values. It has to be noticed that in shared form a negative value is indistinguishable from a positive one. And that in our approach all information related to the bids is kept secret including whether or not it is a supply or demand bid.

Each bid is represented by a tuple $([b_i], [m_i], [p_i], [q_i])$ where $b_i$ is the bid identifier, $m_i$ is the market where the bid is made, $p_i$ its limit price and $q_i$ its quantity. The transmission network is represented by the capacity matrix $N$. We will make repeated use of the following two subroutines.

- **conditional assignment**: This functionality serves as a replacement of a flow control instruction for branching. Although branching on encrypted data is not possible, the functionality can be emulated for assignments. Following [6] we represent the operator by: $[z] \leftarrow_{[c]} [x] : [y]$. Where much like in previous works e.g. [6,32,34] $[z]$ would take the value $[x]$ if $[c]$ is 1 and $[y]$ otherwise. This can be achieved simply by doing the following $[z] \leftarrow ([x] - [y]) \times [c] + [y]$.
- **market identification**: Part of the data that composes a bid is the identification of the market it belongs to. Users are required to input a single identification tag. During our algorithm, we transform this to a unary expansion defined as $Z_{i,m} = 1$ if $m = m_i$ and 0 otherwise. This enables us to reduce the number of equality tests when performing the market identification for a bid. This transformation can be achieved following protocol:

---

**Protocol 1.** unary expansion for market identification

---

**Input**: vector of all markets $M$, bid $[i] \in B$.
**Output**: zero-one matrix $[Z]$ of size $n \times m$
1 for $i \leftarrow 1$ to $m$ do
2 |   $[Z]_{i,j} \leftarrow j == [m]_i$;
3 end
4 return $[Z]$;

---

## 5.2   Secure Auction with Transmission Constraints

The protocol is defined as follows:

**Prerequisites.** The number of bids or at least an upper bound on the size of the vector is assumed to be public. We assume the topology and capacities of the transmission network to be public.

**1.** Bids are sorted in ascending order of price.

**2.** The structure of the graph $G = (V, A)$ is public. The capacity of each edge is initialized with the following value. The capacities between market vertices are set to the capacity matrix $C$. The capacity of each edge $(s, j)$ is set to 0. The capacity of each edge $(j, t)$ is set to the sum of the quantities of all demand bids submitted to market $j$. This is simply done by exploring all the bids and using the market identification protocol 1.

**3.** Evaluate the viability of each of the bids from the recently sorted vector $[B]$ in ascending order. For a given bid, we do this by increasing the capacity of edge $(s, j)$ where $j$ is the market of the bid by its quantity $|q_{b_i}|$. We then compute the maximum $(s, t)$-flow in the graph $G$ to determine whether the bid can improve the solution. The increment of the maxflow compared to the previous iteration is the amount adjudicated to the bid. Finally, the capacity of edge $(s, j)$ is increased by the same increment. Protocol 2 shows a detailed description of this procedure.

**4.** Finally the bids then are permuted randomly, to hide their order. This is necessary to avoid leaking the result of the initial sorting from step 1.

On the prerequisites, several parties constantly submit bids in shared form, we believe it is safe to assume this will not occur simultaneously. Precomputed permutation matrices can be generated. A simple vector multiplication of the corresponding row of the matrix would suffice in this case to place the incoming data in their corresponding permuted position in the vector. Once all data is received, the existing vectors can be easily combined, the result is a single permuted vector. In case this approach is not feasible, the algorithm designer could make use of one of the suggested permutation mechanisms instead. Permuted bids would allow us to make use of Hamada et al. [35] technique of **shuffling before sorting**. This improves considerably the performance of sorting protocols and allows them to achieve $\mathcal{O}(n \times \log n)$ complexity.

Furthermore, we introduce step *3* to serve as an evaluation and allocation mechanism. It can be seen as some heuristic tool that allows us to identify the impact of the bid on the result. Protocol 2 let us explore the inner works of Step *3* in detail. *Line 2* allows us to explore all previously sorted bids in order. *Lines 3 to 5* augment the corresponding edge capacity from the source to the corresponding market with the volume of the bid. *On Line 6*, $\nu$ stores the maximum amount of flow that can be allocated with the new volume. On the final section of the protocol (*Lines 7 to 13*) the difference between previous and present flow gap is calculated. Moreover, the flow added to the graph at the beginning of the iteration is replaced by the gap variation. This value has to be stored as well as the amount of capacity assigned to the bid and the value of the maximum flow for future iterations.

Moreover, at the last and *4* step, data can be edited at will by the algorithm designer. What information is taken to later be presented depends solely on the application's nature. The permutation, although capable to hide the sorting should be ignored in case the final answer also contemplates to open the prices of the bids as well. This is because any party could later sort the bids accordingly.

Please note that our protocol complexity grows linearly with respect of the number of bids $n$ and polynomially by the number of markets $m$.

---

**Protocol 2.** Implementation of secure auction.

---

**Input:** Capacity matrix $[C]_{ij}$. Vector of $n$ bid tuples $([b], [m], [p], [q])$. Matrix of market identification $[Z]_{ij}$ $\forall i \in N$ and $\forall j \in M$

**Output:** Flow Matrix $F$, the list of bids and their accepted quantities $[x]$

1  $[\nu] \leftarrow [0]$
2  **for** $i \leftarrow 1$ **to** $n$ **do**
3  $\quad$ **for** $j \leftarrow 1$ **to** $m$ **do**
4  $\quad\quad |\quad [C]_{sj} \leftarrow_{[Z]_{ij}} [C]_{sj} + |[q_{b_i}]| : [C]_{sj};$
5  $\quad$ **end**
6  $\quad [\nu'] \leftarrow \texttt{maxflow}([G]);$
7  $\quad [\phi] \leftarrow ([\nu'] - [\nu]);$
8  $\quad [x_{b_i}] \leftarrow [\phi];$
9  $\quad$ **for** $j \leftarrow 1$ **to** $m$ **do**
10  $\quad\quad |\quad [C]_{sj} \leftarrow_{[Z]_{ij}} [C]_{sj} - |[q_{b_i}]| + [\phi] : [C]_{sj};$
11  $\quad$ **end**
12  $\quad [\nu] \leftarrow [\nu'];$
13  **end**

---

Finally, note that at the end of the protocol, the adjudicated quantities $x_i$ together with the bid identifier will be disclosed.

**Complexity.** Oblivious shuffling can be achieved (theoretically) in $\mathcal{O}(n \log n)$, and sorting the bids is then $\mathcal{O}(n \log n)$. At step 3, a max flow problem on $m + 2$ vertices has to be executed $n$ times. Using the $\mathcal{O}(m^4)$ max-flow algorithm by Aly et al. [32], this gives an overall bound of $\mathcal{O}(nm^4)$ for Step 3. So in total this yields an overall complexity (communication rounds) of $\mathcal{O}(n(m^4 + \log n))$.

Since the number of markets is usually small (e.g. 1 to 5) for the application at hand, the quartic exponent is not too much of an issue in practice. The fact that the complexity is close to linear in the number of bids is on the other hand vital.

## 5.3  Security and Correctness

In principle, all steps of the algorithm could be implemented with perfect (i.e. information theoretic) security against passive and active adversaries when implemented with no leakage. This follows from the fact that there exists such protocols for sorting [28, 29, 31], max-flow [32, 33] and oblivious shuffling [25–27] that provide this level of security under the information theoretic model. This is also true for multiplications and comparisons. Moreover, the data-obliviousness nature of the protocols implies that for the protocol simulation, the corresponding simulators of all other protocols and their atomic operations (e.g. secure additions multiplications) could be invoked in a predefined execution order, hence, modeling it as an arithmetic circuit.

However, to improve performance, we have decided to weaken the security requirement in the following sense. Firstly, the security of the sorting scheme we use directly depends on the security of the random shuffling implemented. Secondly, for the max-flow problems, instead of running the algorithm for the maximum theoretical number of iterations, we stop the algorithm as soon as optimality is reached. This leaks the number of iterations. Finally, correctness follows from the fact the scheme is a secure implementation of Algorithm 1.

# 6  Computational Experimentation

We have tested our protocol with our custom-made MPC Toolkit library implemented in C++. It implements all the primitives and building blocks described above, but also the underlying MPC crypto-primitives. It also provide our own communication support and use NTL and GMP libraries for the underlying modulo arithmetic. We report below on the most relevant aspects of the implementation. A more thorough and detailed description can be found in [36].

## 6.1  Prototype Capabilities and Technical Characteristics

Table 1 give the implemented protocols for the usual basic operations. The more complex procedures described in the previous sections are built upon these.

**Table 1.** List of primitives used by the Secure Auction protocol implementation

| Building block | Algorithm |
|---|---|
| Sharing | Shamir secret sharing [12] |
| Multiplication | Gennaro et al. [19] |
| Equality test (Statistical) | Limpaa and Toft [24] |
| Inequality test (Statistical) | Catrina and Hoogh [34] |
| Random bit gen. | Damgård et al. [21] |

These are considered core functionalities. The architecture from the library is to provide a basic and decoupled processing unit similar to a small engine. This small engine implements the functionalities from Table 1. Furthermore, it separates computational and cryptographic tasks from communicational tasks. Each engine runs these two sets of tasks in different threads that communicate with each other to coordinate. Basic requirements to obtain the best performance from the engine include 2 CPU threads and ≈500 KB in RAM for the basic use of the primitives. Our configuration gives each computational party 2 similar CPU threads with unlimited access to a memory pool of up 42 GB with each player having a single engine's instance.

**On Security.** The library and prototype were built under the private channel model. Depending on the functionality used, the library provides statistical and perfect security against semi-honest adversaries with minority coalition. For instance, the inequality tests used in our tests brings statistical security meanwhile addition and multiplication perfect security. As mentioned before, statistical security for such method is given as a function of parameters $k$ and the bit-size of the input by parameter $l$. The prototype was pre-configured to use $k = 29$ and $l = 32$. However, because of technical issues, shares themselves can only use up to 63 bits. This means in practice that under the scenario where only primitives with perfect security are used, the size of $l$ could grow up to 63 bits.

## 6.2   Numerical Results

The computational experiments were done using historical data from the Belgian day-ahead market. The data set is composed of a total of 1945 bids (demand and supply). The origin of the data is one hour of a day trade from the Belpex market (12 pm). We have created two data sets by randomly partitioning this set of bids into 2 and 4 markets. Additionally, we would like to note that in our experimentation we consider a 3 computational parties case.

We ran our instances on an Intel Xeon CPUs X5550 (2.67 GHz) and 42 GB of memory, running Mac OS X 10.10. All processes have the same computational power at their disposal (memory and CPU power). Table 2 shows number of communication rounds, comparisons and CPU time (10 executions average).

From these tests, $\approx 21 \times 10^6$ communicational rounds were dedicated to randomization processes for the comparison mechanisms e.g. random bit generations. The use of well studied results like PRSS [37] would limit the use of these communicational rounds and in general terms would allow us to achieve even better computational times. Furthermore, Catrina and Hoogh comparison method depends on the computation of $l$ random bits for its calculations. An offline phase can be considered where this random numbers are pre-computed before the bids arrive to the server, and then distributed to the computational parties for its use. In this case the Secure Auction Mechanism would be executed in an online phase that no longer has to care about random number generation improving the performance for comparisons. Table 2 shows our numerical results and estimated the impact of the use of online/offline phases.

**Table 2.** Overall results

| Markets and perm. method | | Com. rounds | Comparisons | CPU time | Online phase |
|---|---|---|---|---|---|
| 2 Markets | Batcher | $\approx 31.4 \cdot 10^6$ | 226021 | 2056 s | 613 s |
| | Merge | $\approx 31.4 \cdot 10^6$ | 226021 | 2049 s | 606 s |
| 4 Markets | Batcher | $\approx 71.9 \cdot 10^6$ | 537627 | 4702 s | 1276 s |
| | Merge | $\approx 71.9 \cdot 10^6$ | 537627 | 4694 s | 1268 s |

When the number of markets increases from 2 to 4, we observe an increase of more than twice the number of rounds and comparisons. The same follows on computational time, taking in average (10 execution rounds) around 4700 s to complete execution.

On memory, the application did not surpass the 2.5 MB per execution. During its life-cycle, some increment in memory consumption levels was registered during data generation phases. The phenomenon is especially evident in the data preprocessing phase. This is of course, because some data is generated and stored for later use. Less significantly changes are also present. This is explained by the continuous fragmentation of the memory throughout the repeated max-flow problems, where objects of different sizes are continuously created and then destroyed. Nonetheless, the increase of memory usage remains very modest. Figure 2 shows the typical memory usage of the application during its execution.

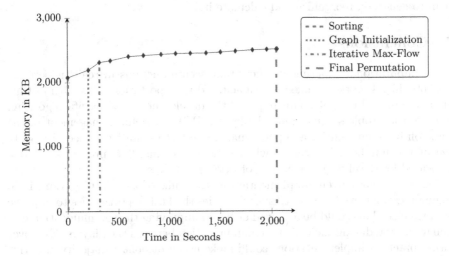

**Fig. 2.** Secure auction protocol life cycle

Finally, we found that the bottleneck of the application are the communications. Data transmission and related tasks are responsible of the 1705 s (83%) of the total computational time. Only a fraction of the time, 351 s (17%), was dedicated to other tasks e.g. share generation, basic arithmetic operations and other algorithmic tasks.

From these results we can conclude the following: **(i)** Realistic computational times were indeed achieved for the data in question, with limited computational power. With the online/offline case, an hour of trade was solved in less than an hour of computations for both market configurations. Given that many of the processes of our protocol are sequential in nature, a computer with a better benchmarked CPU under the same basic configuration would yield better results. **(ii)** Memory is not a decisive factor in this case. Memory increases monotonically but modestly during the execution because of noise. **(iii)** The process can be further accelerated by pre-computing the random values that are needed by the protocol. In our case $\frac{3}{4}$ of communicational rounds that are used for comparisons are dedicated to randomization processes. Even with the use of PRSS, these operations would represent an important proportion of the workload. This is why an offline phase where these values are preprocessed could prove more useful. For instance, to have dedicated servers calculating in shared form random bits and numbers and store them, such that they can just be fetched when any online process needs them. This would imply a reduction in the 2 markets case of $\approx 1450$ s. This would allow us to solve the problem in $\approx 610$ s, a little more than 10 min. When 4 markets are consider instead, the times are reduced to $\approx 1270$ which is little more than 20 min. (iv) Moreover, even though we have put in place a light and dedicated communications setting, the performance of the prototype is largely dependent on the performance of the communications implemented. It was 4.8 times more expensive (in terms of running time) to transmit the data than to generate, reorganize and calculate it.

## 7    Conclusions

Our computational experiments show that secure auctions in realistic settings ($\approx 2000$ bids, 4 markets linked by capacitated transportation links, 30 min time limit) are indeed possible. This required the development of a specific algorithm to solve the problem (more amendable to MPC), a careful management of the trade-off between security and performance (perfect vs. statistical security, leakage of the number of iteration when solving the max-flow problems), and a dedicated low-level implementation of MPC primitives.

Since, in our current implementation, the bulk of the running time is in communications, we feel that this is where lies the best opportunities to improve performance. This could be achieved either in improving the communication efficiency, or by reducing the need for communication between the players. Moreover future practical implementations could make use of dishonest majority or active security protocols for usability.

**Acknowledgements.** This research was supported by the WIST Walloon Region project CAMUS and the Belgian IAP Program P7/36 initiated by the Belgian State, Prime Minister's Office, Science Policy Programming. Both authors were also supported by the Marie Curie ITN "MINO" from the European Commission. The authors are grateful to Olivier Pereira and Ignacio Aravena for their feedback. The scientific responsibility is assumed by the authors.

## References

1. Klemperer, P.: What really matters in auction design, from auctions: theory and practice. In: Auctions: Theory and Practice. Introductory Chapters. Princeton University Press (2004)
2. Yao, A.C.C.: Protocols for secure computations (extended abstract). In: 23rd Annual Symposium on Foundations of Computer Science, pp. 160–164. IEEE (1982)
3. Shoup, V.: NTL: a library for doing number theory. http://www.shoup.net/ntl/
4. Bogetoft, P., et al.: Secure multiparty computation goes live. In: Dingledine, R., Golle, P. (eds.) FC 2009. LNCS, vol. 5628, pp. 325–343. Springer, Heidelberg (2009). doi:10.1007/978-3-642-03549-4_20

5. Geisler, M.: Cryptographic protocols: theory and implementation. Ph.D. thesis, Aarhus University Denmark, Department of Computer Science (2010)
6. Aly, A., Van Vyve, M.: Securely solving classical network flow problems. In: Lee, J., Kim, J. (eds.) ICISC 2014. LNCS, vol. 8949, pp. 205–221. Springer, Cham (2015). doi:10.1007/978-3-319-15943-0_13
7. Franklin, M.K., Reiter, M.K.: The design and implementation of a secure auction service. IEEE Trans. Softw. Eng. **22**, 302–312 (1996)
8. Harkavy, M., Tygar, J.D., Kikuchi, H.: Electronic auctions with private bids. In: Proceedings of the 3rd Conference on USENIX Workshop on Electronic Commerce, WOEC 1998, vol. 3, p. 6. USENIX Association, Berkeley (1998)
9. Kikuchi, H., Hotta, S., Abe, K., Nakanishi, S.: Distributed auction servers resolving winner and winning bid without revealing privacy of bids. In: Seventh International Conference on Parallel and Distributed Systems: Workshops, pp. 307–312 (2000)
10. Peng, K., Boyd, C., Dawson, E.: Optimization of electronic first-bid sealed-bid auction based on homomorphic secret sharing. In: Dawson, E., Vaudenay, S. (eds.) Mycrypt 2005. LNCS, vol. 3715, pp. 84–98. Springer, Heidelberg (2005). doi:10.1007/11554868_7
11. Nojoumian, M., Stinson, D.R.: Efficient sealed-bid auction protocols using verifiable secret sharing. In: Huang, X., Zhou, J. (eds.) ISPEC 2014. LNCS, vol. 8434, pp. 302–317. Springer, Cham (2014). doi:10.1007/978-3-319-06320-1_23
12. Shamir, A.: How to share a secret. Commun. ACM **22**, 612–613 (1979). ACM, New York
13. Catane, B., Herzberg, A.: Secure second price auctions with a rational auctioneer. In: The 10-th SECRYPT International Conference on Security and Cryptography (2013)
14. Madani, M., Van Vyve, M.: A new formulation of the European day-ahead electricity market problem and its algorithmic consequences. CORE Discussion Papers 2013074, Université catholique de Louvain, Center for Operations Research and Econometrics (CORE) (2013)
15. Madani, M., Van Vyve, M.: Computationally efficient MIP formulation and algorithms for European day-ahead electricity market auctions. Eur. J. Oper. Res. **242**, 580–593 (2015)
16. Whitney, H.: On the abstract properties of linear dependence. Am. J. Math. **57**, 509–533 (1935)
17. Ben-Or, M., Goldwasser, S., Wigderson, A.: Completeness theorems for non-cryptographic fault-tolerant distributed computation. In: Proceedings of the Twentieth Annual ACM Symposium on Theory of Computing, STOC 1988, pp. 1–10. ACM, New York (1988)
18. Chor, B., Goldwasser, S., Micali, S., Awerbuch, B.: Verifiable secret sharing and achieving simultaneity in the presence of faults. In: 26th Annual Symposium on Foundations of Computer Science, pp. 383–395, October 1985
19. Gennaro, R., Rabin, M.O., Rabin, T.: Simplified VSS and fast-track multiparty computations with applications to threshold cryptography. In: Proceedings of the Seventeenth Annual ACM Symposium on Principles of Distributed Computing, PODC 1998, pp. 101–111. ACM, New York (1998)
20. Beimel, A.: Secret-sharing schemes: a survey. In: Chee, Y.M., Guo, Z., Ling, S., Shao, F., Tang, Y., Wang, H., Xing, C. (eds.) IWCC 2011. LNCS, vol. 6639, pp. 11–46. Springer, Heidelberg (2011). doi:10.1007/978-3-642-20901-7_2

21. Damgård, I., Fitzi, M., Kiltz, E., Nielsen, J.B., Toft, T.: Unconditionally secure constant-rounds multi-party computation for equality, comparison, bits and exponentiation. In: Halevi, S., Rabin, T. (eds.) TCC 2006. LNCS, vol. 3876, pp. 285–304. Springer, Heidelberg (2006). doi:10.1007/11681878_15
22. Nishide, T., Ohta, K.: Multiparty computation for interval, equality, and comparison without bit-decomposition protocol. In: Okamoto, T., Wang, X. (eds.) PKC 2007. LNCS, vol. 4450, pp. 343–360. Springer, Heidelberg (2007). doi:10.1007/978-3-540-71677-8_23
23. Catrina, O., de Hoogh, S.: Improved primitives for secure multiparty integer computation. In: Garay, J.A., De Prisco, R. (eds.) SCN 2010. LNCS, vol. 6280, pp. 182–199. Springer, Heidelberg (2010). doi:10.1007/978-3-642-15317-4_13
24. Lipmaa, H., Toft, T.: Secure equality and greater-than tests with sublinear online complexity. In: Fomin, F.V., Freivalds, R., Kwiatkowska, M., Peleg, D. (eds.) ICALP 2013, Part II. LNCS, vol. 7966, pp. 645–656. Springer, Heidelberg (2013). doi:10.1007/978-3-642-39212-2_56
25. Laur, S., Willemson, J., Zhang, B.: Round-efficient oblivious database manipulation. In: Lai, X., Zhou, J., Li, H. (eds.) ISC 2011. LNCS, vol. 7001, pp. 262–277. Springer, Heidelberg (2011). doi:10.1007/978-3-642-24861-0_18
26. Keller, M., Scholl, P.: Efficient, oblivious data structures for MPC. In: Sarkar, P., Iwata, T. (eds.) ASIACRYPT 2014, Part II. LNCS, vol. 8874, pp. 506–525. Springer, Heidelberg (2014). doi:10.1007/978-3-662-45608-8_27
27. Czumaj, A., Kanarek, P., Kutylowski, M., Lorys, K.: Delayed path coupling and generating random permutations via distributed stochastic processes. In: Proceedings of the Tenth Annual ACM-SIAM Symposium on Discrete Algorithms, SODA 1999, pp. 271–280. Society for Industrial and Applied Mathematics, Philadelphia (1999)
28. Goodrich, M.T.: Randomized shellsort: a simple data-oblivious sorting algorithm. J. ACM (JACM) 58, 27:1–27:26 (2011). ACM, New York
29. Jónsson, K.V., Kreitz, G., Uddin, M.: Secure multi-party sorting and applications. In: IACR Cryptology ePrint Archive, vol. 2011, p. 122 (2011)
30. Goodrich, M.T.: Zig-zag sort: a simple deterministic data-oblivious sorting algorithm running in o(n log n) time. In: Proceedings of the 46th Annual ACM Symposium on Theory of Computing, STOC 2014, pp. 684–693. ACM, New York (2014)
31. Hamada, K., Ikarashi, D., Chida, K., Takahashi, K.: Oblivious radix sort: an efficient sorting algorithm for practical secure multi-party computation. In: IACR Cryptology ePrint Archive, vol. 2014, p. 121 (2014)
32. Aly, A., Cuvelier, E., Mawet, S., Pereira, O., Van Vyve, M.: Securely solving simple combinatorial graph problems. In: Sadeghi, A.-R. (ed.) FC 2013. LNCS, vol. 7859, pp. 239–257. Springer, Heidelberg (2013). doi:10.1007/978-3-642-39884-1_21
33. Blanton, M., Steele, A., Alisagari, M.: Data-oblivious graph algorithms for secure computation and outsourcing. In: Proceedings of the 8th ACM SIGSAC Symposium on Information, Computer and Communications Security, ASIA CCS 2013, pp. 207–218. ACM, New York (2013)
34. Catrina, O., de Hoogh, S.: Secure multiparty linear programming using fixed-point arithmetic. In: Gritzalis, D., Preneel, B., Theoharidou, M. (eds.) ESORICS 2010. LNCS, vol. 6345, pp. 134–150. Springer, Heidelberg (2010). doi:10.1007/978-3-642-15497-3_9
35. Hamada, K., Kikuchi, R., Ikarashi, D., Chida, K., Takahashi, K.: Practically efficient multi-party sorting protocols from comparison sort algorithms. In: Kwon, T., Lee, M.-K., Kwon, D. (eds.) ICISC 2012. LNCS, vol. 7839, pp. 202–216. Springer, Heidelberg (2013). doi:10.1007/978-3-642-37682-5_15

36. Aly, A.: Network flow problems with secure multiparty computation. Ph.D. thesis, Universté catholique de Louvain, IMMAQ (2015)
37. Cramer, R., Damgård, I., Ishai, Y.: Share conversion, pseudorandom secret-sharing and applications to secure computation. In: Kilian, J. (ed.) TCC 2005. LNCS, vol. 3378, pp. 342–362. Springer, Heidelberg (2005). doi:10.1007/978-3-540-30576-7_19

# How to Challenge *and* Cast Your e-Vote

Sandra Guasch[1]([✉]) and Paz Morillo[2]

[1] Scytl Secure Electronic Voting, Barcelona, Spain
sandra.guasch@scytl.com
[2] Universitat Politecnica de Catalunya, Barcelona, Spain
paz@ma4.upc.com

**Abstract.** An electronic voting protocol provides cast-as-intended verifiability if the voter can verify that her encrypted vote contains the
voting options that she selected. There are some proposals of protocols
with cast-as-intended verifiability in the literature, but all of them have
drawbacks either in terms of usability or in terms of security. In this
paper, we propose a new voting scheme with cast-as-intended verifiability which allows to audit the vote to be cast, while providing measures
for avoiding coercion by allowing the voter to create fake proofs of the
content of her vote. We provide an efficient implementation and formally
analize its security properties.

## 1 Introduction

In remote e-voting schemes the vote is encrypted at the same voter device used
to choose the selections and cast the vote. This way voter choices remain secret
during their transmission and storage in the remote voting server. Encrypted
voting options cast by the voters are anonymized prior to decryption at the
counting phase, in order to maintain voter privacy.

This introduces new concerns on e-voting systems: how can voters be sure
that (i) the vote that their device encrypted contains their selections, (ii) the
vote which was stored in the remote voting server is the same that their device
encrypted and (iii) the anonymization and decryption processes were done correctly? To provide assurance to the voters that the vote casting, vote storage and
vote counting processes were done following the specified protocol, the notions
of cast-as-intended verifiability, recorded-as-cast verifiability and counted-as-
recorded verifiability have been introduced in the literature.

There are some satisfying solutions for both recorded-as-cast verifiability and
counted-as-recorded verifiability. Recorded-as-cast verifiability can be achieved
by publishing all encrypted votes received at the remote voting server in a
Bulletin Board [17], where voters can check for their cast votes, and making sure
that only the votes which are in the Bulletin Board are tallied. For examples
of protocols providing counted-as-recorded verifiability, see [27] or [12], where
verifiable mix-nets and verifiably homomorphic tally schemes are introduced,
respectively.

However, proposed schemes achieving cast-as-intended verifiability still have
some drawbacks, either in usability or security terms. For example, some of these

© International Financial Cryptography Association 2017
J. Grossklags and B. Preneel (Eds.): FC 2016, LNCS 9603, pp. 130–145, 2017.
DOI: 10.1007/978-3-662-54970-4_8

systems, known as *challenge-or-cast*, do not allow to audit the same vote to be cast. In case such systems allowed to verify the same ballot to be cast, they would fail on fulfilling other security requirements for electronic voting systems such as protection against voter coercion and vote selling, given that their verification involves providing the randomness of the encrypted vote.

In this paper, we propose a new voting scheme which provides cast-as-intended verifiability. In our scheme, the voter can audit the same encrypted vote that she will later cast, what we think is an improvement from the point of view of soundness of the verification and of the usability of the system: it represents a more straightforward process for average voters to audit the vote that is going to be cast. Still, measures are applied in order to ensure that this verification does not provide the voter with a receipt that can be used to sell her vote. We call this variant **challenge-*and*-cast**.

**Related Work.** There have been several proposals of cast-as-intended verification schemes during the last two decades. In Helios [2], the voter's device encrypts a vote and the voter is allowed to challenge the encryption and obtain the randomness used for encrypting the voting options, to check that the encrypted vote was constructed correctly. However, in order to prevent vote selling, the vote has to be encrypted again with new randomness, after auditing. In particular, this means that the voter's device has a small probability of cheating, which decreases with the number of challenged encryptions.

Other methods to provide cast-as-intended verification are those based in return codes, such as [18]. In these schemes, a secondary channel is used to deliver reference codes assigned to voting options to each voter before the voting phase. During voting, the remote voting server, computes return codes from received votes and sends them back to the voters, who verify that they match the expected reference codes. These solutions are more usable than previous proposals, but they require a secondary channel, which may not always be available.

Some code voting schemes (Surevote [8], Pretty Good Democracy [26]) or verifiable DRE-based schemes (MarkPledge [24], Moran-Naor's receipt-free voting system [23]) also provide cast-as-intended verifiability. However, they present their own limitations: while the first category relies on the voter having to enter one randomized code for each voting option she selects, with the corresponding drawbacks on usability, the second one requires specific hardware (such as printers with protected output trays) which cannot be assumed to be available in remote voting scenarios.

Finally, there are systems such as [10] which use trapdoor commitments, as our solution, in order to provide receipt-freeness in blind signature voting schemes. However they struggle on the way of providing the voter with the trapdoor key. Although we also use trapdoor commitments in our scheme, we have naturally associated the trapdoor key to a voting credential needed to cast a ballot, in order to improve the usability and understandability of the scheme. Moreover, the protocol we present here does not aim to solve the problem of receipt-freeness. Getting a receipt of your vote is a possibility inherent to most the electronic voting systems where the vote is encrypted at the voting device, such as Helios [2]. Instead, our motivation is to provide a method for cast-as-intended verification which does not involve providing a receipt to the voter (or that at least allows to fake it for a possible coercer). A future work will consist on analyzing how this cast-as-intended verification method can be combined with other systems providing receipt-freeness or even coercion-resistance, such as JCJ [21].

**Overview.** The solution is the following: the voting device encrypts the vote and shows the resulting ballot to the voter, together with a zero-knowledge proof of knowledge (ZKPK) of the encryption randomness instead of revealing the plain value, as in the challenge-or-cast mechanisms. After the voter agrees on the proof, the ballot is cast and published on the bulletin board, so that the voter can check that her ballot has been correctly received at the voting platform. The voter agreement of the proof is represented with an authentication of the ballot, and only authenticated ballots are accepted in the system (posted on the bulletin board).

The cast-as-intended verification is still sound compared to prior systems, thanks to the properties of the proofs of knowledge: the verification of the proof will succeed only in case the voter's device is honest (i.e., the device is encrypting the voting options selected by the voter). In case of a dishonest device, the probability of the proof being successfully verified (and thus, the voter being cheated without notice) is negligible. At the same time, the scheme provides protection in front of vote selling/voter coercion scenarios thanks to the fact that it generates a ZKPK instead of providing the value itself. With the proof itself, the voter can be easily coerced or she can sell her vote. However, we take advantage of the fact that ZKPKs can be simulated to give a chance to the voter to cheat the coercers/vote buyers: In our scheme, the voter is allowed to generate *fake* proofs that will look like good proofs to anyone else.

This paper is organized as follows: Sect. 2 gives an introduction to the techniques used for the simulation of the proofs of the ballot content; Sect. 3 presents the syntax and description of the protocol, as well as the trust assumptions; Sect. 4 provides an efficient instantiation; a discussion about the voter experience using this protocol is provided in Sect. 5. Finally, an extension for multiple voting is provided in Sect. 6. The annexes contain some security definitions of the scheme and the result of the security analysis.

## 2    Proof Simulation

The scheme uses Designated Verifier Proofs [20], which allow a designated proof verifier to get convinced of a statement, while she is able to simulate proofs for other statements (which are not true) to other verifiers. In our scheme, the prover is the voting device, who proves knowledge of the encryption randomness, and the designated verifier is the voter. Other verifiers such as possible coercers or vote buyers cannot be convinced by the proof. Designated Verifier Proofs use trapdoor commitments, also known as chameleon commitments [7]. The trapdoor information is only available to the designated verifier of the proof, who can use it to generate simulated proofs for other verifiers. In non-interactive settings, such as in non-interactive zero-knowledge proofs of knowledge (NIZKPKs), Chameleon hashes [22] are used rather than chameleon commitments.

**Chameleon Hashes.** A chameleon hash function is a trapdoor collision-resistant hash function. Without knowledge of the trapdoor, the chameleon hash behaves as an ordinary collision-resistant hash function. However, using the trapdoor, collisions can be found efficiently.

A chameleon hash function is composed by three p.p.t. algorithms: $\mathsf{Gen}_{ch}$ takes as input a security parameter $1^k$, outputs an evaluation key $\mathsf{ek}_{ch}$ and a trapdoor key $\mathsf{tk}_{ch}$, and defines a message space $\mathcal{M}_{ch}$, a randomness space $\mathcal{R}_{ch}$ and a hash space $\mathcal{Y}_{ch}$; $\mathcal{H}_{ch}$ takes as input an evaluation key $\mathsf{ek}_{ch}$, a message $m \in \mathcal{M}_{ch}$ and a random value $\mathsf{r}_{ch} \in \mathcal{R}_{ch}$ and outputs a hash value $\mathsf{c}_{ch} \in \mathcal{Y}_{ch}$; $\mathcal{H}_{ch}^{-1}$ takes as input the trapdoor $\mathsf{tk}_{ch}$, two messages $m, m' \in \mathcal{M}_{ch}$ and a random $\mathsf{r}_{ch} \in \mathcal{R}_{ch}$, and returns a value $\mathsf{r}_{ch}' \in \mathcal{R}_{ch}$ such that $\mathcal{H}_{ch}(\mathsf{ek}_{ch}, m, \mathsf{r}_{ch}) = \mathcal{H}_{ch}(\mathsf{ek}_{ch}, m', \mathsf{r}_{ch}')$.

Chameleon hashes have the following properties:

COLLISION RESISTANCE. Provides that, given only the evaluation key $\mathsf{ek}_{ch}$, the probability of finding $(m, \mathsf{r}_{ch}) \neq (m', \mathsf{r}_{ch}')$ such that $\mathcal{H}_{ch}(\mathsf{ek}_{ch}, m, \mathsf{r}_{ch}) = \mathcal{H}_{ch}(\mathsf{ek}_{ch}, m', \mathsf{r}_{ch}')$ is negligible in polynomial time.

TRAPDOOR COLLISION. Provides that there is an efficient algorithm $\mathcal{H}_{ch}^{-1}$ which finds two pairs $(m, \mathsf{r}_{ch}) \neq (m', \mathsf{r}_{ch}')$ for which $\mathcal{H}_{ch}(\mathsf{ek}_{ch}, m, \mathsf{r}_{ch}) = \mathcal{H}_{ch}(\mathsf{ek}_{ch}, m', \mathsf{r}_{ch}')$, using the trapdoor key $\mathsf{tk}_{ch}$.

UNIFORMITY. For any message $m \in \mathcal{M}_{ch}$, and any $\mathsf{r}_{ch}$ uniformly distributed in $\mathcal{R}_{ch}$, the hash value $\mathsf{c}_{ch}$ is uniformly distributed in $\mathcal{Y}_{ch}$. Therefore the probability of an adversary of distinguishing between the hash value of $m$ and $m'$, both in $\mathcal{M}_{ch}$ is negligible in polynomial time.

## 2.1  A Simulatable NIZK Proof Using Chameleon Hashes

Although examples of simulatable NIZKPK proofs are given by the authors in [20], here we provide a formal description of the algorithms that will be used in further sections, in order to prove their properties and those of the scheme where they are used.

In a $\Sigma$-protocol, in order to prove that a statement $x$ belongs to $\mathcal{L}_\mathcal{R}$, a prover $P$ and a verifier $V$ engage in an interactive protocol where first, $P$ sends a commitment message $a$ to $V$; then $V$ replies with a random challenge $e$; finally, $P$ sends an answer $z$ to $V$. Interactive zero-knowledge protocols such as $\Sigma$ proofs can be turned into non-interactive using the Fiat-Shamir [16] transformation, where a hash function is used to compute the random challenge $e$.

The transformation into a (trapdoor) simulatable NIZKPK works by substituting the challenge $e$ with the result of a chameleon hash: $P$ chooses a random value $r_{ch}$ and evaluates the chameleon hash function $\mathcal{H}_{ch}$ on the message $m = H(x, a)$ using the randomness $r_{ch}$, where $H$ is a regular collision-resistant hash function. The challenge of the $\Sigma$-protocol is then defined as $e = \mathcal{H}_{ch}(H(x, a); r_{ch})$. In addition, $P$ also sends the randomness $r_{ch}$ which he used in the computation of the chameleon hash.

This non-interactive protocol allows to simulate valid proofs by means of the trapdoor key of the chameleon hash scheme: indeed, given a trapdoor $tk_{ch}$ for the chameleon hash, the simulator can compute the triplet $(a^*, e^*, z^*)$ as the simulator of the $\Sigma$-protocol would do. Then, by using the trapdoor of the chameleon hash, the simulator will be able to find a random value $r_{ch}{}^*$ such that $e^* = \mathcal{H}_{ch}(H(x^*, a^*); r_{ch}{}^*)$. The uniformity property of the chameleon hash scheme guarantees that simulated proofs have the same distribution than honest proofs.

Concretely, the trapdoor-simulatable NIZKPK scheme to be used in our protocol uses a $\Sigma$-protocol, a chameleon hash scheme ($\mathsf{Gen}_{ch}$, $\mathcal{H}_{ch}$, $\mathcal{H}_{ch}^{-1}$) and two hash functions $H_1 : \{0,1\}^* \to \mathcal{M}_{ch}$ and $H_2 : \{0,1\}^* \to \mathcal{CH}$ (the challenge space). Then, the NIZK proof is given by the following algorithms:

- GenCRS: on input a security parameter, it runs $\mathsf{Gen}_{ch}$ and outputs $\mathsf{crs} = \mathsf{ek}_{ch}$ and $\mathsf{tk} = \mathsf{tk}_{ch}$.
- NIZKProve: on input the common reference string $\mathsf{crs}$, a statement $x$ and a witness $w$, it follows the next steps:
  1. Run the first phase of the prover $P$ of the $\Sigma$-protocol, which outputs a commitment $a$.
  2. Sample a random $r_{ch} \in \mathcal{R}_{ch}$ and compute $e = H_2(\mathcal{H}_{ch}(H_1(x, a), r_{ch}))$.
  3. Run the second phase of the prover $P$ of the $\Sigma$-protocol, obtaining an answer $z$.
  4. Define the proof $\pi = (a, e, r_{ch}, z)$.
- NIZKVerify: on input a proof $\pi$ and a statement $x$, return 1 if $e = H_2(\mathcal{H}_{ch}(H_1(x, a), r_{ch})$ and the verification checks of the $\Sigma$-protocol pass on $(a, e, z)$, 0 otherwise.
- NIZKSimulate: on input a statement $x$ and a trapdoor $\mathsf{tk}$, the simulator runs the following steps:
  1. Run the simulator $\mathcal{S}$ of the $\Sigma$-protocol to obtain a triplet $(a^*, e^*, z^*)$.
  2. Use the trapdoor $tk_{ch}$ to obtain a value $r_{ch}{}^*$ s.t. $e^* = H_2(\mathcal{H}_{ch}(H_1(x, a^*), r_{ch}{}^*))$
  3. Output a simulated proof $\pi^* = (a^*, e^*, r_{ch}{}^*, z^*)$

A NIZKPK satisfies the properties of completeness, knowledge soundness and zero-knowledge [13, 28].

## 3   Protocol Syntax

In this section we define a syntax for the proposed voting protocol. We use as a basis the syntax defined in [11, 31] for analyzing the properties of the Helios voting protocol [2], and add an auditing phase for the cast as intended verification functionality.

The following are the participants of the voting protocol: the *Election Authorities* configure the election and tally the votes to produce the election result; the *Registrars* registers the voters and provide them with information for participating in the election; *Voters* participate in the election by providing their choices; the *Voting Device* generates and casts a vote given the voting options selected by the voter; an *Audit Device* is used by the voter to verify cryptographic evidences; the *Bulletin Board Manager* receives and publishes the votes cast by the voters in the bulletin board BB; finally the *Auditors* are responsible of verifying the integrity of the procedures run in the counting phase.

Consider that the list of voting options $V = \{v_1, \ldots, v_n\}$ in the election is defined in advance. The counting function $\rho : (V \cup \{\perp\})^* \to R$, where $\perp$ denotes an invalid vote and $R$ is the set of results, is a multiset function which provides the set of cleartext votes cast by the voters in a random order [5].

The voting protocol uses an encryption scheme with algorithms (Gen$_e$, Enc, Dec, EncVerify), a signature scheme (Gen$_s$, Sign, SignVerify) and a mix- net with algorithms Mix and MixVerify. It additionally uses a trapdoor-simulatable NIZKPK scheme denoted by the algorithms (GenCRS, NIZKProve, NIZKVerify, NIZKSimulate).

- Setup($1^\lambda$) chooses $p$ and $q$ for the ElGamal encryption scheme and runs Gen$_e$. Then it sets the election public key $pk = (pk_e, \mathbb{G})$ and the election private key $sk = (sk_e, pk_e)$. Finally it generates the empty list of credentials ID.
- Register($1^\lambda$, id) takes the public parameters defined by $pk$, runs GenCRS from the NIZKPK scheme and Gen$_s$ from the signature scheme, and sets $pk_{id} = (crs, pk_s)$ and $sk_{id} = (tk, sk_s)$.
- CreateVote($v_i, pk_{id}$) runs Enc from the encryption scheme with inputs $pk$ and $v_i$ and obtains the ciphertext $c_s$. Then it parses $c_s$ as $(c_1, c_2, h, z)$ and $pk_{id}$ as $(crs, pk_s)$, and runs NIZKProve from the NIZKPK scheme, using as input crs, the statement $(c_1, c_2/v_i)$ and the witness $r$, where $r$ is the random element in $\mathbb{Z}_q$ used during encryption. The result is set to be $\sigma$, while the ballot $b$ takes the value of $c_s$.
- AuditVote($v_i, b, \sigma, pk_{id}$) parses $b$ as $(c_1, c_2, h, z)$ and $pk_{id}$ as $(crs, pk_s)$, then runs NIZKVerify from the NIZKPK scheme with inputs the proof $\sigma$, the common reference string crs and the statement $(c_1, c_2/v_i)$. It outputs the result of the proof verification.
- CastVote($b, sk_{id}$, id) runs Sign with inputs the voter's signing private key $sk_s$ and the ballot $b$ to be signed together with the voter identity id. The output is the authenticated ballot $b_a = (id, b, \psi)$.
- FakeProof($b, sk_{id}, pk_{id}, v_j$) parses $b$ as $(c_1, c_2, h, z)$, $pk_{id}$ as $(crs, pk_s)$ and $sk_{id}$ as $(tk, sk_s)$. Then it runs NIZKSimulate from the NIZKPK scheme for the statement $(c_1, c_2/v_j)$. Then the simulated encryption proof data $\sigma'$ is the simulated proof $\pi^*$.
- ProcessBallot(BB, $b_a$) parses $b_a$ as $(id, b, \psi)$ and $b$ as $(c_1, c_2, h, z)$. Then it proceeds to perform some validations: It checks that there is not already an entry in the bulletin board for the same id and that this id is present in the list ID, or with the same ciphertext $(c_1, c_2)$. It also runs EncVerify to verify the

proof $(h, z)$ and the voter's signature running SignVerify (for which it picks the corresponding public key $pk_{id}$ from the list ID). If any of these validations fail, the process stops and outputs 0. Otherwise it outputs 1.

- VerifyVote(BB, $b$, id) checks that there is an entry in the bulletin board for the identity id. In the affirmative case, it parses the authenticated ballot $b'_a$ as $(id, b', \psi')$ and checks that all the fields in $b'$ are equal to all the fields in $b$.
- Tally(BB, $sk$) runs ProcessBallot over the individual entries of the ballot box. For those who passed the verifications, it parses each one as $(id, (c_1, c_2, h, z), \psi)$, it takes the pairs $(c_1, c_2)$ and runs $\mathsf{Mix}((c_1^1, c_2^1), \ldots, (c_1^n, c_2^n))$, which denotes a verifiable mixnet such as [3] or [32]. Then the ciphertexts are decrypted running the Dec algorithm and a proof of correct decryption is produced. The outputs are the list of decrypted votes $r$ and the proofs of correct mixing and decryption, $\Pi$.
- VerifyTally(BB, $r$, $\Pi$) in the first place performs the same validations than the ProcessBallot algorithm over the ballots in BB: for each one, it checks that there is only one entry in the ballot box per id and per $(c_1, c_2)$. In case it founds any coincidence, it halts and outputs $\perp$. Otherwise, it continues with the validations and discards all the ballot box entries for which EncVerify or SignVerify output 0. Finally it verifies the proofs $\Pi$ of correct mixing and decryption, using the ciphertexts of the entries which have passed the validation and the result $r$.

The voting protocol algorithms are organised in the following phases:

**Configuration phase:** In this phase, the election authorities set up the public parameters of the election such as the list of voting options $\{v_i\} \in V$ and the result function $\rho$. They also run the Setup algorithm and publish the resulting election public key $pk$ and the empty credential list ID in the bulletin board. The private key $sk$ is kept in secret by the electoral authorities.

**Registration phase:** In this phase the registrars register the voters to vote in the election. For each voter with identity id, the registrars run Register and update the credential list ID in the bulletin board with the pair $(id, pk_{id})$. The key pair $(pk_{id}, sk_{id})$ is provided to the voter.

**Voting phase:** In this phase the voter chooses a voting option $v_i \in V$ and interacts in the following way with the voting device, in order to cast a vote:

1. The voter provides her identity id and the voting option $v_i$ to the voting device, which gathers the corresponding public key $pk_{id}$ from the bulletin board and runs the CreateVote algorithm. The outputs $b$ and $\sigma$ are provided to the voter.
2. The voter uses an audit device to run AuditVote using $b$ and $\sigma$ provided by the voting device. The voter may enter $pk_{id}$ herself, or her identity id so that the audit device picks the corresponding public key $pk_{id}$ from the list ID. A positive result means that $b$ is encrypting the voter's selection $v_i$ and the voter can continue the process. Otherwise, the voter is instructed to abort the process and choose another voting device to cast her vote, since the one she is using is corrupted and did not encrypt what the she selected.

3. As a sign of approval of the generated ballot, the voter provides her private key $sk_{id}$ to the voting device, which proceeds to run CastVote. The resulting authenticated ballot is sent to the bulletin board manager.
4. Then the voting device runs FakeProof using a voting option $v_j \in V$ as input (supposedly the one requested by the coercer/vote buyer, otherwise it may be a random value from the set $V$), and provides the simulated encryption data $\sigma'$ to the voter.

The bulletin board manager runs the ProcessBallot algorithm. If the result is positive, the authenticated ballot $b_a$ is posted in the bulletin board. Otherwise, the bulletin board is left unchanged, and the voter receives a negative response. From that point, the voter can run VerifyVote to check that her vote has been posted in the bulletin board.

From this point, the voter can provide the ballot $b$ and the simulated encryption data $\sigma'$ to a coercer, who might want to check that a ballot for the requested voting option $v_j$ is present in the bulletin board by running the AuditVote and VerifyVote algorithms.

**Counting phase:** in this phase, the election authorities provide the election private key $sk$ and run the Tally algorithm on the contents of the bulletin board. The obtained result $r$ and the proof $\Pi$ are posted in the bulletin board. The auditors then run the VerifyTally algorithm. In case the verification is satisfactory, the election result is considered to be correct. Otherwise, an investigation is opened in order to detect any manipulation that could lead to a corrupted result.

## 3.1  Trust Model

Security definitions and analysis results are provided in the Annex, while complete demonstrations are included in the full version [19]. However, here we informally introduce the trust assumptions we make on the scheme regarding privacy and integrity:

We assume that voters follow the protocol in the correct way. We also assume the voter to follow the audit processes indicated and complain in case of any irregularity.

In order to simplify the analysis, we consider that the election authorities, and the registrars as well, behave properly in the sense that they generate correct and valid key pairs, and that they do not divulge the secret keys to unintended recipients. Multiparty computation techniques such as [25] or [14] can be used in order to distributely generate secrets among a set of trustees, ensuring their privacy and a correct generation in case a subset of them is honest.

From the point of view of privacy, the voting device is trusted not to leak the randomness used for the encryption of the voter's choices. While this assumption may seem too strong, it is in fact needed in any voting scheme where the voting options are encrypted at the voting device (no pre-encrypted ballots are used) and the vote is not cast in an anonymous way. However, for the point of view of integrity, we consider that a malicious voting device may ignore the selections made by the voter and put another content in the ballot to be cast.

As in similar schemes such as Helios [2] or Wombat [1], the audit device is trusted both from the point of view of privacy (it is assumed not to divulge the voter's selections) and from the point of view of integrity (it is assumed to honestly transmit the result of the proofs verification to the voter).

The bulletin board manager is trusted to accept and post on the bulletin board all the correct votes. No assumptions are done in the topic of privacy. Finally, auditors are assumed to honestly transmit the result of their verification. However, we assume them to be curious and try to find out the content of voter's votes from the information they get.

## 4   Concrete Instantiation

In this section, we provide a concrete instantiation based on ElGamal over a finite field.

**Encryption Scheme.** The Signed ElGamal encryption scheme [30] is used in our instantiation of the protocol. It is a combination of the ElGamal encryption scheme [15] and a proof of knowledge of the encryption randomness, which is based in the Schnorr signature scheme [29] (sometimes we will refer to this proof of knowledge as the Schnorr proof). In our notation, $(c_1, c_2)$ represent the single ElGamal ciphertext, while $(h, z)$ represent the Schnorr signature.

According to the work in [6], this variant of ElGamal is NM-CPA secure.

**Chameleon Hash.** The following instantiation of a chameleon hash ($\mathsf{Gen}_{ch}$, $\mathcal{H}_{ch}, \mathcal{H}_{ch}^{-1}$) based on the discrete logarithm problem [22] is used: $\mathsf{Gen}_{ch}$ receives a group $\mathbb{G}$ of prime order $q$ of elements in $\mathbb{Z}_p^*$ with generator $g$. An element $x$ is sampled uniformly from $\mathbb{Z}_q$ and $h = g^x$ is computed. Then, the evaluation key $\mathsf{ek}_{ch}$ is defined as $\mathsf{ek}_{ch} = (\mathbb{G}, g, h)$ and the trapdoor key $\mathsf{tk}_{ch}$ is defined as $\mathsf{tk}_{ch} = (\mathsf{ek}_{ch}, x)$. The message space and the randomness space are $\mathbb{Z}_q$ and the hash space is $\mathbb{G}$. The algorithm $\mathcal{H}_{ch}$ is defined for $(m, \mathsf{r}_{ch}) \in \mathbb{Z}_q \times \mathbb{Z}_q$ to output $\mathsf{c}_{ch} = g^m \cdot h^{\mathsf{r}_{ch}}$. Finally, $\mathcal{H}_{ch}^{-1}(m, \mathsf{r}_{ch}, m')$ outputs $\mathsf{r}_{ch}' = (m - m') \cdot x^{-1} + \mathsf{r}_{ch}$.

**$\Sigma$-proof.** We use a simulatable NIZKPK based on a $\Sigma$-proof which proves that a specific plaintext corresponds to a given ciphertext. The $\Sigma$-proof computed over an ElGamal ciphertext of the form $(c_1, c_2) = (g^r, pk_e^r \cdot m)$ is as follows:

1. Prover computes $(a_1, a_2) = (g^s, pk_e^s)$, where $s$ is a random element $\in \mathbb{Z}_q$, and provides them to the verifier.
2. Verifier provides a challenge $e$.
3. Prover provides to the verifier $z = s + re$. The verifier checks that $g^z = a_1 \cdot c_1^e$ and that $h^z = a_2 \cdot (c_2/m)^e$.

This $\Sigma$-proof can be simulated in the following way: the simulator samples a random $z^* \in \mathbb{G}$, a random $e^* \in \mathbb{Z}_q$ and computes $a_1^* = g^{z^*} \cdot c_1^{-e^*}$ and $a_2^* = h^{z^*} \cdot (c_2/m)^{-e^*}$. The resulting $(a^*, e^*, z^*)$ values have the same distribution than the original ones.

**Simulatable NIZKPK.** The algorithms of the NIZKPK scheme are then defined by using the discrete log-based chameleon hash scheme and the $\Sigma$-proof defined above, as well as two hash functions $H_1, H_2$ mapping inputs to $\mathbb{Z}_q$, as follows:

- GenCRS runs $\mathsf{Gen_{ch}}$ and outputs $\mathsf{crs} = (\mathbb{G}, g, h)$ and $\mathsf{tk} = (\mathsf{crs}, x)$;
- NIZKProve receives $\mathsf{crs}$, the statement $x = (c_1, c_2/m)$ and the witness $r$, and computes: (1) the commitment $(a_1, a_2) = (g^s, pk_e^s)$, (2) the non-interactive challenge $e = H_2(g^{(H_1(x,a))} \cdot h^{\mathsf{r_{ch}}})$, where $\mathsf{r_{ch}}$ is picked at random from $\mathbb{Z}_q$, (3) the answer $z = s + re$, and (4) provides the proof $\pi = (a, e, \mathsf{r_{ch}}, z)$;
- NIZKVerify checks that $g^z = a_1 \cdot c_1^e$, $h^z = a_2 \cdot (c_2/m)^e$, and that $e = H_2(g^{(H_1(x,a))} \cdot h^{\mathsf{r_{ch}}})$;
- NIZKSimulate receives as input a statement $x^* = (c_1, c_2/m^*)$ and the trapdoor $\mathsf{tk}$, and does the following: takes at random $z^* \in \mathbb{G}$ and random pair $(\alpha, \beta) \in \mathbb{Z}_q$, and sets $e^* = H_2(g^\alpha \cdot h^\beta)$. Then it computes $a_1^* = g^{z^*} \cdot c_1^{-e^*}$ and $a_2^* = h^{z^*} \cdot (c_2/m^*)^{-e^*}$, and finally it obtains $\mathsf{r_{ch}}^* = (\alpha - H_1(x^*, a^*)) \cdot x^{-1} + \beta$. The simulated proof is then $\pi^* = (a^*, e^*, \mathsf{r_{ch}}^*, z^*)$.

The full version of this paper [19] provides a proof that the described simulatable NIZK proof fulfills the properties of completeness, knowledge soundness and zero-knowledge of NIZKPKs.

Additionally, we use the *RSA Full Domain Hash (RSA-FDH)* [4] algorithm for the signature scheme ($\mathsf{Gen_s}, \mathsf{Sign}, \mathsf{SignVerify}$), and a proof of correct decryption based on the Chaum-Pedersen protocol [9], as described in [12].

### 4.1  Performance

This instantiation is simple and efficient. For a *k-out-of-n* voting scheme, where $k$ options can be encrypted into one ElGamal ciphertext, the encryption of the voter selections using the Signed ElGamal encryption scheme requires 3 exponentiations. The computation of the NIZKPK requires 6 additional exponentiations (2 of them for the computation of the chameleon hash), and 6 more for verification. Each proof simulation costs 6 exponentiations.

An important detail is that, for efficiency purposes, the prime group and the generator of such group used in all these primitives must be the same.

## 5  Voting Experience

It is important to recall the criticity of the voter's trapdoor key. A voter who has not access to it will not be able to simulate a proof. Thus, the cast-as-intended verification mechanism will no longer protect the privacy of the voter. On the other hand, the voter device has to learn the trapdoor key only after it has already generated a honest proof for the voter. Otherwise, the device could simulate a proof the voter expects to be honest, and the scheme would no longer be cast-as-intended verifiable.

In order to present an easy and intuitive voting process for the voter, we have related the private information she uses to authenticate her vote (for example, her private signing key) with the trapdoor key which is used to generate false proofs. We think that it is meaningful that the voter provides both secrets at the same time, as a confirmation that she agrees to cast that vote (which she is expected to do only after verifying the honest proof). Before the voter provides these secrets, the voting device can neither cast a valid vote, nor cheat the voter by generating a fake proof.

Therefore, at the voter registration stage each voter may be issued both key pairs (the signing key pair to authenticate their vote, and the evaluation/trapdoor key pair for the NIZKPK scheme), where the private keys are password-protected. Later on, during the voting stage, the voter's selections are encrypted by the voting device, and the resulting ciphertext and the proof of content are shown to the voter, who then can use an audit device to check that the ciphertext contents match her selections (for example, her smartphone). After a positive audit, the voter enters her password into the voting device, which recovers both private keys, using the private signing key part to digitally sign the vote to be cast, and the NIZKPK trapdoor key part to generate one or several fake proofs for alternative voting options which may be defined by the voter. The fake proofs have to be presented in the same way than the honest one, so that they cannot be distinguished by a potential coercer. Finally, the vote is sent to the bulletin board manager which publishes it the bulletin board, so that the voter can check that her audited vote has been correctly received.

## 6   Protocol Extension for Multiple Voting

The possibility of multiple voting may be interesting in case something goes wrong or for anti-coercion measures. However, it has to be taken into account that in this case the voting device learns the trapdoor key after the first vote, and could cheat the voter in further ballot generations.

An approach for allowing multiple voting consists on delegating the generation of simulated proofs to the bulletin board manager, who keeps the voters' trapdoor keys and provides simulated proofs to the voting devices *only* when receiving confirmed ballots (which means that voters already verified their contents and agreed with them). Although this does not endanger the voter's privacy, a collusion of the bulletin board manager and the voting device may defeat the property of cast-as-intended verifiability by simulating proofs in advance or refuse to generate them. A distributed setting, where multiple bulletin board managers hold shares of the voters' trapdoor keys generated with a threshold scheme can be used to enforce this property, even if a subset of the bulletin board managers are malicious.

# A    Security Definitions and Analysis Results

## A.1    Definitions

In this section we define the notions of ballot privacy, and cast as intended verifiability for an electronic voting scheme such as that described in Sect. 3. We take as basis the definitions from [5] and then adapt them to the particularities of our scheme. Other definitions such as strong consistency or strong correctness are available in the full version [19].

**Ballot Privacy.** It is defined by means of an experiment where an adversary is presented with two experiments and has to be able to distinguish between them. In each experiment the adversary has indirect access to a ballot box which receives the ballots created by honest voters, as well as ballots cast by the adversary itself on behalf of corrupted voters. In the case of honest voters, we let the adversary choose two possible votes which they will use to create their ballots. Which vote is used to cast a voter's ballot that goes to a specific ballot box depends on the experiment that is taking place.

At the end of the experiment, the adversary is presented with the result of tallying the ballot box, which is the same regardless of the experiment. As noted in [5], revealing the true tally in each experiment would easily allow the adversary to distinguish between both ballot boxes. Additionally, for the votes cast by honest voters, we provide the resulting encryption proof data to the adversary in order to model a coercer which uses it to learn something about the vote. We will use a simulation functionality to generate fake proofs when required.

$\mathbf{Exp}_{A,V}^{priv,\beta}$:

1. **Setup phase:** The challenger $C$ sets up two empty bulletin boards $BB_0$ and $BB_1$ and runs the $\mathsf{Setup}(1^\lambda)$ algorithm to obtain the election key pair $(pk, sk)$ and the empty list of credentials ID. $A$ is given access to $BB_0$ when $\beta = 0$ and to $BB_1$ when $\beta = 1$.
2. **Registration phase:** The adversary may make the following query:
   - $\mathcal{O}\mathsf{Register}(\mathtt{id})$: $A$ provides an identity $\mathtt{id} \notin \mathsf{ID}$. $C$ runs $\mathsf{Register}(1^\lambda, \mathtt{id})$, provides the voter key pair $(pk_{\mathtt{id}}, sk_{\mathtt{id}})$ to $A$, and adds $(\mathtt{id}, pk_{\mathtt{id}})$ to ID.
3. **Voting phase:** The adversary may make the following types of queries:
   - $\mathcal{O}\mathsf{VoteLR}(\mathtt{id}, v_0, v_1)$: this query models the votes cast by honest voters. $A$ provides an identity $\mathtt{id} \in \mathsf{ID}$ and two possible votes $v_0, v_1 \in V$. The challenger $C$ does the following:
     - It picks the corresponding $pk_{\mathtt{id}}$ from ID and executes $\mathsf{CreateVote}(v_0, pk_{\mathtt{id}})$ and $\mathsf{CreateVote}(v_1, pk_{\mathtt{id}})$ which produce the ballots $b^0$ and $b^1$ respectively and their encryption proof data $\sigma_0$ and $\sigma_1$.
     - Then it executes $\mathsf{CastVote}(b^0, sk_{\mathtt{id}}, \mathtt{id})$, $\mathsf{CastVote}(b^1, sk_{\mathtt{id}}, \mathtt{id})$ to obtain the authenticated ballots $b_a^0$ and $b_a^1$, and $\mathsf{ProcessBallot}(BB_0, b_a^0)$ and $\mathsf{ProcessBallot}(BB_1, b_a^1)$. If both processes return 1, the ballot boxes $BB_0$ and $BB_1$ are updated with $b_a^0$ and $b_a^1$ respectively. Otherwise, $C$ stops and returns $\bot$.

- Finally, $C$ executes FakeProof($b^\beta, sk_{id}, pk_{id}, v_{\overline{\beta}}$) and provides $\sigma_\beta$ and the simulated encryption proof data $\sigma_\beta^*$ to $A$.
  - $O$Cast($b_a$): this query models the votes cast by corrupted voters. $A$ provides an authenticated ballot $b_a$, and then $C$ executes ProcessBallot with $b_a$ and each ballot box. If both algorithms return 1, both ballot boxes are updated with $b_a$. Otherwise, $C$ halts and none of the ballot boxes are updated.
4. **Counting phase:** The challenger runs Tally($BB_0, sk$) and obtains the result $r$ and the tally proof $\Pi$, which are provided to $A$ in case $\beta = 0$. In case $\beta = 1$, $C$ runs SimProof($BB_1, r$) to obtain $\Pi^*$, and provides $(r, \Pi^*)$ to $A$.
5. **Output:** The output of the experiment is the guess of the adversary for the bit $\beta$.

We say that a voting protocol as defined in Sect. 3 has ballot privacy if there exists an algorithm SimProof such that for any probabilistic polynomial time (p.p.t.) adversary $A$, the following advantage is negligible in the security parameter $\lambda$:

$$\mathsf{Adv}_A^{\mathsf{priv}} = |\Pr[\mathsf{Exp}_{A,V}^{\mathsf{priv},0} = 1] - \Pr[\mathsf{Exp}_{A,V}^{\mathsf{priv},1} = 1]|$$

**Cast-as-Intended Verifiability.** A voting system is defined to be cast-as-intended verifiable if a corrupt voting device is unable to cast a vote on behalf of a voter, with a voting option different than the one chosen by the voter, without being detected. In our definition, we consider an adversary who posts ballots in the bulletin board on behalf of honest and corrupt voters. In case of honest voters, they follow the protocol and perform some validations before approving the ballot to be cast. Corrupt voters provide their approval without doing any prior verification.

$\mathsf{Exp}_{A,V}^{\mathsf{Cal}}$:

1. **Setup phase:** The challenger $C$ runs the Setup($1^\lambda$) algorithm and provides the election key pair $(pk, sk)$ to $A$. Then it publishes the empty lists of voter credentials $ID_h$ and $ID_c$ such that $ID = (ID_h \cup ID_c)$. Finally $A$ is given read access to BB.
2. **Registration phase:** The adversary may make the following queries:
   - $O$RegisterHonest(id): $A$ provides an identity id $\notin$ ID. The challenger $C$ runs Register($1^\lambda$, id), and adds (id, $pk_{id}$) to $ID_h$.
   - $O$RegisterCorrupt(id): $A$ provides an identity id $\notin$ ID. The challenger $C$ runs Register($1^\lambda$, id), and adds (id, $pk_{id}$) to $ID_c$.
3. **Voting phase:** The adversary may make the following types of queries:
   - $O$VoteHonest(id, $v_i, b, \sigma$): this query models the votes cast by honest voters. $A$ provides an identity id $\in$ $ID_h$, a ballot $b$, an encryption proof data $\sigma$ and the voting option $v_i$. The challenger $C$ runs AuditVote($v_i, b, \sigma, pk_{id}$), and only if the result is 1 it provides $sk_{id}$ to $A$.

- $\mathcal{O}\mathbf{VoteCorrupt}(b, \mathtt{id})$: this query models the votes cast by corrupted voters. $\mathcal{A}$ provides a ballot $b$ and an identity $\mathtt{id} \in \mathsf{ID}_c$. $\mathcal{C}$ answers with $sk_{\mathtt{id}}$.

4. **Output:** The adversary submits an authenticated ballot $b'_a = (\mathtt{id}', b', \psi')$. The output of the experiment is 1 if the following conditions hold:
   - $\mathtt{id}' \in \mathsf{ID}_h$
   - $\mathsf{ProcessBallot}(\mathsf{BB}, b'_a) = 1$
   - $\mathsf{VerifyVote}(\mathsf{BB}, b', \mathtt{id}') = 1$
   - $\mathsf{Extract}(b'_a; sk) \neq v'_i$, where $v'_i$ is the voting option submitted by the adversary in the $\mathcal{O}\mathsf{VoteHonest}$ query.

We say that a voting protocol as defined in Sect. 3 has cast-as-intended verifiability if, given an $\mathsf{Extract}$ algorithm for which the protocol is consistent with respect to $\rho$, the following advantage is negligible in the security parameter $\lambda$ for any probabilistic polynomial time (p.p.t.) adversary $\mathcal{A}$:

$$\mathsf{Adv}_{\mathcal{A}}^{\mathsf{Cal}} = |\Pr[\mathsf{Exp}_{\mathcal{A},V}^{\mathsf{Cal},0} = 1]|$$

## A.2 Security Analysis Results

In this section we provide the results of our security analysis, which is available in the full version of this paper [19].

**Theorem 1.** *Let* $(\mathsf{Gen}_e, \mathsf{Enc}, \mathsf{Dec})$ *be an NM-CPA secure encryption scheme and* $(\mathsf{GenCRS}, \mathsf{NIZKProve}, \mathsf{NIZKVerify}, \mathsf{NIZKSimulate})$ *a NIZKPK which provides zero-knowledge. Then the protocol presented in Sect. 3 satisfies the ballot privacy property.*

**Theorem 2.** *Let* $(\mathsf{Gen}_e, \mathsf{Enc}, \mathsf{Dec}, \mathsf{EncVerify})$ *be a probabilistic encryption scheme,* $(\mathsf{GenCRS}, \mathsf{NIZKProve}, \mathsf{NIZKVerify}, \mathsf{NIZKSimulate})$ *a NIZKPK which is sound and* $(\mathsf{Gen}_s, \mathsf{Sign}, \mathsf{SignVerify})$ *an unforgeable signature scheme. Then the protocol presented in Sect. 3 satisfies the cast-as-intended verifiability property.*

# References

1. Wombat voting system (2015). http://www.wombat-voting.com/
2. Adida, B.: Helios: web-based open-audit voting. In: van Oorschot, P.C. (ed.) USENIX Security Symposium, pp. 335–348. USENIX Association (2008)
3. Bayer, S., Groth, J.: Efficient zero-knowledge argument for correctness of a shuffle. In: Pointcheval, D., Johansson, T. (eds.) EUROCRYPT 2012. LNCS, vol. 7237, pp. 263–280. Springer, Heidelberg (2012). doi:10.1007/978-3-642-29011-4_17
4. Bellare, M., Rogaway, P.: Random oracles are practical: a paradigm for designing efficient protocols. In: Proceedings of CCS 1993, NY, USA, pp. 62–73 (1993)
5. Bernhard, D., Cortier, V., Galindo, D., Pereira, O., Warinschi, B.: A comprehensive analysis of game-based ballot privacy definitions. IACR Cryptology ePrint Archive 2015, 255 (2015)

6. Bernhard, D., Pereira, O., Warinschi, B.: On necessary and sufficient conditions for private ballot submission. IACR Cryptology ePrint Archive 2012, 236 (2012)
7. Brassard, G., Chaum, D., Crépeau, C.: Minimum disclosure proofs of knowledge. J. Comput. Syst. Sci. **37**(2), 156–189 (1988)
8. Chaum, D.: Surevote: Technical report (2001). http://www.iavoss.org/mirror/wote01/pdfs/surevote.pdf
9. Chaum, D., Pedersen, T.P.: Wallet databases with observers. In: Brickell, E.F. (ed.) CRYPTO 1992. LNCS, vol. 740, pp. 89–105. Springer, Heidelberg (1993). doi:10.1007/3-540-48071-4_7
10. Chen, X., Wu, Q., Zhang, F., Tian, H., Wei, B., Lee, B., Lee, H., Kim, K.: New receipt-free voting scheme using double-trapdoor commitment. Inf. Sci. **181**(8), 1493–1502 (2011)
11. Cortier, V., Galindo, D., Glondu, S., Izabachène, M.: Election verifiability for helios under weaker trust assumptions. In: Kutyłowski, M., Vaidya, J. (eds.) ESORICS 2014. LNCS, vol. 8713, pp. 327–344. Springer, Cham (2014). doi:10.1007/978-3-319-11212-1_19
12. Cramer, R., Gennaro, R., Schoenmakers, B.: A secure and optimally efficient multi-authority election scheme. In: Fumy, W. (ed.) EUROCRYPT 1997. LNCS, vol. 1233, pp. 103–118. Springer, Heidelberg (1997). doi:10.1007/3-540-69053-0_9
13. Damgård, I.: Commitment schemes and zero-knowledge protocols. In: Damgård, I.B. (ed.) EEF School 1998. LNCS, vol. 1561, pp. 63–86. Springer, Heidelberg (1999). doi:10.1007/3-540-48969-X_3
14. Damgård, I., Mikkelsen, G.L.: Efficient, robust and constant-round distributed RSA key generation. In: Micciancio, D. (ed.) TCC 2010. LNCS, vol. 5978, pp. 183–200. Springer, Heidelberg (2010). doi:10.1007/978-3-642-11799-2_12
15. ElGamal, T.: A public key cryptosystem and a signature scheme based on discrete logarithms. In: Blakley, G.R., Chaum, D. (eds.) CRYPTO 1984. LNCS, vol. 196, pp. 10–18. Springer, Heidelberg (1985). doi:10.1007/3-540-39568-7_2
16. Fiat, A., Shamir, A.: How to prove yourself: practical solutions to identification and signature problems. In: Odlyzko, A.M. (ed.) CRYPTO 1986. LNCS, vol. 263, pp. 186–194. Springer, Heidelberg (1987). doi:10.1007/3-540-47721-7_12
17. Gharadaghy, R., Volkamer, M.: Verifiability in electronic voting - explanations for non security experts. In: Proceedings of EVOTE 2010. LNI, vol. 167, pp. 151–162. GI (2010)
18. Gjøsteen, K.: Analysis of an internet voting protocol. IACR Cryptology ePrint Archive 2010, 380 (2010)
19. Guasch, S., Morillo, P.: How to challenge *and* cast your e-vote. IACR Cryptology ePrint Archive (2016). To be published
20. Jakobsson, M., Sako, K., Impagliazzo, R.: Designated verifier proofs and their applications. In: Maurer, U. (ed.) EUROCRYPT 1996. LNCS, vol. 1070, pp. 143–154. Springer, Heidelberg (1996). doi:10.1007/3-540-68339-9_13
21. Juels, A., Catalano, D., Jakobsson, M.: Coercion-resistant electronic elections. In: Proceedings of WPES 2005, pp. 61–70. ACM (2005)
22. Krawczyk, H., Rabin, T.: Chameleon hashing and signatures. IACR Cryptology ePrint Archive 1998, 010 (1998)
23. Moran, T., Naor, M.: Receipt-free universally-verifiable voting with everlasting privacy. In: Dwork, C. (ed.) CRYPTO 2006. LNCS, vol. 4117, pp. 373–392. Springer, Heidelberg (2006). doi:10.1007/11818175_22
24. Neff, C.A.: Practical high certainty intent verification for encrypted votes (2004)

25. Pedersen, T.P.: A threshold cryptosystem without a trusted party. In: Davies, D.W. (ed.) EUROCRYPT 1991. LNCS, vol. 547, pp. 522–526. Springer, Heidelberg (1991). doi:10.1007/3-540-46416-6_47

26. Ryan, P.Y.A., Teague, V.: Pretty good democracy. In: Christianson, B., Malcolm, J.A., Matyáš, V., Roe, M. (eds.) Security Protocols 2009. LNCS, vol. 7028, pp. 111–130. Springer, Heidelberg (2013). doi:10.1007/978-3-642-36213-2_15

27. Sako, K., Kilian, J.: Receipt-free mix-type voting scheme. In: Guillou, L.C., Quisquater, J.-J. (eds.) EUROCRYPT 1995. LNCS, vol. 921, pp. 393–403. Springer, Heidelberg (1995). doi:10.1007/3-540-49264-X_32

28. Santis, A.D., Persiano, G.: Zero-knowledge proofs of knowledge without interaction (extended abstract). In: FOCS, pp. 427–436. IEEE Computer Society (1992)

29. Schnorr, C.P.: Efficient identification and signatures for smart cards. In: Brassard, G. (ed.) CRYPTO 1989. LNCS, vol. 435, pp. 239–252. Springer, New York (1990). doi:10.1007/0-387-34805-0_22

30. Schnorr, C.P., Jakobsson, M.: Security of signed ElGamal encryption. In: Okamoto, T. (ed.) ASIACRYPT 2000. LNCS, vol. 1976, pp. 73–89. Springer, Heidelberg (2000). doi:10.1007/3-540-44448-3_7

31. Smyth, B., Frink, S., Clarkson, M.R.: Computational election verifiability: definitions and an analysis of helios and JCJ. IACR Cryptology ePrint Archive 2015, 233 (2015)

32. Wikström, D.: A commitment-consistent proof of a shuffle. IACR Cryptology ePrint Archive 2011, 168 (2011)

# Multiparty Computation

# VD-PSI: Verifiable Delegated Private Set Intersection on Outsourced Private Datasets

Aydin Abadi[⊠], Sotirios Terzis, and Changyu Dong

Department of Computer and Information Sciences,
University of Strathclyde, Glasgow, UK
{aydin.abadi,sotirios.terzis,changyu.dong}@strath.ac.uk

**Abstract.** Private set intersection (PSI) protocols have many real world applications. With the emergence of cloud computing the need arises to carry out PSI on outsourced datasets where the computation is delegated to the cloud. However, due to the possibility of cloud misbehavior, it is essential to verify the integrity of any outsourced datasets, and results of any delegated computation. Verifiable Computation on private datasets that does not leak any information about the data is very challenging, especially when the datasets are outsourced independently by different clients. In this paper we present VD-PSI, a protocol that allows multiple clients to outsource their private datasets and delegate computation of set intersection to the cloud, while being able to verify the correctness of the result. Clients can independently prepare and upload their datasets, and with their agreement can verifiably delegate the computation of set intersection an unlimited number of times, without the need to download or maintain a local copy of their data. The protocol ensures that the cloud learns nothing about the datasets and the intersection. VD-PSI is efficient as its verification cost is linear to the intersection cardinality, and its computation and communication costs are linear to the (upper bound of) dataset cardinality. Also, we provide a formal security analysis in the standard model.

## 1 Introduction

Private set intersection (PSI) allows parties to compute the intersection of their datasets without revealing anything about the data beyond the intersection [12]. PSI has a variety of real world applications like privacy preserving data mining [2], homeland security [8], etc. Over the years, due to its importance researchers have designed a number of PSI protocols [10,19,21–24,29,31]. However, these typically require parties to jointly compute the intersection with locally available datasets. With the growing impact of cloud computing on businesses, due to its economic benefits [26], the need arises to delegate PSI computation on outsourced datasets to the cloud [1,19].

Cloud computing offers flexible and cost effective storage and computation resources to clients. Nevertheless, past real-world incidents [5] and recent research (see [4,18] for surveys) have shown that the cloud cannot be fully trusted

© International Financial Cryptography Association 2017
J. Grossklags and B. Preneel (Eds.): FC 2016, LNCS 9603, pp. 149–168, 2017.
DOI: 10.1007/978-3-662-54970-4_9

and it may misbehave by exposing or tampering with clients' sensitive data, or fiddling with computation results. These misbehaviors can have a serious impact on businesses. So, it is essential for clients not only to protect the confidentiality of their outsourced data, but also to verify the integrity of the data and the result of the computation delegated to the cloud. In other words, there is a pressing need for *verifiable delegated PSI on outsourced private datasets*.

Verifying the integrity of computation while preserving the confidentiality of the data is particularly challenging. This is even more the case when the data are outsourced independently by different owners, and the data integrity is also a concern. Beyond protecting the confidentiality, and verifying the integrity of any outsourced data and delegated computation, there is a need for a mechanism that ensures outsourced data cannot be used without the owner's permission. But, this mechanism should not restrict the particular clients that may come together to compute the intersection of their datasets, by requiring that they are specified in advance; also it should not constraint the number of clients that come together or the number of intersections that may be performed.

In this paper we present VD-PSI, a protocol that supports efficient verifiable delegated PSI on outsourced private datasets and satisfies the above requirements. VD-PSI allows the result recipient to check whether the computation was performed correctly on the requested intact datasets, without having to keep a local copy of the data, or having any knowledge of the other clients' data. The protocol imposes minimal computational overheads to the verifier (i.e. at most linear to the intersection cardinality). It allows clients to independently prepare and upload their private datasets. It ensures that outsourced datasets can only be used with the owner's permission. It supports multiple clients who can verifiably delegate PSI computation an unlimited number of times with no need to download or re-encode their outsourced data. Moreover, it achieves all that while ensuring that the result recipient learns nothing beyond the intersection about the other clients' datasets, and the cloud learns nothing about the datasets and the intersection. The computation and communication costs of VD-PSI are linear to the (upper bound of) set cardinality.

The rest of the paper starts with a survey of related work in Sect. 2, while Sect. 3 defines our security model and key concepts we rely on. Section 4 presents the design of our protocol and its extensions, while Sect. 5 proves its security. Section 6 presents an analysis of the protocol's overheads and a comparison to work closest to it. Finally, Sect. 7 concludes the paper and identifies directions for future work.

## 2    Related Work

Verifiable delegated PSI can be built either on top of generic verifiable computation protocols or as a standalone operation specific verifiable protocol. Verifiable computation (VC) protocols allow a computationally weak client to securely delegate computation of a function to a powerful but untrusted server. In this setting, the client can detect if the server provides an incorrect result.

We first consider generic VC protocols. A number of protocols such as [15,16] are designed to address the VC problem, where [16] is based on the concept of ringers, and [15] uses the argument system and relies on private information retrieval. However, they do not preserve the privacy of client data. As a result, the server may misbehave and expose sensitive client data, i.e. the input and output of the computation. Other protocols like [13] which uses fully homomorphic encryption (FHE) and Yao's garbled circuits, and [11] based on FHE and a homomorphic hashing technique, preserve the privacy of client data; but, they have been designed for single-client scenarios.

There are practical scenarios in which multiple clients, who mutually distrust each other, want to verifiably delegate computation to a server. In this case, the computation should be verifiable and a client's data should be protected from the other clients who receive the result. These requirements integrate secure multiparty computation (MPC) with VC. In secure MPC protocols, clients (jointly) perform some computation without revealing to each other their private inputs. There are two protocols for such scenarios, [7] based on Yao's garbled circuits, FHE and non-interactive proxy oblivious transfer, and [17] based on the same building blocks plus multi-sender attribute-based encryption. These protocols do not require clients to directly interact with each other at setup. Nonetheless, they do not support outsourced data as they require each client to know the public keys of all other clients when preparing its private data. Consequently, changing the participating clients requires outsourced data to be downloaded and re-prepared.

The protocol in [25] also supports verifiable multi-client delegated generic computation, and allows clients to independently outsource their private data. In this protocol, clients do not need to interact during setup, but they have to interactively decrypt the result when receiving it. Although this protocol satisfies all the requirements set out in Sect. 1, it is not computationally efficient as it is based on (multi-key) fully homomorphic encryption and expensive generic zero-knowledge proofs. Moreover, the protocol is not suitable when the number of inputs is large, as in order to verify the result correctness a client needs to access all the (hash values of) encrypted inputs.

We now turn our attention to protocols designed specifically for PSI. PSI was first introduced in [12] based on additive homomorphic encryption and polynomial representation of sets. Over the years, some efficient protocols, like [10,28,29], have been proposed. However, they are interactive in the sense that the clients jointly compute the intersection of their sets. Thus, they need to have a local copy of their sets to compute the set intersection. A number of protocols that support delegation of PSI to a server are proposed in [1,19,21,22,24,31]. Among them only [1], which is mainly based on point-value polynomial representation of sets and additive homomorphic encryption, supports delegation of both storage and the computation to the cloud, and is fully private. However, it only considers a semi-honest adversary. As a result, the clients cannot verify the correctness of the computation. The only protocols that support verifiable delegated PSI are in [19,31]. In the former, a client encrypts his data and uses tags based on bilinear maps for verification. However, as it is shown in [1], it is not fully private and leaks information about the intersection to the server. The latter is based on a pseudo-random function, whose key is generated jointly by the clients prior to encoding the data and detects server misbehavior at the cost of replicating a number of times all elements of the sets. Although the protocol is efficient, it does not support outsourced data.

From the above discussion, it should be clear that neither PSI protocols nor most of generic computation protocols can meet all our requirements. Only [25] meets all the requirements, but it is not efficient. So, the quest for *efficient verifiable delegated PSI on outsourced private datasets* remains open.

# 3    Preliminaries

## 3.1    Security Model

We consider a static adversary who controls one of the parties at a time. The definition and model are according to [14]. Without loss of generality we consider the three party case where a cloud $C$, and two clients, $A$ and $B$ are involved. We allow an adversary who corrupts $C$ to be malicious. So, it may arbitrarily deviate from the prescribed protocol, but it does not collude with the clients. This is a reasonable assumption as it is usually a well-established company and does not want to jeopardize its reputation by colluding with others. The non-colluding assumption is well-accepted and widely used in the literature [17,19]. Moreover, we allow an adversary who corrupts a client to be semi-honest.

We define a three-party protocol $\pi$ computing function $F$ where $F : \Lambda \times 2^u \times 2^u \to \Lambda \times \Lambda \times f_\cap$. Here, $\Lambda$ denotes the empty string, $2^u$ denotes the powerset of the set universe and $f_\cap$ denotes the set intersection function. For every tuple of inputs $\Lambda, S_A$ and $S_B$ belonging to $C, A$ and $B$ respectively, the function outputs nothing to $C$ and $A$, and outputs $f_\cap(S_A, S_B) = S_A \cap S_B$ to $B$. To show the protocol is secure, we define an ideal model, which satisfies all the security needs. In the ideal model, there is an incorruptible trusted third party ($TTP$) which helps with the functionality. The protocol is said to be secure if for every adversary in the real model there is an adversary in the ideal model that can simulate the real adversary.

**Real Model:** Here, protocol $\pi$ is executed between parties $A$, $B$, $C$ and an adversary denoted by $R$ that is allowed to corrupt one party. In the beginning of the protocol, each party $I \in \{A, B\}$ receives its private input $S_I$, the protocol's public parameters, random coins $r$, and an auxiliary input $z$, while the cloud $C$ receives the public parameters, a set of random coins $r$, and an auxiliary input $z$. At the end of the execution, an honest party outputs whatever is prescribed by the protocol and the adversary outputs its view. The joint output of the real model execution of $\pi$ between the parties in the presence of the adversary $R$ is defined as $\mathsf{REAL}_{\pi,R(z)}(\Lambda, S_A, S_B)$.

**Ideal Model:** The ideal model takes place between parties $A$, $B$, $C$ and a simulator $SIM$ that is allowed to corrupt at most one party at a time.

Each party receives the same input as the corresponding party in the real model. An honest party always sends its input to the $TTP$. The corrupted party may abort or send arbitrary input. The cloud, $C$, receives $d$ (i.e. $d \geq |S_I|, I \in \{A, B\}$) from the $TTP$. The $TTP$ computes the set intersection and sends the result to $B$. If the $TTP$ receives an abort message as an input, it sends $B$ the special symbol $\bot$. The joint output of the parties in the ideal model in the presence of $SIM$ is defined as $\mathsf{IDEAL}_{F,SIM(z)}(\Lambda, S_A, S_B)$.

**Definition 1.** *Let $\pi$ be a protocol and $F$ a deterministic function defined as above. Protocol $\pi$ is said to securely compute $F$ in the presence of static adversaries if for every probabilistic polynomial time (PPT) adversary $R$ in the real model, there exists a PPT adversary $SIM$ in the ideal model such that $\forall I, I \in \{A, B, C\}$:*

$$\mathsf{IDEAL}_{F,SIM_I(z)}(\Lambda, S_A, S_B) \overset{c}{\equiv} \mathsf{REAL}_{\pi,R_I(z)}(\Lambda, S_A, S_B)$$

### 3.2 Additively Homomorphic Encryption

A semantically secure additively homomorphic encryption has the following properties:

(a) Given two ciphertexts $E_{pk}(a), E_{pk}(b)$, $E_{pk}(a) \cdot E_{pk}(b) = E_{pk}(a + b)$.
(b) Given a ciphertext $E_{pk}(a)$ and a constant $b$, $E_{pk}(a)^b = E_{pk}(a \cdot b)$.

One such scheme is the Paillier public key cryptosystem [27]. It works as follows:

**Key Generation:** Choose two random large primes $q_1$ and $q_2$ according to a given security parameter, and set $N = q_1 \cdot q_2$. Let $u$ be the Carmichael value of $N$, i.e. $u = lcm(q_1 - 1, q_2 - 1)$ where $lcm$ stands for the least common multiple. Choose a random $g \in \mathbb{Z}_{N^2}^*$, and ensure that $s = (L(g^u \bmod N^2))^{-1} \bmod N$ exists where $L(x) = \frac{(x-1)}{N}$. The public key is $pk = (N, g)$ and the secret key is $sk = (u, s)$.

**Encryption:** To encrypt a plaintext $m \in \mathbb{Z}_N$, pick a random value $r \in \mathbb{Z}_N^*$, and compute the ciphertext: $C = E_{pk}(m) = g^m \cdot r^N \bmod N^2$.

**Decryption:** To decrypt a ciphertext $C$, $D_{sk}(C) = L(C^u \bmod N^2) \cdot s \bmod N = m$.

### 3.3 Representing Sets by Polynomials

Polynomial representation of sets was introduced in [12] and is widely used [1,9,23]. For the universe of set elements, $\mathcal{U}$, we can define a public finite field $R = \mathbb{F}_p$ that is big enough to encode all elements in $\mathcal{U}$. Also, the field is big enough that when an element is picked uniformly at random from it, the probability that the value belongs to the universe is negligible. Then, we can define a polynomial ring $R[x]$, which consists of all polynomials with coefficients from $R$. We can represent a set, $S$, by polynomial $\rho(x) = \prod_{i=1}^{d}(x - s_i)$, where $s_i \in S, |S| = d$ and $\rho(x) \in R[x]$. The polynomial has the property that every element $s_i \in S$ is a root of it. Furthermore, we can always encode every $s_i$ as $s_i' = s_i || h(s_i)$, where $h$ is a cryptographic hash function, so that given $s_j' = a || b$ and $h$'s output size, one can parse $s_j'$ into $a$ and $b$, and check $b \overset{?}{=} h(a)$.

For two sets $S_A$ and $S_B$ represented by polynomials $\rho_A$ and $\rho_B$ respectively, polynomial $\rho_A \cdot \rho_B$ represents the set union, $S_A \cup S_B$, and $gcd(\rho_A, \rho_B)$ represents the set intersection, $S_A \cap S_B$, where $gcd$ stands for the greatest common divisor. For two degree $d$ polynomials $\rho_A$ and $\rho_B$, and two degree $d$ polynomials $\gamma_A$ and $\gamma_B$ picked uniformly at random from $R[x]$, it is proven in [23] that $\gamma_A \cdot \rho_A + \gamma_B \cdot \rho_B = \mu \cdot gcd(\rho_A, \rho_B)$ where $\mu$ is a uniformly random polynomial. This means that if $\rho_A$ and $\rho_B$ are polynomials representing sets $S_A$ and $S_B$, then the polynomial $\rho_C = \gamma_A \cdot \rho_A + \gamma_B \cdot \rho_B$ contains only information about $S_A \cap S_B$ and no information about other elements in $S_A$ or $S_B$. Given polynomial $\rho_C$, to find the intersection, one can extract the polynomial's roots[1] and consider the roots that have the above structure $(s_i || h(s_i))$ as the intersection.

Based on the theorem of the interpolating polynomial, for a set $\{(x_1, y_1), ..., (x_n, y_n)\}$ with $x_i$ distinct, there exists a unique polynomial $\rho(x)$ of degree at most $n - 1$ such that $\forall i, 1 \leq i \leq n : y_i = \rho(x_i)$. Therefore, $\rho(x)$ can be represented by the $n$ pairs $(x_i, y_i)$. If the $x_i$ values are fixed and public, we can represent the polynomial as a vector of y-coordinates, $\vec{y} = [y_1, ..., y_n]$.

Polynomial arithmetic in point-value representation can be done by adding or multiplying the corresponding y-coordinates. The key benefit of point-value representation is that multiplication complexity is $O(d)$; whereas, multiplying polynomials in coefficient form has $O(d^2)$ complexity. We can convert a polynomial in point-value form to regular coefficient form, using polynomial interpolation [3].

## 4    The Proposed Scheme: VD-PSI

### 4.1    An Overview of VD-PSI

We give an overview of the protocol and depict the interaction between parties in Fig. 1. Without loss of generality, we consider two clients $A$ and $B$. At setup, each client independently encodes, blinds, and stores his dataset in the cloud. Later on, when client $B$ becomes interested in the intersection of his dataset and client $A$'s, he obtains her permission by sending a message to her. Client $A$ authorizes the computation by using the message sent by client $B$ to compute a new message that she sends to the cloud. The cloud uses the message and the clients' outsourced datasets to compute the intersection, and sends the result to client $B$. Client $B$, decodes the cloud's response, retrieves the intersection and checks its correctness. If the result was correct the client accepts it.

The main novelty of VD-PSI is a lightweight verification mechanism that allows a client to efficiently verify the correctness of the result without having access to his own outsourced dataset and having any knowledge of the other

---

[1] To find the roots of a polynomial over a finite field, we can first factorize it to get a set of monic polynomials (see [20] for some algorithms), then find the monic polynomials' roots.

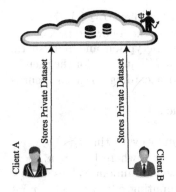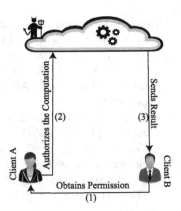

**Fig. 1.** The left-hand side figure: party interaction at data outsourcing phase; the right-hand side figure: party interaction at computation delegation phase.

client's dataset. To achieve this, when the clients decide to delegate the computation of the set intersection, they agree on a secret value $\beta$ and encode $\beta$ in a way that reveals nothing to the cloud, then send the encoded $\beta$ to the cloud. When computing the intersection, the cloud uses the clients' outsourced datasets and the encoded $\beta$. If the cloud computes honestly, value $\beta$ will be inserted into the intersection. Since the outsourced data is blinded, when client $B$ receives the result from the cloud, he needs to unblind it to get the intersection. If the cloud misbehaves or tampers with the result, then after unblinding client $B$ gets a random set, which will not contain $\beta$. Thus, by checking whether $\beta$ is included in the result set, client $B$ knows whether the result set is correct. The verification is very lightweight because the only overhead is to check whether $\beta$ is included in the result set.

### 4.2 VD-PSI Protocol

Without loss of generality, first we consider the two-client case, where client $A$, client $B$ and a cloud engage in the protocol. We denote the multiplicative inverse and additive inverse of value $h_i$, by $(h_i)^{-1}$ and $(-h_i)$, respectively. We use $E_{pk_I}(h_i)$ and $D_{sk_I}(h_i)$ to say that value $h_i$ is encrypted using client $I$'s public key, and decrypted using his secret key, respectively.

1. **Cloud-Side Setup.** The cloud picks a public parameter $d$ that is an upper bound of the set cardinality. It constructs a finite field $\mathbb{F}_p$, where $p$ is a large prime number. It also constructs a vector $\vec{x}$ containing $n = 2d + 3$ distinct non-zero $x_i$ values randomly picked from $\mathbb{F}_p$. It picks a pseudo-random function $f : \{0,1\}^m \times \{0,1\}^l \to \mathbb{F}_p$, which takes an $l$-bit key (i.e. where $l$ is the security parameter) and an $m$-bit message, and maps the message to an element in the field pseudo-randomly. The cloud publishes the description of the field, the value $n$, the vector $\vec{x}$ along with the pseudo-random function $f$.

2. **Client-Side Setup and Data Outsourcing.** Let client $I \in \{A, B\}$ have a set $S_I$, where $S_I \subset \mathcal{U}$ and $|S_I| \leq d$. Both clients do the following tasks:

(a) Compute a key pair $(pk_I, sk_I)$ for Paillier encryption and publish the public key $pk_I$. Pick two random private keys, $k_r^{(I)}$ and $k_z^{(I)}$ for the pseudo-random function $f$. All keys are generated according to given security parameters.

(b) Generate a polynomial representation of the set. $\forall s_i^{(I)} \in S_I$:
$$\tau_I(x) = \prod_{i=1}^{|S_I|} (x - s_i^{(I)}).$$

(c) Convert the polynomial into point-value form by evaluating $\tau_I(x)$ at every element $x_i$ in vector $\vec{x}$. This yields values $\tau_I(x_i)$, where $1 \leq i \leq n$.

(d) Blind every $\tau_I(x_i)$ by first computing pseudo-random values $r_i^{(I)} = f(k_r^{(I)}, i)$ and $z_i^{(I)} = f(k_z^{(I)}, i)$, and then computing $o_i^{(I)} = r_i^{(I)} \cdot (\tau_I(x_i) + z_i^{(I)})$.

(e) Send the blinded dataset $\vec{o}^{(I)} = [o_1^{(I)}, ..., o_n^{(I)}]$ to the cloud.

3. **Set Intersection: Computation Delegation.** In this phase, client $B$ is interested in the intersection of his set and client $A$'s.

(a) Client $B$ picks a uniformly random value $\beta \xleftarrow{R} \mathbb{F}_p^*$ that will be inserted into the two datasets and chooses three fresh keys $k_a^{(B)}$, $k_b^{(B)}$ and $k_{r'}^{(B)}$ that are used to blind the messages sent by client $A$ to the cloud.

(b) Client $B$ constructs a vector $\vec{e}^{(B)}$ that will be used by client $A$ to ask the cloud to insert $\beta$ to her dataset and switch her blinding factors. $\forall i, 1 \leq i \leq n$: $e_i^{(B)} = E_{pk_B}(\sigma(x_i) \cdot r_i'^{(B)} \cdot r_i^{(B)})$, where $\sigma(x_i) = (x_i - \beta)$, values $r_i^{(B)}$ are the blinding factors used by client $B$ in step 2d and $r_i'^{(B)} = f(k_{r'}^{(B)}, i)$.

(c) Client $B$ sends to client $A$: $\vec{e}^{(B)}$, $\beta$, $k_a^{(B)}$, $k_b^{(B)}$, $k_{r'}^{(B)}$, $k_z^{(B)}$, and his ID, $\mathbf{ID}^{(B)}$.

(d) Client $A$ generates $\vec{v}^{(A)}$ and $\vec{v}^{(B)}$ that allow the cloud to multiply each client dataset by a random polynomial and insert $\beta$ to it. Also, $\vec{v}^{(A)}$ allows the cloud to switch the blinding factors of client $A$'s dataset. $\forall i, 1 \leq i \leq n$:

$$v_i^{(A)} = (e_i^{(B)})^{\omega_A(x_i) \cdot (r_i^{(A)})^{-1}}$$
$$= E_{pk_B}(r_i^{(B)} \cdot r_i'^{(B)} \cdot \omega_A(x_i) \cdot \sigma(x_i) \cdot (r_i^{(A)})^{-1})$$
$$v_i^{(B)} = \omega_B(x_i) \cdot \sigma(x_i) \cdot r_i'^{(B)}$$

where $r_i'^{(B)} = f(k_{r'}^{(B)}, i)$, key $k_{r'}^{(B)}$ was sent by client $B$ in step 3c, $r_i^{(A)}$ are the blinding values used by client $A$ in step 2d, $\omega_A(x)$ and $\omega_B(x)$ are two random polynomials of degree $d + 1$ and $\sigma(x) = (x - \beta)$.

(e) Client $A$ generates $\vec{v}'^{(A)}$ and $\vec{v}'^{(B)}$ to allow the cloud to preserve the correctness of the result. $\forall i, 1 \leq i \leq n$:

$$v_i'^{(A)} = (e_i^{(B)})^{\omega_A(x_i) \cdot (-z_i^{(A)}) + a_i}$$
$$= E_{pk_B}((-z_i^{(A)}) \cdot r_i^{(B)} \cdot r_i'^{(B)} \cdot \omega_A(x_i) \cdot \sigma(x_i) + c_i)$$
$$v_i'^{(B)} = (e_i^{(B)})^{\omega_B(x_i) \cdot (-z_i^{(B)}) + b_i}$$
$$= E_{pk_B}((-z_i^{(B)}) \cdot r_i^{(B)} \cdot r_i'^{(B)} \cdot \omega_B(x_i) \cdot \sigma(x_i) + d_i)$$

where $c_i = a_i \cdot r_i^{(B)} \cdot r_i'^{(B)} \cdot \sigma(x_i)$, $d_i = b_i \cdot r_i^{(B)} \cdot r_i'^{(B)} \cdot \sigma(x_i)$, $a_i = f(k_a^{(B)}, i)$, $b_i = f(k_b^{(B)}, i)$, the keys $k_a^{(B)}$ and $k_b^{(B)}$ sent by client $B$ in step 3c, and $z_i^{(I)}$ are the values used by client $I \in \{A, B\}$ in step 2d.

(f) Client $A$ sends to the cloud: $\vec{v}^{(A)}, \vec{v}'^{(A)}, \vec{v}^{(B)}, \vec{v}'^{(B)}, \mathbf{ID}^{(B)}, \mathbf{ID}^{(A)}$, and a request message **Compute**.

4. **Set Intersection: Cloud-Side Computation**

   (a) When the cloud receives client $A$'s message, it uses $\vec{v}^{(A)}$, $\vec{v}'^{(A)}$ and client $A$'s outsourced dataset $\vec{o}^{(A)}$ to switch the dataset blinding factors, insert $\beta$ to the dataset, and multiply it by a random polynomial; this results $\vec{t}^{(C_1)}$.
   $$\forall i, 1 \le i \le n : t_i^{(C_1)} = (v_i^{(A)})^{o_i^{(A)}} \cdot v_i'^{(A)} =$$
   $$E_{pk_B}(r_i^{(B)} \cdot r_i'^{(B)} \cdot \omega_A(x_i) \cdot \sigma(x_i) \cdot \tau_A(x_i) + c_i).$$

   (b) The cloud uses $\vec{o}^{(B)}, \vec{v}^{(B)}, \vec{v}'^{(B)}$ to insert $\beta$ into client $B$'s dataset, and multiply it by a random polynomial. This yields $\vec{t}^{(C_2)}$.
   $$\forall i, 1 \le i \le n : t_i^{(C_2)} = v_i'^{(B)} \cdot E_{pk_B}(v_i^{(B)} \cdot o_i^{(B)}) =$$
   $$E_{pk_B}(r_i^{(B)} \cdot r_i'^{(B)} \cdot \omega_B(x_i) \cdot \sigma(x_i) \cdot \tau_B(x_i) + d_i).$$

   (c) The cloud combines the values computed in steps 4b and 4a to produce the final result $\vec{t}^{(C_3)}$.
   $$\forall i, 1 \le i \le n : t_i^{(C_3)} = t_i^{(C_1)} \cdot t_i^{(C_2)} =$$
   $$E_{pk_B}(r_i^{(B)} \cdot r_i'^{(B)} \cdot (\omega_B(x_i) \cdot \sigma(x_i) \cdot \tau_B(x_i) + \omega_A(x_i) \cdot \sigma(x_i) \cdot \tau_A(x_i)) + c_i + d_i).$$

   (d) The cloud sends to client $B$ vector $\vec{t}^{(C_3)}$.

5. **Set Intersection: Client-Side Result Verification and Retrieval**

   (a) Client $B$ obtains $\vec{g}$ by decrypting the cloud's response $\vec{t}^{(C_3)}$, and unblinding the decrypted values using his knowledge of $(-c_i), (-d_i), (r_i^{(B)})^{-1}$ and $(r_i'^{(B)})^{-1}$. $\forall i, 1 \le i \le n$:

   $$g_i = (D_{sk_B}(t_i^{(C_3)}) + (-c_i) + (-d_i)) \cdot (r_i^{(B)})^{-1} \cdot (r_i'^{(B)})^{-1}$$
   $$= \omega_B(x_i) \cdot \sigma(x_i) \cdot \tau_B(x_i) + \omega_A(x_i) \cdot \sigma(x_i) \cdot \tau_A(x_i).$$

   (b) Client $B$ interpolates a polynomial, $\phi(x)$, using the $n$ point-value pairs $(x_i, g_i)$, extracts its roots, and checks whether $\beta$ is among them. If it is, he considers the rest of the roots as elements of the intersection; otherwise, he aborts.

**Remark 1.** In step 2d, client $I \in \{A, B\}$ blinds his private data $\tau_I(x_i)$ as $o_i^{(I)} = r_i^{(I)} \cdot (\tau_I(x_i) + z_i^{(I)})$ to preserve their privacy and to detect unauthorized modifications. If the client does not blind $\tau_I(x_i)$, the cloud can interpolate the polynomial $\tau_I(x)$ and find the client's set elements. After blinding, every $o_i^{(I)}$ is a uniformly random value and does not leak any information about $\tau_I(x_i)$. If the cloud changes a subset of elements in $\vec{o}^{(I)}$, in step 5b the corresponding values in $\vec{g}$ become uniformly random. As a result, the polynomial interpolated using the $n$ pairs of $(x_i, g_i)$ will not have root $\beta$ (with a high probability), and the client will detect the misbehavior. The same also occurs if the cloud deviates from the protocol.

**Remark 2.** We set $n = 2d + 3$, because in step 5b, polynomial $\phi(x)$ is of degree $2d + 2$ and at least $2d + 3$ pairs of $(x_i, y_i)$ are required to interpolate it. Therefore, given $n$ pairs of $(x_i, y_i)$, computed correctly, client $B$ can always interpolate $\phi(x)$.

**Remark 3.** In Sect. 3.3, we saw that the set of all roots of polynomial $\omega_B(x) \cdot \tau_B(x) + \omega_A(x) \cdot \tau_A(x)$ is $S_A \cap S_B$. Note that $\beta$ is also a root of the polynomial $\phi(x) = \sigma(x) \cdot (\omega_B(x) \cdot \tau_B(x) + \omega_A(x) \cdot \tau_A(x))$, where $\sigma(x) = x - \beta$. Hence, in the protocol, a correctly computed result always contains value $\beta$.

**Remark 4.** Since for each computation, the fresh random polynomials $\omega_A(x)$ and $\omega_B(x)$ are used, the result recipient cannot find out anything beyond the intersection about the other client's set. Also, the cloud cannot learn the exact number of elements in the set; it only knows the upper bound of the set cardinality (i.e. $d$).

**Remark 5.** Every client $I$, after outsourcing his private dataset needs to keep locally only two secret keys, $k_r^{(I)}$ and $k_z^{(I)}$. Moreover, client $B$ who is interested in the result generates keys $k_a^{(B)}$, $k_b^{(B)}$, $k_{r'}^{(B)}$ and value $\beta$ on the fly for each run of the protocol and he can discard them after it ends. Furthermore, given $p$ each client $I$ can always generate his own public key $N_I$ independently, such that $N_I > p + 2p^2 + p^3$ to preserve the computation correctness (i.e. to prevent any overflow during homomorphic operations). To determine the lower bound of $N_I$, we can calculate the maximal value that message $m_i$ in $E(m_i)$ may have as a result of homomorphic operations in the protocol (here, by $E(m_i)$ we mean encryption of message $m_i$). To do so, we start from step 3b and calculate the upper bound of value $m_i$ in each step (note that $o_i^{(I)} \in \mathbb{F}_p$). We continue this up to step 4d and then we set the lower bound of $N_I$ to the maximal upper bound of $m_i$, that is $p + 2p^2 + p^3$.

**Remark 6.** We stress that the clients' outsourced datasets remain unchanged. Also, at the end of protocol all parties can discard all intermediate messages received.

## 4.3   Multiple Clients

With minor modifications two-client VD-PSI can be turned into $q$-client VD-PSI, where $q > 2$. Below we outline how this can be done. We denote the result recipient by client $B$ and the other clients by $A_j$ ($\forall j, 1 \leq j \leq m$), where $m = q-1$.

More specifically, in step 3c, client $B$ sends to every client $A_j$ the same message. Each client $A_j$ takes the same steps described above, except step 3d, where she replaces $\vec{v}^{(B)}$ with $\vec{v}_j^{(B)}$, $v_{j,i}^{(B)} = E_{pk_B}(\omega_B^j(x_i) \cdot \sigma(x_i) \cdot r_i'^{(B)})$, where $\omega_B^j(x)$ is the random polynomial picked by client $A_j$.

In step 4b, the cloud computes $\vec{t}^{(C_2)}$, by selecting one of the clients, say client $A_k$, and only using her vectors $\vec{v}_k^{(B)}$, $\vec{v}_k'^{(B)}$, discarding $\vec{v}_j^{(B)}$, $\vec{v}_j'^{(B)}$ generated by the other clients $A_j, \forall j, 1 \leq j \leq m, j \neq k$. As a result $\forall i, 1 \leq i \leq n$: $t_i^{(C_2)} = v_{k,i}'^{(B)} \cdot (v_{k,i}^{(B)})^{o_i^{(B)}} = E_{pk_B}(r_i^{(B)} \cdot r_i'^{(B)} \cdot \omega_B^k(x_i) \cdot \sigma(x_i) \cdot \tau_B(x_i) + d_i)$.

In step 4c, the cloud computes $\vec{t}^{(C_3)} = \vec{t}^{(C_2)} \cdot \prod_{1 \leq j \leq m} \vec{t}_j^{(C_1)}$, $\forall i, 1 \leq i \leq n$:

$$t_i^{(C_3)} = E_{pk_B}(m \cdot c_i + d_i + (r_i^{(B)} \cdot r_i'^{(B)} \cdot (\omega_B^k(x_i) \cdot \sigma(x_i) \cdot \tau_B(x_i) + \sum_{1 \leq j \leq m} \omega_A^j(x_i) \cdot \sigma(x_i) \cdot \tau_A^j(x_i)))) \text{ and sends it to client } B.$$

Finally, in step 5a, client $B$ computes $\vec{g}$ as follows. $\forall i, 1 \leq i \leq n$:

$$g_i = (D_{sk_B}(t_i^{(C_3)}) + m \cdot (-c_i) + (-d_i)) \cdot (r_i^{(B)})^{-1} \cdot (r_i'^{(B)})^{-1}$$

The rest of the steps remain unchanged.

**Remark 1:** In the multi-client case, each client encrypts elements of vector $\vec{v}_j^{(B)}$; whereas, in the two client case it does not need to do that. Nonetheless, regardless of the number of clients, every client's computation complexity is linear to the set cardinality.

**Remark 2:** Verification complexity at the verifier side is independent of the number of clients. Also, the number of messages every client, except the client who is interested in result, sends and receives is independent of the number of clients, too. The client who is interested in the result sends the same message to all other clients.

**Remark 3:** The security model we consider in this paper can be easily extended to the multi-client case, security analysis of the multi-client case remains the same as the two client case and we do not include it for the sake of brevity.

### 4.4 Reducing Authorizer's Required Storage Space

In VD-PSI, we can leverage a hash table to reduce the storage space that client $A$ needs to authorize the computation. In the following, we briefly outline how this can be done. For the sake of simplicity we consider the two-client case, but the adjustments can also be directly applied to the multi-client setting.

Hash tables have been utilized in the literature to improve the performance of PSI protocols, e.g. [12,28]. In general, in order for clients to use a hash table, its parameters including a random hash function, the number of bins in the hash table and the bin's maximum size are picked. The number of bins in the hash table should be set such that given the maximum set cardinality, $d$, with a high probability each bin receives at most a specific number of elements, $d'$. Given the maximum number of elements $d$ and the bin's maximum size $d'$, we can calculate the number of bins by analyzing hash tables under the balls into bins model [6,30].

In the following, we outline how a hash table can be used in our protocol. In the beginning, hash table parameters are picked and made public by the cloud. In the client-side setup phase, each client first maps its set elements to the hash table bins, pads each bin up to $d'$ elements with random values (if a bin receives less than $d'$ elements) and then encodes the elements of each bin in the same way as they do in VD-PSI. In this case, the clients (when they delegate the computation) insert a random $\beta_j$ in each outsourced bin $\text{HT}_j$, to ensure the operation on each bin is performed correctly. In order for the clients to generate $\beta_j$, they can use a shared key, $\beta k$, where $\beta_j = f(\beta k, j)$. Client $B$ keeps the key that allows it to regenerate $\beta_j$ in the verification phase. When it receives the result from the cloud, it checks whether each bin $\text{HT}_j$ contains $\beta_j$. This setting enables client $B$, in step 3c, to send only one bin at a time to client $A$ who operates on the bin and forwards it to the cloud who similarly operates on each bin and sends the result to client $B$. As a result, the storage space client $A$ needs to authorize the computation reduces from $O(d)$ to $O(d')$, where $d' < d$.

## 5    Proof of Security

In this section we sketch the security proof of the protocol. To this end, first we show that the cloud's misbehavior can be detected with high probability, then we provide the main theorem.

Recall, the client encodes his set as blinded y-coordinates having the following form: $o_i = r_i \cdot (\tau(x_i) + z_i)$, where $o_i \neq 0$, $r_i = f(k_r, i)$ and $z_i = f(k_z, i)$. If $o_i = 0$ the client replaces $k_r$ and $k_z$ with new random keys and encodes $\tau(x_i)$ again until $\forall i, 1 \leq i \leq n : o_i \neq 0$. Note, $o_i$ is uniformly distributed in $\mathbb{F}_p^*$. We can show that if the cloud applies any change to $o_i$, this will make the y-coordinate a uniformly random value.

**Lemma 1.** *Given $o_i = r_i \cdot (\tau(x_i) + z_i)$, where $r_i$ and $z_i$ are two independent pseudo-random values that are unknown to the cloud, if the cloud changes $o_i$ to $o'_i$, then $\tau'(x_i) = r_i^{-1} \cdot o'_i - z_i$ becomes a uniformly random value.*

*Proof.* When $o_i \neq o'_i$, $\tau'(x_i)$ is a uniformly random value in $\mathbb{F}_p$, because $r_i$ and $z_i$ are picked uniformly at random and independently of each other.    □

In step 5a of the protocol, client $B$ after decrypting the server's response obtains blinded values of the form $p_i = e_i \cdot g_i + z_i$, where $e_i$ and $z_i$ are pseudo-random values. If the cloud misbehaves (e.g. deviates from the protocol, modifies the outsourced client datasets, etc.), some $p_i$ are changed to $p'_i$, and Lemma 1 implies that $g'_i = e_i^{-1} \cdot (p'_i - z_i)$ will be a uniformly random value. So, any cloud misbehavior turns some of the values $g_i$ into uniformly random values.

Now, we show that given a set of y-coordinates some of which are uniformly random values, the polynomial that client $B$ interpolates from them (see step 5b in the protocol), will not contain the specific root $\beta$ with a high probability.

**Lemma 2.** *Let polynomial $\tau(x)$ be interpolated from $S = \{(x_1, y_1), ..., (x_n, y_n)\}$, and have a root $\beta$ such that $\forall j, 1 \leq j \leq n : \beta \neq x_j$. Let $S' = \{(x_1, y'_1), ..., (x_n, y'_n)\}$, where at least one of $y'_j$ is a uniformly random value and the rest of them are equal to the y-coordinates in $S$ (i.e. $y'_i = y_i$). Let polynomial $\tau'(x)$ be interpolated from $S'$. The probability that $\tau'(x)$ has the root $\beta$ is negligible.*

*Proof.* Given $S'$, we interpolate a unique polynomial $\tau'(x)$ of degree at most $n - 1$. According to the Lagrange interpolation, the polynomial is

$$\tau'(x) = \sum_{1 \leq j \leq n} y'_j \cdot \prod_{\substack{1 \leq k \leq n \\ j \neq k}} \frac{x - x_k}{x_j - x_k}$$

We evaluate $\tau'(x)$ at $\beta$:

$$\tau'(\beta) = \sum_{1 \le j \le n} y'_j \cdot \prod_{\substack{1 \le k \le n \\ j \ne k}} \frac{\beta - x_k}{x_j - x_k}$$

As $\forall j, 1 \le j \le n : \beta \ne x_j$, we would have $\prod_{\substack{1 \le k \le n \\ j \ne k}} \frac{\beta - x_k}{x_j - x_k} \ne 0$. Since, at least one

of $y'_j$ is uniformly random, value $y'_j \cdot \prod_{\substack{1 \le k \le n \\ j \ne k}} \frac{\beta - x_k}{x_j - x_k}$ is uniformly random. Therefore,

$\tau'(\beta)$ is uniformly random. Thus, $Pr[\tau'(\beta) = 0] = \frac{1}{p}$ which is negligible. $\qquad\square$

Now we are ready to prove that the client can detect cloud misbehavior with high probability.

**Theorem 1.** *Let clients $A$ and $B$ have sets $S^{(A)}$ and $S^{(B)}$ respectively; also let $S_\cap = S^{(A)} \cap S^{(B)}$. In the protocol if the cloud sends $S'$ (where $S' \ne S_\cap$) to the client, the client can detect it with high probability.*

*Proof.* Due to Lemma 1, server misbehavior turns some of the y-coordinates (representing $S_\cap$) into uniformly random values. Also, in the protocol, $\beta$ is chosen uniformly at random from $\mathbb{F}_p^*$, so the probability that $\beta = x_k$ for some $k, 1 \le k \le n$, is negligible; due to Lemma 2, if the client interpolates a polynomial by using a set of y-coordinates where at least one of them is a uniformly random value, the probability that the polynomial would have $\beta$ as a root is negligible. Thus, if the server computes an incorrect intersection the client can detect this with high probability through the absence of $\beta$ from the intersection. $\qquad\square$

Finally, we prove our main theorem.

**Theorem 2.** *If the homomorphic encryption scheme is semantically secure, then the protocol is secure in the presence of (1) a malicious cloud and honest clients, (2) a semi-honest client and honest cloud.*

*Proof.* We consider three cases where each party is corrupted at a time.

**Case 1: Cloud is corrupted.** We construct a simulator $SIM_C$ in the ideal model that uses the adversary $R_C$ as a subroutine. Simulator $SIM_C$ executes the following tasks.

(a) Picks two random sets $S_E$ and $S_D$ and chooses the keys $k_r^{(E)}$, $k_z^{(E)}$, $k_r^{(D)}$, $k_z^{(D)}$, $k_b^{(E)}$, $k_a^{(E)}$, $k_{r'}^{(E)}$.

(b) Generates polynomials $\tau_E(x)$ and $\tau_D(x)$ representing the sets. Then, evaluates the polynomials at every element in $\vec{x}$ and blinds the evaluated values. This results in two vectors, $\vec{o}^{(E)}$ and $\vec{o}^{(D)}$. $\forall o_i^{(I)} \in \vec{o}^{(I)}, o_i^{(I)} = r_i^{(I)} \cdot (\tau_I(x_i) + z_i^{(I)})$, $r_i^{(I)} = f(k_r^{(I)}, i)$, $z_i^{(I)} = f(k_z^{(I)}, i)$, where $I \in \{D, E\}$.

(c) Picks a random value $\beta'$, and constructs polynomial $\sigma'(x) = (x - \beta')$. Then, picks two random polynomials, $\omega_E$ and $\omega_D$, of degree $d + 1$. Then, computes $\vec{v}^{(E)}$ and $\vec{v}^{(D)}$ as follows. $\forall i, 1 \le i \le n$:

$$v_i^{(D)} = E_{pk_E}(r_i^{(E)} \cdot r_i^{\prime(E)} \cdot \omega_D(x_i) \cdot \sigma'(x_i) \cdot (r_i^{(D)})^{-1})$$
$$v_i^{(E)} = \omega_E(x_i) \cdot r_i^{\prime(E)} \cdot \sigma'(x_i)$$

where $r_i'^{(E)} = f(k_{r'}^{(E)}, i)$.

(d) Computes $\vec{v}'^{(E)}$ and $\vec{v}'^{(D)}$; $\forall i, 1 \leq i \leq n, a_i^{(E)} = f(k_a^{(E)}, i), b_i^{(E)} = f(k_b^{(E)}, i)$:

$$v_i'^{(D)} = E_{pk_E}((-z_i^{(D)}) \cdot r_i^{(E)} \cdot r_i'^{(E)} \cdot \omega_D(x_i) \cdot \sigma'(x_i) + c_i^{(E)})$$

$$v_i'^{(E)} = E_{pk_E}((-z_i^{(E)}) \cdot r_i^{(E)} \cdot r_i'^{(E)} \cdot \omega_E(x_i) \cdot \sigma'(x_i) + d_i^{(E)})$$

where $I \in \{D, E\}, z_i^{(I)} = f(k_z^{(I)}, i), c_i^{(E)} = a_i^{(E)} \cdot r_i^{(E)} \cdot r_i'^{(E)} \cdot \sigma'(x_i), d_i^{(E)} = b_i^{(E)} \cdot r_i^{(E)} \cdot r_i'^{(E)} \cdot \sigma'(x_i)$.

(e) Invokes $R_C$ and feeds it with $\vec{o}^{(D)}, \vec{o}^{(E)}, \vec{v}^{(D)}, \vec{v}^{(E)}, \vec{v}'^{(D)}, \vec{v}'^{(E)}$, $\mathbf{ID}^{(D)}, \mathbf{ID}^{(E)}$, and message **Compute**. Then, receives $\vec{t}^{(C)}$ from $R_C$ and decrypts the elements. Next, removes the blinding factors. This yields $\vec{g}'$; $1 \leq i \leq n, g_i' \in \vec{g}' : g_i' = \tau_E(x_i) \cdot \sigma'(x_i) \cdot \omega_E(x_i) + \tau_D(x_i) \cdot \sigma'(x_i) \cdot \omega_D(x_i)$.

(f) Interpolates a polynomial using the $n$ point-value pairs $(x_i, g_i')$. Extracts the roots of the polynomial. Checks whether $\beta'$ is among the roots. If it is not, aborts and instructs the $TTP$ to send abort message $\perp$ to client $B$. Otherwise, asks $TTP$ to send the result to the client.

(g) Outputs whatever the adversary outputs and terminates.

First, we consider the adversary's output. In the real model the elements in $\vec{o}^{(A)}, \vec{o}^{(B)}, \vec{v}^{(B)}$ are blinded by the outputs of a pseudo-random function using random secret keys of length $l$. The same is true in the ideal model for the elements in $\vec{o}^{(E)}, \vec{o}^{(D)}, \vec{v}^{(E)}$. Since the outputs of the pseudo-random function are computationally indistinguishable, the distributions of $\vec{o}^{(A)}, \vec{o}^{(B)}, \vec{v}^{(B)}$ and $\vec{o}^{(E)}, \vec{o}^{(D)}, \vec{v}^{(E)}$ are computationally indistinguishable, too. If the homomorphic encryption is semantically secure then $\vec{v}^{(A)}, \vec{v}'^{(A)}, \vec{v}'^{(B)}$ and $\vec{v}^{(D)}, \vec{v}'^{(D)}, \vec{v}'^{(E)}$ are computationally indistinguishable. Moreover, in both models, the protocol outputs $\Lambda$ (i.e. empty) to the adversary. Therefore, we conclude that the adversary's outputs in both models are computationally indistinguishable.

Now we consider client $B$'s output. We show the honest client $B$ aborts with the same probability in both models. In the ideal model, if the cloud misbehaves, $SIM_C$ would detect it with a high probability according to Theorem 1. In this case it will send $\perp$ to the client and accordingly the client will abort. Note that in this case $SIM_C$ has not found the value $\beta'$ in the intersection. In the real model, since the client knows the value $\beta$ he can do the same checks that $SIM_C$ does. So, in both models the client aborts with the same probability if the cloud misbehaves. Finally, since client $A$ has no output, her output is identical in both models.

From the above we conclude that:

$$\mathsf{IDEAL}_{F, SIM_{C(z)}}(\Lambda, S_A, S_B) \overset{c}{\equiv} \mathsf{REAL}_{\pi, R_{C(z)}}(\Lambda, S_A, S_B).$$

**Case 2: Client $B$ is corrupted.** In this case we consider a semi-honest adversary that controls client $B$. In the real execution, the joint outputs of the parties include only client $B$'s view containing vector $\vec{t}^{(C_3)}$, where the vector comprises the set intersection. Now we construct a simulator, $SIM_B$ in the ideal model. The simulator executes the following tasks.

(a) Invokes adversary $R_B$, and receives $\vec{e}^{(B)}, S_B, \beta, k_a^{(B)}, k_b^{(B)}, k_{r'}^{(B)}, k_z^{(B)}$ from it.

(b) Sends $S_B$ to $TTP$ and receives the result $f_\cap(S_A, S_B)$. Picks two random sets $S_E$ and $S_D$, where $S_E \cap S_D = f_\cap(S_A, S_B)$. Constructs two polynomials $\tau_E(x)$ and $\tau_D(x)$ representing set $S_E$ and $S_D$, respectively.

(c) Picks two uniformly random polynomials, $\omega_E(x)$ and $\omega_D(x)$ of degree $d+1$.

(d) Generates $\vec{t}$ containing $t_i$ such that
$$t_i = (e_i^{(B)})^{\omega_E(x_i)\cdot\tau_E(x_i)+\omega_D(x_i)\cdot\tau_D(x_i)+a_i^{(B)}+b_i^{(B)}} \text{ where } a_i^{(B)} = f(k_a^{(B)}, i), \; b_i^{(B)} = f(k_b^{(B)}, i).$$

(e) Feeds $\vec{t}$ to $R_B$. Outputs whatever the adversary outputs.

Since the other parties have output $\Lambda$ (i.e. no output), we only need to consider the adversary's view. Given the output vector, the adversary decrypts and unblinds the elements. Next it interpolates a polynomial which is of the form $\omega_E \cdot \tau_E + \omega_D \cdot \tau_D = \mu \cdot gcd(\tau_E, \tau_D)$, where $\mu$ is a uniformly random polynomial, and $gcd(\tau_E, \tau_D)$ represents the intersection of the sets (see Sect. 3.3). Therefore, the result polynomial only contains the information of the set intersection and has the same distribution in both models, as the uniformly random polynomials $\omega_A$ and $\omega_B$ are chosen by an honest party. Also, the value $\beta$ has the same distribution in both models.

From the above argument we conclude that:

$$\mathsf{IDEAL}_{F,SIM_{B(z)}}(\Lambda, S_A, S_B) \overset{c}{\equiv} \mathsf{REAL}_{\pi, R_{B(z)}}(\Lambda, S_A, S_B).$$

**Case 3: Client $A$ is corrupted.** This is a trivial case, because client $A$ has no output, and she receives a set of uniformly random values and a vector of encrypted values using semantically secure encryption scheme. A simulator can always be constructed. □

# 6   Evaluation

We evaluate VD-PSI by comparing its properties to those protocols that support verifiable delegated PSI and preserve the privacy of the intersection in the cloud [19,25]. We also compare the protocols in terms of communication, computation and verification complexity. Table 1 summarises the results.

**Properties.** All the three protocols support multiple clients. In [25] the clients can securely delegate an arbitrary computation to the cloud an unlimited number of times. Nevertheless, every client needs to receive all the (hash values of encrypted) inputs of the computation to verify the result. Therefore, the protocol is not suitable for cases where the number of clients or the size of datasets is large. In [19] the clients need to interact with each other in order to jointly generate a key for the pseudo-random function used to encode the datasets. Also, the clients need to re-encode their datasets each time they compute the intersection. So, the protocol does not support outsourcing of the datasets.

In VD-PSI, the clients can independently prepare and outsource the datasets to the cloud. Furthermore, once the clients upload their datasets, they can

**Table 1.** Comparison of the properties of verifiable delegated PSI protocols. We denote the upper bound of set cardinality by $d$, set intersection cardinality by $k$, sum of the cardinality of all sets by $m$, and the security parameter by $\lambda$.

| Property | VD-PSI | [19] | [25] |
|---|---|---|---|
| Computation integrity verification | ✓ | ✓ | ✓ |
| Multiple clients | ✓ | ✓ | ✓ |
| Non-interactive setup | ✓ | × | ✓ |
| Many set intersections without re-preparation | ✓ | × | ✓ |
| Supporting arbitrary computation | × | × | ✓ |
| Using expensive generic proof systems (e.g. Zero Knowledge) | × | × | ✓ |
| Overall communication complexity | $O(d)$ | $O(d)$ | $O(m)$ |
| Overall computation complexity | $O(d)$ | $O(d)$ | $O(m)$ |
| Verification computation complexity | $O(k)$ | $O(\lambda k)$ | $O(m)$ |

securely delegate PSI to the cloud an unlimited number of times. As a result, they do not need to download and re-encode the outsourced datasets every time they delegate the computation.

Thus, VD-PSI and [25] support verifiable delegated PSI over outsourced private datasets; whereas, [19] does not, as it lacks some of the properties.

**Communication Complexity.** In VD-PSI the communication complexity for client $B$ who receives the result is $O(d)$, where $d$ is the set cardinality upper bound; as client $B$ sends to client $A$ vector $\vec{e}^{(B)}$ containing $n = 2d+3$ encrypted values (see step 3c). The communication complexity for client $A$ who grants the computation is $O(d)$, because the client sends to the cloud $\vec{v}^{(A)}, \vec{v}'^{(A)}, \vec{v}'^{(B)}, \vec{v}^{(B)}$ where each of the first three vectors contains $n$ encrypted elements and the last one contains $n$ random elements of the field (see step 3f). The communication complexity for the cloud is $O(d)$, as it sends to client $B$ vector $\vec{t}^{(C_3)}$ that contains $n$ encrypted elements (see step 4d). Hence, the overall communication complexity of our protocol is $6n$, which is $O(d)$.

The protocol in [19] has also $O(d)$ communication complexity. In [25], two protocols dealing with a malicious adversary are proposed. The overall communication complexity of each protocol is linear to the total number of computation inputs $m$, i.e. $O(m)$. In one of the protocols, the cloud broadcasts all the encrypted inputs to the clients; while in the other, the cloud broadcasts the hash value of the encrypted inputs.

Although all the three protocols have overall communication complexity linear to the dataset size, most messages in VD-PSI are ciphertexts of Paillier encryption, in [25] ciphertexts of fully homomorphic encryption, and in [19] ciphertexts of symmetric key encryption.

**Computation Complexity.** Since computation complexity of VD-PSI is dominated by the exponentiation operations, we evaluate its computational cost by counting the number of such operations. Client $B$ in step 3b carries out $n$ exponentiations to encrypt the elements of $\vec{e}^{(B)}$. Furthermore, in step 5a he performs $n$ exponentiations to decrypt the elements of $\vec{t}^{(C_3)}$. Client $A$ carries out $n$ exponentiations in steps 3d and $2n$ exponentiations in step 3e. The cloud carries out $2n$ exponentiations in step 4a, $2n$ exponentiations in step 4b, and $n$ exponentiations in step 4c. In total, $10n$ exponentiation operations are carried out, so the overall computation complexity is $O(d)$. In VD-PSI a verifier only checks whether $\beta$ is among the elements of the intersection. Therefore, the verification computation complexity is at most linear to the intersection cardinality, i.e. $O(k)$.

The computation complexity of the two protocols dealing with a malicious adversary in [25] is dominated by fully homomorphic encryption operations. In each protocol, the overall number of such operations is linear to the size of the inputs $m$. So, the overall computation complexity for each protocol is $O(m)$. Moreover, in order for each client to verify the computation correctness, he needs to access all the (encrypted) inputs and perform generic proof system operations linear to the number of inputs. Therefore, the verification complexity at the verifier side is $O(m)$, too. While, in [19] each participant has overall computation complexity $O(d)$. In order for the client to verify the integrity of the result, he checks whether $\lambda$ copies of all intersection elements exist in the result. So, its verification complexity is $O(\lambda k)$ where $\lambda$ and $k$ are the security parameter and intersection cardinality, respectively.

Thus, all the schemes have overall linear computation complexity; while, VD-PSI uses Paillier encryption, [25] uses fully homomorphic, and [19] uses symmetric key encryption. The verification mechanisms in [25] is based on expensive generic proof systems, while [19] and VD-PSI use lightweight mechanisms.

**Remark.** In VD-PSI after the client outsources its dataset, it has to keep locally only two secret keys. During the computation, the client who is interested in the result generates four values that he needs to keep until he retrieves the result. At the end of the protocol he can discard the four values. In contrast, a variant of the protocol in [25] requires the client to have the hash value of his encrypted inputs for verification. This introduces a storage overhead linear to the number of his outsourced inputs. Similar to VD-PSI, the clients in [19] need to locally store only the secret keys for a pseudo-random function in order to verify the computation result.

In conclusion, although [19] is faster than VD-PSI (and [25]), VD-PSI enjoys two properties that [19] lacks. First, VD-PSI supports non-interactive setup at client-side. Second, it allows clients to upload their datasets once but verifiably delegate the computation to the cloud an unlimited number of times. These properties are vital, because in the real world individuals and businesses can upload their datasets to the cloud at different points in time without necessarily knowing the other cloud users. Also, the users can fully benefit from the cloud's storage and computation capabilities. Compared to [25], VD-PSI offers the same security properties much more efficiently. Thus, VD-PSI allows businesses to get the full benefits of the cloud in a more cost-effective way.

## 7    Conclusions and Future Work

Integrity and privacy of data and computation results are major concerns for clients using the cloud. In this work we proposed VD-PSI, an efficient protocol that allows a client to delegate both storage and computation of private set intersection to the cloud who may misbehave. VD-PSI allows a result recipient to efficiently detect if the cloud tampers with the datasets, or deviates from the protocol, even though the client does not know its own outsourced dataset and the other clients' datasets. The protocol allows clients to independently prepare and store their private datasets in the cloud, and later on ask the cloud to compute the intersection of their outsourced datasets. It ensures that the cloud can compute the intersection only when all the clients agree. Clients can delegate PSI computation over their outsourced datasets an unlimited number of times with no need to download and re-prepare the datasets. We have shown that our protocol is secure in the presence of a malicious cloud and semi-honest clients. Its communication and computation complexity is linear to set cardinality upper bound, and its verification mechanism is lightweight. Overall, VD-PSI is a clear step forward towards efficient verifiable delegated PSI on outsourced private datasets.

In the future we would like to investigate how to further improve the efficiency of the protocol and how to support other privacy preserving delegated set operations on outsourced private datasets such as set difference, set union and subset.

**Acknowledgments.** We would like to thank the anonymous reviewers. This work was partially supported by an EPSRC Doctoral Training Grant studentship and an EPSRC research grant (EP/M013561/1).

## References

1. Abadi, A., Terzis, S., Dong, C.: O-PSI: delegated private set intersection on outsourced datasets. In: Federrath, H., Gollmann, D. (eds.) SEC 2015. IAICT, vol. 455, pp. 3–17. Springer, Cham (2015). doi:10.1007/978-3-319-18467-8_1
2. Aggarwal, C.C., Yu, P.S. (eds.): Privacy-Preserving Data Mining - Models and Algorithms, Advances in Database Systems, vol. 34. Springer, New York (2008)
3. Aho, A.V., Hopcroft, J.E.: The Design and Analysis of Computer Algorithms, 1st edn. Addison-Wesley Longman Publishing Co., Inc., Boston (1974)
4. Ardagna, C.A., Asal, R., Damiani, E., Vu, Q.H.: From security to assurance in the cloud: a survey. ACM Comput. Surv. **48**(1), 2:1–2:50 (2015)
5. BBC-NEW: The interview: a guide to the cyber attack on Hollywood. http://www.bbc.co.uk/news/entertainment-arts-30512032
6. Berenbrink, P., Czumaj, A., Steger, A., Vöcking, B.: Balanced allocations: the heavily loaded case. In: Proceedings of the Thirty-Second Annual ACM Symposium on Theory of Computing, Portland, OR, USA, 21–23 May 2000, pp. 745–754 (2000)

7. Choi, S.G., Katz, J., Kumaresan, R., Cid, C.: Multi-client non-interactive verifiable computation. In: Sahai, A. (ed.) TCC 2013. LNCS, vol. 7785, pp. 499–518. Springer, Heidelberg (2013). doi:10.1007/978-3-642-36594-2_28

8. Cristofaro, E., Kim, J., Tsudik, G.: Linear-complexity private set intersection protocols secure in malicious model. In: Abe, M. (ed.) ASIACRYPT 2010. LNCS, vol. 6477, pp. 213–231. Springer, Heidelberg (2010). doi:10.1007/978-3-642-17373-8_13

9. Dong, C., Chen, L., Camenisch, J., Russello, G.: Fair private set intersection with a semi-trusted arbiter. In: Data and Applications Security and Privacy XXVII - 27th Annual IFIP WG 11.3 Conference, DBSec 2013, USA, pp. 128–144 (2013)

10. Dong, C., Chen, L., Wen, Z.: When private set intersection meets big data: an efficient and scalable protocol. In: Proceedings of the 20th ACM Conference on Computer and Communications Security, pp. 789–800 (2013)

11. Fiore, D., Gennaro, R., Pastro, V.: Efficiently verifiable computation on encrypted data. In: Proceedings of the 21st ACM Conference on Computer and Communications Security, Scottsdale, AZ, USA, pp. 844–855 (2014)

12. Freedman, M.J., Nissim, K., Pinkas, B.: Efficient private matching and set intersection. In: Cachin, C., Camenisch, J.L. (eds.) EUROCRYPT 2004. LNCS, vol. 3027, pp. 1–19. Springer, Heidelberg (2004). doi:10.1007/978-3-540-24676-3_1

13. Gennaro, R., Gentry, C., Parno, B.: Non-interactive verifiable computing: outsourcing computation to untrusted workers. In: Rabin, T. (ed.) CRYPTO 2010. LNCS, vol. 6223, pp. 465–482. Springer, Heidelberg (2010). doi:10.1007/978-3-642-14623-7_25

14. Goldreich, O.: The Foundations of Cryptography - Volume 2, Basic Applications. Cambridge University Press, New York (2004)

15. Goldwasser, S., Kalai, Y.T., Rothblum, G.N.: Delegating computation: interactive proofs for muggles. In: Proceedings of the 40th Annual ACM Symposium on Theory of Computing, Canada, pp. 113–122 (2008)

16. Golle, P., Mironov, I.: Uncheatable distributed computations. In: Naccache, D. (ed.) CT-RSA 2001. LNCS, vol. 2020, pp. 425–440. Springer, Heidelberg (2001). doi:10.1007/3-540-45353-9_31

17. Gordon, S.D., Katz, J., Liu, F.-H., Shi, E., Zhou, H.-S.: Multi-client verifiable computation with stronger security guarantees. In: Dodis, Y., Nielsen, J.B. (eds.) TCC 2015. LNCS, vol. 9015, pp. 144–168. Springer, Heidelberg (2015). doi:10.1007/978-3-662-46497-7_6

18. Huang, W., Ganjali, A., Kim, B.H., Oh, S., Lie, D.: The state of public infrastructure-as-a-service cloud security. ACM Comput. Surv. 47(4), 68:1–68:31 (2015)

19. Kamara, S., Mohassel, P., Raykova, M., Sadeghian, S.: Scaling private set intersection to billion-element sets. In: Proceedings of the 18th International Conference on Financial Cryptography and Data Security, pp. 863–874 (2014)

20. Kedlaya, K.S., Umans, C.: Fast polynomial factorization and modular composition. SIAM J. Comput. 40(6), 1767–1802 (2011)

21. Kerschbaum, F.: Collusion-resistant outsourcing of private set intersection. In: Proceedings of the 27th ACM Symposium on Applied Computing, Riva, Trento, Italy, pp. 1451–1456 (2012)

22. Kerschbaum, F.: Outsourced private set intersection using homomorphic encryption. In: Computer and Communications Security, ASIACCS 2012, pp. 85–86 (2012)

23. Kissner, L., Song, D.: Privacy-preserving set operations. In: Shoup, V. (ed.) CRYPTO 2005. LNCS, vol. 3621, pp. 241–257. Springer, Heidelberg (2005). doi:10.1007/11535218_15

24. Liu, F., Ng, W.K., Zhang, W., Giang, D.H., Han, S.: Encrypted set intersection protocol for outsourced datasets. In: IEEE International Conference on Cloud Engineering, IC2E 2014, pp. 135–140. IEEE Computer Society, Washington, DC (2014)
25. López-Alt, A., Tromer, E., Vaikuntanathan, V.: On-the-fly multiparty computation on the cloud via multikey fully homomorphic encryption. In: Symposium on Theory of Computing Conference, USA, pp. 1219–1234 (2012)
26. Marston, S., Li, Z., Bandyopadhyay, S., Ghalsasi, A.: Cloud computing - the business perspective. In: Proceedings of the 44th Hawaii International International Conference on Systems Science (HICSS-44 2011), USA, pp. 1–11 (2011)
27. Paillier, P.: Public-key cryptosystems based on composite degree residuosity classes. In: Stern, J. (ed.) EUROCRYPT 1999. LNCS, vol. 1592, pp. 223–238. Springer, Heidelberg (1999). doi:10.1007/3-540-48910-X_16
28. Pinkas, B., Schneider, T., Segev, G., Zohner, M.: Phasing: private set intersection using permutation-based hashing. In: Proceedings of the 24th USENIX Security Symposium, USENIX Security 15, Washington, D.C., USA, 12–14 August 2015, pp. 515–530 (2015)
29. Pinkas, B., Schneider, T., Zohner, M.: Faster private set intersection based on OT extension. In: Proceedings of the 23rd USENIX Security Symposium, San Diego, CA, USA. USENIX (2014)
30. Raab, M., Steger, A.: "Balls into Bins" — a simple and tight analysis. In: Luby, M., Rolim, J.D.P., Serna, M. (eds.) RANDOM 1998. LNCS, vol. 1518, pp. 159–170. Springer, Heidelberg (1998). doi:10.1007/3-540-49543-6_13
31. Zheng, Q., Xu, S.: Verifiable delegated set intersection operations on outsourced encrypted data. IACR Cryptology ePrint Archive, p. 178 (2014)

# Confidential Benchmarking
# Based on Multiparty Computation

Ivan Damgård[1], Kasper Damgård[2(✉)], Kurt Nielsen[3],
Peter Sebastian Nordholt[2], and Tomas Toft[4]

[1] Department of Computer Science, Aarhus University, Aarhus, Denmark
[2] The Alexandra Institute, Aarhus, Denmark
kasper.damgaard@alexandra.dk
[3] Department of Food and Resource Economics,
University of Copenhagen, Copenhagen, Denmark
[4] Partisia, Aarhus, Denmark

**Abstract.** We report on the design and implementation of a system
that uses multiparty computation to enable banks to benchmark their
customers' confidential performance data against a large representative
set of confidential performance data from a consultancy house. The system ensures that both the banks' and the consultancy house's data stays
confidential, the banks as clients learn nothing but the computed benchmarking score. In the concrete business application, the developed prototype helps Danish banks to find the most efficient customers among
a large and challenging group of agricultural customers with too much
debt. We propose a model based on linear programming for doing the
benchmarking and implement it using the SPDZ protocol by Damgård
et al., which we modify using a new idea that allows clients to supply
data and get output without having to participate in the preprocessing
phase and without keeping state during the computation. We ran the
system with two servers doing the secure computation using a database
with information on about 2500 users. Answers arrived in about 25 s.

## 1 Introduction

This paper presents a system and a business case based on advanced cryptography for improved credit rating in Danish banks. The system collects data from
different sources and compute performance scores of a given banks own customers relative to a larger number of similar customers outside of the bank. The
system maintains the confidentiality of all of the customers' data by the use
of secure multiparty computation that allows the merged raw data to remain
encrypted at all time.

We gratefully acknowledge financial support from the Center for research in the
Foundations of Electronic Markets (CFEM) funded by the Danish Council for Strate-
gic Research, the FP7 EU-project PRACTICE, the MPCPRO project supported by
ERC and the CTIC center, supported by the Danish National Research Foundation.

J. Grossklags and B. Preneel (Eds.): FC 2016, LNCS 9603, pp. 169–187, 2017.
DOI: 10.1007/978-3-662-54970-4_10

The business case focuses on farmers as a business segment that is particularly challenging for Danish banks. The basic problem is that a large number of farmers have had too high debt ratios and too low earnings for years and the banks have been reluctant to realise the losses[1]. One would like to avoid a chain reaction that may affect the individual bank's own credit rating and hereby it's ability to lend money on the interbank market. So on the one hand, a number of banks have too many farmers with potential losses as customers and on the other hand, status quo worsens the situation for this group of customers that need to invest to stay competitive. To control the situation and to avoid an escalation, the banks are forced to pick the right farmers among this group of risk-prone customers. This requires more analysis than the traditional credit scores. The banks need to look beyond the debt and find the better performing farmers that are more likely to pay back the loans. To do this one needs accounting and production data from a large range of peer farmers. Since farmers are not required to publish accounting data, a number of banks in particular the small and medium sized banks, lack the basic data for sound in-house analysis of their own customers relative performance.

However, there is a consultancy house in the market that possesses accounting data from a large number of farmers. This creates an opportunity to score the bank's customers relative to the sector as a whole and not just the banks own portfolio which may not be representative for the business segment.

Hereby, the business case has a characteristic property that it shares with many similar cases: the inputs we need to solve the problem are held by different parties and privacy issues prevent them from pooling the information. In our case, the consultancy house that has the farmers accounting data is of course required to keeps its database confidential. On the other hand, banks are not allowed to give away data on their customers including the identity of its customers. In fact, even ignoring regulations, it would be particularly problematic in our case if the bank were to send data on a customer $C$ in the clear to the consultancy house. If $C$'s data are already in the database, it is very likely that the consultancy house could find out which customer the bank wants to evaluate, and this is of course a breach of confidentiality.

Agreeing on a trusted third party who can perform the computation may be both difficult and expensive, hence a different solution is desirable. Secure multiparty computation (MPC) provides a solution – two or more parties can compute any function on private inputs such that the only new information leaked is the intended output of the function [Yao82, GMW87, BOGW88, CCD88]. However, though any function is computable in theory, specialized protocols for concrete problems are typically proposed to achieve acceptable efficiency. This is also the case here, where we implement a secure Linear Program (LP)-solver and demonstrate its applicability.

Conceptually, MPC can be seen as an implementation of a Trusted Third Party (TTP) that receives the input and confidentially computes the result (in this case the result of the benchmarking), while not revealing anything else about

---

[1] The banks are typically the lenders with the utmost priority in case of default.

the inputs. As such, the MPC approach is analogous to paying a consultancy house to act as a TTP. However, the economic argument for using MPC is that while a consultancy house is likely to charge the parties substantial fees for every analysis, the cost of developing software for MPC only has to be paid once and can be amortised over many applications of the system.

Linear programming (LP) is one of the basic and most useful optimization problems known. The goal is to find an assignment to variables, $x = (x_1, \ldots, x_n)$, subject to $m$ linear constraints

$$C \cdot x \leq b$$

maximizing (or minimizing) a linear function, $f(x)$. LP is widely used in Operational Research and applied Micro Economics to solve real life problems such as resource allocation, supply chain management or benchmarking as in this paper.

We note that similar business cases for confidential benchmarking have been considered before [KT06, Ker08a, Ker08b], as well as the idea of using LP to solve the problem [KSZ+11].

The remainder of this paper is structured as follows. Section 2 describes the application scenario and the linear program to be solved. Sections 3 and 4 describe the applied protocol and implementation respectively and concluding remarks are given in Sect. 5.

## 2   Application Scenario and Benchmarking Model

Credit rating of a firm is all about estimating the ability that the firm can fulfill its financial commitments based on historical data. Traditional credit rating models such as the original Altman's Z-score aim at predicting the probability that a firm will go into bankruptcy. Using various statistical methods the most relevant explanatory variables are selected and the credit rating model is estimated, see e.g. [Mes97] for a general introduction.

The traditional credit scoring divides customers into groups depending on their overall credit worthiness. While new customers may simply be rejected based on a bad credit score, existing customers that end up with a bad credit score, cannot be rejected without a risk of losses. When larger groups of customers experience a drop in their credit worthiness the banks itself may get exposed by a drop in credit rating. This was indeed the case with the global financial crisis that was created over a number of years and ignited by Lehman Brothers' bankruptcy in 2008. The present problem where a large group of Danish farmers have low credit worthiness, goes back to excessive lending prior to 2008.

In general, farming requires large investments to generate profit. The Danish farmers have historically been highly efficient and to a large extent adapted to the relatively high operational costs, not least the high wages (see e.g. [ANB12]). The otherwise successful substitution away from increasing labor costs has resulted in high debt/equity ratios. This challenges the Danish banks with many farmers as customers that on the one hand require large investments to become competitive and on the other hand suffer from high debt/equity ratios. According to BankResearch.dk that continuously evaluate the Danish banks, 7 of the 8 worst scoring banks are among the 30 Danish banks that are most exposed in the agricultural sector in 2014. These 30 banks are all small and medium sized banks and have from 10 to 35% of total loans and guarantees in agriculture or fishery. This development emphasises the fact that when selecting the right farmers for future loans, one needs an analysis that is based on a larger number of comparable farms than what is found in the individual banks' own portfolios.

In close collaboration with the consultancy house that represents the majority of the farmers and selected small and medium sized banks, a prototype software has been developed. The consultancy house has detailed account and production data that are not publicly available. The added security allows us to create a richer data foundation by merging the confidential data from the accounting firm with additional confidential data from the individual banks. The secure LP solver allows us to conduct state-of-the-art relative performance analysis directly on the richer, though secret data set. The resulting benchmarks is used to evaluate new individual customers as well as the banks' portfolios - in either case the analysis reflects performance relative to the agricultural sector as a whole.

In general terms, benchmarking is the process of comparing the performance/activities of one unit against that of best practice. We apply Data Envelopment Analysis (DEA), which is a so-called frontier-evaluation technique that supports best practice comparisons (or efficiency analysis) in a realistic multiple-inputs multiple-outputs framework. Instead of benchmarking against engineering standards or statistical average performances, DEA invokes a minimum of a priori assumptions and evaluates the performance against that of specific peer units. For these reasons, DEA has become a popular benchmarking approach.

DEA was originally proposed by [CcR78, CcR79], and has subsequently been refined and applied in a large number of research papers and by consultants in a broad sense. A 2008 bibliography lists more than 4000 DEA references, and more than 1600 of these are published in good quality scientific journals [EPT08].

Most often, DEA is used to get *general insight*, e.g. about the variation in performance or the productive development in a given sector. However, DEA have also proven useful in *incentive provision*, e.g. for regulation or as part of an auction market cf. [ABT05, BN08, NT07]. Finally, DEA has also been applied as a direct alternative to traditional credit rating models in predicting the risk of failures [CPV04, PAS04, PBS09]. DEA can be formulated as an LP-problem and therefore in general be solved by the Secure LP-solver described in this paper.

To formally define the DEA methodology used for this analysis, consider the set of $n$ observed farms. All farms are using $r$ inputs to produce $s$ outputs, where the *input-output vector* for farm $i$ is defined as: $(x_i, y_i) \in \mathbb{R}_+^{r+s}$. We let $x_i^k$ denote farm $i$'s consumption of the $k$'th input and $y_i^l$ its production of the $l$'th output.

The DEA input efficiency score under variable returns to scale (cf. [BCc84]) for farm $i$ is called $\theta_i^*$ and is defined as:

$$\theta_i^* = \max \theta_i$$

$$\text{s.t.} \sum_{j=1}^{n} \lambda_j x_j^k \leq x_i^k, k = 1, \ldots, r \qquad (1)$$

$$\sum_{j=1}^{n} \lambda_j y_j^l \geq \theta_i y_i^l, l = 1, \ldots, s$$

$$\sum_{j=1}^{n} \lambda_j = 1, \lambda_j \geq 0, j = 1, \ldots, n.$$

The interpretation is that the efficiency score of farm $i$ is the largest possible factor by which farm $i$ can expand all outputs while still maintaining present input consumption. We use the reverse output efficiency score $1/\theta_i^*$ to fix the score between 0 and 1. As an example, the interpretation of a reverse output score of 80% is that the farm uses only 80% of its potential as estimated by comparing to the other farms (the estimated best practice benchmark). Apart from evaluating individual farmers we use distribution plots to evaluate the individual bank's portfolio of farmers. For further details on the use of DEA, the reader is referred to the textbooks by e.g. [BO11, CST07].

The software described below is in the process of being tested by the end-users i.e. selected banks[2]. The system is able to do several different types of analyses and these have been designed in collaboration with the consultancy house and tested by consultants that are familiar with the evaluated farmers. Here we concentrate on one of the benchmarking analyses that is used on all of the 4 major group of farmers (milk, pig, plant and fur production). The initial data provided by the consultancy house consists of approx. 7500 accounts across the four types of farms in total and provide a representative and sound foundation for the analysis.

The applied benchmarking model reported on in this paper focuses on the farms abilities to transform the basic inputs labour, capital (divided into three sub-groups) and variable inputs into gross output, i.e., profit. The model has been developed, discussed and tested together with the involved consultancy house.

- $x_i^1$: Labour (wages for paid labor + 450000 DKK to the owner)
- $x_i^2$: Value of land
- $x_i^3$: Liquid capital
- $x_i^4$: Other capital assets
- $x_i^5$: All variable costs (excluding internal transfer)
- $y_i^1$: Gross output (including EU subsidies and other income)

---

[2] An early stage demo version of the software has been tested and resulted in valuable feedback for the development of the prototype.

The resulting benchmarking scores from the 7500 farmers, supports the basic argument, that additional analyses are required in selecting the best performing farmers among the many with too much debt. Table 1 shows how the benchmarking scores are distributed within segments of the farmers' debt/equity ratios. The result shows that the vast majority have a debt/equity ratio larger than 50% and that farmers with similar debt/equity ratio have widely spread benchmarking scores. However, there is a tendency to a higher benchmarking score for farmers with higher debt/equity scores i.e. among the most risky customers seen from the banks' perspective. Although traditional credit ratings involve other elements than what is captured by the debt/equity ratio, the results do indicate that the suggested benchmarking analysis is able to identify the better performing farmers among many risky customers with too much debt.

**Table 1.** Debt/equity ratio and distribution of benchmark scores

| Debt/equity ratio | Number of farmers | Average score | Standard deviation (score) |
|---|---|---|---|
| 50%–60% | 632 | 41.6% | 20.6% |
| 60%–70% | 1363 | 40.0% | 18.6% |
| 70%–80% | 2014 | 43.0% | 17.2% |
| 80%–90% | 1807 | 47.8% | 15.6% |
| 90%–100% | 1234 | 48.3% | 15.1% |

We have described how the confidential benchmarking system can be used by banks to evaluate potential new customers, as well as all farmers in their existing portfolios. In addition, the situation allows us to provide a different type of analysis, namely a quick stress test of a bank's portfolio: for all the banks that participate, it holds that the 7500 accounts in the database include a significant share of the bank's agricultural customers. So we can give the bank an idea of how well its customers are doing by comparing those that are in the database with the total population. We do this by first having the database *locally* compute the benchmark score for all farmers in the database. This does not require MPC and can be done quite efficiently. Now, only the bank knows the identity of its customers and this is considered to be confidential information. Therefore the bank uploads a list of id numbers that are secret shared across the two servers, and then, inside a secure computation, we can select the bank's portfolio of farmers and return a summary based on their precomputed scores. Hereby, the initial stress test of the portfolios can be done without delays from the otherwise time intensive LP solving. Note also that since this computation touches every entry in the database, no information is released on which entries belong to customers of the bank in question.

# 3    Using the SPDZ Protocol for Benchmarking

The scenario in which we want to implement Multiparty Computation (MPC) is composed of the following players: clients, who supply input and get outputs and servers who execute the actual computation. We assume that any number of clients and up to $n - 1$ of the $n$ servers may be maliciously corrupted.

In relation to the case outlined in the previous section, a client would typically be a bank who wants to get the score for a certain customer. One special client (who only supplies input) would be the consultancy house who has the database. The servers would be run by different parties with an interest in the system. For the deployment of the present prototype, the two organisations involved in the development of the system (the Alexandra Institute and Partisia), each control one of the two servers involved in the secure computations. Based on discussion with the involved business partners, we expect that the consultancy house and the Danish Bankers Association will control the two servers in a commercial setup.

We use the SPDZ protocol from [DPSZ12] to do the computation. This protocol is indeed capable of general secure computation and can tolerate that all but one of the servers doing the computation are corrupt. Tolerating a dishonest majority actually requires the use of heavy public-key crypto machinery. However, one of the main ideas in SPDZ is to push the use of this into a preprocessing phase that can be done ahead of time (without knowing the inputs), and then use preprocessed material to do the actual computation very efficiently.

However, it is not clear how to integrate the clients. In SPDZ, it is assumed that each player plays both the role of a server and of a client who can supply input and get output. To do this, SPDZ requires that all players take part in the preprocessing stage. But in our scenario, we want to separate the client and server roles and we definitely do not want to demand from our clients that they do the preprocessing: in our application, it may not even be known who the clients are at preprocessing time. We would also like that the clients do not need to keep state while the computation is running as this simplifies the implementation of client software[3]. We explain our solution below after we explain some more details of the SPDZ protocol:

SPDZ can securely evaluate any arithmetic circuit over a finite field $\mathbb{F}$, and we will assume $\mathbb{F}$ is the field with $p$ elements for a prime $p$ is the following. Each value $a$ that occurs in the computation (as input, output or intermediate result) is represented in a certain format denoted by $\langle a \rangle$. The idea is that each server holds part of the data that represents $a$. More specifically, each server $S_i$ holds a *share* $a_i$ of $a$, such that $a = a_1 + \cdots + a_n$ and the $a_i$'s are randomly chosen such that even given $n - 1$ of them, $a$ remains unknown. The servers also hold

---

[3] In [JNO14], a generic client solution was proposed that works for any MPC protocol, but it requires the client to keep state. In principle, one can always store client state info on the servers, but since our servers are malicious it needs to be authenticated and secret shared or encrypted, and this adds further complications to the implementation.

data that can be used to authenticate the value of $a$ if we want to retrieve it in the clear, but the details of this are not important here.

SPDZ includes protocols for operating securely on these representations of field values, i.e., from $\langle a \rangle, \langle b \rangle$, the servers can compute $\langle a + b \rangle$ or $\langle ab \rangle$ without revealing anything about $a$ or $b$. Similarly we add or multiply by a publicly known constant. The main role of the preprocessing is to supply shared randomness that facilitates secure multiplication, but it can also easily be configured to supply any number of representations $\langle r \rangle$, where $r \in \mathbb{F}$ is a random value that is unknown to all players, this will be very important in the following.

The overall idea of the computation phase in SPDZ is then to first construct representations in the right form of the input values, do the required arithmetic operations to come up with representations of the desired outputs, and then open these to reveal the results to the players who are to receive output.

## 3.1    Allowing Clients to Give Input and Get Output

Let us first discuss how to give output to a client $C$, assuming that the servers have managed to compute a representation of an output value $\langle y \rangle$. As mentioned, this means that each server $S_i$ holds $y_i$ where $y = \sum_i y_i$.

So this may seem easy: each $S_i$ sends $y_i$ privately to $C$, who adds all values received to get $y$. However, this will of course not work, even a single malicious server could lie about its value and make $C$ obtain an incorrect result. In the original SPDZ protocol, this type of problem is solved by having the servers collaborate to authenticate the sum of the values supplied. But $C$ cannot take part in and be convinced by such a procedure unless he took part in the preprocessing stage, and we want to avoid this.

So instead we propose to encode the output value in such a way that any modification by malicious servers can be detected by the client[4]. As a first attempt, suppose the servers retrieve a random representation $\langle r \rangle$ from the preprocessing, then they compute securely $\langle w \rangle = \langle yr \rangle$ and finally send all shares to $y, r$ and $w$ privately to $C$. He can now reconstruct and check that indeed $yr = w$ and will reject the output if not. Recall that if we want to tolerate a dishonest majority of servers, we cannot guarantee that players will always terminate with correct output, as servers may for instance just stop playing. So simply aborting if something is wrong is the best we can do.

One can think of $w$ as an authentication tag and $r$ as a key, so this is an authentication scheme similar to the one already used in SPDZ. As we show below, this will indeed ensure that any attempt to change $y$ will be detected except with probability $1/p$, where we assume that $p$ is large enough that this is negligible. However, there is still a subtle problem: $y$ is supposed to be private, known only to the client. Now, a malicious server could (for instance) change $r$ and leave the other values alone. It is easy to see that then the client will

---

[4] This is actually the notion of a strong AMD code [CDF+08], the construction we give here is slightly different from previous ones, though, and fits better into our protocol.

abort if $y \neq 0$ but will accept if $y = 0$. The adversary can observe this and get information on $y^5$. A way to solve this problem is to also authenticate the key $r$ in exactly the same way as we authenticated $y$. It may seem that we are just pushing the problem in front of us, but note that $r$ is guaranteed to be random (contrary to $y$). So while the adversary can still make a guess at $r$ and get to see if his guess was correct, the probability of guessing correctly is negligible, so we can ignore this possibility.

The protocol is specified in detail in Fig. 1 and we have the following result on its security:

---

**Protocol *Output Delivery*.**

Given $\langle y \rangle$ where we want to reveal $y$ to $C$ and only to $C$.

1. The servers do the following: Retrieve unused random $\langle r \rangle$, $\langle v \rangle$ from the preprocessed material and compute $\langle w \rangle = \langle yr \rangle$, $\langle u \rangle = \langle vr \rangle$.
   Each server $S_i$ sends its shares $y_i, r_i, w_i, v_i, u_i$ privately to $C$.
2. $C$ does the following: compute $y = \sum_i y_i, r = \sum_i r_i, w = \sum_i w_i, u = \sum_i u_i, v = \sum_i v_i$. Check that $w = yr$ and $u = vr$. If not, abort, else output $y$.

---

**Fig. 1.** Protocol for giving output to $C$

**Lemma 1.** *The protocol in Fig. 1 satisfies the following. Privacy: if $C$ is honest, the adversary's view of the protocol can be simulated with statistically close distribution without knowing $y$. Correctness: an honest $C$ will accept a value different from $y$ with probability at most $1/p$.*

*Proof.* As for correctness, assume for contradiction that $C$ accepts $y' \neq y$. Let $w', r', v', u'$ be the other values reconstructed by $C$. Since $C$ accepts we have $w' = y'r'$. Also, by correctness of the original SPDZ protocol, we know that $w = yr$. We can write $y' = y + \alpha, w' = w + \beta, r' = r + \gamma$ where $\alpha, \beta, \gamma$ are errors introduced by the adversary sending incorrect shares. Inserting this into $w' = y'r'$, we get $w + \beta = (y + \alpha)(r + \gamma)$. Using $w = yr$, this can be simplified to

$$\beta = y\gamma + \alpha r + \alpha\gamma$$

But since $y \neq y'$ implies $\alpha \neq 0$, this equation determines $r$ uniquely, so the adversary must effectively guess $r$ to make $C$ accept an incorrect value. This happens with probability at most $1/p$ since $r$ is unknown a priori.

As for privacy, note that the adversary's view includes the correct shares for corrupt servers of $y, r, w, u$ and $v$ and the share they send to $C$. The only new information the adversary learns is whether the protocol aborts. We show that

---

$^5$ This problem does not occur in the original SPDZ protocol, since there the values that are opened are public.

from shares and messages sent by corrupt servers, one can predict whether the protocol aborts, except with negligible probability, and hence the adversary's view can be simulated without knowing $y$. To see this, we reuse the notation from the proof of correctness, and also define $u' = u + \delta, v' = v + \epsilon$. We can then see in the same way as above that $C$ will find that $u' = v'r'$ if and only if

$$\delta = v\gamma + \epsilon r + \epsilon\gamma.$$

Of course, the error terms $\alpha, \beta, \gamma, \epsilon, \delta$ can be computed from the adversaries view and we claim that if they are not all 0, $C$ will abort except with negligible probability. So this gives the prediction we were after (note that, of course, if all error terms are 0, $C$ will accept).

Note first that $r$ plays the role as the authenticated message in the equation $u = vr$, and we already argued that $C$ will abort almost always if the message is changed. It follows that if $\alpha \neq 0$ or $\gamma \neq 0$, $C$ aborts almost always. So assume therefore that $\alpha = \gamma = 0$. Our equations simplify to $\beta = 0$ and $\delta = \epsilon r$. Clearly, $C$ aborts if $\beta \neq 0$. Further, if $\epsilon \neq 0$, we can only get $C$ to accept if $r = \delta/\epsilon$ which happens with negligible probability since $r$ is random. So we can assume that $\epsilon = 0$ and then it follows that $\delta = 0$ as well, since otherwise $C$ always aborts.

Before we consider supplying inputs, note that a client can easily broadcast a message to the servers, by simply sending the same message to them all. Then the servers can compare what they received and abort if there is a disagreement. Again, we cannot avoid the possibility of aborting if the client and a majority of servers are malicious.

Now suppose $C$ wants to contribute input value $x$. For this, we use a pre-processed random $\langle s \rangle$. We now use the previous protocol to reveal $s$ to (only) $C$, who can then broadcast $x - s$. The servers can now use a SPDZ subprotocol to add the publicly known value $x - s$ into $\langle s \rangle$ to obtain $\langle x \rangle$. The protocol is specified in detail in Fig. 2.

---

Protocol *Input Supply*.

$C$ holds value $x$ that he wants to supply as input top the servers.

1. The servers do the following: Retrieve an unused random $\langle s \rangle$ from the preprocessed material and use the Output delivery protocol to give $s$ to $C$.
2. $C$ broadcasts $x - s$ to the servers, and the servers compute $(x - s) + \langle s \rangle = \langle x \rangle$.

---

**Fig. 2.** Protocol for $C$ to supply input

For the security of the input protocol, note that if $C$ is honest, then the adversary learns nothing about $x$ because $s$ is uniformly random and hence $x - s$ is uniform as well. By the security of the SPDZ protocol the representation produced by the servers will contain the value $x$ intended by $C$. If $C$ is corrupt, the representation produced will contain a well defined value namely one that is determined by $s$ and the value $C$ broadcasts.

## 3.2    Using SPDZ for Linear Programming

In order to use the SPDZ protocol for Linear Programming as required in the application, we apply the well known Simplex algorithm. For this we need to do integer arithmetic and comparison on sufficiently large integers. To do this we choose the modulus $p$ large enough compared to the actual data, then we can do additions and multiplications by doing them mod $p$ but avoid overflow.

For divisions, two approaches have been proposed in the literature: Toft [Tof09b] suggests using a variant of the Simplex algorithm, where it is ensured that whenever we need to compute $a/b$, it will always be the case that $b$ divides $a$. This means we can do the division by multiplying by $b^{-1}$ mod $p$ which is much easier than a standard division. The downside of this idea is that the involved numbers (and hence the required modulus size) grows with the size of the Linear Programming problem we solve. Catrina and de Hoogh [Cd10] suggest to use instead fixed point rational numbers throughout. This means we can make do with smaller integers and division is now relatively easy. The catch is that we have to live with rounding errors in the result (where Toft's approach is exact), and that the other arithmetic operations become somewhat more complicated.

In our case we found that the problem size we were dealing with could be made small enough to allow us to use Toft's approach, which is simpler to implement. More specifically, we exploit the fact that one of the parties (the consultancy house) possesses the database with data on all the farmers we are comparing bank customers to. Therefore, prior to the secure computation, we can do a computation locally on the data base, that selects the most efficient farmers. More precisely, if we see the farmers as points in a multidimensional space, we identify those farmers that define the convex hull of all the points. Now, we only need to enter these farmers into the secure computation, since the answer to the linear programming problem will be the same. As a result, we had problems with 8 constraints and between 45 and 70 variables. To avoid overflow, we had to use a modulus $p$ with 512 bits.

We also note that there are several different flavours of Simplex to choose from. In particular, Simplex works by initially setting up a Pivot table containing the input values. This table is then iteratively updated until it contains the solution. There are several different rules for how this update can be done, in particular, we considered Bland's rule and Danzig's rule. To explain the difference in geometric terms, the current state of the computation defines a corner of a polytope in a multidimensional space. The update corresponds to selecting an edge on the polytope, and walk along this edge to obtain a better solution than the one defined by the current position. Bland's rule selects the first edge that will improve the current solution, while Danzig's rule considers all edges and selects the one that will give the largest improvement of the current solution. Clearly Danzig's rule requires more computation per iteration and is less "MPC-friendly" because we need several comparisons which are quite heavy. Nevertheless, in our experience, the number of iterations you get is so much smaller that Danzig's rule gives us better performance[6]. More details on this can be found in Sect. 4.2.

Finally, the comparisons are done using ideas from [DFK+06, Tof09a].

Our implementation leaks the number of iterations done in Simplex. This can be partially solved by doing dummy iterations, but this will of course slow down the system. We chose to put priority on getting answers as fast as possible.

# 4    Prototype and Performance

To demonstrate the potential of doing secure benchmarking a demo application was implemented which was tested by selected Danish banks. After initial positive feedback on the demo from the banks an extended prototype has now been built and a second round of testing at Danish banks is scheduled for the end of October 2015. In this section we will give an overview of the prototype and report on the observed performance.

## 4.1    Prototype

In the prototype secure computation is done between two servers. For convenience, in the prototype setup the two servers are controlled by the authors, however, in a real world setup the servers are assumed to be controlled by two distinct non-colluding parties. Namely, the consultancy house owning the database with the farmers' accounting information and a representative of the banks using the system (e.g., the Danish Bankers Association). The individual banks using the system are regarded as clients, i.e., they simply interact with the system to supply input and read output, but do not directly control the server representing them in the secure computation[7].

To initialise the system the consultancy house uploads its database to its secure computation server, which computes the reduced version of the dataset including only the relevant efficient accounts and adds this to the database. As discussed in Sect. 3 this corresponds to computing the convex hull of the points defined by the individual farmers. The two servers then run a protocol to secret share the database in the SPDZ internal format, and store the resulting secret shared database. Once the database is uploaded the consultancy house no longer needs to interact with the system and can go offline. This initialisation process is illustrated in Fig. 3.

---

[6] In theory, Danzig's rule can lead to a cycle, so that the algorithm will not terminate, but this is rare in practice, and never occurred in our testing.

[7] Alternatively, one could let each bank control their own secure computation server communicating directly with the consultancy house controlled server. This setup up was used for the initial demo system, but the current setup was deemed more scalable as it only requires two secure computation servers.

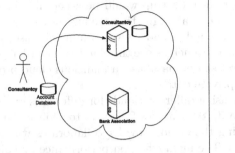
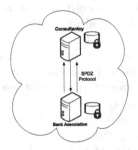

(a) The consultancy house uploading database | (b) Servers sharing database

**Fig. 3.** Initialising the secure benchmarking system

Once the system is initialized, the banks can login and start submitting analyses to be performed on the system, using a simple web-interface executed in the browser. Since banks are simply clients, once they have submitted an analysis to be performed, they no longer need to interact with the system and can go offline. The secure computation servers will then perform the requested analysis and store the resulting output in the secret shared database. Later the bank can login and request the output of the analysis that has been run. The interactions of a bank with the system are illustrated in Fig. 4.

The web-interface used by the banks is connected directly to the two secure computation servers (over https) and runs the input/output protocols described above locally. This means that each server only ever sees the input and output of an analysis in secret shared form. In other words, as long as the bank can trust the two servers to not collude and at least one server to be honest the privacy and correctness of his inputs and outputs are guaranteed.

## 4.2 Performance

The MPC computation needed for the benchmarking analysis (i.e., the Simplex algorithm as described above) was implemented using the FRESCO[8] framework, a Java framework for secure computation applications which contains an implementation of of the on-line phase of the SPDZ protocol. Below, we first give times for the on-line phase and then consider the preprocessing in Sect. 4.3.

Each server is deployed in the cloud on a separate Amazon EC2 instance. Each instance is a standard general purpose *m4.large* instance, with 8 GB RAM and 2 cores, running on a 2.4 GHz Intel Xeon processor. The servers are deployed in the same Amazon *availability zone* and *region*, essentially meaning they run in the same datacenter. This is a benefit for performance as it means there is rather low network latency between the servers. This is significant for protocols such as SPDZ with high round-complexity.

---

[8] https://github.com/aicis/fresco.

It is not entirely clear whether such a set-up would be acceptable in a real business application of the system: One can argue that having the server of each organization hosted by at the same cloud provider (Amazon in this case) places too much trust in the cloud provider. Namely, since the cloud provider has access to both servers including the secret shared database, a malicious cloud provider could potentially reconstruct all private data.

One can reduce these risks by using different clouds for different servers and an organisation could even share its data across 2 servers to reduce the trust in the cloud provider (by requiring the cloud provider collaborates with other cloud providers to break security). The main effect on performance by going to such a solution comes from increased latency of communication. We ran a small number of experiments to see how increased latency affected our prototype, and found that a 10-fold increase in latency gave a 3 fold increase in overall run time. So we estimate that while using different clouds would slow down the system significantly, it would not render it useless.

The prototype allows banks to benchmark a potential costumer's financial data against farmers in four different segments of agriculture: pigs, plants, milk and fur. For these segments the database we benchmark against holds 1786, 2645, 2258 and 358 accounts respectively. After we crop the datasets to only include the relevant efficient accounts, this is reduced to databases of 70, 63,

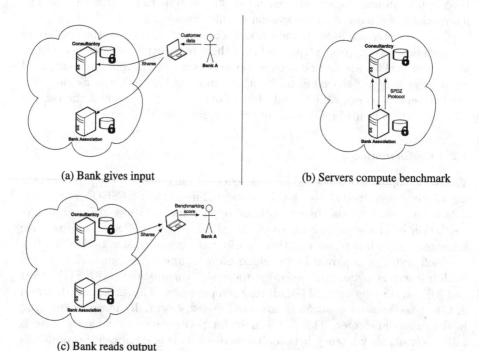

(a) Bank gives input

(b) Servers compute benchmark

(c) Bank reads output

**Fig. 4.** Interactions with the benchmarking system

47 and 45 accounts respectively. In Table 2 we give the average running time in seconds for the analysis on each of the different segments. We see the running time in all segments is around 22–26 s even when running on this rather modest hardware, which should be tolerable for a real world system.

**Table 2.** Time to do analysis for different agricultural segments

| Segment | Accounts (reduced) | Av. time (sec) | Std. dev. (sec) |
|---------|--------------------|----------------|-----------------|
| Pigs    | 70                 | 23             | 4               |
| Plants  | 63                 | 22             | 4               |
| Milk    | 47                 | 26             | 8               |
| Fur     | 45                 | 22             | 6               |

Surprisingly we see that we get the longest running times when benchmarking against the relatively small dataset of the milk segment. We also see a rather large standard deviation in the running time of 4–8 s (i.e., up to 30% in the milk segment). This variation is not due to secure computation it self but rather a property of the Simplex algorithm used to do the benchmarking analysis. Namely, the fact that the Simplex algorithm depending on the data we analyse may use a varying number of iterations to find an optimal value. Thus for evaluating the efficiency of the underlying Simplex implementation the time pr. iteration is really more relevant. We show these times in Table 3, which shows, as expected, that running times pr. iteration goes up the larger the dataset and datasets of similar size have about the same running time.

**Table 3.** Time for the a single Simplex iteration on different agricultural segments

| Segment | Accounts (reduced) | Av. num of iterations | Av. time pr. iteration (sec) | Std. dev. (sec) |
|---------|--------------------|-----------------------|------------------------------|-----------------|
| Pigs    | 70                 | 13                    | 1.80                         | 0.02            |
| Plants  | 63                 | 12                    | 1.78                         | 0.02            |
| Milk    | 47                 | 18                    | 1.47                         | 0.03            |
| Fur     | 45                 | 15                    | 1.46                         | 0.01            |

The numbers in Tables 2 and 3 are for our implementation of Simplex using Danzig's rule. As mentioned above we also considered the variation of the Simplex algorithm using Bland's rule. In Table 4 we give times for this variation. As explained above we see that using Bland's results in considerably faster iteration times, roughly around 20% faster than iterations using Danzig's rule. However, for our analysis the increased speed of iterations is cancelled out by having to do many more iterations to finish the analysis. Specifically, using Bland's instead of Danzig's rule increases the average amount of iterations by 33% in the milk segment and more than 150% in the plant segment. While this discourages us from using Bland's rule in our prototype, it may still be worth considering in other applications were if it would cause a less dramatic increase in the number of required iterations. Also, since there is a number of alternative heuristics for the Simplex updating rule it may be interesting to investigate their performance, to see if we could achieve both fast and few iterations.

**Table 4.** Time for Simplex iterations using Bland's rule

| Segment | Accounts (reduced) | Av. num of iterations | Av. time pr. iteration (sec) | Std dev. (sec) |
|---------|--------------------|-----------------------|------------------------------|----------------|
| Pigs    | 70                 | 23                    | 1.43                         | 0.01           |
| Plants  | 63                 | 31                    | 1.35                         | 0.01           |
| Milk    | 47                 | 24                    | 1.19                         | 0.05           |
| Fur     | 45                 | 23                    | 1.14                         | 0.01           |

One may wonder how the performance scales as datasets grow beyond those naturally occuring in the context of this prototype. We did not experiment with this.

However, recall that the dataset we compute on is reduced to only include the efficient accounts. We conjecture that with the applied benchmarking approach (DEA) the number of efficient accounts is, for all practical applications, significantly smaller than the total number of accounts, as is the case in this paper. Thus, even for much larger datasets the reduced dataset including only efficient accounts, will not be much larger than those used in this prototype (given the same LP-problem, i.e., the benchmarking model). The basic arguments for this conjecture are (1) that only the farmers that represent best practice is relevant in the LP-problem and (2) that the number of observations that represent best practice is driven by the dimensionality of the LP-problem (number of inputs and outputs in the analysis), the total number of observations (in this case accounts) and the basic assumption about the technology (restrictions on the $\lambda$ in the LP-problem). The more dimensions the more efficient observations (the model simply allows for more diversity) and the more observations the better representation of the diversity of the observations.

## 4.3 Preprocessing

For the prototype, we do not actually run the preprocessing that is required for the SPDZ protocol, but work with a fixed set of preprocessed data the we reuse (while this is of course not secure, it gives reliable performance data for the on-line phase). But we can compute how much time the preprocessing would take: first, we have counted the number of multiplications we do while executing a Simplex iteration, which is about 4000 multiplications. Then, from the performance numbers in [DKL+13], we can extrapolate and estimate the actual time their implementation would take for our case. For covert security and probability 1/5 to cheat successfully we get about 20 s per iteration and about 2 min for full active security.

### 4.4 Future Directions

The next step we consider for this prototype, is to bring in multiple data-providers. I.e., make also the consultancy house be a client among several clients contributing to the database against which we do our benchmarks. The data providers may add rows (more observations e.g. farms) or columns (more variables). More rows may come directly from the banks as well as other consultancy houses and accounting firms. More columns may e.g. be details about the debt (e.g. from the banks) or additional background information from Danish Statistics to give a few examples.

A more representative dataset (more rows) will improve the quality of the benchmarks and more importantly make the service more user friendly as less additional information is required. A more rich dataset (more columns) will allow for more analysis that better describe best practice and the performance of the farmers in this case.

This general approach with data from multiple sources merged into a larger database using MPC, is computationally more challenging. One challenge is to reduce the joint dataset to only the efficient observations which can no longer be done in the clear, but must be done in MPC.

More work on optimizing performance is also an obvious future direction. More experiments are needed to find the right levels of, e.g., parallelisation and hardware to be used.

## 5   Conclusion

We have presented a practical implementation of a system for confidentially benchmarking farmers against a large representative population of other farmers, using MPC and linear programming. The prototype has been developed and tested in collaboration with Danish banks and a consultancy house specialised in the agricultural sector. The system creates new information that helps Danish banks selecting the better performing farmers among the many with bad credit rating.

We have presented some add-ons to the SPDZ protocol making it more useful in a client-server scenario. The results obtained demonstrate that MPC can be useful in providing data that are useful and could not have been obtained in other ways without violating requirements for confidentiality.

# References

[ABT05]  Agrell, P.J., Bogetoft, P., Tind, J.: DEA and dynamic yardstick competition in Scandinavian electricity distribution. J. Prod. Anal. **23**(2), 173–201 (2005)

[ANB12]  Asmild, M., Nielsen, K., Bogetoft, P.: Are high labour costs destroying the competitiveness of Danish dairy farmers? Evidence from an international benchmarking analysis. MSAP Working Paper Series (2012)

[BCc84]  Banker, R.D., Charnes, A., Cooper, W.W.: Some models for estimating technical and scale inefficiencies in data envelopment analysis. Manage. Sci. **30**, 1078–1092 (1984)

[BN08]  Bogetoft, P., Nielsen, K.: DEA based auctions. Eur. J. Oper. Res. **184**, 685–700 (2008)

[BO11]  Bogetoft, P., Otto, L.: Benchmarking with DEA, SFA, and R. Springer, New York (2011)

[BOGW88]  Ben-Or, M., Goldwasser, S., Wigderson, A.:. Completeness theorems for non-cryptographic fault-tolerant distributed computation (extended abstract). In: Proceedings of the 20th ACM STOC, Chicago, Illinois, USA, 2–4 May, pp. 1–10. ACM Press (1988)

[CCD88]  Chaum, D., Crépeau, C., Damgård, I.: Multiparty unconditionally secure protocols (extended abstract). In: Proceedings of the 20th ACM STOC, Chicago, Illinois, USA, 2–4 May, pp. 11–19. ACM Press (1988)

[CcR78]  Charnes, A., Cooper, W.W., Rhodes, E.: Measuring the efficiency of decision making units. Eur. J. Oper. Res. **2**, 429–444 (1978)

[CcR79]  Charnes, A., Cooper, W.W., Rhodes, E.: Short communication: measuring the efficiency of decision making units. Eur. J. Oper. Res. **3**, 339 (1979)

[Cd10]  Catrina, O., de Hoogh, S.: Secure multiparty linear programming using fixed-point arithmetic. In: Gritzalis, D., Preneel, B., Theoharidou, M. (eds.) ESORICS 2010. LNCS, vol. 6345, pp. 134–150. Springer, Heidelberg (2010). doi:10.1007/978-3-642-15497-3_9

[CDF+08]  Cramer, R., Dodis, Y., Fehr, S., Padró, C., Wichs, D.: Detection of algebraic manipulation with applications to robust secret sharing and fuzzy extractors. In: Smart, N. (ed.) EUROCRYPT 2008. LNCS, vol. 4965, pp. 471–488. Springer, Heidelberg (2008). doi:10.1007/978-3-540-78967-3_27

[CPV04]  Cielen, A., Peeters, L., Vanhoof, K.: Bankruptcy prediction using a data envelopment analysis. Eur. J. Oper. Res. **154**(2), 526–532 (2004)

[CST07]  Cooper, W.W., Seiford, L.M., Tone, K.: Data Envelopment Analysis: A Comprehensive Text with Models, Applications, References and DEA-Solver Software, 2nd edn. Springer, New York (2007)

[DFK+06]  Damgård, I., Fitzi, M., Kiltz, E., Nielsen, J.B., Toft, T.: Unconditionally secure constant-rounds multi-party computation for equality, comparison, bits and exponentiation. In: Halevi, S., Rabin, T. (eds.) TCC 2006. LNCS, vol. 3876, pp. 285–304. Springer, Heidelberg (2006). doi:10.1007/11681878_15

[DKL+13]  Damgård, I., Keller, M., Larraia, E., Pastro, V., Scholl, P., Smart, N.P.: Practical covertly secure MPC for dishonest majority – or: breaking the SPDZ limits. In: Crampton, J., Jajodia, S., Mayes, K. (eds.) ESORICS 2013. LNCS, vol. 8134, pp. 1–18. Springer, Heidelberg (2013). doi:10.1007/978-3-642-40203-6_1

[DPSZ12]  Damgård, I., Pastro, V., Smart, N., Zakarias, S.: Multiparty computation from somewhat homomorphic encryption. In: Safavi-Naini, R., Canetti, R. (eds.) CRYPTO 2012. LNCS, vol. 7417, pp. 643–662. Springer, Heidelberg (2012). doi:10.1007/978-3-642-32009-5_38

[EPT08]  Emrouznejad, A., Parker, B.R., Tavares, G.: Evaluation of research in efficiency and productivity: a survey and analysis of the first 30 years of scholarly literature in DEA. Socio-Econ. Plann. Sci. **42**, 151–157 (2008)

[GMW87]  Goldreich, O., Micali, S., Wigderson, A.: How to play any mental game or a completeness theorem for protocols with honest majority. In: Aho, A., (ed.) Proceedings of the 19th ACM STOC, New York City, New York, USA, 25–27 May, pp. 218–229. ACM Press (1987)

[JNO14]  Jakobsen, T.P., Nielsen, J.B., Orlandi, C.: A framework for outsourcing of secure computation. In: Proceedings of the 6th edition of the ACM Workshop on Cloud Computing Security, pp. 81–92. ACM (2014)

[Ker08a]  Kerschbaum, F.: Building a privacy-preserving benchmarking enterprise system. Enterp. IS **2**(4), 421–441 (2008)

[Ker08b]  Kerschbaum, F.: Practical privacy-preserving benchmarking. In: Jajodia, S., Samarati, P., Cimato, S. (eds.) SEC 2008. ITIFIP, vol. 278, pp. 17–31. Springer, Boston, MA (2008). doi:10.1007/978-0-387-09699-5_2

[KSZ+11]  Kerschbaum, F., Schröpfer, A., Zilli, A., Pibernik, R., Catrina, O., de Hoogh, S., Schoenmakers, B., Cimato, S., Damiani, E.: Secure collaborative supply-chain management. IEEE Comput. **44**(9), 38–43 (2011)

[KT06]  Kerschbaum, F., Terzidis, O.: Filtering for private collaborative benchmarking. In: Müller, G. (ed.) ETRICS 2006. LNCS, vol. 3995, pp. 409–422. Springer, Heidelberg (2006). doi:10.1007/11766155_29

[Mes97]  Mester, L.J.: What's the point of credit scoring? Bus. Rev. **3**, 3–16 (1997)

[NT07]  Nielsen, K., Toft, T.: Secure relative performance scheme. In: Deng, X., Graham, F.C. (eds.) WINE 2007. LNCS, vol. 4858, pp. 396–403. Springer, Heidelberg (2007). doi:10.1007/978-3-540-77105-0_44

[PAS04]  Paradi, J.C., Asmild, M., Simak, P.C.: Using DEA and worst practice DEA in credit risk evaluation. J. Prod. Anal. **21**(2), 153–165 (2004)

[PBS09]  Premachandra, I.M., Bhabra, G.S., Sueyoshi, T.: DEA as a tool for bankruptcy assessment: a comparative study with logistic regression technique. Eur. J. Oper. Res. **193**(2), 412–424 (2009)

[Tof09a]  Toft, T.: Constant-rounds, almost-linear bit-decomposition of secret shared values. In: Fischlin, M. (ed.) CT-RSA 2009. LNCS, vol. 5473, pp. 357–371. Springer, Heidelberg (2009). doi:10.1007/978-3-642-00862-7_24

[Tof09b]  Toft, T.: Solving linear programs using multiparty computation. In: Dingledine, R., Golle, P. (eds.) FC 2009. LNCS, vol. 5628, pp. 90–107. Springer, Heidelberg (2009). doi:10.1007/978-3-642-03549-4_6

[Yao82]  Yao, A.C.-C.: Protocols for secure computations (extended abstract). In: Proceedings of the 23rd FOCS, Chicago, Illinois, 3–5 November, pp. 160–164. IEEE Computer Society Press (1982)

# Efficiently Making Secure Two-Party Computation Fair

Handan Kılınç[1,2(✉)] and Alptekin Küpçü[2]

[1] EPFL, Lausanne, Switzerland
handan.kilinc@epfl.ch
[2] Koç University, İstanbul, Turkey
akupcu@ku.edu.tr

**Abstract.** Secure two-party computation cannot be fair against malicious adversaries, unless a trusted third party (TTP) or a gradual-release type super-constant round protocol is employed. Existing optimistic fair two-party computation protocols with constant rounds are either too costly to arbitrate (e.g., the TTP may need to re-do almost the whole computation), or require the use of electronic payments. Furthermore, most of the existing solutions were proven secure and fair via a partial simulation, which, we show, may lead to insecurity overall. We propose a new framework for fair and secure two-party computation that can be applied on top of any secure two party computation protocol based on Yao's garbled circuits and zero-knowledge proofs. We show that our fairness overhead is minimal, compared to all known existing work. Furthermore, our protocol is fair even in terms of the work performed by Alice and Bob. We also prove our protocol is fair and secure simultaneously, through one simulator, which guarantees that our fairness extensions do not leak any private information. Lastly, we ensure that the TTP never learns the inputs or outputs of the computation. Therefore, even if the TTP becomes malicious and causes unfairness by colluding with one party, the security of the underlying protocol is still preserved.

## 1 Introduction

In two-party computation (2PC), Alice and Bob intend to evaluate a shared function with their private inputs. The computation is called secure when the parties do not learn anything beyond what is revealed by the output of the computation. Yao [38] introduced the concept of secure 2PC and gave an efficient protocol; but this protocol is not secure against malicious parties who try to learn extra information from the computation by *deviating* from the protocol. Many solutions [19,26,31,37] are suggested to strengthen Yao's protocol against malicious adversaries.

When one considers malicious adversaries, fairness is an important problem. A fair computation should guarantee that Alice learns the output of the function *if and only if* Bob learns. This problem occurs since in the protocol one party learns the output earlier than the other party; therefore (s)he can abort the protocol after learning the output, before the other party learns it.

© International Financial Cryptography Association 2017
J. Grossklags and B. Preneel (Eds.): FC 2016, LNCS 9603, pp. 188–207, 2017.
DOI: 10.1007/978-3-662-54970-4_11

There are two main methods of achieving fairness in 2PC: using gradual release [23,33,34] or a trusted third party (TTP) [6,25]. The *gradual release* based protocols [2,5,12] let the parties gradually (bit by bit, or piece by piece) and verifiably reveal the result. Malicious party will have one bit (or piece) advantage if the honest party starts to reveal the result first. Yet, if the malicious party has more computational power, he can abort the protocol earlier and learn the result via brute force, while the honest party cannot. In this case, fairness is not achieved. Another drawback is the necessity of many rounds.

The *TTP approach* employs a third party that is trusted by both Alice and Bob. A simple solution would be to give the inputs to the TTP, who computes the outputs and distributes fairly. In terms of efficiency and feasibility though, the TTP should be used in the *optimistic* model [1], where he gets involved in the protocol *only* when there is a dispute between Alice and Bob. It is very important to give the TTP the minimum possible workload because otherwise the system will have a bottleneck. Another important concern is *privacy*. In an optimistic solution, if there is no dispute, the TTP should not even know a computation took place, and even with a dispute, the TTP should never learn the inputs or outputs, or even identities. **We achieve all these efficiency and privacy requirements on the TTP.**

Another problem regarding fairness in secure two-party computation is the **proof methodology**. In previous works [6,23,34], fairness and security (with abort) were proven *separately*, only partially simulating the protocol (*partial simulation*). However, it is important to simulate everything together to ensure that the fairness solution *does not leak* any information beyond the original secure two-party computation requirement. Therefore, as in the security of the secure two-party computation, there should be ideal/real world simulation (see Sect. 2) that covers **both fairness and security** (*full simulation*). In other words, **the simulator should learn the output in the real world only after it is guaranteed that both parties can learn the output in the real world** to achieve ideal and real world indistinguishability of the outputs.

**Our Contributions:** The main achievement of this work is an efficient framework for making secure 2PC protocols fair, such that it guarantees fairness and security together, and can work on top of secure two party computation protocols extending Yao's garbled circuits to the malicious setting via zero-knowledge proofs (e.g., [6,15,19]). Note that the state-of-the-art optimistic fairness solution [6] is also based on zero-knowledge proofs.

- We use a simple-to-understand ideal world definition to achieve fairness and security together, and **prove our protocol's security and fairness with full simulation** which means proving security and fairness together.
- We show that proving security and fairness separately via only partial simulation is not necessarily secure (see Sect. 5).
- Our framework employs a trusted third party (TTP) for fairness, in the *optimistic* model. The **TTP's load is very light**: verification of signatures and commitments, and decryption only. If there is no dispute, the TTP does *not* even know a computation took place, and even with a dispute, the TTP *never*

learns the inputs, outputs, or even identities of Alice and Bob. So, a semi-honest TTP is enough in our construction to achieve fairness.

- If the **TTP becomes malicious** (e.g., colludes with one of the parties), it **does not violate the security** of the underlying 2PC protocol; only the fairness property of the protocol is contravened.
- Our framework is also fair about the work done by Alice and Bob, since both of them perform the same steps in the protocol.
- The principles for fairness in our framework can be adopted by any 2PC protocol based on Yao's garbled circuits, employing zero knowledge proofs for the malicious setting, thereby achieving fairness with little overhead.
- We compare our framework with related fair secure two-party computation work and show that we achieve better efficiency and security.

**Related Works:** Cachin and Camenisch [6] present a state-of-the-art fair two-party computation protocol in the optimistic model. The protocol consists of two intertwined verifiable secure function evaluations. In the case of an unfair situation, the honest party interacts with the TTP. **The job of the TTP** can be as bad as almost repeating the whole computation, **linear in the circuit size**, creating a bottleneck in the system. Lindell [25] constructs a framework that can be adopted by any two-party functionality with the property that either both parties receive the output, or one party receives the output while the other receives a digitally-signed check (i.e., monetary compensation). However, one may argue that one party obtaining the output and the other obtaining the money may not always be considered fair, since *we do not necessarily know how valuable the output would be before the evaluation*. Kılınç and Küpçü [20] construct a fair *multi-party* computation (MPC) protocol in the optimistic model. While 2PC can be a special case of MPC, our solutions are optimized for the two-party case and hence are more efficient compared to applying their work to the two-party setting (e.g., they increase input and output sizes).

A detailed analysis of more related works is in the full version of the paper [21].

## 2    Definitions and Preliminaries

**Yao's Two-Party Computation Protocol:** We informally review Yao's construction [38], which is secure in the presence of *semi-honest* adversaries. Such adversaries follow the instructions of the protocol, but try to learn more information. The main idea in Yao's protocol is to compute a circuit without revealing any information about the value of the wires, except the output wires.

The protocol starts by agreeing on a circuit that computes the desired functionality. One party, called the *constructor*, generates two keys for every wire except the output wires. One key represents the value 0, and the other represents the value 1. Next, the constructor prepares a table for each gate that includes four double-encryptions with the four possible input key pairs (i.e., representing $00, 01, 10, 11$). The encrypted value is another key that represents these two input keys' output (e.g., for an AND gate, if keys $k_{a,0}$ and $k_{b,1}$ representing 0 and 1 are used as inputs of Alice and Bob, respectively, the gate's output key $k'$, which is encrypted under $k_{a,0}$ and $k_{b,1}$, represents the value $0 = 0 \ AND \ 1$.). Output gates contain double-encryptions of the actual output bits (no more keys are necessary, since the output will be learned anyway). All tables together are called the *garbled circuit*.

The other party is the *evaluator*. The constructor and the evaluator perform oblivious transfer (OT), where the constructor is the sender and the evaluator is the receiver, who learns the keys that represent his own input bits. Afterward, the constructor sends his input keys to the evaluator. The evaluator evaluates the garbled circuit by decrypting the garbled tables in topological order, and learns the output bits. The evaluator can decrypt one row of each gate's table, since he just knows one key for each wire. Since all he learns for the intermediary values are random keys and only the constructor knows which values these keys represent, the evaluator learns nothing more than what he can infer from the output. The evaluator finally sends the output to the constructor, who also learns nothing more than the output, since the evaluator did not send any intermediary values and they used OT for the evaluator's input keys.

**Secure Two-Party Computation (2PC):** Alice and Bob want to compute a function $f : \{0,1\}^* \times \{0,1\}^* \rightarrow \{0,1\}^* \times \{0,1\}^*$. Alice has her private input $x$, and Bob has his private input $y$. In the end of computation of $f(x,y)$, Alice obtains the output $f_a(x,y)$ and Bob obtains the output $f_b(x,y)$. The computation is secure if the privacy, correctness, independence of inputs, guaranteed output delivery, fairness [27] are achieved by the computation.

Because of the impossibility result on the fairness property without honest majority [8], fairness in a secure computation is not considered in the 2PC literature. Security is formalized with the ideal/real simulation paradigm. For every real world adversary, there must exist an adversary in the ideal world such that the execution in the ideal and real worlds are indistinguishable (e.g., [14]).

**Definition 1 (Ideal World).** *It consists of the corrupted party $C$, the honest party $H$, and the universal trusted party $\mathfrak{U}$ (not the TTP). The ideal protocol is:*

1. *$\mathfrak{U}$ receives input $x$ or the message* ABORT *from $C$, and $y$ from $H$. If the inputs are invalid or $C$ sends the message* ABORT*, then $\mathfrak{U}$ sends $\perp$ to both of the parties and halts.*
2. *Otherwise $\mathfrak{U}$ computes $f(x,y) = (f_c(x,y), f_h(x,y))$. Then, he sends $f_c(x,y)$ to $C$ and $f_h(x,y)$ to $H$.*

*The outputs of the parties in an ideal execution between the honest party $H$ and an adversary $\mathcal{A}$ controlling $C$, where $\mathfrak{U}$ computes $f$, is denoted* $\mathsf{IDEAL}_{f,\mathcal{A}(w)}(x,y,s)$ *where $x,y$ are the respective inputs of $C$ and $H$, $w$ is an auxiliary input of $\mathcal{A}$, and $s$ is the security parameter.*

The standard secure two-party ideal world definition [16,27] lets the adversary $\mathcal{A}$ to ABORT *after* learning his output but *before* the honest party learns her output. Thus, proving protocols secure using the old definition would not meet the fairness requirements.

**Definition 2 (Real World).** *The real world consists of, besides the parties, an adversary $\mathcal{A}$ that controls one of the parties, and the* TTP *who is involved in the protocol when there is unfair behavior. The pair of outputs of the honest party and the adversary $\mathcal{A}$ in the real execution of the protocol $\pi$, possibly employing the* TTP, *is denoted* $\mathsf{REAL}_{\pi,\mathsf{TTP},\mathcal{A}(w)}(x,y,s)$, *where $x, y, w$ and $s$ are like above.*

Note that $\mathfrak{U}$ and TTP are *not* related to each other. TTP is part of the *real* protocol to solve the fairness problem when it is necessary, but $\mathfrak{U}$ is not real.

**Definition 3 (Fair and Secure Two-Party Computation).** *Let $\pi$ be a probabilistic polynomial time (PPT) protocol and let $f$ be a PPT two-party functionality. We say that $\pi$ computes $f$ **fairly and securely** if for every non-uniform PPT real world adversary $\mathcal{A}$ attacking $\pi$, there exists a non-uniform PPT ideal world adversary $S$ so that for every $x, y, w \in \{0,1\}^*$, the ideal and real world outputs are computationally indistinguishable:*

$$\{\mathsf{IDEAL}_{f,S(w)}(x,y,s)\}_{s\in\mathbb{N}} \equiv_c \{\mathsf{REAL}_{\pi,\mathsf{TTP},\mathcal{A}(w)}(x,y,s)\}_{s\in\mathbb{N}}$$

For optimistic protocols, to simulate the complete view of the adversary, **the simulator also needs to simulate the behavior of the TTP** for the adversary. This simulation also needs to be indistinguishable.

The closest such definition was given by Cachin and Camenisch [6]. Their definition's advantage is that it also considers misbehaving TTP, but their ideal world contacts the real world TTP, mixing both worlds. Thus, it does not fit the optimistic usage of TTP. We prefer to use the Definition 3, which is more intuitive and general (it can even include gradual release since it is not specific to only the protocols with TTP), to prove our proposed protocol in Sect. 4 because we use the TTP in the optimistic model and we assume that the TTP is semi-honest while proving the protocol.

Note that in our ideal world, the moment the adversary sends his input, $\mathfrak{U}$ computes the outputs and performs fair distribution. Thus, the adversary can either abort the protocol before any party learns anything useful, or cannot prevent fairness. This is represented in our proof with a **simulator who learns the output only when it is *guaranteed* that both parties can learn the output.** Also observe that, under this ideal world definition, **if the simulator learns the output in the ideal world but the adversary aborts in the real world, that simulation would be *distinguishable*.**

Suppose that Alice is malicious and $S$ simulates the behavior of honest Bob in the real world and the behavior of malicious Alice in the ideal world. Assume $S$ learns the output of Alice from $\mathfrak{U}$ in order to simulate the real protocol *before* it is guaranteed that in a real protocol both of the parties could receive their outputs. Further suppose that the adversarial Alice then aborts the protocol so that $S$ does not receive his output in the real world. Thus, in the real world the real Bob would have aborted, whereas the ideal Bob outputs the result of the computation. Clearly, the ideal and real worlds are *distinguishable* in this case. The proofs in [6,23,34] unfortunately fall into this pitfall.

**Definition 4** *(Verifiable Escrow). An escrow is a ciphertext under the public key of the TTP. A verifiable escrow [1, 7] enables the recipient to verify, using only the public key of TTP, that the plaintext satisfies some relation. A public non-malleable label can be attached to a verifiable escrow [36].*

**Communication Model:** We do *not* need private and authenticated channels between the TTP and the parties. When there is dispute between the two parties, the TTP resolves the conflict *atomically*, which means the TTP interacts with either Alice or Bob at a given time, until that resolution is complete. We assume that the adversary cannot prevent the honest party from reaching the TTP eventually. We do not assume anything else about the communication model; our protocol's needs are minimal.

## 3  Our Solution

**Failed Approaches and Major Issues:** It looks like adding *fairness* to a 2PC protocol based on gabled circuits and zero knowledge using TTP does not need a lot of work. However, if we care efficiency of the protocol and resolution protocols with the TTP, it is challenging. Consider a very simple solution regarding constructor C, evaluator E, and the TTP. Assume that C constructs the circuit such that the output is not revealed directly, but instead the output of the circuit is an encrypted version of the real output, and C knows the key. Thus, after evaluation, E will learn this encrypted output, and C and E need to perform a fair exchange of this encrypted output and the key. This approach increases the circuit size, obviously. Besides, when a dispute occurs and E goes to the TTP for resolution, she cannot efficiently prove to the TTP that she evaluated C's garbled circuit correctly. Indeed, in the solution of Cachin and Camenisch [6], the *resolution* may require work proportional to the circuit size.

Alternatively, instead of encrypting the output, C constructs a garbled circuit where the outputs are encoded with some random values (like an encryption but without increasing the circuit size) in a secret table. So, in the end of the circuit evaluation, E learns some random values such that their corresponding bits are only known by C. Then, they can fairly exchange the table and the output. However, it can be hard to ensure that E sends the correct table and construct proper resolution protocols with TTP.

Because of these issues, we employ the dual-constructor methodology [29,30], where both C and E construct circuits that output random numbers.

**Our Solution:** We show how to efficiently add fairness to any zero knowledge based secure 2PC protocol $\Gamma$ using our framework. The key points are:

- Alice and Bob employ **dual garbling technique** [29], where Alice and Bob both act as the constructor and the evaluator, with almost equal responsibilities. **The circuit constructed by Alice *only* outputs Alice's output and the circuit constructed by Bob outputs Bob's output.**
  The garbled circuit is prepared as the underlying protocol $\Gamma$ with minor differences in the construction of the input and output gates. The modification on

the input gates allow us to **check input equality** between the two circuits. Modifications on the output gates are to **hide the actual output**.

– Alice and Bob exchange the garbled circuits and evaluate each others' circuits. In the end of evaluation, **Alice learns the output labels of Bob and Bob learns the output labels of Alice, both in a hidden way**. Therefore, they need to exchange the outputs fairly after this point.

– Before **fair exchange**, they execute **input equality test** protocol to see if both of them used the same inputs for the both circuits. It is ok to abort if the test fails, because they test for input equality, not output.

– If the equality test is successful, they **verifiably escrow the other party's output labels**. This is essentially a guarantee for the other party that if this party does not send the output labels later on, (s)he can contact the TTP to get them.

– Now, they exchange output labels so that each party can individually translate them back to the actual outputs, since they come from circuits that they themselves created. If there is a dispute about the fairness, they go to the TTP for the resolution.

Overview of the resolution protocols is the following:

**Alice/Bob Resolve:** We describe the resolution for Bob, though it is completely symmetric for Alice. Remember that Bob is equipped with a verifiable escrow. But, for the TTP to decrypt it for him, Bob must prove that he acted properly. He provides output labels of Alice, and proves that they are evaluated from Alice's garbled circuit. If so, the TTP provides the decryption for Bob, who can use it to translate back to his output bits.

**Alice Abort:** Alice may try to abort the protocol and block resolution attempts with the TTP, should she not receive Bob's verifiable escrow. When she contacts the TTP, if Bob has resolved before, she obtains her output labels from the TTP. Otherwise, the TTP marks the protocol as aborted, and would deny any resolution attempt by Alice or Bob.

Note that the **TTP only sees random output labels**, but not their translation tables. Furthermore, since each circuit only evaluates to one party's output, even if the TTP colludes with the malicious party and provides the other party's output labels, those are still meaningless without the corresponding bits. Thus, a **malicious TTP may only break fairness, but not security**.

**Why Target Zero-Knowledge Proof based Garbled Circuit Protocols?** We claimed that our framework can be applied on top of any zero-knowledge proof based garbled circuit protocols. There are two reasons for this:

1. As explained above, parties commit to output labels, for enabling efficient resolutions with the TTP (one of the major problems in previous work). They must prove to each other that they committed to the correct labels as in the garbled circuits. If the underlying protocol, for example, encrypts the garbled tables using AES, then such a proof cannot be efficiently done (without cut-and-choose), whereas if the underlying encryption scheme is number-theoretic

(such as simplified Camenisch-Shoup [7,19]), then using sigma protocols [10], the correctness proofs may be done very efficiently.

2. Item 1 above leaves out the cut-and-choose way of proving. The problem is that, if cut-and-choose is employed, then there will be multiple circuits, rather than one. In our solution, parties create verifiable escrows, and the TTP may need to decrypt them. Verifiable escrow is a primitive that inherently uses zero-knowledge proofs. It is unclear how to combine the verifiable escrow idea with cut-and-choose, where multiple circuits exist, especially when the TTP needs to be able to verify and decrypt them.

In essence, one may think of our solution as a framework that can be applied on top of 2PC schemes that employ a single circuit, and use number-theoretic constructions (of encryption) for efficiency.

## 4   Making Secure 2PC Fair (Full Protocol)

**Notation:** Alice and Bob will evaluate a function $f(x,y) = (f_a(x,y), f_b(x,y))$, where Alice has an input $x$ and gets an output $f_a(x,y)$, and Bob has an input $y$ and gets an output $f_b(x,y)$, $f : \{0,1\}^\ell \times \{0,1\}^\ell \to \{0,1\}^\ell \times \{0,1\}^\ell$, where $\ell$ is a positive integer. For simplicity, we assume Alice and Bob have $\ell$-bit inputs and outputs each. Alice's input bits are $x = \{x_1, x_2, ..., x_\ell\}$ and Bob's input bits are $y = \{y_1, y_2, ..., y_\ell\}$. They use a 2PC protocol $\Gamma$ for the secure computation.

We use $\mathfrak{C}$ to represent circuit. $\mathfrak{C}_a$ outputs the Alice's output and $\mathfrak{C}_b$ outputs Bob's output. Similarly, the garbled circuit that is generated by Alice is $GC_a$ and the one generated by Bob is $GC_b$. We use apostrophe (') for the values that are generated by Bob. When we say Alice's input wires, it means that Alice provides the input for these wires. Similarly, Alice's output wires correspond to Alice's output. Bob's input and output wires have the matching meaning. An *Input Gate* is a gate that has an input wire of Alice or Bob. Similarly, an *Output Gate* is a gate that has a wire of Alice's or Bob's output.

$E_k$ shows an encryption with the key $k$. Therefore, $E_{k_1} E_{k_2}(m_1, m_2)$ means that $m_1$ and $m_2$ are both encrypted by the two keys $k_1$ and $k_2$.

Any commitments that have efficient zero knowledge proofs can be used in this framework. To exemplify the protocol we notate commitments as in Fujisaki-Okamoto commitments [11,13] and Pedersen commitments [32].

We give a review of the random numbers that are used for fairness in Table 1. The protocol steps are described in detail below (and in Fig. 1).

The TTP generates the group $\mathcal{G}_1$ that is used in $\Gamma$ and picks generators $g, h \in \mathcal{G}_1$, secret and public key pair $sk_{TTP}, pk_{TTP}$ for the verifiable escrow scheme. Additionally, he chooses a cyclic group $\mathcal{G}_2$ whose order is a large prime $q$ and randomly selects its generators $g_0, g_1, g_2$ (for the equality test). He also picks a one-way function $\phi()$. Then, he announces his public key $PK_{TTP} = [pk_{TTP}, (\mathcal{G}_1, g, h), (\mathcal{G}_2, q, g_0, g_1, g_2), \phi()]$.

Both Alice and Bob know $PK_{TTP}$ and agree on a circuit $\mathfrak{C}$ that computes $f(x,y)$ and the protocol identifier $id$ before the protocol begins.

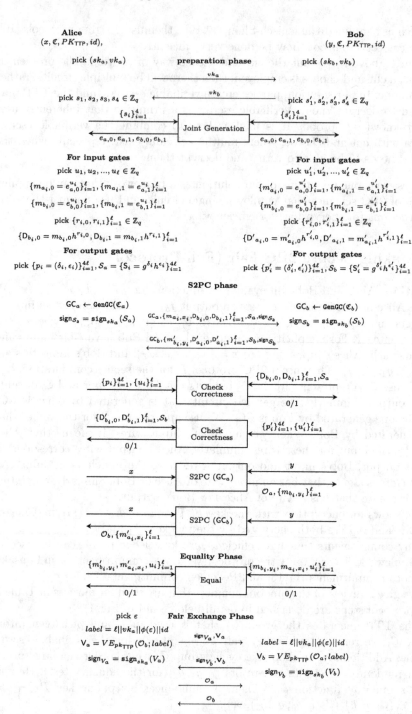

**Fig. 1.** Our framework to make a S2PC protocol fair. GenGC generates garbled circuit.

**Table 1.** The review of the random numbers used for fairness in our framework.

| Name | Form | Relation |
|------|------|----------|
| Equality-test constants | $e = g^\rho$ | There are four kinds of them, where each represents 0 or 1 and right or left. |
| Input-gate randoms | $u$ | Each input gate has them. They are private; just known by the constructors. |
| Equality-test numbers | $m = e^u$ | For each input-gate random $u$, there are four kinds of them, where each represents 0 or 1 and right or left according to $e$. |
| Output labels | $(\delta, \varepsilon)$ | They are randomly chosen pairs, each representing a row of the garbled output gates |

## Preparation Phase:

1. Alice and Bob generate private-public key pairs $(sk_a, vk_a)$ and $(sk_b, vk_b)$, respectively, for an unforgeable signature scheme. They exchange the signature verification keys $vk_a$ and $vk_b$.
   They jointly generate four equality-test constants $e_{a,0}, e_{a,1}, e_{b,0}$ and $e_{b,1}$ as described [21]. Equality test constants represent 0 and 1 for the left $(a)$ and the right $(b)$ wires of the input gates.
2. Alice and Bob separately generate the random numbers and commitments for the input and the output gates as shown in Fig. 1.
   The computations of Alice and Bob for each *input gate* $i$ are the following: input-gate numbers ($u_i$ resp. $u'_i$), the equality-test numbers ($\{t \in \{0,1\}, z \in \{a,b\} : m_{z_i,t} = e^{u_i}_{z,t}\}$ resp. $\{t \in \{0,1\}, z \in \{a,b\} : m'_{z_i,t} = e^{u'_i}_{z,t}\}$), and the commitments ($\{t \in \{0,1\} : D_{b_i,t} = m_{b_i,t} h^{r_{i,t}}\}$ resp. $\{t \in \{0,1\} : D'_{a_i,t} = m'_{a_i,t} h^{r'_{i,t}}\}$). They are used in the input equality test to show the same inputs are used for both garbled circuits.
   They generate output labels (($\delta_j, \epsilon_j$) resp. ($\delta'_j, \epsilon'_j$)) for each row of garbled-output gate $j$ and their commitments ($S_j$ resp. $S'_j$) for the *output gates*. The sets of the commitments are $\mathcal{S}_a = \{S_j\}$ resp. $\mathcal{S}_b = \{S'_j\}$. The output labels are as unique identifiers for the rows of the constructor's garbled-output gates. Only the constructor knows which row they represent, which means only the constructor knows which output bit they correspond to. This makes sure that the evaluator cannot learn the output directly.

## S2PC Phase:

1. [**Garbled Circuits:**] Alice and Bob construct their garbled circuits by following the rules of the underlying $\Gamma$ protocol with little differences on the garbled tables of the input and the output gates.
   **Input Gates:** The difference is that each garbled-table row of an input gate $i$ includes one more encryption besides the encryption of the output key. It is the encryption of either $r'_{i,0}$ or $r'_{i,1}$ representing the input of 0 and 1 for the

wire of Alice in $GC_b$ and either $r_{i,0}$, or $r_{i,1}$ representing the input of 0 and 1 for the wire of the Bob in $GC_a$. See Table 2 for the details.

*Remark:* Alice and Bob just encrypt the partial decommitments of $D_{b_i,0}, D_{b_i,1}$ and $D'_{a_i,t}, D'_{a_i,1}$, respectively because they only need to learn equality-test numbers ($m$ values) that represent their input bits. They do *not* want to reveal input-gate numbers ($u$ values) since it causes the evaluator to learn the constructor's input.

*Remark:* Note that there can be just *one* input wire of a gate (e.g., NOT gate for negation). In this case, there will be two equality-test numbers which represent 0 and 1 for this gate. Alternatively, they can agree to construct a circuit using only NAND gates [6].

**Output Gates:** Each row of the garbled output gate includes the encryption of corresponding output labels instead of encryption of real output bits (see Table 2). This is to hide the actual output from the evaluator.

2. [**Exchange:**] They exchange the constructed garbled tables along with the commitments, the signature of all commitments of the output labels ($\text{sign}_{S_a}$ resp. $\text{sign}_{S_b}$) and equality-test numbers that represents their input bits as in Fig. 1.

3. [**Check Correctness:**] They prove to each other that they performed the input and the output gates' construction honestly, via efficient zero-knowledge proofs (see the full version of the paper [21]):

   - *Proof of Input Gates* to prove that the garbled input gates contain the correct decommitment values. This is basically done in three steps:
     Firstly, prover proves that (s)he knows the decommitmets of all commitments denoted by D [7]. Secondly, prover proves that each commitment pair $D_{z,0}$ and $D_{z,1}$ commits the same value under the different bases $e_{z,0}$ and $e_{z,1}$ respectively. If the prover is Alice then $z = b_i$, if the prover is Bob then $z = a_i$. Lastly, the prover proves that each input-garbled table includes the double-encryption of partial decommitment of $D_{z,0}$ and $D_{z,1}$.
   - *Proof of Output Gates* to prove that the garbled output gates encrypt the committed output labels.

   If there is a problem in the proofs, they abort. Otherwise, they continue.

4. [**S2PC:**] Alice and Bob execute $\Gamma$, and evaluate the garbled circuit they were given. While executing $\Gamma$, Alice and Bob prove that they correctly construct their garbled circuits that evaluate $f$ by zero-knowledge proofs described in the protocol $\Gamma$. If all zero-knowledge proofs are verified, at the end of the evaluation, Alice learns the set $\mathcal{O}_b$ representing $f_b$, Bob learns the set $\mathcal{O}_a$ representing $f_a$, each including $\ell$ output labels. Besides, each party learns the set that includes equality-test numbers that represents her/his input (from the decryption of input-garbled gates). Otherwise, they abort.

**Equality Phase:** *This phase is necessary to test whether or not Alice and Bob used the same input bits for both circuit evaluations.* We use unfair version of equality test by Boudot et al. [3]; the unfair version is sufficient for our purpose.

Alice and Bob want to check, if $x_i^* = x_i$ and $y_i^* = y_i$ for the encryptions $E_{k'_{a_i,x_i}}(E_{k'_{b_i,y_i}}(k'))$ and $E_{k_{a_i,x_i^*}}(E_{k_{b_i,y_i^*}}(k))$ in each garbled input gate $i$, such

**Table 2.** The garbled Input and Output Gate for an OR gate constructed by Alice. Encryption scheme is same as the underlying protocol $\Gamma$.

| Row | Garbled input gate | Garbled output gate |
|-----|--------------------|--------------------|
| 00 | $E_{k_{a_i},0}E_{k_{b_i},0}(r_{i,0},k_0)$ | $E_{k_a,0}E_{k_b,0}(\delta_j,\varepsilon_j)$ |
| 01 | $E_{k_{a_i},0}E_{k_{b_i},1}(r_{i,1},k_1)$ | $E_{k_a,0}E_{k_b,1}(\delta_{j+1},\varepsilon_{j+1})$ |
| 10 | $E_{k_{a_i},1}E_{k_{b_i},0}(r_{i,0},k_1)$ | $E_{k_a,1}E_{k_b,0}(\delta_{j+2},\varepsilon_{j+2})$ |
| 11 | $E_{k_{a_i},1}E_{k_{b_i},1}(r_{i,1},k_1)$ | $E_{k_a,1}E_{k_b,1}(\delta_{j+3},\varepsilon_{j+3})$ |

that the first one was decrypted by Alice and the second one was decrypted by Bob. For this purpose, Alice and Bob will use the equality-test numbers $\{m_{z_i,t}, m'_{z_i,t}\}_{z\in\{a,b\},t\in\{0,1\}}$.

Assume Alice decrypted a row for an input gate $i$ and learned equality-test numbers $m'_{a_i,x_i}$ and she knows $m'_{b_i,y_i}$ since Bob sent his equality-test numbers that represents his input in the exchange step of the S2PC phase. Also assume Bob decrypted the corresponding garbled gate and similarly learned $m_{b_i,y_i^*}$ and he knows $m_{a_i,x_i^*}$ since Alice sent it in the exchange step of the S2PC phase. If they both used consistent input bits for both $GC_a$ and $GC_b$, then we expect to see that the following equation is satisfied:

$$(m'_{a_i,x_i} m'_{b_i,y_i})^{u_i} = (m_{a_i x_i^*} m_{b_i,y_i^*})^{u'_i} \tag{1}$$

The left hand side of the Eq. (1) is composed of values Alice knows since she learned $m'$ values and generated $u_i$ herself. Similarly, the right hand side values are known by Bob since he learned $m$ values and generated $u'_i$ himself. This equality should hold if $x_i^* = x_i$ and $y_i^* = y_i$ since $m'_{a_i,x_i} = e_{a,x_i^*}^{u_i}$, $m'_{b_i,y_i^*} = e_{b,y_i^*}^{u'_i}$ and $m_{a_i,x_i} = e_{a,x_i}^{u_i}$, $m_{b_i,y_i} = e_{b,y_i}^{u_i}$.

After computing their side locally in Eq. (1) for each input gate, they concatenate the results in order to hash them, where the output range of the hash function is $\mathbb{Z}_q$. Then Alice and Bob execute *Proof of Equality* protocol in [3] with the hashes.

If the equality test succeeds, they continue with the next phase.

*Remark:* Remember that the constructor did not prove that (s)he added equality-test numbers to the correct row of the encryption table. Suppose that the constructor encrypted the equality-test number that represents 0 where the evaluator's encryption key represents 1. In this case, it is sure that the equality test will fail, but the important point is that the constructor *cannot* understand which row is decrypted by the evaluator, and thus does not learn any information because he cannot cheat just in one row. If he cheats in one row, he has to change one of the other rows as well, as otherwise he fails the "Proof of Input Gates". Thus, even if the equality test fails, the evaluator might have decrypted any one of the four possibilities for the gate, and thus might have used any input bit. This also means that the equality test can be simulated, and hence reveals nothing about the input.

Note that there are some techniques to check input equality in the literature as in [23, 26, 28–30, 35] but they are based on cut-and-choose. Since the underlying protocol $\Gamma$ does not use cut-and-choose to guarantee the security, the equality test we used is more suitable here.

**Fair Exchange Phase:** In this phase, Alice and Bob exchange the outputs. Remember that the outputs are indeed randomized, and only the constructor knows their meaning. Thus, if they do not perform this fair exchange, no party learns any information about the real output (unless they resolve with the TTP, in which case they both learn their outputs).

1. Alice first picks a value $\omega$ from the domain of the one way-function $\phi$ and computes $\phi(\omega)$. Next, she creates a verifiable escrow $V_a$ including $\mathcal{O}_b$ with non-malleable label $(\ell||vk_a||\phi(\varepsilon)||id)$ as in Fig. 1. Finally, she signs $V_a$ with $sk_a$ and sends the signature $\text{sign}_{V_a}$ and $V_a$.

   With the verifiable escrow, she proves that there are $\ell$ different decommitments in the escrow that correspond to $\ell$ of the commitments in $\mathcal{S}_b$ [4,9,18]. Since Alice can just decrypt one row for every gate and so she only has one pair of keys for each gate, this proof shows that Alice decrypted Bob's garbled output tables correctly, and the verifiable escrow has the evaluation result of $GC_b$. If $V_a$ or $\text{sign}_{V_a}$ fails to verify, or if the label is not correct, then Bob aborts. Otherwise, Bob continues with the next step.

   *Remark:* $\omega$ is used in the Alice Abort protocol with the TTP to prevent Bob from claiming to be Alice and aborting after Bob Resolve. Since only Alice knows $\varepsilon$ that is a pre-image of $\phi(\varepsilon)$, Bob cannot convince the TTP.
2. Bob creates a verifiable escrow $V_b$ including $\mathcal{O}_a$ with non-malleable label the same as Alice created. He signs $V_b$ with $sk_b$ and sends the signature $\text{sign}_{V_b}$ and $V_b$.

   With the verifiable escrow, he proves that there are $\ell$ different decommitments in the escrow that correspond to $\ell$ of the commitments in $\mathcal{S}_a$ [4,9,18]. If $V_a$ or $\text{sign}_{V_a}$ fails to verify, or if the label is not correct, then Alice runs "Alice Abort" protocol with the TTP. Otherwise, Alice continues with the next step.
3. Alice sends $\mathcal{O}_b$ to Bob.
4. Bob checks if the output labels in $\mathcal{O}_b$ are correct. The output labels are correct if $\ell$ of them are the pairs that are generated by Bob. If they are correct, then he sends $\mathcal{O}_a$. If at least one of the output labels is not correct, then he does "Bob Resolve" with the TTP.
5. Alice checks if the output labels in $\mathcal{O}_a$ are correct. If they are not correct, then she does "Alice Resolve" with the TTP. Otherwise the protocol ends.

**Alice and Bob Resolve (See Fig. 2):** We explain Bob Resolve below. Alice Resolve is the same where the verifiable escrow, the signatures and $\mathcal{O}$ are Bob's values.

Bob contacts with the TTP and sends the values $V_a, \text{sign}_{V_a}, \mathcal{S}_a, \text{sign}_{\mathcal{S}_a}, \mathcal{O}_a$. He sends $\text{sign}_{\mathcal{S}_a}$ to prove that $\mathcal{S}_a$ is generated by the same party who generates

$V_a$. The TTP checks if all signatures are correct and the decommitments in $\mathcal{O}_a$ correspond to $\ell$ of the commitments in $\mathcal{S}_a$. If there is no problem, then the TTP decrypts $V_a$ with $sk_{TTP}$ and sends the values inside $V_a$ to Bob. Since Bob knows the meaning of the output labels of the garbled circuit he constructed, he effectively learns his output. The TTP remembers Alice's output $\mathcal{O}_a$, given and proven by Bob, in his database.

**Alice Abort (See Fig. 3):** When Alice contacts the TTP for abort, she sends $V_a$ and $\mathrm{sign}_a$, together with $\varepsilon$. The TTP checks that the signature is valid and $\phi(\varepsilon)$ matches the label of $V_a$. If Bob did resolve before, the TTP sends $\mathcal{O}_a$ as in Fig. 3 so that Alice can also learn her output. Otherwise, the protocol is aborted and the TTP will not honor resolution requests for this exchange.

Remark that Alice and Bob **do not** re-do the zero-knowledge proofs in the S2PC phase to the TTP because $\mathrm{sign}_{V_a}$ and $\mathrm{sign}_{V_b}$ show that both Alice and Bob execute everything correctly until the end of Equality Phase.

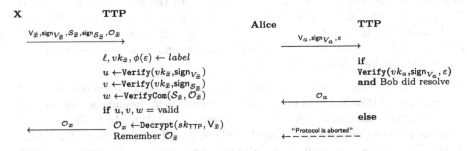

**Fig. 2.** X resolve where X $\in$ {Alice, Bob}. If X is Alice, $\bar{x}$ is $b$, otherwise $\bar{x}$ is $a$.

**Fig. 3.** Alice Abort

**Theorem 1** *Let $f : \{0,1\}^* \times \{0,1\}^* \rightarrow \{0,1\}^* \times \{0,1\}^*$ be any probabilistic polynomial time (PPT) two-party functionality. The protocol above for computing $f$ is secure and fair according to Definition 3, assuming that the TTP is semi-honest, the subprotocols that are stated in the protocol are all secure (sound and zero-knowledge), all commitments are hiding and binding [11,13], the signature scheme used is unforgeable [17], and the $\Gamma$ is a 2PC protocol secure against malicious adversaries based on Yao's garbled circuits and zero knowledge proofs.*

**Proof Sketch.** A full proof exists in the full version of the paper [21]. The important point in our proof is that after learning the input of the adversary in the real world, the simulator does *not* learn the output of the adversary from the ideal world universal party $\mathfrak{U}$ until it is guaranteed that both parties can obtain their outputs.

**Malicious Alice:** Simulator $S_B$ creates a key pair on behalf of the TTP and shares the public key with Alice. $S_B$ prepares the circuit as the simulator of $\Gamma$

with a random input $y'$ and simulates all the proofs, including the equality test. $S_B$ extracts the input $x$ of Alice as in the simulation of $\Gamma$. Here, he does not send the input of Alice directly to the ideal world trusted party $\mathfrak{U}$. He waits until it is guaranteed that Bob can also obtain his input. If, before $V_a$ is received properly, the values Alice sends are not correct or equality test is not successful, he sends ABORT to $\mathfrak{U}$. If $S_B$ receives the correct $V_a$, he sends Alice's input to $\mathfrak{U}$ and receives Alice's output. At this point, he sends $V_b$ to Alice. Afterward, if he does not receive his correct output from Alice, he simulates *Bob Resolve* by decrypting $V_a$. If Alice performs *"Alice Abort"*, then there are two options: if $S_B$ already obtained the output from $\mathfrak{U}$, $S_B$ sends output labels of Alice so that she resolves her output; otherwise, $S_B$ sends ABORT to $\mathfrak{U}$.

**Malicious Bob:** Simulator $S_A$ behaves almost the same as $S_B$. Since $S_A$ does not know the actual output of Bob, she puts random values in $V'_a$ and sends it to Bob, simulating the proof. Then $S_A$ waits for $V_b$: If Bob does not send valid values but performs *"Bob Resolve"*, then $S_A$ gives Bob's input that she extracted to $\mathfrak{U}$ and learns Bob's output so that $S_A$ is able to simulate *"Bob Resolve"*. If Bob does not send valid values and does not perform *"Bob Resolve"*, then $S_A$ sends ABORT to $\mathfrak{U}$ (simulating *"Alice Abort"*). If Bob sends $V_b$, then $S_A$ gives Bob's input to $\mathfrak{U}$ and $\mathfrak{U}$ sends back Bob's output, and finally $S_A$ sends to Bob the correct output labels accordingly.

**TTP Analysis:** As we claim, a semi-honest TTP is sufficient in our protocol because the TTP only learns output labels where their meaning is only known by the circuit constructors (Alice or Bob), and a signature. In addition, (s)he does *not* receive anything else related to the input of Alice or Bob. Therefore, if the TTP follows the protocol but also tries to learn extra information about the parties (input or output), (s)he cannot succeed.

Even if the TTP is malicious, (s)he can only break the fairness property of the protocol. A malicious TTP can collude with Alice or Bob. As seen in Theorem 1, the protocol preserves the privacy if the TTP is malicious since the TTP does not have more power than Alice or Bob. He only knows his secret key which is only used in the Fair Exchange phase.

Malicious TTP also cannot break the correctness property. In the honest Bob case (same in honest Alice case), he cannot receive wrong output since Alice can only learn one output label per gate, so (s)he can use only them. It means TTP cannot give different ones (because (s)he only knows those that Alice provides) to Bob. Thus, the TTP cannot break the correctness property.

## 5   Proving Security and Fairness Together

In this section we show the importance of proving with *full simulation* according to Definition 3. First, we define what we mean by *partial simulation* more formally and then we give contrived versions of several protocols ([6,22,34]) including ours that are obviously insecure, but can be proven fair and secure with partial simulation while it cannot be proven fair and secure with full simulation.

**Definition 5 (Partial Simulation).** *Let $f, h, g$ be the PPT functionalities where $f = g \circ h$, $h(x, y) = (h_b, h_a)$ and $g(h_b, h_a) = (f_a, f_b)$ and let $\pi_f, \pi_h, \pi_g$ be the PPT protocols to compute $f, h, g$, respectively where the first input and output of a functionality correspond to one party (Alice) and the second input and output of a functionality correspond to other party (Bob). The **partial simulation** paradigm says that $\pi_f$ computes $f$ **fairly and securely** if there exists a PPT protocol $\pi_h$ that is secure under simulation with abort [14] and there exists a PPT protocol $\pi_g$ which achieves fairness [1, 24].*

Almost all previous works (See Table 3) prove their fairness and security with partial simulation: prove security with the unfair simulation paradigm (with abort) (corresponding to proving $\pi_h$ to be a secure 2PC protocol with abort), and argue fairness (of the $\pi_g$ part, either using TTP or gradual release) separately. This is risky. Consider the following three contrived protocols where Alice and Bob want to compute functionality $f = (f_a, f_b)$ fairly and securely:

- A modification on our protocol is that the TTP gives Alice's output *along with the input of Bob* whenever Alice contacts for resolution or abort, if Bob have done "Bob Resolve" before (honest Bob is required to provide his input to the TTP in "Bob Resolve"). Here, $h = (h_a, h_b)$ is a functionality where $h_a = \mathcal{O}_a$ and $h_b = \mathcal{O}_b$ ($\pi_h$ is our protocol until the fair exchange phase, where parties only obtain random output labels), and $g$ is a functionality where $g(\mathcal{O}_a, \mathcal{O}_b) = (f_x, f_y)$ ($\pi_g$ is the fair exchange phase of our protocol with new "Alice Abort" and "Alice Resolve".). It is very easy to simulate $\pi_h$ with abort, since parties essentially learn nothing. Also, it is easy to argue about fairness of this $\pi_g$ without simulation, since at the end of resolutions, either both parties obtain their outputs or no one learns anything useful.
- The protocol which is the same as Cachin and Camenisch's protocol [6] where the only difference is that the TTP gives the other parties' inputs to the party in the resolution protocols (with similar reasoning as above).
- The modified versions of Kiraz and Schoenmakers [23] or Ruan et. al [34] protocols where the only difference is Alice sends her *input* to Bob and vice versa at the end of the gradual release.

In [23,34] partial simulation is provided only until the beginning of the gradual release phase, then fairness is argued via the fairness of the gradual release. Similarly, in [6] the partial simulation is provided for a functionality computation, then the fairness is discussed based on the parties' and TTP's behaviors. Using the same type of reasoning, their and our contrived versions can be proven fair and secure via partial simulation, and fairness can be argued since at the end of the gradual release or TTP resolutions, either both parties obtain their outputs or no one does. But, it is clear that the contrived protocols leak the inputs to the other party, becoming insecure. Observe that they can *never* be fully simulated, because *the simulator will not have access to the honest party's input* and so it cannot provide indistinguishability of ideal and real worlds.

Consequently, it is risky to argue fairness separate from the ideal/real world simulation. We do not claim that previous protocols [6,23,34] have security problems, but we want to emphasize that the partial simulation technique does *not* cover all security aspects of a protocol and should not be preferred anymore. Therefore, they should be proven with the full simulation technique.

**Importance of the Timing of the Simulator contacting the Universal Trusted Party:** The proofs of the protocols [6,23,34] are also problematic since the simulator learns the output of the computation from $\mathfrak{U}$ *before* it is guaranteed that the other party can also obtain the output. This behavior of the simulator *violates the indistinguishibility of the ideal and real worlds* because if the simulator does not receive his/her output in the real world while the parties already obtained the outputs in the ideal world, then the outputs in ideal and real worlds are distinguishable, and the simulation fails. Therefore, **the simulator must obtain the output from the universal trusted party in the ideal world,** *only after* it is guaranteed that both parties can obtain the output in the real world.

# 6    Conclusion

Table 3 presents a comparison with the most related works.

**Table 3.** Comparison of our protocol with previous works. CC denotes cut-and-choose, ZK denotes efficient zero-knowledge proofs of knowledge, GR denotes gradual release, OFE denotes efficient optimistic fair exchange, superscript $I$ denotes *inefficient* TTP, superscript $P$ denotes necessity of using a *payment* system, NS denotes *no* ideal-real simulation proof given, PS indicates *partial simulation* proof, and finally FS indicates *full simulation* proof including fairness. A check mark ✓ is put for easily identifying better techniques.

| | [33] | [34] | [23] | [25] | [6] | Ours |
|---|---|---|---|---|---|---|
| Malicious behavior | CC | CC | CC | CC/ZK | ZK | ZK |
| Fairness | GR | GR | GR | $OFE^P$ | $OFE^I$ | OFE ✓ |
| Proof technique | NS | PS | PS | FS ✓ | PS | FS ✓ |

✓ All our overhead (TTP, Alice, Bob) are dependent only on the input and output size, and **independent** of the circuit size, in contrast to [6].

✓ We require a **constant** number of rounds for fairness, contrary to gradual release based solutions [23,33,34].

✓ We do **not** necessitate a payment framework. Our fairness definition is that either both parties obtain the output, or no one does, as opposed to [25].

✓ Even if the TTP becomes malicious and colludes with one participant, he **cannot violate the security of the protocol.** On the other hand, in [25], while the Bank cannot violate 2PC security, it can maliciously deal with the balances, possibly causing a lot of headache.

✓ Finally, our protocol is proven secure in the **ideal/real simulation** paradigm (not in [33]) with **output indistinguishability** (not in [6,23,34]), and by proving fairness and security simultaneously via a **full simulation proof** (none except [25]).

**Acknowledgements.** The authors acknowledge the support of TÜBİTAK, the Scientific and Technological Research Council of Turkey, under project number 111E019, and European Union COST Action IC1306.

# References

1. Asokan, N., Shoup, V., Waidner, M.: Optimistic fair exchange of digital signatures. IEEE J. Sel. Areas Commun. **18**, 591–610 (2000)
2. Boneh, D., Naor, M.: Timed commitments. In: Bellare, M. (ed.) CRYPTO 2000. LNCS, vol. 1880, pp. 236–254. Springer, Heidelberg (2000). doi:10.1007/3-540-44598-6_15
3. Boudot, F., Schoenmakers, B., Traoré, J.: A fair and efficient solution to the socialist millionaires' problem. Discrete Appl. Math. **1–2**, 23–36 (2001)
4. Bresson, E., Stern, J.: Proofs of knowledge for non-monotone discrete-log formulae and applications. In: Chan, A.H., Gligor, V. (eds.) ISC 2002. LNCS, vol. 2433, pp. 272–288. Springer, Heidelberg (2002). doi:10.1007/3-540-45811-5_21
5. Brickell, E.F., Chaum, D., Damgård, I.B., Graaf, J.: Gradual and verifiable release of a secret (extended abstract). In: Pomerance, C. (ed.) CRYPTO 1987. LNCS, vol. 293, pp. 156–166. Springer, Heidelberg (1988). doi:10.1007/3-540-48184-2_11
6. Cachin, C., Camenisch, J.: Optimistic fair secure computation. In: Bellare, M. (ed.) CRYPTO 2000. LNCS, vol. 1880, pp. 93–111. Springer, Heidelberg (2000). doi:10.1007/3-540-44598-6_6
7. Camenisch, J., Shoup, V.: Practical verifiable encryption and decryption of discrete logarithms. In: Boneh, D. (ed.) CRYPTO 2003. LNCS, vol. 2729, pp. 126–144. Springer, Heidelberg (2003). doi:10.1007/978-3-540-45146-4_8
8. R. Cleve: Limits on the security of coin flips when half the processors are faulty. In: STOC (1986)
9. Cramer, R., Damgård, I., Schoenmakers, B.: Proofs of partial knowledge and simplified design of witness hiding protocols. In: Desmedt, Y.G. (ed.) CRYPTO 1994. LNCS, vol. 839, pp. 174–187. Springer, Heidelberg (1994). doi:10.1007/3-540-48658-5_19
10. Damgård, I.: On Sigma protocols. http://www.daimi.au.dk/~ivan/Sigma.pdf
11. Damgård, I., Fujisaki, E.: A statistically-hiding integer commitment scheme based on groups with hidden order. In: Zheng, Y. (ed.) ASIACRYPT 2002. LNCS, vol. 2501, pp. 125–142. Springer, Heidelberg (2002). doi:10.1007/3-540-36178-2_8
12. Damgård, I.B.: Practical and provably secure release of a secret and exchange of signatures. J. Cryptology **8**, 201–222 (1995)
13. Fujisaki, E., Okamoto, T.: Statistical zero knowledge protocols to prove modular polynomial relations. In: Kaliski, B.S. (ed.) CRYPTO 1997. LNCS, vol. 1294, pp. 16–30. Springer, Heidelberg (1997). doi:10.1007/BFb0052225
14. Goldreich, O.: Foundations of Cryptography: Volume 2, Basic Applications. Cambridge University Press, New York (2004)
15. Goldreich, O., Micali, S., Wigderson, A.: Proofs that yield nothing but their validity or all languages in NP have zero-knowledge proof systems. J. ACM **38**, 728 (1991)

16. Goldwasser, S., Lindell, Y.: Secure computation without agreement. In: Malkhi, D. (ed.) DISC 2002. LNCS, vol. 2508, pp. 17–32. Springer, Heidelberg (2002). doi:10. 1007/3-540-36108-1_2
17. Goldwasser, S., Micali, S., Rivest, R.: A digital signature scheme secure against adaptive chosen-message attacks. SIAM J. Comput. **17**, 281–308 (1988)
18. Henry, R., Goldberg, I.: Batch proofs of partial knowledge. In: Jacobson, M., Locasto, M., Mohassel, P., Safavi-Naini, R. (eds.) ACNS 2013. LNCS, vol. 7954, pp. 502–517. Springer, Heidelberg (2013). doi:10.1007/978-3-642-38980-1_32
19. Jarecki, S., Shmatikov, V.: Efficient two-party secure computation on committed inputs. In: Naor, M. (ed.) EUROCRYPT 2007. LNCS, vol. 4515, pp. 97–114. Springer, Heidelberg (2007). doi:10.1007/978-3-540-72540-4_6
20. Kılınç, H., Küpçü, A.: Optimally efficient multi-party fair exchange and fair secure multi-party computation. In: Nyberg, K. (ed.) CT-RSA 2015. LNCS, vol. 9048, pp. 330–349. Springer, Cham (2015). doi:10.1007/978-3-319-16715-2_18
21. Kılınç, H., Küpçü, A.: Efficiently making secure two-party computation fair. Cryptology ePrint Archive, Report 2014/896
22. Kiraz, M.S., Schoenmakers, B.: A protocol issue for the malicious case of Yao's garbled circuit construction. In: Proceedings of 27th Symposium on Information Theory in the Benelux (2006)
23. Kiraz, M.S., Schoenmakers, B.: An efficient protocol for fair secure two-party computation. In: Malkin, T. (ed.) CT-RSA 2008. LNCS, vol. 4964, pp. 88–105. Springer, Heidelberg (2008). doi:10.1007/978-3-540-79263-5_6
24. Küpçü, A., Lysyanskaya, A.: Usable optimistic fair exchange. Comput. Netw. **56**, 50–63 (2012)
25. Lindell, A.Y.: Legally-enforceable fairness in secure two-party computation. In: Malkin, T. (ed.) CT-RSA 2008. LNCS, vol. 4964, pp. 121–137. Springer, Heidelberg (2008). doi:10.1007/978-3-540-79263-5_8
26. Lindell, Y., Pinkas, B.: An efficient protocol for secure two-party computation in the presence of malicious adversaries. In: Naor, M. (ed.) EUROCRYPT 2007. LNCS, vol. 4515, pp. 52–78. Springer, Heidelberg (2007). doi:10.1007/ 978-3-540-72540-4_4
27. Lindell, Y., Pinkas, B.: Secure multiparty computation for privacy-preserving data mining. J. Privacy Confidentiality **1**, 59–98 (2009)
28. Lindell, Y., Pinkas, B.: Secure two-party computation via cut-and-choose oblivious transfer. J. Cryptology **25**, 680–722 (2012)
29. Mohassel, P., Franklin, M.: Efficiency tradeoffs for malicious two-party computation. In: Yung, M., Dodis, Y., Kiayias, A., Malkin, T. (eds.) PKC 2006. LNCS, vol. 3958, pp. 458–473. Springer, Heidelberg (2006). doi:10.1007/11745853_30
30. Mohassel, P., Riva, B.: Garbled circuits checking garbled circuits: more efficient and secure two-party computation. In: Canetti, R., Garay, J.A. (eds.) CRYPTO 2013. LNCS, vol. 8043, pp. 36–53. Springer, Heidelberg (2013). doi:10.1007/ 978-3-642-40084-1_3
31. Nielsen, J.B., Orlandi, C.: LEGO for two-party secure computation. In: Reingold, O. (ed.) TCC 2009. LNCS, vol. 5444, pp. 368–386. Springer, Heidelberg (2009). doi:10.1007/978-3-642-00457-5_22
32. Pedersen, T.P.: Non-interactive and information-theoretic secure verifiable secret sharing. In: Feigenbaum, J. (ed.) CRYPTO 1991. LNCS, vol. 576, pp. 129–140. Springer, Heidelberg (1992). doi:10.1007/3-540-46766-1_9
33. Pinkas, B.: Fair secure two-party computation. In: Biham, E. (ed.) EUROCRYPT 2003. LNCS, vol. 2656, pp. 87–105. Springer, Heidelberg (2003). doi:10.1007/ 3-540-39200-9_6

34. Ruan, O., Chen, J., Zhou, J., Cui, Y., Zhang, M.: An efficient fair UC-secure protocol for two-party computation. Secur. Commun. Netw. **7**, 1253–1263 (2013)
35. shelat, A., Shen, C.: Two-output secure computation with malicious adversaries. In: Paterson, K.G. (ed.) EUROCRYPT 2011. LNCS, vol. 6632, pp. 386–405. Springer, Heidelberg (2011). doi:10.1007/978-3-642-20465-4_22
36. Shoup, V., Gennaro, R.: Securing threshold cryptosystems against chosen ciphertext attack. In: Nyberg, K. (ed.) EUROCRYPT 1998. LNCS, vol. 1403, pp. 1–16. Springer, Heidelberg (1998). doi:10.1007/BFb0054113
37. Woodruff, D.P.: Revisiting the efficiency of malicious two-party computation. In: Naor, M. (ed.) EUROCRYPT 2007. LNCS, vol. 4515, pp. 79–96. Springer, Heidelberg (2007). doi:10.1007/978-3-540-72540-4_5
38. Yao, A.C.: Protocols for secure computations. In: FOCS (1982)

# Fast Optimistically Fair Cut-and-Choose 2PC

Alptekin Küpçü[1] and Payman Mohassel[2(✉)]

[1] Koç University, İstanbul, Turkey
akupcu@ku.edu.tr
[2] Yahoo Labs, Sunnyvale, USA
payman.mohassel@gmail.com

**Abstract.** Secure two party computation (2PC) is a well-studied problem with many real world applications. Due to Cleve's result on general impossibility of fairness, however, the state-of-the-art solutions only provide security with abort. We investigate fairness for 2PC in presence of a trusted Arbiter, in an optimistic setting where the Arbiter is not involved if the parties act fairly. Existing fair solutions in this setting are by far less efficient than the fastest unfair 2PC.

We close this efficiency gap by designing protocols for fair 2PC with covert and malicious security that have competitive performance with the state-of-the-art unfair constructions. In particular, our protocols only requires the exchange of a few extra messages with sizes that only depend on the output length; the Arbiter's load is independent of the computation size; and a malicious Arbiter can only break fairness, but not covert/malicious security even if he colludes with a party. Finally, our solutions are designed to work with the state-of-the-art optimizations applicable to garbled circuits and cut-and-choose 2PC such as free-XOR, half-gates, and the cheating-recovery paradigm.

**Keywords:** Secure two-party computation · Covert adversaries · Cut-and-choose · Garbled circuits · Fair secure computation · Optimistic fair exchange

## 1 Introduction

In electronic commerce, privacy and fairness are two sought-after properties as depicted in work related to contract signing and fair exchange [5,6,8,9,14,21,49]. Fair exchange is used in electronic payments to buy or barter items [12,43] and contract signing is often used to ensure fairness: either all parties sign and agree on the contract, or the contract is invalid.

Fair secure two-party computation (2PC), a fundamental problem in cryptography, can be used to address both the privacy and fairness concerns, simultaneously. Alice and Bob would like to jointly compute a function of their private inputs, such that nothing other than the output leaks, and either both parties

---

A. Küpçü—We thank TÜBİTAK, the Scientific and Technological Research Council of Turkey, project 111E019, and European Union COST Action IC1306.

J. Grossklags and B. Preneel (Eds.): FC 2016, LNCS 9603, pp. 208–228, 2017.
DOI: 10.1007/978-3-662-54970-4_12

learn the output or either do (*e.g.* two banks trying to calculate a joint credit score for a customer, without giving away critical private information). Unfortunately, however, there is a significant efficiency gap between secure 2PC that achieve fairness and their unfair counterparts that have been the subject of many recent implementations and optimizations.

**2PC Without Fairness:** Yao [61] introduced the first 2PC with security against honest-but-curious adversaries [46] and a large body of recent work has focused on making 2PC practical in presence of stronger (covert and malicious) adversaries [7,23,45,47,50,54].

The *cut-and-choose* paradigm is a popular method for enhancing the security of Yao's garbled circuit protocol to the case of *malicious* (or covert) adversaries where the players can deviate arbitrarily. In a nutshell, in this paradigm, one player (Alice) garbles many circuits while the other player (Bob) checks a randomly chosen subset (to ensure that the garbling was done correctly) and evaluates the rest. Until recently, many existing solutions (*e.g.* [47,48,51,52,59,60]) required garbling at least $3s$ circuits to detect cheating with probability $1 - 2^{-s}$. The high number of garbled circuits is due to the fact that all these constructions ask that the evaluator computes a "majority output" and, for it to be valid, require that more than half of the evaluated circuits are correct. For the majority output to be valid, parties also need to enforce equality of the garbler's input to the majority of the circuits evaluated. This is often handled via a procedure called **input-consistency** check.

The recent work of Lindell [45] shows how to reduce the number of garbled circuits by a factor of 3.[1] In this approach, the second player evaluates the unchecked circuits, but is content with computing only one correct output (instead of a majority output) due to a **cheating-detection** component. This allows one to reduce the number of circuits to $s$ and still achieve $1 - 2^{-s}$ security.

A more modest security guarantee for 2PC is **covert security**, proposed by Aumann and Lindell [7], which provides a practical alternative to the malicious setting. In this setting, the adversary can cheat with some small but non-negligible probability. The rationale is that a reputable real-world entity will not risk getting caught with non-negligible probability due to loss of reputation or the legal/economical costs. The protocols in the covert setting are more efficient than their malicious counterparts. For instance, in the cut-and-choose paradigm, one can settle for only garbling $s = 5$ circuits if $1 - 1/s = 4/5$ probability of getting caught is prohibitive enough. Back to our two banks computing a customer's credit score scenario, the financial losses when a bank gets caught cheating can be seen as prohibitive as a negligible probability of cheating.

**2PC with Fairness:** All the above-mentioned work focus on security with abort, where the malicious party is allowed to abort the protocol *after* he learns the output of the computation, but *before* the honest party obtains the output, because it is known that achieving general fairness is impossible [20]. This limits the real world applicability of the most efficient solutions. An interested

---

[1] An alternative approach for reducing the number of circuits by a factor of 1.5 was introduced by [27].

corporation is less likely to adopt 2PC solutions if it has to risk being at a competitive disadvantage by revealing the outcome of the computation to a competitor without learning it itself.

There are two main approaches for achieving fairness in general-purpose 2PC.[2] (i) **Gradual release**-based approaches let Alice and Bob reveal each other's output piece by piece, using super-constant rounds [33,55,57,58]. (ii) **Arbiter**-based approaches achieve constant round complexity by assuming that a trusted third party is available when needed [18,31,32,44]. **Optimistic** approaches employ the Arbiter only if there is a dispute among the parties [5].

The most relevant work to ours is that of Cachin and Camenisch [18], and the follow up work of [31], in the same optimistic Arbiter-based setting. Both constructions utilize zero-knowledge proofs that require public-key operations, and hence have a high computational cost compared to the state-of-the-art cut-and-choose 2PC. Furthermore, in [18], the Arbiter may need to redo almost the whole computation in case of a malicious behavior, which creates a bottleneck in the system.

Lindell's optimistic framework [44], on the other hand, necessitates an electronic payment system. It is possible that one party obtains the output of the computation, whereas the other obtains a payment. [1,2,15,30,37,43] also employ such penalty-based fairness models. These constructions are incomparable to ours as they work in a different setting and make different assumptions. See Table 1 for a list of the main differences between these work and ours.

**Table 1.** Comparison to the most related previous work.

| [18] | [44] | [31] |
|---|---|---|
| Resolutions with Arbiter take time proportional to the circuit size | Requires a payment system and employs penalty-based fairness | Efficiently adds fairness, but to zero-knowledge based 2PC protocols only |

**Our Contribution:** In this paper we investigate fairness for 2PC in presence of a trusted Arbiter in an optimistic setting, where the Arbiter is not involved if the parties act fairly. We design efficient protocols for fair 2PC with security against covert and malicious adversaries. Our constructions follow the cut-and-choose paradigm, and for the first time, close the efficiency gap between fair 2PC and the state-of-the-art unfair solutions, in this setting. In particular:

✓ The overhead of our protocols against state-of-the-art unfair solutions is small; only a constant number of extra rounds and a few messages with sizes that *only* depend on the output length.

✓ The Arbiter's load is minimal, and *independent* of the size of computation.

---

[2] A different line of work focuses on achieving fairness not in general but for specific applications [3,16,17,22,25].

✓ A malicious Arbiter can *only* break fairness, but not covert/malicious security even if he colludes with a party. We prove this via a simulator for the usual security with abort definition, when the adversary is also controlling the Arbiter.

✓ Our protocols are *compatible* with optimizations applicable to cut-and-choose 2PC such as free-XOR [36], FleXor [35], and half-gates [62]. It also utilizes the cheating-recovery paradigm, and hence uses a reduced number of garbled circuits. These render our protocols *the most efficient* fair secure computation protocols to date.

✓ Our work is the first to consider fairness in the covert adversary model.

## 2 Overview of Our Constructions

We review the high level ideas behind our covert and malicious 2PC constructions next, emphasizing the non-trivial parts. Our starting point in each case is the state-of-the-art protocol with security with abort (in the cut-and-choose paradigm). We then show how to enhance and modify each at very low cost in order to obtain fairness in the presence of an Arbiter.

Some of our techniques are similar to that of Kılınç and Küpçü [31] who also provide an efficient solution for fair 2PC in the same setting. Similar to ours, their solution employs commitments to output labels, and verifiable escrows. But they instantiate these using zero-knowledge proofs of knowledge. In fact, verifiable escrow inherently employs zero-knowledge proofs. When one switches to the cut-and-choose setting, it is unclear how to deal with the multitude of such commitments and verifiable escrows, and still preserve correctness and efficiency. Our solutions are the first to combine optimistic Arbiter-based fairness and the cut-and-choose paradigm efficiently.

### 2.1 Fair Covert 2PC

There are various ways of combining fairness and covert security in a simulation-based definition. In this paper we consider the natural notion where both fairness and correctness/privacy are guaranteed with a reasonable (not all-but-negligible) probability $1 - \epsilon$ but both fairness and correctness/privacy are lost with probability $\epsilon$ against active cheating. A related notion to fairness in the covert setting is $1/p$ security [24, 28]. In that line of work [10, 11, 26, 53], the ideal world provides complete fairness (as in our case for malicious adversaries), but the simulation only needs to achieve $1/p$ indistinguishability between the ideal and real worlds. Our approach is slightly different: we directly take the covert adversary model [4, 7], and modify it to preserve fairness unless the adversary cheats and remains undetected. Note that the $1/p$ security does not explicitly model detection of the adversary's misbehavior. It is an interesting question to understand the relation between the two notions. Next, we review the main technical difficulties in our covert construction.

**Security with Abort.** Recall the covert 2PC protocol of Aumann and Lindell [7]. Alice generates $s$ garbled circuits $\mathsf{GC}_1, \ldots, \mathsf{GC}_s$. Then, the parties perform $\ell$ (number of input bits) oblivious transfers (OTs) for Bob to learn his garbled inputs (this is intentionally done for all $s$ circuits and before the opening). Alice sends the $s$ garbled circuits to Bob. Parties then perform a coin-toss to choose a random index $e \in \{1, \ldots, s\}$. Alice opens the secrets for all garbled circuits and OTs except for the $e^{th}$ one. Bob checks correctness of the opened circuits and the corresponding OTs, and aborts if cheating is detected. Else, Alice sends her garbled inputs for the $e^{th}$ circuit. Bob evaluates the circuit and learns his own output. He also obtains the garbled values for Alice's output, which he sends to her for translation.

It is easy to see that the above construction is not fair. We now highlight the main changes we make to this protocol to achieve fairness.

**Delay Evaluator's Output Translation.** Note that Bob can abort the protocol immediately after learning his output and without forwarding Alice's output to her. Therefore, we modify the protocol so that Alice does *not* send to Bob the translation table for his output (mapping output labels to actual bits) *until* he sends Alice's garbled output to her. But note that this trivial change fails since now Alice can abort before sending the translation table to Bob.

Hence, we need to ensure that if Alice aborts at this stage, Bob has enough information to invoke an output resolution protocol with the Arbiter and show evidence that he has been following the steps of the protocol and hence deserves to know the output. After checking Bob's claim, the Arbiter should be able to provide him with sufficient information to decode his output.

**Prove Bob's Honesty to the Arbiter.** Notice that efficiently proving this is a non-trivial task. For example, in [18], the Arbiter and the resolving party re-perform almost the whole computation for this purpose. In our case, Bob's proof of following through with the protocol will be the garbled output he computes for Alice's output. Note that due to the *output-authenticity* property of the garbling scheme, Bob cannot forge this value except if he honestly computes the output. In order to enable the Arbiter to check the validity of Bob's claimed output label, Alice will send hashes of her output labels (in permuted order) to Bob along with the garbled circuits, and a signature for the $e^{th}$ one. Bob verifies validity of these hashes for the opened circuits. Now when he goes to the Arbiter, he shows both the output labels he obtained for Alice's output, and the signed hashes for the $e^{th}$ circuit. The Arbiter can verify that the two are consistent, by ensuring that there is one output label provided per pair.

**Equip the Arbiter with the Translation Table for Bob's Output.** Furthermore, the Arbiter should have sufficient information to pass along to Bob for decoding his output. Hence, Alice encrypts the translation table for Bob's output under the Arbiter's public key and sends it to Bob along with the garbled circuits, and a signature for the $e^{th}$ one. Bob checks validity of these encryptions for the opened circuits. Once Bob's claim of behaving honestly is verified, the Arbiter can decrypt the translation table, and send it to Bob for him to decode his output. The signature is needed to make sure that Bob is sending a legitimate decoding table for decryption. Since Bob verified the opened ones, he is ensured, with good probability, that the $e^{th}$ decoding table is proper.

**Simulation-Based Proof with Fairness.** One important difference between our proof and those of standard 2PC is that in our case the ideal trusted party must only be contacted by the simulator once it is certain that both parties can obtain the output, as first observed by Kılınç and Küpçü [31] for indistinguishability of the ideal and real world outputs. Therefore, to overcome this difficulty, Alice also commits to Bob's output translation tables as $c_i^B$ using a trapdoor commitment, and opens them for the opened circuits. Bob ensures that the committed and encrypted translation tables are the same (in fact, we encrypt the commitment openings). For the $e^{th}$ circuit, she opens $c_e^B$ at the last step of the protocol. The reason we need these commitments is that, unlike standard covert 2PC, the Alice simulator in the proof for the case of corrupted Bob does not have $f_B(x_A, x_B')$ when sending the garbled circuits (since in the fair protocol neither party may learn the output at this stage), and hence cannot embed the output in the $e^{th}$ one at that stage. With trapdoor commitments, at a later stage, she is able to open the translation to something different in order to ensure the "fake" evaluation circuit evaluates to the correct output $f_B(x_A, x_B')$. The hiding property of the commitment scheme ensures indistinguishability of the simulator's actions.

**Handle Premature Resolutions.** The parties have the right to contact the Arbiter. But they may choose to do so at a stage other than the prescribed one. For example, Bob may invoke the output resolution before he sends Alice's output labels to her. This behavior is mitigated by requiring that Bob provides the Arbiter with Alice's output labels that match the signed decoding table. Due to output authenticity of the garbling scheme and unforgeability of the signature scheme, Bob cannot cheat against the Arbiter and must provide correct labels. Later on, Alice can recover her output through her own output resolution protocol. A timeout mechanism ensures that Bob must contact the Arbiter during a predefined time[3], and immediately after that Alice can contact the Arbiter, without waiting indefinitely.

**A Note on Synchronicity.** Observe that we employ a timeout for resolutions with the Arbiter. Katz et al. [29] define a very nice framework for integrating synchronicity in the Universal Composability [19] framework. They provide a clock functionality which allows all honest parties to proceed further once a particular clock signal is reached, allowing for synchronous protocols. In that setting, they show input completeness and guaranteed termination can be achieved together (though not necessarily fairness). In our protocols, the only place we employ loosely synchronized clocks is for resolutions with the Arbiter. The remaining (optimistic) part of the protocol employs no synchronicity assumptions (just local network timeouts). There are two main reasons we choose to proceed this

---

[3] Such timeout mechanisms are easy to implement and standard in the optimistic fair exchange literature (see e.g. [5,43]).

way: (1) Due to a result by Küpçü and Lysyanskaya [41] (see also [40]), if one would like to employ multiple autonomous (independent) entities to replace a single trusted Arbiter, we are forced to employ timing models. (2) Optimistic fair exchange literature shows that the timeout-based resolutions can be exchanged with slightly more expensive protocols (with one more round) that provide fairness without requiring timeouts (see e.g. [5,43]). We believe a similar methodology may be employed here to replace the timeouts, and leave such an extension to our protocols as future work.

**Proof overview.** We obtain security against malicious Bob as follows: The simulator acts as Alice, except that she commits to and encrypts random values instead of actual output decoding table in $c_e^B, d_e^B$. Towards the end, if the simulator obtains proper output labels for Alice's output from the adversarial Bob, then she contacts the ideal trusted party to learn Bob's output and simulate opening of $c_e^B$ to the actual values. Hiding commitments ensure indistinguishability of Alice's behavior. If, instead of sending them directly to Alice, Bob contacts the Arbiter and performs a proper resolution, the simulator simulates the Arbiter, and upon receiving proper output labels for Alice, contacts the ideal trusted party for obtaining Bob's output. She then sends the corresponding decoding table as if it was the decryption of $d_e^B$. Semantic security ensures indistinguishability of Alice's and Arbiter's behavior.

For security against covert Alice, different from the unfair scenario, the simulator contacts the ideal trusted party if Alice acts properly, and obtains Alice's output. He sends the corresponding labels back to Alice. He simulates by himself Bob's Arbiter resolution should Alice not respond back with Bob's output labels' openings. If Alice later contacts the Arbiter for resolution, he returns back Alice's output labels again.

## 2.2    Fair Malicious 2PC

**Security with Abort.** Our starting point is the cut-and-choose 2PC of Lindell [45], which contains a *cheating-detection* component to remove the requirement that majority of the circuits are correct, and hence reduce the number of circuits by a factor of 3.

In this protocol, Alice garbles $s$ circuits $GC_1, \ldots, GC_s$ with the exception that she uses *the same output labels for all circuits*. Parties also perform $\ell$ OTs for Bob to learn his input labels. Bob then chooses a random subset of these circuits to be evaluated, and the rest are to be opened and checked for correctness later. Bob evaluates the evaluation circuits. Since output labels are reused for all circuits, Bob expects to retrieve the same labels from all evaluations. If this is indeed the case, he only needs to ensure that one of the evaluations was correct in order to make sure he has the correct output. If Bob obtains different labels for at least a single output wire, he uses the two distinct labels $W_0$ and $W_1$ corresponding to values 0 and 1, as his proof of Alice's cheating.

At this stage, parties engage in a cheating-detection phase, which itself is a malicious cut-and-choose 2PC for evaluating a cheating-detection (CD) circuit. This cut-and-choose is performed using $3s$ circuits (and a majority output), but since the CD circuit is significantly smaller, this will be a small overhead, independent of the actual circuit's size. The CD circuit takes $W_0$ and $W_1$ as Bob's input (his evidence of Alice's cheating), and takes Alice's input $x_A$ to the original computation as her input. If Bob's two labels are valid proofs (Alice embeds the output labels in the CD circuits, and the CD circuit checks whether Bob's two labels are among them), he learns Alice's input $x_A$ and can compute $f(x_A, x_B)$ on his own. Otherwise he learns a random value. It is important that Alice does not know whether Bob learned the output by evaluating the computation circuits or the cheating-detection circuits. Alice then opens the check circuits and Bob aborts if any of the checks fail. Else, he sends Alice's output labels to her.

**Handle Alice's Input Consistency.** Deviating from [45], we handle the consistency of Alice's inputs using the technique of [60], as it seems more suitable for the tweaks we need to make to input-consistency. In this approach a universal hash function (UH) is evaluated on her input inside the circuits, and Bob verifies that the output of this function is the same in all circuits. Alice's input is padded with a short random string $r_x$ in order to increase its entropy and reduce the amount of information that can be learned about the input from the output of the UH. Let $\ell$ be the input length and $s'$ be a security parameter. [60] shows that a random matrix of dimensions $s' \times (\ell + 2s' + \log s')$ over $GF(2)$ can be used as a UH, where the evaluation consists of multiplying this matrix with the input vector (and getting a vector of length $s'$).

**Delay Bob's Output via a One-time Pad.** Similar to the covert 2PC, it is easy to see that the above construction is not fair. In particular, Bob can abort the protocol immediately after learning his output and without forwarding Alice's output to her. But unlike our fair covert 2PC, delaying the transmission of the output translation table is *not* sufficient for preventing Bob from learning his output early. Since the same output labels are used for all circuits and a fraction of them are opened, Bob can reconstruct the translation table on his own after the opening phase, and learn his output.

To overcome this issue, we encrypt Bob's output using a one-time pad $pad_B$ that is Alice's additional input to the computation circuit. In particular, the circuit returns $f_B(x_A, x_B) \oplus pad_B$ as Bob's output, and the $pad_B$ itself is only revealed in the final step of the protocol. Alice's output in the circuit is also encrypted using a separate pad $pad_A$ of her choice, to prevent Bob from learning her output even after the opening.

**Commit to the Consistent Pad.** Note that simply revealing the $pad_B$ to Bob does not provide Bob with sufficient guarantee that it is the same $pad_B$ Alice used in the computation. Hence, for each circuit Alice sends a trapdoor commitment $c_i^B$ to the translation table $\mathsf{PadDec}_i$ for the input wires associated with $pad_B$. She also encrypts the opening of this commitment as $d_i^B$ using the Arbiter's public key, and signs it for resolution purposes. For the opened circuits, $c_i^B$ and $d_i^B$ are opened and checked. In the final stage, in order to reveal $pad_B$, Alice opens $c_i^B$ for the evaluated circuits. But, we are not done yet. Bob learns one or more pad values used in the evaluation circuits, and needs to determine which is the correct one for decrypting his output. To facilitate this, we apply a separate UH to $pad_B$ (i.e. $M_p \cdot (pad_B \| r_p)$ for a random matrix $M_p$) in the computation circuits, which Bob uses in the final stage to determine the "correct" pad among those retrieved. Without this, we could not have guaranteed correctness.

**Simulate with Fairness.** For simulation purposes, similar to the fair covert 2PC, the fact that the simulator can open $c_i^B$ to an arbitrary pad in the final stage allows the simulation to go through by postponing the query to the ideal trusted party for obtaining the output, until we are sure both parties can learn the output. Remember that such a simulation is a necessity for simulating fair secure computation protocols properly [31].

**Commit to Alice's Output Early.** Similar to the fair covert 2PC, we also need to ensure that if Alice aborts before revealing $pad_B$, Bob has enough information to invoke an output resolution protocol with the Arbiter and show evidence that he has been following the steps of the protocol. In the covert protocol, we used the output-authenticity property of the garbling scheme for this purpose, but in the current protocol, output-authenticity is lost after the opening stage, since all circuits use the *same output labels*. To circumvent this issue, we have Bob commit to the output labels for Alice's output *before* the opening stage, and have Alice sign the commitment. In case of a resolution, Bob opens the signed commitment for the Arbiter, who checks its correctness and consistency with a signed translation table provided by Alice, and only then decrypts $d_i^B$ escrows for Bob to learn the pads and obtain his output.

**Fix Cheating-Detection.** Note that in regular cheating-detection, Bob only learns $x_A$ and hence the plaintext version of Alice's output $f_A(x_A, x_B)$. But, Bob needs to commit to the output labels for Alice's output, and because the output translation table of Alice corresponds to a padded output, knowing $f_A(x_A, x_B)$ is not sufficient for simulation. Therefore, we need to modify the CD circuit as well. We fix this by having the CD circuit also output $pad_A$. Bob can now compute $f_A(x_A, x_B) \oplus pad_A$, and use Alice's output translation table $\mathsf{GDec}^A$ to determine which evaluated circuit returned the correct output (we know there is at least one such circuit with all but negligible probability). He commits to those labels as Alice's output labels.

**Proof overview.** Our proofs are very similar in essence to the above malicious Bob case. Simulator Alice would commit to and encrypt random values, and later when she obtains the actual output from the ideal trusted party, she would simulate opening them to the correct values. For malicious Alice case, simulator Bob also commits to random labels for Alice's outputs, and later simulates opening them to proper labels.

# 3  Preliminaries

Bellare et al. [13] introduce the notion of a **garbling scheme** Garble as a cryptographic primitive. Besides the standard privacy guarantees, we heavily take advantage of the *output-authenticity* of a garbling scheme, which intuitively guarantees that the evaluator cannot forge valid output labels except by honestly evaluating the garbled circuit.

In a standard oblivious transfer (OT) protocol [56], the receiver has a selection bit $\sigma$, and the sender has two messages $a_0, a_1$. At the end of the protocol, the receiver learns $a_\sigma$ while the sender does not learn anything. In a **committing oblivious transfer** [34,59], at the end of the interaction, the receiver also receives a commitment to the sender's input messages, and the sender obtains the opening to those commitments. As a result, the receiver can ask the sender to open his messages at a later stage. Efficient constructions for committing OT were proposed in [52,59].

The **optimistic fair exchange** literature includes many implementation details we skip here for the sake of clarity (see e.g. [5,41,42]). If Alice already registered her signature verification key with the Arbiter, our protocol can be employed as is. But, if we want anonymity, then the Arbiter must have a way of obtaining this verification key. The standard mechanism is to put it into the label of a labeled encryption scheme. In our case, Alice can generate a new key pair for each computation (or even circuit) and put the verification key into the label of $d_i^B$ encryptions, and Bob can verify the signatures using this verification key. The Arbiter can then also use this key for verification. Details such as these and how to handle timeouts without tight synchronization are well-discussed in the previous work [5,38,39,43], and hence we do not repeat for the sake of space.

## 4 Protocols

Due to the page limitations, we defer the security definitions of ideal and real worlds for fair secure two party computation, as well as full security proofs via simulation to the full version [63]. Both protocols remain secure in the unfair sense even if the Arbiter actively cheats and colludes with one of the parties.

In Figs. 1 and 2 we provide a full description of our fair covert 2PC, and Figs. 8 and 9 show the resolutions with the Arbiter for Bob and Alice, respectively. Figures 3, 4, 5, 6 and 7 describe the full protocol fairly secure against malicious parties, and Figs. 10 and 11 show the resolutions with the Arbiter for Bob and

**Table 2.** Overhead for fairness (Covert). Round is a single message. $s$ is the statistical security parameter, $m$ is Bob's output length.

| Extra rounds | Extra messages' size | Operation type |
|---|---|---|
| 1 | $O(sm)$ | Public Key |

**Table 3.** Overhead for fairness (Malicious). Round is a single message. $s$ is the statistical security parameter, $m$ is the output length, $t$ is a security parameter for input consistency.

| Extra rounds | Extra input length | Extra messages' size | Operation type |
|---|---|---|---|
| 3 | $O(m+t)$ | $O(s(m+t))$ | Public Key |

**Alice's input:** $x_A \in \{0,1\}^{\ell}$. **Bob's input:** $x_B \in \{0,1\}^{\ell}$.

**Common input:** Alice and Bob agree on the description of a circuit $C$, where $C(x_A, x_B) = f(x_A, x_B) = (f_A(x_A, x_B), f_B(x_A, x_B))$, and a second-preimage resistant hash function $H : \{0,1\}^* \to \{0,1\}^{\ell}$.

$s$ is a statistical security parameter that is inversely proportional to the bound on the cheating probability. $L$ is a computational security parameter, so, for example, each key label is $L$-bits long. Let $\mathsf{TCommit}(\cdot)$ be a trapdoor commitment scheme.

**Setup:** Let $(PK_T, SK_T)$ be the Arbiter's key pair for a public key encryption, and $(SK_A, VK_A)$ be the signing-verification key-pair for a digital signature scheme for Alice. At the beginning of the protocol, both parties obtain the Arbiter's public key from the Arbiter. Alice sends her verification key to Bob and the Arbiter.

**Output:** Alice learns an $m$-bit string $f_A(x_A, x_B)$ and Bob learns an $m$-bit string $f_B(x_A, x_B)$.

---

**Alice Prepares the Garbled Circuits.**

1. For $1 \le i \le s$, Alice computes $\mathsf{GC}_i \leftarrow \mathsf{Garble}(C)$.
2. Let $\mathsf{in}_b^{A,i,j}$ denote the key for bit $b$ for Alice's $j^{th}$ input wire in the $i^{th}$ garbled circuit for $b \in \{0,1\}$, $1 \le i \le s$, and $1 \le j \le \ell$. $\mathsf{in}_b^{B,i,j}$ is defined similarly for Bob's input labels.
3. Let $\mathsf{out}_b^{A,i,j}$ denote the key for bit $b$ for Alice's $j^{th}$ output wire in the $i^{th}$ garbled circuit. $\mathsf{out}_b^{B,i,j}$ is used for Bob's output labels.
4. Alice lets $\mathsf{GDec}_i^B = \{\mathsf{out}_0^{B,i,j}, \mathsf{out}_1^{B,i,j}\}_{j=1}^m$ be the decoding table for Bob's output.
5. Alice computes $\mathsf{GDec}_i^A = \{H(\mathsf{out}_{b_{i,j}}^{A,i,j}), H(\mathsf{out}_{\neg b_{i,j}}^{A,i,j})\}_{j=1}^m$ for random bits $b_{i,j}$ as the output validity-checking table for her output. [This table is randomly permuted based on the bits $b_{i,j}$ such that in case of output resolution, the Arbiter can check validity of output labels without learning their actual value.]
6. She computes $c_i^B = \mathsf{TCommit}(\mathsf{GDec}_i^B)$ as the commitment to Bob's output decoding table. Let $\mathsf{GDecOpen}_i^B$ be the opening of this commitment. She encrypts this opening as $d_i^B = E_{PK_T}(\mathsf{GDecOpen}_i^B)$ using the Arbiter's public key. [$\mathsf{GDec}_i^A$ and $d_i^B$ will be used by the Arbiter to verify Bob's honesty, and give back Bob's output decoding table, respectively. $c_i^B$ will be employed by Bob to ensure that Alice behaves honestly at the last step. Note that $\mathsf{GDec}_i^A$ is computed using a second-preimage resistant hash function, whereas $c_i^B$ is computed via trapdoor commitments.]
7. Alice signs those as $\sigma_i = Sign(SK_A, (sid, \mathsf{GDec}_i^A, d_i^B))$. [This signature will tie the two decryption tables to the same circuit, and be checked by the Arbiter. $sid$ is the unique session identifier.]

**Oblivious Transfer for Bob's Input.**

1. Alice and Bob engage in $\ell$ committed OTs, where in the $j^{th}$ OT, Bob's input is $x_{B,j}$ and Alice input is a pair where the first component is $[\mathsf{in}_0^{B,1,j}, \ldots, \mathsf{in}_0^{B,s,j}]$ and the second component is $[\mathsf{in}_1^{B,1,j}, \ldots, \mathsf{in}_1^{B,s,j}]$. As a result, Bob learns $\mathsf{in}_{x_{B,j}}^{B,i,j}$ for $1 \le i \le s$, $1 \le j \le \ell$.

**Alice Sends the Circuits.**

1. Alice sends $\{\mathsf{GC}_i, \mathsf{GDec}_i^A, c_i^B, d_i^B\}_{i=1}^s$ to Bob.

---

**Fig. 1.** Optimistic fair **Covert** 2PC

Alice, respectively. The vertical lines in the figures represent parts that would not have existed in the unfair counterpart. Tables 2 and 3 summarize the overhead of adding fairness in covert and malicious protocols, respectively.

---

**OT-based Challenge Generation.**

1. Bob picks a random challenge index $e$, lets $b_e = 0$, and $b_i = 1$ for all $i \neq e$.
2. Alice and Bob run $s$ OTs where Bob's input (as the receiver) in the $i^{th}$ OT is $b_i$ while Alice (as the sender) inputs a pair where the first component is her garbled inputs $\{in_{X_{A,j}}^{A,i,j}\}_{j=1}^{\ell}$ along with $\sigma_i$, and the second component is the openings for $GC_i, GDec_i^A, c_i^B, d_i^B$ and the input and randomness she used in the $i^{th}$ committed OT above. In other words, for $i \neq e$ Bob learns openings for everything about the circuits, and for $i = e$ he learns Alice's input labels and her signature.

**Bob Verifies Check Circuits.**

1. For $i \neq e$, Bob uses the openings he obtained in the challenge generation phase to check the correctness of $GC_i$. He verifies the consistency of $c_i^B$ with $d_i^B$ both of which he has openings for. He checks that $GDec_i^B$ is consistent with $GC_i$.
2. For $i = e$, he verifies the signature $\sigma_e$.

**Bob Evaluates.**

1. Note that Bob has Alice's input labels for the $e^{th}$ circuit via the OT-based challenge generation and his own input labels via the committed OT. He evaluates $GC_e$.

**Output Exchange.**

1. Bob tells Alice that he is done with the evaluation.
2. Alice responds by sending $\sigma_t = Sign(SK_A, (sid, deadline))$. Bob checks the timeout and the session identifier are consistent with the agreed upon values, and aborts otherwise.
3. Denote the labels for Alice's output by $\{out_{out_{A,j}}^{A,e,j}\}_{j=1}^{m}$. Bob sends these to Alice, along with $\sigma_e$ so that Alice will learn the evaluated circuit identifier $e$, and then she translates them to her actual output on her own. If Alice does not receive the correct labels in time, she contacts the Arbiter for resolution.
4. Alice opens $c_e^B$ to the decoding table $GDec_e^B$, which Bob uses to decode his actual output. If Bob does not receive the correct decoding table in time, he contacts the Arbiter for resolution.

---

**Fig. 2.** Optimistic fair **Covert** 2PC (cnt'd)

---

**Alice's input:** $x_A \in \{0,1\}^{\ell}$. **Bob's input:** $x_B \in \{0,1\}^{\ell}$.
**Common input:** Alice and Bob agree on the description of a circuit $C$, where $C(x_A, x_B) = f(x_A, x_B) = (f_A(x_A, x_B), f_B(x_A, x_B))$, and a second-preimage resistant hash function $H : \{0,1\}^* \rightarrow \{0,1\}^{\ell}$.
$s$ is a statistical security parameter that represents the bound on the cheating probability. $L$ is a computational security parameter, so, for example, each key label is $L$-bits long. $s'$ is a statistical security parameter associated with the input-consistency matrix. Let $t = 2s' + \log s'$, and $\ell' = 2m + \ell + 2t$.
Let $\mathsf{TCommit}(\cdot)$ be a trapdoor commitment scheme, and $\mathsf{Commit}(\cdot)$ be a regular commitment scheme.

---

**Fig. 3.** Optimistic fair **Malicious** 2PC inputs

**Setup:** Let $(PK_T, SK_T)$ be the Arbiter's key pair for a public key encryption, and $(SK_A, VK_A)$ be the signing-verification key-pair for a digital signature scheme for Alice. At the beginning of the protocol, both parties obtain the commitment parameters, and the Arbiter's public key from the Arbiter. Alice sends her verification key to Bob and the Arbiter.

**Output:** Alice learns an $m$-bit string $out_A = f_A(x_A, x_B)$ and Bob learns an $m$-bit string $out_B = f_B(x_A, x_B)$.

---

### Alice Prepares Input/Output Labels.

1. Alice chooses $s$ PRF seeds $sd_1^A, \ldots, sd_s^A$, and commits to them using $\mathsf{Commit}(sd_1^A), \ldots, \mathsf{Commit}(sd_s^A)$. All the randomness Alice will use for generating the $i^{th}$ garbled computation circuit and its input labels will be derived from $sd_i^A$. Similarly, she chooses $3s$ PRF seeds $sd_1'^A, \ldots, sd_{3s}'^A$, and commits to them, where the randomness she uses for generating the $i^{th}$ garbled cheating-detection (CD) circuit and its input labels will be derived from $sd_i'^A$.

2. Alice chooses $r_x, r_p \in_R \{0, 1\}^t, pad_A, pad_B \in_R \{0, 1\}^m$ and sets $x_A^C = pad_B \| r_p \| x_A \| pad_A \| r_x$. She will be using $x_A^C$ as her input to the computation circuits instead of $x_A$. We denote the $j^{th}$ bit of $x_A^C$ by $x_{A,j}^C$.

3. Alice chooses $\mathsf{in}_b^{A,i,j} \in_R \{0, 1\}^L$ for $b \in \{0, 1\}$, $1 \le i \le s$ and $1 \le j \le \ell'$. $\mathsf{in}_b^{A,i,j}$ would be the $b$-key for Alice's $j^{th}$ input wire in the $i^{th}$ computation garbled circuit.

4. Alice sends $\mathsf{Commit}(H(\mathsf{in}_{x_{A,1}^C}^{A,i,1} \| \cdots \| \mathsf{in}_{x_{A,\ell'}^C}^{A,i,\ell'}))$ for $1 \le i \le s$, i.e. commitments to encoding of her inputs. This is intended to commit Alice to her inputs before the matrices associated with input-consistency are chosen.

5. Alice lets her input to the CD circuit be $x_A^{CD} = x_A \| pad_A \| r_x$. She chooses random labels for the associated input wires in the CD circuits and commits to the encoding of her inputs as she did for the computation circuits.

6. Alice chooses $W_b^{A,j} \in_R \{0, 1\}^L$ for $j \in \{1, \ldots, m\}$ and $b \in \{0, 1\}$. Similarly, she chooses $W_b^{B,j} \in \{0, 1\}^L$. These correspond to labels for output wires corresponding to Alice's and Bob's output (padded with Alice's pads), respectively, and unlike the covert protocol, will be the *same* across all $s$ circuits.

7. Alice lets $\mathsf{GDec}^B = \{H(W_0^{B,j}), H(W_1^{B,j})\}_{j=1}^m$ be the decoding table for Bob's output. She also lets $\mathsf{GDec}^A = \{H(W_0^{A,j}), H(W_1^{A,j})\}_{j=1}^m$. The translation table for other outputs of the circuit (i.e. outputs of the UH functions) will be created in the standard way and with different labels for each circuit.

8. Alice lets $\mathsf{PadDec}_i = \{\mathsf{in}_0^{A,i,j}, \mathsf{in}_1^{A,i,j}\}_{j=1}^{m+t}$ for the $i^{th}$ circuit (note that the first $m+t$ input wires are associated with Alice's $pad_B$ and $r_p$). This is essentially a decoding table for input wires for Alice's $pad_B$ and $r_p$. Alice then commits to this table $c_i^B = \mathsf{TCommit}(\mathsf{PadDec}_i)$ using the trapdoor commitment scheme, and encrypts its opening as $d_i^B = E_{PK_T}(\mathsf{PadDecOpen}_i)$ using the Arbiter's public key.

**Fig. 4.** Optimistic fair **Malicious** 2PC

**Alice Prepares the Garbled Circuits.**

1. Alice and Bob jointly choose random binary matrices $M_x \in_R \{0,1\}^{s' \times \ell + m + t}$, $M_p \in_R \{0,1\}^{s' \times m + t}$. Let $C'(x_A^C, x_B) = (f_A(x_A, x_B) \oplus pad_A, (f_B(x_A, x_B) \oplus pad_B, M_x \cdot (x_A \| pad_A \| r_x), M_p \cdot (pad_B \| r_p)))$. In other words, the circuit pads Alice and Bob's output with separate pads generated by Alice, and also outputs the result of applying the $M_x$ and $M_p$ to $x_A$ and $pad_B$ for input-consistency checks.

2. For $1 \leq i \leq s$, Alice computes $\mathsf{GC}_i \leftarrow \mathsf{Garble}(C')$ with the consideration that she uses the input and output labels she generated above for the garbling.

3. Denote by $CD$ the cheating detection circuit. Alice's input to this circuit is $x_A^{CD} = x_A \| pad_A \| r_x$. Bob's input is an $L$-bit string $pc$, his (potential) proof of Alice's cheating. $CD$'s computation is as outlined in Lindell [45] with the exception that in case of detected cheating $x_A$ and $pad_A$ are both revealed to Bob. In particular, $CD$ has the labels $\{W_0^{B,j}, W_1^{B,j}\}_{j=1}^m$ and $\{W_0^{A,j}, W_1^{A,j}\}_{j=1}^m$ embedded in it and checks whether $pc$ is the XOR of the 0-key and the 1-key for any of the wires. If so, it outputs to Bob $x_A \| pad_A$. Otherwise, it outputs a random string. $CD$ also outputs $M_x \cdot (x_A \| pad_A \| r_x)$ to Bob. Alice has no output.

4. For $1 \leq i \leq 3s$, Alice computes $\mathsf{GCD}_i \leftarrow \mathsf{Garble}(CD)$ with the consideration that she uses the input labels she generated above for garbling. The translation tables for $\mathsf{GCD}_i$ are generated in the standard way.

**Oblivious Transfer for Bob's Input to Computation Circuits.** Alice and Bob engage in $\ell$ committed OTs, where in the $j^{th}$ OT, Bob's input is $x_{B,j}$ and Alice's input is a pair where the first component is $[\mathsf{in}_0^{B,1,j}, \ldots, \mathsf{in}_0^{B,s,j}]$ and the second component is $[\mathsf{in}_1^{B,1,j}, \ldots, \mathsf{in}_1^{B,s,j}]$. As a result, Bob learns $\mathsf{in}_{x_{B,j}}^{B,i,j}$ for $1 \leq i \leq s$, $1 \leq j \leq \ell$.

**Alice Sends the Garbled Circuits.** Alice sends $\{\mathsf{GC}_i, c_i^B, d_i^B\}_{i=1}^s$ and $\mathsf{GDec}^A$, $\mathsf{GDec}^B$, and $\sigma_{out^A} = Sign(SK_A, (sid, \mathsf{GDec}^A))$ to Bob (where $sid$ is the unique session identifier). She also sends $\{\mathsf{GCD}_i\}_{i=1}^{3s}$ and the associated output translation tables.

**Challenge Generation.** Alice and Bob jointly run a simulatable coin-toss to generate a uniformly random $s$-bit string $b$ and a uniformly random $3s$-bit string $b'$. Define the evaluation set $\mathbb{E}$ where $i \in \mathbb{E}$ if and only if $b_i = 0$, and the evaluation set $\mathbb{E}'$ similarly with respect to $b'$. Both parties learn $\mathbb{E}$ and $\mathbb{E}'$. Circuits are *not* opened immediately, though.

**Fig. 5.** Optimistic fair **Malicious** 2PC (cnt'd)

**Bob Evaluates Computation Circuits in $\mathbb{E}$.**

1. Alice sends her garbled input labels for $x_A^C$ for all $\mathsf{GC}_i, i \in \mathbb{E}$, by opening the commitments she made to them earlier. Alice also sends $\sigma_{i,pad} = Sign(SK_A, (sid, d_i^B))$ for $i \in \mathbb{E}$. Bob uses these input labels and those of his own from the committed OTs to evaluate all $\mathsf{GC}_i$ where $i \in \mathbb{E}$.

2. If there is at least one circuit with a valid output, and all circuits with a valid output return the same output labels $W_{o_{A,1}}^{A,1}, \ldots, W_{o_{A,m}}^{A,m}$ and $W_{o_{B,1}}^{B,1}, \ldots, W_{o_{B,m}}^{B,m}$, Bob lets $C_A = \mathsf{TCommit}(W_{o_{A,1}}^{A,1}, \ldots, W_{o_{A,m}}^{A,m})$. Note that through these, Bob can learn $o_A = out_A \oplus pad_A$ and $o_B = out_B \oplus pad_B$, but since he does not know the pads, these are useless. Bob lets $pc$ be a random $L$-bit string.

3. If there are at least two circuits with valid but different outputs, Bob chooses the first output wire with different labels and denotes the two labels by $W$ and $W'$. $pc = W \oplus W'$ will constitute Bob's input to the cheating detection circuits.

4. If all circuits are evaluated to *invalid* output labels (i.e. the obtained labels are not consistent with $\mathsf{GDec}^A$ and $\mathsf{GDec}^B$) or if the output of the UHs in any two circuits are different Bob does not abort (until after the opening stage) but instead commits to a random string of appropriate length in $C_A$.

**Evaluating Cheating-Detection Circuits in $\mathbb{E}'$.**

1. Alice and Bob engage in $L$ committed OTs, where in the $j^{th}$ OT, Bob's input is $pc_j$ and Alice's input is a pair where the first component is the $3s$ input labels corresponding to 0 and the second component is the $3s$ labels corresponding to 1.

2. Alice sends her garbled input labels for $x_A^{CD}$ for $\mathsf{GCD}_i$ where $i \in \mathbb{E}'$, by opening the commitments she made to them earlier.

3. Bob uses the input labels to evaluate all $\mathsf{GCD}_i$ with $i \in \mathbb{E}'$, and uses the translation tables to translate to plaintext outputs. If any two UH outputs are different or if they are different from those output in the computation circuits Bob postpones aborting until the opening stage, commits to a random string of appropriate length for $C_A$.

4. Else, he considers the majority output as the correct output. If Bob had a valid proof of cheating $pc$, he learns $x_A \| pad_A$. He computes $o_A = f_A(x_A, x_B) \oplus pad_A$ on his own. He then chooses a $\left\{ W_{o_{A,j}}^{A,j} \right\}_{j=1}^m$ from the evaluation circuits that is consistent with $GDec^A$ and $o_A$, and lets $C_A = \mathsf{TCommit}(W_{o_{A,1}}^{A,1}, \ldots, W_{o_{A,m}}^{A,m})$ (with high probability there is at least one). [Note that in case Alice's opening of the check circuits are problematic, Bob will never decommit anyways.]

**Bob Commits to Alice's Garbled Output.**

1. Bob sends $C_A$ as his commitment to Alice's output labels.

2. Alice sends back $\sigma_{o_A} = Sign(SK_A, (sid, deadline, C_A))$. Bob can use this in case of resolution to prove to the Arbiter that he computed Alice's output honestly.

**Fig. 6.** Optimistic fair **Malicious** 2PC (cnt'd)

**Alice Opens Everything for Check Circuits.**

1. For $i \notin \mathbb{E}$, Alice opens $sd_i^A$ to open all secrets of $\mathsf{GC}_i$. She also opens $c_i^B, d_i^B$, and the randomness used in committed OTs for Bob's input. Bob checks correctness of opened circuits and their consistency with $\mathsf{GDec}^A, \mathsf{GDec}^B$. He also verifies correctness $c_i^B, d_i^B$ and the opened $\mathsf{PadDec}_i$. He aborts if any of the checks fail.

2. For $i \notin \mathbb{E}'$, Alice opens $sd_i'^A$ to open all secrets of $\mathsf{GCD}_i$. He also reveals the randomness used in committed OTs for Bob's input. Bob checks the correctness of the opened circuits and the OTs, and aborts in case of a fail.

**Output Exchange.**

1. Bob opens $C_A$ to Alice's output labels. Alice translates these to her actual output $out_A$ using $pad_A$ and the translation table, on her own. In case of a problem, Alice resolves with the Arbiter.

2. Alice opens $c_i^B$ for $i \in \mathbb{E}$. This allows Bob to learn the values Alice used for $pad_B, r_p$ in all evaluated circuits. For each such value he computes $M_p \cdot (pad_B \| r_p)$ and checks if the result is equal to the unique UH output he obtained when evaluating the circuits. He chooses a pad meeting this requirement and uses it to decode his final output $out_B$. In case of a problem, Bob resolves with the Arbiter.

**Fig. 7.** Optimistic fair **Malicious** 2PC (cnt'd)

1. Bob sends $\mathsf{GDec}_e^A, d_e^B, \sigma_e, \sigma_t$ to the Arbiter. He also sends labels for Alice's output i.e. $\left\{ \mathsf{out}_{out_{A,j}}^{A,e,j} \right\}_{j=1}^m$.

2. The Arbiter verifies the signatures, checks that the time is earlier than the deadline in $\sigma_t$ and the session identifiers are matching. He also makes sure $\mathsf{out}_{out_{A,j}}^{A,e,j}$ values are consistent with $\mathsf{GDec}_e^A$. Essentially, one output label per pair must be provided. He aborts if any of the checks fail.

3. In case of no fails, the Arbiter decrypts $d_e^B$ and sends $\mathsf{GDecOpen}_e^B$ to Bob. He stores $\left\{ \mathsf{out}_{out_{A,j}}^{A,e,j} \right\}_{j=1}^m$ for Alice.

4. Bob checks that $\mathsf{GDecOpen}_e^B$ is the correct opening for $c_e^B$,[a] and uses $\mathsf{GDec}_e^B$ in the opening to translate his output labels to actual outputs.

---

[a]This check is necessary against potentially malicious Arbiter to preserve correctness.

**Fig. 8.** Resolution for Bob (for optimistic fair **Covert** 2PC)

1. If Alice contacts the Arbiter *before* the timeout and Bob has *not* contacted the Arbiter yet, the Arbiter tells Alice to come after the timeout.

2. If Alice contacts the Arbiter *after* the timeout and Bob has *not* contacted the Arbiter yet, the protocol is aborted and no party obtains the actual output.

3. Else (Bob already contacted the Arbiter and resolved), the Arbiter sends $\left\{ \mathsf{out}_{out_{A,j}}^{A,e,j} \right\}_{j=1}^m$ obtained via Bob's resolution to Alice (after making sure she is the same Alice, e.g. by asking for the input to a one way function whose output was in the associated signature given by Bob, see e.g. [5]).

4. Alice translates $\left\{ \mathsf{out}_{out_{A,j}}^{A,e,j} \right\}_{j=1}^m$ to actual outputs on her own.

**Fig. 9.** Resolution for Alice (for optimistic fair **Covert** 2PC)

1. Bob sends $\mathsf{GDec}^A, \sigma_{\mathsf{GDec}^A}, C_A, \sigma_{o_A}$ to the Arbiter. He also sends $d_i^B, \sigma_{i,pad}$ for all $i \in \mathbb{E}$ to the Arbiter. He also opens $C_A$ to $W_{o_{A,1}}^{A,j}, \ldots, W_{o_{A,m}}^{A,j}$.
2. The Arbiter verifies the signature, checks that the time is earlier than the deadline in the signature and the session identifiers match. He also makes sure the opened values $W_{o_{A,1}}^{A,j}, \ldots, W_{o_{A,m}}^{A,j}$ are consistent with $C_A$ and $\mathsf{GDec}^A$. Essentially, one output label per pair must be provided. He aborts if any of the checks fail.
3. In case of no fails, the Arbiter decrypts $d_i^B$ for $i \in \mathbb{E}$ and sends $\mathsf{PadDecOpen}_i$ to Bob. He stores $W_{o_{A,1}}^{A,1}, \ldots, W_{o_{A,m}}^{A,m}$ for Alice.
4. Bob checks that $\mathsf{PadDecOpen}_i^B$ is the correct opening for $c_i^B$, for $i \in \mathbb{E}$, and then uses $\mathsf{PadDec}_i$ values to obtain his actual output $out_B$ as in the last step of the main protocol.

**Fig. 10.** Resolution for Bob (for optimistic fair **Malicious** 2PC)

1. If Alice contacts the Arbiter *before* the timeout and Bob has *not* contacted the Arbiter yet, the Arbiter tells Alice to come after the timeout.
2. If Alice contacts the Arbiter *after* the timeout and Bob has *not* contacted the Arbiter yet, the protocol is aborted and no party obtains the actual output.
3. Else (Bob already contacted the Arbiter and resolved), the Arbiter sends $W_{o_{A,1}}^{A,1}, \ldots, W_{o_{A,m}}^{A,m}$ obtained via Bob's resolution to Alice.
4. Alice translates $W_{o_{A,1}}^{A,1}, \ldots, W_{o_{A,m}}^{A,m}$ to her actual outputs on her own.

**Fig. 11.** Resolution for Alice (for optimistic fair **Malicious** 2PC)

**Acknowledgements.** We thank TÜBİTAK, the Scientific and Technological Research Council of Turkey, project 111E019, and European Union COST Action IC1306.

# References

1. Andrychowicz, M., Dziembowski, S., Malinowski, D., Mazurek, L.: Fair two-party computations via bitcoin deposits. In: Böhme, R., Brenner, M., Moore, T., Smith, M. (eds.) FC 2014. LNCS, vol. 8438, pp. 105–121. Springer, Heidelberg (2014). doi:10.1007/978-3-662-44774-1_8
2. Andrychowicz, M., Dziembowski, S., Malinowski, D., Mazurek, L.: Secure multiparty computations on Bitcoin. In: IEEE Security and Privacy (2014)
3. Asharov, G.: Towards characterizing complete fairness in secure two-party computation. In: Lindell, Y. (ed.) TCC 2014. LNCS, vol. 8349, pp. 291–316. Springer, Heidelberg (2014). doi:10.1007/978-3-642-54242-8_13
4. Asharov, G., Orlandi, C.: Calling out cheaters: covert security with public verifiability. In: Wang, X., Sako, K. (eds.) ASIACRYPT 2012. LNCS, vol. 7658, pp. 681–698. Springer, Heidelberg (2012). doi:10.1007/978-3-642-34961-4_41
5. Asokan, N., Shoup, V., Waidner, M.: Optimistic fair exchange of digital signatures. IEEE Sel. Areas Commun. **18**, 591–610 (2000)
6. Ateniese, G.: Efficient verifiable encryption (and fair exchange) of digital signatures. In: ACM CCS (1999)

7. Aumann, Y., Lindell, Y.: Security against covert adversaries: efficient protocols for realistic adversaries. J. Cryptol. **23**, 281–343 (2010)
8. Avoine, G., Vaudenay, S.: Optimistic fair exchange based on publicly verifiable secret sharing. In: Wang, H., Pieprzyk, J., Varadharajan, V. (eds.) ACISP 2004. LNCS, vol. 3108, pp. 74–85. Springer, Heidelberg (2004). doi:10.1007/978-3-540-27800-9_7
9. Bao, F., Deng, R., Mao, W.: Efficient and practical fair exchange protocols with off-line TTP. In: IEEE Security and Privacy (1998)
10. Beimel, A., Lindell, Y., Omri, E., Orlov, I.: $1/p$-Secure multiparty computation without honest majority and the best of both worlds. In: Rogaway, P. (ed.) CRYPTO 2011. LNCS, vol. 6841, pp. 277–296. Springer, Heidelberg (2011). doi:10.1007/978-3-642-22792-9_16
11. Beimel, A., Omri, E., Orlov, I.: Protocols for multiparty coin toss with dishonest majority. In: Rabin, T. (ed.) CRYPTO 2010. LNCS, vol. 6223, pp. 538–557. Springer, Heidelberg (2010). doi:10.1007/978-3-642-14623-7_29
12. Belenkiy, M., Chase, M., Erway, C., Jannotti, J., Küpçü, A., Lysyanskaya, A., Rachlin, E.: Making p2p accountable without losing privacy. In: WPES (2007)
13. Bellare, M., Hoang, V.T., Rogaway, P.: Foundations of garbled circuits. In: ACM CCS (2012)
14. Ben-Or, M., Goldreich, O., Micali, S., Rivest, R.L.: A fair protocol for signing contracts. IEEE Trans. Inf. Theor. **36**, 40–46 (1990)
15. Bentov, I., Kumaresan, R.: How to use bitcoin to design fair protocols. In: Garay, J.A., Gennaro, R. (eds.) CRYPTO 2014. LNCS, vol. 8617, pp. 421–439. Springer, Heidelberg (2014). doi:10.1007/978-3-662-44381-1_24
16. Boudot, F., Schoenmakers, B., Traoré, J.: A fair and efficient solution to the socialist millionaires' problem. Discret. Appl. Math. **111**(1–2), 23–36 (2001)
17. Brandão, L.T.A.N.: Secure two-party computation with reusable bit-commitments, via a cut-and-choose with forge-and-lose technique. In: Sako, K., Sarkar, P. (eds.) ASIACRYPT 2013. LNCS, vol. 8270, pp. 441–463. Springer, Heidelberg (2013). doi:10.1007/978-3-642-42045-0_23
18. Cachin, C., Camenisch, J.: Optimistic fair secure computation. In: Bellare, M. (ed.) CRYPTO 2000. LNCS, vol. 1880, pp. 93–111. Springer, Heidelberg (2000). doi:10.1007/3-540-44598-6_6
19. Canetti, R.: Universally composable security: a new paradigm for cryptographic protocols. In: FOCS (2001)
20. Cleve, R.: Limits on the security of coin flips when half the processors are faulty. In: STOC (1986)
21. Dodis, Y., Lee, P.J., Yum, D.H.: Optimistic fair exchange in a multi-user setting. In: Okamoto, T., Wang, X. (eds.) PKC 2007. LNCS, vol. 4450, pp. 118–133. Springer, Heidelberg (2007). doi:10.1007/978-3-540-71677-8_9
22. Dong, C., Chen, L., Camenisch, J., Russello, G.: Fair private set intersection with a semi-trusted arbiter. In: Wang, L., Shafiq, B. (eds.) DBSec 2013. LNCS, vol. 7964, pp. 128–144. Springer, Heidelberg (2013). doi:10.1007/978-3-642-39256-6_9
23. Frederiksen, T.K., Jakobsen, T.P., Nielsen, J.B., Nordholt, P.S., Orlandi, C.: MiniLEGO: efficient secure two-party computation from general assumptions. In: Johansson, T., Nguyen, P.Q. (eds.) EUROCRYPT 2013. LNCS, vol. 7881, pp. 537–556. Springer, Heidelberg (2013). doi:10.1007/978-3-642-38348-9_32
24. Gordon, S., Katz, J.: Partial fairness in secure two-party computation. J. Cryptol. **25**(1), 14–40 (2012)
25. Gordon, S.D., Hazay, C., Katz, J., Lindell, Y.: Complete fairness in secure two-party computation. J. ACM **58**, 24 (2011)

26. Gordon, S.D., Katz, J.: Partial fairness in secure two-party computation. In: Gilbert, H. (ed.) EUROCRYPT 2010. LNCS, vol. 6110, pp. 157–176. Springer, Heidelberg (2010). doi:10.1007/978-3-642-13190-5_8

27. Huang, Y., Katz, J., Evans, D.: Efficient secure two-party computation using symmetric cut-and-choose. In: Canetti, R., Garay, J.A. (eds.) CRYPTO 2013. LNCS, vol. 8043, pp. 18–35. Springer, Heidelberg (2013). doi:10.1007/978-3-642-40084-1_2

28. Katz, J.: On achieving the best of both worlds in secure multiparty computation. In: STOC (2007)

29. Katz, J., Maurer, U., Tackmann, B., Zikas, V.: Universally composable synchronous computation. In: Sahai, A. (ed.) TCC 2013. LNCS, vol. 7785, pp. 477–498. Springer, Heidelberg (2013). doi:10.1007/978-3-642-36594-2_27

30. Kiayias, A., Zhou, H.-S., Zikas, V.: Fair and robust multi-party computation using a global transaction ledger. Cryptology ePrint Archive, Report 2015/574 (2015)

31. Kılınç, H., Küpçü, A.: Efficiently making secure two-party computation fair. In: FC (2016)

32. Kılınç, H., Küpçü, A.: Optimally efficient multi-party fair exchange and fair secure multi-party computation. In: Nyberg, K. (ed.) CT-RSA 2015. LNCS, vol. 9048, pp. 330–349. Springer, Cham (2015). doi:10.1007/978-3-319-16715-2_18

33. Kiraz, M.S., Schoenmakers, B.: An efficient protocol for fair secure two-party computation. In: Malkin, T. (ed.) CT-RSA 2008. LNCS, vol. 4964, pp. 88–105. Springer, Heidelberg (2008). doi:10.1007/978-3-540-79263-5_6

34. Kiraz, M.S., Schoenmakers, B., Villegas, J.: Efficient committed oblivious transfer of bit strings. In: Garay, J.A., Lenstra, A.K., Mambo, M., Peralta, R. (eds.) ISC 2007. LNCS, vol. 4779, pp. 130–144. Springer, Heidelberg (2007). doi:10.1007/978-3-540-75496-1_9

35. Kolesnikov, V., Mohassel, P., Rosulek, M.: FleXOR: flexible garbling for XOR gates that beats Free-XOR. In: Garay, J.A., Gennaro, R. (eds.) CRYPTO 2014. LNCS, vol. 8617, pp. 440–457. Springer, Heidelberg (2014). doi:10.1007/978-3-662-44381-1_25

36. Kolesnikov, V., Schneider, T.: Improved garbled circuit: free XOR gates and applications. In: Aceto, L., Damgård, I., Goldberg, L.A., Halldórsson, M.M., Ingólfsdóttir, A., Walukiewicz, I. (eds.) ICALP 2008. LNCS, vol. 5126, pp. 486–498. Springer, Heidelberg (2008). doi:10.1007/978-3-540-70583-3_40

37. Kosba, A., Miller, A., Shi, E., Wen, Z., Papamanthou, C.: Hawk: the blockchain model of cryptography and privacy-preserving smart contracts. Cryptology ePrint Archive, Report 2015/675 (2015)

38. Küpçü, A.: Efficient cryptography for the next generation secure cloud. Ph.D. thesis, Brown University (2010)

39. Küpçü, A.: Efficient Cryptography for the Next Generation Secure Cloud: Protocols, Proofs, and Implementation. Lambert Academic Publishing, Saarbrücken (2010)

40. Küpçü, A.: Distributing trusted third parties. ACM SIGACT News Distrib. Comput. Column **44**, 92–112 (2013)

41. Küpçü, A., Lysyanskaya, A.: Optimistic fair exchange with multiple arbiters. In: Gritzalis, D., Preneel, B., Theoharidou, M. (eds.) ESORICS 2010. LNCS, vol. 6345, pp. 488–507. Springer, Heidelberg (2010). doi:10.1007/978-3-642-15497-3_30

42. Küpçü, A., Lysyanskaya, A.: Usable optimistic fair exchange. In: Pieprzyk, J. (ed.) CT-RSA 2010. LNCS, vol. 5985, pp. 252–267. Springer, Heidelberg (2010). doi:10.1007/978-3-642-11925-5_18

43. Küpçü, A., Lysyanskaya, A.: Usable optimistic fair exchange. Comput. Netw. **56**, 50–63 (2012)

44. Lindell, A.Y.: Legally-enforceable fairness in secure two-party computation. In: Malkin, T. (ed.) CT-RSA 2008. LNCS, vol. 4964, pp. 121–137. Springer, Heidelberg (2008). doi:10.1007/978-3-540-79263-5_8

45. Lindell, Y.: Fast cut-and-choose based protocols for malicious and covert adversaries. In: Canetti, R., Garay, J.A. (eds.) CRYPTO 2013. LNCS, vol. 8043, pp. 1–17. Springer, Heidelberg (2013). doi:10.1007/978-3-642-40084-1_1

46. Lindell, Y., Pinkas, B.: A proof of yaos protocol for secure two-party computation. In: ECCC (2004)

47. Lindell, Y., Pinkas, B.: An efficient protocol for secure two-party computation in the presence of malicious adversaries. In: Naor, M. (ed.) EUROCRYPT 2007. LNCS, vol. 4515, pp. 52–78. Springer, Heidelberg (2007). doi:10.1007/978-3-540-72540-4_4

48. Lindell, Y., Pinkas, B.: Secure two-party computation via cut-and-choose oblivious transfer. In: Ishai, Y. (ed.) TCC 2011. LNCS, vol. 6597, pp. 329–346. Springer, Heidelberg (2011). doi:10.1007/978-3-642-19571-6_20

49. Micali, S.: Simple and fast optimistic protocols for fair electronic exchange. In: PODC (2003)

50. Mohassel, P., Franklin, M.: Efficient polynomial operations in the shared-coefficients setting. In: Yung, M., Dodis, Y., Kiayias, A., Malkin, T. (eds.) PKC 2006. LNCS, vol. 3958, pp. 44–57. Springer, Heidelberg (2006). doi:10.1007/11745853_4

51. Mohassel, P., Franklin, M.: Efficiency tradeoffs for malicious two-party computation. In: Yung, M., Dodis, Y., Kiayias, A., Malkin, T. (eds.) PKC 2006. LNCS, vol. 3958, pp. 458–473. Springer, Heidelberg (2006). doi:10.1007/11745853_30

52. Mohassel, P., Riva, B.: Garbled circuits checking garbled circuits: more efficient and secure two-party computation. In: Canetti, R., Garay, J.A. (eds.) CRYPTO 2013. LNCS, vol. 8043, pp. 36–53. Springer, Heidelberg (2013). doi:10.1007/978-3-642-40084-1_3

53. Moran, T., Naor, M., Segev, G.: An optimally fair coin toss. In: Reingold, O. (ed.) TCC 2009. LNCS, vol. 5444, pp. 1–18. Springer, Heidelberg (2009). doi:10.1007/978-3-642-00457-5_1

54. Nielsen, J.B., Nordholt, P.S., Orlandi, C., Burra, S.S.: A new approach to practical active-secure two-party computation. In: Safavi-Naini, R., Canetti, R. (eds.) CRYPTO 2012. LNCS, vol. 7417, pp. 681–700. Springer, Heidelberg (2012). doi:10.1007/978-3-642-32009-5_40

55. Pinkas, B.: Fair secure two-party computation. In: Biham, E. (ed.) EUROCRYPT 2003. LNCS, vol. 2656, pp. 87–105. Springer, Heidelberg (2003). doi:10.1007/3-540-39200-9_6

56. Rabin, M.O.: How to exchange secrets with oblivious transfer. IACR Cryptology ePrint Archive, 2005:187 (2005)

57. Ruan, O., Chen, J., Zhou, J., Cui, Y., Zhang, M.: An efficient fair UC-secure protocol for two-party computation. Secur. Commun. Netw. **7**, 1253–1263 (2013)

58. Ruan, O., Zhou, J., Zheng, M., Cui, G.: Efficient fair secure two-party computation. In: IEEE APSCC (2012)

59. Shelat, A., Shen, C.: Two-output secure computation with malicious adversaries. In: Paterson, K.G. (ed.) EUROCRYPT 2011. LNCS, vol. 6632, pp. 386–405. Springer, Heidelberg (2011). doi:10.1007/978-3-642-20465-4_22

60. Shelat, A., Shen, C.-H.: Fast two-party secure computation with minimal assumptions. In: ACM CCS (2013)

61. Yao, A.C.-C.: How to generate and exchange secrets. In: FOCS (1986)

62. Zahur, S., Rosulek, M., Evans, D.: Two halves make a whole. In: Oswald, E., Fischlin, M. (eds.) EUROCRYPT 2015. LNCS, vol. 9057, pp. 220–250. Springer, Heidelberg (2015). doi:10.1007/978-3-662-46803-6_8
63. Alptekin, K., Mohassel, P.: Fast optimistically fair cut-and-choose 2PC. Cryptology ePrint Archive, Report 2015/1209 (2015)

# Mobile Malware

# CuriousDroid: Automated User Interface Interaction for Android Application Analysis Sandboxes

Patrick Carter[1]([envelope]), Collin Mulliner[1], Martina Lindorfer[2], William Robertson[1], and Engin Kirda[1]

[1] Northeastern University, Boston, MA, USA
{pdc,crm,wkr,ek}@ccs.neu.edu
[2] SBA Research, Vienna, Austria
mlindorfer@iseclab.org

**Abstract.** Mobile computing has experienced enormous growth in market share and computational power in recent years. As a result, mobile malware is becoming more sophisticated and more prevalent, leading to research into dynamic sandboxes as a widespread approach for detecting malicious applications. However, the event-driven nature of Android applications renders critical the capability to automatically generate deterministic and intelligent user interactions to drive analysis subjects and improve code coverage. In this paper, we present CuriousDroid, an automated system for exercising Android application user interfaces in an *intelligent, user-like* manner. CuriousDroid operates by decomposing application user interfaces on-the-fly and creating a context-based model for interactions that is tailored to the current user layout. We integrated CuriousDroid with Andrubis, a well-known Android sandbox, and conducted a large-scale evaluation of 38,872 applications taken from different data sets. Our evaluation demonstrates significant improvements in both end-to-end sample classification as well as increases in the raw number of elicited behaviors at runtime.

**Keywords:** User Interface Analysis · Android · Dynamic analysis

## 1 Introduction

Mobile computing has experienced enormous growth since the introduction of Apple's iPhone in 2007. A 2011 poll conducted by the Pew Research Center showed that 85% of Americans owned a cell phone, of which more than 50% were smartphones [22]. The Android operating system was released in 2008 and has since gained a significant share of the market, comprising 85% of smartphone shipments in the second quarter of 2014, up from 75% just over a year before [24]. With the growing number of mobile users worldwide, the increasing power of these devices, and the corresponding growth of the mobile economy, mobile malware has similarly grown in both sophistication and prevalence [11].

© International Financial Cryptography Association 2017
J. Grossklags and B. Preneel (Eds.): FC 2016, LNCS 9603, pp. 231–249, 2017.
DOI: 10.1007/978-3-662-54970-4_13

In response, considerable research has focused on dynamic analysis sandboxes as a general approach for detecting malicious applications [21,23,26]. In contrast to static approaches [8–10], dynamic analysis is able to precisely characterize the runtime behavior of an application under test, or AUT, over concrete inputs, as well as deal with several techniques that pose significant difficulty for static analysis such as static code obfuscation, dynamic code loading, and the use of native code.

Despite its advantages, dynamic analysis can fail to provide useful insight into test subject behavior due to incomplete coverage. One feature of the Android platform that exacerbates this problem is the event-driven nature of its applications, where security-relevant code is often only executed in response to external stimuli such as interactions with the user interface. Current standard practice, therefore, is to use standard off-the-shelf tools such as the Monkey [4] or MonkeyRunner [3], which provide random sequences of user inputs and execute pre-scripted UI tests, respectively. Both of these tools are problematic in the context of large-scale dynamic analysis for different reasons: pre-scripting user interactions simply does not scale, and on the other hand random inputs lead to low code coverage.

In this paper, we introduce CuriousDroid, an automated system for driving Android application user interfaces in an *intelligent, user-like* manner. CuriousDroid operates by decomposing application user interfaces on-the-fly and creating a context-based model for interactions with an application. Unlike the Monkey, it is designed to deliver user interactions based upon actual application layouts discovered at draw-time. It significantly improves upon the capabilities of the MonkeyRunner since it can determine a set of natural, user-like interactions without prior knowledge of the application. Using structural decomposition of on-screen layouts and automated identification and classification of interactive views, CuriousDroid is able to generate a series of interactions that emulate typical human interaction.

In this paper, we show that CuriousDroid would be highly useful in a malware triage role, greatly reducing the burden on manual analysts in terms of numbers of new malicious samples to analyze. In particular, one of our evaluation data sets contained 8,827 applications that could not be classified as either benign or malicious. Using CuriousDroid to reclassify the data set resulted in 2,246 likely malicious applications, a significant reduction.

While prior work has examined more sophisticated user input generation [5,6,15,16,20,27], we distance ourselves from these efforts by precisely quantifying the effects of human-like user interactions for large-scale dynamic analysis, as well as requiring no modifications to the operating system nor any static analysis component.

To summarize, this paper makes the following contributions.

- We introduce CuriousDroid, a system for automatically generating user-like UI interactions for Android applications. CuriousDroid uses dynamic instrumentation, application layout decomposition, and heuristic input generation to explore Android applications in an intelligent, user-like manner.

- We integrated CuriousDroid with the well-known Andrubis malware analysis sandbox, replacing the Monkey with CuriousDroid to drive the UI of analysis subjects.
- We conducted a large-scale evaluation of CuriousDroid using 38,872 applications from different data sets. Our evaluation demonstrates that our system improves the analysis results of Andrubis, eliciting behaviors that were not observed when relying upon random UI interactions.

## 2  Background and Motivation

Android is an open source mobile operating system that has enjoyed enormous success in recent years. The backbone of the OS is a modified Linux kernel targeted towards embedded devices with limited power, memory, and storage. Applications are written primarily in Java with the option of utilizing the Java Native Interface (JNI) via Android's Native Development Kit (NDK) to leverage existing libraries and optimize for performance.

Android applications can consist of four basic component types: `Activity`, `Service`, `BroadcastReceiver`, and `ContentProvider`. Activities provide the basic UI structure of an application, where each screen displayed to the user corresponds to an `Activity`. Services are meant to run in the background, separate from the main UI thread and are useful for operations that should not affect the UI thread, e.g., downloading content. Broadcast receivers are used to listen for system-wide events such as incoming SMS, phone calls, or emails. Content providers allow applications to make data available for use by other applications.

**Activities.** Activities are the most important component of the system in terms of the UI. An application consists of one or more activities, only one of which can be visible to the user at any given time. Normally, applications specify the UI design for each activity using resource files. Whenever the Android framework wants to display a given activity, the resource file is loaded and displayed to the user. Additionally, an application can create and add UI elements programmatically during runtime. These UI elements are not part of the resource files contained in an Android application package (APK).

To cover both statically- and dynamically-generated UI elements, CuriousDroid analyzes an application's UI at runtime. Our runtime analysis is based on dynamic instrumentation of the target application. Using dynamic instrumentation, we hook the functionality that is responsible for managing the application's UI. Dynamic instrumentation has the further benefit that we do not have to modify the Android framework, source code, or the application binary.

**Dynamic Analysis and UI Exploration.** Because Android applications are event-driven and many important events occur through UI interactions, performing a dynamic analysis of Android applications using the Monkey as a driver – which simply generates random event sequences – is problematic. Consider an activity that requires a user to enter an email address and password to register an account before using the application. If the application performs any kind of input validation on those fields, as is often the case, it is highly unlikely that the

Monkey would be able to provide a value that satisfies the validity check, if it is able to enter any input into the required fields at all.

CuriousDroid is intended to remedy this problem by driving Android applications using intelligent, user-like interactions in order to increase the likelihood that any malicious behavior contained therein will be identified by the analysis as a whole.

## 3    System Overview

Since Android applications are mostly UI-driven, applications only execute the majority of their code after receiving external input, such as from a human user. Without realistic inputs tailored to the current application UI context, dynamic analyses might not explore interesting, security-relevant code, leading to inaccurate classification results. CuriousDroid aims to solve this problem by interacting with applications as normal users would, with the goal of increasing application coverage and eliciting more runtime behaviors in order to improve the results of the entire analysis.

To that end, CuriousDroid iterates over Android activities in three phases: *user interface decomposition*, *input inference*, and *input generation*. For each activity discovered by the system, the hierarchy of views contained in the activity is extracted using dynamic instrumentation. Then, the system uses a number of heuristics to infer the types of user inputs, or interactions, the views expect (if any). Finally, suitable inputs are generated. Any observed transitions to subsequent activities are added to a work queue for later processing. Activities that have previously been explored are recorded and, if encountered again, CuriousDroid attempts to explore a different path from that point in the UI. CuriousDroid intercepts events that might lead to early termination of the exploration, for instance when the Back button is pressed and the current activity is at the top of the activity stack. An overview of this process is shown in Fig. 1a.

Supporting this process are two components: the UIAnalyzer and InputDriver. The UIAnalyzer uses dynamic instrumentation to inject itself into the target application, and is responsible for analyzing the UI, inferring context, and tracking visited activities. The InputDriver is executed as a separate process, and is responsible for sending user inputs to AUT.

We designed CuriousDroid to be agnostic of its environment – that is, it is intended to run on any device or emulator with minimal effort. As one of the goals of CuriousDroid is to provide a generic automated UI interaction tool that can be deployed on any kind of Android application or malware analysis platform, our system does not require modification of the Android platform or the application that is tested (aside from automated dynamic instrumentation). The only requirement is that a device be rooted.

## 4    User Interface Decomposition

User interface decomposition is the first phase of CuriousDroid for a given activity, where the goal is to recover the hierarchy of user interface views contained in

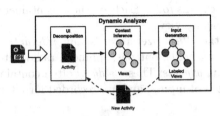

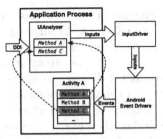

(a) CuriousDroid overview. Application activity user interfaces are decomposed into view hierarchies. Individual views are labeled with the class of expected input using input inference. For each labeled view, an appropriate input is then generated. If a transition to a new activity is observed after submitting this input, the new activity is scheduled for analysis. This process iterates until a fixpoint is reached – i.e., no new activities are observed.

(b) Components comprising CuriousDroid. The UIAnalyzer is injected directly into the AUT using DDI, and hooks application event callbacks to interpose on UI-related operations in order to extract view hierarchies. The InputDriver resides in an external process that receives sequences of user interactions to drive the AUT.

**Fig. 1.** CuriousDroid overview and components.

an activity. As stated in Sect. 3, CuriousDroid uses dynamic instrumentation to interpose on event callback invocations in order to extract this information. In the following, we describe the instrumentation framework used to accomplish this, and then outline how view hierarchies are recovered.

### 4.1 Dynamic Dalvik Instrumentation

CuriousDroid leverages the Dynamic Dalvik Instrumentation (DDI) framework [18] to instrument Android applications. This framework allows for in-memory injection of arbitrary code into application processes, enabling dynamic hooking and interposition on both managed and native code, including transitions between application and Android framework code.

In particular, DDI is used to inject the aforementioned UIAnalyzer component into the process corresponding to the AUT. The UIAnalyzer consists of a native library that in turn executes the AUT within the process. Once the application's code has been loaded into memory, the DVM API is used to instrument specific application methods concerned with UI-related events. Figure 1b depicts this process.

### 4.2 User Interface Analysis

For each activity, the UIAnalyzer decomposes the current view hierarchy. Starting from the root view (`PhoneWindowDecorView`) below which all other views in the activity are attached, all of its descendants are recursively explored using class introspection for identification and attribute extraction. Typically, the direct descendants of the root view are instances of one or more container views such as LinearLayout, GridLayout, or RelativeLayout. Each of these containers holds either further nested layouts or concrete views.

As the view hierarchy is explored, the UIAnalyzer records any *interactive* views that it discovers, such as editable text fields, buttons, spinners, radio buttons, and checkboxes, which we refer to as *widgets*. These *widgets* often contain attributes that indicate the expected types of inputs, and are recorded for later use as described in the next section.

# 5    Input Inference

The second phase of CuriousDroid's user interface exploration is input inference, where the goal is to determine the type of interaction a widget expects. The point of input inference is to ensure that CuriousDroid drives the execution of the application in a way similar to how the developers would expect a human to do so. The underlying assumption is that blindly exercising an application's UI, while perhaps useful for simple or widget-less activities, will not cover as much of the UI – and, therefore, application code. Likewise, attempting to exhaustively explore all possible targeted interactions within an activity can quickly become intractable for complicated activities.

To that end, one concrete aim of input inference is to not only identify the set of widgets that require input in order to trigger behavior or launch further activities, but also to tailor *meaningful* input for each identified widget. For example, instead of simply providing random text to a text field, CuriousDroid attempts to identify the class of input a field requires, such as an email address or phone number, and generates a realistic input drawn from the inferred class.

However, inferring expected classes of input for each widget is not sufficient to properly explore an activity. Indeed, the ordering of inputs is also important because a basic requirement of many widgets is that they are populated with a (well-formed) value before performing an action or launching a new activity. Therefore, CuriousDroid also needs to infer this partial ordering on all widgets in the current UI layout so that such constraints are satisfied.

## 5.1    Widget Orderings

The UIAnalyzer considers four widget attributes when determining an ordering of widgets to exercise in a UI layout: widget type, the nextFocus property (if present), widget screen position, and widget text labels. These attributes, taken together, allow the UIAnalyzer to construct a simple, yet accurate, model of how a user might interact with any given UI. Figure 2 presents an overview of the ordering inference process for an example activity UI layout.

The incorporation of widget type information into the ordering inference process is motivated by the fact that exercising certain widgets implies a transition to another activity. The most straightforward concrete example of this is an OK or Cancel button that submits or dismisses a form, respectively.

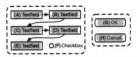

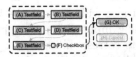

(a) The example activity layout as displayed to the user. Dashed lines indicate a **nextFocus** relationship between widgets.

(b) The UIAnalyzer places widgets into two equivalence classes: buttons, and everything else.

(c) **nextFocus** relationships for (A–E) are overlaid onto the current ordering.

(d) Position-based heuristics indicate that the next link should be the checkbox (F).

(e) Label extraction identifies (G) as the correct button to exercise. At this point, a candidate ordering has been inferred.

**Fig. 2.** Inference of an ordering on user inputs for an example activity UI layout.

Since most or all of the other widgets must generally be populated prior to successful submission of a form (or to trigger behavior that changes the state of the current activity), it follows that this class of widget – in particular, OK buttons – must be exercised last. Therefore, the first step in the ordering inference is to group widgets into two classes: buttons, and everything else (Fig. 2b).

The optional widget **nextFocus** property provides developers with a mechanism for encoding within UI layouts exactly the ordering that users are intended to follow when interacting with an activity. This manifests in the user experience as an automatic shift of focus from one widget to another when the Next button on the keyboard is pressed. The UIAnalyzer considers the presence of this property as ground truth of the intended interaction with an activity, and so the next step of the inference process is to incorporate this ordering information (Fig. 2c).

The UIAnalyzer assumes that widgets are exercised in a top-to-bottom, left-to-right order, and uses screen coordinates of the remaining, unordered non-button widgets to heuristically include them into the current ordering (Fig. 2d).

Finally, the terminal user input is selected from the button class of widgets. Here, the UIAnalyzer uses each button's label as an indicator of whether it is likely to produce some update to the activity's state and, potentially, produce a transition to another activity (Fig. 2e).

## 5.2    Expected Input Classes

Given an inferred ordering of widgets to exercise, the next step is to decide *what* inputs the UIAnalyzer should provide. For this, three attributes are taken into account: widget hints, labels, and contextual information. Most developers add hints to editable text fields that indicate the type of input that is expected, such as an email address, phone number, postal code, or name.

In the absence of such information, label text is extracted from either the widget directly – e.g., placeholder text – or from label widgets directly adjacent to the widget in question. In our observations, these labels are almost as accurate as explicit hint properties. The labels are then matched against manually-compiled keyword lists to map them to a canonical class identifier. For instance, a Register label on a button would map to the OK class, and a Mobile label on a text field would map to the Phone class. The text contained in these keyword-lists is translated to several languages, including English, Russian, Korean, Japanese, and Chinese.

For those widgets that the UIAnalyzer is successfully able to identify a corresponding input class, an appropriate input is generated. The text is drawn from lists corresponding to a specific class of input – for example, in the case of editable text fields, the UIAnalyzer contains lists for names, addresses, phone numbers, passwords, and many more.

If the input inference process is unable to determine an input class for a widget, a random interaction will be supplied. In the case of one or more image buttons lacking any descriptive text, a single button is randomly chosen.

## 6    Input Generation

Given an inferred widget ordering and expected input classes for each widget, the next stage of the UI exploration for each activity is to actually drive the current UI. To that end, the UIAnalyzer communicates with the InputDriver, providing it with ordering and input class information. The InputDriver translates this information into concrete user input events, which it then injects directly to the Android event drivers. An overview of this is shown in Fig. 1b.

### 6.1    Input Translation

Translating an interaction to a set of input commands first requires determining the type of interaction that is expected. Currently, CuriousDroid can generate both taps and swipes. To click a button, it is only necessary to inject one tap at the button's on-screen position. To enter text into a widget, the InputDriver takes the desired text as input and maps the location of each character to a position – or positions – on the virtual keyboard. Multiple positions could be required for characters that require multiple taps, such as capitals, numbers, and special characters.

The InputDriver defines a function called genericPress that takes as parameters the desired $(x, y)$ coordinates of the tap, and the amount of time in microseconds to wait before initiating the tap, and returns each of the values needed to populate an event structure for the touchscreen event driver.

In addition to the function described above, the InputDriver also provides functions for the menu button, the back button, and a function that returns random events for fuzzing. After the formatted command string for all interactions has been completely generated, the command string is ready for injection into the AUT.

## 6.2  Input Injection

Input injection is achieved via two approaches: *event injection* and *random event generation*. Event injection writes the commands from the UIAnalyzer to the Android touchscreen event driver, while the random event generation function creates random taps and swipes to write to the event drivers. Similar to RERAN [12], the InputDriver can speed up or slow down the execution of an application; however, we choose to execute at a speed resembling human usage.

In the case that an activity does not contain (known) widgets in its layout, our interactions will not induce the execution of a new activity. It is therefore necessary to have a fallback mechanism that attempts to get an application out of a "stalled" execution state. We have implemented that system from within the InputDriver module.

In particular, if a preset period of time has elapsed and no observable action has occurred in response to an input sequence, the InputDriver initiates the random event generation process. The process assumes the application is in a stalled state and attempts to perturb it by sending random events to the system driver. If this fails to advance the execution of the application, it presses the Back button, reverting the state of the application to the previous activity.

## 7  Evaluation

In this section, we evaluate the efficacy of CuriousDroid as a driver for dynamic analysis. In particular, we compare the results of standard Andrubis [1,14], a well-known dynamic analysis sandbox for Android applications, to the results of composing Andrubis with CuriousDroid, and show significant improvements in the analysis results.

### 7.1  Andrubis

Andrubis is a large-scale public malware analysis system for Android applications. It provides a comprehensive analysis report that includes results from static code analysis as well as runtime behavior using dynamic analysis in the QEMU emulator, on both the Dalvik VM and system level.

Static analysis of the application's manifest and certificate yields meta information such as requested permissions, services, broadcast receivers, activities, package name, SDK version, and information about the author. Furthermore, static code analysis extracts APIs calls and identifies the permissions actually used in the application's bytecode in contrast to the permissions required in the manifest.

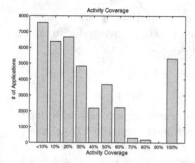

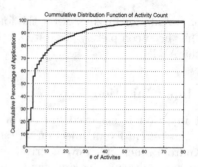

**Fig. 3.** Activity coverage by Curious-Droid for all applications.

**Fig. 4.** Cumulative distribution function for application activity counts. The steep curve indicates the majority of applications contain fewer than 10 activities.

During dynamic analysis, Andrubis monitors applications through an instrumented Dalvik VM. It records data leaks, filesystem activity, phone activity such as sending SMS and making phone calls, network activity, and the dynamic loading of DEX code as well as native code through JNI. In order to drive program execution, by default Andrubis utilizes the pseudorandom user interaction sequences generated by the Monkey.

In addition to the analysis report, Andrubis provides a *malice score* for each application [13]. Based on static and dynamic features learned from a set of known benign and malicious applications, Andrubis leverages an SVM-based classifier to assign scores on a scale from 0 to 10, with 0 being benign and 10 being malicious.

## 7.2  Experimental Setup

Our evaluation was performed over a data set of 51,571 randomly selected Android applications from five categories: applications that received a borderline classification from standard Andrubis, those that contain SMS-related code, those that perform dynamic code loading, those that perform native library loading, and those that interact with the network. Except for the first category, each of these represents a specific behavior that is potentially (and often) indicative of malware [28].

We found that out of the 51,571 applications tested, 12,699 drew no activities. In this case, CuriousDroid was not invoked and we were unable to collect results for those runs. Therefore, only the 38,872 remaining applications were considered in our evaluation.

## 7.3  Activity Coverage

A natural measure of CuriousDroid's effectiveness in exploring application user interfaces is in terms of activity coverage, as activities are the main container for

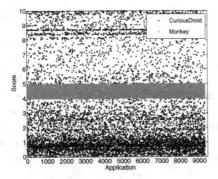

**Fig. 5.** Effect of CuriousDroid on borderline Andrubis scores. Scores from modified Andrubis are in black, and standard Andrubis in gray. Note the significantly greater spread of scores due to incorporating CuriousDroid during UI exploration.

UI layouts on Android. The list of activities for an application is extracted from its manifest by Andrubis during static analysis. In addition, CuriousDroid logs each activity it visits during its exploration. We compare these lists of activities to calculate our total activity coverage.

Figure 3 shows the activity coverage for all applications in the data set. In this figure, coverage is binned in 10-percent increments. We note, in Fig. 4, that the majority of applications contain fewer than 10 activities, but as many as 284 have been found in a single application. Applications with such a large number of activities are guaranteed to produce low coverage numbers primarily due to the analysis time limit enforced by CuriousDroid.

### 7.4 Borderline Classification

To measure the impact of CuriousDroid on Andrubis' application classifier, we analyzed 8,827 applications from the data set that received a score on the interval [4, 5] – i.e., a borderline score that is neither definitively benign nor malicious. As described above, Andrubis' classifier constructs a feature vector from a mix of static and dynamic features. CuriousDroid has no impact on the static analysis performed by Andrubis, so the static features used in our analysis are the same as in the original Andrubis analysis. Therefore, any change in an application's score can be attributed to a change in dynamic features observed during UI exploration. Figure 5 plots both the original scores assigned by standard Andrubis as well as the scores generated when incorporating CuriousDroid for this test set.

We note that CuriousDroid produces a significant increase in the quality of Andrubis' classifier as measured by score spread. There is an observable density of scores around 1.0, which demonstrates that the additional runtime behavior elicited by CuriousDroid was able to allow a relabeling from unknown to benign for many applications. Also observable are three smaller bands around 8.5, 8.75, and 10, which demonstrates that a (relatively) smaller group of applications could be reclassified from unknown to malicious due to CuriousDroid.

We plot the number of dynamic features used by Andrubis during classification in Fig. 6. On average, more than nine additional dynamic features were used when incorporating CuriousDroid. The average number of dynamic features used by CuriousDroid increased to 30.8 from 21.6 with the Monkey. Additionally, the total number of features generated increased by an average of more than 27 features per application, all of which we can assume are dynamic. The average total number of features used increased from 58.6 with the Monkey to 68.4 with CuriousDroid, in line with the increase in the number of dynamic features used.

### 7.5   Observed Dynamic Behaviors

The remaining four application categories described in the experimental setup refer to a specific behavior that static analysis indicated the application had the capability to perform. However, the applications we consider in each of these categories did not exhibit these behaviors during dynamic analysis using standard Andrubis. An overview of the results of composing Andrubis with CuriousDroid in this respect is shown in Table 1. In the following, we discuss each of the categories separately.

**SMS.** The SMS category is a set of applications chosen because they were statically determined to possess the capability to send or receive SMS messages. Not only do they request the SEND_SMS permission, but they are also found to have actual method calls that send or receive SMS messages. We chose this as a search parameter because it is possible for an application to request a permission that the developer never intends to use, especially in the case of code re-use. We found that CuriousDroid was able to trigger the sending of SMS messages in 440 of the 6,871 applications analyzed. Furthermore, many of the numbers to which messages were sent were short numbers, indicating a higher likelihood that these messages were sent to premium numbers. Such behavior is often indicative of malware.

**Dynamic Code Loading.** There are times when utilizing dynamic code loading is useful or necessary – e.g., when the primary application DEX file has more than 64 K method references [7]. Andrubis is able to detect dynamic code loading during static analysis. The resulting test set consisted of 8,371 applications, in which CuriousDroid were able to trigger the loading of dynamic code in 358, representing a total of 4.28% of the set.

**Native Library Loading.** Android provides developers with an API for loading and running native code using JNI. This functionality is particularly important to developers who need direct access to the GPU or CPU for performance or power-saving purposes. However, malware can exploit the JNI interfaces to hide certain behaviors, such as communicating with remote servers, installation of rootkits, or general obfuscation [28].

Therefore, we analyzed a set of 7,669 applications containing native libraries that were not loaded during dynamic analysis using standard Andrubis.

**Table 1.** Dynamic application behavior elicited due to CuriousDroid. By comparison, Andrubis used with the Monkey produced *no* behavior in each category.

| Category | # Apps | # Triggered | % Triggered |
|---|---|---|---|
| SMS | 6871 | 440 | 6.40% |
| Dynamic code | 8371 | 358 | 4.28% |
| Native code | 7669 | 1945 | 25.36% |
| Networking | 7134 | 2650 | 37.15% |

CuriousDroid triggered the loading of these libraries in 1,945 applications, constituting 25.36% of the applications in the set.

**Networking.** The last test set was composed of applications that requested the INTERNET permission, commonly used in both benign and malicious applications. Network connectivity allows applications to access resources over the Internet. This could be as benign as checking account credentials or downloading legitimate content or advertisements. This permission, however, is also often used for nefarious behavior such as downloading dynamic code, drive-by downloads, or connecting to a command-and-control server for mobile bots.

Of the original 10,000 applications tested, 2,866 were found to have drawn zero activities. Therefore, we limited our analysis to the remaining 7,134. CuriousDroid triggered network traffic in 2,650 applications, representing an improvement of 37.15% of the total set.

## 7.6   Case Study

In the final experiment, we specifically investigated the 440 samples that only send SMS messages when executed by CuriousDroid. Using their MD5, we searched sites such as AndroTotal [17] to determine if a sample is known, determining that 20 samples were not previously known. 15 samples sent SMS messages to premium numbers, while five samples sent messages to regular phone numbers.

We further investigated one of the SMS samples in more detail. We selected the sample based on its change in malice score from 0.8743 to 8.6093 when driven using CuriousDroid. The application asks the user to accept an update of the program's database. If the user accepts, the application starts a larger download. During the download, the application sends five SMS messages to different short codes. CuriousDroid was able to trigger sending the SMS messages because it intelligently drove the UI by pressing the correct button. If the user does not accept the update download, the application immediately terminates without sending the SMS messages.

# 8   Discussion

Upon inspection of our initial test set, we discovered 12,699 applications where zero activities were drawn. We randomly chose a subset of applications to manually inspect in an emulator and found several reasons for this phenomenon.

The most obvious cause for zero-activity coverage is that some applications simply crash upon startup. Of these, many applications received a score of 9.0 or higher by Andrubis. We postulate that many malicious applications run their payload at startup, and have no intention of ever displaying this bootstrapping activity to the user. In one instance, we observed an application that crashed on startup, but on a second execution opened a dialog box requesting the user download and install an update from a third-party website.

On the other end of the spectrum, we noticed that most applications that achieved 100% coverage had very few activities. Malware is very likely packaged with simple applications, perhaps containing just one or two activities, although we see evidence that simply running an application containing malware is not necessarily enough to trigger the payload. We can infer from Sect. 7.5 that stimulating a UI with intelligent interactions is more likely to trigger malicious behavior.

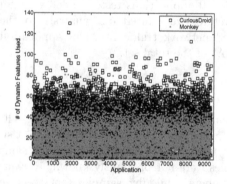

**Fig. 6.** Number of observed dynamic features for each application in the test set. Again, CuriousDroid elicits significantly more behavior than the Monkey.

When an application transitions from one activity to another, it calls the `startActivityForResult` family of methods which takes an intent as an argument. Applications are not limited to starting activities contained within their own application, and can additionally open activities belonging to other applications such as a browser or email application. CuriousDroid examines the intents passed to `startActivityForResult` and determines whether or not the target activity belongs to the current application. If it does not, it blocks the method call to ensure that the AUT retains focus. Doing so can have unforeseen consequences, sometimes resulting in an application crash. However, in most cases the application remains in the current activity until perturbed by the random event generator.

In a similar situation, when the Back button is pressed, the current activity's finish method is invoked. If the current activity is not the root of the activity stack, this is not a problem. However, in the event that the current activity is the root activity of the application, making a call to finish causes the application to exit. In an effort to keep the AUT in focus, we block all finish calls originating from the root activity. This can cause an application crash – which occurs more often in applications written for older SDK versions – when the root activity changes from one activity to another. When this happens, we have observed on occasion that the call to the current root activity's finish method occurs before the new root activity has been created. If the new root activity has not yet been set, we block the call to the previous root activity's finish call, causing an application crash.

## 9   Related Work

Recent work in Android dynamic analysis has taken numerous, diverse approaches. A recent study [19] performed a comprehensive analysis of 16 dynamic analysis platforms. Some systems rely on a blend of static and dynamic analysis, while others only provide a mechanism for examining dynamic properties and do not include a way to execute applications. Some only rely on fuzz testing, or random interactions, to drive execution, while others attempt to exercise the UI in a more deterministic fashion. We consider several systems that employ these techniques and show how CuriousDroid distinguishes itself from these systems.

To avoid detection, malware can implement sandbox evasion. A recent effort studied the characteristics of different Android sandboxes and how these can be evaded [25]. Since CuriousDroid can be also deployed on a real device, it can be used to analyze evasive malware that attempts to fingerprint emulated environments.

**Dynodroid** [16] provides a system for interacting with UI widgets dynamically. The authors implement a mechanism that attempts to generate a sequence of intelligent UI interactions and system events by observing the UI's layout, composing and selecting a set of interactions, and executing those actions. Dynodroid leverages the Hierarchy Viewer [2], a tool packaged with the Android platform to infer a UI model during execution, to determine an activity's layout. We note that it was necessary to make changes to the SDK source code to enable this capability. Finally, and perhaps most importantly, Dynodroid requires that a tester has access to the source code of an application, as use of the Android instrumentation framework is necessary. In contrast, CuriousDroid can be used to test any APK file without source code since it dynamically instruments the application bytecode.

**SmartDroid** [27] uses a hybrid approach, leveraging both static and dynamic analysis, to discover and exercise UI trigger conditions. Using static analysis, SmartDroid constructs a desired activity switch path that leads to the sensitive API calls it wishes to exercise. During dynamic analysis, SmartDroid traverses the view tree of an activity and triggers the event listeners for each UI element. If the event listener invokes the start of a new activity, SmartDroid determines if that activity is on the activity switch path. If not, it blocks the call to that activity and continues to traverse the current activity's view tree until the correct element is stimulated. SmartDroid requires not only modifications to the SDK, but a modified emulator as well. In addition, relying on static analysis to reveal sensitive behaviors will exclude calls to dynamically loaded code or native libraries.

**Swifthand** [6] is an automated GUI testing tool for Android that leverages machine learning techniques to create a model of an application which it can leverage to generate user inputs in an attempt to visit unexplored areas of the application. Swifthand requires modifications of applications through static instrumentation of the binary and it is unclear to us whether or not this process is entirely automated. It makes no attempt to derive context from an application based on the UI, as a human would. The average runtime required by Swifthand tests was three hours per application, making it unsuited for large-scale testing. Finally, only 10 applications were included in the test set. Such as small set does not provide adequate insight into the efficacy of the tool at scale.

**A3E** [5] provides another system for UI exploration of Android applications with two separate approaches: "Targeted Exploration" which uses a CFG generated during static analysis to develop a strategy for exploration by targeting specific activities, and "Depth-first Exploration" which attempts to mimic user interactions to drive execution in a more systematic, albeit slower, way. A3E is not suitable for large-scale testing due to the long testing time required for each application. A3E was tested on only 25 applications, and has an average runtime of 87 min per application for targeted exploration method and 104 min per application for the depth-first exploration.

**AppsPlayground** [20], in addition to acting as a malware detection system, employs a technique for automatically executing Android applications. Similar to CuriousDroid, AppsPlayground attempts to determine context from the UI in order to more intelligently direct an applications execution. This includes inserting relevant text into text boxes, as well as clicking the most appropriate buttons. We employ a similar technique to AppsPlayground, using hints and keywords from UI elements to determine context.

We note that AppsPlayground requires modification of the SDK and OS and can only be used with an emulator. CuriousDroid has been tested on physical devices as low as API level 4, up to API level 16, and requires no modifications to the OS or SDK. We leverage the techniques used in RERAN [12] to pass interactions to the device, such as taps, swipes, and hardware button pushes. This means that when text is entered into a field, it is passed in as a series of actual taps to keys on the virtual keyboard. In contrast, AppsPlayground uses a modified version of the MonkeyRunner to pass interactions to the application.

AppsPlayground was tested on just under 4,000 applications, only three of which were known malware samples. Finally, the authors of AppsPlayground provided no measurements of the end-to-end time required to test an application. Therefore we are unable to determine the suitability of AppsPlayground as a system for large-scale measurement.

## 10    Conclusion

In this paper, we introduced CuriousDroid, an automated system to drive Android applications in an *intelligent, user-like* manner. Our system is generic and can be deployed in any Android sandbox and even on real Android devices. To evaluate our system, we integrated it into the well-known Andrubis sandbox. We evaluated CuriousDroid using 38,872 applications that we randomly selected from different categories. The results of our evaluation demonstrate that our system was able to elicit significantly more runtime behavior over the standard combination of Andrubis and random input generated by the Monkey, improving Andrubis' ability to categorize previously borderline applications as either definitively benign or malicious. This capability in particular suggests that Curious-Droid would prove very helpful for malware triage, greatly reducing the numbers of applications that would require manual analysis to classify.

**Acknowledgements.** This material is based upon work supported by the National Science Foundation under Grant No. CNS-1409738. The research leading to these results has received funding from the FFG – Austrian Research Promotion under grant COMET K1 and has been carried out within the scope of u'smile, the Josef Ressel Center for User-Friendly Secure Mobile Environments.

## References

1. Andrubis. http://anubis.iseclab.org/
2. Hierarchy Viewer. http://developer.android.com/tools/help/hierarchy-viewer.html
3. MonkeyRunner. http://developer.android.com/tools/help/monkeyrunner_concepts.html
4. UI/Application Exerciser Monkey. http://developer.android.com/tools/help/monkey.html
5. Azim, T., Neamtiu, I.: Targeted and depth-first exploration for systematic testing of Android apps. In: International Conference on Object Oriented Programming Systems Languages & Applications (OOPSLA) (2013)
6. Choi, W., Necula, G., Sen, K.: Guided GUI testing of Android apps with minimal restart and approximate learning. In: International Conference on Object Oriented Programming Systems Languages & Applications (OOPSLA) (2013)
7. Chung, F.: Android Developers Blog (2011). http://android-developers.blogspot.com/2011/07/custom-class-loading-in-dalvik.html. Accessed 5 May 2014
8. Egele, M., Brumley, D., Fratantonio, Y., Kruegel, C.: An empirical study of cryptographic misuse in Android applications. In: ACM Conference on Computer and Communications Security (CCS) (2013)

9. Enck, W., Ongtang, M., McDaniel, P.D., et al.: Understanding Android security. IEEE Secur. Priv. (Oakland) **7**, 50–57 (2009)
10. Felt, A.P., Chin, E., Hanna, S., Song, D., Wagner, D.: Android permissions demystified. In: ACM Conference on Computer and Communications Security (CCS) (2011)
11. Felt, A.P., Finifter, M., Chin, E., Hanna, S., Wagner, D.: A survey of mobile malware in the wild. In: ACM Workshop on Security and Privacy in Smartphones and Mobile Devices (SPSM) (2011)
12. Gomez, L., Neamtiu, I., Azim, T., Millstein, T.: RERAN: timing- and touch-sensitive record and replay for Android. In: International Conference on Software Engineering (ICSE) (2013)
13. Lindorfer, M., Neugschwandtner, M., Platzer, C.: MARVIN: efficient and comprehensive mobile app. Classification through static and dynamic analysis. In: Annual International Computers, Software & Applications Conference (COMPSAC) (2015)
14. Lindorfer, M., Neugschwandtner, M., Weichselbaum, L., Fratantonio, Y., van der Veen, V., Platzer, C.: ANDRUBIS - 1,000,000 apps later: a view on current Android malware behaviors. In: Workshop on Building Analysis Datasets and Gathering Experience Returns for Security (BADGERS) (2014)
15. Liu, B., Nath, S., Govindan, R., Liu, J.: DECAF: detecting and characterizing ad fraud in mobile apps. In: USENIX Conference on Networked Systems Design and Implementation (NSDI) (2014)
16. MacHiry, A., Tahiliani, R., Naik, M.: Dynodroid: an input generation system for Android apps. In: Foundations of Software Engineering (2013)
17. Maggi, F., Valdi, A., Zanero, S.: AndroTotal: a flexible, scalable toolbox and service for testing mobile malware detectors. In: ACM Workshop on Security and Privacy in Smartphones and Mobile Devices (SPSM) (2013)
18. Mulliner, C.: Dynamic Dalvik Intrumentation (DDI). https://github.com/crmulliner/ddi
19. Neuner, S., Van der Veen, V., Lindorfer, M., Huber, M., Merzdovnik, G., Mulazzani, M., Weippl, E.R.: Enter sandbox: Android sandbox comparison. In: IEEE Mobile Security Technologies Workshop (MoST) (2014)
20. Rastogi, V., Chen, Y., Enck, W.: AppsPlayground: automatic security analysis of smartphone applications. In: Conference on Data and Application Security and Privacy (CODASPY) (2013)
21. Reina, A., Fattori, A., Cavallaro, L.: A system call-centric analysis and stimulation technique to automatically reconstruct Android malware. In: European Workshop on Systems Security (EuroSec) (2013)
22. Smith, A.: Americans and mobile computing: key trends and consumer research (2011). http://www.slideshare.net/PewInternet/americans-and-mobile-computing-key-trends-in-consumer-research. Accessed 7 May 2014
23. Spreitzenbarth, M., Freiling, F., Echtler, F., Schreck, T., Hoffmann, J.: Mobile-sandbox: having a deeper look into Android applications. In: Symposium on Applied Computing (SAC) (2013)
24. Strategy Analytics: Android captures record 85 percent share of global smartphone shipments in Q2 2014 (2014). http://www.prnewswire.com/news-releases/strategy-analytics-android-captures-record-85-percent-share-of-global-smartphone-shipments-in-q2-2014-269301171.html
25. Vidas, T., Christin, N.: Evading Android runtime analysis via sandbox detection. In: ACM Symposium on Information, Computer and Communications Security (ASIACCS) (2014)

26. Yan, L.K., Yin, H.: DroidScope: seamlessly reconstructing the OS and Dalvik semantic views for dynamic Android malware analysis. In: USENIX Security Symposium (2012)
27. Zheng, C., Zhu, S., Dai, S., Gu, G., Gong, X., Han, X., Zou, W.: SmartDroid: an automatic system for revealing UI-based trigger conditions in Android applications. In: ACM Workshop on Security and Privacy in Smartphones and Mobile Devices (SPSM) (2012)
28. Zhou, Y., Jiang, X.: Dissecting Android malware: characterization and evolution. In: IEEE Symposium on Security and Privacy, Oakland (2012)

# DroydSeuss: A Mobile Banking Trojan Tracker (Short Paper)

Alberto Coletta[1](✉), Victor van der Veen[2], and Federico Maggi[1]

[1] Politecnico di Milano, Milan, Italy
alberto.coletta@mail.polimi.it, federico.maggi@polimi.it
[2] Vrije Universiteit, Amsterdam, The Netherlands
vvdveen@cs.vu.nl

**Abstract.** After analyzing several Android mobile banking trojans, we observed the presence of repetitive artifacts that describe valuable information about the distribution of this class of malicious apps. Motivated by the high threat level posed by mobile banking trojans and by the lack of publicly available analysis and intelligence tools, we automated the extraction of such artifacts and created a malware tracker named DroydSeuss. DroydSeuss first processes applications both statically and dynamically, extracting relevant strings that contain traces of communication endpoints. Second, it prioritizes the extracted strings based on the APIs that manipulate them. Finally, DroydSeuss correlates the endpoints with descriptive metadata from the samples, providing aggregated statistics, raw data, and cross-sample information that allow researchers to pinpoint relevant groups of applications.

We connected DroydSeuss to the VirusTotal daily feed, consuming Android samples that perform banking-trojan activity. We manually analyzed its output and found supporting evidence to confirm its correctness. Remarkably, the most frequent itemset unveiled a campaign currently spreading against Chinese and Korean bank customers.

Although motivated by mobile banking trojans, DroydSeuss can be used to analyze the communication behavior of any suspicious application.

## 1 Introduction

With the widespread use of mobile devices as a second factor of authentication, malware authors equipped their *banking trojans* (e.g., ZeuS, SpyEye, Carberp, and derivatives), to leverage dedicated companion mobile malware trojan apps. With apps known in the underground as ZitMo, SpitMo, and CitMo, attackers create a man-in-the-middle between the banking website and the victim, effectively bypassing two factor authentication.

Cyber criminals strive to streamline the generation and distribution of mobile bankers as much as possible, using so-called *crimeware kits*, in order to reach large pools of victims. However, the more a cyber gang needs to automate their operations, the more likely their "dev ops" will leave traces that allow to identify groups

J. Grossklags and B. Preneel (Eds.): FC 2016, LNCS 9603, pp. 250–259, 2017.
DOI: 10.1007/978-3-662-54970-4_14

of related apps. To our knowledge, however, most of the analysts' work is still done manually. Moreover, there is no mobile equivalent of the ZeuS Tracker [1], which turns out to be extremely useful to security and malware researchers. Motivated by this, we created the DroydSeuss mobile malware tracker.

Our work is inspired by observations made during manual reverse engineering efforts. First, traces of C&C endpoints (e.g., phone number, domain name, URL) are typically visible in (byte)code, at runtime, or both, depending on the sophistication of the sample. Generally, finding both static and dynamic evidence of the same endpoint is a good indicator that the sample supports some configuration mechanism, which may reveal that it was generated semi-automatically (e.g., by a crimeware kit). Second, certain static features of the malicious app (e.g., prefixes of package name) that recur frequently, *together* with the same C&C endpoints is a further indicator that the malicious sample may be part of a campaign.

DroydSeuss runs each malware sample in an instrumented environment to track statically and dynamically allocated strings that are likely to be C&C endpoints. DroydSeuss has prioritization heuristics that assign an increasing level of importance to the candidate endpoints. In addition, DroydSeuss analyzes the itemsets containing (1) the extracted endpoints and (2) descriptive metadata from the samples (e.g., prefix of the package name). The outcome is a rank of itemsets that provide succinct insights such as *package name X is almost always related to phone-based C&C endpoints in country Y*.

We manually inspected the top 10 most frequent itemsets of each endpoint type (i.e., web and phone-based) and in all cases except one, we found contextual evidence from online resources that backed our findings. Interestingly, the left-out case led us to a very active, mobile-only banking trojan campaign targeting Korean and Chinese customers, of which no public evidence was available so far.

In summary, our work makes the following contributions:

- We propose a simple but effective pattern-elicitation technique based on frequent itemset mining which unveils growing campaigns and allows researchers to pin-point relevant groups of samples.
- We design and implement the *first* mobile malware tracker that leverages frequent itemset mining, along with classic static- and dynamic-data extraction techniques, to track phone- and web-based C&C endpoints.
- We release our tracker to the public at http://droydseuss.necst.it where it has been running since October 2014; during this time frame, it correctly brought to our attention groups of trojans that would otherwise have required manual analysis in order to understand their importance.

## 2   DroydSeuss' Approach

The rationale behind DroydSeuss is twofold. First, evidence of interesting C&C endpoints can appear statically, dynamically, or both, depending on the sophistication of the sample. Second, metadata that recur frequently together with the same C&C endpoint indicates that there may be a crimeware kit or a campaign involved.

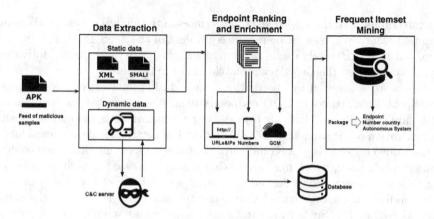

**Fig. 1.** Data processing pipeline of DroydSeuss.

The remainder of this section describes how we implemented the aforementioned rationale in order to elicit relevant information that helps the analyst finding interesting groups of samples and, possibly, campaigns, starting from a feed of malicious apps. Figure 1 summarizes how **Phase 1** and **Phase 2** implement the first rationale, whereas **Phase 3** implements the second rationale.

## 2.1  Phase 1: Data Extraction

We are interested in capturing two categories of C&C endpoints: *web based* ones (e.g., IPs, URLs) and *phone based* ones. In addition, we also track recent trojans that take advantage of the Google Cloud Messaging (GCM) system [8] for push communication. While regular expressions for domain names, URLs and IPs are rather easy to write, parsing phone numbers is not straightforward. For this, we used the Python port of the `libphonenumber` library.

**Static Data.** As a preliminary step, we use `apktool` to unpack the APK archives, disassemble the Dalvik bytecode into an ASCII representation of the Smali assembly code and extract the manifest and resource files. Starting from static resources and Smali assembly files, this sub-phase is implemented as a set of regular expressions and post-processing scripts.

The following snippet, obtained from a real-world malicious APK, exemplifies how phone numbers and URL paths are saved in resource files.

**XML resource file found in an iBanking sample.**

```
<resources>
  <string name="def_tel_number">+43676800XXXX</string>
  <string name="urlPostData">/iBanking/sms/index.php</string>
  <string name="urlPostSms">/iBanking/sms/saveSMS.php</string>
  <string name="urlCommand">/iBanking/sms/sync.php</string>
  <string name="urlSmsList">/iBanking/getList.php</string>
  <string name="urlSendFile">/iBanking/sendFile.php</string>
  <string name="urlPing">/iBanking/sms/ping.php</string>
</resources>
```

Additionally, we parse Smali string constants denoted by the `const-string` instruction and check whether the manifest declares the GCM permission. An example of such string constant is shown in the following snippet.

**C&C phone number declared in a malicious APK.**

```
const-string v4, "+43676800XXXX"
```

**Dynamic Data.** In this sub-phase, we run the APK file in an instrumented sandbox. For our proof-of-concept implementation of DroydSeuss we leverage TraceDroid [20], which produces detailed, readable and easily parsable traces with deserialized arguments and return values.

We are particularly interested in stimulating the typical behaviours involved in botnet communication. To this end, TraceDroid triggers a number of special events (e.g., device reboot, phone call, network disconnect, etcetera). Furthermore, the sandbox launches all the activities and starts all the services declared in the app manifest. Finally, it runs the Android UI Exerciser Monkey that generates pseudo-random streams of user events such as clicks, touches and gestures.

The following listing shows an excerpt output resulting from the analysis of a real banker. The sub-phase continues by applying a set of regular expressions on the (string-typed) input arguments and return values of every API invocation to capture potential endpoints.

**TraceDroid output file**

```
public java.lang.StringBuilder
      java.lang.StringBuilder("http://dubleautoriza.net").append((java.lang.String)
      "/iBanking/sms/ping.php")
return (java.lang.StringBuilder) "http://dubleautoriza.net/iBanking/sms/ping.php"
public java.lang.String
      java.lang.StringBuilder("http://dubleautoriza.net/iBanking/sms/ping.php").toString()
return (java.lang.String) "http://dubleautoriza.net/iBanking/sms/ping.php"
new org.apache.http.client.methods.HttpPost((java.lang.String)
      "http://dubleautoriza.net/iBanking/sms/ping.php")
```

The following APIs are processed in a special way because they are directly connected with endpoint activity (see Sect. 2.2):

- `SmsManager`'s functions are interesting because they can be used to send text messages to a specified number.
- `URL.openConnection` is interesting because it specifies an URL to connect to. Also `apache.*` methods are tracked for the same purpose.
- `GoogleCloudMessaging.register` (and deprecated versions) are used for GCM-related operations. We are interested in extracting the sender ID, which uniquely identifies the server-side message sender.

## 2.2 Phase 2: Endpoint Ranking and Enrichment

In this phase, DroydSeuss ranks endpoints according to various heuristics. We define three rank levels, in order from the least to the most important:

1. **Suspicious**, if an endpoint is matched only during static analysis.

2. **Significant**, if a web endpoint is matched during dynamic analysis, yet in ancillary functions (e.g., string manipulation). This specific rank level allows to reveal cases such as the concatenation of a domain name with the paths.
3. **Important**, if the endpoint is matched during dynamic analysis in an API function which indicates that the malware has actually used the endpoint.

Additionally, we enrich extracted endpoints with the following details:

- **Geolocalization.** We use a free service [3] for IPs and the `pycountry` library for phone numbers.
- **Autonomous System.** We associate the IPs to their respective autonomous system using the Cymru service [4], which exposes a DNS-based API.
- **Phone number type.** Using `libphonenumber`, we determine whether the phone number is a fixed line, mobile, fixed line or mobile, toll free, premium rate, shared cost, VOIP, personal number, pager, UAN or voicemail.

### 2.3 Phase 3: Frequent Itemset Mining

In this phase, DroydSeuss implements our second rationale to elicit recurrent relations between the endpoints ranked as C&C (highest rank level) and the APK metadata. In principle, any metadata can be used but, based on the results of previous work [13] and on our results, we concentrate on the package name.

We leverage a fast, simple but effective frequent itemset mining technique. In essence, we count the occurrences of ⟨endpoint feature, package name prefix⟩ tuples, where *endpoint feature* ∈ {country, ASN, domain, IP} and *package name prefix* is the shortest prefix with at least two elements (e.g., `com.ann88.*`) (from hereinafter, for brevity, we use the terms *package name* and *package name prefix* as synonyms). Finally, we count occurrences of each itemset in our dataset of APKs, that is $\#\langle e, p \rangle$ $\forall e, p$, where $e$ and $p$ are the actual values of the endpoint feature and package name. To obtain the *frequency* [11] $\phi$ of each itemset we calculate:

$$\phi\langle e, p \rangle = 2 \cdot \frac{\#\langle e, p \rangle}{\#(p) + \max_p \#(p)}, \tag{1}$$

where $\#(p)$ is the number of APKs with that package name—we do not count multiple occurrences of a package within the same APK. We normalize $\phi \in [0, 1]$ by multiplying by a factor 2. Moreover, summing the count of the most frequent package name $\max_p \phi(p)$ gives more weight to really frequent packages and, on the other hand, avoids assigning high frequencies to itemsets generated by only few packages.

## 3     Experimental Results

Although providing a complete evaluation for an intelligence system that can potentially produce novel knowledge is a difficult task, we want to obtain quantitative and qualitative indicators about its performance, correctness and usefulness for the analyst.

## 3.1  Dataset and Setup

For the purpose of this evaluation we used 4,293 samples of banking trojans, downloaded nightly through the VirusTotal Intelligence API, that match the following malware families: ZitMo, SpitMo, CitMo, iBanking and FakeBank.

As Fig. 2 shows, DroydSeuss has been running for almost 12 months since its release in late October 2014. Since January 10, we started monitoring web-based endpoints by sending an HTTP HEAD request and keeping track of whether they responded. On average, a little over 10% of the contacted endpoints responded.

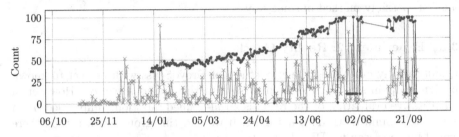

**Fig. 2.** Daily number of downloaded/processed samples (blue) and number of responding web-based endpoints (red). (Color figure online)

## 3.2  Experiment 1: False Positives

As the feed of samples includes only known malicious APKs, we expect a low fraction of benign domains. This is important because the assumption behind any malware tracker is that the activity performed by the sample is malicious or otherwise interesting for the malware analyst.

As of October 9, 2015, the fraction of benign domains in the feed of samples tracked by DroydSeuss is minuscule, summarized in Table 1. We obtained these numbers by using the Alexa Top 1M domain list [2] as a whitelist.

We manually analyzed the benign domains and found that the ones classified as *important* were `baidu.com` and `cl.ly`. The sample contacting `baidu.com` was using the following URL templates:

http://www.baidu.com/index.php?m=Api&a=SMSReceiver&imsi=CENSORED&
number=CENSORED&from=86279&content=CENSORED

**Table 1.** Rate of benign (Alexa Top 1M) domain names found in the samples.

|  | Important | Significant | Suspicious |
|---|---|---|---|
| Distinct | 2/410 (0.48%) | 8/597 (1.34%) | 57/571 (9.98%) |
| Overall (distinct per sample) | 2/1453 (0.13%) | 109/3052 (3.57%) | 277/12636 (2.19%) |

Manual inspection of the sample confirmed that it was a data-stealing trojan that sent stolen data encoded as `baidu.com` URLs. In a similar vein, `cl.ly` URLs point to a legitimate file-hosting service, which is being used by the miscreants to host malicious APKs. This may appear strange, but using existing, popular services as the backend of a (mobile) botnet essentially creates a covert channel, making it hard for the analysts to separate between legitimate and non-legitimate traffic. In fact, although not prevalent, botnets that follow this approach have recently appeared in the wild [7]. In conclusion, although whitelisting the known benign domains is tempting, we believe that they should be reported to the analyst, possibly marked in some way.

### 3.3   Experiment 2: Reality Check

Quantitatively evaluating the correctness of DroydSeuss with respect to known benign endpoints is feasible, as discussed in the previous section. However, a quantitative evaluation of the recall is an ill-defined question, simply because a complete ground truth does not exist. If we had this ground truth, then there would be no reason for DroydSeuss to exist.

We opted for a qualitative evaluation that we carried out by manually Googling for endpoints which DroydSeuss assigned high rankings to and inspecting the search results. In addition, we used threat investigation channels such as private mailing lists, CERTs, and other sources of contextual information that corroborate the correctness of our findings.

**Endpoints from Most Frequent Itemsets.** We took the domain names of the C&C appearing in the highest ranked itemsets (top 10) and searched for evidence to support their relevance. Over the past year, `*.vicp.co` (78.96%), `smsgrabber.url.ph`, `y30icv.com` and `124ffsaf.com` are the most relevant ones.

The latter search key lead us to a Trusteer report [10] that confirmed that it was indeed used to collect data stolen from SpyEye bots. `smsgrabber.url.ph` was part of the C&C infrastructure used by the iBanking Malware in late 2014, as confirmed by a technical report by F5 [16]. Interestingly, according to Google Safe Browsing, `*.y30icv.com` is not engaged in any malicious activity, although according to our analysis it is clearly pointing to C&C and APK-hosting server.

As we found no public reports about `*.vicp.co`, we extended our search using PassiveTotal [5] and a private mailing list used by experts to exchange fresh, threat-related information. It was found that we spotted an actively spreading trojan campaign started in December 2014, targeting Korean and Chinese customers. According to the intelligence information at our disposal and to ZeuS Tracker, none of these subdomains were used for non-mobile malicious purposes. In conclusion, the campaign that was brought to our attention, thanks to the frequent itemset mining system of DroydSeuss, is a very relevant one and seems to be exclusively targeting mobile customers. Our findings were later confirmed by the NASK/CERT Polska.

**Phone Numbers from Most Frequent Itemsets.** Among the most frequent itemsets we found numbers such as +467694XXXX, used as C&C in ZitMo campaigns [19], +79252XXXX, included in a spyware kit [14] or +447781XXXX, used by an iBanking campaign [12] and further confirmed by the NASK/CERT Polska. A curious case is +49157061XXXX, a German number used as a C&C endpoint by 20 samples. According to a (cached) WHOIS record, this phone number was of the admin contact the kundencenter-accountservice.com domain name. A further search revealed that the number was used in the past to host a PayPal phishing campaign [18].

**GCM Endpoints.** Among the samples that used GCM endpoints (i.e., sender ID 738965552XXXX, a C&C server address 94.75.**.** and the respective domain name), we found one blog post [6] and a project deliverable [9]. The blog post was written by the AndroTotal group and required to manually reverse engineer the samples and extract the concise relevant information extracted automatically by DroydSeuss. Similarly, the project deliverable described the results of an analysis of the sample carried out manually in order to recognize whether the APK was malicious or not.

To summarize, the evidence reported by DroydSeuss led us to finding either (1) automatically generated analysis reports that confirmed their correctness, or (2) manually written technical reports that certainly required human effort. Therefore, we can argue that DroydSeuss extracts data that is correct and useful for analysts. Of course, this manual effort was required only once to confirm our findings.

### 3.4 Experiment 3: Runtime Performance

From analyzing 100 apps, we conclude that DroydSeuss completes the analysis of one APK in about 5 min on average. The heaviest part is dynamic analysis with an average of 4'40". Static data extraction and ranking are negligible.

## 4 Limitations and Future Work

The itemset mining process may be subject to specific evasion attempts. By randomizing the *entire* package name an attacker could make DroydSeuss generate one low-frequency itemset per distinct APK. However, this would be against the attacker's goals who wants to mimic the official apps. Indeed, recent work [13] showed that, according to the cyber criminals' modus operandi, the package name is suitable as a lightweight identifier. As a mitigation, other features could be used together with the package name to better characterize a sample.

Since Android malware's sophistication is relatively low compared to PC-based malware, DroydSeuss does not trace native code. Future work should focus on whether this is necessary and, if it is, how this can be implemented efficiently.

DroydSeuss inherits the limitations of dynamic analysis. A sample may not show its (malicious) behavior because some code paths are not reached, it recognizes that it is running in an emulator [17,21] or it employs advanced timing attacks. Our experience indicates that samples need to contact the C&C at least once, which is enough for our purposes. Notwithstanding, as a mitigation, our sandbox strives to stimulate the execution by injecting various events and we also used a patched emulator that resembles a smartphone-like hardware profile.

In addition to addressing the first two limitations, we foresee another research direction. While searching for qualitative evidence to support our findings, we understood that infection campaigns against desktop computers could be used as an early-warning indicator of upcoming mobile infection campaigns. Indeed, we foresee an approach that tracks the HTML content injected by ZeuS (desktop) and checks whether it contains signs of URLs or QR-codes pointing the user to download an APK. Moving from this observation, more advanced pre-infection indicators could be derived in order to alert mobile customers.

## 5  Conclusions

The community of malware researchers relies on publicly available feeds. Droyd-Seuss is a first step towards a public tracker of mobile botnets in the spirit of ZeuS Tracker. The Android Malware Trckr appeared some months [15] after DroydSeuss, showing once again the importance of such data feeds.

With this work, we showed that the simple yet effective ranking mechanisms that DroydSeuss conveys, can correctly pinpoint relevant active campaigns, concluding that our approach works.

**Acknowledgments.** The authors are thankful to the reviewers and to MIUR FACE Project No. RBFR13AJFT and Reply CV for supporting this work.

## References

1. Zeus tracker. https://zeustracker.abuse.ch/
2. Alexa top 1M (2015). http://s3.amazonaws.com/alexa-static/top-1m.csv.zip
3. HostIP (2015). www.hostip.info
4. IP to ASN mapping (2015). http://www.team-cymru.org/IP-ASN-mapping.html
5. PassiveTotal (2015). https://www.passivetotal.org
6. Andrototal.org: (Another) Android trojan scheme using Google Cloud Messaging (2015). http://blog.andrototal.org/post/89637972097/another-android-trojan-scheme-using-google-cloud
7. Lehtiö, A.: C&C-as-a-service: abusing third-party web services as C&C channels (2015). https://www.virusbtn.com/conference/vb2015/abstracts/R-Lehtio.xml
8. Chebyshev, V., Unuchek, R.: Mobile malware evolution: 2013 (2014). http://securelist.com/analysis/kaspersky-security-bulletin/58335/mobile-malware-evolution-2013

9. Delosières, L., Baltatu, M.: D2.3 lightweight malware detector. Technical report, Enhanced Network Security for Seamless Service Provisioning in the Smart Mobile Ecosystem (2012). http://www.nemesys-project.eu/nemesys/files/document/deliverables/NEMESYS_Deliverable_D2.3.pdf
10. Heyman, A.: First SpyEye attack on Android mobile platform now in the wild (2011). http://www.trusteer.com/cn/node/360
11. Hipp, J., Güntzer, U., Nakhaeizadeh, G.: Algorithms for association rule mining - a general survey and comparison. SIGKDD Explor. Newsl. 2(1), 58–64 (2000). http://doi.acm.org/10.1145/360402.360421
12. Kafeine: Nitmo? no!dotsjust "iBanking" used by a (the?) neverquest/vawtrak team (2013). http://malware.dontneedcoffee.com/2013/12/nitmo-no-just-ibanking-used-by-the.html
13. Lindorfer, M., et al.: AndRadar: fast discovery of Android applications in alternative markets. In: Dietrich, S. (ed.) DIMVA 2014. LNCS, vol. 8550, pp. 51–71. Springer, Cham (2014). doi:10.1007/978-3-319-08509-8_4
14. Loetprasoetsit, A.: Csd 2013 sso_session_2_14112013 (2013). http://www.slideshare.net/nozumutee/csd-2013-ssosession214112013
15. Siewierski, L.: Tweet by maldr0id (2015). https://twitter.com/maldr0id/status/595953612032991232
16. Meller, I.: F5SOC iBanking malware analysis report. Technical report. https://devcentral.f5.com/d/f5soc-ibanking-malware-analysis-report
17. Petsas, T., Voyatzis, G., Athanasopoulos, E., Polychronakis, M., Ioannidis, S.: Rage against the virtual machine: hindering dynamic analysis of Android malware. In: Proceedings of the Seventh European Workshop on System Security, EuroSec 2014, pp. 5:1–5:6. ACM, New York (2014). http://doi.acm.org/10.1145/2592791.2592796
18. PhishReported: Submission #1531388 - http://kundencenter-accountservice.com (2015). http://www.phishtank.com/phish_detail.php?phish_id=1531388
19. Spasojevic, B.: Android.zeusmitmo (2012). http://www.symantec.com/security_response/writeup.jsp?docid=2012-080818-0448-99&tabid=2
20. Van Der Veen, V.: Dynamic analysis of Android malware. Ph.D. thesis (2013). http://tracedroid.few.vu.nl/thesis.pdf
21. Vidas, T., Christin, N.: Evading Android runtime analysis via sandbox detection. In: Proceedings of the 9th ACM Symposium on Information, Computer and Communications Security, ASIA CCS 2014, pp. 447–458. ACM, New York (2014). http://doi.acm.org/10.1145/2590296.2590325

# DroidAuditor: Forensic Analysis of Application-Layer Privilege Escalation Attacks on Android (Short Paper)

Stephan Heuser[1(✉)], Marco Negro[2], Praveen Kumar Pendyala[1],
and Ahmad-Reza Sadeghi[1]

[1] Intel CRI-SC, TU Darmstadt, Darmstadt, Germany
{stephan.heuser,praveen.pendyala,ahmad.sadeghi}@trust.cased.de
[2] University of Padua, Padua, Italy
mnegro@studenti.math.unipd.it

**Abstract.** Smart mobile devices process and store a vast amount of security- and privacy-sensitive data. To protect this data from malicious applications mobile operating systems, such as Android, adopt fine-grained access control architectures. However, related work has shown that these access control architectures are susceptible to application-layer privilege escalation attacks. Both automated static and dynamic program analysis promise to proactively detect such attacks. Though while state-of-the-art static analysis frameworks cannot adequately address native and highly obfuscated code, dynamic analysis is vulnerable to malicious applications using logic bombs to avoid *early* detection.

In contrast, the *long-term* observation of application behavior could help users and security analysts better understand malicious apps. In this paper we present the design and implementation of DroidAuditor, which observes application behavior on real Android devices and generates a graph-based representation. It visualizes this *behavior graph*, which enables users to develop an intuitive understanding of application internals. Our solution further allows security analysts to query the behavior graph for malicious patterns. We present the design of the DroidAuditor framework and instantiate it using the Android Security Modules (ASM) access control architecture. We evaluate its capability to detect application-layer privilege escalation attacks, such as confused deputy and collusion attacks. In addition, we demonstrate how our architecture can be used to analyze malicious spyware applications.

## 1 Introduction

Smart mobile devices, such as smartphones and tablets, host a vast number of third-party applications of varying quality and trustworthiness. These applications access, store and process security- and privacy-sensitive data, ranging from personal contacts, location information to high-profile enterprise assets, which makes these devices valuable targets for attacks. Unsurprisingly, the number of newly discovered malware families targeting these devices is rising [11].

© International Financial Cryptography Association 2017
J. Grossklags and B. Preneel (Eds.): FC 2016, LNCS 9603, pp. 260–268, 2017.
DOI: 10.1007/978-3-662-54970-4_15

To mitigate such attacks operating systems for smart mobile devices use fine-grained access control architectures. For example, Android uses *permissions* to restrict access to privacy- and security-sensitive data. However, related work has shown that Android's access control model is susceptible to application-layer privilege escalation attacks, ranging from insufficiently protected system settings [7] to accessing the Internet [10] or sending SMS [4] without holding corresponding permissions.

The systematic detection, analysis and mitigation of such attacks is an active area of research today: On one hand, system-centric access control architectures [3,8] attempt to mitigate these attacks using carefully designed use-case specific policies. On the other hand, both static and dynamic program analysis promise to proactively detect such attacks, but either do not adequately address native and highly obfuscated code, or are susceptible to malware using logic bombs [12] to avoid early detection.

This inability to proactively and reliably detect application-layer privilege escalation attacks mandates tools for long-term observation and analysis of application behavior. In this paper, we present DroidAuditor, a forensic application behavior analysis toolkit targeting application-layer privilege escalation attacks. DroidAuditor adopts the *Android Security Modules (ASM)* [8] access control architecture to observe application behavior at all layers of the Android operating system. Our solution organizes these observations in a *behavior graph* and generates an interactive visualization. It further allows forensic analysts to query this graph for suspicious patterns using a graph query language.

Our main contributions are as follows:

- We present the design and implementation of DroidAuditor, a solution for application behavior analysis using interactive behavior graphs.
- We evaluate DroidAuditor's capabilities by analyzing application-layer privilege escalation attacks as well as malicious spyware apps.
- We show that sophisticated access control frameworks, such as the ASM framework, are a valid basis for application behavior analysis.

DroidAuditor differs from related work on application behavior analysis in two major aspects: First, to the best of our knowledge, it is the first solution that adopts a modular access control framework for application behavior analysis. Second, the behavior graph generated by DroidAuditor serves as an important building block for further research on application behavior analysis, which we describe in more detail in our technical report [9] due to space constraints.

## 2 Background

Android is a Linux-based operating system for smart mobile devices. It hosts system and third-party applications, which consist of the following main components: *Activities* (GUI elements), *Services* (background tasks without any user interface), *ContentProviders* (data stores with SQL semantics) and *Broadcast-Receivers* (mailboxes for messages *(Intents)* from other components). Applications are executed in isolated least-privilege sandboxes, and they share data and functionality via inter-process communication (IPC). Standard operating system components located on the middleware and application layer provide access to security- and privacy-sensitive resources, such as location information or contacts data. To control access to these components Android uses *permissions* granted by the user to applications.

However, this permission-based access control model is prone to application-layer privilege escalation attacks, such as confused deputy and collusion attacks [4]. In a confused deputy attack, an adversary abuses non-malicious but vulnerable software components via IPC to perform privileged security- and privacy-sensitive operations: On Android, for example, only apps holding the INTERNET permission are able to open network sockets. However, any app can contact arbitrary web servers by deputizing the web browser via IPC [10]. In contrast, in a collusion attack multiple seemingly benign applications operate in concert to share their permissions towards a common goal. Colluding applications coordinate their attack via overt (e.g., Android's Binder IPC mechanism) or covert communication channels, such as shared system settings or files.

## 3    Adversary Model and Objectives

The main goals of DroidAuditor are the systematic monitoring of application behavior and the detection as well as forensic analysis of potential application-layer privilege escalation attacks. The adversary is capable of deploying one or more malicious applications on a target device, for example via social engineering or by gaining temporary physical access to the device. We place no restrictions on the type of code the adversary executes and thus allow managed bytecode as well as native and self-modifying code. Since DroidAuditor is a system-centric application behavior analysis framework, we have to assume that malicious applications do not gain administrative device management privileges, and that the trusted computing base of the Android device (bootloader, operating system kernel, middleware layer and system applications) remains intact. Otherwise, no correct app behavior analysis can be guaranteed. Finally, we assume that all DroidAuditor software components are trusted.

## 4    DroidAuditor

The high-level idea of DroidAuditor is to observe application behavior using the system-centric Android Security Modules (ASM) access control framework [8]. DroidAuditor stores these observations in a *behavior graph*, where vertices represent applications and resources, and edges represent data- or control flows.

Consider the following confused deputy attack: A malicious Android application holds the READ_CONTACTS permission and abuses the web browser to exfiltrate sensitive contacts information to a remote server without holding the INTERNET permission. Figure 1 shows this attack as a behavior graph: Upon start (Step 1) the malicious app reads sensitive data from the contacts database (Step 2). It then starts the web browser via an Intent (Step 3) and instructs it to

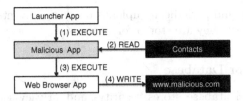

**Fig. 1.** Example confused deputy attack, where a malicious app deputizes the web browser to exfiltrate sensitive contacts information.

exfiltrate contacts data on its behalf. The web browser opens a network socket to a remote server and uploads the collected contacts information (Step 4).

DroidAuditor generates such behavior graphs using three main components (see Fig. 2). On the mobile device, the ASM for DroidAuditor is notified by the ASM framework whenever Android applications access security- or privacy-critical resources (Steps 1 – 4). The DroidAuditor ASM forwards these events to the DroidAuditor Database via an authenticated and encrypted channel (Step B), where they are stored in the behavior graph. Finally, security analysts can interact with the behavior graph using the DroidAuditor Client (Step C).

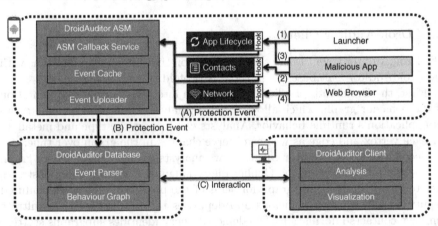

**Fig. 2.** DroidAuditor high-level architecture.

## 4.1   DroidAuditor ASM

The Android Security Modules framework places hooks in all security- and privacy-sensitive kernel- and middleware-layer operating-system components. These hooks generate aforementioned protection events, which the ASM framework forwards to all installed security modules. Each module can then decide whether to allow or deny the corresponding operations. Our DroidAuditor Android Security Module however does not enforce any access control rules, but collects protection events to obtain a *global view* of all privacy- and security-critical operations performed by *all* applications. Accordingly, it allows every access control query and periodically uploads protection events to the DroidAuditor Database, where they are stored for analysis.

## 4.2   DroidAuditor Database

The DroidAuditor Database stores security- and privacy-sensitive protection events for offline analysis. It parses events uploaded by the DroidAuditor ASM and generates the *behavior graph* $G = \langle V, E \rangle$: The vertex set $V = A \cup R$ is composed of two subsets $A$ and $R$, which represent applications $A$ and resources $R$. For each application vertex $a \in A$ the DroidAuditor Database stores an identifier as well as additional metadata, for instance the permissions the application holds. Each resource vertex $r \in R$ models a security- or privacy-sensitive operating system resource. Important examples are Android's ContactsProvider, LocationManagerService or CameraService, as well as files and network sockets.

Every edge $e \in E$ is directional and describes a data- or control flow between two vertices $v_i, v_j \in V$. Each edge contains descriptive metadata, such as the time and date a flow was observed. Edges are grouped into categories, which model Android component interaction as well as file system and network operations (CREATE, READ, WRITE, UPDATE, DELETE, EXECUTE).

## 4.3   DroidAuditor Client

The DroidAuditor Client is a desktop application that interacts in real-time with the DroidAuditor Database. Its purpose is twofold:

First, the DroidAuditor Client generates an interactive visual representation of the behavior graph, which allows forensic analysts to intuitively understand an application's runtime behavior. Analysts can inspect the type and metadata for each vertex and edge as well as observe changes in the graph over time.

Second, the DroidAuditor Client allows analysts to query the behavior graph for specific patterns using the Cypher query language.[1] Listing 1 demonstrates how to query the behavior graph for signs of the previously described confused deputy attack, where a malicious app deputizes the web browser to exfiltrate sensitive contacts information. The depicted query identifies subgraphs starting with apps reading the Contacts resource (Lines 1–2). We only consider applications which then execute the Android web browser (Line 3) and do not hold the INTERNET permission (Line 5). Finally, this query expects the web browser to write data to a network socket (Line 4). Matching subgraphs are highlighted using the visualization plugin.

```
1   MATCH confuseddeputy = (contacts:Resource {type:'contacts'})
2   - [event1:READ] -> (app1:App {systemApp:false})
3   - [event2:EXECUTE] -> (app2:App {package:'com.android.browser'})
4   - [event3:WRITE] -> (socket:Resource {type:'socket'})
5   WHERE NOT 'internet' IN app1.permissions
```

**Listing 1.** Cypher query to detect the confused deputy attack.

---

[1] http://neo4j.com/developer/cypher-query-language/.

# 5  Evaluation

DroidAuditor inherits the performance and energy consumption overhead of the underlying Android Security Modules framework, which has been scrutinized in [8]. In this work we primarily focused on DroidAuditor's effectiveness to analyze malicious application behavior. To this end, we implemented the DroidAuditor architecture using the Java programing language. We place the DroidAuditor ASM on a Nexus 4 smartphone running the ASM architecture version 4.4.4 r2. The Neo4J-based DroidAuditor graph database[2] and the DroidAuditor client communicate opportunistically when Wifi connectivity is available using the Kryonet[3] network communication stack. Real-world DroidAuditor deployments however should consider more firewall-friendly communication channels, such as HTTPS. The behavior graph is visualized using the GraphStream[4] library. We then deployed applications which implement confused deputy and collusion attacks as well as malicious spyware applications on the device and analyzed their behavior.

## 5.1  Application-Layer Privilege Escalation Attacks

**Confused Deputy Attacks.** We implemented the confused deputy attack described in Sect. 4, where a malicious app not holding the INTERNET permission deputizes the web browser to exfiltrate sensitive contacts data to a remote server. We then verified that the query described previously in Listing 1 indeed correctly identifies this confused deputy attack.

**Collusion Attacks.** We further implemented two variants of a collusion attack, where two malicious apps coordinate their actions towards a common goal, which in our example is to exfiltrate the SMS database over the Internet. The first malicious application only possesses the READ_SMS permission, and the second application only the INTERNET permission.

*Collusion via Binder IPC.* In a simple collusion attack two malicious apps communicate using overt channels, such as Android's Binder IPC mechanism. Listing 2 shows a Cypher query which targets this behavior. We query the behavior graph for non-system apps (Line 3), which do not hold the INTERNET permission (Line 5) and read from the SMS database (Line 1 and 2). We search for paths leading to another non-system app, which writes data to a remote server (Line 3 and 4). The corresponding subgraph is highlighted in Fig. 3(a).

```
1   MATCH collusion1 = (sms:Resource {type:'sms'})
2   - [event1:READ] -> (app1:App {systemApp:false})
3   - [event2:EXECUTE] -> (app2:App {systemApp:false})
4   - [event3:WRITE] -> (socket:Resource {type:'socket'})
5   WHERE NOT 'internet' IN app1.permissions
```

**Listing 2.** Cypher Query to detect the collusion attack depicted in Fig. 3(a).

---

[2] http://www.neo4j.com.

[3] https://github.com/EsotericSoftware/kryonet.

[4] http://graphstream-project.org/.

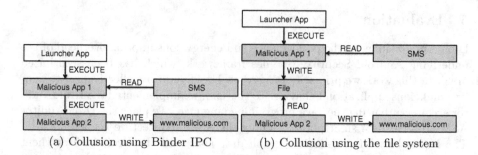

(a) Collusion using Binder IPC    (b) Collusion using the file system

**Fig. 3.** Example collusion attacks where two malicious apps coordinate their behavior to exfiltrate the SMS database.

*Collusion via File-based Communication.* In this obfuscated collusion attack two applications share a file on the file system to exchange sensitive data. Note that no direct inter-process communication between both apps occurs in this scenario. Starting from the previous query in Listing 2, we add a file resource node to the query which matches files written to and read from the two colluding applications. Listing 3 shows the resulting query, and Fig. 3(b) depicts a visualization of the discovered subgraph.

```
1    MATCH collusion2 = (sms:Resource {type:'sms'})
2    - [event1:READ] -> (app1:App {systemApp:false})
3    - [event2:WRITE] -> (file:Resource {type:'file'})
4    - [event3:READ] -> (app2:App {systemApp:false})
5    - [event4:WRITE] -> (socket:Resource {type:'socket'})
6    WHERE NOT 'internet' IN app1.permissions
```

**Listing 3.** Cypher Query to detect the collusion attack depicted in Fig. 3(b).

DroidAuditor can similarly be used to detect signs of collusion attacks via other operating-system resources, such as domain or network sockets, Content-Providers or Services. However, it should be noted that DroidAuditor is limited by the granularity of the underlying ASM framework, which is unable to observe app collusion via hardware side channels, such as the CPU cache.

## 5.2    Identifying Spyware Applications

To demonstrate that DroidAuditor is a valid basis for generic application behavior analysis beyond application-layer privilege escalation attacks we installed two popular spyware applications, namely "TheTruthSpy"[5] and "LetMeSpy"[6], on a DroidAuditor device. By analyzing the behavior graph we found that these apps silently access privacy-sensitive resources, such as the CallLog and SMS/MMS ContentProviders as well as location data, and upload this data to a remote server. We further noticed that these apps only have very limited user interfaces (Activities), which are exclusively used for initial configuration.

---

[5] http://thetruthspy.com/.

[6] http://www.letmespy.com/.

To detect such behavior, we first labeled all privacy-sensitive resources in the behavior graph. In Listing 4, we query the graph for non-system apps accessing these resources (Lines 1 and 2) and writing data to a remote server (Line 3). The WHERE clause (Line 4) limits our query to apps which silently access privacy-sensitive resources. A visualization of the behavior graph and corresponding DroidAuditor client screenshots can be found in our technical report [9].

```
1  MATCH spyware1 = (res:Resource {privacySensitive:true})
2  - [event1:READ] -> (app:App {systemApp:false})
3  - [event2:WRITE] -> (socket:Resource {type:'socket', addr:'69.64.81.49'})
4  WHERE NOT event1.foregroundApp = app.package
```

**Listing 4.** Cypher query to detect the behavior of the TheTruthSpy app.

## 6 Related Work

Our DroidAuditor architecture shares functionality with dynamic program analysis solutions [2,6,13–16], which observe app behavior in instrumented Android environments. Common techniques adopted by these frameworks are system call tracing, dynamic taint analysis and virtual machine introspection. While taint analysis can provide fine-grained tracing of privacy sensitive data while it is processed on a device, current designs do not adequately handle native code. Further, all approaches adopting dynamic program analysis are prone to logic bombs, where apps delay their malicious behavior to avoid detection [12]. DroidAuditor avoids these limitations by observing application behavior on real Android devices without imposing restrictions on the analyzed applications.

Some work has proposed the use of IPC call chain verification [1,5,7] to mitigate application-layer privilege escalation attacks. Other work more related to DroidAuditor [3] records app interaction in a graph structure and enforces access control policies targeting confused deputy and collusion attacks. Since DroidAuditor is based on the system-centric ASM access control framework, it is conceivable to implement this functionality by generating the behavior graph on the mobile device itself and applying a corresponding access control policy.

## 7 Conclusion

In this paper, we presented DroidAuditor, a toolkit for forensic long-term application behavior analysis. DroidAuditor uses the system-centric ASM mandatory access control framework to generate a graph-based model of application behavior. The preliminary evaluation of our proof-of-concept implementation demonstrates that modular access control frameworks are a valid building block for application behavior analysis and motivate us to extend our work in multiple directions: First, we plan to conduct a usability study to better understand how users interact with DroidAuditor. Second, we are implementing a policy enforcement architecture based on DroidAuditor's behavior graph by storing and evaluating the behavior graph on the mobile device. Finally, we aim to integrate dynamic taint analysis into DroidAuditor, which would allow us to support more precise data flow analysis for applications which do not contain native code.

# References

1. Backes, M., Bugiel, S., Gerling, S.: Scippa: system-centric IPC provenance on android. In: 30th Annual Computer Security Applications Conference, pp. 36–45. ACM (2014)
2. Blsing, T., Batyuk, L., Schmidt, A.-D., Camtepe, S., Albayrak, S.: An android application sandbox system for suspicious software detection. In: 5th International Conference on Malicious and Unwanted Software, pp. 55–62 (2010)
3. Bugiel, S., Davi, L., Dmitrienko, A., Fischer, T., Sadeghi, A.-R., Shastry, B.: Towards taming privilege-escalation attacks on android. In: 19th Annual Network & Distributed System Security Symposium (2012)
4. Davi, L., Dmitrienko, A., Sadeghi, A.-R., Winandy, M.: Privilege escalation attacks on android. In: Burmester, M., Tsudik, G., Magliveras, S., Ilić, I. (eds.) ISC 2010. LNCS, vol. 6531, pp. 346–360. Springer, Heidelberg (2011). doi:10.1007/978-3-642-18178-8_30
5. Dietz, M., Shekhar, S., Pisetsky, Y., Shu, A., Wallach, D.S.: Quire: lightweight provenance for smart phone operating systems. In: 20th USENIX Security Symposium, USENIX (2011)
6. Enck, W., Gilbert, P., Chun, B.-G., Cox, L.P., Jung, J., McDaniel, P., Sheth, A.N.: TaintDroid: an information flow tracking system for real-time privacy monitoring on smartphones. Commun. ACM 57(3), 99–106 (2014)
7. Felt, A.P., Wang, H.J., Moshchuk, A., Hanna, S., Chin, E.: Permission re-delegation: attacks and defenses. In: 20th USENIX Security Symposium, USENIX (2011)
8. Heuser, S., Nadkarni, A., Enck, W., Sadeghi, A.-R.: ASM: a programmable interface for extending android security. In: 23rd USENIX Security Symposium, USENIX (2014)
9. Heuser, S., Negro, M., Pendyala, P.K., Sadeghi, A.-R.: DroidAuditor: Forensic Analysis of Application-Layer Privilege Escalation Attacks on Android. Technical report, TU Darmstadt (2016)
10. Lineberry, A., Richardson, D.L., Wyatt, T.: These Aren't the Permissions You're Looking For. DefCon 18 (2010)
11. McAfee. Threats report May 2015. http://www.mcafee.com/us/resources/reports/rp-quarterly-threat-q1-2015.pdf, May 2015
12. Rasthofer, S., Asrar, I., Huber, S., Bodden, E.: How current android malware seeks to evade automated code analysis. In: Akram, R.N., Jajodia, S. (eds.) WISTP 2015. LNCS, vol. 9311, pp. 187–202. Springer, Cham (2015). doi:10.1007/978-3-319-24018-3_12
13. Rastogi, V., Chen, Y., Enck, W.: AppsPlayground: automatic security analysis of smartphone applications. In: Third ACM Conference on Data and Application Security and Privacy, pp. 209–220. ACM (2013)
14. Spreitzenbarth, M., Freiling, F., Echtler, F., Schreck, T., Hoffmann, J.: Mobile-sandbox: having a deeper look into android applications. In: 28th Annual ACM Symposium on Applied Computing, pp. 1808–1815. ACM (2013)
15. Tam, K., Khan, S.J., Fattori, A., Cavallaro, L.: CopperDroid: automatic reconstruction of android malware behaviors. In: 22nd Annual Network & Distributed System Security Symposium (2015)
16. Yan, L.K., Yin, H.: DroidScope: seamlessly reconstructing the OS and dalvik semantic views for dynamic android malware analysis. In: 21st USENIX Security Symposium, USENIX (2012)

# Social Interaction and Policy

# Discrete Choice, Social Interaction, and Policy in Encryption Technology Adoption (Short Paper)

Tristan Caulfield[1]([✉]), Christos Ioannidis[2], and David Pym[1]

[1] University College London, London, UK
{t.caulfield,d.pym}@ucl.ac.uk
[2] Aston Business School, Birmingham, UK
c.ioannidis@aston.ac.uk

**Abstract.** We introduce a model for examining the factors that lead to the adoption of new encryption technologies. Building on the work of Brock and Durlauf, the model describes how agents make choices, in the presence of social interaction, between competing technologies given their relative cost, functionality, and usability. We apply the model to examples about the adoption of encryption in communication (email and messaging) and storage technologies (self-encrypting drives) and also consider our model's predictions for the evolution of technology adoption over time.

## 1 Introduction

In recent years, especially in the light of Edward Snowden's revelations, awareness of the need for enhanced privacy and confidentiality for both communications and devices has increased. In response to this, many new technologies, including various forms of encryption, have been introduced. However, the adoption of these new technologies is not guaranteed: their use depends on a number of factors, including how effective they are, how much they cost, how easy they are to use, and the social and policy contexts within which they are introduced.

The use of encryption for electronic communications and data storage is accelerating and people are increasingly shifting to new technologies for interpersonal communications. Such behavioural changes are indicative of the existence of agents revising their choices between technological alternatives to achieve their communications goals. The aim of the paper is to provide a theoretical framework which can capture such changes in the choice of technologies in the presence of external impulses emanating from either policy or other external events.

We introduce a model, based on work by Brock and Durlauf [1], that incorporates these factors into a utility-theoretic framework that describes how agents make choices between competing technologies. We use this model to analyse the adoption of encryption in a range of communication and storage technologies. We consider three examples: first, email, where we look at the use of PGP/GPG encryption; second, messaging applications, where we examine the adoption of

© International Financial Cryptography Association 2017
J. Grossklags and B. Preneel (Eds.): FC 2016, LNCS 9603, pp. 271–279, 2017.
DOI: 10.1007/978-3-662-54970-4_16

WhatsApp compared to traditional SMS messaging; and, finally, the adoption of self-encrypting drives over standard, non-encrypted drives.

The Brock and Durlauf model captures social interactions between non-cooperative decision-making agents. This reflects the reality of decisions about the use of encryption: agents—either individuals or organizations—make decisions independently and without coordination and yet their decisions can have an effect on the utility of other agents. For example, the utility of encrypted communications technology to a user changes with the number of other users; it is low if there is nobody to communicate with, and higher if it can be used to communicate with a larger number of others.

Besides the social interactions, the Brock and Durlauf model uses the relative profitability of technologies as the main factor that determines adoption. This single factor would not give great insight into the adoption of encryption technologies. To this end, we introduce some modifications to the model that allow us to examine the influence on utility—and hence, adoption—of different technology attributes: functionality, monetary cost, and usability. These are sufficient to demonstrate the model; other attributes may also be of interest for different applications. These are multiple attributes in the sense of [4].

Other work has also looked at the adoption of security technologies. Rosasco and Larochelle [14] look at the adoption of SSH over telnet, and considers the cost and functionality of the technologies. Ozment and Schechter [13] use a model, which includes a social component, to suggest strategies to promote the adoption of DNSSEC.

In conclusion, our model is a tool for thinking about the different factors that determine adoption, such as attributes of the technologies themselves, technological innovation, or policy. Understanding how these factors affect adoption is important for decision-makers—those designing a technology, deciding whether to adopt it, or seeking to promote or inhibit adoption through policy.

## 2   Technology Adoption Model

We start with the discrete choice model of Brock and Durlauf [1], which, in this context, describes a system where $M$ technologies are competing in a market for adoption by $N$ agents. The model assigns a share of the market to each technology, based on its profitability. This profitability also includes a social component: a technology can be more profitable if more agents are using it. There can also be additional factors, such as taxes, policy, or technological innovation, but we start with the simple model and introduce the other factors below, before continuing with our extensions to apply the model to encryption technology.

The utility an agent receives from technology $c$ in time period $t$ is

$$u_{c,t} = \lambda_c + \rho_c x_{c,t}, \tag{1}$$

where the profitability of technology $c$ is given by $\lambda_c$ and the number of agents choosing $c$ at time $t$ is $x_{c,t}$. The value $\rho_c$ (where $\rho_c > 0$) defines the intensity of the social component, the term $\rho_c x_{c,t}$. The greater the value of $\rho_c$, the more agents' utilities and subsequently choices are influenced by the choices of others. Each agent $i$ experiences a random utility $\tilde{u}_{i,t} = u_{i,t} + \epsilon_{i,t}$, where the noise, $\epsilon_{i,t}$, is independently identically distributed across agents, and known to the agent at decision time. As the number of agents tends to infinity and when the noise has a double exponential distribution, the probability of adoption of technology $c$ converges to

$$x_{c,t} = \frac{e^{\beta u_{c,t-1}}}{\sum_{j=1}^{M} e^{\beta u_{j,t-1}}}. \tag{2}$$

Here, the parameter $\beta$ is the intensity of choice, and is inversely related to the variance of the noise $\epsilon_{i,t}$. When $\beta \to \infty$, there is no noise and all agents choose their optimal technology. When $\beta \to 0$, agents pick technologies randomly, and the share of each technology tends towards $1/M$. Essentially, with higher values of $\beta$, the equilibria points in the model become more extreme; that is, they tend towards 'corner solutions' with only one surviving technology.

In this model, agents know only the social term $\rho_c x_{c,t}$ in (1), which represents the decisions of other agents and benefits associated with them. Agents are making a choice between tech options with different profitability to themselves, using knowledge about market penetration in the last period.

Now let's consider a model with two competing technologies, $c$, a new technology, and $d$, an existing technology. Because there are just two, we need only one variable, $x$, which is the share of agents using technology $c$, to keep track of the state: $x_c = x$ and $x_d = 1 - x$. For simplicity, we also assume that the technologies experience equal increasing return on adoption; that is, $\rho_c = \rho_d = \rho$. From (2), the probability of adoption (and market share) of technology $c$ in time $t$ is then

$$x_t = \frac{e^{\beta(\lambda_c + \rho x_{t-1})}}{e^{\beta(\lambda_c + \rho x_{t-1})} + e^{\beta(\lambda_d + \rho(1 - x_{t-1}))}} = \frac{1}{1 + e^{\beta(\lambda + \rho(1 - 2x_{t-1}))}} = f(x_{t-1}). \tag{3}$$

The model is driven by the difference of utilities between the two technologies, $u_{d,t} - u_{c,t} = \lambda + \rho(1 - 2x_t)$, where $\lambda = \lambda_d - \lambda_c$. If the difference is positive, agents will prefer technology $d$; if it is negative, they will prefer technology $c$. More pronounced differences will result in ever-increasing shares for the preferred technology.

**Policy.** We can extend the above model with an additional component that represents a policy about the choice between the two technologies. The policy is imposed by some external source, and takes the form of a penalty or incentive on one of the technologies.

As an example, assume that technology $d$ is currently more profitable (and hence more popular) than technology $c$. A policy-maker, such as a government or industry-regulator, wishes to encourage the adoption of $c$ and may introduce a tax on $d$ or impose some regulatory restriction on its use. We represent this by adding a factor, $\tau$, to the model: $u_{d,t} - u_{c,t} = \lambda_0 + \rho(1 - 2x_t) - \tau(1 - x)$.

As the adoption of $c$ grows, although the taxation decreases (and vice versa) the social reinforcement from the increased adoption will still lead to an increased market share for $c$.

**Technological Progress.** In the previous sections, the values $\lambda_c$ and $\lambda_d$ have been static, meaning that the cost difference between the two technologies remains constant over time. We can model a change in this difference over time by considering how past investment in each of the technologies affects its current profitability. We consider the impact of the cumulative investment on each technology and postulate that such impact follows the time-dependent learning curve stated as follows:

$$\lambda_{c,t} = \lambda_{c0} + \psi_c \left( \sum_{j=1}^{t} x_j \right)^{\zeta_c} \quad \text{and} \quad \lambda_{d,t} = \lambda_{d0} + \psi_d \left( \sum_{j=1}^{t} (1 - x_j) \right)^{\zeta_d} . \quad (4)$$

Here, $\psi_d$ and $\psi_c$ are values that determine how effective investment is in making technological progress, and $\zeta_d$ and $\zeta_c \in [0, 1]$ determine the shapes of the learning curves for each of the technologies.

Now the difference in profitability depends on time,

$$\lambda_t = \lambda_{d,t} - \lambda_{c,t} = \lambda_0 + \psi_d \left( \sum_{j=1}^{t} (1 - x_j) \right)^{\zeta_d} - \psi_c \left( \sum_{j=1}^{t} x_j \right)^{\zeta_c} , \quad (5)$$

as does the difference in utility, $u_{d,t} - u_{c,t} = \lambda_t + \rho(1 - 2x_t)$, and the share of technology $c$, $x_t = \frac{1}{1+e^{\beta[\lambda_{t-1}+\rho(1-2x_{t-1})]}} = f_{t-1}(x_{t-1})$.

As an example, in the first, simple model without policy or technological progress, a new technology that starts with little market share is unlikely ever to gain very much. However, if we model the technological change, and the new technology has higher values of $\psi$ and $\zeta$ than the existing technology, it can eventually become more profitable over time, acquiring increasing market share as a progressively increasing number of agents adopt it because of increases in their personal profitability.

**Switching Costs.** In the models so far, every agent makes a decision about which technology to use in every time period. In reality, this is not the case because there are costs associated with switching. We can model this by assuming that a proportion, $\alpha$, of agents do not switch technologies in each time period:

$$f_{\tau,\alpha}(x) = \alpha x + (1 - \alpha) \frac{1}{1 + e^{\beta[\lambda_0 + \rho(1 - 2x) - \tau(1 - x)]}}.$$

**The Cryptographic Utility Function.** Improvement in utility in the basic model is based on a single value, $\lambda$, which is the difference in profitabilities between the two technologies. This value, along with social externalities, policy, and technological progress then determines the adoption of the technologies.

We introduce to the model a richer concept of utility so as to be able to express the differences between encryption technologies in greater detail. Instead of a single attribute determining the utility—its profitability, in the basic model—we use a set of different attributes, $A$ (see [3] for this multi-attribute utility-theoretic [4] set-up in the context of security). Thus, $\lambda$ becomes the difference between the values, $v_a$, of the attributes, $a \in A$, for the two technologies $c$ and $d$: $\lambda = \sum_{a \in A}(v_{a,d} - v_{a,c})$.

We also wish to be able to express policies about each of the different attributes, so we change $\tau$ to be a function which describes the policy for each attribute. The difference in utilities is then given by $u_{d,t} - u_{c,t} = \lambda_0 + \rho(1 - 2x_t) + \sum_{a \in A}\tau_a(x)$.

Finally, we describe the development of each attribute individually as investment could affect each of the attributes in different ways. The updated model allowing for technological progress is

$$\lambda_t = \lambda_{d,t} - \lambda_{c,t} = \lambda_0 + \sum_{a \in A}\left[\psi_{a,d}\left(\sum_{j=1}^{t}(1 - x_j)\right)^{\zeta_{a,d}} - \psi_{a,c}\left(\sum_{j=1}^{t}x_j\right)^{\zeta_{a,c}}\right]. \quad (6)$$

**Attributes for Encryption Technologies.** We use a set of three attributes that capture the aspects of the technologies that we wish to discuss. These attributes are appropriate to demonstrate the model with the examples we use; other technologies and applications of the model might use different attributes.

First, monetary cost: this is different from the notion of profitability in the basic model, as this (profitability) acts as an aggregate term which includes all of the other attributes; here, we just want to consider how expensive a technology is. Second, usability: there has been a lot of research into the usability of various encryption technologies and how the ease of their use has a large role in determining whether or not people choose to use them. Finally, functionality: this expresses the range of functions that a technology or product covers that benefit the user, not just in terms of encryption. For example, consider two competing products: one has a great number of features that are useful to the user, but offers no encryption, and one that has encryption, but lacks some of the other features. The latter product, although it has increased functionality by offering encryption, may have a lower total functionality.

## 3   Three Examples

In this section, we briefly introduce three examples of encryption technologies that we use to demonstrate different aspects of the model. Here, we only look at static situations; in Sect. 4, next, we explore the dynamics of these examples. Models are implemented in the julia language [10].

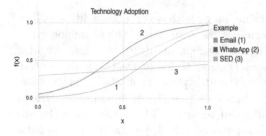

**Table 1.** Model parameters

|  | $\rho$ | Cost | Usability | Funct. |
|---|---|---|---|---|
| *Default tech* | – | 1.0 | 1.0 | 1.0 |
| GPG/PGP | 1.0 | 1.0 | 0.6 | 1.1 |
| WhatsApp | 1.0 | 1.05 | 1.0 | 1.1 |
| SED | 0.1 | 0.85 | 0.9 | 1.1 |

**Fig. 1.** Adoption: all three examples.

The models depend critically on choices of values for a number of parameters. Where possible, our choices have been informed by available data; where not, we have estimated sensible values based on our modelling experience and knowledge of the situations. Clearly, further systematic exploration of the parameter spaces and their sensitivity would be valuable.

In each of the examples, a new technology is compared to a default, incumbent technology. The attribute values for the default technology are all 1. The values for each example are shown in Table 1. Values above 1 are better than the incumbent technology; values below are worse. We use a value of $\beta = 3.4$ in all examples.

The first two examples look at email encryption, comparing standard email to email encrypted with PGP/GPG [6], and messaging apps, comparing normal SMS messaging to the WhatsApp messenger. Both of these examples have a high social component, $\rho$: the utility of the technology increases as more people use it, and suffers when there are few other users. This is contrasted with the third example, which compares standard hard drives to self-encrypting drives. Here, $\rho$ is low, as whether or not others are using the technology does not have a large influence on its utility.

Now looking at costs, encryption software is available for free, so we give it the same value as normal email. WhatsApp is potentially less costly than traditional SMS messaging, which can charge for every message sent, well above the equivalent cost of the data [7], and self-encrypting drives are more expensive than normal drives.

Usability for encrypted email is much lower than standard email. As studies have shown [12], it can be quite difficult for people to correctly encrypt their messages; more recently, Edward Snowden described GPG as 'damn near unusable' [9]. We assume that usability for WhatsApp is similar to regular messaging, and that self-encrypting drives, with the overhead of key management, are less usable than standard drives.

Finally, the functionality of all of the new technologies is greater than the incumbents. Encrypted email is encrypted, as are self-encrypting drives, and WhatsApp has additional features such as sending pictures and video messages.

Each of these examples have different equilibria, based on (5), which are shown in Fig. 1. For email (1), there is only one equilibrium point, where the share of encrypted email is close to zero. For WhatsApp (2), there are three equilibria: two stable equilibria, one high and one low, and a third, unstable equilibrium at $x \approx 0.3$.

If WhatsApp starts from a small market share, it will grow until it reaches the lower adoption share stable equilibrium. If there is some change or shock—a sudden increase in profitability or usage, for example—that increases its market share beyond the unstable equilibrium point, then its share will continue to grow until it reaches the higher point and will dominate the market. This is not the case for encrypted email where the low usability means that, although its value increases with the number of people using it, without some 'external impulse' that changes the utility, the level of adoption will always return to the single, low equilibrium point.

Finally, Fig. 1 (3) shows the equilibrium of the self-encrypting drive example. There is only one equilibrium (at $x \approx 0.35$) and, because of the low $\rho$, the value of the technology does not change a great amount based on the level of adoption, which is mainly driven by the characteristics of the technology.

## 4  Dynamics of the Model and Discussion

So far, the models have been deployed to display the equilibria which can be used for the comparative statics of technology adoption. We proceed by extending the email encryption example to study the evolution of technology adoption over time, in the presence of both exogenous policy influences and endogenous technology changes.

The policy influences take the form of functions that influence the behaviour of agents by changing the value of the utility of the different technologies. Technology changes are modelled within the existing model structure as either changes in the returns on investment over time, or instantaneous shocks to utility-attribute parameters.

We analyse two dynamic aspects of the email encryption example. First, the effect of events such as the Snowden revelations on its use, and, second, how increases in the usability of the encryption software can increase its adoption.

On 5 June 2013, the first of the newspaper articles containing information disclosed by Edward Snowden was published. The documents he released shed light on the expansive electronic surveillance programs being run by the American and British governments. These revelations led to an increased desire to protect the privacy of electronic communications. This can be seen directly in Fig. 2, which shows the total number of PGP/GPG keys registered on public keyservers daily over several years [8]. The vertical line indicates the date of the first Snowden article, immediately after which the rate at which keys were added markedly increased.

While this doesn't determine the exact number of people using encrypted email—people can have multiple keys, some keys may be abandoned, etc.—it clearly demonstrates that the revelations had an impact. We can model this as a revelation of government policy: it adds additional costs to using regular email. We can implement this as a function for the functionality attribute

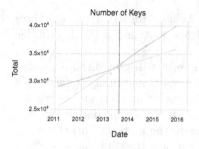

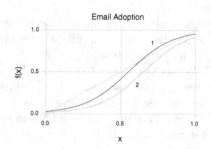

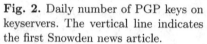

**Fig. 2.** Daily number of PGP keys on keyservers. The vertical line indicates the first Snowden news article.

**Fig. 3.** Email adoption (1) with and (2) without government surveillance policy.

$\tau_{functionality}(x) = -0.2$, which returns a constant value, rather than being dependent on the share of adoption: insecure email is less useful, no matter how many people are using it.

Figure 3 shows the effects of the policy compared to the previous case without such policy (essentially, $\tau_{functionality}(x) = 0$). There are now two stable equilibria, instead of just one. Unlike before, if, somehow, there was now a sudden large increase in encrypted email use—to over 62 percent adoption, the location of the unstable equilibrium—the system would change to the higher stable equilibrium and encrypted email use would be dominant. However, a sudden increase of such size is not likely, and the probable result is that the system stays at the lower equilibrium, which has shifted slightly higher (from $x \approx 0.013$ to $x \approx 0.028$), showing a small increase in the adoption of encrypted email.

These developments are assuming that there is no innovation around encrypted email and the technology and user experience stay constant. In reality, the usability of encryption software is being improved. For example, Google and Yahoo are working on a web browser plugin that provides end-to-end encryption for their respective webmail services [2,11]. This plugin also manages key distribution, aiming to make things easier for users than PGP/GPG's Web of Trust model. Other services, such as Keybase [5], which uses social network identities as a means of verifying the identity of a key's owner, are also attempting to improve key distribution. How much efforts such as these will increase the use of email encryption largely depends on how much they improve usability.

We can use the technological progress model to look at how investment in improving usability will affect adoption. Figure 4 shows the adoption over time for four different scenarios. The first two have a low rate of return for investment in usability, one with the government policy and one without ($\psi_{usability,c} = 0.05, \zeta_{usability,c} = 0.1$). The second two have a very high rate of return on investment, again with and without policy ($\psi_{usability,c} = 0.2, \zeta_{usability,c} = 0.3$). In all cases, the values for non-encryption are the same: $\psi_{usability,d} = 0.01, \zeta_{usability,d} = 0.01$. We use $\alpha = 0.99$ for the switching rate.

In the high-return cases, the investment causes the system to switch to an equilibrium with high adoption of email encryption. The transition happens

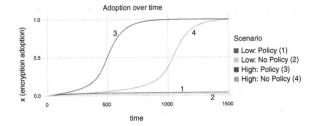

**Fig. 4.** Email adoption over time

much sooner with the government policy than without. In both of the low-return cases, encryption never gets a large market share.

# References

1. Brock, W.A., Durlauf, S.N.: Discrete choice with social interactions. Rev. Econ. Stud. **68**(2), 235–260 (2001)
2. Google Online Security Blog: Making End-to-End Encryption Easier to Use (2014). http://googleonlinesecurity.blogspot.co.uk/2014/06/making-end-to-end-encryption-easier-to.html. Visited 20 Sep 2015
3. Ioannidis, C., Pym, D., Williams, J.: Investments and trade-offs in the economics of information security. In: Dingledine, R., Golle, P. (eds.) FC 2009. LNCS, vol. 5628, pp. 148–166. Springer, Heidelberg (2009). doi:10.1007/978-3-642-03549-4_9
4. Keeney, R.L., Raiffa, H.: Decisions with Multiple Objectives: Preferences and Value Trade-offs. Wiley, Hoboken (1976)
5. Keybase (2015). https://keybase.io/. Visited 20 Sep 2015
6. OpenPGP.org (2015). http://www.openpgp.org. Visited 30 Sep 2015
7. Shambare, R.: The adoption of WhatsApp: breaking the vicious cycle of technological poverty in South Africa. J. Econ. Behav. Stud. **6**(7), 542–550 (2014)
8. SKS Keyservers: History of Number of OpenPGP Keys (2015). https://sks-keyservers.net/status/key_development.php. Visited 30 Sep 2015
9. The Guardian: Snowden Implores Hackers to Focus on Protecting Users' Rights (2014). http://www.theguardian.com/technology/2014/jul/21/edward-snowden-hackers-encryption-patriot. Visited 7 Oct 2015
10. The julia language (2015). http://julialang.org/. Visited 30 Sep 2015
11. User-Focused Security: End-to-End Encryption Extension for Yahoo Mail (2015). http://yahoo.tumblr.com/post/113708033335/user-focused-security-end-to-end-encryption. Visited 30 Sep 2015
12. Whitten, A., Tygar, J.D.: Why Johnny can't encrypt: a usability evaluation of PGP 5.0. In: Proceedings 8th Conference on USENIX Security Symposium, vol. 8, SSYM 1999, pp. 14–14. USENIX Association, Berkeley (1999)
13. Ozment, A., Schechter, S.E.: Bootstrapping the adoption of internet security protocols. In: WEIS (2006). http://www.econinfosec.org/archive/weis2006/docs/46.pdf. Visited 02 Jan 2016
14. Rosasco, N., Larochelle, D.: How and why more secure technologies succeed in legacy markets: lessons from the success of SSH. In: Jean Camp, L., Lewis, S. (eds.) Economics of Information Security, pp. 247–254. Kluwer, Boston (2004)

# Cryptanalysis

# Failures of Security APIs: A New Case

Abdalnaser Algwil and Jeff Yan[✉]

School of Computing and Communications, Lancaster University, Lancaster, UK
{a.algwil,jeff.yan}@lancaster.ac.uk

**Abstract.** We report novel API attacks on a Captcha web service, and discuss lessons that we have learned. In so doing, we expand the horizon of security APIs research by extending it to a new setting. We also show that system architecture analysis is useful both for identifying vulnerabilities in security APIs and for fixing them.

**Keywords:** API attacks · Architecture analysis for security · Captcha · Web security

## 1 Introduction

A security API is an Application Programming Interface that facilitates less trusted or even untrusted code to interact with a trusted computer. A classic example of security APIs are those that enable interactions between a banking computer (less trusted) and a cryptographic Hardware Security Module (trusted) attached to it. Security APIs differ from general programming APIs in that the former enforces a security policy, and typically the policy is about preventing some information flow while allowing tight and dynamic interactions between the untrusted computer and the trusted one. Even if the less trusted or untrusted code is malicious, ideally it should not be able to break the security of the trusted computer.

Security APIs started to get going as a research subject in 2000 with Ross Anderson's seminal paper [1]. A research community has formed, and interesting results emerged. However, most security API attacks published to date are about HSMs and cryptographic key management APIs, e.g. [2–4,8,9]. An exception is Robert Watson's work [12] that exploited concurrency vulnerabilities in system call wrappers to launch API attacks on operating systems.

In this paper, we report novel API attacks on CCaptcha (http://crecaptcha.org), an Internet service that is created to generate Captchas for any websites. A CCaptcha server (trusted) generates automated Turing tests using sensitive materials, and verifies each test result for the websites in the wild. The websites (untrusted) interact with the CCaptcha server via a set of APIs defined by the service provider. This gives us an opportunity for studying security APIs in a new setting, which expands the horizon of security APIs research.

We will show a number of API attacks. For example, one allows us to download all sensitive materials that the service uses for constructing Captchas; one

J. Grossklags and B. Preneel (Eds.): FC 2016, LNCS 9603, pp. 283–298, 2017.
DOI: 10.1007/978-3-662-54970-4_17

allows us to launch an effective dictionary attack on the service; and the third allows us to bypass this Captcha entirely. Two of the attacks defeat entirely or nearly so the purpose of deploying this service.

Our attacks work on both versions of the CCaptcha service, one released in 2010 and the other in the summer of 2014 (i.e. the latest version). It is clear that the service provider has invested some serious efforts in its design and implementation. But we argue that the designers did not seem to consider system architecture issues carefully, and this is a main reason that their security APIs fail. We discover our attacks by analysing the service's architecture, interactions among individual system components, as well as a limited amount of dynamic code available to a client.

This work also contributes to Captcha research. On the one hand, prior art did not examine Captcha security from the angle of security APIs, as conventional Captcha designs rarely provide the possibility to articulate or enforce a security policy.

On the other hand, text Captchas have been widely deployed, but many designs have been broken [5,10,11,13,14]. It is intellectually interesting and practically relevant to explore alternative designs, which are currently an active research topic. Initially disclosed in a USA patent application [7], CCaptcha is an interesting alternative scheme. The design is based on Chinese language, but due to its clever idea, it is universally usable, even to those who are illiterate in Chinese, which is quite counterintuitive. In a user study run by the inventors, foreigners without Chinese language knowledge achieved a high accuracy in solving this Captcha as native speakers did [6]. Our work is the first security analysis of CCaptcha.

## 2   CCaptcha

*Concept.* As shown in Fig. 1, a CCaptcha challenge (or puzzle) is composed of 10 images. The bigger image at the top-left corner is a target Chinese character that can be decomposed into multiple elementary radicals. The nine smaller images on the right are candidate radicals. Some of them are real radicals from

Fig. 1. CCaptcha: an example

the target character, but others are faux ones. Thin lines and small dots in the background are not part of the character or radicals, but clutters. To pass a test, a user has to click typically three real radicals on the right panel. Selecting any faux radical will fail the test.

Each time when a character or radical is used in a puzzle, it will undergo random distortions such as rotation, scaling and warping, and then random background clutters will be added. The inventors applied OCR software to recognize such distorted characters and radicals, but to no avail. Whether their recognition experiment is rigorous or not is beyond the scope of our paper. However, human users can easily solve such tests via pattern recognition, and they do not have to be literate in Chinese.

***Random guess attacks.*** With random guessing, an attacker has about 1.19% chance (i.e., $1/C_3^9$) to break this scheme. If necessary, a user can be asked to solve 2 challenges or more in a row, and this will reduce the random guess success to $\sim 0.014\% = (1.19\%)^2$, or less. Alternatively, if the number of real radicals used, the number of all candidate radicals, or both, is slightly increased, it will reduce the random guess success, too. It will further decrease the success probability of random guess attacks by applying all these countermeasures together. Therefore, random guess attacks are not a serious issue for this Captcha.

***System architecture.*** CCaptcha is implemented as a web service, and it provides both Captcha creation and validation services to web sites, where a CCaptcha challenge (or puzzle) can be easily embedded in each web page by installing a PHP library.

The service provider does not explicitly describe the system architecture for CCaptcha. By studying the limited amount of documents available online and by experimenting with the service, we reconstruct its system architecture diagram. Figure 2 attempts to capture the workflow envisaged by the designers.

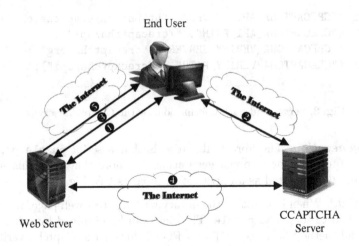

**Fig. 2.** CCaptcha web service: a reconstructed system architecture

Interactions among an end user, a web server and the CCaptcha service can be summarized as follows:

1. A user requests to fetch a page from the web server, and the server sends her the page in which a CCaptcha script is embedded;
2. Driven by the script, her browser retrieves a puzzle from the CCaptcha server;
3. The user submits her puzzle solution to the web server;
4. The web server forwards this solution to the CCaptcha Server, and the CCaptcha Server verifies it and sends back a verification result;
5. Following the result, the web server accepts or denies the user's request.

## 3    API Attacks on CCaptcha

Here we present API attacks that we have uncovered. They include information leakages, a dictionary attack and several oracle attacks. Some of the attacks are built upon each other, but some are standalone attacks on their own.

### 3.1    Information Leakage

The CCaptcha service provides a PHP library `labcrecaptcha.php`, which wraps its APIs and provides a simple mechanism to embed a Ccaptcha puzzle on any web page. Our analysis starts with this library and follows up with leads exposed.

***Paths.*** At the beginning of the library, as shown in Fig. 3, we find the location and path where the CCaptcha APIs are served:

$$\text{https://crecaptcha.org/crecaptcha/api/}$$

```
define("CRECAPTCHA_API_SERVER", "https://crecaptcha.org");
define("CRECAPTCHA_API_PATH", "/crecaptcha/api");
define("CRECAPTCHA_VERIFY_SERVER", "crecaptcha.org");
define("CRECAPTCHA_VERIFY_PATH", "/crecaptcha/api");
```

**Fig. 3.** Server and path information for the CCaptcha service

***Puzzle generation.*** The library also reveals that a script `puzzle.php` is the interface responsible for Captcha generation. We note that once this script is called, a puzzle is created as an array of 10 integers (see Fig. 4).

***Hidden field.*** When integrating the library with our test web page, we discover a hidden field `crecaptcha_puzzle`. This field can be obtained by using a PHP super-global method such as GET and POST during the Captcha verification process.

```
var CrecaptchaConfiguration = {
server : ' https://www.crecaptcha.org/crecaptcha/api' ,
ishint : 3,
hardlevel : 1,
skin : 1,
puzzle : new Array(' 10089' ,' 18429' ,' 253' ,' 136' ,' 18591' ,
                    ' 20469' ,' 19901' ,' 17288' ,' 271' ,' 20461' )};
document.write(' <s' + ' cript type="text/javascript" src="' +
 CrecaptchaConfiguration.server+' /crecaptcha.js"></s' +' cript>' );
```

**Fig. 4.** Captcha generation

We note that this hidden field stores 10 integers separated by comma, for example,

> crecaptcha_puzzle = "10089, 18429, 253, 136, 18591, 20469,
> 19901, 17288, 271, 20461"

We also note that these numbers are the same as those stored in the puzzle array.

It turns out that these numbers are distinct IDs of the images used to compose a CCaptcha puzzle, with the first number identifying the target character and the others identifying nine candidate radicals respectively. As illustrated in Fig. 5, a puzzle is generated by fetching 10 images via their IDs, and then composing the images accordingly.

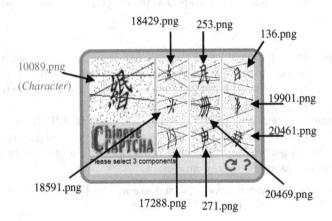

**Fig. 5.** Images used in a puzzle (1 character + 9 radicals) and their numeric IDs

Each time when a character or radical is used to compose a puzzle, it will undergo different distortions and be rendered as a different image. That is, the generator will not reuse any image, but create a different image for the same character or radical each time. However, the numeric ID always remains the same for all the different image versions rendered for the same character or radical. That is to say, there is a fixed one-to-one relationship between a character/radical and its image ID. This means that with the knowledge of an image's ID, we will know the image's content without applying any computer vision or pattern recognition algorithms.

*Database leakage.* A further analysis of `puzzle.php` source code (Fig. 4) reveals a JavaScript file `crecaptcha.js`. By examining this JS script (see Fig. 6), we discover that a PHP script `image.php` is responsible for retrieving image files from the CCaptcha server.

```
_create_image_tag: function (i, c, width, height) {
  output = '<img src="' + CrecaptchaConfiguration.server +
        '/image.php?c=' + c + '" alt="" style="width:' +
        width + ';height:' + height + ';border: 0px;" />' ;
  if (i > 0 && i < 10){
     output = '<a href="javascript:Crecaptcha.click_option('
           + i.toString() + ');">' + output + '</a>' ;
  }
  return output;
},
```

**Fig. 6.** Source code snippet from `crecaptcha.js`: `image.php` fetches images from the CCaptcha server

The script `image.php` enables us to fetch any radical and character by sending their numeric ID to the server. For example, as shown in Fig. 7, https://crecaptcha.org/crecaptcha/api/image.php?c=1 returns us the character/radical of ID 1.

By sending a sequence of numbers starting from 1 to 72154, we manage to fetch 66,111 unique characters/radicals from the server – all the components used for CCaptcha generation. Note that a majority of numbers between 13060 and 19783 are not assigned to any images.

*Note*: all the scripts that we have analysed are available on the client side, and they are readily accessible merely via a browser.

### 3.2  A Dictionary Attack

The information leakages discussed above can be exploited to launch two attacks: (1) a machine learning attack that trains an automatic Captcha solving algorithm with the leaked database, and (2) an effective dictionary attack that solves the CCaptcha tests with a high success rate.

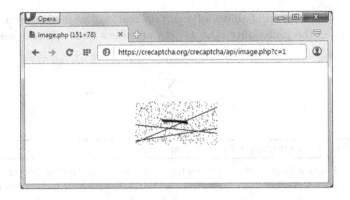

**Fig. 7.** Retrieving an image from the CCaptcha database

The first attack is beyond the scope of this paper, and we discuss only the dictionary attack here. The idea is as follows. We build a dictionary with entries being each character along with its valid radicals, and we store their image IDs in the dictionary. To solve a new puzzle, we simply pick up its target character's ID from the traffic, use that ID to look up the dictionary, and then identify valid radicals among nine candidates in the puzzle.

We have a simple but effective method for dictionary construction. By exploiting the ID leakage vulnerability, we know which character/radical is which, with the knowledge of their ID alone. If we analyse multiple puzzles generated for the same target character, we will know that if a radical occurs every time or most of the time in the puzzles, it will be a valid one with a high probability.

A general description of our dictionary construction is given as follows. First we launch a large number of requests to the server to collect $\theta$ different puzzles for each character. For a certain character, we can sort all candidate radicals by their occurrence frequency in the $\theta$ puzzles. If a radical occurs at least $k$ times, we keep it in the dictionary as a real radical for the character. This process will be applied to all characters until our dictionary is stabilized. More details are given in Algorithm 1.

Next we discuss how to determine $\theta$ (the number of tables) and $k$ (occurrence threshold) with the following analysis.

***Parameter configurations.*** We know that a puzzle typically has 3 real radicals and 6 fake ones. It is reasonable to assume that they are randomly selected by the system from the real radical set (of a certain character) and the fake radical set, respectively. Also assume that a certain character has $m$ real radicals (e.g. $m = 4$ for character 42328 and $m = 3$ for character 30646 in Fig. 10). Therefore, for $\theta$ trails, the probability that a real radical has been selected $k$ times, denoted by $P_1$, follows the binomial distribution:

$$P_1 = C_r^n \rho_1^k (1 - \rho_1)^{\theta - k},$$

where $\rho_1 = 3/m$ is the probability of a certain real radical having been selected in a trial. Then the probability that a real radical has been selected less than $k$ times is:

$$P_R = P(\#real < k) = \sum_{i=0}^{k-1} C_i^\theta \rho_1^i (1 - \rho_1)^{\theta-i}. \tag{1}$$

---

**Algorithm 1.** Dictionary Construction

---

**input** : Puzzles from Chinese Characters Database in CCaptcha Server
**output**: Dictionary contains each Chinese character along with its correct
        radicals

$DB_{CCs}$ : *Chinese Characters Database in CCaptcha Server*;
P: *Puzzle (1 character + 9 radicals$_{\{3real+6faux\}}$)*;
P[*char*] : *Target Character ID (i.e. Big image)*;
P[$R_j$] : *Radical ID (i.e. small Image), where* $j = 1, 2, 3, \ldots, 9$;
$T_n$ : *Table to store puzzles (P), where* $n = 1, 2, 3, \ldots, \theta$;
$\theta$ : *Number of tables (e.g. 5)*;
$k$ : *Threshold of a radical occurrence*;
$NoR$ : *Number of table Records*;
$P_{T_n}$ : *Stored Puzzle in table n ($T_n$)*;
$C_{T_n}$ : *Target Character ID in stored puzzle in table n ($T_n$)*;
$R_{T_n}$ : *Radical IDs in stored puzzle in table n ($T_n$)*;
All_Radicals : $P_{T_1}[R] + P_{T_2}[R] + P_{T_3}[R] + \cdots + P_{T_\theta}[R]$;
candidate_radicals : *IDs of correct radicals that compose the Target character*;

**do**
    P $\leftarrow$ *send a request to CCaptcha Server and fetch a new puzzle*;
    **for** $n \leftarrow 1$ **to** $\theta$ **do**
        **if** (IsFound(P[*char*], $T_n$) $\neq$ true) **then**
            *insert* P *into* $T_n$ ;
            break; *// for*
        **end**
    **end**
**while** ($NoR(T_\theta) < NoR(DB_{CCs})$);

Dictionary $\leftarrow$ { };

**for** *all records in* $T_1$ **do**
    $C_{T_1} \leftarrow P_{T_1}[char]$;
    All_Radicals $\leftarrow P_{T_1}[R]$;
    **for** $n \leftarrow 2$ **to** $\theta$ **do**
        $R_{T_n} \leftarrow$ GetRadicals ($T_n$ , $C_{T_1}$);
        *Merge* $R_{T_n}$ *with* All_Radicals;
    **end**
    *count all of the matching values in* All_Radicals;
    candidate_radicals $\leftarrow$ All_Radicals[R] *where their frequency* $> k$;
    *insert*($C_{T_1}$, candidate_radicals) *into* Dictionary ;
**end**

---

Similarly, we can model the probably distribution of the fake radicals. Assume that there are $M$ fake radicals that can be chosen from, where $M = z - m$, and $z = 1366$ (the total number of radicals used in the system). After $\theta$ trials, the probability that a fake radical has been selected at least $k$ times is

$$P_F = P(\#fake \geq k) = 1 - \sum_{i=0}^{k-1} C_i^\theta \rho_2^i (1 - \rho_2)^{\theta-i}, \tag{2}$$

where $\rho_2 = 6/M$.

In building our dictionary, we repeat the random selecting process $\theta$ times, and then select radicals occurred at least $k$ times as the real ones. Note that $P_R$ and $P_F$ are two important metrics determining the effectiveness of the dictionary. By definition, it is preferable to set parameters that yield small $P_R$ and $P_F$.

We have empirical evidence that $\rho_2$ is relatively small but $\rho_1$ relatively large: by sending millions of requests to grab puzzles from the CCaptcha server, we establish that not all 66111 characters, but only 50313 of them, are used as a target character in a puzzle, where there are at least 3 valid radicals. We also establish that for all the 50313 characters, $m \in \{3, 4, 5, 6, 7\}$.

Therefore, according to Eq. 2, and Eq. 1, $P_R$ and $P_F$ can be very small if we choose a large $\theta$ and an appropriate $k$. However, a large $\theta$ would result in a high computational cost. To balance the trade-off between accuracy and efficiency, we decide to set $\theta = 5$ and $k = 3$, which as shown later will yield a reasonable accuracy with a low computational cost.

Given the distribution of character number with respect to $m$, we can also calculate $P_R^{Overall}$ and $P_F^{Overall}$, defined as follows:

$$P_R^{Overall} = \sum_{m=3}^{m=7} \frac{\# \, character(m)}{N} P_R(m)$$

$$P_F^{Overall} = \sum_{m=3}^{m=7} \frac{\# \, character(m)}{N} P_F(m),$$

where $N = \sum_3^7 \# \, character(m) = 50313$.

Table 1 shows various probabilities as calculated, and it clearly indicates that with $\theta = 5$ and $k = 3$, an effective dictionary can be built, since $P_R^{Overall}$ and $P_F^{Overall}$ are low, which suggests that real radicals tend to occur more than $k$ times while fake radicals tend to occur less than k times.

**An example of dictionary building** is given in Fig. 8, where we use the character 11148 and $\theta = 5$. Each puzzle is stored in a different table that contains the character alongside with 9 candidate radicals. We put together the 5 puzzles and count the occurrences of each candidate radical. Radical 136 occurs 5 times, 18461 occurs 4 times, and both 18445 and 63470 occur 3 times, and therefore all of them are determined as real radicals for the character. Figure 9 shows all the corresponding images identified by their IDs, confirming the correctness of our algorithm.

**Table 1.** The probabilities of $P_R$ & $P_F$ ($\theta = 5$; $k = 3$)

| – | # character(m) | $P_R(m)$ | $P_F(m)$ |
|---|---|---|---|
| $m = 3$ | 25088 | 0.0 % | 0.00008474 % |
| $m = 4$ | 18780 | 10.35 % | 0.00008493 % |
| $m = 5$ | 5907 | 31.74 % | 0.00008511 % |
| $m = 6$ | 525 | 50.00 % | 0.00008530 % |
| $m = 7$ | 13 | 63.21 % | 0.00008549 % |
| $P_{R\,or\,F}^{Overall}$ | | **8.13 %** | **0.00008486 %** |

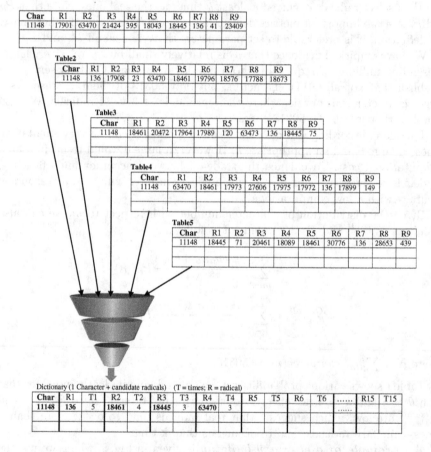

| Char | R1 | R2 | R3 | R4 | R5 | R6 | R7 | R8 | R9 |
|---|---|---|---|---|---|---|---|---|---|
| 11148 | 17901 | 63470 | 21424 | 395 | 18043 | 18445 | 136 | 41 | 23409 |

Table2

| Char | R1 | R2 | R3 | R4 | R5 | R6 | R7 | R8 | R9 |
|---|---|---|---|---|---|---|---|---|---|
| 11148 | 136 | 17908 | 23 | 63470 | 18461 | 19796 | 18576 | 17788 | 18673 |

Table3

| Char | R1 | R2 | R3 | R4 | R5 | R6 | R7 | R8 | R9 |
|---|---|---|---|---|---|---|---|---|---|
| 11148 | 18461 | 20472 | 17964 | 17989 | 120 | 63473 | 136 | 18445 | 75 |

Table4

| Char | R1 | R2 | R3 | R4 | R5 | R6 | R7 | R8 | R9 |
|---|---|---|---|---|---|---|---|---|---|
| 11148 | 63470 | 18461 | 17973 | 27606 | 17975 | 17972 | 136 | 17899 | 149 |

Table5

| Char | R1 | R2 | R3 | R4 | R5 | R6 | R7 | R8 | R9 |
|---|---|---|---|---|---|---|---|---|---|
| 11148 | 18445 | 71 | 20461 | 18089 | 18461 | 30776 | 136 | 28653 | 439 |

Dictionary (1 Character + candidate radicals)    (T = times; R = radical)

| Char | R1 | T1 | R2 | T2 | R3 | T3 | R4 | T4 | R5 | T5 | R6 | T6 | ...... | R15 | T15 |
|---|---|---|---|---|---|---|---|---|---|---|---|---|---|---|---|
| 11148 | 136 | 5 | 18461 | 4 | 18445 | 3 | 63470 | 3 | | | | | ...... | | |

**Fig. 8.** The dictionary construction process for a character

***Experiment results.*** We spent about two weeks building a dictionary with $\theta = 5$ tables, i.e. 5 different puzzles for each character. Figure 10 visualizes a small part of the dictionary. With this dictionary, we tested on 2000 new puzzles that were randomly generated by the service, and completely solved 1833 of

11148 (character)    136 (5 times)    18461 (4 times)   18445 (3 times)   63470 (3 times)

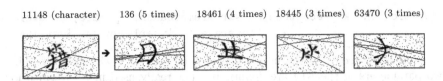

**Fig. 9.** An example on a character with the classified real radicals

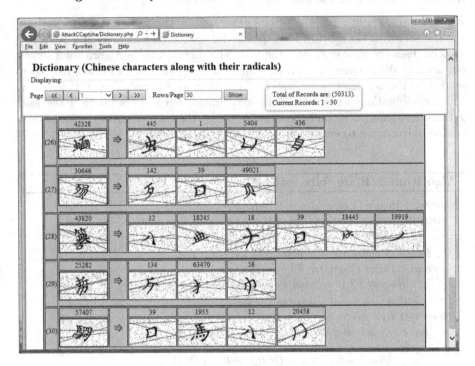

**Fig. 10.** Dictionary visualization

them, achieving a success rate of 91.65%. For 152 failed cases, 2 out of the 3 real radicals were successfully identified by our dictionary attack. It takes on average about 0.093 seconds to solve a puzzle on a standard desktop computer.

To increase the success of our dictionary attack, we can further suppress $P_R^{Overall}$ and $P_F^{Overall}$ by increasing $\theta$ (the number of tables) and choosing an appropriate threshold $k$. For example, when we set $\theta = 10$ and $k = 5$, $P_R^{Overall}$ becomes 3.10% and $P_F^{Overall}$ becomes 0.000000041%, which are both much lower than the previous configurations. The dictionary attack's success will be improved accordingly.

### 3.3    Verification Abuse

Further investigation into the CCaptcha library "*labcrecaptcha.php*" reveals that a script named "*verify.php*" is responsible for Captcha verification. The key API is defined as follows:

```
function check_crecaptcha_answer($remoteaddr, $puzzle, $answer,
                                 $useragent, $userlanguage, $setting)
```

It returns *'Success'* if the user's answer is correct, and *'Failure'* otherwise. Two parameters of the API are defined but not really used in the verification process, and they are *remote address* and *user agent*. We find that adversaries can abuse this API for the following oracle attacks.

***Bypass the service.*** For any puzzle generated by the service, an attacker can ask the server to do a brute force search for the correct answer, and then the attacker uses the answer to pass the test. The pseudocode in Algorithm 2 shows our attack. We enumerate each combination of 3 candidate radicals, and then send it to the service one by one. It takes at most 84 trials (i.e., $C_3^9$) to know which combination is correct. In our experiment, our success rate is 100% and it takes less than 30 seconds on average to get the correct answer. This attack enables adversaries to entirely bypass the CCaptcha test.

---

**Algorithm 2.** Brute Force Search

---

**input** : Puzzle (1 character + 9 radicals$_{\{3\,real+6\,faux\}}$)
**output**: Correct solution (IDs of correct radicals that compose the Target character)

P: *Puzzle (1 character + 9 radicals$_{\{3real+6faux\}}$)*;
P[*char*] : *Target Character ID (i.e. Big image)*;
P[$R_n$] : *Radical ID (i.e. small Image), where $n = 1, 2, 3, \ldots, 9$*;

P $\leftarrow$ *grab a new puzzle needed to solve*;
**for** $i \leftarrow 1$ **to** 7 **do**
    **for** $j \leftarrow i + 1$ **to** 8 **do**
        **for** $k \leftarrow j + 1$ **to** 9 **do**
            Possible_Solution = {P[$R_i$], P[$R_j$], P[$R_k$]} ;
            Result = **check_crecaptcha_answer** (P, Possible_Solution,...);
            **if** (Result = *success*) **then**
                Correct_Solution = Possible_Solution;
                **Exit**;
            **end**
        **end**
    **end**
**end**

---

***Improve dictionary quality.*** We can also improve our dictionary (constructed in Sect. 3.2) by abusing the API to ensure the correctness of dictionary entries, e.g. by filtering out fake radicals.

We first run Algorithm 1 to build our dictionary, which mainly keeps track of radicals appearing more than 3 times in five puzzles. Since only 5 tables are used for dictionary construction, we also keep track of each radical that appears only twice. Next, for each dictionary entry, we sent a series of requests to the verification script, each request including a character together with three candidate radicals, and the **check_crecaptcha_answer** API will tell us whether they are the right combination.

This way, we have successfully eliminated each radical that accidentally repeats at least 3 times but is not part of the correct combination. On the other hand, we have also found that some radicals appear only twice, but are real roots from target characters.

However, this enhancement method hardly produces a perfect dictionary for a simple reason: when we choose small numbers for k and $\theta$, some real radicals will never be observed in the say 5 tables.

***Build an optimal dictionary.*** We can also build an attack dictionary by abusing the verification API alone. To do so, we ask the service to perform a brute force search for each character. That is, at most 84 requests will identify 3 real radicals for a character, creating a dictionary entry. The dictionary constructed this way will be optimal, but it will take a long time, much longer than required for building the improved dictionary described earlier.

## 4   Countermeasures

The vulnerabilities we have discussed are mostly due to architecture flaws in the system design, and they can be addressed by carefully thinking about architecture issues.

All the information leakage vulnerabilities can be prevented by significantly restructuring the division of labour between the CCaptcha server and the code executed on an end user's computer (i.e. the client). Specifically, generating Captchas can be entirely done by the server without interacting with the client. The server randomly picks a target character, and assembles it with nine candidate radicals into a big image like the one shown in Fig. 1. Then, the image is sent to the client, which will display the image to the end user, collect her inputs in the form of a series of coordinate pairs describing where she has clicked on the image, and then send the inputs to the server. Next, the server interprets which candidate radicals the user has clicked, and determines whether the clicked radicals are real ones or not.

The one-to-one relationship between a character (or a radical) and its image ID is a devastating vulnerability. It could be fixed by hashing the ID with a random number to give each image a completely different name each time. However, this quick hack solution is not needed anymore if the new architecture discussed above is in place.

Our dictionary attack was built on both the leaked database and the one-to-one mapping between characters (or radicals) and their IDs. With both of the problems being fixed, the dictionary attack will no longer work.

Verification abuse has not only contributed to improve our dictionary attack, but it can be used as a standalone attack by itself. The root causes of verification abuse are two serious flaws in the architecture design:

1. No mechanism is in place to identity a web server that interacts with the CCaptcha server, and thus any third party can request the CCaptcha server for Captcha generation and verification.
2. No mechanism is in place to vouch and verify the authenticity of each Captcha puzzle, and the CCaptcha server fails to tell whether a puzzle is issued by itself or not.

Such critical flaws have allowed us to launch various oracle attacks. Even when we sent millions of requests to the server, we have experienced little obstruction.

To fix these problems, we recommend an improved system architecture, which is shown in Fig. 11.

First, the CCaptcha service should provide each website a unique pair of API keys: one is a site key that uniquely identifies a website, the other a secret key that is known only to the website and the CCaptcha server. An end user will get the site key from the web server (step 1 in Fig. 11), and use the key to retrieve a Captcha from the CCaptcha server (step 2-A). The secret key is used for authenticated communication between the web server and the CCaptcha server in the verification stage (step 4-A) to prevent the verification abuse.

The CCaptcha service can introduce an enrolment process, in which the pair of API keys is generated upon a website's registration with the service. Second, a unique ID (token) should accompany each new puzzle issued by the Captcha generator (step 2-B). Each token should be used only once. This token should also accompany the solution when the latter is sent from the web server to the CCaptcha server in the verification process (step 4-A). Using this token, the CCaptcha server can determine whether a puzzle is authentic or issued by a party impersonating the Captcha generator. Additionally, the end of the puzzle's life should be associated with the end of the token's life in the verification process.

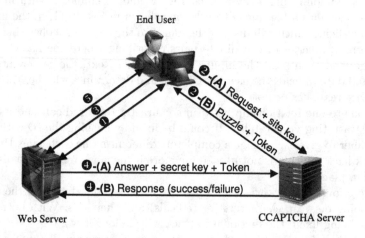

**Fig. 11.** A revised system architecture

When adversaries have a website and an end user both under their control, they will have legitimate access to the API keys and can misuse them. For example, the adversaries can act first as a legitimate web server and register for free access to an API key pair, and they can act thereafter as a legitimate end-user. A simple, cheap but imperfect solution we suggest is for the CCaptcha server to monitor the number of requests from each website, and to apply rate control when traffic anomalies are detected.

## 5  Lessons

It is notoriously hard to design security APIs. With nearly thirty years of research in cryptographic protocols, it is still a challenge to get a novel design right. Security APIs are much harder to design than cryptographic protocols. Therefore, it is crucial to understand failures of security APIs, and learn from them.

We conclude this paper by summarising lessons that we have learned both from identifying the API attacks on CCaptcha, and from fixing the vulnerabilities.

*Lesson 1: Security policies were not articulated by the designers.* Otherwise, entirely bypassing the service should probably have never happened in the first place.

In this specific context, at least three security policies are relevant:

1. Do not trust client;
2. No leakage of sensitive materials;
3. No bypass of the service without solving an automated Turing test.

*Lesson 2: System architecture is highly relevant to security APIs, but it was not carefully considered, and not articulated either.*

Probably the most important lesson we have learned is the following. A careful analysis of system architecture is useful and effective for identifying vulnerabilities in security APIs and for figuring out suitable countermeasures. To the best of our knowledge, this insight was never spelled out in the literature.

To extrapolate it a little further, we believe that for any complex system (including a system of systems) where multiple components interact with each other, an architecture analysis will prove an effective method both for identifying security vulnerabilities in the system and for fixing them. This analysis can be applied in many stages of the system's life circle such as design, implementation and testing.

This method of 'architecture analysis for security' deserves further study and is our ongoing research.

**Acknowledgement.** We thank Butler Lampson for inspiring conversations, Yu Guan for assistances, and anonymous reviewers for helpful comments.

# References

1. Anderson, R.: The correctness of crypto transaction sets. In: Christianson, B., Malcolm, J.A., Crispo, B., Roe, M. (eds.) Security Protocols 2000. LNCS, vol. 2133, pp. 128–141. Springer, Heidelberg (2001). doi:10.1007/3-540-44810-1_18
2. Berkman, O., Ostrovsky, O.M.: The unbearable lightness of PIN cracking. In: Dietrich, S., Dhamija, R. (eds.) FC 2007. LNCS, vol. 4886, pp. 224–238. Springer, Heidelberg (2007). doi:10.1007/978-3-540-77366-5_20
3. Bond, M.: Understanding Security APIs. Ph.D. thesis, University of Cambridge (2004)
4. Bond, M., Anderson, R.: API level attacks on embedded systems. IEEE Comput. Mag. **34**, 67–75 (2001)
5. Bursztein, E., Martin, M., Mitchell, J.C.: Text-based CAPTCHA strengths and weaknesses. In: Proceedings of the 18th ACM Conference on Computer and Communications Security. ACM (2011)
6. Chen, L.: Personal Communications (2014)
7. Chen, L., Juang, D., Zhu, W., Yu, H., Chen, F.: CAPTCHA AND reCAPTCHA WITH SINOGRAPHS. Patent US20120023549 A1 (2012)
8. Clulow, J.: On the security of PKCS #11. In: Walter, C.D., Koç, Ç.K., Paar, C. (eds.) CHES 2003. LNCS, vol. 2779, pp. 411–425. Springer, Heidelberg (2003). doi:10.1007/978-3-540-45238-6_32
9. Cortier, V., Steel, G.: A generic security API for symmetric key management on cryptographic devices. In: Backes, M., Ning, P. (eds.) ESORICS 2009. LNCS, vol. 5789, pp. 605–620. Springer, Heidelberg (2009). doi:10.1007/978-3-642-04444-1_37
10. Gao, H., Wang, W., Qi, J., Wang, X., Liu, X., Yan, J.: The robustness of hollow CAPTCHAs. In: Proceedings of the 2013 ACM SIGSAC Conference on Computer & Communications Security - CCS 2013, New York, USA, pp. 1075–1086 (2013)
11. Gao, H., Yan, J., et al.: A simple generic attack on text Captchas. In: Proceedings Network and Distributed System Security Symposium (NDSS), San Diego, USA (2016)
12. Watson, R.N.M.: Exploiting concurrency vulnerabilities in system call wrappers. In: First USENIX Workshop on Offensive Technologies (WOOT 07) (2007)
13. Yan, J., El Ahmad, A.S.: Breaking visual CAPTCHAs with naïve pattern recognition algorithms. In: 23rd Annual Computer Security Applications Conference - ACSAC 2007, USA (2007)
14. Yan, J., El Ahmad, A.S.: A low-cost attack on a Microsoft Captcha. In: Proceedings of the 15th ACM Conference on Computer and Communications Security - CCS 2008, New York, USA, pp. 543–554 (2008)

# Explicit Optimal Binary Pebbling for One-Way Hash Chain Reversal

Berry Schoenmakers[✉]

TU Eindhoven, Eindhoven, The Netherlands
berry@win.tue.nl

**Abstract.** We present explicit optimal binary pebbling algorithms for reversing one-way hash chains. For a hash chain of length $2^k$, the number of hashes performed in each output round does not exceed $\lceil k/2 \rceil$, whereas the number of hash values stored (pebbles) throughout is at most $k$. This is optimal for binary pebbling algorithms characterized by the property that the midpoint of the hash chain is computed just once and stored until it is output, and that this property applies recursively to both halves of the hash chain.

We introduce a framework for rigorous comparison of explicit binary pebbling algorithms, including simple speed-1 binary pebbling, Jakobsson's speed-2 binary pebbling, and our optimal binary pebbling algorithm. Explicit schedules describe for each pebble exactly how many hashes need to be performed in each round. The optimal schedule turns out to be essentially unique and exhibits a nice recursive structure, which allows for fully optimized implementations that can readily be deployed. In particular, we develop the first *in-place* implementations with minimal storage overhead (essentially, storing only hash values), and fast implementations with minimal computational overhead. Moreover, we show that our approach is not limited to hash chains of length $n = 2^k$, but accommodates hash chains of arbitrary length $n \geq 1$, without incurring any overhead. Finally, we show how to run a cascade of pebbling algorithms along with a bootstrapping technique, facilitating sequential reversal of an unlimited number of hash chains growing in length up to a given bound.

## 1 Introduction

Originally introduced by Lamport to construct an identification scheme resisting eavesdropping attacks [Lam81, Hal94], one-way hash chains have become a truly fundamental primitive in cryptography.[1] The idea of Lamport's asymmetric identification scheme is to let the prover generate a hash chain as a sequence of successive iterates of a one-way hash function applied to a random seed value, revealing only the last element of the hash chain to the verifier upon registration. Later, during successive runs of the identification protocol, the remaining

---

[1] Bitcoin's block chain [Nak08] is probably the best-known example of a hash chain nowadays. Unlike in our setting, however, block chains are costly to generate due to the "proof of work" requirement for the hash values linking the successive blocks.

© International Financial Cryptography Association 2017
J. Grossklags and B. Preneel (Eds.): FC 2016, LNCS 9603, pp. 299–320, 2017.
DOI: 10.1007/978-3-662-54970-4_18

elements of the hash chain are output by the prover in reverse order, one element on each run.

Due to the one-way property of the hash function, efficient reversal of a hash chain is non-trivial for long chains. Jakobsson introduced a simple and efficient pebbling algorithm for reversal of one-way hash chains [Jak02], inspired by the pebbling algorithm of [IR01] for efficient key updates in a forward-secure digital signature scheme. Pebbling algorithms for one-way hash chain reversal strike a balance between storage requirements (measured as the number of hash values stored) and computational requirements (measured as the maximum number of hashes performed in any round). The performance constraint is that each next element of the reversed hash chain should be produced within a limited amount of time after producing the preceding element—without this performance constraint, the problem would indeed be easy, see Appendix A. For a hash chain of length $n = 2^k$, Jakobsson's algorithm stores $O(\log n)$ hash values only and the number of hashes performed in each round is limited to $O(\log n)$ as well.

The problem of efficient hash chain reversal was extensively studied by Coppersmith and Jakobsson [CJ02]. They proved nearly optimal complexity for a binary pebbling algorithm storing at most $k + \lceil \log_2(k+1) \rceil$ hash values and performing at most $\lfloor \frac{k}{2} \rfloor$ hashes per round. Later, it was observed by Yum et al. that a greedy implementation of Jakobsson's original algorithm actually stores no more than $k$ hash values, requiring no more than $\lceil \frac{k}{2} \rceil$ hashes per round [YSEL09].

In this paper we consider the class of *binary* pebbling algorithms, covering the best algorithms of [Jak02,CJ02,YSEL09] among others. A binary pebbling algorithm is characterized by the property that the *midpoint* of the hash chain is computed just once and stored until it is output; moreover, this property applies recursively to both halves of the hash chain. In particular, this means that after producing the last element of the hash chain as the first output, a binary pebbling algorithm stores the $k$ elements at distances $2^i - 1$, for $1 \le i \le k$, from the end of the hash chain. Optimal binary pebbling achieves the lowest space-time product of $\frac{1}{2}k^2$ among all published results,[2] but see Sect. 8.

We introduce a simple yet general framework for rigorous analysis of efficient binary pebbling algorithms for hash chain reversal, and we completely resolve the case of binary pebbling by constructing an *explicit* optimal algorithm. The storage required by our optimal algorithm does not exceed the storage of $k$ hash values and the number of hashes performed in any output round does not exceed $\lceil \frac{k}{2} \rceil$. This matches the performance of the greedy algorithm of [YSEL09], which is an optimal binary pebbling algorithm as well. However, we give an exact schedule for all hashes performed by the algorithm (rather than performing these hashes in a greedy fashion). We also believe that our approach is much more accessible than previous ones, leading to high quality algorithms that can readily be deployed.

Our optimal schedule is defined explicitly, both as a recursive definition and as a closed formula, specifying exactly how many hashes should be performed

---

[2] E.g., using the space-time trade-offs of [Sel03] and [Kim03], one cannot go below $\min_{b>1} b/(\log_2 b)^2 k^2 \approx 0.89 k^2$ and $\min_{b>1} (b-1)/(\log_2 b)^2 k^2 \approx 0.74 k^2$, respectively.

in a given round for each pebble. Furthermore, we will argue that the optimal schedule is essentially unique. Apart from the insightful mathematical structure thus uncovered, the explicit optimal schedule enables the development of fully optimized solutions for one-way hash chain reversal. We construct the first in-place (or, *in situ*) hash chain reversal algorithms which require essentially no storage beyond the hash values stored for the pebbles; at the same time, the computational overhead for each round is limited to a few basic operations only beyond the evaluation of the hash function. Finally, as another extreme type of solution, we show how to minimize the computational overhead to an almost negligible amount of work, at the expense of increased storage requirements.

Concretely, for hash chains of length $2^{32}$ using a 128-bit one-way hash, our in-place algorithm only stores 516 bytes (32 hash values and one 32-bit counter) and performs, at most 16 hashes per round. Our results are therefore of particular importance in the context of lightweight cryptography. See, e.g., the references in [PCTS02, YSEL09, MSS13] for a glimpse of the extensive literature on hash chains, covering an extensive range of lightweight devices such as wireless sensors, RFID tags, and smart cards. Moreover, we note that our results are also interesting in the context of post-quantum cryptography, as the security of one-way hash chains is not affected dramatically by the potential of quantum computers.

## 2   One-Way Hash Chains

Throughout, we will use the following notation for (finite) sequences. We write $A = \{a_i\}_{i=1}^{n} = \{a_1, \ldots, a_n\}$ for a sequence $A$ of length $n$, $n \geq 0$, with $\{\}$ denoting the empty sequence. We use $|A| = n$ to denote the length of $A$, and $\#A = \sum_{i=1}^{n} a_i$ to denote the weight of $A$. We write $A \parallel B$ for the concatenation of sequences $A$ and $B$, and $A + B$ for element-wise addition of sequences $A$ and $B$ of equal length, where $+$ takes precedence over $\parallel$. Constant sequences are denoted by $c = c^{*n} = \{c\}_{i=1}^{n}$, suppressing the length $n$ when it is understood from context; e.g., $A+c$ denotes the sequence obtained by adding $c$ to all elements of $A$. We will use similar notation for arrays; specifically, for an array $a$ of length $n$, we write $a[j, k)$ for the segment $\{a[i]\}_{i=j}^{k-1}$, $0 \leq j \leq k \leq n$, and so on.

Let $f$ be a cryptographic hash function. The length-$2^k$ **(one-way) hash chain** $f_k^*(x)$ for a given seed value $x$ is defined as the following sequence:

$$f_k^*(x) = \{f^i(x)\}_{i=0}^{2^k-1}.$$

For authentication mechanisms based on hash chains, we need an efficient algorithm for producing the sequence $f_k^*(x)$ *in reverse*. The problem arises from the fact that computation of $f$ in the forward direction is easy, while it is *intractable* in the reverse direction. So, given $x$ it is easy to compute $y = f(x)$, but given $y$ it is hard to compute any $x$ at all such that $y = f(x)$. For long hash chains the straightforward solutions of either (i) storing $f_k^*(x)$ and reading it out in reverse or (ii) computing each element of $f_k^*(x)$ from scratch starting from $x$ are clearly too inefficient.

## 3   Binary Pebbling

We introduce a framework that captures the essence of binary pebbling algorithms as follows. We will define a pebbler as an algorithm proceeding in a certain number of rounds, where the initial rounds are used to compute the hash chain in the forward direction given the seed value $x$, and the hash chain is output in reverse in the remaining rounds, one element at a time.

For $k \geq 0$, we define pebbler $P_k(x)$ below as an algorithm that runs for $2^{k+1} - 1$ rounds in total, and outputs $f_k^*(x)$ in reverse in its last $2^k$ rounds. It is essential that we include the initial $2^k - 1$ rounds in which no outputs are produced as an integral part of pebbler $P_k(x)$, as this allows us to define and analyze binary pebbling in a fully recursive manner. In fact, in terms of a given **schedule** $T_k = \{t_r\}_{r=1}^{2^k-1}$ with $\#T_k = 2^k - 1$, a **binary pebbler** $P_k(x)$ is completely specified by the following recursive definition, see also Figs. 1 and 2:

> **Rounds** $[1, 2^k)$: set $y_i = f^{2^k-2^i}(x)$ for $i = k, \dots, 0$ using $t_r$ hashes in round $r$.
> **Round** $2^k$: output $y_0$.
> **Rounds** $(2^k, 2^{k+1})$: run $P_{i-1}(y_i)$ in parallel for $i = 1, \dots, k$.

We will refer to rounds $[1, 2^k)$ as the **initial stage** of $P_k$ and to rounds $[2^k, 2^{k+1})$ as its **output stage**. Running pebblers in parallel means that pebblers take turns to execute for one round each, where the order in which this happens within a round is irrelevant.

The behavior of $P_0$ and $P_1$ is fixed since $T_0 = \{\}$ and $T_1 = \{1\}$, respectively. Pebbler $P_0(x)$ runs for one round only, in which $y_0 = x$ is output, using no hashes at all. Similarly, $P_1(x)$ runs for three rounds, performing one hash in its first round to compute $y_1 = x$ and $y_0 = f(x)$, outputting $f(x)$ in its second round, and then running $P_0(y_1)$ in the third round, which will output $x$. More generally, the following theorem shows that correct behavior follows for any $P_k$ independent of the particular schedule $T_k$, and furthermore that the total number of hashes performed by $P_k$ is fixed as well.

**Theorem 1.** *Any $P_k(x)$ produces $f_k^*(x)$ in reverse in its output stage, performing $k2^{k-1}$ hashes ($2^k - 1$ in its initial stage and $(k-2)2^{k-1}+1$ in its output stage).*

*Proof.* The proof is by induction on $k$. For $k = 0$, we have that $P_0(x)$ outputs $f_0^*(x) = x$ in its one and only round, using 0 hashes.

For $k \geq 1$, we see that $P_k(x)$ first outputs $y_0 = f^{2^k-1}(x)$ in round $2^k$, which is the last element of $f_k^*(x)$. Next, $P_{i-1}(y_i)$ run in parallel for $i = 1, \dots, k$. The induction hypothesis yields that each $P_{i-1}(y_i)$ produces $f_{i-1}^*(f^{2^k-2^i}(x))$ in reverse in its last $2^{i-1}$ out of $2^i - 1$ rounds. Hence, in round $2^k + 1$, $P_0(y_1)$ outputs $\{y_1\} = f_0^*(f^{2^k-2}(x))$. In the next two rounds, $P_1(y_2)$ outputs $f_1^*(f^{2^k-4}(x))$ in reverse. And so on until finally $P_{k-1}(y_k)$ outputs $f_{k-1}^*(f^{2^{k-1}}(x))$ in reverse in the last $2^{k-1}$ rounds of $P_k(x)$. The total number of hashes performed by $P_k$ is $2^k - 1 + \sum_{i=1}^{k}(i-1)2^{i-2} = k2^{k-1}$, using that $P_{i-1}$ performs $(i-1)2^{i-2}$ hashes per the induction hypothesis.                    □

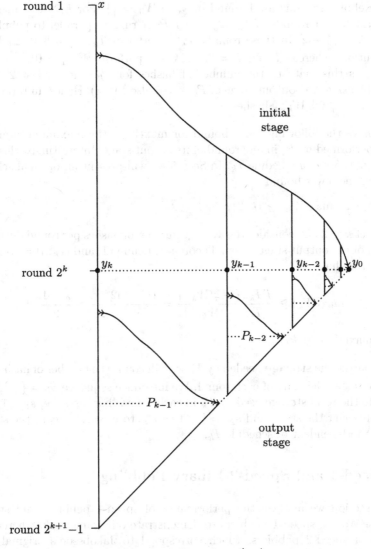

**Fig. 1.** Binary pebbler $P_k(x)$, where $y_i = f^{2^k - 2^i}(x)$ for $i = k, \ldots, 0$.

Schedule $T_k$ specifies the number of hashes for the initial stage of $P_k$. To analyze the **work** done by $P_k$ in its output stage, we introduce sequence $W_k$ of length $2^k - 1$ to denote the number of hashes performed by $P_k$ in each of its last $2^k - 1$ rounds—noting that by definition no hashes are performed by $P_k$ in round $2^k$. The following recurrence relation for $W_k$ will be used throughout our analysis.

**Lemma 1.** $W_0 = \{\}, \quad W_k = T_{k-1} + W_{k-1} \parallel 0 \parallel W_{k-1}.$

*Proof.* Pebbler $P_0$ runs for 1 round only, so $W_0 = \{\}$. For $k \geq 1$, we see that in the last $2^k - 1$ rounds of $P_k$, a pebbler $P_{k-1}$ runs in parallel to pebblers $P_i$ for $i = 0, \ldots, k - 2$. In these rounds, $P_{k-1}$ performs $T_{k-1} \parallel 0 \parallel W_{k-1}$ hashes by definition, whereas $P_i$ for $i = 0, \ldots, k - 2$ perform $W_{k-1} \parallel 0^{*2^{k-1}}$ hashes in total, as this matches the number of hashes for $P_{k-1}$ in its last $2^{k-1} - 1$ rounds (consider the output stage of $P_{k-1}$, see also Fig. 1). Hence, in total $W_k = T_{k-1} + W_{k-1} \parallel 0 \parallel W_{k-1}$ hashes.                                      $\square$

We have the following lower bound for $\max(W_k)$, the maximum number of hashes performed by $P_k$ in any round of its output stage. Interestingly, this lower bound holds for *any* schedule $T_k$. In Sect. 5 we will present an optimal schedule achieving the lower bound.

**Theorem 2.** $\max(W_k) \geq \lceil k/2 \rceil$, *for* $k \geq 2$.

*Proof.* Let $k \geq 2$ and consider the average number of hashes per round during the first half of the output stage. From Theorem 1, Lemma 1, and $|T_{k-1}| = |W_{k-1}| = 2^{k-1} - 1$, we have

$$\max(W_k) \geq \frac{\#T_{k-1} + \#W_{k-1}}{|T_{k-1} + W_{k-1}|} = \frac{(k-1)2^{k-2}}{2^{k-1} - 1} > \frac{k-1}{2}.$$

Hence, $\max(W_k) \geq \lceil k/2 \rceil$.                                      $\square$

To analyze the **storage** needed by $P_k$ we will count the number of hash values stored by $P_k$ at the start of each round. We introduce sequence $S_k = \{s_r\}_{r=1}^{2^{k+1}-1}$ to denote the total storage used by $P_k$ in each round. For instance, $s_1 = 1$ as $P_k$ only stores $x$ at the start, and $s_{2^k} = k + 1$ as $P_k$ stores $y_0, \ldots, y_k$ at the start of round $2^k$ independent of schedule $T_k$.

## 4   Speed-1 and Speed-2 Binary Pebbling

In this section we analyze the performance of speed-1 pebblers and speed-2 pebblers. We use speed-1 pebblers to demonstrate our framework, whereas the analysis of speed-2 pebblers, which correspond to Jakobsson's original algorithm [Jak02], will be used in the analysis of our optimal pebblers in the next section.

We define **speed-1** pebblers by setting $T_k = 1^{*2^k-1}$, hence one hash evaluation in each initial round of $P_k$. To define **speed-2** pebblers we set $T_0 = \{\}$ and $T_k = 0^{*2^{k-1}-1} \parallel 2^{*2^{k-1}-1} \parallel 1$ for $k \geq 1$, hence a speed-2 pebbler is idle in the first part of the initial stage and then hashes twice in each round until the end of the initial stage. As can be seen from Theorem 4 below, the storage requirements are reduced by a factor of 2 for speed-2 pebblers over speed-1 pebblers.

**Theorem 3.** *Both speed-1 and speed-2 pebblers* $P_k$ *use up to* $\max(W_k) = k - 1$ *hashes in any output round, for* $k \geq 1$.

*Proof.* For a speed-1 pebbler, Lemma 1 implies $\max(W_k) = k - 1$ for $k \geq 1$, as all elements of $T_{k-1}$ are equal to 1.

For a speed-2 pebbler we prove by induction on $k$ that $\max(W_k) = k - 1$. This clearly holds for $k = 1, 2$. For $k \geq 3$, we have, using Lemma 1,

$$T_{k-1} = 0^{*2^{k-2}-1} \qquad \| \; 2^{*2^{k-2}-1} \; \| \; 1$$
$$W_{k-1} = 0 \; \| \; T_{k-2} + W_{k-2} \; \| \; 0 \; \| \; W_{k-2}.$$

Therefore,

$$\max(W_k) = \max(T_{k-1} + W_{k-1}) = \max(W_{k-1}, 2 + W_{k-2}),$$

noting that the last element of $W_{k-2} = 0$. Applying the induction hypothesis twice, we conclude $\max(W_k) = \max(k - 2, k - 1) = k - 1$.  □

**Lemma 2**

$$S_0 = \{1\},$$
$$S_k = (1^{*2^k} \; \| \; S_{k-1}) + (0 \; \| \; 1^{*2^{k-1}-1} \; \| \; S_{k-1} \; \| \; 0^{*2^{k-1}}), \textit{ for a speed-1 } P_k,$$
$$S_k = (1^{*2^k} \; \| \; S_{k-1}) + (0^{*2^{k-1}} \; \| \; S_{k-1} \; \| \; 0^{*2^{k-1}}), \qquad \textit{for a speed-2 } P_k.$$

*Proof.* $P_0(x)$ only needs to store $x$ during its one and only round, therefore $S_0 = \{1\}$. For $k \geq 1$, any $P_k(x)$ also needs to store $x$ throughout all of its rounds, where $P_{k-1}(y_k) = P_{k-1}(x)$ takes over the storage of $x$ during the output stage. This accounts for the term $1^{*2^k} \; \| \; S_{k-1}$.

In addition, a speed-1 pebbler needs to store a hash value from round 2 until it reaches $y_{k-1}$ in round $2^{k-1}$. From thereon, the total additional storage corresponds to running a speed-1 pebbler $P_{k-1}(y_{k-1})$. This accounts for the term $0 \; \| \; 1^{*2^{k-1}-1} \; \| \; S_{k-1} \; \| \; 0^{*2^{k-1}}$.

A speed-2 pebbler needs no additional storage during its first $2^{k-1}$ rounds. Then it needs to store an additional hash value from round $2^{k-1}+1$ on. By taking $0^{*2^{k-1}} \; \| \; S_{k-1} \; \| \; 0^{*2^{k-1}}$ as additional term, we account for both the additional hash value stored by a speed-2 pebbler during rounds $(2^{k-1}, 2^{k-1} + 2^{k-2}]$ and the storage corresponding to a speed-2 pebbler $P_{k-1}(y_{k-1})$, running from round $2^{k-1} + 1$.  □

**Theorem 4.** *A speed-1 pebbler $P_k$ uses up to $\max(S_k) = \max(k + 1, 2k - 2)$ storage, and a speed-2 pebbler $P_k$ uses up to $\max(S_k) = k + 1$ storage.*

*Proof.* Using that $s_{2^k} = k + 1$, we write $S_k = A_k \; \| \; k{+}1 \; \| \; B_k$, where $|A_k| = |B_k| = 2^k - 1$.

For a speed-1 pebbler $P_k$, it can easily be checked that $\max(S_k) = \max(k + 1, 2k - 2)$ holds for $k = 0, 1$. To prove this for $k \geq 2$, we note that it suffices to show $\max(A_k, B_k) = 2k - 2$, as $\max(S_k) = \max(A_k, k + 1, B_k)$. Lemma 2 implies

$$A_k = 1 \; \| \; 2^{*2^{k-1}-1} \qquad \| \; 1 + A_{k-1}$$
$$B_k = A_{k-1} + B_{k-1} \; \| \; k \; \| \; B_{k-1},$$

so we have that $\max(A_k, B_k) = \max(A_{k-1} + B_{k-1}, k) = \max(2k - 2, k) = 2k - 2$ follows if we can show $\max(A_k + B_k) = 2k$, for $k \geq 1$. We prove the latter by induction on $k$. For $k = 1$, it is clearly true as $A_1 = B_1 = \{1\}$. For $k \geq 2$, we see that $\max(A_k + B_k) = \max(2 + A_{k-1} + B_{k-1}, k + 2) = \max(2k, k + 2) = 2k$ follows from the induction hypothesis, also using that the first element of $A_{k-1} + B_{k-1}$ is equal to $k$.

For a speed-2 pebbler $P_k$, we note that $\max(S_k) = k + 1$ follows from the fact that $A_k + B_k = k + 1$, which we show by induction on $k$. For $k = 0$, $A_k + B_k = k + 1$ is vacuously true, as $A_0, B_0$ are empty sequences. For $k \geq 1$, we see from Lemma 2 that

$$A_k = 1^{*2^{k-1}} \qquad \| \ 1 + A_{k-1}$$
$$B_k = A_{k-1} + B_{k-1} \ \| \ k \ \| \ B_{k-1}.$$

From the induction hypothesis we have $A_{k-1} + B_{k-1} = k$, hence it follows that $A_k + B_k = k + 1$. □

## 5   Optimal Binary Pebbling

In this section, we will reduce the maximum number of hashes per round from $k - 1$ for a speed-2 pebbler $P_k$ to $\lceil k/2 \rceil$ for an optimal pebbler $P_k$, without increasing the storage requirements. We do so by letting our optimal pebblers $P_k$ be idle for the first $2^{k-1} - 1$ rounds, just as speed-2 pebblers do. During rounds $[2^{k-1}, 2^k)$, an optimal pebbler will work at varying speeds, roughly as follows: the average speeds in each quarter are 2, 1, 2, and 3 hashes per round, respectively. To streamline the presentation, we will at first allow "$\frac{1}{2}$ hashes" in the definition of our optimal schedule. At the end of this section, we will show how to round the schedule to integer values without affecting optimality.

We define the **optimal** schedule $T_k$ as follows:

$$T_0 = \{\}, \quad T_k = 0^{*2^{k-1}-1} \ \| \ U_k \ \| \ V_k,$$

where

$$U_1 = \{1\}, \quad U_k = \tfrac{1}{2} + U_{k-1} \ \| \ 1^{*\lfloor 2^{k-3} \rfloor},$$
$$V_1 = \{\}, \quad V_k = \tfrac{1}{2} + U_{k-1} \ \| \ \tfrac{1}{2} + V_{k-1}.$$

For example, $T_1 = \{1\}$, $T_2 = \{0, \frac{3}{2}, \frac{3}{2}\}$, and $T_3 = \{0, 0, 0, 2, 1, 2, 2\}$.

Optimality is proved in the next two theorems. Subsequently, we will argue that optimal schedule $T_k$ is essentially unique.

**Theorem 5.** *An optimal pebbler $P_k$ uses up to $\max(W_k) = k/2$ hashes in any output round, for $k \geq 2$.*

*Proof.* We use Lemma 1 without explicitly referring to it.

Since $\max(W_k) = \max(T_{k-1} + W_{k-1})$, we obtain $\max(W_k) = k/2$, if we prove by induction on $k$ that

$$T_k + W_k = T_{k-1} + W_{k-1} \ \| \ \tfrac{k+1}{2}^{*2^{k-1}}.$$

This property clearly holds for $k = 1, 2$. For $k \geq 3$, the definition of $T_k$ implies that the property is in fact equivalent to

$$(U_k \parallel V_k) + (0 \parallel W_{k-1}) = \tfrac{k+1}{2} {}^{*2^{k-1}}. \tag{1}$$

From the definition of $U_k, V_k$ and the induction hypothesis for $T_{k-2} + W_{k-2}$ we obtain

$$U_k \parallel V_k = \tfrac{1}{2} + U_{k-1} \qquad \parallel 1^{*2^{k-3}} \parallel \tfrac{1}{2} + (U_{k-1} \parallel V_{k-1}),$$
$$0 \parallel W_{k-1} = 0 \parallel T_{k-3} + W_{k-3} \parallel \tfrac{k-1}{2}{}^{*2^{k-3}} \parallel 0 \parallel W_{k-2}.$$

Since $0 \parallel T_{k-3} + W_{k-3}$ is equal to the first half of $0 \parallel W_{k-2}$, we get from the induction hypothesis that indeed all elements of $(U_k \parallel V_k) + (0 \parallel W_{k-1})$ are equal to $\tfrac{k+1}{2}$. □

Let $\mathrm{len}(x) = \lceil \log_2(x+1) \rceil$ denote the bit length of nonnegative integer $x$. The next two lemmas give closed formulas for the optimal schedule $T_k$ and its partial sums. Lemma 4 will be used to prove Theorem 6, but these formulas also provide the basis for our efficient in-place implementation of optimal binary pebbling.

**Lemma 3.** *For optimal schedule* $T_k = \{t_r\}_{r=1}^{2^k - 1}$, *we have for* $2^{k-1} \leq r < 2^k$:

$$t_r = \tfrac{1}{2} \left( k + 1 - \mathrm{len}\left((2r) \bmod 2^{\mathrm{len}(2^k - r)}\right) \right).$$

*Proof.* The proof is by induction on $k$. For $0 \leq k \leq 2$, the formula is easily checked. For $k \geq 3$, we distinguish two cases.

*Case* $2^{k-1} \leq r < 2^{k-1}+2^{k-2}$. We first note that $(2r) \bmod 2^{\mathrm{len}(2^k-r)} = 2r-2^k$. If $r \geq 2^{k-1} + 2^{k-3}$, we have $t_r = 1$ by definition and we see the formula for $t_r$ yields 1 as well as $\mathrm{len}(2r - 2^k) = k - 1$. Otherwise $r < 2^{k-1} + 2^{k-3}$, hence we have $t_r = t_{r+2^{k-2}}$. So, this case reduces to the case below by noting that also $(2(r + 2^{k-2})) \bmod 2^{\mathrm{len}(2^k - (r+2^{k-2}))} = 2r - 2^k$.

*Case* $2^{k-1} + 2^{k-2} \leq r < 2^k$. From the definition of the optimal schedule we see that in this case $t_r = \tfrac{1}{2} + t'_{r-2^{k-1}}$, where $T_{k-1} = \{t'_z\}_{z=1}^{2^{k-1}-1}$. From the induction hypothesis we get:

$$t'_{r-2^{k-1}} = \tfrac{1}{2} \left( k - \mathrm{len}((2(r - 2^{k-1})) \bmod 2^{\mathrm{len}(2^{k-1}-(r-2^{k-1}))}) \right).$$

Rewriting this formula for $t'_{r-2^{k-1}}$ we obtain

$$t_r = \tfrac{1}{2} + \tfrac{1}{2} \left( k - \mathrm{len}((2r - 2^k) \bmod 2^{\mathrm{len}(2^k - r)}) \right).$$

Noting that $\mathrm{len}(2^k - r) \leq k$, we see that the formula holds for $t_r$ as well. □

**Lemma 4.** *For optimal schedule* $T_k = \{t_r\}_{r=1}^{2^k - 1}$, *we have for* $0 \leq j \leq 2^{k-1}$:

$$\sum_{r=2^k-j}^{2^k-1} t_r = \tfrac{1}{2}\left(j(k - m) + (m + 3 - l)2^l - 2^m\right) - 1,$$

*where* $l = \mathrm{len}(j)$ *and* $m = \mathrm{len}(2^l - j)$.

*Proof.* The proof is by induction on $j$. For $j = 0$, both sides are equal to 0. For $1 \le j \le 2^{k-1}$, Lemma 3 implies that

$$t_{2^k-j} = \tfrac{1}{2}\left(k+1 - \operatorname{len}((-2j) \bmod 2^l)\right).$$

Combined with the induction hypothesis for $j - 1$ we obtain

$$\sum_{r=2^k-j}^{2^k-1} t_r = \tfrac{1}{2}\left(j(k-m') + m'+1 - \operatorname{len}((-2j) \bmod 2^l) + (m'+3-l')2^{l'} - 2^{m'}\right)-1,$$

where $l' = \operatorname{len}(j-1)$ and $m' = \operatorname{len}(2^{l'} - j + 1)$. We distinguish two cases.

*Case $l' = l - 1$.* This means that $j = 2^{l-1}$, and hence $m = l$ and $m' = 1$. We are done as both sides are equal to $\tfrac{1}{2}j(k+4-l) - 1$.

*Case $l' = l$.* This means that $2^{l-1} < j < 2^l$, hence $0 < 2^{l+1} - 2j < 2^l$. This implies $\operatorname{len}((-2j) \bmod 2^l) = m + 1$, so we see that both sides are equal if $m = m'$. If $m' = m + 1$, we see that $2^l - j = 2^m - 1$ and that therefore both sides are equal as well. $\qquad\square$

**Theorem 6.** *An optimal pebbler $P_k$ uses up to $\max(S_k) = k + 1$ storage.*

*Proof.* We prove that the storage requirements of an optimal pebbler do not exceed the storage requirements of a speed-2 pebbler, hence that $\max(S_k) = k+1$ for an optimal pebbler as well.

Consider the rounds in which a speed-2 pebbler and an optimal pebbler store the values $y_i = f^{2^k-2^i}(x)$ for $i = k, \ldots, 1$. We claim that an optimal pebbler will never store $y_i$ before a speed-2 pebbler does. Clearly, a speed-2 pebbler stores $y_i$ in round $2^k - 2^{i-1}$ for $i = k, \ldots, 1$. However, in round $2^k - 2^{i-1}$ an optimal pebbler still has to compute at least as many hashes as a speed-2 pebbler needs to reach $y_0$:

$$\sum_{r=2^k-2^{i-1}}^{2^k-1} t_r = 2^{i-2}(k+4-i) - 1 \ge 2^i - 1,$$

using Lemma 4 for $j = 2^{i-1}$. $\qquad\square$

The above analysis implies that the optimal schedule $T_k$ is essentially unique. That is, if we require that the bounds stated in Theorems 5 and 6 must be met, optimal schedule $T_k$ is basically the only solution within our framework for binary pebbling. Clearly, like for any schedule in our framework, we have $T_0 = \{\}$ and $T_1 = \{1\}$. For $k \ge 2$, we first note that optimal schedule $T_k$ must start with $2^{k-1} - 1$ zeros in order to meet the bound of Theorem 6. More precisely, by writing $S_k = A_k \parallel k+1 \parallel B_k$ with $|A_k| = |B_k| = 2^k - 1$, as we also did in the proof of Theorem 4, and noting that $\max(B_k) = k$, we observe that this bound for $B_k$ is met only if optimal pebbler $P_k$ does not perform any hashes in its first $2^{k-1} - 1$ rounds. Next, by inspecting the proof of Theorem 5 we actually see that the number of hashes performed by an optimal pebbler $P_k$ in each of the last $2^{k-1}$ rounds of its initial stage is determined uniquely as well. A simple calculation shows that Eq. (1) necessarily holds for any optimal schedule: $\#U_k + \#V_k + \#W_{k-1} = (k+1)2^{k-2}$ hashes to be performed in $2^{k-1}$ rounds requires exactly $(k+1)/2$ hashes to be performed in each of these rounds. Hence, using induction on $k$, we see that $U_k$ and $V_k$ are determined uniquely by Eq. (1).

As a final step we will round the optimal schedule $T_k$ to integer values, without affecting optimality. For example, we round $T_2 = \{0, \frac{3}{2}, \frac{3}{2}\}$ to $\{0, 1, 2\}$ or to $\{0, 2, 1\}$. In general, we make sure that if an element is rounded up then its neighbors are rounded down, and vice versa. The rounding also depends on the parity of $k$ to alternate between rounding up and rounding down. Hence, we define the **rounded** optimal schedule by:

$$t_r = \left\lfloor \tfrac{1}{2} \left( (k+r) \bmod 2 + k + 1 - \mathrm{len}((2r) \bmod 2^{\mathrm{len}(2^k - r)}) \right) \right\rfloor, \qquad (2)$$

for $2^{k-1} \leq r < 2^k$. Accordingly, we see that optimal pebbler $P_k$ will use up to $\max(W_k) = \lceil k/2 \rceil$ hashes in any output round, matching the lower bound of Theorem 2.

# 6   Optimized Implementations

A hash chain is deployed as follows as part of an authentication mechanism like Lamport's asymmetric identification scheme. Given a random seed value $x$, the initial stage of any type of binary pebbler $P_k(x)$ is simply performed by iterating the hash function $f$ and storing the values $y_i = f^{2^k - 2^i}(x)$ for $i = k, \ldots, 0$. The value of $y_0$ is then output, e.g., as part of the registration protocol for Lamport's scheme. The other hash values $y_1, \ldots, y_k$ are stored for the remainder of the output stage, e.g., for use in later runs of Lamport's identification protocol.

The initial stage is preferably executed inside the secure device that will later use the hash chain for identification. However, for lightweight devices such as smart cards, RFID tags, sensors, etc., the initial stage will typically be run on a more powerful device, after which the hash values $y_1, \ldots, y_k$ will be inserted in the lightweight device and the hash value $y_0$ can be used for registration.

To implement the output stage of pebbler $P_k$ one needs to handle potentially many pebblers all running in parallel. The pseudocode in [Jak02, CJ02, YSEL09] suggests rather elaborate techniques for keeping track of the (state of) pebbles. On the contrary, we will show how to minimize storage and computational overhead by exploiting specific properties of Jakobsson's speed-2 pebbling and our optimal pebbling algorithm. In particular, we present in-place hash chain reversal algorithms, where the entire state of these algorithms (apart from the hash values) is represented between rounds by a single $k$-bit counter *only*.

We introduce the following terminology to describe the state of a pebbler $P_k$. This terminology applies to both speed-2 pebblers and optimal pebblers. Pebbler $P_k$ is said to be **idle** if it is in rounds $[1, 2^{k-1})$, **hashing** if it is in rounds $[2^{k-1}, 2^k]$, and **redundant** if it is in rounds $(2^k, 2^{k+1})$. An idle pebbler performs no hashes at all, while a hashing pebbler will perform at least one hash per round, except for round $2^k$ in which $P_k$ outputs its $y_0$ value. The work for a redundant pebbler $P_k$ is taken over by its child pebblers $P_0, \ldots, P_{k-1}$ during its last $2^k - 1$ output rounds.

The following theorem provides the basis for our in-place algorithms by showing precisely how the state of all pebblers running in parallel during the output stage of $P_k$ can be determined from the round number. Let $x_i \in \{0, 1\}$ denote the $i$th bit of nonnegative integer $x$, $0 \le i < \text{len}(x)$.

**Theorem 7.** *For a speed-2 or optimal pebbler $P_k$ in output round $2^{k+1} - c$, $1 \le c \le 2^k$, we have for every $i$, $0 \le i \le k$, exactly one non-redundant pebbler $P_i$ present if and only if bit $c_i = 1$, and if present, $P_i$ is in round $2^i - (c \bmod 2^i)$.*

*Proof.* The proof is by induction on $c$. For $c = 2^k$, only $c_k = 1$, which corresponds to $P_k$ being the only pebbler around. Also, $P_k$ is in its $2^k$th round.

For $1 \le c < 2^k$, write $c' = c + 1$ and let $i' \ge 0$ be maximal such that $c' \bmod 2^{i'} = 0$. Hence $c'_{i'} = 1$. By the induction hypothesis for $c'$, pebbler $P_{i'}$ is in its first output round $2^{i'}$. So, in the next round $P_{i'}$ becomes redundant, and is replaced by child pebblers $P_{i'-1}, \ldots, P_0$ which will all be in their first round. As $c = c' - 1$, this corresponds to the fact that $c_{i'} = 0$ and $c_{i'-1} = \cdots = c_0 = 1$, also noting that $2^i - (c \bmod 2^i) = 1$ for $i = i' - 1, \ldots, 0$.

For $i > i'$, we have $c_i = c'_i$. All non-redundant pebblers in round $2^{k+1} - c'$ remain so in round $2^{k+1} - c$, and for these pebblers the round number becomes $2^i - (c' \bmod 2^i) + 1 = 2^i - (c \bmod 2^i)$, as required. $\qquad\square$

As a corollary, we see that a non-redundant pebbler $P_i$ is hashing precisely when $c_{i-1} = 0$, and $P_i$ is idle otherwise, since for $c_i = 1$ we have that $c_{i-1} = 0$ if and only if $2^i - (c \bmod 2^i) \ge 2^{i-1}$. This holds also for $i = 0$ if we put $c_{-1} = 0$.

## 6.1    In-place Speed-2 Binary Pebbling

We present an in-place implementation of a speed-2 pebbler $P_k$ for which the overall storage is limited to the space for $k$ hash values and one $k$-bit counter $c$. As explained above, we will assume that hash values $y_1, \ldots, y_k$ are given as input and that $y_0$ has been output already. Thus, $P_k$ has exactly $2^k - 1$ output rounds remaining. We use $c$ to count down the output rounds.

The basis for our in-place algorithm is given by the next theorem.

**Theorem 8.** *For a speed-2 pebbler $P_k$ in output round $2^{k+1} - c$, $1 \le c \le 2^k$, each non-redundant pebbler $P_i$ present stores $e + 1$ hash values, where $e$ is maximal such that $c_{i-1} = \ldots = c_{i-e} = 0$ with $0 \le e \le i$.*

*Proof.* From Theorem 7 it follows that non-redundant pebbler $P_i$ is in round $r = 2^i - (c \bmod 2^i)$. Since $0 \le e \le i$ is maximal such that $c_{i-1} = \ldots = c_{i-e} = 0$, we have that $2^i - 2^{i-e} < r \le 2^i - 2^{i-e-1}$. This implies that $P_i$ stores $e + 1$ hash values in round $r$, as Lemma 2 says that for a speed-2 pebbler $P_i$ the storage requirements throughout its first $2^i$ rounds are given by sequence $D_i$, where $D_0 = \{1\}$ and $D_i = 1^{*2^{i-1}-1} \parallel 1 + D_{i-1}$. $\qquad\square$

---

**Algorithm 1.** In-place speed-2 binary pebbler $P_k(x)$.

---

**Initially:** array $z[0, k)$ where $z[i-1] = f^{2^k - 2^i}(x)$ for $i = 1, \ldots, k$.
**Round** $r$, $2^k < r < 2^{k+1}$:

1: output $z[0]$
2: $c \leftarrow 2^{k+1} - r$
3: $i \leftarrow \text{pop}_0(c)$
4: $z[0, i) \leftarrow z[1, i]$
5: $i \leftarrow i + 1;\ c \leftarrow \lfloor c/2 \rfloor$
6: $q \leftarrow i - 1$
7: **while** $c \neq 0$ **do**
8: $\quad z[q] \leftarrow f(z[i])$
9: $\quad$ **if** $q \neq 0$ **then** $z[q] \leftarrow f(z[q])$
10: $\quad i \leftarrow i + \text{pop}_0(c) + \text{pop}_1(c)$
11: $\quad q \leftarrow i$

---

Theorem 8 suggests an elegant approach to store the hash values of a speed-2 pebbler $P_k$ throughout its output stage. We use a single array $z$ of length $k$ to store all hash values as follows. Initially, $z[0] = y_1, \ldots, z[k-1] = y_k$, and counter $c = 2^k - 1$. This corresponds to $P_k$ being at the start of its output stage, where it starts to run $P_i(y_{i+1})$ in parallel, for $i = 0, \ldots, k - 1$, each of these (non-redundant) pebblers $P_i$ storing exactly one hash value in array $z$. In general, in output round $2^{k+1} - c$ of $P_k$, we let each non-redundant $P_i$ store its hash values in segment $z[i - e, i]$ (corresponding to $c_{i-e} = 0, \ldots, c_{i-1} = 0$ and $c_i = 1$). As a result, the non-redundant pebblers jointly occupy consecutive segments of array $z$, storing exactly $\text{len}(c)$ hash values in total.

Algorithm 1 describes precisely what $P_k$ does in round $r$, $2^k < r < 2^{k+1}$. Note that we set $c = 2^{k+1} - r$ at the start of round $r$. Based on Theorem 7, we process the bits of $c$ as follows, using operations $\text{pop}_0(c)$ and $\text{pop}_1(c)$ to count and remove all trailing 0s and 1s from $c$, respectively.

Let $i' \geq 0$ be maximal such that $c \bmod 2^{i'} = 0$. Hence $c_{i'} = 1$. From Theorem 7, we see that $P_{i'}$ is in its first output round $2^{i'}$, hence $P_{i'}$ becomes redundant in the next round, and each of its children will take over one hash value. The hash values $y_0, \ldots, y_{i'}$ computed by $P_{i'}$ in its initial stage are stored in $z[0], \ldots, z[i']$. So, we output $z[0] = y_0$ for $P_{i'}$ and move $y_1, \ldots, y_{i'}$ to entries $z[0], \ldots, z[i' - 1]$. This makes entry $z[i']$ available. We distinguish two cases.

*Case* $\text{len}(c - 1) = \text{len}(c) - 1$. In this case no new hash values need to be stored, and $z[i']$ will be unused from this round on.

*Case* $\text{len}(c-1) = \text{len}(c)$. Let $i'' \geq i'+1$ be maximal such that $c \bmod 2^{i''} = 2^{i'}$. Hence $c_{i''} = 1$. We claim that $P_{i''}$ is the unique pebbler that needs to store an additional hash value. Pebbler $P_{i''}$ is in round $2^{i''} - (c \bmod 2^{i''}) = 2^{i''} - 2^{i'}$, so it is $2^{i'}$ rounds from the end of its initial stage. We store its additional hash value in $z[i']$.

This explains Algorithm 1. In the first iteration of the loop in lines 7–11, we have that $q = i'$ holds at line 8. Each hashing pebbler performs two hashes, except when a pebbler is at the end of its initial stage (corresponding to $q = 0$).

---

**Algorithm 2.** In-place optimal binary pebbler $P_k(x)$.

---

**Initially:** array $z[0, k)$ where $z[i-1] = f^{2^k - 2^i}(x)$ for $i = 1, \ldots, k$.
**Round** $r$, $2^k < r < 2^{k+1}$:

1: output $z[0]$
2: $c \leftarrow 2^{k+1} - r$
3: $i \leftarrow \text{pop}_0(c)$
4: $z[0, i) \leftarrow z[1, i]$
5: $i \leftarrow i + 1; c \leftarrow \lfloor c/2 \rfloor$
6: $m \leftarrow i; s \leftarrow 0$
7: **while** $c \neq 0$ **do**
8:     $l \leftarrow i$
9:     $i \leftarrow i + \text{pop}_0(c)$
10:     $j \leftarrow (-r) \bmod 2^i$
11:     $p \leftarrow (i + j) \bmod 2$
12:     $h \leftarrow \lfloor (p + j(i - m) + (m + 3 - l)2^l - 2^m)/2 \rfloor$
13:     $q \leftarrow \text{len}(h) - 1$
14:     **for** $d \leftarrow 1$ **to** $\lfloor (p + i + 1 - s)/2 \rfloor$ **do**
15:         $y \leftarrow z[q]$
16:         **if** $h = 2^q$ **then** $q \leftarrow q - 1$
17:         $z[q] \leftarrow f(y)$
18:         $h \leftarrow h - 1$
19:     $m \leftarrow i; s \leftarrow m + 1$
20:     $i \leftarrow i + \text{pop}_1(c)$

---

Essentially no processing is done for idle pebblers, due to the use of operation $\text{pop}_1(c)$ in line 10.

## 6.2    In-place Optimal Binary Pebbling

In this section we turn the algorithm for speed-2 pebbling into one for optimal pebbling by making three major changes. See Algorithm 2.

First, we make sure that the number of hashes performed by each hashing pebbler $P_i$ is in accordance with Eq. (2). The actual hashing by $P_i$ is done in the loop in lines 14–18. Theorem 7 states that the round number for $P_i$ is given by $2^i - (c \bmod 2^i)$, hence by $2^i - j$ if we set $j = (-r) \bmod 2^i$ in line 10. By ensuring that $l = \text{len}(j)$ and $m = \text{len}(2^l - j)$ holds as well, we have that the number of hashes as specified by Eq. (2) can be computed as $\lfloor (p + i + 1 - s)/2 \rfloor$, where $p = (i + j) \bmod 2$ and $s = (m + 1) \bmod (l + 1)$ (actually using that $\text{len}((2^l - 2j) \bmod 2^l) = \text{len}(2^{l+1} - 2j) \bmod (l + 1)$ holds for $j \geq 1$).

Second, we make sure that each hashing pebbler $P_i$ will store the correct hash values for $y_i, \ldots, y_0$. To this end, note that Lemma 4 tells precisely how many hashes $P_i$ still needs to compute at the start of round $j$. Thus we set $h$ to this value (plus one) in line 12, and test in line 16 if the current hash value must be stored (that is, whether $h$ is an integral power of 2).

Finally, we make sure that hashing pebbler $P_i$ will use the correct entries of array $z$. Since $h$ records the number of hashes that $P_i$ still needs to compute

---

**Algorithm 3.** Fast optimal binary pebbler $P_k(x)$.

---

**Initially:** array $z[0, k)$ where $z[i-1] = f^{2^k - 2^i}(x)$ for $i = 1, \ldots, k$;
    array $a[0, \lfloor k/2 \rfloor)$, $v = 0$.

**Round** $r$, $2^k < r < 2^{k+1}$:

1:   output $z[0]$
2:   $c \leftarrow 2^{k+1} - r$
3:   $i \leftarrow \mathrm{pop}_0(c)$
4:   $z[0, i) \leftarrow z[1, i]$
5:   $i \leftarrow i + 1$; $c \leftarrow \lfloor c/2 \rfloor$
6:   **if** $c$ odd **then** $a[v] \leftarrow (i, 0)$; $v \leftarrow v + 1$
7:   $u \leftarrow v$
8:   $w \leftarrow (r \bmod 2) + i + 1$
9:   **while** $c \neq 0$ **do**
10:     $w \leftarrow w + \mathrm{pop}_0(c)$
11:     $u \leftarrow u - 1$; $(q, g) \leftarrow a[u]$
12:     **for** $d \leftarrow 1$ **to** $\lfloor w/2 \rfloor$ **do**
13:       $y \leftarrow z[q]$
14:       **if** $g = 0$ **then** $q \leftarrow q - 1$; $g = 2^q$
15:       $z[q] \leftarrow f(y)$
16:       $g \leftarrow g - 1$
17:     **if** $q \neq 0$ **then** $a[u] \leftarrow (q, g)$ **else** $v \leftarrow v - 1$
18:     $w \leftarrow (w \bmod 2) + \mathrm{pop}_1(c)$

---

(plus one), it follows that the current hash value for $P_i$ is stored in entry $z[q]$, where $q = \mathrm{len}(h) - 1$. Hence, we set $q$ to this value in line 13.

This explains the design of Algorithm 2. Note that only one bit length computation is used per hashing pebbler (cf. line 13).

## 6.3 Optimal Binary Pebbling with Minimal Computational Overhead

Even though the computational overhead for our in-place implementation is small, it may still be relatively large if hash evaluations themselves take very little time. For instance, if the hash function is (partly) implemented in hardware. Using Intel's AES-NI instruction set one can implement a 128-bit hash function that takes a few cycles only (e.g., see [BÖS11], noting that for one-way hash chains no collision-resistance is needed such that one can use Matyas-Meyer-Oseas for which the key is fixed). Therefore, we also provide an implementation minimizing the computational overhead at the expense of some additional storage.

We will keep some state for each pebbler, or rather for each *hashing* pebbler only. Although an optimal pebbler $P_k$ will store up to $k$ hash values at any time, we observe that no more than $\lceil k/2 \rceil$ hashing pebblers will be present at any time. As in our in-place algorithms we will thus avoid any storage (and processing) for idle pebblers, as can be seen from Algorithm 3.

A segment $a[0, v)$ of an array $a$ of length $\lfloor k/2 \rfloor$ suffices to store the states of all hashing pebblers, where initially $v = 0$. In each round, at most one idle pebbler $P_i$ will become hashing, and if this happens pebbler $P_i$ is added to array $a$, cf. line 6. Later, once pebbler $P_i$ is done hashing, it will be removed again from array $a$, cf. line 17.

For each hashing pebbler we store two values called $q$ and $g$ such that $q$ matches the value of variable $q$ in Algorithm 2 and $g$ matches the value of $h - 2^q$ in Algorithm 2. Hence, we use $g$ to count down to zero starting from the appropriate powers of 2, cf. line 14. Finally, variable $w$ is introduced such that its value matches the value of $p + i + 1 - s$ in Algorithm 2. As a result, Algorithm 3 limits the computations for each hashing pebbler to a few elementary operations only.

Note that Algorithm 3 is actually quite intuitive and remarkable at the same time. E.g., by focusing on variable $w$, one can easily see that the total number of hashes performed by $P_k$ in any output round does not exceed $\lceil k/2 \rceil$.

# 7    Extensions

In this section we briefly discuss three extensions, omitting details.

First, we show how to accommodate hash chains of arbitrary length $n$ by generalizing the initialization of Algorithms 1, 2, and 3 from $n = 2^k$ to any $n \geq 1$, without incurring any overhead. That is, given a seed value $x$, we will iterate the hash function $f$ for exactly $n - 1$ times and output $f^{n-1}(x)$ (e.g., as part of the registration protocol for Lamport's scheme). At the same time, we will store precisely those intermediate hash values in array $z$ such that the state becomes equivalent to the state of binary pebbler $P_k$ at round $2^{k+1} - (n - 1)$, where $2^{k-1} < n \leq 2^k$.

We demonstrate this for in-place speed-2 pebbling, by extending Theorem 8 to the following theorem, which exactly describes the state of speed-2 pebbler $P_k(x)$ at round $c = n - 1$.

**Theorem 9.** *For a speed-2 pebbler $P_k(x)$ in output round $2^{k+1} - c$, $1 \leq c \leq 2^k$, each idle $P_i$ stores the hash value $f^{c-(c \bmod 2^i)-2^i}(x)$ and each hashing $P_i$ stores the following $e + 1$ hash values:*

$$f^{c-(c \bmod 2^i)-2^i}(x), \ldots, f^{c-(c \bmod 2^i)-2^{i-e+1}}(x), f^{c-\max(1,3(c \bmod 2^i))}(x),$$

*where $e$ is maximal such that $c_{i-1} = \ldots = c_{i-e} = 0$ with $0 \leq e \leq i$.*

Based on this theorem array $z$ can be initialized simply by inspecting the bits of $c$ (most-significant to least-significant) while iterating $f$. The remaining $n - 1$ output rounds are then executed exactly as in Algorithm 1. A slightly more complicated approach applies to our optimal pebbling algorithm, for which we omit the details.

Next, we show how to construct a *cascade* of pebblers $P_k(x)$, $P_k(x')$, $P_k(x'')$, and so on, for seed values $x, x', x'', \ldots$, such that the initial stage of $P_k(x')$ is run in parallel to the output stage of $P_k(x)$ (more precisely, in parallel to rounds $(2^k, 2^{k+1})$ of $P_k(x)$), and so on. Hence, as soon as $P_k(x)$ is done, $P_k(x')$ will continue with producing hash chain $f_k^*(x')$ in reverse. In general, this combination corresponds exactly to running the output stage of a $P_{k+1}$ pebbler over and over again. Therefore, the maximum number of hashes in any round will be limited to $\max(W_{k+1})$. Using our optimal pebbler, we thus get no more than $\lceil (k+1)/2 \rceil$ hashes per round. Moreover, we only need to store a maximum of $k + 1$ hash values at any time (conceptually, the value $y_{k+1}$ that a $P_{k+1}$ pebbler would store is not present), hence essentially for free; this can even be reduced to $\lceil k/2 \rceil$ per round at the expense of increasing the maximum storage to $k + 2$ hash values.

To make such a cascade useful, the hash values $f^{2^k-1}(x')$, $f^{2^k-1}(x'')$, ... need to be authenticated. A straightforward way is to run the registration protocol once $f^{2^k-1}(x')$ is output, and so on. A more refined way is to apply known techniques for "re-initializing" hash chains [Goy04, ZL05], hence using a one-time signature to authenticate $f^{2^k-1}(x')$, for which the public key is incorporated in the previous seed value $x$.

In fact, this approach can be extended to eliminate initialization altogether, basically by starting with a $P_{k+1}$ pebbler in its first output round, where each $y_i$ is assigned a seed value incorporating a one-time public key. Setting $y_i = f^{2^{k'}-2^i}(x)$ for $i = k', \ldots, 0$ for some small $k'$, and using such seed values for the remaining $y_i$'s, this *bootstrapping* technique can be tuned for optimal performance.

Finally, we show how to eliminate the shifting done in line 4 of Algorithms 1, 2, and 3, which forms a potential bottleneck as naively copying up to $k - 1$ hash values may be relatively expensive. A standard technique to avoid such excessive copying is to use an auxiliary array of "pointers" $d[0, k)$ such that $d[i]$ points to the entry in $z[0, k)$ that should actually be used, but this would break the in-place property. Fortunately, it turns out that permutation $d$ can be characterized nicely as a function of the round number, thus allowing us to efficiently restore the in-place property, without copying even a single hash value throughout our algorithms.

## 8    Concluding Remarks

We have completely resolved the case of binary pebbling of hash chains by constructing an explicit optimal schedule. A major advantage of our optimal schedule is that it allows for very efficient *in-place* pebbling algorithms. This compares favorably with the greedy pebbling algorithms of [YSEL09], which require a substantial amount of storage beyond the hash values themselves. The pseudocode of Algorithms 1, 2, and 3 is readily translated into efficient program code, applying further optimizations depending on the target platform. [3]

The security of one-way hash chains for use in authentication mechanisms such as Lamport's asymmetric identification scheme does not depend on the collision resistance of the hash function. Therefore, it suffices to use 128-bit hash

---

[3] Sample code (in Python, Java, C) available at www.win.tue.nl/~berry/pebbling/.

values—rather than 256-bit hash values, say. Using, for instance, the above mentioned Matyas-Meyer-Oseas construction one obtains a fast and simple one-way function $f : \{0,1\}^{128} \to \{0,1\}^{128}$ defined as $f(x) = \text{AES}_{\text{IV}}(x) \oplus x$, where IV is a 128-bit string used as fixed "key" for the AES block cipher.[4] Consequently, even for *very long* hash chains of length $2^{32}$, our in-place optimal pebbling algorithm will just store 516 bytes (32 hash values and one 32-bit counter) and perform at most 16 hashes per identification round. Similarly, *long* hash chains of length $2^{16}$ would allow devices capable only of lightweight cryptography to run 65535 rounds of identification (e.g., more than twice per hour over a period of three years), requiring only 258 bytes of storage and using at most 8 hashes per round.

Reversal of a length-$n$ hash chain using optimal binary pebbling requires $\log_2 n$ storage and $\frac{1}{2} \log_2 n$ time per round, yielding $\frac{1}{2} \log_2^2 n$ as space-time product. Coppersmith and Jakobsson [CJ02] derived a lower bound of approximately $\frac{1}{4} \log_2^2 n$ for the space-time product.[5] Whether this lower bound is achievable is doubtful, because the lower bound is derived *without* taking into account that the maximum number of hashes during any round needs to be minimized. We like to mention, however, that by means of "Fibonacci" pebbling we can actually achieve $\frac{1}{2\sqrt{5}} \log_\phi^2 n \approx 0.46 \log_2^2 n$ as space-time product, where $\phi$ is the golden ratio. Omitting details, we consider hash chains of length $n = F_k$, the $k$th Fibonacci number, e.g., for even $k$, storing $k/2$ elements at distances $F_{2i} - 1$, for $1 \leq i \leq k/2$, from the end of the hash chain, and using $k/\sqrt{5}$ time per round.

As another direction for further research we suggest to revisit the problem of efficient Merkle tree traversal studied in [Szy04], which plays a central role in hash-based signature schemes [Mer87, Mer89]; in particular, it would be interesting to see whether algorithms for generating successive authentication paths can be done in-place. More generally, research into optimal (in-place) algorithms for hash-based signatures is of major interest both in the context of lightweight cryptography (e.g., see [PCTS02, MSS13]; more references in [YSEL09]) and in the context of post-quantum cryptography (e.g., see [BDE+13]).

**Acknowledgments.** It is my pleasure to thank both Niels de Vreede and Thijs Laarhoven for many discussions on variants of the problem, and to thank Niels especially for suggesting the bootstrapping approach (see Sect. 7). Moreover, the anonymous reviewers are gratefully acknowledged for their comments.

---

[4] More precisely, function $f$ should be one-way on its iterates [Lev85, Ped96].

[5] Incidentally, this lower bound had been found already in a completely different context [GPRS96]; see Appendix A.

# A  Rushing Binary Pebbling

The problem studied in the area of algorithmic (or, automatic, computational) differentiation [GW08] is similar to the task for our pebbler $P_k(x)$ of computing the hash chain $f_k^*(x)$ and outputting this sequence in reverse. The critical difference, however, is that in the context of algorithmic differentiation the goal is basically to minimize the *total time* for performing this task (or, equivalently, to minimize the *amortized time* per output round). This contrasts sharply with the goal in the cryptographic context, where we want to minimize the *worst case time* per output round while performing this task.

Below we show that it is easy to achieve logarithmic space and logarithmic amortized time per output round for binary pebbling algorithms. This result is comparable to what is achieved by means of checkpointing for the reverse (or, adjoint, backward) mode of algorithmic differentiation in [Gri92]; in fact, without the performance constraint unique for the cryptographic setting, as initiated by Jakobsson [Jak02, CJ02], it is even possible to attain the lower bound of [GPRS96]. Therefore, the solutions achieved in the area of algorithmic differentiation (and in related areas such as reversible computing [Per13], for that matter) do not carry over to the cryptographic setting.

In fact, logarithmic amortized time per output round is achieved by *any* binary pebbler $P_k$ as follows directly from Theorem 1: any $P_k$ performs $\#W_k = (k-2)2^{k-1} + 1$ hashes in total during its output stage consisting of $2^k$ rounds, hence the amortized number of hashes per output round is equal to $\#W_k/2^k \approx k/2 - 1$. This holds for any schedule $T_k$ satisfying $\#T_k = 2^k - 1$.

To achieve logarithmic space as well, we choose $T_k$ such that the storage requirements for $P_k$ are minimized. This can simply be done by postponing the evaluation of all hashes to the last round of the initial stage of $P_k$. Concretely, we define a **rushing** pebbler $P_k$ by setting $T_0 = \{\}$ and $T_k = 0^{*2^k-2} \parallel 2^k - 1$ for $k \geq 1$. Hence, a rushing pebble performs all $2^k - 1$ hashes in the last round of its initial stage; see also Fig. 2.

As a consequence, a rushing pebbler minimizes its storage requirements at the cost of some computationally very expensive rounds, as follows.

**Theorem 10.** *A rushing pebbler $P_k$ uses up to* $\max(W_k) = 2^{k-1} - 1$ *hashes in any output round, for $k \geq 1$.*

**Lemma 5.** *For a rushing pebbler $P_k$, we have:*

$$S_0 = \{1\}, \quad S_k = (0^{*2^k-1} \parallel 1 \parallel S_{k-1}) + (1^{*2^{k-1}} \parallel S_{k-1} \parallel 0^{*2^{k-1}}).$$

**Theorem 11.** *A rushing pebbler $P_k$ uses up to* $\max(S_k) = k + 1$ *storage.*

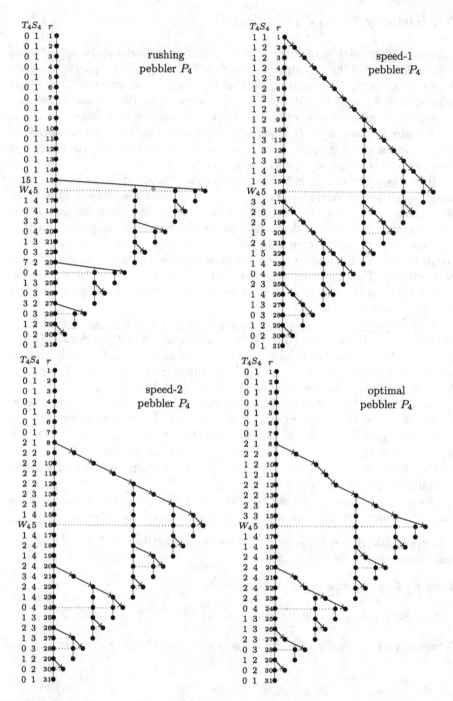

**Fig. 2.** Schedule $T_4$, work $W_4$, storage $S_4$ for binary pebblers $P_4$ in rounds 1–31. Bullets represent stored values, arrows represent hashing, vertical lines represent copying.

# References

[BDE+13] Buchmann, J., Dahmen, E., Ereth, S., Hülsing, A., Rückert, M.: On the security of the Winternitz one-time signature scheme. Int. J. Appl. Crypt. **3**(1), 84–96 (2013)

[BÖS11] Bos, J.W., Özen, O., Stam, M.: Efficient hashing using the AES instruction set. In: Preneel, B., Takagi, T. (eds.) CHES 2011. LNCS, vol. 6917, pp. 507–522. Springer, Heidelberg (2011). doi:10.1007/978-3-642-23951-9_33

[CJ02] Coppersmith, D., Jakobsson, M.: Almost optimal hash sequence traversal. In: Blaze, M. (ed.) FC 2002. LNCS, vol. 2357, pp. 102–119. Springer, Heidelberg (2003). doi:10.1007/3-540-36504-4_8

[Goy04] Goyal, V.: How to re-initialize a hash chain. eprint.iacr.org/2004/097

[GPRS96] Grimm, J., Potter, L., Rostaing-Schmidt, N.: Optimal time and minimum space-time product for reversing a certain class of programs. In: Berz, M., Bischof, C.H., Corliss, G., Griewank, A. (eds.) Computational Differentiation Techniques. Applications, and Tools, pp. 95–106. SIAM, Philadelphia (1996)

[Gri92] Griewank, A.: Achieving logarithmic growth of temporal and spatial complexity in reverse automatic differentiation. Optim. Methods Softw. **1**(1), 35–54 (1992)

[GW08] Griewank, A., Walther, A.: Evaluating Derivatives: Principles and Techniques of Algorithmic Differentiation, 2nd edn. SIAM, Reading (2008)

[Hal94] Haller, N.: The S/KEY one-time password system. In: Proceedings of the Symposium on Network and Distributed System Security (NDSS), pp. 151–157. Internet Society, February 1994. en.wikipedia.org/wiki/S/KEY

[IR01] Itkis, G., Reyzin, L.: Forward-secure signatures with optimal signing and verifying. In: Kilian, J. (ed.) CRYPTO 2001. LNCS, vol. 2139, pp. 332–354. Springer, Heidelberg (2001). doi:10.1007/3-540-44647-8_20

[Jak02] Jakobsson, M.: Fractal hash sequence representation and traversal. In: Proceedings of IEEE International Symposium on Information Theory (ISIT 2002), p. 437. IEEE Press (2002). Full version eprint.iacr.org/2002/001

[Kim03] Kim, S.-R.: Improved scalable hash chain traversal. In: Zhou, J., Yung, M., Han, Y. (eds.) ACNS 2003. LNCS, vol. 2846, pp. 86–95. Springer, Heidelberg (2003). doi:10.1007/978-3-540-45203-4_7

[Lam81] Lamport, L.: Password authentication with insecure communication. Commun. ACM **24**(11), 770–772 (1981)

[Lev85] Levin, L.: One-way function and pseudorandom generators. In: Proceedings of the 17th Symposium on Theory of Computing (STOC 1985), pp. 363–365 (1985)

[Mer87] Merkle, R.C.: A digital signature based on a conventional encryption function. In: Pomerance, C. (ed.) CRYPTO 1987. LNCS, vol. 293, pp. 369–378. Springer, Heidelberg (1988). doi:10.1007/3-540-48184-2_32

[Mer89] Merkle, R.C.: A certified digital signature. In: Brassard, G. (ed.) CRYPTO 1989. LNCS, vol. 435, pp. 218–238. Springer, New York (1990). doi:10.1007/0-387-34805-0_21

[MSS13] Mourier, N., Stampp, R., Strenzke, F.: An implementation of the hash-chain signature scheme for wireless sensor networks. In: Avoine, G., Kara, O. (eds.) LightSec 2013. LNCS, vol. 8162, pp. 68–80. Springer, Heidelberg (2013). doi:10.1007/978-3-642-40392-7_6

[Nak08]  Nakamoto, S.: Bitcoin: a peer-to-peer electronic cash system, 31 October 2008. bitcoin.org/bitcoin.pdf

[PCTS02]  Perrig, A., Canetti, R., Tygar, J.D., Song, D.: The TESLA broadcast authentication protocol. RSA CryptoBytes 5(2), 2–13 (2002)

[Ped96]  Pedersen, T.P.: Electronic payments of small amounts. In: Lomas, M. (ed.) Security Protocols 1996. LNCS, vol. 1189, pp. 59–68. Springer, Heidelberg (1997). doi:10.1007/3-540-62494-5_5

[Per13]  Perumalla, K.: Introduction to Reversible Computing. Chapman and Hall/CRC, Boca Raton (2013)

[Sel03]  Sella, Y.: On the computation-storage trade-offs of hash chain traversal. In: Wright, R.N. (ed.) FC 2003. LNCS, vol. 2742, pp. 270–285. Springer, Heidelberg (2003). doi:10.1007/978-3-540-45126-6_20

[Szy04]  Szydlo, M.: Merkle tree traversal in log space and time. In: Cachin, C., Camenisch, J.L. (eds.) EUROCRYPT 2004. LNCS, vol. 3027, pp. 541–554. Springer, Heidelberg (2004). doi:10.1007/978-3-540-24676-3_32

[YSEL09]  Yum, D.H., Seo, J.W., Eom, S., Lee, P.J.: Single-layer fractal hash chain traversal with almost optimal complexity. In: Fischlin, M. (ed.) CT-RSA 2009. LNCS, vol. 5473, pp. 325–339. Springer, Heidelberg (2009). doi:10.1007/978-3-642-00862-7_22

[ZL05]  Zhao, Y., Li, D.: An improved elegant method to re-initialize hash chains, January 2005. eprint.iacr.org/2005/011

# Factoring as a Service

Luke Valenta, Shaanan Cohney, Alex Liao, Joshua Fried, Satya Bodduluri,
and Nadia Heninger[✉]

University of Pennsylvania, Philadelphia, USA
nadiah@cis.upenn.edu

**Abstract.** The difficulty of integer factorization is fundamental to modern cryptographic security using RSA encryption and signatures. Although a 512-bit RSA modulus was first factored in 1999, 512-bit RSA remains surprisingly common in practice across many cryptographic protocols. Popular understanding of the difficulty of 512-bit factorization does not seem to have kept pace with developments in computing power. In this paper, we optimize the CADO-NFS and Msieve implementations of the number field sieve for use on the Amazon Elastic Compute Cloud platform, allowing a non-expert to factor 512-bit RSA public keys in under four hours for $75. We go on to survey the RSA key sizes used in popular protocols, finding hundreds or thousands of deployed 512-bit RSA keys in DNSSEC, HTTPS, IMAP, POP3, SMTP, DKIM, SSH, and PGP.

## 1 Introduction

A 512-bit RSA modulus was first factored by Cavallar et al. in 1999, which took about seven calendar months in a distributed computation using hundreds of computers and at least one supercomputer [8]. The current public factorization record, a 768-bit RSA modulus, was reported in 2009 by Kleinjung et al. and took about 2.5 calendar years and a large academic effort [22].

Despite these successes, 512-bit RSA keys are still regularly found in use. Several implementations of the number field sieve have been published, including CADO-NFS [34], Msieve [28], and ggnfs [26], allowing even enthusiastic amateurs to factor 512-bit or larger RSA moduli. In 2009, Benjamin Moody factored a 512-bit RSA code signing key used on the TI-83+ graphing calculator using 2.5 calendar months of time on a single computer, and a distributed effort then factored several more 512-bit TI-68k and TI-Z80 calculator signing keys [33]. The NFS@Home project has organized several large distributed factorizations since 2009 [9]. In 2012, Zachary Harris factored the 512-bit DKIM RSA keys used by Google and several other major companies in 72 h per key using CADO-NFS and Amazon's Elastic Compute Cloud (EC2) service [37].

The persistence of 512-bit RSA is likely due in part to the legacy of United States policies regarding cryptography. In the 1990s, international versions of cryptographic software designed to comply with United States export control regulations shipped with 40-bit symmetric keys and 512-bit asymmetric keys, and export-grade cipher suites with these key sizes were built into protocols like

© International Financial Cryptography Association 2017
J. Grossklags and B. Preneel (Eds.): FC 2016, LNCS 9603, pp. 321–338, 2017.
DOI: 10.1007/978-3-662-54970-4_19

SSL. Restrictions were later raised or lifted on open-source and mass-market software with cryptographic capabilities, but as of 2015, the United States Commerce Control List still includes systems "designed or modified to use 'cryptography' employing digital techniques performing any cryptographic function other than authentication, digital signature, or execution of copy-protected 'software' and having ... an 'asymmetric algorithm' where the security of the algorithm is based on ... factorization of integers in excess of 512 bits (e.g., RSA)" [7].

Factoring a 512-bit RSA key using the number field sieve is still perceived by many as a significant undertaking. In 2015, Beurdouche et al. [6] discovered the FREAK attack, a flaw in many TLS implementations that allows man-in-the-middle attacks to downgrade connections to 512-bit export-grade RSA cipher suites. In evaluating the prospect of a fully exploitable vulnerability, the paper states "we observe that 512-bit factorization is currently solvable at most in weeks." Subsequently, Bhargavan, Green, and Heninger developed a FREAK attack proof-of-concept in part by configuring CADO-NFS to run more efficiently on Amazon EC2. This setup was reported to factor a 512-bit key in approximately 7 h on EC2, with a few additional hours for startup and shutdown [5].

In this paper, we present an improved implementation which is able to factor a 512-bit RSA key on Amazon EC2 in as little as four hours for \$75. Our code is available at https://github.com/eniac/faas.

We gain these improvements by optimizing existing implementations for the case of factoring in the cloud. In particular, we rewrote the distributed portion of the number field sieve to use the Slurm job scheduler [35], allowing us to more effectively scale to greater amounts of computational resources. We describe our implementation and parallelizations in Sect. 3. We then performed extensive experiments on both CADO-NFS and Msieve to determine optimal parameter settings for the network interconnect speeds and resource limits achievable on Amazon EC2. Our experiments are detailed in Sect. 4.

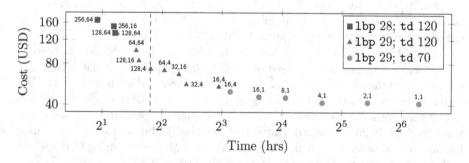

**Fig. 1. A time/cost curve for 512-bit factorization.** Each point above is annotated with the instances used for sieving and linear algebra, respectively, and represents an experimental estimate. There are diminishing returns from imperfect parallelization in linear algebra. The dotted line shows the fastest time we were able to achieve; larger experiments usually encountered node instability.

Figure 1 summarizes the time and cost to factor a 512-bit RSA key using current optimal parameters with varying amounts of resources, and the average cost we paid between May and September 2015 for EC2 resources. By tuning the parameters for factoring, one can achieve different points in the trade-off between overall clock time and overall cost. Using more machines gives a faster overall factoring time, but has diminishing returns because of imperfect parallelism. Linear algebra time was measured empirically and sieving was measured once for each parameter set and extrapolated to different numbers of instances.

The order of magnitude of the costs we give lines up with previous reports and estimates of factoring on EC2, and we achieve a significant speedup in overall running time. Performing a computation of this magnitude reliably remains a challenging endeavor. Our paper can also be viewed as a case study on the successes and challenges in trying to replicate a high-performance computing environment in the Amazon EC2 cloud.

In order to measure the impact of fast 512-bit factorization, in Sect. 5 we analyze existing datasets and perform our own surveys to quantify 512-bit RSA key usage in modern cryptographic public key infrastructures. We find thousands of DNSSEC records signed with 512-bit keys, millions of HTTPS, SMTP, IMAPS, and POP3S servers still supporting RSA_EXPORT cipher suites for TLS, and a long tail of 768-bit, 512-bit, and shorter RSA keys in use across DKIM, SSH, IPsec VPNs, and PGP.

## 2    Background

In this paper, we focus on the impact of factoring on the security of RSA public keys [32], though integer factorization has many applications across mathematics. Factoring the modulus of an RSA public key allows an attacker to compute the corresponding private key, and thus to decrypt any messages encrypted to that key, or forge cryptographic signatures using the private key.

### 2.1    Number Field Sieve

The general number field sieve is the fastest known algorithm for factoring generic integers larger than a few hundred bits [25]. Its running time is described using $L$-notation as $L_N[1/3, 1.923] = \exp\left(1.923(\log N)^{1/3}(\log\log N)^{2/3}\right)$–subexponential, but super-polynomial [21] in the size of $N$, the integer to be factored. A gentle introduction to the big ideas behind sieving algorithms for integer factorization and can be found in Pomerance's 1996 survey [30], and more in-depth information on the number field sieve can be found in the books by Lenstra, Lenstra, Manasse, and Pollard [25] and Crandall and Pomerance [12].

In this section, we give a brief overview of the structure of the algorithm, in order to identify potential implementation optimizations and barriers to parallelization. The number field sieve has four main computational stages: *polynomial selection, sieving, linear algebra,* and *square root* (Fig. 2).

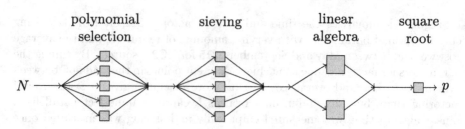

**Fig. 2. The number field sieve.** The number field sieve factoring algorithm consists of several main stages. Sieving and linear algebra are the most computationally intensive stages. Sieving is embarrassingly parallel, while parallelizing linear algebra can encounter communication bottlenecks.

The first stage of the algorithm, *polynomial selection*, searches for a polynomial $f(x)$ and integer $m$ satisfying $f(m) \equiv 0 \bmod N$, where $N$ is the integer to factor. $f(x)$ defines the number field $\mathbb{Q}(x)/f(x)$ to be used in the rest of the algorithm. A good choice of polynomial in this stage can significantly speed up the rest of the computation, by generating smaller elements in the sieving phase. Several techniques exist for choosing the polynomial, but in general many different polynomials are tested and the best one is passed on to the next stage. The polynomial selection stage is embarrassingly parallel.

The next stage of the algorithm, *sieving*, factors ranges of integers and number field elements to find many relations of elements and saves those whose prime factors have size less than some size bound $B$, called the smoothness bound. CADO-NFS uses the *large prime variant* of sieving, and the large prime bound parameters `lbp` control the log of the smoothness bounds. Decreasing these bounds increases the difficulty of sieving, since relations are less likely to factor completely into smaller factors. The sieving stage is also embarrassingly parallel, since candidate relations can be evaluated independently in small batches.

In the third stage, *linear algebra*, the coefficient vectors of the relations are used to construct a large sparse matrix with entries over $\mathbb{F}_2$. Before beginning this stage, some preprocessing on the relations is used to decrease the dimension of the resulting matrix. In general, more relations collected during sieving will produce a smaller matrix and reduce the runtime for linear algebra. The goal of the linear algebra stage is to discover a linear dependency among the rows. This is accomplished via the Block Wiedemann [10] or Block Lanczos [27] algorithms, which are specialized for sparse linear algebra. This step can be parallelized, but the parallelization requires much more communication and synchronization.

The final stage involves computing the *square root* of a number field element corresponding to a dependency in the matrix. In practice, many dependencies will be tested since not all of them will lead to a nontrivial factor; the square roots can be computed and tested in parallel. This step takes only a few minutes.

*Discrete log.* There is also a number field sieve algorithm for discrete logarithms with a nearly identical structure. Many of the implementation improvements that we describe here also apply to discrete log. However a 512-bit prime-field discrete log is significantly more burdensome than a 512-bit factorization, in large part because the linear algebra stage involves arithmetic over a large-characteristic finite field. Adrian et al. [1] describe 512-bit discrete log computations in practice; we estimate that a single equivalent discrete log computation performed on Amazon EC2 would cost approximately $1400 and take 132 h.

## 2.2   Amazon EC2

Amazon Elastic Compute Cloud (EC2) is a service that provides virtualized computing resources that can be rented by the hour. Several competitors exist, including Google Compute Engine. We specialize our results to Amazon largely out of convenience and because when we began this project some tools were specialized to Amazon's infrastructure.

Amazon EC2 bills for computing resources by the *instance-hour*. An *instance* is a single virtualized machine associated with resources including processing cores, memory, and disk storage. Amazon offers many different instance types. We chose the largest type of compute-optimized instance available as of August 2015, the c4.8xlarge instance. This instance type has two Intel Xeon E5-2666 v3 processor chips, with 36 vCPUs in a NUMA configuration with 60 GB of RAM.

There are multiple pricing structures available to purchase instance-hours. For our purposes, one can purchase fixed-rate *on-demand* instances, or bid a variable rate for *spot instances* which may be terminated depending on demand. The difference can be significant: for a c4.8xlarge instance, the on-demand price as of September 2015 is $1.763, while the average spot price we paid between May and September 2015 was $0.52. We used spot instances for our experiments. Amazon raised our account limit to allow us to launch up to 200 instances.

The c4.8xlarge instance type supports Enhanced Networking with 10 GbE interconnect between instances. Machines can be rented in different *availability zones* located around the world, and within an availability zone one can request machines to be co-located in a single *placement group* to minimize latency. We measured the interconnect bandwidth of instances in the same availability zone and placement group at 9.46 Gbit/s, and between instances not in the same placement group at 4–5 Gbit/s. We enabled enhanced networking and launched instances used for linear algebra in one placement group.

The networking environment of Amazon EC2 is distinct from a traditional HPC cluster. The connection was not saturated during our linear algebra optimization tests in Sect. 4 below. However, our measured interconnect latency, at 151 μs, is significantly greater than most HPC standards. For reference, Infini-Band FDR has latency requirements of 7 μs at 10 Gbit speeds.

Kleinjung, Lenstra, Page, and Smart [23] estimated in 2012 that factoring 512-bit RSA on Amazon EC2 would cost $107 for sieving and $30 for linear algebra. Their estimates were obtained from experiments on truncated sieving jobs and simplified linear algebra. In comparison, we focused on building a system to reliably perform full 512-bit factorizations as quickly as possible given the current state of the EC2 platform. Paterson, Poettering, and Schuldt [29] used EC2 to perform large-scale cryptanalytic experiments for the RC4 stream cipher.

# 3 Implementation

In order to speed up factoring, we wanted to maximize parallelism. In the polynomial selection and sieving stages, parallelization is straightforward, because the tasks can be split into arbitrarily small pieces to be executed independently, with only a relatively small amount of sequential work to process the results together at the end. Our improvements in these stages come from reliably distributing these tasks across cluster resources in a scalable way. Scaling the linear algebra stage is more complex, because the communication overhead results in diminishing returns from additional resources. We performed extensive experiments to characterize the trade-offs and guide parameter selection.

## 3.1 Managing Amazon EC2 Resources with Ansible

We used Ansible [13], a cluster management tool, to set up and configure an EC2 cluster and to scale the cluster appropriately at each stage of factorization. After the sieving stage, we terminate nodes not required for linear algebra. Ansible can launch and configure a cluster of 50 on-demand instances in under 5 min, and 50 spot instances in 10–15 min.

## 3.2 Parallelizing Polynomial Selection and Sieving with Slurm

The polynomial selection and sieving stages generate thousands of individual tasks to be distributed to cluster compute nodes. This requires a job distribution framework that is fast and scalable to many machines. The CADO-NFS implementation is distributed with a Python script to coordinate each stage, including a job distribution system over HTTP designed to require minimal setup from participating computers. Unfortunately this implementation did not scale well to simultaneously tracking thousands of tasks. We experimented with Apache Spark [36] to manage data flow, but Spark was not flexible enough for our needs, and our initial tests suggested that a Spark-based job distribution system was more than twice as slow as the system we were aiming to replace.

Ultimately we chose Slurm (Simple Linux Utility for Resource Management) [35] for job distribution and management during polynomial selection and sieving. Slurm can resubmit failed or timed-out tasks, monitors for and deals with failed nodes, has low startup overhead, and scales well to large clusters.

Our implementation uses a management thread to submit polynomial selection and sieving tasks asynchronously in batches to the Slurm controller, which then handles distribution and execution. This thread rate limits batch sizes in order to get around Slurm's job submission rate of a thousand jobs per second [4]. We found that scheduling two jobs per vCPU yielded faster sieving times than one job per vCPU, since the latter did not always fully saturate CPU usage.

## 3.3 Parallelizing Linear Algebra with MPI

After sieving has completed, the relations that have been produced are processed to generate a large, sparse matrix. The runtime of this linear algebra phase depends on the dimension of the matrix and the number of nonzero entries per matrix row, called the *density*, so the preprocessing stage attempts to produce a matrix that is as small as possible by filtering and combining relations. The parameters that control the effectiveness of the dimension reduction are the number of relations collected and the allowed density of the matrix.

The parallelization of the linear algebra stage is more complex than sieving or polynomial selection. In general, the matrix is divided up into an $n \times n$ grid. In each iteration, each worker operates on its own grid element, gathers results from each of the other workers using the Message Passing Interface (MPI), and combines the results into its own grid element. We used OpenMPI 1.8.6 [18].

*Comparing CADO-NFS and Msieve linear algebra.* We compared the linear algebra implementations of CADO-NFS, which implements the Block Wiedemann algorithm, and Msieve, which implements the Block Lanczos algorithm for linear algebra. Although Block Wiedemann is designed to parallelize well on independent resources, Msieve was significantly faster on our EC2 configuration. Both implementations support MPI out of the box. For a 512-bit factorization with an identical set of 53 million relations, we found that CADO-NFS without MPI completed the linear algebra stage in 350 min, while Msieve without MPI completed linear algebra in 140 min. When parallelized across multiple EC2 instances, CADO-NFS's runtime did not decrease significantly, whereas Msieve's did. We decided to use Msieve's implementation for linear algebra.

Unfortunately, the input and output formats used by CADO-NFS and Msieve are not compatible, so using Msieve's linear algebra meant we also needed to use Msieve's matrix preprocessing and final square root phases or rewrite these stages ourselves. We compromised by parallelizing Msieve's square root implementation to test multiple dependencies simultaneously, so that the square root phase finishes in approximately 10 min.

# 4   Experiments

We performed several experiments to explore the effects of different parameter settings on running time. All of the experiments in this section were carried out on the same arbitrarily chosen 512-bit RSA modulus. There will be some variation in running time across different moduli. In order to understand this variation, we measured the CPU time required to sieve 54.5 million relations for five different randomly generated RSA moduli with the parameters lbp 29 and target density 70 on a cluster with 432 CPUs. We observed a median of 2770 CPU hours with a standard deviation of 227 CPU hours in the sample set.

## 4.1   Large Prime Bounds

The large prime bounds lbp specify the log of the smoothness bound for relations collected in the sieving stage. Decreasing the large prime bound will decrease the dimension of the matrix and therefore decrease the linear algebra running time,

**Table 1. Large prime bounds.** Decreasing the large prime bound parameter increases the amount of work required for sieving, but decreases the work required for linear algebra. This is an advantageous choice when large amounts of resources can be devoted to sieving.

| lbp | Relations | Matrix rows | Matrix size | Sieve CPU-hours | Linalg instance-hours |
|-----|-----------|-------------|-------------|-----------------|------------------------|
| 28  | 28.2M     | 4.96M       | 1.48 GB     | 3271.1          | 5.4                    |
| 29  | 44.8M     | 5.68M       | 1.71 GB     | 2369.2          | 8.5                    |

but will increase sieving time because relations with smaller prime factors are less common. The lbp parameter provides the first step for tuning the trade-off between sieving and linear algebra time to optimize for different-sized clusters.

We experimented with lbp values 28 and 29. At lbp 27, CADO-NFS was unable to gather enough relations even after increasing the sieving area. At lbp 30, linear algebra will dominate the computation time even for small clusters.

Table 1 shows the effect of the changing the large prime bound for one experimental setup. Both of the runs used the minimum number of relations required to build a full matrix with target density 70 (see Sect. 4.2), and linear algebra was completed on a single machine with 36 vCPUs. Decreasing lbp from 29 to 28 causes the sieving CPU time to increase by 38% even though fewer relations are collected, but the linear algebra time decreases by 36%.

## 4.2    Target Density

The target density parameter specifies the average number of sparse nonzero entries per matrix row that Msieve will aim for in matrix construction. Linear algebra time is dependent on the product of the density and dimension, and can be decreased by raising the target density to lower the dimension. Figure 3a shows how increasing the target density decreases linear algebra time for a fixed set of input relations on a cluster of 16 instances.

For a 512 bit number with 53 million relations (more than 20 million relations over the minimum), a matrix with target density 70 took 15 min to construct and 68 min for the linear algebra computation. For the same set of relations, a matrix with target density of 120 took 17 min to construct and 55 min for linear algebra, a 19% reduction in linear algebra time. However, there were diminishing returns to increases in target density: increasing the target density from 120 to 170 reduced the overall time by only 4%.

The drawback to increasing target density is that more relations are needed from the sieving stage to construct the matrix. Figure 3b shows how the minimum number of relations required increases sharply as target density is increased beyond a particular threshold. When large amounts of resources are available for sieving, the increased work required to collect additional relations can be compensated for by a larger decrease in linear algebra time. For a given cluster size, there is an optimal target density that takes into account these trade-offs.

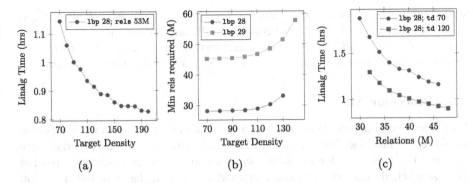

**Fig. 3. Target density and oversieving.** Increasing the target density parameter decreases linear algebra time, but requires more relations to construct the matrix. Collecting additional relations beyond the minimum also produces a better matrix and decreases linear algebra time. This trade-off can be advantageous if more resources can be devoted to sieving, as sieving parallelizes well.

### 4.3 Oversieving

Oversieving means generating excess relations during the sieving phase. This can help to produce an easier matrix for the linear algebra phase, reducing linear algebra runtime. We ran experiments varying cluster configurations, target densities, and large prime bounds to determine an oversieving curve for each. Figure 3c shows two representative oversieving curves for a 16-node linear algebra cluster with lbp 28 and target densities 70 and 120, respectively. For the target density 70 curve, the linear algebra time for the minimum number of relations required to construct the matrix, 30 million, was 112 min. At 32 million relations, the linear algebra time was reduced to 101 min, an 11% improvement. However, as Fig. 3c shows, there are diminishing returns to oversieving, while the work required to produce additional relations scales close to linearly. Optimal oversieving amounts are dependent on the cluster configuration.

### 4.4 MPI Grid Size

The grid size parameter directly controls the number of work units that MPI can assign to cluster resources. We experimented with both fine-grained grids matching the number of work units to the total number of vCPUs, and coarse-grained grids matching work units to instances. The optimum turned out to be somewhere in the middle: a single multithreaded work unit was not able to occupy all of the 36 vCPUs on a single instance, while the other extreme is likely to become limited by communication overhead since the Block Lanczos algorithm requires each node to gather results from every other node at each iteration.

In order to determine the optimal grid size, we tested a range of grid sizes for cluster sizes of 1, 4, 16, and 64 instances. The best performance for clusters with 1 and 4 instances was $4 \times 4$ and $8 \times 8$, respectively, where each cluster had 16 work units in total. For the clusters with 16 and 64 instances, the optimal grid size was $8 \times 8$ and $16 \times 16$, where each cluster had 4 work units in total. The differences as cluster size grows are likely due to communication bottlenecks.

## 4.5   Processor Affinity

The default parameters of OpenMPI dictate that each of the work units is bound to a specific machine, but when multiple work units are assigned to the same instance they compete for the same processor and memory resources, creating processor scheduling overhead and increased variance in the work unit iteration times. Each work unit must iterate together, so the time per iteration is dictated by the slowest work unit. Since the c4.8xlarge EC2 instances have two processor sockets and a NUMA memory layout, the distribution of the threads of a work unit across two processors means longer intra-process communication times and slower memory access times. We used the rankfile/process affinity parameter in OpenMPI to bind each of the work units on a single instance to its own subset of processor cores and saw an improvement of 1–2% in linear algebra time.

We also tested binding each thread of each of the work units to individual cores, but this did not improve running times.

## 4.6   Block Size

The default block size in Msieve is 8192 bytes. Theoretically, matching the block size used in Msieve with the size of the L1 cache of the processor should yield better performance by decreasing cache and memory access times. However, for the parameters lbp 28 and target density 70, increasing the block size from 8K to 16K increased computation time from 67 min to 69 min, and increasing the block size from 8K to 32K increased computation time from 67 min to 73 min. We decided to leave the block size unchanged.

## 4.7   Putting It All Together

To generate the data points in Fig. 1, we individually timed each sieving job together with system overhead. For each set of parameters, we combined the linear algebra running time from the experiments in this section with the total measured running time to complete enough sieving jobs to generate the required number of relations. We then added a measured estimate of costs for the remaining steps of factoring to get our total running time estimates. We were able to reliably achieve running times under four hours for factoring, but in several attempts to verify lower overall times, we encountered issues where some EC2 instances in our cluster ran more slowly than others or became unresponsive. These issues become more pronounced with larger cluster sizes. Our sieving setup can deal gracefully with slow nodes, but linear algebra is more fragile and is currently limited by the slowest node.

# 5   512-Bit Keys Still in Use

In this section, we survey RSA key lengths across public key infrastructures for a variety of protocols, finding that 512-bit RSA keys are surprisingly persistent.

## 5.1   DNSSEC

DNSSEC [3] is a DNS protocol extension that allows clients to cryptographically authenticate DNS records. DNS records protected by DNSSEC include a public key record (usually RSA) and a signature that can be chained up to a trusted root key. DNSKEY records can contain either a zone-signing key (ZSK), used to sign DNS records, or a key-signing key (KSK), used to sign DNSKEY records. RFC 4033 [3] specifies that zone-signing keys may have shorter validity periods, and key-signing keys should have longer validity periods. RFC 6781 [24], published by the IETF in 2012 on DNSSEC Operational Practices, states that "it is estimated that most zones can safely use 1024-bit keys for at least the next ten years."

An attacker who knows the private key to a zone-signing key or key-signing key could mount an active attack to forge DNS responses for any descendants below that location in the chain.

We analyzed several DNSSEC datasets. The most comprehensive is a collection of DNS records collected by Rapid7 which we downloaded from Scans.io. They performed biweekly DNS lookups on approximately 529 million domains starting in June 2014 and continuing to present. The number of lookups varies by as much as 61 million domains across scans, and the number of domains with valid DNSSEC records fluctuated between 3.7 million and 1.1 million and decreased over time compared to total domains. The relative fraction of DNSSEC key sizes did not change much over time. The distribution is shown in Fig. 4a.

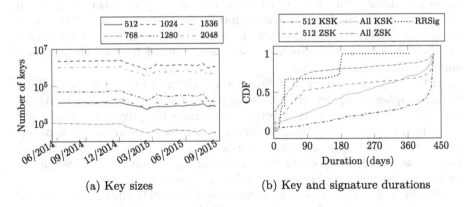

(a) Key sizes                          (b) Key and signature durations

**Fig. 4. DNSSEC key sizes and duration.** The ratios of RSA key lengths has remained relatively stable over time, although the total number of DNSSEC keys collected fluctuated across scans. The number of 512-bit keys remained around 10,000, or 0.35% of the total. Many DNSSEC keys are rotated infrequently, and 512-bit keys are rotated less frequently than longer keys.

In order to measure the completeness of the Rapid7 dataset, we compared to a second dataset of anonymized 512-bit DNSSEC keys for all .com, .net, and .org domains between February 22, 2015 and September 3, 2015 from the SURFnet DNS measurement infrastructure of van Rijswijk-Deij, Jonker, Sperotto, and Pras [31] which was provided to us by the researchers. The SURFnet data contained 2,116 distinct public keys of which 1,839 (86%) were present in the Rapid7 scans from the same time period. To measure how many 512-bit keys are in active use, SURFnet provided a set of all 512-bit DNSkey records collected using their passive DNS monitoring system for a one-month period between September 12, 2015 and October 13, 2015. The set included 1,239 records covering 613 distinct domains and contained 705 distinct keys.

Finally, we performed DNS lookups on eleven thousand zones not contained in the Rapid7 dataset that were required for signature validation. 56% of domains with 512-bit keys failed signature verification, most commonly because the TLD signature was not present in the chain of trust.

Many keys were never rotated at all over the 431-day period spanned by the Rapid7 dataset, and signatures were renewed more frequently than keys were updated. Figure 4b illustrates signature validity periods and key lifetimes. Signature validity periods are clustered around a few common ranges: 33% of keys were signed for six months, 34% for one month, 25% for three weeks, and 6% for 14 days. 512-bit zone-signing keys and key-signing keys were less frequently rotated than other key sizes.

## 5.2  HTTPS

RSA public keys are used for both encryption and authentication in the TLS protocol. If the client and server negotiate an RSA cipher suite, the client encrypts the premaster secret used to derive the session keys to the RSA public key in the server's certificate. An adversary who compromises the private key can passively decrypt session traffic from the past or future. However, since no 512-bit certificates have currently valid signatures from certificate authorities, these servers are also vulnerable to an active man-in-the-middle attack from an adversary who simply replaces the certificate.

If the client and server negotiate a Diffie-Hellman or elliptic curve Diffie-Hellman cipher suite, the server uses the public key in its certificate to sign its key exchange parameters. An adversary who knows the private key could carry out a man-in-the-middle attack by forging a correct signature on their desired parameters. Since again no 512-bit certificates are currently signed or trusted, such an active adversary could also merely replace the server certificate in the exchange along with the chosen Diffie-Hellman parameters.

Finally, connections to servers supporting RSA_EXPORT cipher suites may be vulnerable to an active downgrade attack if the clients have not been patched against the FREAK attack [6]. Successfully carrying out this attack requires the attacker to factor the server's ephemeral RSA key, which is typically generated when the server application launches and is reused as long as the server is up. "Ephemeral" RSA keys can persist for weeks and are almost always 512 bits.

**Table 2.** HTTPS RSA common key lengths and export RSA support.

| Length | All certificates | Distinct keys | Trusted certificates | Trusted and valid |
|---|---|---|---|---|
| 512 | 303,199 (0.9%) | 32,870 | 0 (0.0%) | 0 (0.0%) |
| 768 | 26,582 (0.1%) | 14,581 | 0 (0.0%) | 0 (0.0%) |
| 1024 | 12,541,661 (36.8%) | 3,196,169 | 4,016 (0.0%) | 4,012 (0.0%) |
| 1536 | 2,537 (0.0%) | 2,108 | 0 (0.0%) | 0 (0.0%) |
| 2048 | 20,782,686 (60.9%) | 6,891,678 | 14,413,589 (42.2%) | 14,411,618 (42.2%) |
| 2432 | 2,685 (0.0%) | 1,191 | 128 (0.0%) | 128 (0.0%) |
| 3072 | 65,765 (0.2%) | 58,432 | 1,787 (0.0%) | 1,787 (0.0%) |
| 4096 | 391,123 (1.1%) | 218,334 | 259,898 (0.8%) | 259,830 (0.8%) |
| 8192 | 2,172 (0.0%) | 971 | 481 (0.0%) | 481 (0.0%) |
| RSA export | 2,630,789 (7.7%) | | | |
| Total | 34,121,474 (100.0%) | | 14,680,782 (43.0%) | 14,678,739 (43.0%) |

We examined IPv4 scan results for HTTPS on port 443 performed using Zmap [17] by the University of Michigan which we accessed via Scans.io and the Censys scan data search interface developed by Durumeric et al. [14]. Table 2 summarizes scans from August 23 and September 1, 2015.

Durumeric, Kasten, Bailey, and Halderman [16] examined the HTTPS certificate infrastructure in 2013 using full IPv4 surveys and found 2,631 browser-trusted certificates with key lengths of 512 bits or smaller, of which 16 were valid. Heninger, Durumeric, Wustrow, and Halderman [20] performed a full IPv4 scan of HTTPS in October 2011 with responses from 12.8 million hosts, and found 123,038 certificates (trusted and non-trusted) containing 512-bit RSA keys. Similar to [20], we observe many repeated public keys.

## 5.3   Mail

Table 3 summarizes several Internet-wide scans targeting SMTP, IMAPS, and POP3S. The scans were performed by the University of Michigan using Zmap between August 23, 2015, and September 3, 2015.

**Table 3.** Mail protocol key lengths.

| | Port | Handshake | RSA_EXPORT | 512-bit certificate key |
|---|---|---|---|---|
| SMTP | 25 | 4,821,615 | 1,483,955 (30.8%) | 64 (0%) |
| IMAPS | 993 | 4,468,577 | 561,201 (12.6%) | 102 (0%) |
| POP3S | 995 | 4,281,494 | 558,012 (13.0%) | 115 (0%) |

We used the Censys scan database interface provided by [14] to analyze the data. While only a few hundred few mail servers served TLS certificates containing 512-bit RSA public keys, 13% of IMAPS and POP3S servers and 30%

of SMTP servers supported **RSA_EXPORT** cipher suites with 512-bit ephemeral RSA, meaning that unpatched clients are vulnerable to the FREAK downgrade attack by an adversary with the ability to quickly factor a 512-bit RSA key.

We also examined DKIM public keys. DomainKeys Identified Mail [2] is a public key infrastructure intended to prevent email spoofing. Mail providers attach digital signatures to outgoing mail, which recipients can verify using public keys published in a DNS text record.

We gathered DKIM public keys from the Rapid7 DNS dataset. However, the published dataset had lowercased the base64-encoded key entries, so we performed DNS lookups on the 11,600 domains containing DKIM records ourselves on September 4, 2015. We made a best-effort attempt to parse the records, but 5% of the responses contained a key that was malformed or truncated and could not be parsed. Of the remainder, 124 domains used 512-bit keys or smaller, including one that used a 128-bit RSA public key. We were able to factor this key in less than a second on a laptop and verify that it is, in fact, a very short RSA public key. Table 4 summarizes the distribution.

**Table 4.** DKIM key sizes.

| Length | Keys |
|---|---|
| 4096 | 5 (0.0%) |
| 2048 | 64 (0.5%) |
| 1028 | 1 (0.0%) |
| 1024 | 10,726 (92.2%) |
| 768 | 126 (1.1%) |
| 512 | 103 (0.9%) |
| 384 | 20 (0.2%) |
| 128 | 1 (0.0%) |
| Parse error | 591 (5.1%) |
| Total | 11,637 |

Durumeric et al. [15] surveyed cryptographic failures in email protocols using Internet-wide scans and data from Google. They examine DKIM use in April 2015 and discovered that 83% of mail received by Gmail contained a DKIM signature, but of these, 6% failed to validate. Of these failures, 15% were due to a key size of less than 1024 bits, and 63% were due to other errors.

## 5.4   IPsec

**Table 5.** IPsec VPN certificate keys

| Length | Keys |
|---|---|
| 4096 | 37 (0.8%) |
| 3072 | 1 (0.0%) |
| 2048 | 2,257 (51.3%) |
| 1024 | 1,804 (41.0%) |
| 768 | 1 (0.0%) |
| 512 | 69 (1.6%) |
| Parse error | 234 (5.3%) |
| Total | 4,403 (100%) |

We conducted two Zmap scans of the full IPv4 space to survey key sizes in use by IPsec VPN implementations that use RSA signatures for identity validation during server-client handshakes. An adversary who compromised the private keys for one of these certificates could mount a man-in-the-middle attack (Table 5).

Our Zmap scans targeted IKEv1 aggressive mode [19], which allows the server to send a certificate after a only a single message is received. The messages we sent contained proposals for DES, 3DES, AES-128, and AES-256 each with both SHA1 and MD5. Our first scan offered a key exchange using Oakley group 2 (a 1024-bit Diffie-Hellman group) and elicited certificates from 4% of the servers that accepted our message. Our second scan offered Oakley group 1 (a 768-bit Diffie-Hellman group) and received responses from 0.2% of hosts. Of the non-responses from both scans, 71% of the servers responded indicating that they did not support our combination of aggressive mode with our chosen parameters, 16% rejected our connection for being unauthorized (not on a whitelist), and the remaining 11% returned other errors.

## 5.5  SSH

SSH hosts authenticate themselves to the client by signing the protocol handshake with their public host key. Clients match the host key to a stored trusted fingerprint. An adversary who is able to compromise the private key for an SSH host key can perform an active man-in-the-middle attack.

Table 6 summarizes host key sizes collected by a Zmap scan of SSH hosts on port 22 mimicking OpenSSH 6.6.1p1. The data was collected in April 2015 by Adrian et al. [1], who provided it to us. A very large number of hosts used 1040-bit keys; these hosts had banners identifying them

Table 6. SSH host key lengths.

| RSA size | Hosts | Distinct |
|---|---|---|
| 512 | 508 (0.0%) | 316 |
| 768 | 2,972 (0.0%) | 2,419 |
| 784 | 3,119 (0.0%) | 223 |
| 1020 | 774 (0.0%) | 572 |
| 1024 | 296,229 (4.4%) | 91,788 |
| 1040 | 2,786,574 (41.3%) | 1,407,922 |
| 1536 | 639 (0.0%) | 536 |
| 2048 | 3,632,865 (53.9%) | 1,752,406 |
| 2064 | 1,612 (0.0%) | 957 |
| 4096 | 15,235 (0.2%) | 1,269 |
| RSA Total | 6,741,352 | 3,258,742 |
| DSA | 692,011 | 421,944 |
| ECDSA | 2,192 | 2,192 |

as using Dropbear, a lightweight SSH implementation aimed at embedded devices. Heninger, Durumeric, Wustrow, and Halderman [20] performed a full IPv4 scan of SSH public keys in February 2012 offering only Diffie-Hellman Group 1 key exchange. Of 10 million responses, they reported that 8,459 used 512-bit RSA host keys and observed many repeated host keys.

Clients can also use public keys to authenticate themselves to a server. An adversary who is able to compromise the private key for a client SSH authentication key can access the server by logging in as the client. Ben Cox [11] collected 1,376,262 SSH public keys that had been uploaded to GitHub by users to authenticate themselves to the service between December 2014 and January 2015 by using GitHub's public API. He collected 1,205,330 RSA public keys, 27,683 DSA public keys, and 1,060 ECDSA public keys. Of the RSA public keys, 2 had 256-bit length, 3 had 512-bit length, and 28 had 768-bit length.

## 5.6  PGP

PGP implements encryption and digital signatures on email or files. RSA public keys can be used for both encryption and signatures. PGP uses a public "web of trust" model: users can distribute their public keys along with signatures attesting trust relationships via a public network of keyservers. An adversary who compromises a PGP public key could use it to impersonate a user with a digital signature or decrypt content encrypted to that user.

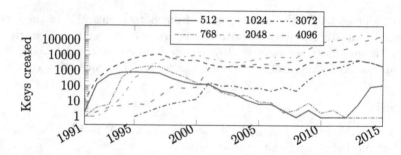

**Fig. 5.** PGP RSA public key lengths by reported creation date.

We downloaded a PGP keyserver bootstrap dataset from keyserver.borgnet. us on October 4, 2015. It contained 4.9 million public keys from 3 million users. Of these, 1.6 million were RSA, 1.7 million were DSA, 1.7 million were ElGamal, 398 were ECDH, 158 were EdDSA, and 513 were ECDSA. 4,688 512-bit RSA keys were present in the dataset; 123 of them listed a creation date in 2015. Figure 5 shows the shift to longer RSA key lengths over time.

## 6    Conclusions

512-bit RSA has been known to be insecure for at least fifteen years, but common knowledge of precisely *how* insecure has perhaps not kept pace with modern technology. We build a system capable of factoring a 512-bit RSA key in under four hours. We then measure the impact of such a system by surveying the incidence of 512-bit RSA in modern cryptographic infrastructure, and find a long tail of too-short public keys and export-grade cipher suites still in use in the wild. These numbers illustrate the challenges of keeping an aging Internet infrastructure up to date with even decades-old advances in cryptanalysis.

**Acknowledgements.** We thank Daniel Bernstein, Tanja Lange, Pierrick Gaudry, Emmanuel Thomé, and Paul Zimmermann for helpful comments and discussion. Nicole Limtiaco, Toma Pigli, Zachary Ives, and Sudarshan Muralidhar contributed to early versions of this project. We thank Osman Surkatty for help with Amazon services. We are grateful to Zakir Durumeric, Roland van Rijswijk-Deij, and Ryan Castellucci for providing data. We thank Ian Goldberg for suggesting additional references [21] and Lionel Debroux for a correction. This work is based upon work supported by the National Science Foundation under grant no. CNS-1408734, a gift from Cisco, and an AWS Research Education grant.

## References

1. Adrian, D., Bhargavan, K., Durumeric, Z., Gaudry, P., Green, M., Halderman, J.A., Heninger, N., Springall, D., Thomé, E., Valenta, L., VanderSloot, B., Wustrow, E., Zanella-Béguelin, S., Zimmermann, P.: Imperfect forward secrecy: how Diffie-Hellman fails in practice. In: 22nd ACM Conference on Computer and Communications Security (CCS 2015) (2015)

2. Allman, E., Callas, J., Delany, M., Libbey, M., Fenton, J., Thomas, M.: DomainKeys identified mail (DKIM) signatures (2007). http://www.ietf.org/rfc/rfc6376.txt

3. Arends, R., Austein, R., Larson, M., Massey, D., Rose, S.: DNS security introduction and requirements. RFC 4033, Internet Society, March 2005. http://www.ietf.org/rfc/rfc4033.txt

4. Auble, D., Jette, M., et al.: Slurm documentation. http://slurm.schedmd.com/. Accessed 19 Sept 2015

5. Beurdouche, B., Bhargavan, K., Delignat-Lavaud, A., Fournet, C., Kohlweiss, M., Pironti, A., Strub, P.Y., Zinzindohoue, J.K.: FREAK: Factoring RSA export keys (2015). https://www.smacktls.com/#freak

6. Beurdouche, B., Bhargavan, K., Delignat-Lavaud, A., Fournet, C., Kohlweiss, M., Pironti, A., Strub, P.Y., Zinzindohoue, J.K.: A messy state of the union: taming the composite state machines of TLS. In: IEEE Symposium on Security and Privacy (2015)

7. Bureau of Industry and Security: Export administration regulations (2015). http://www.bis.doc.gov/index.php/regulations/export-administration-regulations-ear

8. Cavallar, S., et al.: Factorization of a 512-Bit RSA modulus. In: Preneel, B. (ed.) EUROCRYPT 2000. LNCS, vol. 1807, pp. 1–18. Springer, Heidelberg (2000). doi:10.1007/3-540-45539-6_1

9. Childers, G.: NFS@home. http://escatter11.fullerton.edu/nfs/

10. Coppersmith, D.: Solving homogeneous linear equations over GF(2) via block Wiedemann algorithm. Math. Comput. **62**(205), 333–350 (1994)

11. Cox, B.: Auditing GitHub users SSH key quality. https://blog.benjojo.co.uk/post/auditing-github-users-keyscollected

12. Crandall, R., Pomerance, C.B.: Prime Numbers: A Computational Perspective, vol. 182. Springer Science & Business Media, New York (2006)

13. DeHaan, M.: Ansible. http://www.ansible.com

14. Durumeric, Z., Adrian, D., Mirian, A., Bailey, M., Halderman, J.A.: A search engine backed by Internet-wide scanning. In: Proceedings of the 22nd ACM Conference on Computer and Communications Security, October 2015

15. Durumeric, Z., Adrian, D., Mirian, A., Kasten, J., Bursztein, E., Lidzborski, N., Thomas, K., Eranti, V., Bailey, M., Halderman, J.A.: Neither snow nor rain nor MITM... an empirical analysis of email delivery security. In: Proceedings of Internet Measurement Conference (IMC 2015) (2015)

16. Durumeric, Z., Kasten, J., Bailey, M., Halderman, J.A.: Analysis of the HTTPS certificate ecosystem. In: Proceedings of the 13th Internet Measurement Conference, October 2013

17. Durumeric, Z., Wustrow, E., Halderman, J.A.: ZMap: fast Internet-wide scanning and its security applications. In: Proceedings of the 22nd USENIX Security Symposium, August 2013

18. Gabriel, E., et al.: Open MPI: goals, concept, and design of a next generation MPI implementation. In: Kranzlmüller, D., Kacsuk, P., Dongarra, J. (eds.) EuroPVM/MPI 2004. LNCS, vol. 3241, pp. 97–104. Springer, Heidelberg (2004). doi:10.1007/978-3-540-30218-6_19

19. Harkins, D., Carrel, D.: The Internet Key Exchange (IKE). RFC 2409, RFC Editor, November 1998. http://www.rfc-editor.org/rfc/rfc2409.txt

20. Heninger, N., Durumeric, Z., Wustrow, E., Halderman, J.A.: Mining your Ps and Qs: detection of widespread weak keys in network devices. In: Proceedings of the 21st USENIX Security Symposium, August 2012

21. Hughes, E.: How to give a math lecture at a party (2000). https://web.archive. org/web/20010222192642/http://www.xent.com/FoRK-archive/oct00/0429.html
22. Kleinjung, T., et al.: Factorization of a 768-Bit RSA modulus. In: Rabin, T. (ed.) CRYPTO 2010. LNCS, vol. 6223, pp. 333–350. Springer, Heidelberg (2010). doi:10. 1007/978-3-642-14623-7_18
23. Kleinjung, T., Lenstra, A.K., Page, D., Smart, N.P.: Using the cloud to determine key strengths. In: Galbraith, S., Nandi, M. (eds.) INDOCRYPT 2012. LNCS, vol. 7668, pp. 17–39. Springer, Heidelberg (2012). doi:10.1007/978-3-642-34931-7_3
24. Kolkman, O.M., Mekking, W.M., Gieben, R.M.: DNSSEC operational practices, Version 2. RFC 6781, Internet Society, December 2012. http://www.ietf.org/rfc/ rfc6781.txt
25. Lenstra, A.K., Lenstra Jr., H.W., Manasse, M.S., Pollard, J.M.: The number field sieve. In: Lenstra, A.K., Lenstra, H.W. (eds.) The development of the number field sieve. LNM, vol. 1554, pp. 11–42. Springer, Heidelberg (1993). doi:10.1007/ BFb0091537
26. Monico, C.: GGNFS. http://www.math.ttu.edu/~cmonico/software/ggnfs/
27. Montgomery, P.L.: A block Lanczos algorithm for finding dependencies over GF(2). In: Guillou, L.C., Quisquater, J.-J. (eds.) EUROCRYPT 1995. LNCS, vol. 921, pp. 106–120. Springer, Heidelberg (1995). doi:10.1007/3-540-49264-X_9
28. Papadopoulos, J.: Msieve. http://www.boo.net/~jasonp/qs.html
29. Paterson, K.G., Poettering, B., Schuldt, J.C.N.: Big bias hunting in Amazonia: large-scale computation and exploitation of RC4 biases (invited paper). In: Sarkar, P., Iwata, T. (eds.) ASIACRYPT 2014. LNCS, vol. 8873, pp. 398–419. Springer, Heidelberg (2014). doi:10.1007/978-3-662-45611-8_21
30. Pomerance, C.: A tale of two sieves. Not. Am. Math. Soc. (1996). http://www. ams.org/notices/199612/pomerance.pdf
31. van Rijswijk-Deij, R., Jonker, M., Sperotto, A., Pras, A.: The Internet of names: a DNS big dataset. SIGCOMM Comput. Commun. Rev. 45(5), 91–92 (2015)
32. Rivest, R.L., Shamir, A., Adleman, L.: A method for obtaining digital signatures and public-key cryptosystems. Commun. ACM 21(2), 120–126 (1978)
33. Smith, D.: All TI signing keys factored, September 2009. http://www.ticalc.org/ archives/news/articles/14/145/145273.html
34. Team, T.C.D.: CADO-NFS, an implementation of the number field sieve algorithm (2015). http://cado-nfs.gforge.inria.fr/
35. Yoo, A.B., Jette, M.A., Grondona, M.: SLURM: Simple Linux Utility for Resource Management. In: Feitelson, D., Rudolph, L., Schwiegelshohn, U. (eds.) JSSPP 2003. LNCS, vol. 2862, pp. 44–60. Springer, Heidelberg (2003). doi:10.1007/10968987_3
36. Zaharia, M., Chowdhury, M., Franklin, M.J., Shenker, S., Stoica, I.: Spark: cluster computing with working sets. In: Proceedings of the 2nd USENIX Conference on Hot Topics in Cloud Computing, vol. 10, p. 10 (2010)
37. Zetter, K.: How a Google headhunter's e-mail unraveled a massive net security hole. http://www.wired.com/2012/10/dkim-vulnerability-widespread/

# The Self-blindable U-Prove Scheme from FC'14 Is Forgeable (Short Paper)

Eric Verheul[1], Sietse Ringers[2(✉)], and Jaap-Henk Hoepman[1]

[1] Radboud University, Nijmegen, The Netherlands
{e.verheul,jhh}@cs.ru.nl
[2] Johann Bernoulli Institute for Mathematics and Computer Science,
University of Groningen, Groningen, The Netherlands
s.ringers@rug.nl

**Abstract.** Recently an unlinkable version of the U-Prove attribute-based credential scheme was proposed at Financial Crypto'14 [9]. Unfortunately, the new scheme is forgeable: if sufficiently many users work together then they can construct new credentials, containing any set of attributes of their choice, without any involvement of the issuer. In this note we show how they can achieve this and we point out the error in the unforgeability proof.

## 1 Introduction

Attribute-based credential schemes [1,3] provide a very secure and privacy-friendly form of identity management. In these schemes, users are granted by an issuer a credential that contains several attributes (generally elements of $\mathbb{Z}_q := \mathbb{Z}/q\mathbb{Z}$ for some number $q$), and when the user shows his credential to a verifier using a ShowCredential protocol, he can choose to reveal some of these while keeping the other ones hidden from the verifier. Some of these schemes offer anonymity in the form of *multi-show unlinkability*: that is, when a verifier runs the ShowCredential protocol twice and both times the same attributes with the same values were disclosed to it, then it cannot tell whether it was shown one credential twice, or two different credentials that happened to disclose the same attributes.

A well-known and very efficient attribute-based credential scheme is U-Prove [6,10]. However, this scheme offers no multi-show unlinkability. In an attempt to fix this, L. Hanzlik and K. Kluczniak proposed in [9], and presented at Financial Crypto 2014, a new scheme that is based on U-Prove but uses a different signature scheme. This signature scheme is based on the self-blindable construction by Verheul [11], and allows a credential to be blinded; i.e., modified into a new valid credential over the same attributes. Although [9] does contain an argument for the unforgeability of their scheme, we show here that this argument contains an error, and that the proposed construction is forgeable, in the sense that if sufficiently many users collude then they can construct new credentials containing arbitrary attributes of their choice, without involvement of the issuer.

© International Financial Cryptography Association 2017
J. Grossklags and B. Preneel (Eds.): FC 2016, LNCS 9603, pp. 339–345, 2017.
DOI: 10.1007/978-3-662-54970-4_20

## 2   The Credential Scheme

Hanzlik and Kluczniak [9] present their blindable U-Prove scheme as an extension of the original U-Prove scheme, in the following sense: a self-blindable signature (based on [11]) is added to a U-Prove credential. When showing a credential, the user can then choose to either show his credential using the original linkable U-Prove ShowCredential protocol, or using a new protocol that uses the new self-blindable signature and should offer unlinkability. Since we are concerned only with the forgeability of the self-blindable construction, our description of the credential scheme will omit details that are relevant only to the original construction.

The setup is as follows. $q$ is a prime number of length $k$, and $e \colon G_1 \times G_2 \to G_T$ is a bilinear pairing of Type 2 (see [8], [5, Ch. I, X]), where $q$ is the order of $G_1$, $G_2$ and $G_T$. The issuer's public key is

$$(q, e, g_0, \ldots, g_n, p, p', p_0, p_1),$$

where

- $g_0, \ldots, g_n$ are random generators of $G_1$,
- $p$ and $p'$ are random generators of $G_2$,
- $p_0 = (p')^z$,
- $p_1 = p^f$.

The tuple $(f, z) \in \mathbb{Z}_q^2$ is the issuer's secret key.

A credential consists of the tuple

$$((x_1, \ldots, x_n), (h, h_2, h_3, h_4, \alpha, b_1, b_2)),$$

where

- $x_1, \ldots, x_n \in \mathbb{Z}_q$ are the attributes,
- $\alpha, b_0, b_1 \in \mathbb{Z}_q$, chosen by the user during issuing of the credential,
- $h = (g_0 g_1^{x_1} \cdots g_n^{x_n})^\alpha$,
- $h_2 = h^f$,
- $h_3 = h^{b_1} h_2^{b_2}$,
- $h_4 = h_3^z = (h^{b_1} h_2^{b_2})^z$.

The validity of the credential can be checked by

$$e(h, p_1) \stackrel{?}{=} e(h_2, p) \quad \text{and} \quad e(h_3, p_0) \stackrel{?}{=} e(h_4, p').$$

Such a credential can be blinded into a new one as follows. Take random $k, \ell \in \mathbb{Z}_q^*$, and set $(\overline{h}, \overline{h}_2, \overline{h}_3, \overline{h}_4) = (h^k, h_2^k, h_3^{k\ell}, h_4^{k\ell})$. Then

$$((x_1, \ldots, x_n), (\overline{h}, \overline{h}_2, \overline{h}_3, \overline{h}_4, \alpha k, b_1 \ell, b_2 \ell))$$

is a new, valid credential over the same attributes. In [9] a ShowCredential protocol for these credential is provided, in which the credentials are blinded as above. The protocol should offer unlinkability but it is not proven that it does (and we have not checked this).

## 3   Forging New Credentials

### 3.1   Constructing Signatures on the Elements $g_i$

We first show that if sufficiently many users work together, then for each $i$ they can compute a tuple $g_i^f, g_i^z, g_i^{fz}$, even though $f$ and $z$ are private to the issuer. Using these tuples they can easily create new valid credentials over any set of attributes of their choice. Since this will involve many credentials, we will write the elements from the credential of user $j$ with an extra subscript $j$:

$$((x_{1,j}, \ldots, x_{n,j}), (h_j, h_{2,j}, h_{3,j}, h_{4,j}, \alpha_j, b_{1,j}, b_{2,j})) .$$

The element $h_j$ is of the form

$$h_j = (g_0 g_1^{x_{1,j}} \cdots g_n^{x_{n,j}})^{\alpha_j} .$$

By blinding the credential with $k = \alpha_j^{-1}, \ell = 1$ (i.e., we raise all group elements of the credential to the power $\alpha_j^{-1}$; note that these numbers are known to the users), we can remove the number $\alpha$ from our considerations, so we will henceforth simply write

$$h_j = g_0 g_1^{x_{1,j}} \cdots g_n^{x_{n,j}} .$$

Let us write $\widetilde{g}_i = g_i^f$. Then we can write $h_{3,j}$ as

$$h_{3,j} = h_j^{b_{1,j}} h_{2,j}^{b_{2,j}} = g_0^{b_{1,j}} \widetilde{g}_0^{b_{2,j}} g_1^{b_{1,j} x_{1,j}} \widetilde{g}_1^{b_{2,j} x_{1,j}} \cdots g_n^{b_{1,j} x_{n,j}} \widetilde{g}_n^{b_{2,j} x_{n,j}} .$$

Setting $x_{0,j} = 1$ and writing $y_{i,j} = b_{1,j} x_{i,j}$ and $\widetilde{y}_{i,j} = b_{2,j} x_{i,j}$, we get

$$h_{3,j} = g_0^{y_{0,j}} \widetilde{g}_0^{\widetilde{y}_{0,j}} g_1^{y_{1,j}} \widetilde{g}_1^{\widetilde{y}_{1,j}} \cdots g_n^{y_{n,j}} \widetilde{g}_n^{\widetilde{y}_{n,j}} , \tag{1}$$

where all numbers $y_{i,j}$ and $\widetilde{y}_{i,j}$ are known to the user.

We know that $h_{4,j} = h_{3,j}^z$, i.e., the discrete log of $h_{4,j}$ with respect to $h_{3,j}$ is $z$. If we raise $h_{3,j}$ to some power and we simultaneously raise $h_{4,j}$ to the same power, then the resulting two elements will still have $z$ as discrete log. The same holds if we multiply two elements $h_{3,j}$ and $h_{3,j'}$ together. In the remainder of this section we will take a number of powers and products of the elements $h_{3,j}$; whenever we write such a power or product, the same power or product for $h_{4,j}$ is implied.

Observe that when raising $h_{3,1}$ to the power $1/\widetilde{y}_{n,1}$ we obtain a product of the generators $g_i$ to certain exponents, where $\widetilde{g}_n$ now has exponent 1. Thus two users 1 and 2 can work together to form the element $h_{3,1}^{1/\widetilde{y}_{n,1}}/h_{3,2}^{1/\widetilde{y}_{n,2}}$, which is of the form

$$\frac{h_{3,1}^{1/\widetilde{y}_{n,1}}}{h_{3,2}^{1/\widetilde{y}_{n,2}}} = g_0^{v_0} \widetilde{g}_0^{\widetilde{v}_0} g_1^{v_1} \widetilde{g}_1^{\widetilde{v}_1} \cdots g_n^{v_n} ,$$

with $v_i = y_{i,1}/y_{n,1} - y_{i,2}/y_{n,2}$, and similar for $\widetilde{v}_i$. Note that the right hand side no longer contains $\widetilde{g}_n$. If two more users do the same and obtain a similar expression, then the four users can collectively remove $g_n$ in exactly the same fashion, resulting in an expression as above containing only the elements $g_0, \widetilde{g}_0, \ldots, g_{n-1}, \widetilde{g}_{n-1}$.

Continuing in this fashion, $2^{2n+1}$ users can find an element in $G_1$ that is just $g_0$ raised to some power which is known and can easily be removed. If they apply all powers and products in parallel to the corresponding $h_{4,j}$, then they also obtain $g_0^z$. Similarly, they can obtain $\widetilde{g}_0 = g_0^f$, and $\widetilde{g}_0^z = g_0^{fz}$. In fact, they can do this for all elements $g_i, \widetilde{g}_i$, resulting finally in expressions for $g_i^f$, $g_i^z$ and $g_i^{fz}$ for all $i$. Using these elements, anyone can calculate a valid credential over any set of attributes as explained below. The amount of users that need to work together to achieve this ($2^{2n+1}$) is exponential in $n$ (the amount of attributes of the system) but *not* in the security parameter. Therefore, this can be done in polynomial time.

*Remark 1.* An alternative explanation for why this is possible is as follows. Suppose we are given $m$ valid credentials, with $h_{3,j}$ of credential $j$ given by (1). Notice that the operations we apply to the elements $h_{3,j}$ and $h_{4,j}$ above correspond exactly to taking linear combinations of the $h_{3,j}$ and $h_{4,j}$ (although linear combinations are usually written additively instead of multiplicatively). So if we consider the elements $g_i, \widetilde{g}_i$ occurring in $h_{3,j}$ as unknowns, then we can interpret Eq. (1) as one equation in $2n + 2$ unknowns. Thus if we have $m := 2n + 2$ credentials, then we obtain $2n + 2$ equations in as many unknowns.

Using linear algebra over the field $\mathbb{Z}_q = \mathrm{GF}(q)$, then, we can solve this system of linear equations to the $g_i, \widetilde{g}_i, g_i^{fz} = \widetilde{g}_i^z$, as long as the square matrix of the coefficients,

$$M := \begin{pmatrix} y_{0,1} & \cdots & y_{0,2n+2} \\ \widetilde{y}_{0,1} & \cdots & \widetilde{y}_{0,2n+2} \\ \vdots & \ddots & \vdots \\ y_{n,1} & \cdots & y_{n,2n+2} \\ \widetilde{y}_{n,1} & \cdots & \widetilde{y}_{n,2n+2} \end{pmatrix}$$

is invertible (i.e., its determinant $\det M$ is unequal to 0). Since the numbers $y_{i,j}, \widetilde{y}_{i,j}$ are under our control in a chosen-message attack, this should be easy to achieve. If we write $m_{i,j}$ for the $j$-th entry of the $i$-th row of the inverse $M^{-1}$ of $M$, we obtain

$$g_i = \prod_{j=1}^{2n+2} h_{3,j}^{m_{2i+1,j}}, \qquad \widetilde{g}_i = \prod_{j=1}^{2n+2} h_{3,j}^{m_{2i+2,j}},$$

$$g_i^z = \prod_{j=1}^{2n+2} h_{4,j}^{m_{2i+1,j}}, \qquad \widetilde{g}_i^z = \prod_{j=1}^{2n+2} h_{4,j}^{m_{2i+2,j}}.$$

This also shows that the scheme is already completely forgeable (in the sense that new credentials with arbitrary attributes can be computed) with just $2n+2$ collaborating users, instead of $2^{2n+1}$.

## 3.2 Constructing a Forged Credential

Using the elements $g_i, g_i^f, g_i^z, g_i^{fz}$ constructed above, a new credential with attributes $x_1, \ldots, x_n$ may be constructed as follows. Choose $b_1, b_2 \in_R \mathbb{Z}_q$ randomly, and set

$$h = g_0 g_1^{x_1} \cdots g_n^{x_n},$$
$$h_2 = g_0^f (g_1^f)^{x_1} \cdots (g_n^f)^{x_n},$$
$$h_3 = g_0^{b_1} (g_0^f)^{b_2} g_1^{b_1 x_1} (g_1^f)^{b_2 x_1} \cdots g_n^{b_1 x_n} (g_n^f)^{b_2 x_n},$$
$$h_4 = (g_0^z)^{b_1} (g_0^{fz})^{b_2} (g_1^z)^{b_1 x_1} (g_1^{fz})^{b_2 x_1} \cdots (g_n^z)^{b_1 x_n} (g_n^{fz})^{b_2 x_n}.$$

Then

$$h_2 = h^f, \qquad h_3 = h^{b_1} h_2^{b_2}, \qquad h_4 = (h^{b_1} h_2^{b_2})^z$$

as required.

## 4  The Problem in the Unforgeability Argument

An argument for unforgeability is given in [9] in Sect. 4, "Security Analysis". The argument is based on the appendix from [11], in which it is argued that credentials of the form

$$h, \ h_2 = h^f, \ h_4 = (h^{b_1} h_2^{b_2})^z \tag{2}$$

are unforgeable. Here, as above, $f$ and $z$ are the issuer's secret key, and the numbers $b_1, b_2$ are part of the credential (i.e., known to the user). However, the difference with Verheul's system is that there $h$ is randomly chosen from $G_1$, and in particular, no participant of the system knows the discrete log of $h$ with respect to any other element from $G_1$, or any DL-representation of $h$ (i.e., an expression of $h$ in terms of powers of $g_0, \ldots, g_n$, such as (3)). By contrast, in Hanzlik and Kluczniak's U-Prove scheme the user knows numbers $\alpha, x_1, \ldots, x_n$ such that

$$h = (g_0 g_1^{x_1} \cdots g_n^{x_n})^\alpha, \tag{3}$$

where the elements $g_0, \ldots, g_n$ are the same for all users. In this case, the argument from [11] does not apply, so that no argument can be based on it.

In addition, we wish to point out that the argument from the appendix in [11] was meant as a sketch, and in particular, there is the following subtlety. It is argued in the appendix that if an adversary $\mathcal{A}$ manages to forge credentials of the form (2), i.e.

$$(h, h_2, h_4, b_1, b_2) = \mathcal{A}\Big((h_j, h_{2,j}, h_{4,j}, b_{1,j}, b_{2,j})_{j=1,\ldots,m}\Big),$$

where the output $(h, h_2, h_4, b_1, b_2)$ is valid (i.e., satisfying (2)), then either there must exist a $j$ and numbers $k, \ell \in \mathbb{Z}_q$ such that

$$(h, h_2, h_4, b_1, b_2) = (h_j^k, h_{2,j}^k, h_{4,j}^{k\ell}, b_{1,j}\ell, b_{2,j}\ell)$$

or the adversary $\mathcal{A}$ can be used to solve discrete logarithms in $G_1$. However, the argument mentions certain "transformation factors" which are numbers like $k, \ell$ from $\mathbb{Z}_q$, and the algorithm sketched by [11] that uses the adversary $\mathcal{A}$ to compute discrete logarithms would need to know these numbers in order to be able to work. However, it is not clear how to obtain these transformation factors from the adversary $\mathcal{A}$, or even if $\mathcal{A}$ is aware of them. We believe, however, that they can be extracted from the adversary by an extension of the Known Exponent Assumption (see [7], where this assumption was introduced, and for example [2,4]).

# References

1. Alpár, G., Hoepman, J., Siljee, J.: The identity crisis. security, privacy and usability issues in identity management. CoRR abs/1101.0427 (2011). http://arxiv.org/abs/1101.0427

2. Bellare, M., Palacio, A.: The knowledge-of-exponent assumptions and 3-round zero-knowledge protocols. In: Franklin, M. (ed.) CRYPTO 2004. LNCS, vol. 3152, pp. 273–289. Springer, Heidelberg (2004). doi:10.1007/978-3-540-28628-8_17

3. Bichsel, P., Camenisch, J., Dubovitskaya, M., Enderlein, R.R., Krenn, S., Krontiris, I., Lehmann, A., Neven, G., Nielsen, J.D., Paquin, C., Preiss, F.S., Rannenberg, K., Sabouri, A., Stausholm, M.: D2.2 architecture for attribute-based credential technologies. Technical report, final version, ABC4Trust (2014). https://abc4trust.eu/download/Deliverable_D2.2.pdf

4. Bitansky, N., Canetti, R., Chiesa, A., Goldwasser, S., Lin, H., Rubinstein, A., Tromer, E.: The hunting of the SNARK. IACR Cryptology ePrint Archive 2014 (2014). https://eprint.iacr.org/2014/580

5. Blake, I.F., Seroussi, G., Smart, N.P. (eds.): Advances in Elliptic Curve Cryptography. Cambridge University Press, Cambridge (2005)

6. Brands, S.: Rethinking Public Key Infrastructures and Digital Certificates: Building in Privacy. MIT Press, Cambridge (2000)

7. Damgård, I.: Towards practical public key systems secure against chosen ciphertext attacks. In: Feigenbaum, J. (ed.) CRYPTO 1991. LNCS, vol. 576, pp. 445–456. Springer, Heidelberg (1992). doi:10.1007/3-540-46766-1_36

8. Galbraith, S.D., Paterson, K.G., Smart, N.P.: Pairings for cryptographers. Discret. Appl. Math. **156**(16), 3113–3121 (2008)

9. Hanzlik, L., Kluczniak, K.: A short paper on how to improve U-Prove using self-blindable certificates. In: Christin, N., Safavi-Naini, R. (eds.) Financial Cryptography and Data Security. LNCS, pp. 273–282. Springer, Heidelberg (2014)

10. Paquin, C., Zaverucha, G.: U-prove cryptographic specification v1.1 (revision 3), December 2013. http://research.microsoft.com/apps/pubs/default.aspx?id=166969, released under the Open Specification Promise
11. Verheul, E.R.: Self-blindable credential certificates from the weil pairing. In: Boyd, C. (ed.) ASIACRYPT 2001. LNCS, vol. 2248, pp. 533–551. Springer, Heidelberg (2001). doi:10.1007/3-540-45682-1_31

# A Sound for a Sound: Mitigating Acoustic Side Channel Attacks on Password Keystrokes with Active Sounds

S. Abhishek Anand[(⊠)] and Nitesh Saxena

University of Alabama at Birmingham, Birmingham, AL 35294, USA
{anandab,saxena}@cis.uab.edu

**Abstract.** Keyboard acoustic side channel attacks have been shown to utilize the audio leakage from typing on the keyboard to infer the typed words up to a certain degree of accuracy. Researchers have continued to improve upon the accuracy of such attacks by employing different techniques and attack vectors such as feature extraction and classification, keyboard geometry and triangulation.

While research is still ongoing towards further improving acoustic side channel attacks, much work has been lacking in building a working defense mechanism against such class of attacks. In this paper, we set out to propose a practical defense mechanism against keyboard acoustic attacks specifically on password typing and test its performance against several attack vectors. Our defense involves the use of various background sounds to mask the audio leakage from the keyboard thereby preventing the side channel attacks from gaining usable information about the typed password. The background sounds are generated by the device that is used to input the passwords. We also evaluate the usability of our approach and show that the addition of background sounds does not hamper users' capability to input passwords.

## 1 Introduction

Passwords constitute the primary means of user authentication for accessing various online services currently. They are used as a protective measure to limit access to user sensitive data that may include personal details, banking credentials, and restricted work data. They are also used for logging into personal computing systems and website accounts. Given the extensive use of passwords, it is important to pay attention to different strategies attackers may exploit to compromise passwords. Indeed, the security of passwords has often been questioned [1,11,14], and shown to be weak against a variety of attacks such as brute force attacks and keyloggers, as well as side channel attacks like timing attacks [13], acoustic side channel attacks [2–4,6,8,16], vibrational side channel attacks [10] and electromagnetic radiations [7].

In this paper, we focus on the vulnerability of the password entry mechanism on keyboards against acoustic side channel attacks, and propose a viable defense mechanism to mitigate it. Keyboard acoustic side channel attacks belong to a

© International Financial Cryptography Association 2017
J. Grossklags and B. Preneel (Eds.): FC 2016, LNCS 9603, pp. 346–364, 2017.
DOI: 10.1007/978-3-662-54970-4_21

class of attacks known as side channel attacks that exploit the physical implementation of the deployed security measure rather than using brute force method to overcome it or an underlying theoretical weakness in the system that makes it vulnerable. A traditional brute force attack would try to guess the password by trying all possible permutations of alphabets, numbers and allowed special characters for varying lengths. This attack may require extensive computational power yet can be very easy to perform because people often tend to use bits of personal information in the password and make an effort to keep it short that makes it easy to memorize. A key logging attack tracks the keys being pressed without the user knowing they are being monitored. They can be bundled either as a malware like a trojan horse or can be a hardware artifact inside the keyboard.

Side channel attacks, on the other hand, make it harder to defend against as they utilize the implementation of the security algorithm rather than the algorithm itself. For example, a timing attack [13] monitors the IP packets being sent on the network and uses the time duration between successive keystrokes during a user's typing to infer the keys being pressed. A power monitoring attack measures and profiles the power consumed during specific computations to derive the secret information. An electromagnetic attack [7] depend upon the leaked electromagnetic radiation from the system to deduce the password information.

Acoustic side channel attacks [2–4, 6, 8, 16] record the sounds emanating from the keyboard using microphones covertly while the user types the password. Each key press emits a unique sound that makes it possible for the adversary to identify it using its frequency features.[1] While an acoustic side channel attack may not fully recover the keystroke information, various statistical methods make it possible to reconstruct the keystroke information from the partially recovered information. Hidden Markov Models (HMM) and language based models have been used extensively to reconstruct text from identified keystrokes.

Given the ubiquity of low-cost microphones and potential for almost invisible audio monitoring, keyboard acoustic emanations attacks can now be considered a realistic threat. While research is still ongoing towards further improving acoustic side channel attacks, much work has been lacking in building a working defense mechanism against such class of attacks.

**Our Contributions:** In this paper, we set out to propose a practical defense mechanism against keyboard acoustic side channel attacks specifically on password typing and evaluate its performance against several attack vectors as well its usability factors. The main contributions of this paper are summarized below.

1. *Recreation of Prior Attacks:* Before presenting our defense model, we first recreated the keyboard acoustic side channel attack that serves to validate the need for the defense. This also serves to reproduce the prior research results in independent settings.

---

[1] A similar concept is used in a vibrational side channel attack that measures the surface vibrations using accelerometers when the key is pressed.

2. *Design and Implementation of the Defense:* We build a viable defense system that utilizes masking signals to mitigate keyboard acoustic side channel attacks. The defense system is designed to be a part of the device that is the source of acoustic leakage, which would be the keyboard in our case study. The intuition behind our defense model is to actively cloak the acoustic leakage emanating from the keyboard with other sounds that would be playing in the background.

3. *Evaluation of Security:* We evaluate the security of our defense system by testing its ability to reduce the accuracy of the keyboard acoustic side channel attack that we recreated in the initial step of our research by preventing the adversary from gaining usable information about the typed password. Our results show that a masking signal that combines white noise with sounds of previously recorded keystrokes can effectively cloak the acoustic side channel.

4. *Evaluation of Usability:* While designing the defense model duly serves our purpose of defeating keyboard acoustic side channel attacks, we also study the usability of the proposed defense system. We show that the addition of background sounds does not hamper users' capability to input passwords while mitigating the keyboard acoustic side channel attack.

## 2    Related Work

Acoustic side channel attacks have been a long studied topic in the field of security research. Asonov and Agrawal [2] were the first researchers to demonstrate the threat of side channel attacks using acoustic leakage from the keyboard. They used the Fast Fourier Transform (FFT) features of the extracted keystroke as an identifier and use a neural network to classify and recognize the keystrokes. This process involved a training phase that used labeled data pair consisting of a key and its corresponding feature, and a testing phase that took a feature as an input and the output consisted of the closest matching key.

Zhuang et al. [16] extended the work of Asonov and Agrawal by using cepstrum features, in particular Mel-Frequency Cepstrum Coefficients (MFCC) as identifiers for the keystrokes and used unlabeled data in the training phase for the neural network unlike Asonov and Agrawal. Berger et al. [4] used cross correlation between the recorded keystroke signals and Euclidean distance between frequency based features to classify and recognize the keystrokes. They then used dictionary based attack to reconstruct the text from the recovered keystrokes. Halevi and Saxena [8] combined the cross correlation information between the two keystrokes signals and the frequency distance measure from the work done by Berger et al. to create a new feature called time-frequency classification. This new feature was used for identifying different keystrokes and then used for password detection. They also studied the effect of various typing styles (hunt and peck, and touch typing) on keystroke signal similarities and found out that the signal similarity decreases with change in the typing style. These findings showed that the effectiveness of a keyboard eavesdropping attack depends upon the input data, the typing style and the detection technique used for the purpose.

Fiona [6] presented a distance-time based triangulation attack that is able to identify a keystroke by recording the keystroke with multiple microphones. Due to fixed location of each key on the keyboard, the sound recorded by each microphone arrives at a different time and the time delay for each keystroke can be used to distinguish between the keystrokes.

# 3  Attack Background and Recreation

Keyboard acoustic emanations represent a class of attacks that exploit the audio leakage from the system (keyboard) to gain useful information (typed input). In this section, we first review the attack threat model and attack principles. We then go on to recreate the attacks present in the literature, which serves as a means to evaluate our defense mechanism. At last, we review the triangulation attack.

## 3.1  Threat Model

The threat model is similar to the attack models studied in previous work [2–4,6,8,16]. We assume that the adversary has access to the victim's location and implants a covert listening device on or near the victim's keyboard. The adversary can record the keystrokes entered by the victim, retrieve the recording from the covert listening device and process it for information extraction at a later time.

In this threat model, we assume that the user only employs lowercase letters while typing on the keyboard. Also, we assume that attacker already has possession of labeled audio samples for each of the alphabetical keys in a similar typing style as the victim. We will expand on the influence of typing style on the attack's accuracy in the later sections. The attacker can also obtain the samples by gaining access to the keyboard for a short duration and typing on the keyboard to get the samples while recording them.

We only study random passwords as HMM and language-based models and dictionary-based attacks have been shown effective against passwords containing words from the dictionary. Also, random passwords are now gaining momentum in everyday use. We keep the password length to 6 characters.

The final assumption in our threat model is that the attacker has access to the user device and can try out the possible candidates for the passwords at will. The attacker can try to check as many candidate passwords in a single time duration or he may try it over multiple time duration as most authentication systems place a limit over number of attempts.

## 3.2  Attack Foundations and Principles

In this paper, we focus on audio leakage from keyboards that occurs due to the keys being pressed while typing. The audio signal from a key when pressed is shown in Fig. 1. It has a characteristic press region and a release region that corresponds to the key being pushed and released by the finger. The observed duration for a keystroke including the key press and release time is 100 ms that is inline with previous works [2, 16]. The key press region consists of two peaks: touch peak and push peak. The touch peak refers to the finger touching the key and the push peak occurs when the key hits the rubber pad beneath it, when pressed by the finger. The release region contains only the release peak.

The key press and release regions can be used to extract features that would be useful in keystroke recognition. Asonov and Agrawal [2] used the FFT features from the touch peak and used a neural network to classify and recognize them. Zhuang et al. [16] used the cepstrum features from the push peak and used HMM based on English language.

However, this method may not work well with passwords that consist of random characters and not dictionary words. Halevi and Saxena [8] time-frequency classifier combined cross correlation value of two signals and the distance between their FFT features as a point in Euclidean plane and used the distance from origin as the classification parameter.

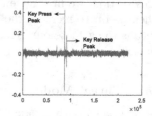

**Fig. 1.** A single keystroke signal

### 3.3   Attack Modeling and Recreation

In order to showcase the effectiveness of our defense, we proceeded to construct a potent acoustic side channel attack based upon the research described above. The first step involved collecting keystroke samples involving straw man typing and compare it against the samples acquired with hunt and peck typing style.

**Keystroke Sample Collection:** We recorded the keystroke sound for each alphabetical key[A–Z] using both typing styles for a total of twenty samples per key with a sampling frequency of 44.1 kHz. Straw man typing style involves hitting the key at the same angle multiple times using the same finger. In hunt and peck style, we use the same finger for key press but the angle at which the finger hits the key is different for each hit.

**Key Detection:** To detect a keystroke, we calculate the FFT coefficient of the signal with a window size of 441 samples and sum up the coefficient between the frequency range 0.4–22 kHz. A threshold is used to determine a peak in key press region and the area around the peak (around 20 ms) is taken out as key press region. For determining the key release region, we repeat the procedure with a smaller window size of 88 samples and a smaller area of 10 ms is extracted a key release region.

**Recognition Technique:** Asonov and Agrawal [2] used FFT features along with neural network for keystroke recognition. Zhuang et al. [16] used cepstrum features (MFCC) in place of FFT to improve upon previous work. Berger et al.

used cross correlation between signals for identifying keystrokes. Halevi and Saxena [8] introduced time-frequency classification method that performed better than other detection techniques when tested with different typing styles and hence we decided to use this method for keystroke recognition.

**Evaluation of the Dataset:** We compared the hunt and peck dataset against straw man dataset using both the push and release region for classifying the keystrokes, and using only the push region. We found out that using only the push region provided a better accuracy rate (17%) against using both the push and release region (12%) for single character detection rate hence we used only the push region of the keystroke for feature extraction in subsequent further experiments.

After we chose the best possible technique that would form the basis our attack, we started with collecting samples of password typing and test them against our attack. The strength of a password depends upon its randomness and its length. Since passwords based upon English language are susceptible to language model based attacks, we only consider passwords containing random letters. The length of the password was chosen to be six as it is the minimum required size of passwords on most of the authentication systems. Due to randomness in the password structure, the length of the password bears no relation to the accuracy of the attack.

Zhuang et al. [16] discussed password stealing using MFCC and a keystroke classifier but they did not include the effect of typing style in their experiments. Halvei and Saxena [8] used hunt and peck style to type random passwords 6 characters long and tested them against the straw man type dataset using time-frequency classification. They got a detection rate of 65% per character. In order to improve their detection rate, they employed the best guesses search method that creates a list of candidate keys as replacement for the detected keys. A candidate key is defined as the key having the closest matching feature (minimum time-frequency distance) with the given key. A list of best 5 candidate keys was built for every key and was used to create a list of possible passwords by replacing the key in question with a candidate key. This method increased the probability of password detection to 88%.

## 3.4   Attack Against Password Typing

We used a different approach for password detection that only depends upon number of collected samples of audio recordings. We collected some samples of the audio recordings of a random password being typed and noted down the most frequently occurring letter for each of the six positions. For example, in the first column of Table 2 (included in the Appendix), none of the detected passwords are a complete match to the original password "gkbxym" that was typed. However, we noticed that for a sample size of 20 recordings of the same password being typed, letter 'g' appears 6 times in our samples at the first position and hence a very strong candidate to be the actual typed letter in that position. The final password after applying this technique on every position is "gkbcyw" and it is incorrect in only two letters when compared to the original password "gkbxym".

We tested 3 random passwords of 6-character length with a sample size of 20 and found out that the average accuracy rate for detecting the correct letter at each position in the password was 66%. We find this detection rate to be high enough to be deemed as a viable attack. The attack is computationally light as it does not require a replacement list for each character and then producing an exhaustive list of all possible passwords by replacing each letter in the detected password. We also believe that given a big enough sample size, the attack may even be able to fully decode the password.

### 3.5    Triangulation Attack

Triangulation attack [6] is an attack mechanism that uses multiple microphones to record the keystrokes and computes the time of arrival at each microphone for each keystroke. The time delay for the arrival of the keystroke signal at each microphone is distinct for each keystroke due to the fixed location of the keys on the keyboard. This leads to a unique constant distance of each key from each microphone that can be used as an identifying feature for that key. However, this method is not much accurate at detecting keys that are located in close proximity to each other on the keyboard, hence other techniques like cross-correlation are applied to overcome this shortcoming.

## 4    Overview of Our Defense

As shown in the earlier section, the acoustic emanations from keyboards present a valid threat to user security and privacy. In order to mitigate this attack, several measures have been conceptualized. Asonov et al. [2] proposed a sound-free (lacking mechanical components) keyboard that would be an obvious choice against such class of attacks. However, this solution is not feasible as it is not inexpensive to design such keyboards and the users must get familiar with using such keyboards. Another proposed solution was to use a homophonic mechanical keyboard that produces similar sounds clicks for each key press. Yet, it is not known if it is possible to construct such keyboards and how they will perform over time given wear and tear. Another potential defense would be to sound-proof the surroundings of the user to prevent acoustic leakage from the keyboard. However, there exists many powerful microphones, such as parabolic and laser microphones, that can overcome the sound proofing. A similar defense system used by military, intelligence and security services is Sensitive Compartmented Information Facility where sensitive information is confined to a secure facility with limited access.

An alternative approach is to reduce the quality of the information that can be extracted from the acoustic signal as suggested by Zhuang et al. [16] rather than cutting off the acoustic leakage itself. The idea is to add some masking noises that will distort the leaking signal enough so that it is almost impractical

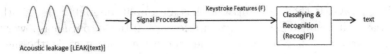

**Fig. 2.** In absence of masking signal

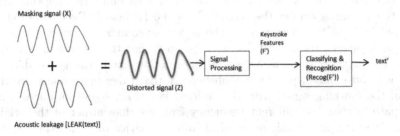

**Fig. 3.** In presence of masking signal

to extract any useful information from the distorted signal. As it can be seen, the idea for using masking signal to mitigate keyboard acoustic side channel attacks has been briefly touched upon in existing literature, but no prior work has been done upon their feasibility (security and usability) in a real-world scenario to the best of our knowledge. Hence, in this work, we will focus on the feasibility of masking signals as a viable defense against keyboard acoustic emanations especially when the typed input is passwords. The defense idea is portrayed in Fig. 3.

Adding masking signal to the acoustic leakage signal poses a two-fold design requirement: (1) the masking signal should be similar to the signal being masked so that it is difficult to separate them out, and (2) the masking signal should not have any degrading effect on the usability of the system (password typing) as a whole.

## 5   Defense Design

The concept of using a masking signal to hide the intended signal is similar to using jamming signal or interference in radio communication though the objective may be different in both scenarios. The purpose of using a jamming signal in radio communication is to block the reception of the transmitted signal, in order to prevent the receiving operator from decoding the signal. The jamming signal, if set to same frequency, modulation and with same or more power than the transmitted signal can override the original signal to the effect that it becomes difficult to separate the two signals. An interference signal causes unintentional distortion to the transmitted signal thereby degrading the quality of the transmitted signal at the receiving operator.

Both of the above observations happen due to the phenomenon called *wave interference*. Two waves when they meet in the same medium superpose to form a resultant wave. If the resultant wave has an amplitude higher than both the parent waves, it is called constructive interference. If the amplitude is lower than both the parents, it is referred to as destructive interference. At the meeting point of the two waves, the total displacement equals the point-wise sum of the displacement of individual waves.

In our defense design, we build a mechanism that emits the masking signal while the victim is typing the password on the keyboard. By emanating the masking signal at the same time as the keystroke sounds, we hope to interfere with the keystroke sound and distort it to an extent that it becomes unfeasible for the attacker to gain any useful information about the typed data. As explained above, any type of wave interference that takes place due to overlapping of the masking signal with the emitted keystroke signal produces a new wave pattern that has different frequency features than either of the original signals. We incorporate this mechanism into the device of the victim's system since it will make it easier to detect the key press event on the keyboard thereby triggering the defense mechanism. It also gives the victim, the control of the defense mechanism so that it can be enabled or disabled as per victim's choice.

As mentioned earlier, the choice of the masking signal is affected by two factors: the similarity of the masking signal to the acoustic leakage signal and the usability of such a signal in a real-world scenario. We discuss both the factors below (and evaluate them in the following two sections):

**Similarity of the Signals:** The masking signal should be closely similar to the signal it is trying to hide. The reason behind this requirement is to make it harder for the adversary to separate the two signals as the signals are too close to each other. In Fig. 2, the acoustic leakage signal is in clear and is picked up by the adversary for signal processing that yields the keystroke features ($F$). The set of obtained features are classified and recognized that yields the text being typed. In the presence of the masking signal, in contrast, the adversary receives the combined distorted signal ($Z$), instead of just the acoustic leakage signal, which is the sum of the acoustic leakage signal and the masking signal. When this signal is picked up for processing by the adversary, the set of features obtained ($F'$), are not the same as the features from the acoustic signal ($F$). This is due to overlapping between the acoustic leakage signal and the masking signal that produces the wave interference phenomenon as explained previously.

For separation of two signals ($A$ and $B$) from the combined signal ($S$), an adversary can filter out one of the signals if the signal is characteristically differing from the other in the frequency spectrum. Suppose signal $A$ is in frequency range 4–6 kHz and signal $B$ is in the range 5–12 kHz. Signal $A$ can be filtered out from the combined signal $C$ ($= A + B$), if the adversary only considers the frequencies in the range 6–12 kHz. The loss of frequency range (5–6 kHz) will not affect the adversary's goal as the adversary can still use the remaining frequency range (6–12 kHz) for the purpose of training, classification and recognition. Similar argument can be made for retaining signal $A$ and discarding signal $B$.

Another method for separating the signals from each other is to use signal inversion. Suppose the adversary records a signal $S$ that is the sum of two separate signals $A$ and $B$. If the adversary has the knowledge of signal $B$, it can invert signal $B$ and add it back to signal $S$. The addition of the inverted signal of $B$ cancels out the original signal $B$ leaving us with only signal $A$.

As demonstrated above, signal inversion is the main principle behind modern noise cancellation technology. However, it requires a prior knowledge of the signal to be removed. If the signal has a recognizable pattern, modern techniques exist in audio processing tools (e.g., Audacity) that can perform noise reduction using the provided pattern on the input signal. However, in our defense, the masking signal is a random signal picked by the device subject to the attack, which will be unpredictable to the attacker.

**Usability of the Masking Signal:** While there exist myriads of choices that can be used as masking signals, their usability should also be evaluated before adopting them in our defense. Any signal that lies in the same frequency range as the one we are trying to hide, can be used as a masking signal. However, such a signal should not be annoying or distracting to the user. The power of the signal also plays a role in usability as more the power of the signal, the better it will be able to override the keyboard acoustic leakage yet it can also affect the usability to the extent that the user may find the masking signal distracting or unbearable.

## 6    Evaluating the Security of the Defense

This section details the experiments carried to explore the feasibility of masking signals against keyboard acoustic side channel attacks. We test three types of masking signals: (1) *white noise,* (2) *fake keystrokes,* and (3) *combined signal* (one combining white noise and fake keystrokes). The masking signal is designed to play in the background while the user types on the keyboard. This ensures that the keystrokes sounds and the masking signal are emitted in the same time frame and any recording done by the adversary includes a combination of both sounds.

Similar to the attack setting, we provide adversary with the most capability. This means that the adversary already possesses a system trained on the same typing style as the victim's typing style. We also allow the adversary to implant a covert listening device to record the victim's keystrokes as they are being typed and provide the adversary access to victim's system to test the possible candidates for the typed passwords. If our proposed defense mechanism is successful in thwarting the attacker with the most capabilities, it would be successful against attacks in real world scenarios where attacker may have to capture the keystroke sound from a greater distance, or the user may be using a different typing style than hunt and peck like touch typing.

In our experiments, the victim entered the password in hunt and peck typing style. The typed password was six characters long and consisted of a random sequence of alphabets only, in line with the attack scenarios. A microphone placed at a distance of 1 ft (about 30 cm) from the keyboard, acts as an adversary by recording the emitted audio. For password entry by the user, a java swing application was designed.

**White Noise:** White noise is a random signal having a uniform frequency spectrum. It has been used extensively as a concentration and relaxation aid. It is also been used for sound masking in office settings due to its ability to hide out annoying or distracting background noises. We proceeded with the white noise as the first choice for our defense model due to its widespread usage and tested its ability to withstand keyboard acoustic side channel attacks.

A sample of white noise was chosen and played in the background while the password was being entered. The audio recording from the adversary was processed and evaluated against the attack mechanism. The attack mechanism was able to detect on an average 2 characters from the possible 6 characters of the password. The results of the experiment are listed under column 2 of Table 2. Since white noise has a distinct pattern, it is possible to separate it from the recorded audio signal. To test the effect of noise removal from the signal, we used the noise reduction option from Audacity on the recorded audio signal. After applying noise reduction, our results showed that there was no increase in the detection rate. A possible explanation for this result is that the removal of noise from the recorded audio signal also affects the keystroke signals embedded in it. It occurs due to degradation in the keystroke features because of imperfection in the noise removal algorithms as the noise profile is not the same throughout the recorded audio signal.

**Fake Keystrokes:** The next obvious choice for a masking signal that could cloak the keyboard acoustic leakage would be an audio consisting of keystrokes. We would hereby refer to the recording of keystrokes as *fake keystrokes* as they are not a part of the current keystrokes emitted during the user's password entry. The *fake keystrokes* are an excellent candidate for a masking signal to be used against keyboard acoustic side channel attacks as they consists of same keystroke features that would be emitted during password entry. This would make it difficult for the attacker to distinguish between the *fake keystrokes* and the actual keystrokes.

In order to use the *fake keystrokes*, the user system needs to possess an audio recording of the keystrokes. This audio recording is obtained from the user by prompting the user to randomly type some text while recording the audio using a microphone. This exercise needs to be performed only once though it would be useful to refresh this audio recording consisting of random keystrokes at some predetermined intervals. This action would take in account the normal wearing down of keys due to regular usage that can affect the emitted keystroke sound. It would also prevent the attacker from building a noise profile by sampling the keystrokes over a period of time and figuring out the frequently occurring keystrokes.

For our experiment, we recorded single instance of a keystroke for each of the alphabetical keys thereby creating a pool of keystroke recordings. The user was asked to enter the password and a *key-press* event was bound to the password entry box. As soon as the user typed the first letter of the password, the system generated a random number between 1 to 26 and played the keystroke audio file corresponding to the generated random number. A *TimerTask* thread was created to perform the above task at a regular interval of 100 ms. Since an average keystroke duration is 100 ms and the average interval between keystrokes is more than 100 ms [2, 16], we chose 100 ms as the interval between subsequent keystrokes. This would allow the *fake keystrokes* to overlap with the actual keystroke thereby producing a distinct keystroke audio signal that would not map to either of the two keystrokes. The interval between the *fake keystrokes* can also be randomized but should not exceed 100 ms.

Figure 4(a) shows a recording of actual keystrokes while the *fake keystrokes* played in the background according to the approach described above and Fig. 4(b) details the spectrogram of the same signal. From Fig. 4(a), we can clearly see the first keystroke which is isolated as the system can not predict its occurrence. However, once the first keystroke was detected, the system started playing the fake keystrokes in the background hiding the actual keystrokes in the process.

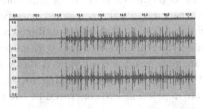

(a) The audio signal (x axis represents the time and y axis represents the normalized amplitude of the signal)

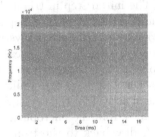

(b) The spectrogram

Fig. 4. Fake Keystrokes as a Masking Signal

Figure 4(b) also shows that the *fake keystrokes* and the actual keystrokes have same power spectral density, which may make it hard to separate the fake keystrokes from the actual keystrokes. All the keyboard acoustic side channel attacks depend upon frequency range and a threshold to detect a key press, and having similar energy and frequency range makes it very difficult for the adversary to separate the two signals. Our results confirm this observation. Column 3 of Table 2 shows the recovered passwords over 20 samples of recording as per the attack scenario with the *fake keystrokes* playing in the background and using the attack technique as detailed in Sect. 3.

**Combined Signal:** While *fake keystrokes* are efficient in masking the keyboard acoustic leakage, a layered approach can improve the efficiency of the defense mechanism by burying the keystroke sound beneath a layer involving multiple masking signals, each of which adds an additional defensive layer above the keystroke sound. We use a combination of white noise and *fake keystrokes* to act as two layers that shield the keyboard acoustic leakage. Since *fake keystrokes* are enough to shield the actual keystrokes, the addition of white noise can serve to either bolster the existing background noise or increase the usability of the masking signal by making it pleasant for the user to hear. Hence, our combined signal consists of fake keystrokes and the white noise mixed together.

Figures 5 and 6 (included in the appendix) refer to the recorded audio signal and the resulting spectrogram when combined signal is used. Column 4 of Table 2 shows the recovered passwords over 20 samples of recording as per the attack scenario with combined signal playing in the background and using the attack technique as detailed in Sect. 3.

**Evaluation Against Triangulation Attack:** The triangulation attack exploits the differences in arrival times of a sound wave at each microphone to identify the keystrokes. Since, the defense model uses the speakers to produce the *fake keystrokes* that are stationary, it is possible that it would be vulnerable to this type of attack.

The initial step in triangulation attack is to detect keystrokes and note the time of arrival at each microphone. The distance approach is used to classify and recognize each detected keystroke. As the *fake keystrokes* have similar acoustic signature to actual key press sound hence they are treated as legitimate keystrokes by the triangulation attack and are processed accordingly. A meticulous attacker may have the ability to detect *fake keystrokes* by looking for similar time of arrival for the keystrokes as all *fake keystrokes* are generated at the same distance from the microphone.

A drawback to the triangulation attack is that it works well for far separated keys but for keys in close proximity, it has to add an additional signal correlation factor for keystroke classification. It was demonstrated in earlier sections that the cross correlation (which was one of the classifying features in time-frequency classification) can not differentiate between fake keystrokes and actual keystrokes. Thus, we believe that the triangulation attack will have low accuracy against our defense model.

## 7   Evaluating the Usability of the Defense

Our user study was designed to test the proposed defense mechanism for its usability among the people while they are engaged in typing passwords. We recruited 10 users (ages 20–35; 8 males and 2 females) by word of mouth. All the recruited users were graduate students from our university. Since our primary goal was to gain qualitative feedback from the users regarding the defense mechanism, and not statistical significance, a small sample size was appropriate for our study. The study was approved by our university's IRB. The participation was consensual and voluntary for the users. No audio was recorded during the study.

We developed four authentication systems that required the user to input a password of their own choosing. The first system was developed without any defense mechanism in place to protect against acoustic eavesdropping. The second system played white noise in the background while the user entered the password. The system began playing the white noise as soon as the user began typing in the password field and stopped when the password was verified. The third system used *fake keystrokes* to play in the background while the fourth system used a combination of white noise with water flowing and *fake keystrokes* as the masking signal.

We used five trials per user and each trial presented the above four systems in a random order. This was done to prevent the user from getting familiar with the pattern of masking signals and hence psychologically ignoring the masking signal. We also noted the number of times the user failed in entering the password which could indicate the distracting effect of the masking signal. At the end of the study, each user was asked to fill a survey form based on System Usability Scale (SUS) [5] questionnaire and a usability score (out of 100) was derived from the submitted response. We also asked an additional question to each user if the masking signal was distracting while typing the password. The response was graded on a scale from "strongly disagree" (*score* = 1) to "strongly agree" (*score* = 5).

**Table 1.** Usability study results

|  | No masking signal | White noise | Fake keystroke | Combined signal |
| --- | --- | --- | --- | --- |
| SUS score | 91.88 (7.65) | 76.25 (15.70) | 69.38 (19.40) | 69.06 (17.92) |
| Distraction score | 1.00 (0.00) | 2.75 (1.03) | 3.62 (1.19) | 3.5 (1.19) |

The SUS scores (mean and standard deviations) from the usability study are listed in Table 1. The scores suggest that the usability drops in the presence of a masking signal. This is a reasonable conclusion as background noises may affect the usability compared to plain password input (without masking signal). Although the usability level drops in comparison to plain password input, the SUS scores are still high enough (around 70 on an average) for the system to be considered usable [9].

When we compared the SUS scores among the different types of masking signals, we found that white noise had the highest mean usability score followed by the combined masking signal. The fake keystrokes had the lowest usability score. All previous observations were also confirmed by the distraction score. The standard deviation for distraction score for no masking signal case was 0 as all users "strongly disagreed" that the absence of any masking signal was annoying. One complaint in the study was from a user who was surprised by the sudden injection of the noise in the background when he started typing the password. We attribute this effect to the unfamiliarity of the user with the system and believe that the users will become more comfortable as they adapt to the system.

We therefore conclude that the combined signal is the best candidate for masking signal from the users' perspective. Since the amount of time required for password entry is short, we believe that an active noise generation does not have a major effect on the users' ability to perform the password entry task.

## 8    Discussion and Future Directions

**Summary of Results:** We studied the effect of acoustic side channel attacks on keyboards during password entry. We chose time-frequency classification technique [8] to extract keystroke features from the acoustic leakage. We also considered the typing style of the user as an important criteria for initializing our dataset. We showed that more than half of the password (66.67 %) can be recovered by the adversary over 20 trials by noting down the most frequently occurring character for each letter position in the typed password.

We introduced a defense mechanism to counteract such attacks thereby preserving the privacy of the user. We used active background sounds to cloak the acoustic leakage from the keyboard. We explored three classes of backgrounds sounds that could be used as masking signals: white noise, *fake keystrokes* and combined signal (a mix of white noise and *fake keystrokes*). We found out that the *fake keystrokes* performed better than white noise at masking the acoustic leakage against our side channel attack.

We also explored the usability of our attack and our user study indicated that white noise was the most preferred background noise that could be played while the password typing was in progress followed by the combined signal and the *fake keystrokes* in the same order. This observation suggests that the combined signal can serve as a middle ground between security and usability of the masking signal since it is at least as secure as *fake keystrokes* but more user friendly.

**Real-World Defense Implementation:** The design of our proposed defense mechanism requires the masking signal generator to be in-built within the users' system. This approach was used to allow the detection of the first key press for the password entry that will act as a trigger for the defense mechanism to start emitting the masking signal. However, in scenarios such as password entry on websites, the trigger can also be bound to the URL of the website, in particular to the login webpage. In our experiments, a Java swing based user interface was constructed to test the defense mechanism. However, the defense mechanism can also be deployed as a browser plugin that can generate the masking signals based on the visited URL. It may also hand over the control to the user who can enable or disable the defense mechanism at will (e.g., by typing in a special character sequence such as "@@" as in an existing password manager application [12].

**Active Sound Generation by Mobile Devices:** Furthering the utilization of the defense mechanism, it can also be deployed as an application on mobile devices like smartphones. The user can place the smartphone near the input device (e.g., a keyboard, or an ATM keypad) and launch the defense application that will start emitting the masking signal while the user can proceed towards password/PIN entry. Thus, we can have a transportable defense mechanism, easy enough to be carried in pockets and can be triggered at will by the users.

**Other Keyboard Input:** While the focus of this paper was oriented towards password typing, any input containing sensitive data can be protected by this defense mechanism. An example is payment information required on various online merchant websites where the user has to enter banking or credit card information. Since the time taken to enter this information is relatively short, the defense mechanism can be used without disturbing surrounding environment. This could also be applicable to general text (email or other conversations, for example). However, given these tasks are longer in time duration, further usability studies need to performed to analyze the effect of background noise generation on arbitrary text input.

**Context-Free Attacks:** Our defense model was evaluated against the category of attack that rely upon the similarity of features among keystroke signals [2–4,6,8,16]. It may not be effective against the context-free attack [15] as this attack identifies each keystroke in an independent manner and does not depend upon similarity of keystroke signals. Instead, it locates the most probable origin of the signal and maps it on the keyboard. A signal originating outside the keyboard (e.g., a separate speaker) may fail to map on the reconstructed keyboard. Although context-free attacks may be less practical since they require multiple audio recording devices close to the keyboard, further work can reveal the extent to which our defense mechanism can degrade the accuracy of this attack. A possible modification to strengthen our design against context-free attack may include varying the emanating signal among a number of speakers that surround the device (or embed the speakers within the keyboard itself).

**Other Side Channel Attacks:** The idea of actively generating noise to shield the acoustic leakage from keyboards can also be extended to defending against other side channel attacks. Adding a vibrating element/device to the surface on which the keyboard is placed may be able to lower the accuracy of the vibrational side channel attacks [10]. Similarly, we may inject CPU emanations or printer emanations actively using the speakers to shield against CPU or printer emanation based attacks [3,7]. Further studies should be conducted to validate the defense in the context of these side channel attacks.

## 9    Conclusion

In this paper, we proposed a feasible defense mechanism against acoustic side channel attacks directed towards keyboards and password entry. We showed that it is possible to extract more than half of the password just by using time-frequency features and observing the most frequently occurring characters over a large sample of audio samples captured from the keyboard during password entry. We proceeded to build a defense mechanism based on the notion of bolstering the background noises that can cloak the acoustic leakage from the keyboard making it extremely difficult for the adversary to obtain any useful information about the typed password. We tested different types of signals that could be used a masking signal and evaluated them based on security and usability. The proposed defense mechanism is easy to use and requires minimal user input. It is lightweight and only requires the availability of a speaker that can be used for sound generation.

## Appendix

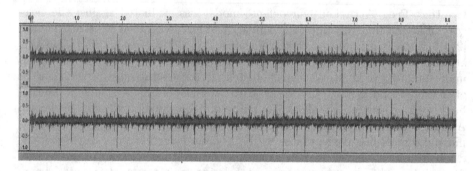

**Fig. 5.** Audio for combined signal (x axis represents the time and y axis represents the normalized amplitude of the signal)

**Table 2.** Password detection samples for the password "gkbxym"

| No masking signal | White noise | Fake keystroke | Combined masking signal |
|---|---|---|---|
| xmbuuu | mvvxhv | utyixf | oifdtv |
| ukcecd | sxlxyz | mfufxf | dfkhjd |
| rlnuzl | vqzbgu | hmysyf | ifdfkd |
| ikkbuc | qjbyfi | vdjfff | sjsifd |
| gkbuys | klvoyv | mfwfff | sjsdfd |
| gknamw | ikubtt | ifffff | vjdkii |
| bvxxtk | ilkvlj | bgfffd | ojsddd |
| ukbvkw | duyeyy | gfvfff | hdsddd |
| bqvzyw | havlyy | gbfiff | ojsddd |
| hkbiui | vtiyir | dfdipi | sjvidd |
| gbmqlp | ngbkym | dddfip | ojsddd |
| vmbqlp | kkckyj | dvdivo | ffbqki |
| asbzyf | sbzuhv | dfvpvs | hdhisd |
| gxbczf | gvxhyi | iiigfd | sdhddd |
| qsbcyi | nivkyj | vfiddv | divvik |
| xsbnfz | kokykt | ddvhdd | iddisd |
| gkmcxg | havkvz | dixpfv | dovdfi |
| jkvcmk | zkpqvk | gfbiff | ojsddi |
| dmszvb | ggyuul | fvdvvi | ifddid |
| ggbvtv | igbiyy | vdmsfd | dafdgk |
| **gkbcyw** | **kkvkyj** | **dfdff** | **ojsddd** |

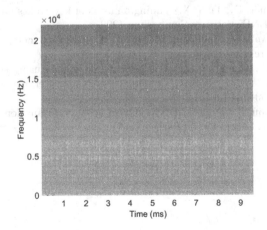

**Fig. 6.** Spectrogram for combined signal

# References

1. Adams, A., Sasse, M.A.: Users are not the enemy. Commun. ACM **42**, 12 (1999)
2. Asonov, D., Agrawal, R.: Keyboard acoustic emanations. In: IEEE Symposium on Security and Privacy (2004)
3. Backes, M., Dürmuth, M., Gerling, S., Pinkal, M., Sporleder, C.: Acoustic side-channel attacks on printers. In: USENIX Security Symposium (2005)
4. Berger, Y., Wool, A., Yeredor, A.: Dictionary attacks using keyboard acoustic emanations. In: ACM Conference on Computer and Communications Security (2006)
5. Brooke, J.: Sus - a quick and dirty usability scale. In: Jordan, P., Thomas, B., Weerdmeester, B., McClelland, I.L. (eds.) Usability Evaluation in Industry. Taylor and Francis, London (1996)
6. Fiona, A.: Keyboard acoustic triangulation attack (2006). http://citeseerx.ist.psu.edu/viewdoc/download?doi=10.1.1.100.3156&rep=rep.1&type=pdf. (Final Year Project)
7. Genkin, D., Shamir, A., Tromer, E.: RSA key extraction via low-bandwidth acoustic cryptanalysis. In: Garay, J.A., Gennaro, R. (eds.) CRYPTO 2014. LNCS, vol. 8616, pp. 444–461. Springer, Heidelberg (2014). doi:10.1007/978-3-662-44371-2_25
8. Halevi, T., Saxena, N.: A closer look at keyboard acoustic emanations: random passwords, typing styles and decoding techniques. In: ACM Symposium on Information, Computer and Communications Security (2012)
9. Lewis, J.R., Sauro, J.: The factor structure of the system usability scale. In: Kurosu, M. (ed.) HCD 2009. LNCS, vol. 5619, pp. 94–103. Springer, Heidelberg (2009). doi:10.1007/978-3-642-02806-9_12
10. Marquardt, P., Verma, A., Carter, H., Traynor, P.: (sp)iphone: decoding vibrations from nearby keyboards using mobile phone accelerometers. In: ACM Conference on Computer and Communications Security (2011)
11. Morris, R., Thompson, K.: Password security: a case history. Commun. ACM **22**, 11 (1979)
12. Ross, B., Jackson, C., Miyake, N., Boneh, D., Mitchell, J.C.: Stronger password authentication using browser extensions. In: USENIX Security Symposium (2005)
13. Song, D., Wagner, D., Tian, X.: Timing analysis of keystrokes and timing attacks on ssh. In: USENIX Security Symposium (2001)
14. Yan, J., Blackwell, A., Anderson, R., Grant, A.: Password memorability and security: empirical results. IEEE Secur. Priv. **2**, 5 (2004)
15. Zhu, T., Ma, Q., Zhang, S., Liu, Y.: Context-free attacks using keyboard acoustic emanations. In: ACM SIGSAC Conference on Computer and Communications Security, pp. 453–464 (2014)
16. Zhuang, L., Zhou, F., Tygar, J.D.: Keyboard acoustic emanations revisited. ACM Trans. Inf. Syst. Secur. **13**, 1 (2009)

# Surveillance and Anonymity

# Leaky Birds: Exploiting Mobile Application Traffic for Surveillance

Eline Vanrykel[1], Gunes Acar[2(✉)], Michael Herrmann[2], and Claudia Diaz[2]

[1] KU Leuven, Leuven, Belgium
eline.vanrykel@gmail.com
[2] imec-COSIC KU Leuven, Leuven, Belgium
{gunes.acar,michael.herrmann,claudia.diaz}@esat.kuleuven.be

**Abstract.** Over the last decade, mobile devices and mobile applications have become pervasive in their usage. Although many privacy risks associated with mobile applications have been investigated, prior work mainly focuses on the collection of user information by application developers and advertisers. Inspired by the Snowden revelations, we study the ways mobile applications enable mass surveillance by sending unique identifiers over unencrypted connections. Applying passive network fingerprinting, we show how a passive network adversary can improve his ability to target mobile users' traffic.

Our results are based on a large-scale automated study of mobile application network traffic. The framework we developed for this study downloads and runs mobile applications, captures their network traffic and automatically detects identifiers that are sent in the clear. Our findings show that a global adversary can link 57% of a user's unencrypted mobile traffic. Evaluating two countermeasures available to privacy aware mobile users, we find their effectiveness to be very limited against identifier leakage.

## 1 Introduction

Documents that have been revealed by the former NSA contractor Edward Snowden shed light on the massive surveillance capabilities of the USA and UK intelligence agencies. One particular document released by the German newspaper *Der Spiegel* describes the ways in which traffic of mobile applications (apps) is exploited for surveillance [16]. The document, which reads "Exploring and Exploiting Leaky Mobile Apps With BADASS," provides a unique opportunity to understand the capabilities of powerful network adversaries. Furthermore, the document reveals that identifiers sent over unencrypted channels are being used to distinguish the traffic of individual mobile users with the help of so-called *selectors*. Similar revelations about the use of Google cookies to target individuals imply that BADASS is not an isolated incident [12,34].

While it is known that a substantial amount of mobile app traffic is unencrypted and contains sensitive information such as users' location or real identities [24,35,43], the opportunities that mobile traffic offers to surveillance agencies

© International Financial Cryptography Association 2017
J. Grossklags and B. Preneel (Eds.): FC 2016, LNCS 9603, pp. 367–384, 2017.
DOI: 10.1007/978-3-662-54970-4_22

may still be greatly underestimated. Identifiers that are being sent in the clear, may allow the adversary to link app sessions of users and thus to learn more information about the surveilled users than he could without. The purpose of this study is to evaluate this risk and to quantify the extent to that it is possible to track mobile app users based on unencrypted app traffic.

To this end we present a novel framework to quantify the threat that a surveillance adversary poses to smartphone users. The framework automates the collection and analysis of mobile app traffic: it downloads and installs Android apps, runs them using Android's *The Monkey* [18] tool, captures the network traffic on cloud-based VPN servers, and finally analyzes the traffic to detect unique and persistent identifiers. Our framework allows large-scale evaluation of mobile apps in an automated fashion, which is demonstrated by the evaluation of 1260 apps. We choose the apps among all possible categories of the Google Play store and of different popularity levels.

Our study is inspired by a recent work by Englehardt et al. [26]. They studied the surveillance implications of cookie-based tracking by combining web and network measurements. The evaluation method they use boils down to measuring the success of the adversary by the ratio of user traffic he can cluster together. We take a similar approach for automated identifier detection but we extend their work to capture non-cookie-based tracking methods that are suitable for user tracking. Moreover, we show how TCP timestamp-based passive network fingerprinting can be used to improve the clustering of the traffic and may allow to detect the boot time of Android devices.

## 1.1   Contributions

**Large-scale, automated study on surveillance implications of mobile apps.** We present an automated analysis of 1260 Android apps from 42 app categories and show how mobile apps enable third party surveillance by sending unique identifiers over unencrypted connections.

**Applying passive network fingerprinting for mobile app traffic exploitation.** We show how a passive network adversary can use TCP timestamps to significantly improve the amount of traffic he can cluster. This allows us to present a more realistic assessment of the threat imposed by a passive adversary. Further, we show how an adversary can guess the boot time of an Android device and link users' traffic even if they switch from WiFi to 3G or vice versa.

**Evaluation of the available defenses for privacy aware users.** We analyze the efficacy of two mobile ad-blocking tools: Adblock Plus for Android [13] and Disconnect Malvertising [14]. Our analysis shows that these tools have a limited effect preventing mobile apps from leaking identifiers.

## 2    Background and Related Work

**Android apps and identifiers.** Android apps and third-parties can access
common identifiers present on the smartphone, such as MAC address, Google
Advertising ID or IMEI number. We call these identifiers *smartphone IDs*. An
overview of the Android smartphone IDs can be found in Table 1. Developers
may also choose to assign IDs to users (instead of using smartphone IDs), for
identifying individual app installations or simply to avoid asking for additional
permissions [11]. We refer to such identifiers as *app assigned IDs*.

Table 1. Unique smartphone identifiers present on Android, an overview.

| Name | Persistence | Permission |
|------|-------------|------------|
| Android ID | Until a factory reset | None |
| MAC Address | Lifetime of the device | ACCESS_WIFI_STATE |
| IMEI | Lifetime of the device | READ_PHONE_STATE |
| IMSI | Lifetime of the SIM card | READ_PHONE_STATE |
| Serial number | Lifetime of the device | None [41] |
| SIM serial number | Lifetime of the SIM card | READ_PHONE_STATE |
| Phone number | Lifetime of the SIM card | READ_PHONE_STATE |
| Google Advertising ID | Until reset by the user | ACCESS_NETWORK_STATE, INTERNET |

**Privacy implications of mobile apps.** Although privacy implications of
Android apps have been extensively studied in the literature [25,28,29], prior
work has mainly focused on the sensitive information that is collected and transmitted to remote servers. Xia et al. showed that up to 50% of the traffic can be
attributed to the real names of users [43]. Enck et al. developed TaintDroid [25],
a system-wide taint analysis system that allows runtime analysis and tracking
of sensitive information flows. While it would be possible to use TaintDroid in
our study, we opted to keep the phone modifications minimal and collect data
at external VPN servers. This allows us to have a more realistic assessment of
application behavior and adversary capabilities.

   Our work differs from these studies, by quantifying the threat posed by a passive network adversary who exploits mobile app traffic for surveillance purposes.
We also show how the adversary can automatically discover user identifiers and
use passive network fingerprinting techniques to improve his attack.

**Passive network monitoring and surveillance.** Englehardt et al. [26] show
how third-party cookies sent over unencrypted connections can be used to *cluster*
the traffic of individual users for surveillance. They found that reconstructing
62–73% of the user browsing history is possible by passively observing network
traffic.

   In addition to using identifiers to track smartphones, an eavesdropping adversary can use passive network fingerprinting techniques to distinguish traffic from

different physical devices. Prior work showed that clock skew [31,33,44], TCP timestamps [23,42] and IP ID fields [21] can be used to remotely identify hosts or count hosts behind a NAT. In this study, we use TCP timestamps to improve the linking of users' mobile traffic in short time intervals. We assume the adversary to exploit TCP timestamps to distinguish traffic of users who are behind a NAT. Moreover, we demonstrate how an adversary can discover the boot time of an Android device by exploiting TCP timestamps.

## 3    Threat Model

In this paper we consider passive network adversaries whose goal is to link app traffic of smartphone users. The adversaries observe unique identifiers that are being transmitted from mobile apps in the clear and apply network fingerprinting techniques. We consider that the adversaries cannot break cryptography or launch MITM attacks such as SSLstrip [32].

We distinguish between two types of passive adversaries: A *global passive adversary*, who can intercept all Internet traffic at all time; and a *restricted passive adversary* who can only observe a limited part of the network traffic. Both adversaries have the capability to collect bulk data. This may be achieved in various ways, such as tapping into undersea fiber-optic cables; hacking routers or switches; intercepting traffic at major Internet Service Providers (ISP) or Internet Exchange Points (IXP)[1].

There can be several models in which an adversary may have limited access to the user's traffic. In this study we evaluate adversaries whose limitation is either *host-based* or *packet-based*. The host-based adversary is only able to see traffic bound to certain hosts; for example, because the adversary is only able to obtain warrants for intercepting traffic within its own jurisdiction. The packet-based adversary may only have access to a certain point in the Internet backbone and thus miss traffic that is being sent along other routes. For both adversaries, we evaluate the success based on different levels of network coverage (Sect. 7.2). We simulate partial network coverage by randomly selecting hosts or packets to be analyzed depending on the model. For instance, for the host-based model with 0.25 network coverage, we randomly pick one-fourth of the hosts and exclude the traffic bound to remaining hosts from the analysis.

## 4    Data Collection Methodology

### 4.1    Experimental Setup

We present the experimental setup[2] that is used for this paper in Fig. 1. It includes a controller PC, two smartphones and two VPN servers for traffic capture. The main building blocks of our framework are as follows:

---

[1] All these methods are feasible, as illustrated by the Snowden revelations [6,8].
[2] The source code of the framework, as well as the collected data will be made available to researchers upon request.

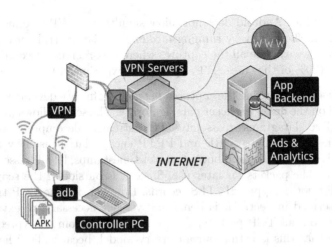

**Fig. 1.** Our setup in this study consists of a Controller PC that manages the experiments, two Android phones that run apps, and two VPN servers that capture the network traffic.

**Controller PC.** The Controller PC runs the software that orchestrates the experiments and the analysis. It has three main tasks: (1) installing apps on the smartphones and ensuring that the experiment runs smoothly, e.g. checking the phone's WiFi and VPN connections, (2) sending SSH commands to the remote VPN servers to start, stop and download the traffic capture, (3) analyzing the collected data.

**Smartphones.** We conducted our experiments with two *Samsung Galaxy SIII Mini* smartphones running Android version 4.1.2. We *rooted* the phones to address issues such as storage and uninstallation problems. Although we considered using the Android emulator as in other works [24,36,38], our preliminary tests [39] showed that the number of transmitted identifiers is significantly less in the emulator compared to the same setting with a real smartphone and the emulator lacks certain identifiers, such as the WiFi MAC address. We also chose not to intercept system API calls or instrument the operating system, such as in [25,27], since we preferred a simpler and more portable solution.

**The Monkey.** We use *The Monkey* [18] tool to automate the experiments and simulate the user interaction at large scale. The Monkey generates a pseudo-random event stream that includes touch, motion and keyboard events.

**Traffic Capture.** The network traffic is captured by two remote VPN servers, using the *dumpcap* [5] command line tool. Using VPN servers, we could capture *all* the network traffic and not only HTTP traffic, which would be the case with an HTTP proxy. Also, since we record the traffic on remote machines, we ensure that there is no packet drop due to lack of buffer space on resource constrained devices [15]. However, we captured traffic locally on the phone during the evaluation of ad-blockers for Android. These tools use a proxy or VPN themselves to block ads. Since Android does not allow simultaneous VPN connections, we captured the traffic locally by running *tcpdump* on the smartphones. To ensure comparability, we exclude all the captures where we observed packet drops from the analysis (20% of the cases, 171 apps in two experiments).

**Traffic parser.** For parsing the captured network traffic, we developed a Python script based on the dpkt [3] packet parsing library. The script allows us to decode IPv4 and IPv6 datagrams, reassemble TCP streams, decompress compressed HTTP bodies and to parse GRE and PPTP encapsulation used by the VPN. We extract HTTP headers and bodies, packet timestamps, IP addresses and port numbers from the packets for later use. Since it is outside of the scope of this study, we did not decrypt SSL/TLS records. However, for the TCP timestamp analysis described in Sect. 6 it is beneficial, yet not necessary, to extract TCP timestamps from all TCP packets, including the ones from encrypted HTTPS traffic. Note that this is within our adversary model, because TCP headers are sent in the clear and thus available to a passive adversary.

Having described the main building blocks of the experimental setup, now we outline the different modes and steps of the experiments:

**Experiment modes.** We run experiments in two different modes to evaluate the difference in identifier transmission; (i) if the app is simply opened and (ii) if the user actually interacts with the app. We refer to the former as *startscreen experiment* and to the latter as *interactive experiment*. The Monkey is used to simulate user interaction in the interactive experiments.

**Evaluation of ad-blocker apps.** We evaluate the effect of apps that block ads and trackers. While those apps are not specifically designed to prevent identifier leakage, they may still reduce the number of identifiers being sent in the clear. Specifically, we repeated the experiment of the top-popularity apps after we installed and activated the ad-blocker apps *Adblock Plus for Android* [13] and *Disconnect Malvertising* [14].

**Steps of the experiment.** Our framework executes the steps of the experiments in an entirely automated fashion. The Controller PC connects the smartphone to the VPN server by running a Python based *AndroidViewClient* [4] script that emulates the touch events necessary to start the VPN connection on the smartphone. Since installing all the apps at once is not possible due to storage constraints, our framework conducts the experiment in cycles. In each cycle we install 20 apps and then run them sequentially[3]. The apps for each cycle are randomly chosen from the entire set of apps, with the condition that each app is only picked once. Before running an app, the Controller PC kills the process of the previous app. This way we are able to prevent the traffic of the previously tested app mistakenly being recorded for the subsequent app. After finished running the 20 apps, the Controller PC runs all 20 apps a second time in the same order. Running each app twice enables the automated detection of

---

[3] We chose 20 since this was the maximum number of apps that can be installed on an Android emulator at once, which we used in the preliminary stages of the study.

identifiers outlined in Sect. 5.1. Finally, the Controller PC completes the current cycle by uninstalling all 20 apps.

## 4.2  Obtaining Android Applications

To obtain the Android apps, we developed scripts for crawling the Google Play store and, subsequently, to download APK files. Our scripts are based on the Python Selenium [17] library, the APK downloader browser extension and webpages [1]. Using this software, we crawled the entire Play Store and obtained information on 1,003,701 different Android apps. For every app we collected information such as number of downloads, rating scores and app category. This allows us to rank the apps of every category according to their popularity.

For every app category we choose 10 apps from three different popularity levels: *top-popularity*, *mid-popularity* and *low-popularity*. While we use the most popular apps for the top-popularity category, we sample the mid-popularity and low-popularity apps from the 25th and 50th percentiles from each category. At the time we conducted the crawl, there were 42 different app categories and we therefore obtained a total of 1260 ($42 \times 10 \times 3$) apps. The average time for evaluating one app is 64 seconds.

# 5  Analysis Methodology

In the following we show how an adversary is able to extract identifiers from network traffic and then use these identifiers to cluster data streams, i.e. linking data streams as belonging to the same user. This is the same that an adversary with the goal of surveilling Internet traffic would do, i.e. extracting and applying a set of *selectors* that match unique and persistent mobile app identifiers.

## 5.1  Identifier Detection

Suitable identifiers for tracking need to be persistent and unique, i.e. the same ID cannot appear on different phones and IDs need to be observable over multiple sessions. Our framework automatically detects such unique identifiers in unencrypted mobile app traffic. While the overall approach is similar to the one in [19,26] we extend the cookie-based identifier detection technique to cover mobile app traffic. We assume that the smartphone IDs (such as Android ID or MAC address) are not known a priori to the adversary. The adversary has to extract IDs based on the traffic traces only. Yet, we use smartphone IDs as the ground truth to improve our automated ID detection method by tuning its parameters.

For finding identifiers, we process HTTP request headers, bodies and URL parameters. Specifically, the steps of the unique identifier detection are as follows:

– Split URLs, headers, cookie contents and message bodies using common delimiters, such as "=", "&", ":", to extract key-value pairs. Decode JSON encoded strings in HTTP message bodies.

- Filter out cookies with expiry times shorter than three months. A tracking cookie is expected to have a longer expiry period [26].
- For each key-value pair, we construct an *identifying rule set* and add it to the potential identifier list. This is the tuple (host, position, key), where *host* is extracted from the HTTP message and *position* indicates whether the key was extracted from a cookie, header or URL.
- Compare values of the same key between runs of two smartphones.
  - Eliminate values if they are not the same length.
  - Eliminate values that are not observed in two runs of the same app on the same smartphone.
  - Eliminate values that are shorter than 10 or longer than 100 characters.
  - Eliminate values that are more than 70% similar according to the Ratcliff-Obershelp similarity measure [22].
- Add (host, position, key) to the rule set.

We tuned similarity (70%) and length limits (10, 100) according to two criteria: minimizing false positives and detecting all the smartphone identifiers (Table 1) with the extracted rule set. We experimented with different limit values and picked the values that gave us the best results based on these criteria. A more thorough evaluation of these limits is omitted due to space constraints, but interested readers can refer to [19,26] for the main principles of the methodology.

## 5.2    Clustering of App Traffic

While the ultimate goal of the adversary is to link different app sessions of the same user by exploiting unique identifiers transmitted in app traffic, the first challenge of the adversary is to identify the traffic of one app. An app may open multiple TCP connections to different servers and linking these connections can be challenging. The user's public IP address is not a good identifier: several users may share the same public IP via a NAT. Moreover, IP addresses of mobile phones are known to change frequently [20].

In this work we consider two different clustering strategies. In the *TCP stream based linking*, the attacker can only link IP packets based on their TCP stream. The adversary can simply monitor creation and tear down of TCP streams and ensure that the packets being sent within one stream are originating from the same phone. The second, more sophisticated strategy employs passive network fingerprinting techniques to link IP packets of the same app session. We will refer this technique as *app session based linking* and outline it in Sect. 6.

Following Englehardt et al. [26] we present linking of the user traffic as a graph building process. We use the term *node* to refer to a list of packets that the adversary is certain that they belong to the same user. As explained above, this is either a TCP stream or an app session. For every node the adversary extracts the identifying rule set (host, position, key) as described in Sect. 5.1. Starting from these nodes, the adversary inspects the content of the traffic and then tries to link nodes together to so-called *components*.

Therefore, the attacker will try to match a node's identifiers to the identifiers of the existing components. We account for the fact that some developers do not use the smartphone ID right away as identifier, but derive an identifier from it by hashing or encoding. Thus the clustering algorithm will also try to match the SHA-1, SHA-256, MD5 and murmur3 hashes and base64 encoded form of the identifiers. For every node, there exist three possibilities when comparing the node's identifiers to a existing component's identifiers:

1. **The node's value (or its derivative) matches the identifiers of an existing component:** The node will be added to the component and the respective identifiers are being merged, i.e. the newly added node may include identifiers not yet included in the component.
2. **None of the node's identifiers or their derivatives can be matched to an existing component:** The node creates its own component which is disconnected from all other components.
3. **The node shares identifiers with multiple components:** These components are merged together and the node is added to this component.

For the remainder of this paper, we refer to the component that contains the highest number of nodes as the *Giant Connected Component* (GCC). Furthermore, we define the ratio of number of nodes in GCC to the number of nodes in the whole graph as the *GCC ratio*. The *GCC ratio* serves as a metric for measuring the adversary's success for linking users' traffic based on the amount of traffic he observes.

### 5.3 Background Traffic Detection

The Android operating system itself also generates network traffic, for example to check updates or sync user accounts. Although we find in our experiments that the Android OS does not send any identifiers in the clear, we still take measures to avoid that this traffic pollutes our experiment data. Particularly, we captured the network traffic of two smartphones for several hours multiple times without running any app. A complete overview of all HTTP queries made during such captures can be found in [40]. We excluded all the HTTP requests to these domains during the analysis stage. Although we excluded background traffic from our analysis, the adversary may try to exploit the background traffic in a real-world attack.

## 6  Linking Mobile App Traffic with TCP Timestamps

In this section we elaborate on the adversary's ability to employ passive fingerprinting techniques to link different IP packets originating from the same smartphone. As mentioned in Sect. 5.2, this gives a significant advantage to the adversary when clustering the user traffic. In particular, the adversary is able to analyze TCP timestamps for this task as they are commonly allowed by the firewalls [33].

TCP timestamps are an optional field in TCP packets that include a 32-bit monotonically increasing counter. They are used to improve the protocol performance and protect against old segments that may corrupt TCP connections [30]. While the exact usage of TCP timestamps is platform dependent, our inspection of the Android source code and capture files from our experiments revealed that Android initializes the TCP timestamp to a fixed value after boot and uses 100 Hz as the timestamp increment frequency [2]. Thus, at any time $t$, TCP timestamp of a previously observed device can be estimated as follows: $TS_t = TS_{prev} + 100 \times (t - t_{prev})$, where $TS_{prev}$ is the timestamp observed at $t_{prev}$ and $(t - t_{prev})$ is the elapsed time. The adversary can therefore link different visits from the same device by comparing the observed TCP timestamps to his estimate. Prior studies have shown that distinguishing devices behind a NAT using TCP timestamps can be done in an efficient and scalable manner [23, 37, 42].

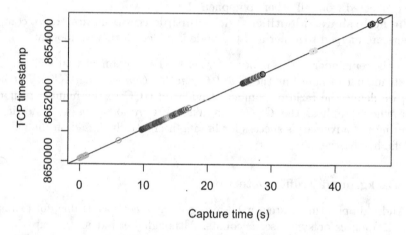

**Fig. 2.** TCP timestamp vs. capture time plot of Angry Birds Space app follows a line with a slope of 100, which is the timestamp resolution used by Android. Different TCP sessions, indicated by different colors, can be linked together by exploiting the linearity of the TCP timestamp values.

Figure 2 demonstrates the linear increase of the TCP timestamps of a phone running the "Angry Bird Space" app. To demonstrate the linkability of TCP streams, every point in Fig. 2 is colored based on its TCP source and destination port. The straight line shows that the adversary can easily link different TCP streams of the same device by exploiting the linearity of the timestamps. The adversary is also able to consider TCP timestamps of encrypted communications, because TCP timestamps are sent unencrypted in the packet headers. This allows adversaries within our threat model to further increase the success of the linking. Furthermore, TCP timestamps can be used to link traffic even if the user switches from WiFi to mobile data connection or vice versa [40]. Finally, the linking is still feasible even if the adversary misses some packets, for instance, due to partial coverage of the network.

**Limitations.** During the background traffic detection experiments, we observed cases in which TCP timestamps are not incremented linearly. Consulting the Android System Clock Documentation, we determined that the CPU and certain system timers stop when the device enters the *deep sleep* state [10]. This power saving mechanism is triggered only when the screen is off and the device is not connected to the power outlet or USB port. Therefore, the phone will never go into deep sleep when a user is interacting with an app and the TCP timestamps will be incremented in a predictable way, allowing the linking of the traffic by app sessions.

**Implications for traffic linking.** We will assume the adversary can use TCP timestamps to cluster packets generated during the use of an app (app session), as the phone never enters *deep sleep* mode when it is in active use. As mentioned in Sect. 5.2, we will refer to this as *app session based linking*.

**Android boot time detection.** In addition to linking packets from different TCP streams, TCP timestamps can also be used to guess the boot time of remote devices [7]. Among other things, boot time can be used to determine if the device is patched with critical updates that require a reboot. Since it is not directly related to traffic linking attack considered in the study, we explain the boot time detection methodology in the unabridged version of this paper [40].

# 7 Results

## 7.1 Identifier Detection Rules

We present in Table 2 an overview of the identifying rule set that we detected by the methodology explained in Sect. 5.1. Recall that identifying rules correspond to "selectors" in the surveillance jargon, which allow an adversary to target a user's network traffic. In total we found 1597 rules with our method, of which 1127 (71%) correspond to a smartphone ID or its derivative. Our results show that the Android ID and Google Advertising ID are the most frequently transmitted smartphone IDs, accounting for 72% (812/1127) of the total. We group the least commonly transmitted smartphone IDs under the *Other Smartphone IDs* column, which include the following: device serial number, IMSI, SIM serial number and registered Google account email. Furthermore, we found 29% of the extracted rules to be app-assigned IDs.

Analyzing the extracted rules for the top-popularity, interactive experiments, we found that 50% of the identifiers are sent in the URI of the HTTP requests (291 rules). In 39% (225) of the rules, the IDs are sent in the HTTP request body, using the POST method. Only 3% (18) of the cases, the identifier was sent in a cookie. The average identifier length in our rule set is 26.4 characters. A sample of identifying rules is given in Table 3.

After extracting identifier detection rules, we apply them to the traffic captured during the experiments. Due to space constraints we present the detailed results on the transmitted IDs in the unabridged version of this paper [40].

**Table 2.** The extracted ID detection rules and corresponding smartphone IDs. *SID*: Smartphone ID, *AAID*: App Assigned ID.

| Exp. mode | App popularity | Android ID | Google Ad ID | IMEI | MAC | Other SIDs | AAIDs | Total ID rules |
|---|---|---|---|---|---|---|---|---|
| Interactive | Top | 165 | 111 | 63 | 29 | 16 | 193 | 577 |
| Startscreen | Top | 115 | 56 | 45 | 19 | 11 | 91 | 337 |
| Interactive | Mid | 56 | 28 | 20 | 6 | 5 | 60 | 175 |
| Startscreen | Mid | 48 | 28 | 16 | 5 | 4 | 40 | 141 |
| Interactive | Low | 73 | 61 | 22 | 15 | 8 | 53 | 232 |
| Startscreen | Low | 47 | 24 | 16 | 7 | 8 | 33 | 135 |
| **Total** | | 504 | 308 | 182 | 81 | 52 | 470 | 1597 |

**Table 3.** Examples rules found in the constructed identifying rule set. The values are modified to prevent the disclosure of real identifiers of the phones used in the study.

| Host | Position | Key | ID | Value |
|---|---|---|---|---|
| data.flurry.com | Body | offset60 | Android ID | AND9f20d23388... |
| apps.ad-x.co.uk | URI | custom_data/meta_udid | Unknown | 19E5B4CEE6F5... |
| apps.ad-x.co.uk | URI | macAddress | WiFi MAC | D0:C4:F7:58:6C:12 |
| alog.umeng.com | Body | header/device_id | IMEI | 354917158514924 |
| d.applovin.com | Body | device_info/idfa | Google Ad ID | 0e5f5a7d-a3e4-.. |

Moreover, analyzing the traffic captures of the top-popularity apps, we found that certain apps send precise location information (29 apps), email address (7 apps) and phone number (2 apps) in the clear. Together with the linking attack presented in this paper, this allows an adversary to link significantly more traffic to real-life identities.

We found that 1076 different hosts were contacted over unencrypted connections during the experiments for the top-popularity apps in the interactive mode. The *data.flurry.com* domain is the most popular third-party domain collecting Android ID from 43 different apps (Table 4). Note that *data.flurry.com* received a notable mention in the slides of the BADASS program [16] for its identifier leakage.

**Table 4.** The most common third-party hosts found to collect at least an identifier over unencrypted connections. The listed hosts are contacted by the highest number of apps (based on 420 top-popularity apps, interactive experiment).

| Host | # Apps | Collected IDs |
|---|---|---|
| data.flurry.com | 43 | Android ID |
| ads.mopub.com | 32 | Google advertising ID |
| apps.ad-x.co.uk | 22 | Google advertising ID, IMEI, Serial number, Android ID |
| alog.umeng.com | 16 | IMEI |
| a.applovin.com | 16 | Google advertising ID |

## 7.2   Traffic Clustering

Here we evaluate the adversary's success in terms of unencrypted app traffic ratio (GCC ratio) that he can link together in different settings. We follow the analysis methodology explained in Sect. 5.2 and present clustering results for 100 randomly selected combinations of 27 apps. We pick 27 apps since it is the average number of apps used per month according to a recent survey [9]. Running 100 iterations with a different combination of (27) apps allowed us to reduce the variance between different runs and account for all the studied apps. We only consider apps that send at least one HTTP request and calculate the GCC ratio based on the unencrypted traffic. For the top-popular apps in interactive mode, these account for 69% of the apps. For simplicity, we will present the clustering results for only one phone and a single run of each app. The results from two phones did not have any significant difference.

**Effect of using TCP timestamps for traffic linking.** The left boxplot in Fig. 3(a), shows that when the adversary does not take TCP timestamps into account (TCP stream based linking), he can cluster 25% of users' unencrypted traffic. However, by exploiting TCP timestamps he can increase the GCC ratio to 57%.

**Effect of app popularity.** Figure 3(b) shows that popularity has a significant impact on the linking success of the adversary. The most popular apps allow the adversary to cluster 57% of the unencrypted traffic, while the apps from the mid-popular and low-popular level result in a GCC ratio of 32% and 28%, respectively.

Due to space constraints, we will only present results for the apps from the top-popularity level in the rest of this section.

**Effect of user interaction.** Figure 3(c) shows the GCC ratio for two different experiment modes, *interaction* and *startscreen*. Although, the number of identifiers sent in two modes are significantly different (577 vs. 337), the graph shows a similar GCC ratio around 53% for two modes. A possible explanation is that the identifiers that enable linking are already sent as soon as the app is started.

**Effect of countermeasures.** Figure 3(d) shows that both ad-blocking apps provide a limited protection against linking of the app traffic. Using Adblock Plus leads to an average linking of 50%. Disconnect Malvertising performs better, with a GCC rate of 38%, reduced from 57%.

**Restricted adversary.** Figure 3(e) shows that an adversary that can only intercept traffic to 50% of the hosts can link up to 38% of the unencrypted mobile app sessions. For the *packet based* restricted adversary model, we observe that an adversary with a limited coverage of 25% of the user's packets can still link 37% of all app sessions together (Fig. 3(f)). In both models restricted adversary's success grows almost linear with his network coverage. Note that packet based restricted adversary can link significantly more traffic than the host-based model

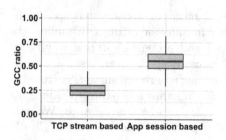

(a) GCC ratio for the top-popularity apps, shown for TCP stream and app session based linking.

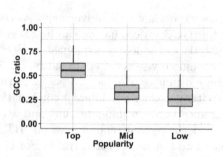

(b) GCC ratio for apps of different popularity levels for interaction mode.

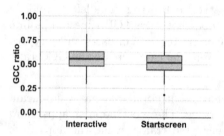

(c) GCC ratio for top-popularity apps, shown for interaction and startscreen mode.

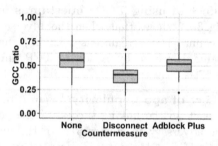

(d) GCC ratio for the top-popularity apps, shown while using different privacy enhancing tools.

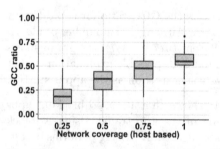

(e) GCC ratio for the top-popularity apps, shown for different network coverage levels of a *host based* restricted adversary.

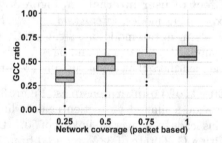

(f) GCC ratio for the top-popularity apps, shown for different network coverage levels of a packet based restricted adversary.

**Fig. 3.** The success of the adversary under different experimental settings and adversary models. The GCC ratio is the proportion of the unencrypted app traffic that the adversary can link together. The results are shown for 100 different randomly selected combinations of 27 apps.

for the same network coverage ratio. This may be due to being able to observe packets from more hosts which will allow to link apps across sessions.

## 8    Limitations

Some apps may not be fully discovered by *The Monkey*, leading to an incomplete view of the network traffic. Also, apps that require user logins may not be sufficiently analyzed by our automated methodology. For those reasons, our results should be taken as lower bounds.

While we assume that the smartphones can be distinguished by their TCP timestamps, some middleboxes may interfere with user traffic. Firewalls, proxies or cache servers may terminate outgoing HTTP or TCP connections and open a new connection to the outside servers. Furthermore, end-user NAT devices may have various configurations and hence behave differently compared to enterprise NATs. In such cases, the adversary's ability to link traffic by TCP timestamps may be reduced.

We used *rooted* Android phones in our experiments. Although rooting the phones may introduce changes in the observed traffic, we assumed the changes to be minimal.

## 9    Conclusion

The revealed slides of the BADASS program have shown that unencrypted mobile app traffic is exploited for mass surveillance. Identifiers sent in the clear by the mobile applications allow targeting mobile users, linking of their traffic and building a database of their online activities.

In this study, we evaluated the surveillance threat posed by a passive network adversary who exploits mobile app traffic for surveillance purposes. We presented a novel framework that automates the analysis of mobile app network traffic. Our framework and methodology is designed to be flexible and can be used in other mobile privacy studies with slight modifications.

Our results show that using TCP timestamps and unique identifiers sent in the unencrypted HTTP traffic, a global adversary can cluster 57% of users' unencrypted mobile app sessions. We demonstrated that a passive adversary can automatically build a rule set that extracts unique identifiers in the observed traffic, which serves as a "selector" list for targeting users.

Our results suggest that popular apps leak significantly more identifiers than the less popular apps. Furthermore, while interacting with the app increases the number of leaked identifiers, solely starting an app amounts to the same attack effectiveness.

We evaluated two countermeasures designed to block mobile ads and found that they provide a limited protection against linking of the user traffic. Encrypting mobile app traffic can effectively protect against passive network adversaries. Moreover, a countermeasure similar to HTTPS Everywhere browser extension can be developed to replace insecure HTTP connections of mobile apps with secure HTTPS connections on the fly.

**Acknowledgment.** We would like to thank Steve Englehardt, Yves Tavernier and anonymous reviewers for their helpful and constructive feedback. This work was supported by the Flemish Government FWO G.0360.11N Location Privacy, FWO G.068611N Data mining and by the European Commission through H2020-DS-2014-653497 PANORAMIX and H2020-ICT-2014-644371 WITDOM.

# References

1. APK Downloader [Latest] Download Directly — Chrome Extension v3 (Evozi Official). http://apps.evozi.com/apk-downloader/
2. Cross Reference: /external/kernel-headers/original/asm-arm/param.h. http://androidxref.com/4.1.2/xref/external/kernel-headers/original/asm-arm/param.h# 18
3. dpkt 1.8.6.2: Python Package Index. https://pypi.python.org/pypi/dpkt
4. dtmilano/AndroidViewClient. https://github.com/dtmilano/AndroidViewClient/
5. dumpcap - The Wireshark Network Analyzer 1.12.2. https://www.wireshark.org/docs/man-pages/dumpcap.html
6. GCHQ taps fibre-optic cables for secret access to world's communications. http://www.theguardian.com/uk/2013/jun/21/gchq-cables-secret-world-communications-nsa
7. Nmap Network Scanning - Remote OS Detection - Usage and Examples. http://nmap.org/book/osdetect-usage.html
8. NSA Prism program taps in to user data of Apple, Google and others. http://www.theguardian.com/world/2013/jun/06/us-tech-giants-nsa-data
9. Smartphones: So many apps, so much time. http://www.nielsen.com/us/en/insights/news/2014/smartphones-so-many-apps-so-much-time.html
10. SystemClock — Android Developers. http://developer.android.com/reference/android/os/SystemClock.html
11. Identifying App Installations — Android Developers Blog (2011). http://android-developers.blogspot.be/2011/03/identifying-app-installations.html
12. 'Tor Stinks' presentation (2013). http://www.theguardian.com/world/interactive/2013/oct/04/tor-stinks-nsa-presentation-document
13. About Adblock Plus for Android (2015). https://adblockplus.org/android-about
14. Disconnect Malvertising for Android (2015). https://disconnect.me/mobile/disconnect-malvertising/sideload
15. Manpage of TCPDUMP (2015). http://www.tcpdump.org/tcpdump_man.html
16. Mobile apps doubleheader: BADASS Angry Birds (2015). http://www.spiegel.de/media/media-35670.pdf
17. Selenium - Web Browser Automation (2015). http://docs.seleniumhq.org/
18. UI/Application Exerciser Monkey — Android Developers (2015). http://developer.android.com/tools/help/monkey.html
19. Acar, G., Eubank, C., Englehardt, S.: The web never forgets: persistent tracking mechanisms in the wild. In: Proceedings of the 2014 ACM SIGSAC Conference on Computer and Communications Security (2014)
20. Balakrishnan, M.: Where's that phone? Geolocating IP addresses on 3G networks. In: Proceedings of the 9th ACM SIGCOMM Conference on Internet Measurement Conference, pp. 294–300 (2009)
21. Bellovin, S.M.: A technique for counting NATted hosts. In: Proceedings of the second ACM SIGCOMM Workshop on Internet Measurement - IMW 2002, p. 267 (2002)

22. Black, P.E.: Ratcliff/Obershelp pattern recognition, December 2004. https://xlinux.nist.gov/dads//HTML/ratcliffObershelp.html
23. Bursztein, E.: Time has something to tell us about network address translation. In: Proceedings of NordSec (2007)
24. Dai, S., Tongaonkar, A., Wang, X., Nucci, A., Song, D.: NetworkProfiler: towards automatic fingerprinting of Android apps. In: 2013 Proceedings IEEE INFOCOM, pp. 809–817, April 2013
25. Enck, W., Cox, L.P., Gilbert, P., Mcdaniel, P.: TaintDroid: an information-flow tracking system for realtime privacy monitoring on smartphones. In: OSDI 2010 Proceedings of the 9th USENIX Conference on Operating Systems Design and Implementation (2010)
26. Englehardt, S., Reisman, D., Eubank, C., Zimmerman, P., Mayer, J., Narayanan, A., Felten, E.W.: Cookies that give you away: the surveillance implications of web tracking. In: Proceedings of the 24th International Conference on World Wide Web, pp. 289–299 (2015)
27. Felt, A.P., Chin, E., Hanna, S., Song, D., Wagner, D.: Android permissions demystified. In: Proceedings of the 18th ACM Conference on Computer and Communications Security, p. 627 (2011)
28. Grace, M., Zhou, W., Jiang, X., Sadeghi, A.: Unsafe exposure analysis of mobile in-app advertisements. In: Proceedings of the fifth ACM Conference on Security and Privacy in Wireless and Mobile Networks 067(Section 2) (2012)
29. Hornyack, P., Han, S., Jung, J., Schechter, S., Wetherall, D.: These aren't the droids you're looking for: Retrofitting Android to protect data from imperious applications. In: Proceedings of the 18th ACM Conference on Computer and Communications Security, pp. 639–652. ACM (2011)
30. Jacobson, V., Braden, R., Borman, D., Satyanarayanan, M., Kistler, J., Mummert, L., Ebling, M.: RFC 1323: TCP extensions for high performance (1992)
31. Kohno, T., Broido, A., Claffy, K.C.: Remote physical device fingerprinting. IEEE Trans. Dependable Secure Comput. 2(2), 93–108 (2005)
32. Marlinspike, M.: New tricks for defeating SSL in practice. BlackHat DC, February 2009
33. Murdoch, S.J.: Hot or not: revealing hidden services by their clock skew. In: Proceedings of the 13th ACM Conference on Computer and Communications Security, pp. 27–36. ACM (2006)
34. Soltani, A., Peterson, A., Gellman, B.: NSA uses Google cookies to pinpoint targets for hacking (2013). https://www.washingtonpost.com/news/the-switch/wp/2013/12/10/nsa-uses-google-cookies-to-pinpoint-targets-for-hacking/
35. Stevens, R., Gibler, C., Crussell, J.: Investigating user privacy in android ad libraries. In: IEEE Mobile Security Technologies (MoST) (2012)
36. Suarez-Tangil, G., Conti, M., Tapiador, J.E., Peris-Lopez, P.: Detecting targeted smartphone malware with behavior-triggering stochastic models. In: Kutyłowski, M., Vaidya, J. (eds.) ESORICS 2014. LNCS, vol. 8712, pp. 183–201. Springer, Cham (2014). doi:10.1007/978-3-319-11203-9_11
37. Tekeoglu, A., Altiparmak, N., Tosun, A.: Approximating the number of active nodes behind a NAT device. In: 2011 Proceedings of 20th International Conference on Computer Communications and Networks (ICCCN), pp. 1–7. IEEE (2011)
38. Tongaonkar, A., Dai, S., Nucci, A., Song, D.: Understanding mobile app usage patterns using in-app advertisements. In: Roughan, M., Chang, R. (eds.) PAM 2013. LNCS, vol. 7799, pp. 63–72. Springer, Heidelberg (2013). doi:10.1007/978-3-642-36516-4_7

39. Vanrykel, E.: Passive network attacks on mobile applications. Master's thesis, Katholieke Universiteit Leuven (2015)
40. Vanrykel, E., Acar, G., Herrmann, M., Diaz, C.: Exploiting Unencrypted Mobile Application Traffic for Surveillance (Technical report) (2016). https://securewww. esat.kuleuven.be/cosic/publications/article-2602.pdf
41. Weinstein, D.: Leaking Android hardware serial number to unprivileged apps (2013). http://insitusec.blogspot.be/2013/01/leaking-android-hardware-serial-number.html
42. Wicherski, G., Weingarten, F., Meyer, U.: IP agnostic real-time traffic filtering and host identification using TCP timestamps. In: 2013 IEEE 38th Conference on Local Computer Networks (LCN), pp. 647–654. IEEE (2013)
43. Xia, N., Song, H.H., Liao, Y., Iliofotou, M.: Mosaic: quantifying privacy leakage in mobile networks. In: SIGCOMM 2013, Proceedings of the ACM SIGCOMM 2013 Conference on SIGCOMM (ii), pp. 279–290 (2013)
44. Zander, S., Murdoch, S.J.: An improved clock-skew measurement technique for revealing hidden services. In: USENIX Security Symposium, pp. 211–226 (2008)

# Footprint Scheduling
# for Dining-Cryptographer Networks

Anna Krasnova[✉], Moritz Neikes[✉], and Peter Schwabe[✉]

Digital Security Group, Radboud University,
Toernooiveld 212, 6525 EC Nijmegen, The Netherlands
anna@mechanical-mind.org, m.neikes@student.ru.nl, peter@cryptojedi.org

**Abstract.** In many communication scenarios it is not sufficient to protect only the content of the communication, it is necessary to also protect the identity of communicating parties. Various protocols and technologies have been proposed to offer such protection, for example, anonymous proxies, mix-networks, or onion routing. The protocol that offers the strongest anonymity guarantees, namely unconditional sender and recipient untraceability, is the Dining Cryptographer (DC) protocol proposed by Chaum in 1988. Unfortunately the strong anonymity guarantees come at the price of limited performance and scalability and multiple issues that make deployment complicated in practice.

In this paper we address one of those issues, namely slot reservation. We propose *footprint scheduling* as a new technique for participants to negotiate communication slots without losing anonymity and at the same time hiding the number of actively sending users. Footprint scheduling is at the same time simple, efficient and yields excellent results, in particular in very dynamic networks with a frequently changing set of participants and frequently changing activity rate.

**Keywords:** DC-net · Scheduling · Anonymity · Slot-reservation

# 1 Introduction

*"We kill people based on metadata"* – this statement by former CIA and NSA director Michael Hayden demonstrates more than clearly that cryptographically protecting only the content of communication is insufficient; secure communication also has to protect the identities of the communicating parties. Various protocols and techniques have been proposed to enable anonymous communication. All of these techniques have to choose a trade-off between efficiency in terms of throughput, latency, and scalability on the one hand and security guarantees

This research was conducted within the Privacy and Identity Lab (PI.lab, http://www.pilab.nl) and funded by SIDN.nl (http://www.sidn.nl/) and by Netherlands Organisation for Scientific Research (NWO) through Veni 2013 project 13114. Permanent ID of this document: 215ad4d1ccbd4ee7a6c763de5d2a8537. Date: October 19, 2015.

J. Grossklags and B. Preneel (Eds.): FC 2016, LNCS 9603, pp. 385–402, 2017.
DOI: 10.1007/978-3-662-54970-4_23

on the other hand. For example, anonymous proxies provide low latency and potentially very good throughput and scalability, but all participants' identities are compromised if one trusted node, the proxy, is compromised. Stronger guarantees are offered by a cascade of proxies in onion-routing networks like Tor [17], which were originally proposed by Syverson, Goldschlag, and Reed in [16]. However, onion-routing networks are possibly susceptible to attacks that correlate traffic entering and leaving the network. See, for example, [11]. Mix-nets, proposed already in 1981 by Chaum in [4] do not have this problem; however, they suffer from increased latency.

The anonymity protocol that offers the strongest guarantees is the *Dining-Cryptographers protocol*, also known as Dining-Cryptographers network or short DC-net, which was introduced by Chaum in [3]. The protocol provides unconditional communication anonymity for senders and recipients, however, at the cost of low throughput and high latency, in particular when scaling to many participants.

**Dining Cryptographers.** To explain how DC-net works, consider an example with 3 participants exchanging 6-bit messages. Figure 1 depicts the example. Each participant has a shared symmetric key with each other participant. Assume that participant $A$ wants to send a message. To do so, she xors her message with all the keys she shares with the other participants. The result is an *output* that $A$ sends out to every participant of the DC-net. The other participants perform the same procedure, but use a zero message instead of a meaningful one. All outputs of all participants are xored together to reveal the meaningful message of the participant $A$, because keys are canceling out (since each symmetric key is used twice). This completes a single *round* of the DC-net, during which one participant can transfer (broadcast) one message; in the next round another participant transmits a message until all participants are done transmitting.

**Collisions and Scheduling.** If two participants send in the same round, their messages collide and become unusable. This can happen accidentally or also

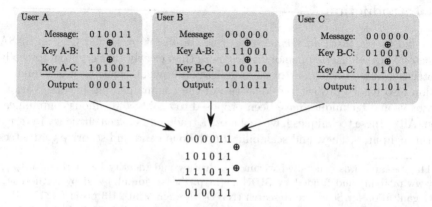

**Fig. 1.** DC-net with tree participants and 6-bit messages

intentionally from a malicious participant who is *disrupting* communication. This raises the central question addressed in this paper: How does each participant know when it is his or her turn to send? Note that many standard slot-reservation protocols as used, for example, in dynamic time-division multiple-access (TDMA) networks are not applicable, because they would compromise anonymity. The task of *slot-reservation* in DC-net is to agree on a sending schedule in a way that each participant knows when to send, but does not learn who is sending in the other slots.

Generally there are three different approaches to solve this problem. The first approach comprises so-called *reservation-map* methods. These methods employ a *scheduling vector* consisting of *slots*; each slot represents a future round with a corresponding index number. To reserve a round, a participant marks the corresponding slot in the scheduling vector as occupied. The second approach is to use *collision-resolution algorithms*. The third approach is to use secure multi-party computation to obtain a secret permutation that assigns rounds to participants.

**Contributions of this Paper.** This paper presents a novel approach that belongs to the class of reservation-map methods. The general problem of this class of methods is that they essentially defer the problem of undetected collisions from the communication phase to a slot-reservation phase. One way to solve this problem is to use many more slots than participants, to keep the probability of collisions low. However, this leaves many communication slots unused and drastically reduces the throughput of the DC-net. We present *footprint scheduling* as a simple and efficient way to implement the slot-reservation phase without the loss of throughput. Footprint scheduling is the first scheduling algorithm to combine reasonable communication overhead that scales logarithmic in the number of participants, absence of computation overhead, and naturally handling participants joining and leaving the network.

**Full Version of this Paper.** The full version of this paper can be found at http://eprint.iacr.org/2015/1213.

**Availability of Results.** To maximize re-usability of our results, we made the software used to produce simulation results publicly available at https://github.com/25A0/DCnet-simulator.

**Notation.** We write $0^B$ for the string that consists of $B$ zeros. All logarithms in this paper are to the base 2.

**Organization of this Paper.** Section 2 reviews the state of the art in scheduling for DC-net. Section 3 introduces footprint scheduling and Sect. 4 describes how to tune the parameters of footprint scheduling and compares its performance to previous approaches. Section 5 describes a protection mechanism against disruption. Section 6 summarizes the key strengths of footprint scheduling.

## 2   Existing Scheduling Methods

In this section we describe the previous approaches to scheduling in DC-net. As listed in the previous section, we group the algorithms into three categories: reservation maps, collision resolution, and secure multi-party computation (MPC).

**Reservation Maps.** Reservation maps were already introduced as one possible way to handle scheduling in the original DC-net paper by Chaum [3]. The idea is to perform a separate scheduling phase to assign rounds to particular participants to avoid collisions. During this phase participants can reserve a round of DC-net by setting a bit of a *scheduling message* at the position corresponding to the round number. Note that also scheduling messages are sent through the anonymous DC-net channel; i.e., they are xored with all the shared keys of the other participants. Disruptions of the scheduling message can be detected with a certain probability by checking if the Hamming weight of the message is smaller or equal than the number of participants. The downside of this approach is that, because of the birthday paradox, the number of bits in the scheduling message must be quadratic in the number of participants to avoid collisions with high probability. Reservation maps are used by Herbivore, an implementation of DC-net presented by Goel, Robson, Polte, and Sirer in [9]. Herbivore optimizes the size of the scheduling message by allowing some collisions during message cycle depending on the message size (collisions for smaller messages are more likely). For performance comparison in Sect. 4 we also performed such optimization, however we decided for optimization that does not depend on the size of the message (See Appendix A in the full version of this paper for details).

The length of the scheduling message can be reduced if instead of bits representing rounds, one would use elements of the additive group of integers modulo $m$ [12]. After all the scheduling messages of participants are added up, elements of value 0 indicate an unreserved round, elements of value 1 indicate a reserved round, all other values indicate collisions.

**Collision Resolution.** The second approach proposed by Chaum in [3] is to use a contention algorithm with discrete time slots and resolve collisions by retransmitting the messages. A common example of such an algorithm is slotted ALOHA [14]. In Slotted ALOHA participants pick a time slot for transmission at will. Whenever a collision happens, participants wait for a random amount of time before they pick a new time slot for retransmission. The simplicity of the protocol is countered by the limitation of the transmission capacity of the network due to collisions.

One way to improve transmission capacity in collision resolution is through a technique called *superposed receiving*. The idea is to derive the retransmission schedule for collided messages from the result of a collision. New transmissions have to wait until a collision has been resolved. In [13, Sect. 3.1.2.3.2], A. Pfitzmann presents such an algorithm, which is an improvement of the tree algorithm that was independently proposed by Capetanakis in [2] and by Tsybakov and

Mikhailov in [18]. Pfitzmann calls this algorithm *tree-like collision resolution with superposed receiving*; in the following, we refer to this algorithm as *Pfitzmann's algorithm*. Let the number of messages that collided be $s$, then the protocol guarantees that the collision will be resolved in exactly $s$ retransmission steps. Additionally, this protocol guarantees fair usage of the channel for all sending participants. Note that this algorithm requires DC-net to be modified to work on integers modulo $m > 2$ instead of simple xors. This makes it possible to compute the "average" of the collided messages (treated as an integer). Participants that sent a message smaller than the average retransmit; participants that sent a larger message wait. As soon as only two messages collided, only one participant retransmits; the other message is recomputed locally. A more detailed description of the algorithm can be found in [19] and [7, Sect. 3.2.2].

Another algorithm, using a similar approach, was presented in [1] by Bos and Boer. It also computes a retransmission schedule for collided messages and requires $s$ retransmissions after $s$ messages collided. However, it has a larger overhead in header messages and is computationally more expensive than Pfitzmann's algorithm.

Note that these superposed-receiving techniques can also be applied to slot reservation as proposed by Waidner in [19]. Pfitzmann's algorithm is then used to resolve collisions of reservation messages. Each reservation message contains the number of the round in which a participant wants to send. With this approach the traffic load does not depend on the length of the messages transmitted through DC-net as in the original Pfitzmann's algorithm.

The first protective measure against disruption during the scheduling phase was presented by Waidner and B. Pfitzmann in [20,21]. The idea is to investigate the reservation phase in case of impossible results of the specific scheduling algorithm used. For example, in Pfitzmann's algorithm, the number of initially collided messages should be not more than the predefined maximum. To enable investigation, all the outputs during the scheduling phase are protected by output commitments. In the special phase called *palaver phase* any participant can start an investigation of the scheduling phase in order to detect disrupters.

**Secure Multi-party Computation.** In [10], Golle and Juels propose two new versions of DC-net that allow detection and identification of disrupters with high probability by using zero-knowledge proofs. They do not consider the problem of collisions (and thus reservation of rounds) in their solution; they comment that "the problem can be avoided through techniques like secure multi-party computation of a secretly distributed permutation of slots among players, but this is impractical".

Studholme and Blake propose in [15] a way to implement such a multi-party computation called *secret shuffle* by organizing a Mix-net with participants of DC-net serving as nodes. Encrypted round-reservation requests are transmitted through this Mix-net to obtain a secretly permuted vector of re-encrypted requests. Re-encryption is performed such that a participant can recognize his own request only after the permutation is completed. His reserved round number can be derived from the position of the request in the vector.

This idea is used in the Master's thesis of Franck [7], in which he derives a fully verifiable variant of DC-net. Later, verifiable DC-net was rediscovered in [6] and implemented under the name Verdict. The advantage of Verdict is that it allows switching between traditional DC-net and verifiable DC-net, depending on the presence of disruption. For scheduling, Verdict uses a similar approach as [7,15] and the same as in another implementation of DC-net by the same group, Dissent [5,22].

In [8], Franck proposes a scheduling for DC-net based on the collision-resolution protocol SICTA. This scheduling protocol is very similar to Pfitzmann's collision resolution algorithm, the only difference being that it operates with multiplication of ciphertexts instead of addition. The author proposes to use this algorithm to produce a secret shuffle of public keys of participants to establish a schedule. The protocol is non-deterministic; it achieves a maximum stable throughput (MST) of 0.924 messages per round. Disruption in the scheduling phase in this protocol is prevented by using zero-knowledge proofs.

## 3   Footprint Scheduling

In this section, we introduce *footprint scheduling*. Footprint scheduling is similar to the map-reservation algorithm described by Chaum [3]; however, it requires significantly shorter reservation vectors and drastically decreases the likelihood of (undetected) collisions in these vectors.

In the map-reservation algorithm, the $A$ active participants (i.e., participants who want to send a message in the next round) of a DC-net with a total of $N$ users can reserve one out of $S$ slots by inverting the corresponding bit in a reservation vector of $S$ bits. The reservation vector is then transmitted through DC-net, and the resulting reservation vector, i.e., the xor of all the individual reservations, is broadcast to all participants. See also Sect. 2. An undetected collision occurs in this vector as soon as an odd number of participants attempts to reserve the same slot. This event is obviously undesirable, since it leads to collisions of messages during the sending phase. To decrease the probability of such an event, the original paper [3] suggests to choose the length of the reservation vector to be quadratic in the number of participants.

**Footprints Instead of Bits.** The first idea of footprint scheduling is to use $B > 1$ bits in the reservation vector to represent each slot of the schedule. The reservation vector is thus extended to a length of $B \cdot S$ bits. A participant attempts to reserve a specific slot by changing the corresponding $B$ bits of the reservation vector to a random value $f \in \{0,1\}^B \setminus \{0\}^B$. This value is called his *footprint* . Figure 2a demonstrates an example of a reservation vector with 3-bit footprints. DC-net will broadcast the xor of all individual reservation vectors to the participants, just as for plain map reservation. If the reservation vector contains the footprint of a participant, it is likely that no other participant tried to reserve that slot. If instead the participant finds a different value, this indicates that at least one other participant tried to reserve the same slot.

| $A$ | 000 | 000 | 000 | 000 | 000 | 000 | 110 | 000 |
|-----|-----|-----|-----|-----|-----|-----|-----|-----|
| $B$ | 000 | 000 | 000 | 101 | 000 | 000 | 000 | 000 |
| $C$ | 000 | 011 | 000 | 000 | 000 | 000 | 000 | 000 |
| $D$ | 000 | 100 | 000 | 000 | 000 | 000 | 000 | 000 |
| $E$ | 000 | 000 | 000 | 000 | 001 | 000 | 000 | 000 |
| $F$ | 000 | 010 | 000 | 000 | 000 | 000 | 000 | 000 |
| $R$ | 000 | 101 | 000 | 101 | 001 | 000 | 110 | 000 |

(a) One scheduling round of footprint scheduling with 3-bit footprint s.

| $A$ | 000 | 000 | 000 | 000 | 000 | 000 | 011 | 000 |
|-----|-----|-----|-----|-----|-----|-----|-----|-----|
| $B$ | 000 | 000 | 000 | 101 | 000 | 000 | 000 | 000 |
| $C$ | 000 | 100 | 000 | 000 | 000 | 000 | 000 | 000 |
| $D$ | 101 | 000 | 000 | 000 | 000 | 000 | 000 | 000 |
| $E$ | 000 | 000 | 000 | 000 | 010 | 000 | 000 | 000 |
| $F$ | 000 | 000 | 000 | 000 | 000 | 000 | 000 | 011 |
| $R$ | 101 | 100 | 000 | 101 | 010 | 000 | 011 | 011 |

(b) The state of the reservation vector after the second scheduling round of footprint scheduling.

Fig. 2. The result of two scheduling rounds in footprint scheduling

In Fig. 2a one can see that participants C, D and F try to reserve the same slot. All three of them can recognize the collision since their original footprint s are not in the result of this round.

**Scheduling Cycles and Message Cycles.** Using $B$ bits per slot in the reservation vector alone would simply blow up the reservation vector by a factor of $B$. This is where footprint scheduling applies a second modification to reservation maps, which allows to drastically reduce the size of $S$ (for example, to $S = 32$ for up to 10,000 participants). The idea is to iterate slot reservation through a *scheduling cycle* consisting of $R$ *scheduling rounds*. In the first round, each participant just attempts to reserve a slot as described above. In each subsequent round, the behavior depends on whether the participant detected a collision in "his" slot in the previous round. If not, he will reserve the same slot again with a fresh random footprint. If the participant detected a collision, he flips a coin to choose between two possible actions. If the coin is 1, the participant backs off and does not continue to attempt to reserve any slot during this scheduling cycle. If the coin is 0, he tosses another coin[1]. If that second coin is 1, he stays in his slot and reserves it again with a fresh random footprint. Otherwise he randomly picks one of the slots that were left empty in the previous round (i.e., the ones that produced a zero xor of all footprints) and places a fresh random footprint in the corresponding slot. If no such empty slot exists, he backs off for the rest of the scheduling cycle.

In the last round of a cycle, all participants that detected a collision in their slot in the second but last round, back off and do not attempt to reserve a slot in the last round. This leaves the corresponding slots empty in the very last round. When the schedule is then executed, all empty slots can be skipped as in plain reservation maps.

Let us return to the example. After the first round, participants A, B and E have successfully reserved slots 7, 4 and 5, respectively. Participants C, D and F

---

[1] Note that tweaking the bias of these coin tosses is necessary to reach peak performance in large networks. The pseudocode description of the algorithm in Appendix A shows optimal probabilities for cases where users are allowed to reserve multiple slots.

know that their reservation collided with reservation attempts by other participants. Slots 1, 3, 5 and 8 appear empty after the first round. Figure 2b demonstrates the reservation vector after the second round. Participants D and F have moved away from slot 2 to one of the empty slots, while participant C stayed in the first slot. Note that participants A, B and E placed a fresh footprint in the slots they successfully reserved during the first round. They will continue to generate new footprints each round to reveal undetected collisions in case they occurred in the previous rounds.

By the end of the scheduling cycle several users hold reservations of slots in the following *message cycle*. The actual transfer of user messages in DC-net happens during this cycle. A message cycle has a maximum of $S$ rounds, the maximum amount of slots users could reserve during the scheduling cycle.

**Combining Scheduling Cycles and Message Cycles.** The short length of a scheduling vector is advantageous since scheduling cycles and message cycles can now be combined to reduce latency in DC-net. For this, one has to have the number of scheduling rounds $R$ be equal to (or smaller than) the number of slots $S$ in the scheduling vector. Then the scheduling vector can be attached as a header to a message in the message cycle to agree on the schedule of the upcoming message cycle.

**Multiple Reservations.** The activity rate of the network participants (i.e. the percentage of users who want to send data) will depend on the application for which a DC-net is used; for an anonymous file sharing application, the activity rate might hit 100% regularly, while a chat application might have a much lower activity rate on average. The algorithm that we described up to this point is not well-suited for networks with a very low activity rate. If there are less than $S$ active participants, and each of them is allowed to reserve exactly one slot, then the remaining slots will be unused. This has two disadvantages: On the one hand, it limits the potential throughput of small, inactive networks. On the other hand, this leaks information about the number of actively sending participants in the network. If only 4 out of 16 slots are reserved at the end of a scheduling cycle, then it is very likely that there are exactly 4 actively sending participants.

Both disadvantages can be solved by allowing all participants to reserve up to $S$ slots. Thus, at the beginning of a scheduling cycle, each participant picks up to $S$ slots at random, and tries to individually reserve each of them, just as described above. It is important to note that different footprints have to be used for each slot.

A pseudocode description of footprint scheduling is given in Appendix A. It also shows the additional steps that have to be taken in order to allow participants to reserve multiple slots.

# 4   Benchmarks and Comparison

This section shows how to optimize the configuration of footprint scheduling, and compares its performance to the performance of other scheduling algorithms. In the first part of this section, we will very briefly inspect the performance of footprint scheduling for different configurations in order to find optimal parameters. After that, we will compare its performance to the performance of Pfitzmann's scheduling algorithm and to Chaum's map-reservation scheduling algorithm.

**Choice of Parameters.** There are three parameters that can be tweaked to minimize scheduling overhead: $B$, the number of bits per slot, $S$, the number of slots, and $R$, the number of scheduling rounds per scheduling cycle. The scheduling overhead is measured in terms of the amount of scheduling data that each participant has to send for each successful reservation that the network achieves. During one scheduling cycle, each participant will send $B \cdot S \cdot R$ bits of scheduling data. At the end of the cycle, there will be $\hat{S}$ successful reservations. Ideally, all $S$ slots were successfully reserved, so that $\hat{S} = S$. But $\hat{S}$ might also be smaller than $S$ if there were undiscovered collisions or unused slots in the schedule. Thus, the overhead $O$ can be measured by

$$O = \frac{S \cdot R \cdot B}{\hat{S}} \ .  \tag{1}$$

Our optimization is mostly based on this formula, and we use simulations to test how different configurations perform. Schedule convergence is an important metric for this optimization. A messaging *slot* has converged if there is at most one participant who tries to reserve this slot. A *schedule* has converged if all $S$ slots have converged. If a slot did not converge by the end of a scheduling cycle, then no participant can successfully send a message in that slot once the schedule is executed. It is thus crucial for the throughput of the algorithm that most of the slots converge.

We will start by minimizing $R \cdot B$. Figure 3 shows how many scheduling rounds are necessary to reach schedule convergence[2] for different values of $B$. Increasing $B$ leads to a decrease in $R$, but it is easy to see that $B \cdot R$ is minimal for $B = 2$, regardless of the choice of $S$. Changing the network size does not affect this outcome.

In the previous simulation, the number of participants was fixed. But in order to determine an optimal value for $R$ in general, we will now look at networks of various sizes. Figure 4 shows the number of scheduling rounds that are necessary to resolve all collisions for $B = 2$ bits and various values of $S$. The number of required rounds is clearly influenced by both, the network size and the number of slots. Although schedules converge faster on average when the number of slots is small, it is not recommended to choose $S < R$: Similar to Pfitzmann's scheduling

---

[2] Note that, while it is easy to detect in a simulation whether all collisions have been resolved, it is not trivial to detect this in practice.

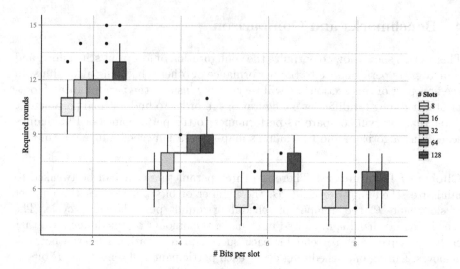

**Fig. 3.** The number of rounds that are necessary to resolve all collisions, for 5000 participants and different values of $B$ and $S$.

algorithm, each message in footprint scheduling depends on the content of the previous message. Therefore, the scheduling data needs to be sent in individual packages. For $B = 2, S = 16$, these packages will only hold 32 bits of data. When this data is sent over the Internet, then the TCP-IP header of at least 32 Byte will add a massive overhead. But if $S \geq R$, then the current message cycle and the scheduling cycle for the following schedule can be interleaved as described in Sect. 3. This will decrease the *relative* overhead of the TCP-IP header and network delay. For this reason, we choose $S = 32$, which requires far less than 32 scheduling rounds, so that scheduling and message data can be interleaved.

Next, we will inspect the relation between the network size and the number of scheduling rounds. The dashed blue line in Fig. 4 shows $log(N)$, with $N$ being the number of participants in the network. For $S = 32$, no more than $log(N)$ rounds are necessary on average for the schedule to converge. Thus, rather than having one fixed value for $R$, we can dynamically determine $R$ based on the current size of the network.

**Performance Comparison.** With this configuration, $S = 32, R = log(N)$, $B = 2$, we will now show how footprint scheduling performs compared to other scheduling algorithms. For this, we will show benchmark results for three scenarios: One with a very high activity rate, as it may occur for torrent downloads and video streaming, one with a very low activity rate, which could simulate instant-messaging, as well as two scenarios with intermediate activity rates.

We will compare the performance of footprint scheduling to the performance of Chaum's reservation map, as well as to the performance of Pfitzmann's collision resolution algorithm. We optimized the ratio between the number of participants and the number of slots for both algorithms using a series of

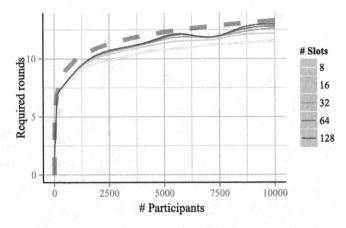

**Fig. 4.** The number of rounds that are necessary to resolve all collisions for various numbers of slots and networks of different sizes. These results were produced with 2 bit footprints.

simulations. We should note that the scheduling overhead of Chaum's reservation map depends heavily on the presence or absence of an estimation of the current activity rate. An abstract description of an algorithm that can be used to predict the activity rate is given in [9, pp. 10–11]. But especially in large networks where message cycles can take multiple minutes, the number of users might change drastically between two subsequent rounds. This makes it particularly difficult to predict the activity rate of the following cycle correctly. In our simulation, we measure the performance of Chaum's algorithm for the case that there is no estimation of the activity rate. Note that footprint scheduling is only configured based on the size of the network; it does not require an estimate of the number of active users. More details on the optimization process can be found in Appendix A in the full version of this paper.

Performance is measured in terms of *scheduling overhead*, as defined in the beginning of this section. Note that the size of the message itself is not taken into account in our simulations because the absolute overhead to reserve a slot is not affected by the message size. Also, while Pfitzmann's algorithm could be used to resolve collisions between actual messages, we implement it for the scheduling purposes, which is in general more efficient for reasonable message sizes.

Before presenting results of simulation, we demonstrate in Table 1 theoretical estimations of scheduling overhead according to the formulas given in Table 2 in Appendix C in the full version of this paper. These formulas are valid in case of no collisions, which means that after completion of the scheduling protocol all slots are reserved successfully. In such conditions footprint scheduling is advantageous in all considered network sizes. However, results of simulations show somewhat different picture, which we discuss below.

In our simulations we do not consider the number of participants in the network to be larger than 10, 000. Significantly larger networks are almost always impractical because the amount of message data that is produced by the entire network grows quadratically with the number of participants.

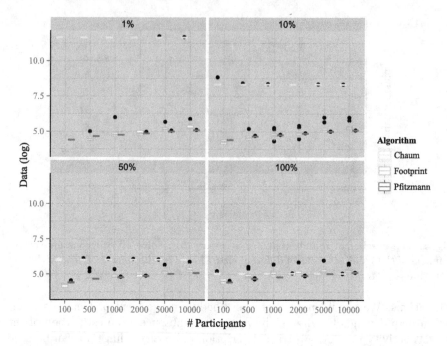

**Fig. 5.** The overhead of all three scheduling algorithm in networks with different activity rates.

Figure 5 shows the performance of the three scheduling algorithms in networks with different activity rates. The scheduling overhead of both, Pfitzmann's algorithm and footprint scheduling, scale with the activity rate of the network. The overhead of Chaum's reservation maps increases with a decrease in the network's activity rate, since the available slots cannot be used as efficiently. Chaum's algorithm does, however, offer the lowest scheduling overhead for large networks. In theory, Pfitzmann's algorithm offers a scheduling overhead in large, active networks that is similar to what Chaum's reservation maps achieves, but we will address in Sect. 6 why Pfitzmann's algorithm is not practical in large networks.

In a network where the activity rate and the network size do not change drastically, the scheduling overhead can be minimized by choosing either Chaum's reservation maps or Pfitzmann's algorithm, depending on the exact characteristics of the network.

However, in a dynamic network where network size and activity rate change over time, footprint scheduling gives a better overall performance: While the activity rate is low, the network can benefit from the reduced scheduling overhead that footprint scheduling offers. In large networks and in networks with a very high activity rate, footprint scheduling still adds a slight increase in the scheduling overhead, compared to Chaum's reservation maps.

**Table 1.** Average scheduling overhead in Bytes (based on the formulas given in Table 2 in Appendix C in the full version of this paper).

| Algorithm | Participants | | | | | | |
|---|---|---|---|---|---|---|---|
| | 100 | 200 | 500 | 1000 | 2000 | 5000 | 10,000 |
| Footprint ($B = 2$) | 13.29 | 15.29 | 17.93 | 19.93 | 21.93 | 24.58 | 26.58 |
| Pfitzmann | 24.93 | 27.93 | 31.9 | 34.9 | 37.9 | 41.86 | 44.86 |
| Herbivore/Chaum ($A = 1\%$) | 3200 | 3200 | 3200 | 3200 | 3200 | 3200 | 3200 |
| Herbivore/Chaum ($A = 10\%$) | 320 | 320 | 320 | 320 | 320 | 320 | 320 |
| Herbivore/Chaum ($A = 50\%$) | 64 | 64 | 64 | 64 | 64 | 64 | 64 |
| Herbivore/Chaum ($A = 100\%$) | 32 | 32 | 32 | 32 | 32 | 32 | 32 |

## 5 Disruptions and footprint Scheduling

Recall that disruptions are collisions that are intentionally induced by a denial-of-service attacker or a participant who attempts to increase his transmission bandwidth on the cost of the bandwidth of other participants. In this section we briefly describe a possible protection against an attacker who attempts to disrupt the scheduling phase of footprint scheduling.

The literature describes two approaches to cope with disruption in DC-net. The first approach is to open up special meaningless (*trap*) messages of participants after (suspected) disruption [1,3,21] and thus reveal which participants did not behave according to the protocol. The second approach is to use zero-knowledge proofs [5,6,8,10]. Our technique follows the first approach since it does not require any of the two computationally-secure variants of DC-net introduced in [10]. Additionally, scheduling messages can be opened without compromising anonymity of participants. This holds if the opened schedule is afterwards discarded and if the sending rates are constant, so sending wishes of a particular participant cannot be learned. One of the ways to achieve constant sending rates is to let users regularly reserve slots for dummy messages. Dummy messages in turn can be used as traps to protect message phase from disruption.

The idea is to use a PRNG with a secret seed for all randomness that is required for footprint scheduling (i.e., slot positions, footprints and random choice to stay in a slot or back off). To prevent cheating, users are obliged to commit to the seed. Note that this is an obvious choice also for efficiency reasons. To protect against disrupters, each participant uses a new random seed for every scheduling cycle and commits to this seed before scheduling.

Whenever the decision is made to open a scheduling cycle, each participant publishes the seed used for this cycle. These seeds are checked against the commitments and then the scheduling vectors of each round are recomputed and compared with the scheduling vectors that were previously obtained from the DC-net output. Note, keys and messages output by each individual participant are not opened and verified at this stage. If these recomputed scheduling vectors match, all participants followed the rules. If not, at least one of the participants did not follow the protocol. In order to find the disrupter, all participants reveal their keys used in the scheduling phase. To prevent disrupters from wrongly accusing honest participants by revealing an incorrect key, one can enforce that participants also commit to those shared keys in advance.

Such a technique provides performance improvements when the scheduling algorithm has a certain chance of undetected collisions (Footprint, Herbivore) for the following reason. Undetected collisions during the scheduling cycle lead to collisions during the message cycle. How can one efficiently distinguish an honest collision of messages due to such a problem and a disruption? Traps (non-meaningful messages that can be opened with no harm to anonymity) will not be helpful to answer this question for every single case of messages colliding. Opening of keys and rounds is too costly for such a check, ideally one would want to apply heavy methods only if it is known that there is a disrupter. Our method allows to perform a quick and efficient check if there was a disruption or not by opening only seeds used for generating footprints, and only after that decide if to open the scheduling cycle, which involves opening keys shared between users and verifying if individual outputs were made correctly.

## 6   Advantages of footprint Scheduling

In this section, we provide a detailed description of the main advantages of the footprint algorithm.

As mentioned earlier, footprint scheduling inherits from the reservation-map algorithm. In particular, footprint scheduling involves no computational overhead for participants. The algorithm improves on reservation maps by reducing the probability of undetected collisions in the reservation vector. In networks with very high activity rate the cost for this improvement can be a very slight increase in scheduling overhead, depending on how many undetected collisions the reservation-map algorithm accepts. If message collisions are prohibitive or if the network does not have a very high activity rate, footprint scheduling noticeably *reduces* the scheduling overhead compared to reservation maps. For details see Sect. 4.

Further, unlike superposed receiving and MPC-based scheduling protocols, footprint scheduling naturally handles events of participants joining or leaving the DC-net during the schedule negotiation. When a participant disconnects, his reservation slot will appear free in the next round. Any participant that is in the process of resolving a collision can now move to this slot. Thus, footprint scheduling re-allocates slots that become available, even in the middle of a schedule cycle. At the same time footprint keeps scheduling and message cycles short, which permits fast joining to the network. That in turn improves anonymity, allowing potentially a bigger anonymity set in the new cycle.

When using Chaum's reservation map, a good estimate of the network's activity rate is necessary in order to optimize the scheduling overhead (for details, see Sect. 4). With footprint scheduling, the success chance of a reservation attempt automatically increases if fewer participants bid for a slot in the next message cycle. Senders will be able to reserve a slot in fewer attempts if the activity of other participants goes down, and it will take more attempts if other participants become more active. This makes it unnecessary to estimate the activity rate.

Just like Pfitzmann's scheduling algorithm, footprint scheduling is an interactive protocol, in the sense that each message in the protocol depends on the content of the previous one. For Pfitzmann's algorithm, the protocol is completed after $A$ successive messages, where $A$ is the number of active network participants. In the case of footprint scheduling, the protocol is completed after $S$ successive messages, where $S \ll A$ for large networks, as we showed in Sect. 4. In practice, network latency alone can be a major obstacle to complete a protocol of $A$ messages in a large network. The following example shows a best-case scenario for a network with 10,000 active participants: Assume that all participants live in major US cities. In this case, the average latency between them will be about 33 ms on average at the time of this writing[3]. Thus, there will be a delay of at least 66 ms between each message. With 10,000 active participants, this means that the protocol is completed after $10,000 \cdot 66\,\text{ms} = 660\,\text{s} = 11\,\text{min}$.

Recall that Pfitzmann's scheduling protocol cannot be completed if a participant leaves before the protocol is completed. It is impractical to demand that not a single participant must leave the network over a period of 11 min, especially when some participants are connected via personal mobile devices like a phone or a laptop. Footprint scheduling does not suffer from this problem since each protocol run is completed much faster, but also since the protocol can be completed even if users disconnect from the network.

Footprint scheduling is also advantageous due to the fact that it hides the number of actively sending users in the network from an eavesdropping adversary. Such information can serve as a marker of upcoming social events; for example, the Tor network showed largely increased activity just before the Arab Spring[4].

One of the advantages of DC-net over Mix-nets (and onion routing) is that it hides the number of actively sending users due to the fact that all the users have to contribute to the network in order to facilitate anonymous sending. Unfortunately, previous efficient scheduling protocols either allow to estimate the number of active users by counting the number of empty slots in the scheduling messages, or they require to know the number of active users to operate.

Footprint scheduling disguises the number of active users as long as each user is allowed to reserve multiple slots. Even very small networks, the number of free slots does not give away the number of active users. An internal observer can gain a rough estimate of the number of active users over a longer period, based on the number of collisions that they experience. However, for an external observer, it is impossible to determine reliably whether there is a collision in any of the slots, since footprints change with every round. Further, for an external observer it is impossible to estimate if there were collisions in any of the slots since footprints change from round to round even if there were no collisions. In footprint scheduling the number of slots as well as discussion rounds does not change with the number of active users. Altogether, this prevents estimation of actively sending participants if footprint scheduling is used.

---

[3] http://ipnetwork.bgtmo.ip.att.net/pws/network_delay.html.

[4] http://www.monitor.upeace.org/innerpg.cfm?id_article=816.

Last but not least, footprint scheduling has an advantage over other map reservation protocols due to fast and efficient method of verifying if a collision in message cycle was caused by an undetected collision in scheduling cycle or by a disruption. For details, see Sect. 5.

## A    Pseudocode Description of footprint Scheduling

---

**Algorithm 1.** Footprint scheduling from the perspective of one participant $A$

---

**Parameters:** Number of footprint bits $B$, number of participants $N$, number of slots $S$ per message cycle

**Output:** A vector $D \in \{0,1\}^S$, indicating for each slot whether it can be used for sending.

$R \leftarrow \log(N)$
$D \leftarrow \{1\}^S$                                      ▷ Vector indicating which slots can be used for sending
$f \leftarrow \{0,1\}^B \setminus \{0\}^B$                              ▷ Set of possible footprints
$F \leftarrow_R f^S$                                         ▷ Vector holding footprints for each slot
$V \leftarrow \text{SLOTRESERVE}(D, F)$                  ▷ First round of the scheduling cycle
**for** $i$ from 1 to $R - 2$ **do**                              ▷ Rounds 1 to $R - 2$
  **for** $j$ from 0 to $s - 1$ **do**
    **if** $D[j] = 0$ **then**
      **continue**
    **end if**
    **if** $V[j] \neq F[j]$ **then**                              ▷ Reservation attempt failed
      $c_1 \leftarrow_R [0,1)$                           ▷ Biased coin toss
      **if** $c_1 < 0.7$ **then**
        $D[j] \leftarrow 0$                           ▷ Back off
      **else**
        $c_2 \leftarrow_R \{0,1\}$
        **if** $c_2 = 1$ **then**                           ▷ Try same slot again
        **else**                                         ▷ Empty slot available?
          $I \leftarrow \{s' | D[s'] = 0 \text{ and } V[s'] = 0\}$
          $D[j] \leftarrow 0$
          **if** $I \neq \emptyset$ **then**                      ▷ Pick empty slot
            $s' \leftarrow_R I$
            $D[s'] \leftarrow 1$
          **end if**
        **end if**
      **end if**
    **end if**
  **end for**                                         ▷ Generate new footprints
  $F \leftarrow_R f^S$
  $V \leftarrow \text{SLOTRESERVE}(D, F)$
**end for**
**for** $j$ from 0 to $s - 1$ **do**                              ▷ Last round
  **if** $V[j] \neq F[j]$ **then**
    $D[j] \leftarrow 0$
  **end if**
**end for**
$F \leftarrow_R f^S$
$\text{SLOTRESERVE}(D, F)$
**return** $D$

---

**Algorithm 2.** Procedure for a slot-reservation attempt in footprint scheduling

**procedure** SLOTRESERVE($D, F$)
  $V_A \leftarrow \{\{0\}^B\}^s$
  **for** $i$ from 0 to $s - 1$ **do**
    **if** $D[i] = 1$ **then** $V_A[i] \leftarrow F[i]$
    **end if**
  **end for**
  Broadcast $V_A$ through DC-net
  Receive $V$ (xor of all individual scheduling vectors) from DC-net
  **return** $V$
**end procedure**

# References

1. Bos, J., Boer, B.: Detection of disrupters in the DC protocol. In: Quisquater, J.-J., Vandewalle, J. (eds.) EUROCRYPT 1989. LNCS, vol. 434, pp. 320–327. Springer, Heidelberg (1990). doi:10.1007/3-540-46885-4_33
2. Capetanakis, J.I.: Tree algorithms for packet broadcast channels. IEEE Trans. Inf. Theory **IT-25**(5), 505–515 (1979)
3. Chaum, D.: The dining cryptographers problem: unconditional sender and recipient untraceability. J. Cryptol. **1**(1), 65–75 (1988). http://www.cs.ucsb.edu/~ravenben/classes/595n-s07/papers/dcnet-jcrypt88.pdf
4. Chaum, D.L.: Untraceable electronic mail, return addresses, and digital pseudonyms. Commun. ACM **24**(2), 84–90 (1981). www.freehaven.net/anonbib/cache/chaum-mix.pdf
5. Corrigan-Gibbs, H., Ford, B.: Dissent: accountable anonymous group messaging. In: Proceedings of the 17th ACM Conference on Computer and Communications Security, pp. 340–350. ACM (2010). http://dedis.cs.yale.edu/dissent/papers/ccs10/dissent.pdf
6. Corrigan-Gibbs, H., Wolinsky, D.I., Ford, B.: Proactively accountable anonymous messaging in verdict. In: Proceedings of the 22nd USENIX Conference on Security, pp. 147–162. USENIX Association (2013). http://dedis.cs.yale.edu/dissent/papers/verdict.pdf
7. Franck, C.: New directions for dining cryptographers. Master's thesis, University of Luxembourg (2008). http://secan-lab.uni.lu/images/stories/christian_franck/FRANCK_Christian_Master_Thesis.pdf
8. Franck, C.: Dining cryptographers with 0.924 verifiable collision resolution (2014). http://arxiv.org/abs/1402.1732
9. Goel, S., Robson, M., Polte, M., Sirer, E.G.: Herbivore: a scalable and efficient protocol for anonymous communication. Technical report 2003-1890, Cornell University (2003). http://www.cs.cornell.edu/People/egs/papers/herbivore-tr.pdf
10. Golle, P., Juels, A.: Dining cryptographers revisited. In: Cachin, C., Camenisch, J.L. (eds.) EUROCRYPT 2004. LNCS, vol. 3027, pp. 456–473. Springer, Heidelberg (2004). doi:10.1007/978-3-540-24676-3_27
11. Murdoch, S.J., Danezis, G.: Low-cost traffic analysis of Tor. In: 2005 IEEE Symposium on Security and Privacy, pp. 183–195. IEEE (2005). https://www.cl.cam.ac.uk/~sjm217/papers/oakland05torta.pdf

12. Pfitzmann, A.: How to implement ISDNs without user observability - Some remarks. Technical report, Department of Computer Science, University of Karlsruhe. Internal report 14/85 (1985)

13. Pfitzmann, A.: Diensteintegrierende Kommunikationsnetze mit teilnehmerüberprüfbarem Datenschutz. Ph.D. thesis, Fakultät für Informatik, Universität Karlsruhe (1990). http://dud.inf.tu-dresden.de/sirene/publ/Pfit_88_0.pdf, http://dud.inf.tu-dresden.de/sirene/publ/Pfit_88_1.pdf, http://dud.inf.tu-dresden.de/sirene/publ/Pfit_88_2.pdf, http://dud.inf.tu-dresden.de/sirene/publ/Pfit_88_3.pdf, http://dud.inf.tu-dresden.de/sirene/publ/Pfit_88_4.pdf, http://dud.inf.tu-dresden.de/sirene/publ/Pfit_88_5.pdf, http://dud.inf.tu-dresden.de/sirene/publ/Pfit_88_6.pdf

14. Roberts, L.G.: Aloha packet system with and without slots and capture. SIGCOMM Comput. Commun. Rev. 5(2), 28–42 (1975). www.freehaven.net/anonbib/cache/chaum-mix.pdf

15. Studholme, C., Blake, I.: Multiparty computation to generate secret permutations. IACR Cryptology ePrint Archive: Report 2007/353 (2007). http://eprint.iacr.org/2007/353

16. Syverson, P.F., Goldschlag, D.M., Reed, M.G.: Anonymous connections and onion routing. In: 1997 IEEE Symposium on Security and Privacy, pp. 44–54. IEEE (1997). www.onion-router.net/Publications/SSP-1997.pdf

17. Tor project: Anonymity online. https://www.torproject.org/. Accessed 17 Mar 2015

18. Tsybakov, B.S., Mikhailov, V.A.: Free synchronous packet access in a broadcast channel with feedback. Probl. Peredachi Informatsii 14(4), 32–59 (1978). http://www.mathnet.ru/php/getFT.phtml?jrnid=ppi&paperid=1558&what=fullt&option_lang=eng. (in Russian)

19. Waidner, M.: Unconditional sender and recipient untraceability in spite of active attacks. In: Quisquater, J.-J., Vandewalle, J. (eds.) EUROCRYPT 1989. LNCS, vol. 434, pp. 302–319. Springer, Heidelberg (1990). doi:10.1007/3-540-46885-4_32

20. Waidner, M., Pfitzmann, B.: The dining cryptographers in the disco: unconditional sender and recipient untraceability with computationally secure serviceability. In: Quisquater, J.-J., Vandewalle, J. (eds.) EUROCRYPT 1989. LNCS, vol. 434, pp. 690–690. Springer, Heidelberg (1990). doi:10.1007/3-540-46885-4_69

21. Waidner, M., Pfitzmann, B.: The dining cryptographers in the disco: unconditional sender and recipient untraceability with computationally secure serviceability. Technical report, Universität Karlsruhe (1998). See also abstract [20]. http://citeseerx.ist.psu.edu/viewdoc/download?doi=10.1.1.74.218&rep=rep1&type=pdf

22. Wolinsky, D.I., Corrigan-Gibbs, H., Ford, B., Johnson, A.: Dissent in numbers: making strong anonymity scale. In: Proceedings of the 10th USENIX Conference on Operating Systems Design and Implementation, pp. 179–192. USENIX Association (2012). http://dedis.cs.yale.edu/dissent/papers/osdi12.pdf

# Web Security and Data Privacy

# How Anywhere Computing Just Killed Your Phone-Based Two-Factor Authentication

Radhesh Krishnan Konoth$^{(\boxtimes)}$, Victor van der Veen, and Herbert Bos

Vrije Universiteit, Amsterdam, The Netherlands
r.k.konoth@vu.nl, {vvdveen,herbertb}@cs.vu.nl

**Abstract.** Exponential growth in smartphone usage combined with recent advances in mobile technology is causing a shift in (mobile) app behavior: application vendors no longer restrict their apps to a single platform, but rather add synchronization options that allow users to conveniently switch from mobile to PC or vice versa in order to access their services. This process of integrating apps among multiple platforms essentially removes the gap between them. Current, state of the art, mobile phone-based two-factor authentication (2FA) mechanisms, however, heavily rely on the existence of such separation. They are used in a variety of segments (such as consumer online banking services or enterprise secure remote access) to protect against malware. For example, with 2FA in place, attackers should no longer be able to use their PC-based malware to instantiate fraudulent banking transactions.

In this paper, we analyze the security implications of diminishing gaps between platforms and show that the ongoing integration and desire for increased usability results in violation of key principles for mobile phone 2FA. As a result, we identify a new class of vulnerabilities dubbed *2FA synchronization vulnerabilities*. To support our findings, we present practical attacks against Android and iOS that illustrate how a Man-in-the-Browser attack can be elevated to intercept One-Time Passwords sent to the mobile phone and thus bypass the chain of 2FA mechanisms as used by many financial services.

**Keywords:** Two-Factor Authentication · Smartphone security · Financial trojans · Synchronization · Anywhere computing

## 1 Introduction

Approaching an impressive 1.25 billion sales in 2014 with an expected audience of over 1.75 billion, smartphones have become an important factor in many people's day-to-day life [17,35]. Daily activities performed on these mobile devices include those that can be done on PC as well: accessing e-mail, searching the web, social networking, or listening to music [19]. To enhance usability, both application developers and platform vendors are making an effort to blur boundaries

---

R.K. Konoth and V. van der Veen—Equal contribution joint first authors.

J. Grossklags and B. Preneel (Eds.): FC 2016, LNCS 9603, pp. 405–421, 2017.
DOI: 10.1007/978-3-662-54970-4_24

between the two platforms. This is reflected in synchronization features like Firefox Sync and Samsung SideSync or sophisticated market places like Google Play and Microsoft's Windows Store that allow users to manage their mobile phone remotely.

A second important trend in web computing is the increasing number of applications that provide the possibility to harden user accounts by enabling *2 Factor Authentication* (2FA) for them. 2FA is a form of multi-factor authentication and provides unambiguous identification of users by means of the combination of two different components, i.e., something the user *knows* (PIN code, password) and something the user *possesses* (bank card, USB stick token). With 2FA enabled, if attackers steal a user's password, they still require access to the second component before they can impersonate the victim.

Not surprisingly, software vendors often embody the second component of 2FA in the form of a mobile phone. To authenticate, the web application sends a one-time-valid, dynamic passcode to the user's mobile phone (for instance via SMS, e-mail, or a dedicated application), which must then be entered along with the user's credentials in order to complete the authentication. Since users usually carry their phone all the time, *Mobile Phone 2FA* does not introduce additional costs and can be implemented relatively easy. Examples of well-known companies that provide mobile phone 2FA include Amazon, Apple, Dropbox, Google, Microsoft, Twitter, Yahoo, and many more, including a large number of financial institutions[1]. The latter is represented by many of the biggest financial organisations in the world such as Bank of America, Wells Fargo, JP Morgan Chan, ICBC in China, and ING in The Netherlands.

In this paper, we analyze the security implications of *Anywhere Computing* and show that seamless platform integration comes at the cost of weakening the (commonly perceived) strong mobile phone 2FA mechanism. We define a new class of vulnerabilities dubbed *2FA synchronization vulnerabilities* and show how these can be exploited by an attacker. In particular, we present reliable attacks against both Android and iOS, two platforms that represent a combined market share of over 90% [6]. Our threat model is the same as that of 2FA: we assume that a victim's PC has been compromised, allowing an attacker to perform Man-in-the-Browser (MitB) attacks. In this scenario, mobile phone 2FA should guarantee that the attacker cannot perform authorized operations without having also access to the user's phone. By exploiting certain 2FA synchronization vulnerabilities, however, we show that mobile phone 2FA as used by many online services for secure authentication, including financial institutions, can be easily bypassed.

In more detail, our first attack utilizes Google Play's remote app installation feature to install a specifically crafted *vulnerable* app onto registered Android devices of the victim which is then silently activated and used to hijack One-Time Passwords (OTPs). Our iOS attack, on the other hand, exploits a new OS X feature that enables the synchronization of SMS messages between iPhone and Mac.

---

[1] http://twofactorauth.org.

Although the security of 2FA implementations has been subject of prior work [16], we believe that our work is the first to address weaknesses relating to ongoing synchronization and usability enhancement efforts.

**Contributions.** In summary, our contributions are the following:

1. We identify a new class of vulnerabilities, *2FA synchronization vulnerabilities*, that weaken the security guarantees of mobile phone 2FA.
2. We present practical attacks against Android and iOS that exploit multiple 2FA synchronization vulnerabilities and show how these can be used to successfully bypass mobile phone 2FA.
3. We discuss the security implications of our findings and provide recommendations for various stakeholders. Based on our findings, we conclude that SMS-based 2FA should be considered unsafe.

The remainder of this paper is organized as follows. In Sect. 2, we outline current efforts deployed by vendors that ease platform integration and provide a definition of *2FA synchronization vulnerabilities*. Section 3 details our attacks against Android and iOS which can be used to bypass mobile phone 2FA. We discuss security implications and recommendations in Sect. 4, followed by a related work study on the evolution of Man-in-the-Browser attacks and 2FA in Sect. 5. We conclude in Sect. 6.

## 2  Synchronization

To maximize connectivity and to ensure that users never miss another status update, vendors continuously come up with ways to close the gap between PC and mobile devices. In this section, we separate these integration techniques into two categories: (i) remote services as provided by mobile operating system vendors and (ii) integration of applications across the different platforms using synchronization features. Finally, we define *2FA synchronization vulnerabilities* in detail and show example vulnerabilities that we later use to break mobile phone 2FA.

### 2.1  Remote Services

Mobile operating system market leader Google provides a *remote install* service in its Play Store that allows users to install Android applications on any of their phones or tablets, from a desktop computer. The process is painless and straightforward: a user (i) logs into the Google Play store, (ii) picks an app of his interest, (iii) hits the *install* button, (iv) accepts the app's permissions, (v) chooses the device on which this app should be installed, and (vi) confirms installation. The app is now automatically pushed and installed onto the selected phone—as soon as it has connectivity. Since all the app's permissions are requested and confirmed in the browser already, the only trace left on the phone is a *<app name>*

*successfully installed* notification message. Similar features have been deployed in app stores of both Microsoft (Windows Phone) and Apple (iOS).

Naturally, platform vendors have adopted security policies to prevent exploitation of this feature. Focussing on Android, for example, Google, deployed two: (i) silent remote install only works for apps on Google Play, which is actively monitored for malware by Google Bouncer; and (ii) newly installed apps default to a *deactivated* state which means that even if the app defines specific event receivers (e.g., on BOOT_COMPLETED to start a service at boot-time, or SMS_RECEIVED to listen for incoming SMS text messages), it cannot use these until the app is explicitly activated by the user. Activation is triggered by starting the app for a first time, either by selecting it from the launcher or by sending it an intent from another app (e.g., by opening a link from the mobile browser) [1].

In addition to remote install, platform vendors also provide features that help users in locating or wiping a lost device [2,5,7].

## 2.2  App Synchronization

Besides remote *services*, developers try to increase usability even further by incorporating cross-platform synchronization features in their *applications*. This is best illustrated by looking at recent changes in browsers. Browsers once were self-contained software pieces that ran on a single device. Popular browsers like Google Chrome or Mozilla Firefox, however, nowadays offer integrated synchronization services. By using these features, users no longer have to configure browsers individually, but can automatically synchronize all their saved passwords, bookmarks, open tabs, browser history and settings across multiple devices [4,8]. It is expected that Microsoft's Edge introduces similar functionality soon [32].

Another example of application synchronization is Apple's Continuity which features, among others, synchronization of SMS text messages between iOS (8.1 and up) and Mac OS X (10.10 Yosemite and later): "with Continuity, all the SMS and MMS text messages you send and receive on your iPhone also appear on your Mac, iPad, and iPod touch" [9].

## 2.3  2FA Synchronization Vulnerabilities

Given the ongoing efforts by both platform vendors and application developers to bridge the gap between the end-user's desktop and his or her mobile devices, we identify a new class of vulnerabilities that, while increasing usability, jeopardize 2FA security guarantees.

**Definition.** *A 2FA synchronization vulnerability is a usability feature that deliberately blurs the boundaries between devices, but, potentially combined with other vulnerabilities, inadvertently weakens the security guarantees of 2FA.*

As an example, consider the previously discussed remote app installation feature: a clear product of a design decision aiming to enhance usability. Although such option successfully improves usability indeed—users can conveniently manage their mobile device from their browser—it comes with an obvious security risk: if attackers manage to get control over a user's browser, they can extend control to the user's mobile devices as well by pushing arbitrary apps to them. We thus identify the remote install feature as a 2FA synchronization vulnerability.

Focussing again on Android, Google's deployed security measures make that without additional vulnerabilities, attackers cannot abuse this synchronization vulnerability alone to bypass mobile phone 2FA. Finding such vulnerabilities is easy though. First, fundamental weaknesses in Google Bouncer expose multiple ways to bypass malware detection, giving attackers a sufficient time window to push malicious apps to Google Play and thus to mobile devices. Second, we identify numerous ways to activate apps after installation, either by exploiting end-users' curiosity (*hey, what is this app?*) or by relying on additional synchronization vulnerabilities, for example in browser apps: previously discussed features can be used by an attacker to synchronize malicious bookmarks or browser tabs that, when opened on the mobile device, can activate deactive apps.

A second attack exploits the clear 2FA synchronization vulnerability introduced in recent Mac OS X releases. If Continuity is enabled, there is no need for attackers to control a victim's phone: they can read SMS messages from an infected Mac directly.

It is important to realize that 2FA synchronization vulnerabilities are not necessarily caused by bad developer habits or configuration mistakes. More often, they will be the result of a design decision-making process. This means that it is much harder to convince vendors of their mistakes: a 2FA synchronization vulnerability does not leak data or enable code execution, but must be considered within the mobile phone 2FA threat model before it becomes a threat.

## 3   Exploiting 2FA Synchronization Vulnerabilities

By exploiting the synchronization vulnerabilities discussed in Sect. 2, we can construct attacks that break mobile phone 2FA. In this section, we present practical implementations of such attacks against the two major mobile operating systems: Google Android and Apple iOS. Additionally, we show that synchronization vulnerabilities also imperil mobile phone 2FA implementations that use a dedicated app to transfer the OTP.

Our attacks operate on the basic threat model of 2FA: we assume that the attacker already has control over the victim's PC, possibly including a MitB, and is specifically interested in bypassing mobile phone 2FA.

### 3.1   Android

The intention of our Android attack is to exploit the remote install feature of Google Play to push a malicious app onto the user's mobile device. This app can then intercept and forward OTPs sent as SMS messages to a server that is controlled by the attacker. Given that the attackers have control over the user credentials (stolen by the MitB), this gives them sufficient means to bypass 2FA.

Google's deployed mitigation techniques slightly complicate our scenario. In order to successfully break 2FA, we need to address two defenses: (i) we need to bypass Google Bouncer before we can publish our SMS stealing app in Google Play, and (ii) we need the user to activate the app before it can intercept and forward SMS messages.

**Bypassing Google Bouncer.** Since Google's remote install feature only allows app installation from trusted sources, attackers first need to get an SMS stealing app published in Google Play. For this, they need to bypass Bouncer, Google's automated malware analysis tool that uses both static and dynamic analysis to identify malicious behavior [26]. Once an application is uploaded to Google Play, Bouncer starts analyzing it for known malware, spyware and trojans.

Although the inner workings of Bouncer are kept confidential, prior work has shown that it is easily circumvented [29,30]. This is confirmed by a recent case study where Avast identified a number of popular Play Store apps that had over a million downloads to be in fact malware [15].

Orthogonal to recent work, our approach to trick Bouncer into accepting rogue apps is publishing a *vulnerable* application [36]. By pushing a poorly coded WebView application, for example, attackers no longer have to hide malicious code from Bouncer, but can simply move it to a web server that will be contacted by the app to display regular data [28]. An alternative, even harder to detect scheme, involves exposing a backdoor in native code via a memory corruption vulnerability [11].

To show the practicality of our attack, we successfully published an SMS 'backup' app in Google Play. Upon SMS reception, our app first writes the message content to a file, followed by loading a remote webpage inside a hidden webview component. The prepared webview component, however, is made vulnerable by exposing a ProcessBuilder class via the addJavascriptInterface API. This allows the remote webpage to execute arbitrary commands within the app's context using JavaScript.

Removing malicious code from the app makes it undetectable for Google Bouncer's static analysis. To also hide from dynamic analysis, we construct the remote webpage in such a way that it does not serve malicious commands when the incoming connection is made from a Google machine. In practice, to avoid accidental misuse, we instructed the webpage to only serve malicious code if accessed from an IP address that is under our control.

**App Activation.** Once installed, Android puts new apps in a *deactivated* state. While deactivated, an app will not run for any reason, except after (i) a manual launch of its main activity via the launcher, or (ii) an explicit intent from another app (e.g., a clicked link from the mobile browser) [22]. Attackers must thus somehow steer their victim into starting the app manually. We identify two reliable approaches to achieve this.

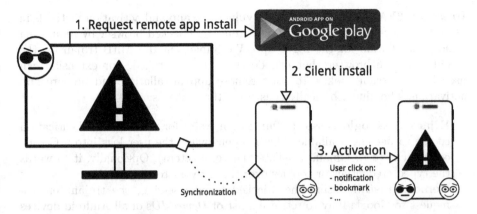

**Fig. 1.** Malicious app installation process. Attackers (i) use their deployed MitB to request the installation of a vulnerable app, stored in Google Play, and replace all the browser's bookmarks with malicious variants. Google then (ii) pushes the app onto the mobile phone of the victim. Finally (iii) the user is steered into activating the app. Activation is achieved by exploiting browser *synchronization* features to synchronize the malicious bookmarks to the phone, or by exploiting the user's curiosity (a click on the *app is installed* notification message).

1. The most naive method is to hide the malicious activity inside an attractive container. By using a challenging or even provocative app name or icon, a user may be tempted into opening the app manually, simply out of curiosity.
2. Armed with both synchronization vulnerabilities and the victim's Google credentials obtained by the MitB, an attacker can manipulate saved bookmarks, recent tabs, or URLs used in e-mail, cloud documents, social media, etcetera, in such a way that, when clicked, they redirect to a malicious webpage. This page, controlled by the attacker, can then send the aforementioned intent to activate the malicious app.

To prevent a user from detecting the rogue app after it has been activated, we complement it with stealth features. Strictly abiding to the Android developers guidelines, we constructed our app in such a way that, once activated, it removes it's main icon from the launcher. Additionally, we use a name masquerading technique to maximize discretion: (i) the app name shown in the notification bar is different from (ii) the name of the app as found in the launcher, which in its turn differs from (iii) the official app name as shown in the *app overview* (accessible from the settings view). This works because (i) during app submission, the Google Developers Console does not check whether the provided app name matches the official app name as found in the uploaded .apk, and (ii) the <activity-alias> tag inside the app's manifest allows us to declare additional activity names.

The process of installing a vulnerable app and activating it is shown in Fig. 1. The stealthy installation via bookmarks (or recent tabs or some other object of synchronization) combined with name obfuscation makes it hard to tell that an app is malicious, even for experienced users.

**Breaking 2FA.** With the malicious/vulnerable app and activation methods in place, attackers can start their attack from the hijacked browser by requesting remote installation for the rogue app. We implemented a MitB trojan for the Google Chrome browser that can do this. Once installed, our extension can use Google session cookies to start remote app installation and prepare app activation. The plugin basically consists of three phases:

1. **Hijack a Google session.** Our plugin waits for a Google authentication cookie to become available. This happens when the user logs into a Google component (e.g., Gmail, YouTube, Drive, etcetera). Optionally, it forwards the typed credentials or cookies over the network to the attacker.

2. **Remote install.** Using the hijacked Google session, the trojan sends a request to Google Play to retrieve a list of *Device ID*s of all Android devices linked to this particular Google account. Next, for each device, the plugin requests remote installation of the vulnerable app. Since app permissions are approved from within the PC-based browser only, the app will be silently installed, leaving only a *<app name> successfully installed* installation notification on the device.

3. **Activation.** In order to allow app activation, our extension rewrites all stored bookmarks and recent tabs so that they point to an attacker-controlled page while the original URL is provided as parameter: `http://mal.icio.us/proxy.php?url=<original_url>`. When opened using the mobile Chrome browser, this page performs a redirect to `rogueapp://<original_url>` which triggers activation of the rogue app. The app then immediately fires another intent that redirects the mobile browser to `<orignal_url>`, leaving practically no footprint.

Once activated, the malicious app can be used in conjunction with the PC-based trojan to successfully bypass mobile phone 2FA. Fraudulent financial

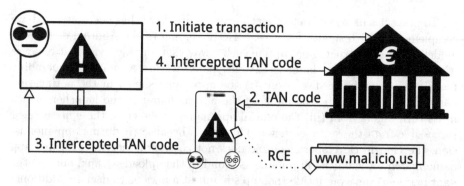

**Fig. 2.** Completing fraudulent transactions while bypassing 2FA. After our app processes the TAN code, it loads a remote webpage into a `WebView` component that allows the attacker to perform Remote Code Execution (RCE). This way, attackers can hide their malicious activity from Google Play.

transactions, for example, can be initiated by attackers once their PC-based trojan has captured banking credentials of their victims. To confirm such transaction, the mobile component intercepts the OTP sent via SMS, and forwards it to the attacker. This attack scenario is depicted in Fig. 2.

### 3.2  iOS

Similar to our Android attack, mobile phone 2FA on the iOS platform can be bypassed by publishing a rogue app to Apple's App Store and installing it from an infected PC via the iTunes remote-install feature. Wang et. al., already demonstrated how a vulnerable app could slip through Apple's strict review process and how such app can be used to access private APIs reserved for system apps to read SMS messages [3,36]. Additionally, Bosman and Bos showed how a vulnerable app and *sigreturn oriented programming* allow to execute any set of system calls needed to pull of any attack [11].

As of iOS 8.3, released in April 2015, however, it is no longer possible to receive a so-called `kCTMessageReceivedNotification` to let an app act on incoming text messages without using a specific entitlement (similar to the Android `RECEIVE_SMS` permission). Since this functionality stems from a so-called private API, requesting such permission violates the App Store Review Guidelines and will result in an app rejection, effectively breaking this type of attack. The recent release of Mac Os X 10.10 Yosemite, however, opens up a new attack scenario.

As outlined in Sect. 2, Mac OS X Continuity features options to synchronize SMS and MMS text messages between multiple Apple devices. When enabled, SMS messages that are received on a linked iPhone, are forwarded and stored in plain-text in the `~/Library/Messages/chat.db` file on the Mac.

**Breaking 2FA.** With Continuity enabled, attackers can break 2FA by instructing their MitB to monitor the `chat.db` database for changes and forward new messages to a remote server immediately after receipt. To show the practicality of this attack, we implemented a Firefox extension that uses the `FileUtils.jsm` API to read contents of synchronized SMS messages as soon as they are delivered to the iPhone.

The Continuity attack is illustrated in Fig. 3.

### 3.3  Dedicated 2FA Apps

Many online and offline applications are in the process of complementing their authentication mechanism with an optional 2FA step, often dubbed Two-Step Verification (2SV). Open source implementations are provided by Google (Google Authenticator) and Microsoft (Azure Authenticator) and can already be enabled for dozens of popular services, including Google, Microsoft Online, Amazon Web Services, Dropbox, Facebook, WordPress, Joomla, and KeePass.

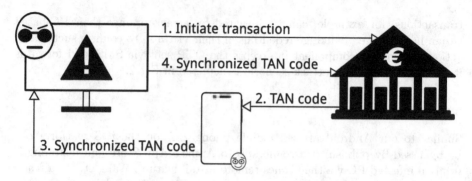

**Fig. 3.** Breaking 2FA on apple continuity. If enabled, Mac OS X 10.10 automatically synchronizes SMS messages between different Apple devices, breaking the second factor.

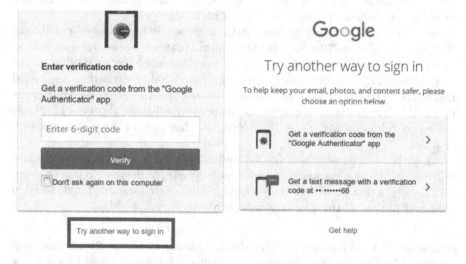

**Fig. 4.** Bypassing dedicated 2FA apps. The screenshot on the left shows Google 2SV requesting a verification code from the Google Authenticator. Note the *Try another way to sign in* option near the bottom of the window. When clicked, the right-hand figure shows the fallback option to get a text message with an OTP sent over SMS. An attacker in control of the PC-browser is therefore able to dicate what 2FA technique is used.

Due to sandboxing techniques, our previously described attacks cannot access OTPs that are generated by 2SV authenticator apps. During the process of setting up an authenticator app, however, users are advised to provide the underlying system a backup phone number. The rationale behind this is that if, for some reason, users fail to access the authenticator app, they can fallback to requesting an OTP sent over SMS.

Assuming that many users provide a backup phone number that is used by the same smartphone that runs the authenticator app, an attacker can easily bypass these dedicated 2FA apps: (i) having access to stolen credentials harvested by the MitB, an attacker initiates the login procedure; (ii) for logins via the Google Authenticator, for example, when prompted to enter a verification code, the attacker instructs the login page to *try another way to sign in*, followed by selecting the *Send a text message to your phone* option. From here, our previously described attacks can be used to completely bypass the 2FA mechanism.

Figure 4 illustrates how an attacker can fallback to SMS based OTPs when using Google Authenticator.

# 4  Discussion

In the previous sections, we showed how an attacker can bypass a variety of mobile phone 2FA mechanisms by exploiting synchronization vulnerabilities. We now study feasibility and practicalities of our attacks in more detail. Additionally, we discuss our efforts regarding responsible disclosure, as well as recommendations for involved parties.

## 4.1  Feasibility

Reviewing our Android attack described in Sect. 3.1, we conclude that exploiting synchronization vulnerabilities to bypass 2FA can be done in a reliable and stealthy way on Google's mobile operating system. Attackers can reduce their footprint to a bare minimum by breaking the attack down in different steps: (i) a **preparation phase** wherein attackers acquire access to infected PCs, possibly via a *Malware as a Service*-provider [14]; (ii) an **app-installation phase** wherein attackers push a vulnerable app to Google Play and instruct their victims to remotely install it. Depending on the target audience of the attacker, this can be done within a time window of only a couple of hours, after which the rogue app can again be removed from Google's servers; (iii) an **app-activation phase** wherein attackers gracefully wait until victims activate the malicious app. Our app-hiding tricks make that attackers can safely wait days so that a large group of victims get to activate the rogue app; and (iv) an **attack phase** wherein attackers perform an automated attack that requires access to OTPs sent over SMS. One typical example of such attack is transferring funds from saving accounts to an account that is controlled by the attackers.

Although more prerequisites must be met for our iOS attacks described in Sect. 3.2, they complement each other nicely: the *vulnerable app* approach does not work on iPhones running the latest iOS version, while our Continuity attack requires that victims *do* use more up to date versions of iOS and Mac OS X. The latter, however, also requires that (i) victims have enabled message synchronization (which setup process requires interaction with both Mac and iPhone), and (ii) both devices are connected to the same wireless network. Although this does not necessarily make the attack less feasible, it may slightly reduce its scalability given that synchronization is off by default and increase the detection rate by attentive users (the content of received SMS messages will pop up on both devices).

Finally, although the remote-install 2FA synchronization vulnerability is also prevalent on the Windows Phone (WP) platform, Microsoft does not (yet) provide an API for reading received SMS messages programmatically. Additionally, to the best of our knowledge, WP does not provide SMS synchronization features like Apple's Continuity. It is because of this that we were unable to break mobile phone 2FA on WP.

## 4.2 Recommendations and Future Work

An important step towards preventing the presented sophisticated MitB-based attacks against mobile phone 2FA, is to raise awareness among the various stakeholders. *Mobile platform vendors* should be aware that the release of new synchronization features may introduce security risks for their end-users. As such, vendors should be extremely careful when enabling new features by default instead of making them optional. It is their obligation to inform *end-users* that enabling or using certain synchronization features might jeopardize security guarantees of mobile phone 2FA. Only then can the user make a considered decision to give up security in favor of usability.

Reviewing our proposed attacks, this means that Apple, for example, should warn users about potential security risks when they set up Continuity. Moreover, if the user decides to enable this feature, synchronizing only messages sent by *trusted* phone numbers — those that are found in the user's contact list — would eliminate our attack scenario, assuming that TAN codes are sent by an unknown sender or SMS gateway. Additionally, we recognize a major task for platform vendors to safeguard their remote-install features. In our view, users should always be forced to explicitly approve new app installations on their mobile device. This way, attackers can no longer silently push apps, but always require manual user-interaction. Ignorant users may still be phished into approving unknown install requests, of course, but such change would eradicate our completely automated attack scenario. We believe that the current app-activation security policy alone as deployed by vendors is too weak, given that additional synchronization vulnerabilities can be used to achieve activation.

Startled users who do not want to wait for a fix from their vendor, can protect themselves from exploitation by using a separate account for each device. This way, remote-install features have zero knowledge about which devices an app can be pushed to. Naturally, the downside of such approach is losing the ability to use synchronization features at all. Authenticator users, in addition, should update their settings so that their backup is a phone number that is attached to a dumb phone. These phones are remarkably harder to get infected.

Besides raising user-awareness, future work should focus on the detection of SMS stealing apps at runtime, given that existing mobile Anti-Virus apps are useless to this respect—they are confined to their own filesystem sandbox and thus cannot access directories of other apps, monitor the phone's file system, or analyze dynamic behavior of installed applications [31]. Instead, system modifications that can monitor the global smartphone state are required. To this, the redesigned permission model of Android Marshmallow in which apps are no longer automatically granted all of their specified permissions at install time, but rather prompt users to grant individual permissions at runtime, is promising. Unfortunately, this model will only be used by applications that are specifically compiled for Marshmallow and can thus still be bypassed.

As an ultimate resort, we recommend that financial institutions consider the removal of mobile 2FA from their business processes and switch to token based 2FA instead—such token must of course be able to show transaction details, so that Man-in-the-Middle attacks can be detected by the user during transaction processing. Naturally, such switch will cause large expenses; each institution will have to consider whether moving away from mobile 2FA is feasible by comparing costs, gained security, and risk analysis results. Even so, given the attack scenarios we conclude that 2FA on smartphones is currently entirely compromised and no safer than single factor authentication.

### 4.3   Responsible Disclosure

To show the practicality of bypassing Google Bouncer, we uploaded a first version of our SMS stealing app to Google Play on July 8, 2015, where it has been publicly available for over two months. The app got removed on September 10, 2015, only a few hours *after* we had shared its name and a video demonstration of our attack with the head of Android Platform Security, while we already reported our attack scenario and recommendations to the Android security team months before the initial publication. Responses so far, unfortunately, indicate that Google believes that our proposed attack is not feasible in practice, despite all evidence to the contrary (including actual demos[2]).

We notified Apple about our findings on November 30, 2015, but we did not receive a technical response.

## 5   Background and Related Work

In this section, we provide a brief historical overview and related work discussion of the two fundamental components covered in this paper: Man-in-the-Browser attacks and Two-Factor Authentication. Additionally, we discuss current, state-of-the-art attacks against mobile-phone 2FA which rely on cross-platform infection. We focus on online banking schemes in particular, as this always was, and still is, one of the services subject to a vast amount of criminal activity.

### 5.1   Man-in-the-Browser

At first, online financial services depended completely on single-factor authentication (e.g., by using a secret key). For attackers, keyloggers were enough to steal credentials of associated users. However, they also generated vast amount of useless data, forcing the attacker to parse a huge amount of log output in

---

[2]  https://youtu.be/k1v_rQgS0d8.

order to retrieve meaningful credentials. Parsing keylog data was considered a challenging and time consuming task for an attacker, as it is hard to automate. As an alternative, cyber criminals deployed phishing campaigns, followed quickly by form grabbing attacks. The latter proved to be an effective and robust mechanism to steal useful information.

Well known banking trojans like Zeus and SpyEye were the first to implement form grabbing by hooking web browser APIs [24,38]. The fundamental idea behind form grabbing is to intercept all form information before it is sent to the network via HTTP requests. Form grabbing can be implemented in different ways: (i) *sniffing* all outgoing requests using a PCAP-based library—something that has the disadvantage of only working for unencrypted data [34]; (ii) *API hooking* the browser's dynamic library to steal all the requests and responses made by the user before they get encrypted [34]; and (iii) using a *malicious plugin* to easily register callbacks within the browser for events like *page load* or *file download* in order to intercept any request or response.

Malicious plugins and API hooking techniques can be used to do more than just form grabbing. Using a plugin, an attacker can modify HTTP responses received by the browser or covertly perform illegitimate operations on behalf of the user. This is commonly known as a Man-in-the-Browser (MitB) attack [21].

Guhring has identified various ways of which a trojan can perform a MitB attack and discusses pros and cons of various countermeasures that could be taken [21]. Boutin studies how webinjects are used by a trojan in the browser and discusses the underground economy behind selling webinjects [12]. Buescher et al., analyzed different types of hooking methods as used by financial trojans [13]. They propose an approach for detecting and classifying trojans by looking at the manipulations they perform on a browser. However, their approach is mainly based on detecting API hooks. As a consequence, MitB attacks that are implemented using plugins cannot be detected using this technique.

## 5.2   Two-Factor Authentication

Most account fraud and identity theft relate to accounts that use only single-factor authentication [20]. To defend against MitB attacks, financial services started using different types of multi-factor authentication mechanisms. The most elementary mechanism is that of a list of Transaction Authorization Numbers (TAN codes) as provided by the online service, from which the user can choose one to perform a secure transaction. A more convenient method that has been adopted by a majority of financial services is generating a new TAN code for each transaction and sending this via an out-of-band channel to the user. Naturally, SMS is a cheap and efficient candidate channel: almost everybody owns a mobile phone.

To defend against MitB attacks that hijack an ongoing transaction by modifying its details (receiver's bank account number or the amount of money transferred), financial services are starting to include transaction details along with the TAN code in the out-of-band SMS message. Users can then verify the transaction by inspecting these details in the SMS and only confirm if these match their expectation.

On August 8, 2001, the Federal Financial Institutions Examination Council agencies (FFIEC) issued guidance entitled *Authentication in an Electronic Banking Environment* [20]. FFIEC encourages financial institutions to use mobile phone-based 2FA as described above to secure their user's transactions.

Aloul et al., show how an app on a trusted mobile device can be used for generating one-time passwords, or how a mobile device itself can be used as a medium for out-of-band communication to financial services [10]. This is what most current deployed 2FA implementations use today. Mulliner analyzes attacks that target SMS interception in general and shows how a smartphone trojan can steal OTPs received via SMS. He proposes to use a dedicated channel which cannot be controlled by normal applications for receiving the OTP [27]. This is based on the assumption that mobile trojans do not have root privileges. Schartner et al., describe an attack against SMS based OTPs in the scenario where a transaction is made from the mobile device itself [33]. Since the transaction involves a single device (smartphone), a malware in the device can sniff both credentials and OTPs received via SMS.

Konoth et al., describe how Google's 2FA implementation can be bypassed using a MitB attack on an untrusted device [25]. Dmitrienko et al., analysed 2FA implementations of major online service providers such as Google, Twitter, Dropbox and Facebook [16]. Their work identifies various weaknesses in existing implementations that allow an attacker to bypass 2FA and also illustrates a general attack against 2FA. However, unlike ours, their attack relies on complex cross-platform infection.

### 5.3   Cross-Platform Infection

Cardtrap.A is the first discovered malware that features a cross-platform infection implementation. The trojan first infects a symbian smartphone. When the user inserts the memory card of the mobile phone into a Windows PC, it attempts to infect the PC [23]. In 2006, researchers found that it is possible for PC malware to infect a smartphone by exploiting Microsoft's ActiveSync synchronization software [18]. Furthermore, Wang et al., explain how a sophisticated adversary can spread malware to another device through a USB connection [37]. Finally, Dmitrienko et al., demonstrated via prototypes the feasibility of both PC-to-mobile and mobile-to-PC cross platform attacks [16].

## 6   Conclusion

With the ongoing integration of platforms—the result of a strong desire for enhanced usability—keeping our web accounts safe has become increasingly challenging. In this paper, we showed how synchronization features and cross-platform services can be used to elevate a regular PC-based Man-in-the-Browser to an accompanying Man-in-the-Mobile threat which can be used to successfully bypass mobile phone 2FA. The root cause is that imprudent synchronization functionality has obliterated the security boundaries on which 2FA solutions depend.

Due to the large number of financial institutions that rely on mobile phone 2FA for secure transaction processing, we expect that cyber criminals extend their activities by implementing attacks similar to ours, putting those institutions and their customers at risk. We hope that this paper helps in identifying issues with respect to cross-platform integration and that both software and platform vendors adopt our recommendations in order to prevent these types of attacks from becoming a major threat in the near future.

**Acknowledgements.** We would like to thank the anonymous reviewers for their valuable comments and input to improve the paper. This work was supported by the MALPAY project and by the Netherlands Organisation for Scientific Research through grants NWO 639.023.309 VICI "Dowsing" and NWO CSI-DHS 628.001.021.

# References

1. Android intents with Chrome. https://developer.chrome.com/multidevice/android/intents
2. Find a lost phone. http://www.windowsphone.com/en-us/how-to/wp8/settings-and-personalization/find-a-lost-phone
3. Get SMS broadcast with text body without Jailbreak BUT private frameworks in IOS. http://stackoverflow.com/questions/26642770/get-sms-broadcast-with-text-body-without-jailbreak-but-private-frameworks-in-ios
4. How do I set up Sync on my computer? http://support.mozilla.org/kb/how-do-i-set-sync-my-computer
5. iCloud: Erase your device. https://support.apple.com/kb/PH2701
6. Mobile/tablet operating system market share. https://www.netmarketshare.com/operating-system-market-share.aspx?qprid=8&qpcustomd=1
7. Remotely ring, lock or erase a lost device. https://support.google.com/accounts/answer/6160500
8. Sync tabs across devices. http://support.google.com/chrome/answer/2591582
9. Use Continuity to connect your iPhone, iPad, iPod touch, and Mac. http://support.apple.com/HT204681
10. Aloul, F., Zahidi, S., Hajj, W.E.: Two factor authentication using mobile phones. In: Proceedings on the International Conference on Computer Systems and Applications (AICCA) (2009)
11. Bosman, E., Bos, H.: Framing signals - a return to portable shellcode. In: Proceedings of the Symposium on Security and Privacy (S&P) (2014)
12. Boutin, J.I.: The evolution of webinjects, September 2014
13. Buescher, A., Leder, F., Siebert, T.: Banksafe information stealer detection inside the web browser. In: Proceedings on the International Conference on Recent Advances in Intrusion Detection (RAID) (2011)
14. Caballero, J., Grier, C., Kreibich, C., Paxson, V.: Measuring pay-per-install: the commoditization of malware distribution. In: Proceedings of the USENIX Security Symposium (USENIX Sec) (2011)
15. Chytry, F.: Apps on Google Play Pose As Games and Infect Millions of Users with Adware, February 2015
16. Dmitrienko, A., Liebchen, C., Rossow, C., Sadeghi, A.-R.: On the (In)security of mobile two-factor authentication. In: Christin, N., Safavi-Naini, R. (eds.) FC 2014. LNCS, vol. 8437, pp. 365–383. Springer, Heidelberg (2014). doi:10.1007/978-3-662-45472-5_24

17. eMarketer: Smartphone Users Worldwide Will Total 1.75 Billion in 2014, January 2014
18. Evers, J.: Virus makes leap from PC to PDA, Feburary 2006
19. Target, E.: 2014 Mobile Behavior Report, February 2014
20. Federal Financial Institutions Examination Council: Authentication in an Internet Banking Environment (2005)
21. Gühring, P.: Concepts against Man-in-the-Browser Attacks, September 2006
22. inazaruk: "Activating" Android applications, December 2011
23. Kawamoto, D.: Cell phone virus tries leaping to PCs, September 2005
24. Kharouni, L.: Automating Online Banking Fraud (2012)
25. Krishnan, R., Kumar, R.: Securing user input as a defense against MitB. In: Proceedings of the International Conference on Interdisciplinary Advances in Applied Computing (ICONIAAC) (2014)
26. Lockheimer, H.: Android and Security, February 2012
27. Mulliner, C., Borgaonkar, R., Stewin, P., Seifert, J.-P.: SMS-based one-time passwords: attacks and defense. In: Rieck, K., Stewin, P., Seifert, J.-P. (eds.) DIMVA 2013. LNCS, vol. 7967, pp. 150–159. Springer, Heidelberg (2013). doi:10.1007/978-3-642-39235-1_9
28. Neugschwandtner, M., Lindorfer, M., Platzer, C.: A view to a kill: webview exploitation. In: Proceedings of the USENIX Workshop on Large-Scale Exploits and Emergent Threats (LEET) (2013)
29. Oberheide, J., Miller, C.: Dissecting the Android Bouncer, June 2012
30. Poeplau, S., Fratantonio, Y., Bianchi, A., Kruegel, C., Vigna, G.: Execute this! Analyzing unsafe and malicious dynamic code loading in android applications. In: Proceedings of the Network and Distributed System Security Symposium (NDSS) (2014)
31. Rafael Fedler, M.K., Schutte, J.: An antivirus API for android malware recognition. In: Proceedings of Malicious and Unwanted Software: "The Americas" (MALWARE), 2013 8th International Conference (2013)
32. Sams, B.: Microsoft confirms Edge will sync passwords, bookmarks, tabs, and more. http://www.neowin.net/news/microsoft-confirms-edge-will-sync-passwords-bookmarks-tabs-and-more
33. Schartner, P., Bürger, S.: Attacking mTAN-Applications like e-Banking and mobile Signatures. Technical report, Univeristy of Klagenfurt (2011)
34. Sood, A.K., Enbody, R.J., Bansal, R.: The art of stealing banking information – form grabbing on fire, November 2011
35. Statista: Global smartphone sales to end users 2007–2014 (2015)
36. Wang, T., Lu, K., Lu, L., Chung, S., Lee, W.: Jekyll on iOS: when benign apps become evil. In: Proceedings of the USENIX Security Symposium (USENIX Sec) (2013)
37. Wang, Z., Stavrou, A.: Exploiting smart-phone USB connectivity for fun and profit. In: Proceedings of the Computer Security Applications Conference (ACSAC) (2010)
38. Wyke, J.: What is Zeus? Sophos, May 2011

# Security Keys: Practical Cryptographic Second Factors for the Modern Web

Juan Lang$^{(\boxtimes)}$, Alexei Czeskis, Dirk Balfanz, Marius Schilder, and Sampath Srinivas

Google, Inc., Mountain View, CA, USA
juanlang@google.com

**Abstract.** "Security Keys" are second-factor devices that protect users against phishing and man-in-the-middle attacks. Users carry a single device and can self-register it with any online service that supports the protocol. The devices are simple to implement and deploy, simple to use, privacy preserving, and secure against strong attackers. We have shipped support for Security Keys in the Chrome web browser and in Google's online services. We show that Security Keys lead to both an increased level of security and user satisfaction by analyzing a two year deployment which began within Google and has extended to our consumer-facing web applications. The Security Key design has been standardized by the FIDO Alliance, an organization with more than 250 member companies spanning the industry. Currently, Security Keys have been deployed by Google, Dropbox, and GitHub. An updated and extended tech report is available at https://github.com/google/u2f-ref-code/docs/SecurityKeys_TechReport.pdf.

## 1 Introduction

Recent account takeovers [1–3] have once again highlighted the challenge of securing user data online: accounts are often protected by no more than a weak password [4] and whatever implicit signals (if any) that the online service provider has collected to distinguish legitimate users from account hijackers.

Academic research has produced numerous proposals to move away from passwords, but in practice such efforts have largely been unsuccessful [5,6]. Instead, many service providers augment password-based authentication with a second factor in the form of a one-time passcode (OTP), *e.g.*, [7,8]. Unfortunately, OTPs as a second factor are still vulnerable to relatively common attacks such as phishing [9]. In addition, OTPs have a number of usability drawbacks (see Sect. 2). These factors limit the success and deployment of OTPs as a reliable and secure second factor.

Meanwhile, secure authentication factors, which use challenge/response-based cryptographic protocols, have their own barriers to deployment. National ID cards [10,11] and smart cards require custom reader hardware and/or driver

J. Grossklags and B. Preneel (Eds.): FC 2016, LNCS 9603, pp. 422–440, 2017.
DOI: 10.1007/978-3-662-54970-4_25

software to be installed prior to use. Depending on the implementation, these systems also make it challenging for users to protect their privacy (see Sect. 2).

In this work, we present Security Keys: second factor devices that improve the state of the art for *practical authentication for real consumers* in terms of privacy, security, and usability. This is evidenced by the fact that Security Keys have been publicly deployed by Google [12], Dropbox [13], and GitHub [14]. Security Keys were designed from the ground up to be practical: simple to implement and deploy, straightforward to use, privacy preserving, and secure against strong attackers. We have shipped support for Security Keys in the Chrome browser, have deployed it within Google's internal sign-in system, and have enabled Security Keys as an available second factor in Google's web services. *In this work, we demonstrate that Security Keys lead to both an increased level of security and user satisfaction as well as cheaper support cost.* The Security Key design has been standardized within an industry alliance, the FIDO Alliance [15] as the Universal Second Factor (U2F) protocol.

## 2    Related Work

We now give an overview of the most relevant related work. For detailed background of the field, please consult a variety of excellent survey works [5,6,16,17].

**One-Time Passcodes.** OTPs are short (typically 6 to 8 digit) codes that are one time use and are sent to the user via SMS or are generated by a separate physical dongle. Though they provide more security than passwords, OTPs have a number of downsides. First, they are vulnerable to phishing and man-in-the-middle attacks [9]. Second, OTPs that are delivered by phones are subject to data and phone availability, while those that are generated by dongles cause the user to have one dongle per web site. Finally, OTPs provide a sub-optimal user experience as they often require the user to manually copy codes from one device to another. *Security Keys are resistant to phishing and man-in-the-middle by design; our preliminary study also shows that they provide a better user experience.*

**Smartphone as Second Factor.** A number of efforts have attempted to leverage the user's phone as a cryptographic second factor, both within academia (*e.g.*, [18]) and in industry (*e.g.*, [19]). While promising, they face a number of challenges: for example, protecting application logic from malware is difficult on a general purpose computing platform. Moreover, a user's phone may not always be reachable: the phone may not have a data connection or the battery may have run out. *Security keys require no batteries and usually have a dedicated tamper-proof secure element.*

**Smart Cards.** Security Keys fit into the "what you have" category of authentication schemes and have a close relationship to smart cards. While Security

Keys can be (and have been) implemented on top of a smart card platform such as JavaCard [20], *Security Keys express a particular protocol for which smart cards are just one possible implementation platform.*

**TLS Client Certificates.** TLS Client Certificates [21] traditionally bear the user's identity and can be used for on-line authentication. When users navigate to a web service that requires TLS client authentication, their browser will prompt the user for their client certificate. Unfortunately, current implementations of TLS client certificates have a poor user experience. Typically, when web servers request that browsers generate a TLS client certificate, browsers display a dialog where the user must choose the certificate cipher and key length—a cryptographic detail that is unfamiliar and confusing to most users.

When web servers request that the browser provide a certificate, the user is prompted to select the client certificate to use; accidentally choosing the wrong certificate will cause the user's identity to leak across sites. In addition, because client certificates are transmitted in the clear, the user's identity is revealed during TLS client certificate transfer to any network adversary. TLS client certificates also suffer from a lack of portability: they are tough to move from one client platform to another. *Security Keys have none of these issues: as we will describe, they are designed to be fool-proof: with users' privacy in mind, to be simple to use, and to be portable.*

**Electronic National Identification Cards.** Some countries have deployed national electronic identification cards. In Estonia, for example, electronic ID cards "are used in health care, electronic banking and shopping, to sign contracts and encrypt e-mail, as tram tickets, and much more besides—even to vote" [11]. Despite their rich capabilities, national identity cards have not become a popular global online authentication mechanism [10]. One possible reason is that current national identity cards require special hardware (a card reader) and thus are hard to deploy. Another possible reason is that national identity cards are by definition controlled by one government, which may not be acceptable to businesses in another country. *Security Keys have no such downsides: they work with pre-installed drivers over commonly available physical media (USB, NFC, Bluetooth) and are not controlled or distributed by any single entity.*

Finally, some approaches can combine multiple elements, *e.g.*, some electronic ID cards combine smart card, TLS client certificate, and government identification.

## 3    Threat Model

We briefly outline major attackers and attacks that we consider in our design.

## 3.1   Attackers

**Web Attackers.** Entities who control malicious websites (*e.g.*, bad.com[1]) are called *web attackers*. We believe that virtually all users might accidentally visit such a malicious site. The attacker may design bad.com to visually mimic a user's bank or e-mail website in an attempt to get (*i.e.*, *phish*) the user's login credentials. As the attackers are quite skilled, and may occupy clever URLs (such as bamk.com[2]), we assume that most users will fall for this trick. That is, they will enter credentials such as their password into the attacker-controlled bad.com.

**Related-Site Attackers.** Some attackers will compromise sites having weak security practices in order to steal the site's user credentials. As users often reuse credentials across sites [22], *related-site attackers* will reuse the stolen credentials on more secure sites in hopes of accessing the user's accounts [23].

**Network Attackers.** Adversaries may be able to observe and modify network traffic between the user and the legitimate site. We call such adversaries *network attackers*. For example, a network attacker might sniff wireless traffic in a coffee shop [24,25]) or a nation-state may interpose on all traffic that traverses their physical borders [26,27]. A man-in-the-middle attacker can defeat the security properties offered by TLS [21], *e.g.*, by forging rogue server TLS certificates [28]. Other network attackers may record traffic and subsequently exploit the TLS cryptographic layer [29,30] to extract authentication data.

**Malware Attackers.** In some cases, attackers may be able to silently install and run arbitrary software on users' computers; such attackers are *malware attackers*. We assume that such software can run with arbitrary privileges and can freely help itself to cookies, passwords, and any other authentication material.

## 3.2   Attack Consequences

We highlight two of the most concerning attack consequences below.

**Session Duplication.** In some cases, an attacker may be able to steal credentials that allow him/her to access the user's account from any computer and at any time. For example, if an attacker is able to steal cookies or passwords, then he/she may be able to log into the victim's account at virtually any subsequent date (assuming the password isn't changed, and the cookie doesn't expire).

---

[1] This is just an example, the real bad.com may not be malicious.

[2] This is just an example, the real bamk.com may not be malicious.

**Session Riding.** If an attacker can only access or modify the user's account when the user is actively using his/her computer, we call this attack *session riding*. For example, if the website always requires the user to begin a new session by providing proof of a hardware device that the attacker does not control, the attacker is only able to *ride* the user's active sessions.

*Security Keys make session duplication and riding much more difficult.*

# 4    System Design

We now give a system overview; for details please consult the official specification on the FIDO Alliance website [15]. In juggling the various requirements, we settled on the following design goals:

- *Easy for Users*: Using Security Keys should be fast, easy, and "brainless". It must be difficult to use Security Keys incorrectly or insecurely.
- *Easy for Developers*: Security Keys must be easy for developers to integrate into their website through simple APIs.
- *Privacy*: Security Keys should not allow tracking of any kind. In addition, if a Security Key is lost, it should be difficult for an attacker to get any useful information from a Security Key.
- *Security*: Security Keys should protect users against password reuse, phishing, and man-in-the-middle attacks.

## 4.1    System Overview

Security Keys are intended to be used in the context of a web application in which the server wishes to verify the user's identity. At a high level, Security Keys support the following commands which are provided to web pages as browser APIs (see Sect. 5).

- *Register*: Given this command, the Security Key generates a fresh asymmetric key pair and returns the public key. The server associates this public key with a user account.
- *Authenticate*: Given this command, the Security Key tests for user presence and exercises its private key to provide a response. The server can verify that the response is valid, and thus authenticate the user.

Figure 1 shows two different Security Keys manufactured by Yubico—one of the several vendors who produce Security Keys. Each devices communicates over a USB interface and has a capacitive touch sensor which must be touched by the user in order to authorize any operation (register or authenticate). Both devices contain a tamper-proof secure element.

## 4.2    Detailed Design

We now focus on the details of both registration and authentication. Full specifications can be found on the FIDO Alliance website [15].

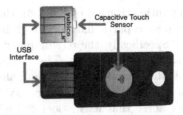

**Fig. 1.** Two Security Keys. Both have a USB interface and a capacitive touch sensor. One also has an NFC interface.

**Registration.** During registration (see Fig. 2), the relying party—the server—produces a random challenge. The user's browser binds the server's challenge into a Client Data structure, to be covered shortly. The browser sends the server's web origin and a hash of the Client Data to the Security Key. In response, the Security Key generates a new key pair along with a key handle, which will also be covered later. The Security Key associates the key pair with the relying party's web origin and then returns the generated public key, key handle, an attestation certificate, and a signature over: 1. the web origin, 2. hash of the client data, 3. public key, and 4. key handle. The web browser then forwards this data, along with the client data, back to the website. The website verifies the signature and associates the public key and key handle with the user's account.

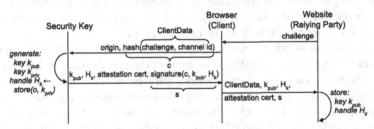

**Fig. 2.** Security Key registration.

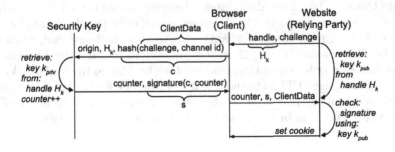

**Fig. 3.** Security Key authentication.

**Authentication.** During authentication (see Fig. 3), the relying party requests that the Security Key exercise a particular key which has previously been registered for a user account. Specifically, the relying party sends the desired key's handle and a challenge to the web browser. The browser generates the client data (see above) and sends the hash of the client data along with the key handle and the web origin to the Security Key. If the Security Key does not recognize the key handle, or doesn't agree that it is associated with the web origin that requested the signature, it rejects the request. Otherwise, it produces a signature of the client data. The Security Key signs two additional attributes: whether a Test of User Presence (TUP) succeeded, and a counter value. The Test of User Presence is described in more detail below. The counter value is a 32-bit counter that is incremented with every signature the Security Key performs; its presence allows the server to detect potential cloning of a Security Key, *e.g.*, when the counter value appears to decrease from one signature to the next. The counter is described in more detail in Sect. 7.2.

The browser passes the signature, along with the TUP and the counter value, to the server. The server then checks the signature against the public key it has registered and authenticates the user if the signature matches.

**Device Attestation.** Each Security Key must provide an attestation certificate during registration. This allows servers to gate the use of a particular security key (for example, if servers trust only certain Security Key suppliers). A related desire is revocability: if a device or model is known to have flaws or have been compromised, a server might wish to not accept it.

Individually identifying devices would reveal a unique identifier for a device across unrelated origins, violating the user's privacy. To achieve both security and privacy, we recommended that devices implement batch attestation: a batch of devices shares a single attestation key (and certificate), such that all devices with a known flaw can be revoked together, and users' privacy is still respected: at worst, a device can be identified as a member of a batch. Alternatives for device attestation are explored further in Sect. 7.1.

**Client Data.** The client data binds the server-provided challenge to the browser's view of its connection to the server. Specifically, the client data includes the type of the request (register or authenticate), the challenge, and, when possible, the TLS channel ID [31,32] of the connection. Binding the TLS channel ID allows the server to detect the presence of a TLS Man in the Middle. When a server receives a signed TLS channel ID, it can compare it with the TLS channel ID it observes in the TLS layer. If they differ, the server will be aware of the presence of a TLS Man in the Middle, and can abort the connection.

**Test of User Presence.** The Test of User Presence (TUP) allows the caller to test whether a human is present during command execution. This serves two purposes: first, it provides a mechanism for human confirmation of commands.

Second, it allows web applications to implement a policy based on that check, e.g. "Transactions for a dollar amount greater than \$1,000 require confirmation,"or "Credentials must be re-presented by a human being after 90 days."

TUP implementation is left up to the device manufacturer. One vendor uses a capacitive touch sensor, others employ a mechanical button, while another makes a device that stays powered up only a short time after insertion into a USB port, requiring the user to reinsert the device for every operation.

**Cryptographic Primitives.** For all signing operations, we chose ECDSA over the NIST P-256 curve. For all hashing operations, we chose SHA-256. The choice of the curve and hash algorithm was made because of their wide availability on embedded platforms. At this time we believe these primitives, which offer 128 bit security, to be sufficiently secure.

# 5   Implementation

We have implemented end-to-end support for Security Keys. This involved building a large number of components; we describe some of them below (others were omitted because of space). Note that all of the components have been open-sourced, are actively maintained, and can be found at https://github.com/ google/u2f-ref-code.

## 5.1   Browser Support

We have implemented and shipped support for Security Keys as part of the Chrome web browser (available since version 41.) The browser support consists of JavaScript APIs that can be called by any web application. In total, the support consists of roughly 8,000 lines of code.

**Register Method.** A web server requests a new Security Key registration by making use of a new browser API:

```
u2f.register()
```

This API accepts a challenge and a list of already-registered key handles. The list of already-registered key handles allows the browser to avoid double registration of the same Security Key. If the browser finds an eligible Security Key, the client sends a *register* command to the Security Key, described in more detail in the next section. Upon successful completion of the register command, the browser sends the Security Key's Registration Message output, along with the client data described in Sect. 4.2, to the server. The server verifies the registration signature and that the client data matches its own view of the request. Finally, the server can check the attestation certificate to verify that it meets the server's requirements. Assuming all parameters match and are found acceptable, the server stores the key handle $H_k$ and the public key $k_{pub}$ for the user's account.

**Sign Method.** A web server requests a signature from a Security Key by making use of a new browser API:

```
u2f.sign()
```

The parameters to the sign API are a challenge, and any registered key handles for the user. The browser then searches for available Security Keys. For each device found, the browser sends a *sign* command, described in more detail in the next section. Upon successful completion of a sign command, the browser provides the signature to the server, along with the client data (Sect. 4.2) and the key handle $H_k$ that produced the signature. The server checks that the signature verifies with the public key $k_{pub}$ it has stored for $H_k$, and that the counter value has increased. The server also verifies the client data against its own view of the request. If all the checks succeed, the user is authenticated.

## 5.2    Security Key Token Implementation

We developed a JavaCard-based implementation of a Security Key. The underlying applet consists of approximately 1,500 lines of Java code. In addition, as we describe shortly, we use traditional cryptographic techniques to support an arbitrary number of keys and origins given the limited storage capabilities of embedded platforms.

Security Keys support two basic operations: *register*, to create a new key pair, and *sign*, to produce a cryptographic signature.

**Register Operation.** The *register* operation takes two parameters, an application parameter—the web origin provided by the browser—and a challenge. The Security Key generates a new key pair $(k_{pub}, k_{priv})$ for the application parameter. It then performs a *store* operation to store both the application parameter and the private key $k_{priv}$. The *store* operation yields a key handle $H_k$ and is discussed more fully shortly. The public key $k_{pub}$ and the key handle $H_k$, along with the challenge parameter and application parameter, are then signed with the device's attestation private key, $Priv_{attest}$. The Security Key provides as output a Registration Message (see Fig. 4), which includes the public key $k_{pub}$ and the key handle $H_k$, as well as the device attestation certificate.

**Sign Operation.** The *sign* operation takes three parameters, an application parameter, a key handle, and a challenge. During authentication, the Security Key first performs a *retrieve* operation to retrieve the stored application parameter and the private key for the key handle. If the Security Key does not recognize the key handle, it rejects the operation. Similarly, if it recognizes the key handle but the retrieved application parameter does not match the application parameter to the sign operation, it rejects the operation with the same error value as if it did not recognize the key handle. In this way, a web site that tries to make use of a key handle that was registered on a different origin cannot learn that

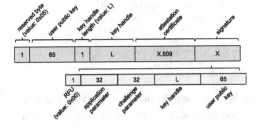

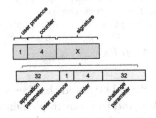

**Fig. 4.** Security Key registration message.

**Fig. 5.** Security Key authentication message.

the key handle is valid for the other origin. The *retrieve* operation is discussed further shortly.

Once the Security Key has retrieved a valid private key $k_{priv}$ for the key handle, and verified that it was generated for the supplied application parameter, it increments the counter value and signs a concatenation of the Test of User Presence indication, the new counter value, and the challenge parameter. It provides the signature $s$ to the browser, along with the Test of User Presence indication and the new counter value. The result of the sign operation is the Authentication Message shown in Fig. 5.

### 5.3    Store and Retrieve Operations

*Store* and *retrieve* can be thought of as database operations: storing a private key yields an index into a table, and this index is returned as the key handle. Retrieving a key handle looks up the value in the table at the given index.

However, a database-like implementation reduces privacy and usability: a predictable index for key handles reveals the number of accounts a Security Key is being used with. Additionally, the users need to be aware of the storage capacity of Security Keys to ensure she doesn't run out of space in the key database.

In our reference implementation, *store* is instead implemented as a key wrapping operation: the private key $k_{priv}$ and the application parameter are encrypted using a secret key $K_{wrap}$ known only to a single Security Key. By implementing *store* and *retrieve* as key wrap/unwrap operations, the Security Key reference implementations can store an unlimited number of key handles: the storage is implemented by the server.

In order to avoid known plaintext attacks, our reference implementations obscure the application parameter with a second secret key, $K_{app}$, also known only to a single Security Key. The obscured application parameter and the private key are then interleaved together, prior to encrypting with the wrapping key. In the reference implementation, two-key 3DES was chosen as the cipher, due to the quality of the implementation on the hardware we used. Algorithmically, our key wrapping implementation is:

```
function STORE(k_priv, app)                function RETRIEVE(H_K, app)
    app' ← Encrypt(app)_{K_app}               app' ← Encrypt(app)_{K_app}
    plaintext ← Interleave(k_priv, app')      plaintext ← Decrypt(H_K)_{K_wrap}
    H_K ← Encrypt(plaintext)_{K_wrap}         (k_priv, app'') ← Deinterleave(plaintext)
    return H_K                                constant-time check(app' == app'')
end function                                  return k_priv
                                           end function
```

It should be noted that key wrapping is an optional optimization vendors may employ, and that our implementation is one approach. The FIDO U2F specifications allow device manufacturers to choose any approach for key wrapping. For example, one vendor's approach is described in [33].

### 5.4    Server Implementation

We implemented, open-sourced, and actively maintain a reference Security Key server. It runs on the Google App Engine platform and consists of approximately 2,000 lines of Java code.

## 6    Evaluation

We evaluate Security Keys using a number of metrics. We begin by comparing the usability, deployability, and security of Security Keys to existing and prior technologies. Next, we discuss the performance of various Security Key hardware devices. Finally, we give an in-depth analysis of our deployment experience including effect on users, support cost, and other relevant variables.

### 6.1    Comparative

We use the rating criteria defined in Bonneau *et al.* [5] to compare Security Keys to passwords alone, as well as to other second factor authentication methods in common use in online accounts today. A summary of the comparison can be seen in Table 1. We use the ratings Bonneau *et al.* assign, with the exception of the phishing protection existing second factor schemes provide. We discuss this more shortly. In short, Security Keys offer similar usability to just passwords while being much more secure. In addition, Security Keys can be deployed for supported browsers with a relatively small server-side change.

**Usability.** Security Keys partially offer the *memorywise-effortless* and *scalable-for-users* benefits because they dramatically reduce the risk of password reuse. They are not *physically-effortless* because they still require a password entry, but the additional burden—a button push—is low. They are both *easy-to-learn* and *efficient-to-use,* and they perform with *infrequent-errors*. These assertions are further supported in Sect. 6.3.

**Table 1.** Comparative evaluation of Security Keys to similar schemes

| Category | Scheme | Memorywise-Effortless | Scalable-for-Users | Nothing-to-Carry | Physically-Effortless | Easy-to-Learn | Efficient-to-Use | Infrequent-Errors | Easy-Recovery-from-Loss | Accessible | Negligible-Cost-per-User | Server-Compatible | Browser-Compatible | Mature | Non-Proprietary | Resilient-to-Physical-Observation | Resilient-to-Targeted-Impersonation | Resilient-to-Throttled-Guessing | Resilient-to-Unthrottled-Guessing | Resilient-to-Internal-Observation | Resilient-to-Leaks-from-Other-Verifiers | Resilient-to-Phishing | Resilient-to-Theft | No-Trusted-Third-Party | Requiring-Explicit-Consent | Unlinkable |
|---|---|---|---|---|---|---|---|---|---|---|---|---|---|---|---|---|---|---|---|---|---|---|---|---|---|---|
| | | Usability | | | | | | | | Deployability | | | | | | Security | | | | | | | | | | |
| (incumbent) | Web passwords | | | ● | | ● | ● | ○ | ● | ● | ● | ● | ● | ● | ● | | ○ | | | | | | ● | ● | ● | ● |
| Hardware tokens | Security Keys | ○ | ○ | | | ● | ● | ● | | ● | ○ | | ○ | ● | ● | ● | ● | ● | ● | ● | ● | ● | ● | ● | ● | ● |
| Hardware tokens | RSA SecurID | | | | | ● | ○ | ○ | | | | | ● | ● | | ● | ● | ● | ● | ● | ● | | ● | | ● | ● |
| Hardware tokens | YubiKey | | | | | ● | ○ | ○ | | ● | | | ● | ● | | ● | ● | ● | ● | ● | | | ● | | ● | ● |
| Phone-based | OTP over SMS | ● | ● | ○ | | ● | | ○ | ○ | ○ | | | ● | ● | ● | ● | ● | ● | ● | ● | ● | | | ○ | ● | ● |
| Phone-based | Google 2-Step | | ○ | | | ● | ○ | ○ | ○ | ○ | | | ● | ● | | ○ | ○ | ● | ● | ● | | | ● | ● | ● | ● |

● = offers the benefit; ○ = almost offers the benefit; *no circle* = does not offer the benefit.

**Deployability.** Security Keys are *accessible*—the physical burden of tapping a button is minimal; visually impaired users within Google successfully use Security Keys. Security Keys nearly offer a *negligible-cost-per-user*: the user only needs one for any number of websites, and they are available from multiple vendors at varying prices. Bonneau *et al.* do not offer guidance to what price is considered "negligible," so we give Security Keys partial credit. Security Keys are partially *browser-compatible*: one major browser has built-in support for them, and we are working toward standardizing support for them.

Security Keys are *mature*: they have been implemented and deployed on several large web properties, discussed further in Sect. 6.3. Finally, they are *non-proprietary*: There are open standards and source for them. They are available from multiple vendors. Support for them is deployed in one major browser [12], with support from another major browser announced [34]. Multiple servers have implemented support for them.

**Security.** Security Keys generate assertions that protect users against phishing and website attackers. While Bonneau *et al.* claim existing second factor schemes provide protection against phishing, they do so under the assumption that relay-based or realtime phishing attacks are hard to mount. We disagree given recent evidence of successful phishing campaigns against accounts protected by OTP credentials [9], hence we downgrade the protection for OTP-based second factors.

Security Keys generate unique key pairs per account and restrict key use to a single origin, protecting users against tracking across websites/linkability. Unlike other hardware 2nd factor solutions such as RSA SecurID, there is no trusted third party involved. Security Keys, when used with TLS Channel ID, also provide resistance against man-in-the-middle attacks by letting servers recognize the presence of two different TLS connections. Finally, Security Keys limit the user's exposure to session riding by requiring that a TUP is performed. Note that Security Keys do not allow transaction confirmation via a trusted display, therefore clever attacker may still alter transaction details (*e.g.*, transfer amounts)—though not without a TUP.

## 6.2   Hardware Performance

The performance of an operation involving a Security Key involves many variables. Nevertheless, our aim was to create a protocol that seems "fast enough" during ordinary use. Our informal guideline was that a sign operation should complete in well under a second, while registration should complete in around a second. Measured times for both operations for commercially available hardware are shown in Table 2. These times show the "raw" performance time—the time it takes for hardware devices to execute each operation.

With these speeds, we believe we achieved an experience whereby users do not find the additional step (beyond a password) onerous. We will expand upon our experience further in the next section.

**Table 2.** Security Key performance. Raw time needed to complete an operation.

| Device | Operation time (*ms*) | |
|---|---|---|
| | Enroll | Sign |
| Happlink FIDO U2F | 1210 | 660 |
| Yubico FIDO U2F | 394 | 192 |
| Yubico YubiKey NEO | 398 | 192 |

## 6.3   Deployment Experience

Because of the usability and security benefits Security Keys provide over OTPs, we have deployed them to more than 50,000 employees, and made them an available option for consumer accounts. Our users have been very happy with the switch: we received many instances of unsolicited positive feedback.

The benefits of Security Keys are difficult to quantify. The first benefit is increased security: users are now protected against phishing, including from well-known campaigns. Unfortunately, the impact of this benefit can only be measured in terms of what did not happen, hence it is hard to quantify. Other impacts include increased productivity due to decreased time spent authenticating, and decreased support cost; we quantify these below.

**Time Spent Authenticating.** We compared the time it takes to authenticate using Security Keys versus other two-factor methods, using two user populations: Google employees and consumers using our web products.

Figure 6 shows the average time spent authenticating, per user, for Google's employees during an arbitrary two-day period. All authentication steps are measured, *i.e.*, a user is entering a password and providing a second factor. In the measurements, Security Keys are compared with OTPs, where the OTP may be provided by one of several sources, the most prevalent being a USB device that acts as a keyboard. The data originated from authentication events in a two-day period and thus could be biased toward those who reauthenticate frequently, and therefore are best trained in the use of their second factor. Because Security Keys were considered equivalent to OTPs during the period of study, Security Key users were not prompted more or less frequently than OTP users, and we do not expect a bias between the two populations as a result.

Total authentication time decreased markedly when using Security Keys; this may account for the overwhelmingly positive reaction. Previously, the dominant OTP mechanism in the company was a USB-based device very similar to a Security Key, but Security Keys are still faster. One possible reason is that most employees received a tiny Security Key that is meant to never be removed from the USB port. Thus, when the user is prompted for a second factor, she need only touch the Security Key's button, rather than having first to find and insert the device. A second reason is that the USB OTP devices act like a keyboard, and require the user to (1) navigate to a form field before touching the device to release the OTP, then (2) press Enter or click a button to a submit a web form. With Security Keys, on the other hand, the JavaScript API returns the result of the Security Key request directly to the page, and the form submission can happen automatically as a result without additional user action.

Figure 6 also shows the average time required to collect a second factor from consumers over several days in 2016. Again, Security Keys were faster for consumers to use than OTPs, whether they were delivered by SMS or via a smartphone app. Earlier in this work, we gave several reasons why this could be: SMS delivery can suffer delays, while OTPs in a smartphone app must be manually typed by users.

**Authentication Failure Rate.** Authentication failures result in increased authentication time and user frustration. In our examination of the time period studied, 3% of OTP-based authentications resulted in failure, while Security Keys did not present any authentication failures.

**Support Cost.** Figure 7 shows the number of support incidents we received for two kinds of authentication second factors for the period in which we transitioned from using OTPs to Security Keys, normalized by the total number of employees, on a linear scale. The number of authentication events per user did not depend on whether the users had Security Keys or OTPs for a second factor, so the number of support events is believed to be representative. There is a gap in data

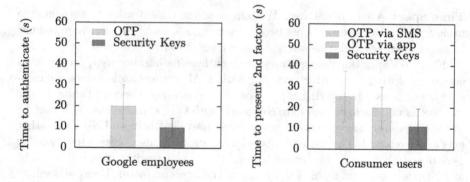

**Fig. 6.** Time spent authenticating

collection, when support data were transitioned for one system to another, and Security Key support incidents were not collected. The approximate percentage of the company actively using Security Keys is also shown.

The number of support incidents per user rose slightly as the rollout of Security Keys expanded, before decreasing again. It's worth noting that the support load was higher for OTP than for Security Keys for all time periods. By end of the period studied, the vast majority of the company had switched from OTP to Security Keys, and new employees were no longer given OTP devices. Our support organization estimates that we save thousands of hours per year in support cost by switching from OTP to Security Key.

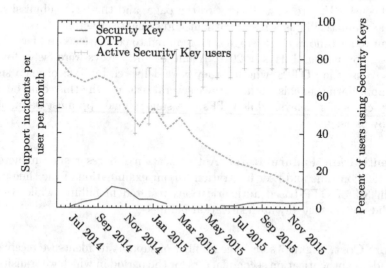

**Fig. 7.** 2nd factor support incidents per employee per month (gaps where data are unavailable)

**Hardware Cost.** For the corporate-wide deployment we studied, the devices purchased had similar per-unit cost to the USB-based OTP devices they replaced. For this deployment, one Security Key was allotted per computer per employee. Roughly, this equated to giving each employee 2 Security Keys, on average. This implies that more was spent on hardware Security Key tokens than for hardware OTP tokens. For the deployment, we found the increased user productivity, and decreased support cost, were worth the increased hardware cost.

For consumers, multiple vendors provide Security Keys at different price points, some as low as $6 USD[3]. Since users only need one device, rather than one device per account or site, the resulting cost in our opinion approaches the "negligible cost per user" suggested by Bonneau *et al.* [5].

# 7  Discussion

## 7.1  Attestation

We chose batch attestation in order to allow servers to assess the trustworthiness of a device, while still affording privacy for the user. There are two other alternatives that offer attestation while protecting users' privacy: employing a trusted third party, and using advanced cryptographic techniques.

In a trusted third party scheme, a device makes an individually identifiable attestation statement to a privacy CA, first proposed by the Trusted Computing Group in their Trusted Platform Module (TPM) 1.1 specifications. A privacy CA provides its own anonymous attestation of the device's trustworthiness to the interested party. However, one challenge is that the privacy CA must always be available and reachable. Another is the distributed trust it requires: Who will run the privacy CA? Can different entities pick a privacy CA that suits them? What happens if each party doesn't trust the same privacy CA? Finally, a privacy CA would learn the identity of many individuals, presenting a single point of failure for compromising user privacy.

Advanced cryptographic techniques such as Direct Anonymous Attestation [35] and Enhanced Privacy ID [36] address many of the shortcomings of a privacy CA scheme, by allowing revocation without involving a trusted third party. We did not choose these approaches because they have not yet been demonstrated to be fast enough on low-cost hardware. For example, Bichsel *et al.* [37] evaluated an implementation of an RSA-based scheme running on JavaCard devices, which runs in roughly 16.5 s. This is well beyond the "around a second" guideline we had for registration operations.

## 7.2  Signature Counter

Our design includes a 32-bit signature counter, but leaves some decisions up to implementers: (1) wrapping behavior and (2) increment amount. Since a TUP is

---

[3] http://smile.amazon.com/s/ref=sr_kk_1?rh=k:u2f.

performed with every signature, a 32-bit counter provides the ability to perform a signature per second for more than 100 years before wrapping, and it seems reasonable that this is outside the lifetime of a Security Key. For the increment amount, an implementer could have a per-key handle counter, or could use a single global counter on a particular device. The latter choice is cheaper and easier to implement, although it presents a minor privacy leak if the counter update amount is predictable. Implementers could choose to increment a global counter by a randomly varying amount, though they would have to take care to avoid early counter wrapping as a result.

## 8    Conclusion

We have presented Security Key, a special-purpose device for improved second factor authentication on the web. Security Keys protect users against password reuse, phishing, and man-in-the-middle attacks by binding cryptographic assertions to website origin and properties of the TLS connection.

Security Keys also score favorably in the usability framework established by Bonneau et al. [5]. This is further substantiated by our preliminary data analysis which quantifies the benefits of Security Keys in a two-year deployment study by measuring reduction in sign-in times experienced by users and reduction in burden on a support organization.

The Security Key protocol has been standardized within the FIDO Alliance organization as the Universal Second Factor (U2F) open standard. We have open-sourced a reference implementation of the standard. Security Keys are supported by the Chrome browser and by the login system of major web service providers such as Google, GitHub, and DropBox. We hope this paper serves as an academic foundation to study and improve Security Keys going forward. Note, an updated and extended tech report is available at https://github.com/google/u2f-ref-code/docs/SecurityKeys_TechReport.pdf.

**Acknowledgements.** Listing all of the people who have contributed to the design, implementation, and evaluation of Security Keys is virtually impossible. We would like to thank the anonymous reviewers, along with the following individuals: Arnar Birgisson, Frank Cusack, Jakob Ehrensvärd, Kenny Franks, Iulia Ion, Benjamin Kalman, Kyle Levy, Brett McDowell, Dan Montgomery, Ratan Nalumasu, Rodrigo Paiva, Nishit Shah, Matt Spear, Jayini Trivedi, Mike Tsao, Mayank Upadhyay, and many Google teams (UX, QA, Legal).

## References

1. Fallows, J.: Hacked! The Atlantic. November 2011
2. Honan, M.: How Apple and Amazon Security Flaws Led to My Epic Hacking. http://www.wired.com/2012/08/apple-amazon-mat-honan-hacking/all/, Accessed 31 Dec 2014
3. Wikipedia: 2014 celebrity photo hack – wikipedia, the free encyclopedia. http://en.wikipedia.org/w/index.php?title=2014_celebrity_photo_hack&oldid=640287871, Accessed 31 Dec 2014

4. Bonneau, J.: The science of guessing: analyzing an anonymized corpus of 70 million passwords. In: 2012 IEEE Symposium on Security and Privacy. May 2012
5. Bonneau, J., Herley, C., van Oorschot, P.C., Stajano, F.: The quest to replace passwords: a framework for comparative evaluation of web authentication schemes. In: 2012 IEEE Symposium on Security and Privacy. May 2012
6. Herley, C., Oorschot, P.C., Patrick, A.S.: Passwords: if we're so smart, why are we still using them? In: Dingledine, R., Golle, P. (eds.) FC 2009. LNCS, vol. 5628, pp. 230–237. Springer, Heidelberg (2009). doi:10.1007/978-3-642-03549-4_14
7. Google Inc: Google 2-Step Verification (2015). https://support.google.com/accounts/answer/180744
8. Bank of America: SafePass Online Banking Security Enhancements (2015). https://www.bankofamerica.com/privacy/online-mobile-banking-privacy/safepass.go
9. Railton, J.S., Kleemola, K.: London Calling: Two-Factor Authentication Phishing From Iran (2015). https://citizenlab.org/2015/08/iran_two_factor_phishing/
10. Harbach, M., Fahl, S., Rieger, M., Smith, M.: On the acceptance of privacy-preserving authentication technology: the curious case of national identity cards. In: Cristofaro, E., Wright, M. (eds.) PETS 2013. LNCS, vol. 7981, pp. 245–264. Springer, Heidelberg (2013). doi:10.1007/978-3-642-39077-7_13
11. Unknown: Estonia takes the plunge: A national identity scheme goes global (2014). http://www.economist.com/news/international/21605923-national-identity-scheme-goes-global-estonia-takes-plunge
12. Shah, N.: Strengthening 2-Step Verification with Security Key (2014). https://googleonlinesecurity.blogspot.com/2014/10/strengthening-2-step-verification-with.html
13. Heim, P., Patel, J.: Introducing U2F support for secure authentication (2015). https://blogs.dropbox.com/dropbox/2015/08/u2f-security-keys/
14. Toews, B.: GitHub supports Universal 2nd Factor authentication (2015). https://github.com/blog/2071-github-supports-universal-2nd-factor-authentication
15. Fast IDentity Online (FIDO): (2015). https://fidoalliance.org/
16. Biddle, R., Chiasson, S., Van Oorschot, P.: Graphical passwords: learning from the first twelve years. ACM Comput. Surv. **44**(4), 19:1–19:41 (2012)
17. Jain, A.K., Flynn, P., Ross, A.A.: Handbook of Biometrics, 1st edn. Springer, New York (2010)
18. Parno, B., Kuo, C., Perrig, A.: Phoolproof phishing prevention. In: Crescenzo, G., Rubin, A. (eds.) FC 2006. LNCS, vol. 4107, pp. 1–19. Springer, Heidelberg (2006). doi:10.1007/11889663_1
19. Toopher Inc.: Toopher - 2 Factor Authentication (2012). http://toopher.com
20. Oracle: Java Card Technology (2014). http://www.oracle.com/technetwork/java/embedded/javacard/overview/index.html
21. Dierks, T., Rescorla, E.: The Transport Layer Security (TLS) Protocol, Version 1.2. http://tools.ietf.org/html/rfc5246, August 2008
22. Gaw, S., Felten, E.W.: Password management strategies for online accounts. In: Proceedings SOUPS 2006, pp. 44–55. ACM Press (2006)
23. Fontana, J.: Stolen passwords re-used to attack Best Buy accounts (2012). http://www.zdnet.com/stolen-passwords-re-used-to-attack-best-buy-accounts-7000000741/
24. Aircrack: Aircrack-ng Homepage (2015). http://www.aircrack-ng.org/doku.php
25. Butler, E.: Firesheep (2010). http://codebutler.com/firesheep
26. Ewen, M.: The NSA Files (2015). http://www.theguardian.com/us-news/the-nsa-files

27. The Register: Microsoft Outlook PENETRATED by Chinese 'man-in-the-middle' (2015). http://www.theregister.co.uk/2015/01/19/microsoft_outlook_hit_by_mitm_attack_says_china_great_fire_org/
28. Adkins, H.: An update on attempted man-in-the-middle attacks. http://googleonlinesecurity.blogspot.com/2011/08/update-on-attempted-man-in-middle.html, August 2011
29. Rizzo, J., Duong, T.: BEAST. http://vnhacker.blogspot.com/2011/09/beast.html, September 2011
30. AlFardan, N.J., Paterson, K.G.: Lucky Thirteen: Breaking the TLS and DTLS Record Protocols (2013). http://www.isg.rhul.ac.uk/tls/TLStiming.pdf
31. Dietz, M., Czeskis, A., Balfanz, D., Wallach, D.S.: Origin-bound certificates: a fresh approach to strong client authentication for the web. In: Proceedings of the 21st USENIX Conference on Security Symposium. Security 2012, Berkeley, CA, USA, USENIX Association (2012). 16–16
32. Popov, A., Balfanz, D., Nystroem, M., Langley, A.: The Token Binding Protocol Version 1.0 (2015). https://tools.ietf.org/html/draft-ietf-tokbind-protocol
33. Nilsson, D.: Yubico's Take On U2F Key Wrapping. https://www.yubico.com/2014/11/yubicos-u2f-key-wrapping/. Accessed 6 Jan 2016
34. Barnes, R.: Intent to implement and ship: FIDO U2F API (2015). https://groups.google.com/forum/#!msg/mozilla.dev.platform/IVGEJnQW3Uo/Eu5tvyLmCgAJ
35. Brickell, E., Camenisch, J., Chen, L.: Direct anonymous attestation. In: Proceedings of the 11th ACM Conference on Computer and Communications Security, CCS 2004, pp. 132–145. ACM, New York (2004)
36. Brickell, E., Li, J.: Enhanced privacy ID: a direct anonymous attestation scheme with enhanced revocation capabilities. In: Proceedings of the 2007 ACM Workshop on Privacy in Electronic Society, WPES 2007, pp. 21–30. ACM, New York (2007)
37. Bichsel, P., Camenisch, J., Groß, T., Shoup, V.: Anonymous credentials on a standard Java Card. In: Proceedings of the 16th ACM Conference on Computer and Communications Security, pp. 600–610. ACM (2009)

# Include Me Out: In-Browser Detection
# of Malicious Third-Party Content Inclusions

Sajjad Arshad[✉], Amin Kharraz, and William Robertson

Northeastern University, Boston, USA
{arshad,mkharraz,wkr}@ccs.neu.edu

**Abstract.** Modern websites include various types of third-party content such as JavaScript, images, stylesheets, and Flash objects in order to create interactive user interfaces. In addition to explicit inclusion of third-party content by website publishers, ISPs and browser extensions are hijacking web browsing sessions with increasing frequency to inject third-party content (e.g., ads). However, third-party content can also introduce security risks to users of these websites, unbeknownst to both website operators and users. Because of the often highly dynamic nature of these inclusions as well as the use of advanced cloaking techniques in contemporary malware, it is exceedingly difficult to preemptively recognize and block inclusions of malicious third-party content before it has the chance to attack the user's system.

In this paper, we propose a novel approach to achieving the goal of preemptive blocking of malicious third-party content inclusion through an analysis of inclusion sequences on the Web. We implemented our approach, called EXCISION, as a set of modifications to the Chromium browser that protects users from malicious inclusions while web pages load. Our analysis suggests that by adopting our in-browser approach, users can avoid a significant portion of malicious third-party content on the Web. Our evaluation shows that EXCISION effectively identifies malicious content while introducing a low false positive rate. Our experiments also demonstrate that our approach does not negatively impact a user's browsing experience when browsing popular websites drawn from the Alexa Top 500.

**Keywords:** Web security · Malvertising · Machine learning

## 1 Introduction

Linking to third-party content has been one of the defining features of the World Wide Web since its inception, and this feature remains strongly evident today. For instance, recent research [28] reveals that more than 93% of the most popular websites include JavaScript from external sources. Developers typically include third-party content for convenience and performance – e.g., many JavaScript libraries are hosted on fast content delivery networks (CDNs) and are likely to already be cached by users – or to integrate with advertising networks, analytics

© International Financial Cryptography Association 2017
J. Grossklags and B. Preneel (Eds.): FC 2016, LNCS 9603, pp. 441–459, 2017.
DOI: 10.1007/978-3-662-54970-4_26

frameworks, and social media. Third-party content inclusion has also been used by entities other than the website publishers themselves. For example, ad injection has been adopted by ISPs and browser extension authors as a prominent technique for monetization [25].

However, the inherent feature of content-sharing on the Web is also an Achilles heel when it comes to security. Advertising networks, as one example, have emerged as an important vector for adversaries to distribute attacks to a wide audience [21,22,29,36,43]. Moreover, users are more susceptible to *malvertising* in the presence of ad injection [17,38,42]. In general, linking to third-party content is essentially an assertion of trust that the content is benign. This assertion can be violated in several ways, however, due to the dynamic nature of the Web. Since website operators cannot control external content, they cannot know *a priori* what links will resolve to in the future. The compromise of linked content or pure malfeasance on the part of third parties can easily violate these trust assumptions. This is only exacerbated by the transitive nature of trust on the Web, where requests for content can be forwarded beyond the first, directly observable origin to unknown parties.

While the same origin policy (SOP) enforces a modicum of origin-based separation between code and data from different principals, developers have clamored for more flexible sharing models provided by, e.g., Content Security Policy (CSP) [7], Cross-Origin Resource Sharing (CORS) [6], and postMessage-based cross-frame communication. These newer standards permit greater flexibility in performing cross-origin inclusions, and each come with associated mechanisms for restricting communication to trusted origins. However, recent work has shown that these standards are difficult to apply securely in practice [34,40], and do not necessarily address the challenges of trusting remote inclusions on the dynamic Web. In addition to the inapplicability of some approaches such as CSP, third parties can leverage their power to bypass these security mechanisms. For example, ISPs and browser extensions are able to tamper with HTTP traffic to modify or remove CSP rules in HTTP responses [17,38].

In this paper, we propose an in-browser approach called EXCISION to automatically detect and block malicious third-party content inclusions as web pages are loaded into the user's browser or during the execution of browser extensions. Our approach does not rely on examination of the content of the resources; rather, it relies on analyzing the sequence of inclusions that leads to the resolution and loading of a terminal remote resource. Unlike prior work [22], EXCISION resolves *inclusion sequences* through instrumentation of the browser itself, an approach that provides a high-fidelity view of the third-party inclusion process as well as the ability to interdict content loading in real-time. This precise view also renders ineffective common obfuscation techniques used by attackers to evade detection. Obfuscation causes the detection rate of these approaches to degrade significantly since obfuscated third-party inclusions cannot be traced using existing techniques [22]. Furthermore, the in-browser property of our system allows users to browse websites with a higher confidence since malicious third-party content is prevented from being included while the web page is loading.

We implemented EXCISION as a set of modifications to the Chromium browser, and evaluated its effectiveness by analyzing the Alexa Top 200 K over a period of 11 months. Our evaluation demonstrates that EXCISION achieves a 93.39% detection rate, a false positive rate of 0.59%, and low performance overhead. We also performed a usability test of our research prototype, which shows that EXCISION does not detract from the user's browsing experience while automatically protecting the user from the vast majority of malicious content on the Web. The detection results suggest that EXCISION could be used as a complementary system to other techniques such as CSP.

The main contributions of this paper are as follows:

- We present a novel in-browser approach called EXCISION that automatically detects and blocks malicious third-party content before it can attack the user's browser. The approach leverages a high-fidelity in-browser vantage point that allows it to construct a precise inclusion sequence for every third-party resource.
- We describe a prototype of EXCISION for the Chromium browser that can effectively prevent inclusions of malicious content.
- We evaluate the effectiveness and performance of our prototype, and show that it is able to automatically detect and block malicious third-party content inclusions in the wild – including malicious resources not previously identified by popular malware blacklists – without a significant impact on browser performance.
- We evaluate the usability of our prototype and show that most users did not notice any significant quality impact on their browsing experience.

## 2    Problem Statement

In the following, we first discuss the threats posed by third-party content and then motivate our work.

### 2.1    Threats

While the inclusion of third-party content provides convenience for web developers and allows for integration into advertising distribution, analytics, and social media networks, it can potentially introduce a set of serious security threats for users. For instance, advertising networks and social media have been and continue to be abused as a vector for injection of malware. Website operators, or publishers, have little control over this content aside from blind trust or security through isolation. Attacks distributed through these vectors – in the absence of isolation – execute with the same privileges as all other JavaScript within the security context of the enclosing DOM. In general, malicious code could launch drive-by downloads [10], redirect visitors to phishing sites, generate fraudulent clicks on advertisements [22], or steal user information [16].

Moreover, ad injection has become a new source of income for ISPs and browser extension authors [25]. ISPs inject advertisements into web pages by tampering with their users' HTTP traffic [9], and browser extension authors have recently started to inject or replace ads in web pages to monetize their work. Ad injection negatively impacts both website publishers and users by diverting revenue from publishers and exposing users to malvertising [38,42]. In addition to ad injection, malicious browser extensions can also pose significant risks to users due to the special privileges they have [19].

## 2.2   Motivation

Publishers can try to isolate untrusted third-party content using iframes (perhaps enhanced with HTML5 sandboxing features), language-based sandboxing, or policy enforcement [1,12,15,23,24]. However, these approaches are not commonly used in practice; some degrade the quality of ads (from the advertiser's perspective), while others are non-trivial to deploy. Publishers could attempt to use Content Security Policy (CSP) [7] to define and enforce access control lists for remote inclusions in the browser. However, due to the dynamic nature of the web, this approach (and similar access control policy-based techniques) has problems. Recent studies [34,40] indicate that CSP is difficult to apply in practice. A major reason for this is the unpredictability of the origins of inclusions for third-party resources, which complicates the construction of a correct, yet tight, policy.

For example, when websites integrate third-party advertisements, multiple origins can be contacted in order to deliver an ad to the user's browser. This is often due to the practice of re-selling ad space (a process known as ad syndication) or through real-time ad auctions. Either of these approaches can result in ads being delivered through a series of JavaScript code inclusions [35]. Additionally, the growing number of browser extensions makes it a non-trivial task for website operators to enumerate the set of benign origins from which browser extensions might include a resource. As an example, for theverge.com website, the number of unique included domains over a period of 11 months increases roughly linearly; clearly, constructing an explicit whitelist of domains is a challenging task.

Even if website publishers can keep pace with origin diversity over time with a comprehensive list of CSP rules, ISPs and browser extensions are able to tamper with in-transit HTTP traffic and modify CSP rules sent by the websites. In addition, in browsers such as Chrome, the web page's CSP does not apply to extension scripts executed in the page's context [2]; hence, extensions are able to include arbitrary third-party resources into the web page.

Given the challenges described above, we believe that existing techniques such as CSP can be evaded and, hence, there is a need for an automatic approach to protect users from malicious third-party content. We do not necessarily advocate such an approach in isolation, however. Instead, we envision this approach as a complementary defense that can be layered with other techniques in order to improve the safety of the Web.

# 3   EXCISION

In this section, we describe EXCISION, our approach for detecting and blocking the inclusion of malicious third-party content in real-time. An overview of our system is shown in Fig. 1. EXCISION operates by extracting resource *inclusion trees* from within the browser. The inclusion tree precisely records the inclusion relationships between different resources in a web page. When the user requests a web page, the browser retrieves the corresponding HTML document and passes it to the rendering engine. The rendering engine incrementally constructs an inclusion tree for the DOM and begins extracting external resources such as scripts and frames as it reaches new HTML tags. For inclusion of a new resource, the rendering engine consults the CSP engine and the *inclusion sequence classifier* in order to decide whether to include the resource. If the resource's origin and type are whitelisted in the CSP rules, the rendering engine includes the resource without consulting the inclusion sequence classifier and continues parsing the rest of the HTML document. Otherwise, it extracts the *inclusion sequence* (path through the page's inclusion tree) for the resource and forwards this to the inclusion sequence classifier. Using pre-learned models, the classifier returns a decision about the malice of the resource to the rendering engine. Finally, the rendering engine discards the resource if it was identified as malicious. The same process occurs for resources that are included dynamically during the execution of extension scripts after they are injected into the page.

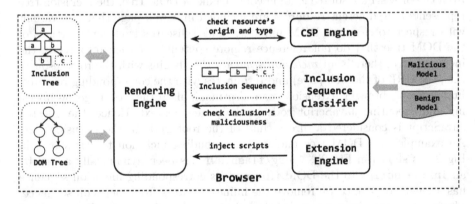

**Fig. 1.** An overview of EXCISION.

## 3.1   Inclusion Trees and Sequences

A website can include resources in an HTML document from any origin so long as the inclusion respects the same origin policy, its standard exceptions, or any additional policies due to the use of CSP, CORS, or other access control framework. A first approximation to understanding the inclusions of third-party content for a given web page is to process its DOM tree [41] while the page loads. However, direct use of a web page's DOM tree is unsatisfactory because the DOM does not

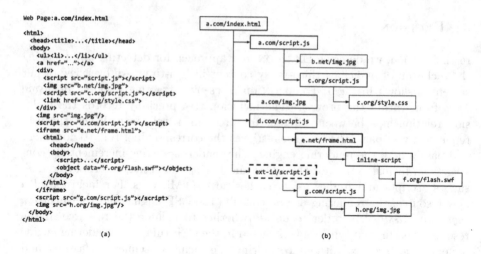

**Fig. 2.** (a) DOM tree, and (b) Inclusion tree

in fact reliably record the inclusion relationships between resources referenced by a page. This follows from the ability for JavaScript to manipulate the DOM at run-time using the DOM API.

Instead, in this work we define an *inclusion tree* abstraction extracted directly from the browser's resource loading code. Unlike a DOM tree, the inclusion tree represents how different resources are included in a web page that is invariant with respect to run-time DOM updates. It also discards irrelevant portions of the DOM tree that do not reference remote content. For each resource in the inclusion tree, there is an *inclusion sequence* that begins with the root resource (i.e., the URL of the web page) and terminates with the corresponding resource. Furthermore, browser extensions can also manipulate the web page by injecting and executing JavaScript code in the page's context. Hence, the injected JavaScript is considered a direct child of the root node in the inclusion tree. An example of a DOM tree and its corresponding inclusion tree is shown in Fig. 2. As shown in Fig. 2b, `f.org/flash.swf` has been dynamically added by an `inline script` to the DOM tree, and its corresponding inclusion sequence has a length of 4 since we remove the inline resources from inclusion sequence. Moreover, `ext-id/script.js` is injected by an extension as the direct child of the root resource. This script then included `g.com/script.js`, which in turn included `h.org/img.jpg`.

## 3.2    Inclusion Sequence Classification

Given an inclusion sequence, EXCISION must classify it as benign or malicious based on features extracted from the sequence. The task of the *inclusion sequence classifier* is to assign a class label from the set {benign,malicious} to a given sequence based on previously learned models from a labeled data set. In our definition, a malicious sequence is one that starts from the root URL of a web page and terminates in a URL that delivers malicious content. For classification, we used hidden Markov models (HMM) [31]. Models are comprised of states, each of which holds transitions to other states based on a probability distribution. Each state can probabilistically emit a symbol from an alphabet. There are other sequence classification techniques such as Naïve Bayes [20], but we used an HMM for our classifier because we also want to model the inter-dependencies between the resources that compose an inclusion sequence.

In the training phase, the system learns two HMMs from a training set of labeled sequences, one for the benign class and one for the malicious class. We estimated the HMM parameters by employing the Baum-Welch algorithm which finds the maximum likelihood estimate of these parameters based on the set of observed sequences. In our system, we empirically selected 20 for the number of states that are fully connected to each other. In the subsequent detection phase, we compute the likelihood of a new sequence given the trained models using the forward-backward algorithm and assign the sequence to the class with the highest likelihood. Training hidden Markov models is computationally expensive. However, computing the likelihood of a sequence is instead very efficient, which makes it a suitable method for real-time classification [31].

## 4    Classification Features

Let $r_0 \rightarrow r_1 \rightarrow \cdots \rightarrow r_n$ be an inclusion sequence as described above. Feature extraction begins by converting the inclusion sequence into sequences of feature vectors. After analyzing the inclusion trees of several thousand benign and malicious websites for a period of 11 months, we identified 12 feature types from three categories. For each feature type, we compute two different features: individual and relative features. An individual feature value is only dependent on the current resource, but a relative feature value is dependent on the current resource and its preceding (or parent) resources. Consequently, we have 24 features for each resource in an inclusion sequence. Individual features can have categorical or continuous values. All continuous feature values are normalized on $[0, 1]$ and their values are discretized. In the case of continuous individual features, the relative feature values are computed by comparing the individual value of the resource to its parent's individual value. The result of the comparison is less, equal, or more. We use the value none for the root resource. To capture the high-level relationships between different inclusions, we only consider the host part of the URL for feature calculation.

### 4.1    DNS-Based Features

The first feature category that we consider is based on DNS properties of the resource host.

**Top-Level Domain.** For this feature, we measure the types of TLDs from which a resource is included and how it changes along the inclusion sequence. For every resource in an inclusion sequence, we assign one of the values in Table 1 as an

**Table 1.** Individual TLD values

| Value | Example |
|---|---|
| none | IPs, Extensions |
| gen | *.com, *.org |
| gen-subdomain | *.us.com |
| cc | *.us, *.de, *.cn |
| cc-subdomain | *.co.uk, *.com.cn |
| cc-int | *.xn--p1ai (ru) |
| other | *.biz, *.info |

**Table 2.** Relative TLD values.

| Value | Example |
|---|---|
| none | root resource |
| {got,lost}-tld | Ext. → *.de, *.us → IP |
| gen-to-{cc,other} | *.org → {*.de, *.info} |
| cc-to-{gen,other} | *.uk → {*.com, *.biz} |
| other-to-{gen,cc} | *.info → {*.net, *.uk} |
| same-{gen,cc,other} | *.com → *.com |
| diff-{gen,cc,other} | *.info → *.biz |

**Table 3.** Individual type values

| Value | Example |
|---|---|
| ipv6 | 2607:f0d0::::4 |
| ipv4-private | 192.168.0.1 |
| ipv4-public | 4.2.2.4 |
| extension | Ext. Scripts |
| dns-sld | google.com |
| dns-sld-sub | www.google.com |
| dns-non-sld | abc.dyndns.org |
| dns-non-sld-sub | a.b.dyndns.org |

**Table 4.** Relative type values.

| Value | Example |
|---|---|
| none | root resource |
| same-site | w.google.com → ad.google.com |
| same-sld | 1.dyndns.org → 2.dyndns.org |
| same-company | ad.google.com → www.google.de |
| same-eff-tld | bbc.co.uk → london.co.uk |
| same-tld | bbc.co.uk → london.uk |
| different | google.com → facebook.net |

individual feature. For the relative feature, we consider the changes that occur between the top-level domain of the preceding resource and the resource itself. Table 2 shows 15 different values of the relative TLD feature.

**Type.** This feature identifies the types of resource hosts and their changes along the inclusion sequence. Possible values of individual and relative features are shown in Tables 3 and 4 respectively.

**Level.** A domain name consists of a set of labels separated by dots. We say a domain name with $n$ labels is in level $n - 1$. For example, www.google.com is in level 2. For IP addresses and extension scripts, we consider their level to be 1. For a given host, we compute the individual feature by dividing the level by a maximum value of 126.

**Alexa Ranking.** We also consider the ranking of a resource's domain in the Alexa Top 1M websites. To compute the normalized ranking as an individual feature, we divide the ranking of the domain by one million. For IP addresses, extensions, and domains that are not in the top 1M, we use the value none.

## 4.2 String-Based Features

We observed that malicious domain names often make liberal use of digits and hyphens in combination with alphabetical characters. So, in this feature category, we characterize the string properties of resource hosts. For IP addresses and extension scripts, we assign the value 1 for individual features.

**Non-alphabetic Characters.** For this feature, we compute the individual feature value by dividing the number of non-alphabetical characters over the length of domain.

**Unique Characters.** We also measure the number of unique characters that are used in a domain. The individual feature is the number of unique characters in the domain divided by the maximum number of unique characters in the domain name, which is 38 (26 alphabetics, 10 digits, hyphen, and dot).

**Character Frequency.** For this feature, we simply measure how often a single character is seen in a domain. To compute an individual feature value, we calculate the frequency of each character in the domain and then divide the average of these frequencies by the length of the domain to normalize the value.

**Length.** In this feature, we measure the length of the domain divided by the maximum length of a domain, which is 253.

**Entropy.** In practice, benign domains are typically intended to be memorable to users. This is often not a concern for attackers, as evidenced by the use of domain generation algorithms [8]. Consequently, we employ Shannon entropy to measure the randomness of domains in the inclusion sequence. We calculate normalized entropy as the absolute Shannon entropy divided by the maximum entropy for the domain name.

### 4.3  Role-Based Features

We observed that identifying the role of resources in the inclusion sequences can be helpful in detecting malicious resources. For example, recent work [29] reveals that attackers misuse ad networks as well as URL shortening services for malicious intent. So far, we consider three roles for a resource: (i) ad-network, (ii) content delivery network (CDN), and (iii) URL shortening service.

In total, we have three features in this category, as each host can simultaneously perform multiple roles. Both individual and relative features in this category have binary values. For the individual feature, the value is Yes if the host has the role, and No otherwise. For the relative feature, we assign a value Yes if at least one of the preceding hosts have the corresponding role, and No otherwise. For extension scripts, we assign the value No for all of the features. To assign the roles, we compiled a list of common hosts related to these roles that contains 5,767 ad-networks, 48 CDNs, and 461 URL shortening services.

## 5  Implementation

In this section, we discuss our prototype implementation of EXCISION for detecting and blocking malicious third-party content inclusions. We implemented

EXCISION as a set of modifications to the Chromium browser[1]. In order to implement our system, we needed to modify Blink and the Chromium extension engine to enable EXCISION to detect and block inclusions of malicious content in an online and automatic fashion while the web page is loading. The entire set of modifications consists of less than 1,000 lines of C++ and several lines of JavaScript.

## 5.1    Enhancements to Blink

Blink is primarily responsible for parsing HTML documents, managing script execution, and fetching resources from the network. Consequently, it is ideally suited for constructing the inclusion tree for a web page, as well as blocking the inclusion of malicious content.

**Tracking Resource Inclusion.** Static resource inclusions that are hard-coded by publishers inside the page's HTML are added to the inclusion tree as the direct children of the root node. For dynamic inclusions (e.g., via the createElement() and write() DOM API functions), the system must find the script resource responsible for the resource inclusion. To monitor dynamic resource inclusions, the system tracks the start and termination of script execution. Any resources that are included in this interval will be considered as the children of that script resource in the inclusion tree.

**Handling Events and Timers.** Events and timers are widely used by web developers to respond to user interactions (e.g., clicking on an element) or schedule execution of code after some time has elapsed. To capture the creation and firing of events and timers, the system tracks the registration of callback functions for the corresponding APIs.

## 5.2    Enhancements to the Chromium Extension Engine

The Chromium extension engine handles the loading, management, and execution of extensions. To access the page's DOM, the extension injects and executes *content scripts* in the page's context which are regular JavaScript programs.

**Tracking Content Scripts Injection and Execution.** Content scripts are usually injected into web pages either via the extension's manifest file using the content_scripts field or at runtime via the executeScript API. Either way, content scripts are considered direct children of the root node in the inclusion tree. Therefore, in order to track the inclusion of resources as a result of content script execution, the extension engine was modified to track the injection and execution of content scripts.

---

[1] While our implementation could be adopted as-is by any browser vendors that use WebKit-derived engines, the design presented here is highly likely to be portable to other browsers.

**Handling Callback Functions.** Like any other JavaScript program, content scripts rely heavily on callback functions. For instance, onMessage and sendMessage are used by content scripts to exchange messages with their background pages. To track the execution of callback functions, two JavaScript files were modified in the extension engine which are responsible for invocation and management of callback functions.

## 6  Evaluation

In this section, we evaluate the security benefits, performance, and usability of the EXCISION prototype. We describe the data sets we used to train and evaluate the system, and then present the results of the experiments.

### 6.1  Data Collection

To collect inclusion sequences, we performed two separate crawls for websites and extensions. The summary of crawling statistics are presented in Table 5.

**Website Crawl.** We built a crawler based on an instrumented version of PhantomJS [3], a scriptable open source browser based on WebKit, and crawled the

**Table 5.** Summary of crawling statistics.

| Item | Website crawl | Extension crawl |
|---|---|---|
| Websites crawled | 234,529 | 20 |
| Unavailable websites | 7,412 | 0 |
| Unique inclusion trees | 47,789,268 | 35,004 |
| Unique inclusion sequences | 27,261,945 | 61,489 |
| Unique URLs | 546,649,590 | 72,064 |
| Unique hosts | 1,368,021 | 1,144 |
| Unique sites | 459,615 | 749 |
| Unique SLDs | 419,119 | 723 |
| Unique companies | 384,820 | 719 |
| Unique effective TLDs | 1,115 | 21 |
| Unique TLDs | 404 | 21 |
| Unique IPs | 9,755 | 3 |

**Table 6.** Data sets used in the evaluation.

| Dataset | No. of inclusion sequences | | No. of terminal hosts | |
|---|---|---|---|---|
| | Web. crawl | Ext. crawl | Web. crawl | Ext. crawl |
| Benign | 3,706,451 | 7,372 | 35,044 | 250 |
| Malicious | 25,153 | 19 | 1,226 | 2 |

home pages of the Alexa Top 200K. We performed our data collection from June 20th, 2014 to May 11th, 2015. The crawl was parallelized by deploying 50 crawler instances on five virtual machines, each of which crawled a fixed subset of the Alexa Top 200 K websites. To ensure that visited websites did not store any data on the clients, the crawler ran a fresh instance of PhantomJS for each visit. Once all crawlers finished crawling the list of websites, the process was restarted from the beginning. To thwart cloaking techniques [18] utilized by attackers, the crawlers presented a user agent for IE 6.0 on Windows and employed Tor to send HTTP requests from different source IP addresses. We also address JavaScript-based browser fingerprinting by modifying the internal implementation of the `navigator` object to return a fake value for the `appCodeName`, `appName`, `appVersion`, `platform`, `product`, `userAgent`, and `vendor` attributes.

**Extension Crawl.** To collect inclusion sequences related to extensions, we used 292 Chrome extensions reported in prior work [42] that injected ads into web pages. Since ad-injecting extensions mostly target shopping websites (e.g., Amazon), we chose the Alexa Top 20 shopping websites for crawling to trigger ad injection by those 292 extensions. We built a crawler by instrumenting Chromium 43 and collected data for a period of one week from June 16th to June 22nd, 2015. The system loaded every extension and then visited the home pages of the Alexa Top 20 shopping websites using Selenium WebDriver [4]. This process was repeated after crawling the entire set of extensions. In addition, our crawler triggered all the events and timers registered by content scripts.

## 6.2   Building Labeled Datasets

To classify a given inclusion sequence as benign or malicious, we trained two hidden Markov models for benign and malicious inclusion sequences from our data set. We labeled collected inclusion sequences as either benign or malicious using VirusTotal [5]. VirusTotal's URL scanning service aggregates reports of malicious URLs from most prominent URL scanners such as Google Safe Browsing [13] and the Malware Domain List. The malicious data set contains all inclusion sequences where the last included resource's host is reported malicious by at least three out of the 62 URL scanners in VirusTotal. On the other hand, the benign data set only contains inclusion sequences that do not contain any host in the entire sequence that is reported as malicious by any URL scanner in VirusTotal. To build benign data set, we considered reputable domains such as well-known search engines and advertising networks as benign regardless of whether they are reported as malicious by any URL scanner in VirusTotal. Table 6 summarizes the data sets. The unique number of inclusion sequences and terminal hosts are shown separately for the website and extension data sets. The terminal hosts column is the number of unique hosts that terminate inclusion sequences.

## 6.3   Detection Results

To evaluate the accuracy of our classifier, we used 10-fold cross-validation, in which we first partitioned each data set into 10 equal-sized folds, trained the models on nine folds, and then validated the resulting models with the remaining fold. The process was repeated for each fold and, at the end, we calculated the average false positive rate and false negative rate. When splitting the data set into training and testing sets, we made sure that inclusion sequences with different lengths were present in both. We also ensured that both sets contained extension-related inclusion sequences.

The results show that our classifier achieved a false positive rate of 0.59% and false negative rate of 6.61% (detection rate of 93.39%). Most of the false positives are due to inclusion sequences that do not appear too often in the training sets. Hence, users are unlikely to experience many false positives in a real browsing environment (as will be shown in our usability analysis in Sect. 6.6).

To quantify the contribution of different feature categories to the classification, we trained classifiers using different combinations of feature categories and compared the results. Figure 3a shows the false positive rate and false negative rate of every combination with a 10-fold cross-validation training scheme. According to Fig. 3a, the best false positive and false negative rates were obtained using a combination of all feature categories.

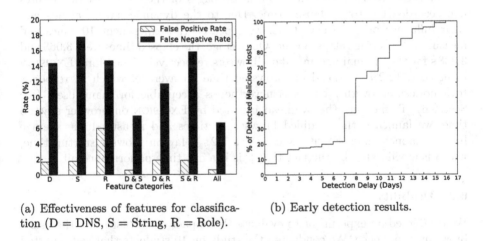

(a) Effectiveness of features for classification (D = DNS, S = String, R = Role).

(b) Early detection results.

**Fig. 3.** Feature category contributions and early detection results.

## 6.4  Comparison with URL Scanners

To evaluate the ability of our system in detecting unreported suspicious hosts, we ran our classifier on inclusion sequences collected from June 1st until July 14th, 2015. We compared our detection results with reports from URL scanners in VirusTotal and detected 89 new suspicious hosts. We believe that these hosts are in fact dedicated malicious hosts that play the role of redirectors and manage malicious traffic flows as described in prior work [21]. These hosts did not deliver malicious resources themselves, but they consistently included resources from other hosts that were flagged as malicious by URL scanners. Out of 89 suspicious domains, nearly 44% were recently registered in 2015, and more than 23% no longer resolve to an IP address.

Furthermore, we detected 177 hosts that were later reported by URL scanners after some delay. Figure 3b shows the early detection results of our system. A significant number of these hosts were not reported until some time had passed after EXCISION initially identified them. For instance, nearly 78% of the malicious hosts were not reported by any URL scanner during the first week.

## 6.5    Performance

To assess the performance of EXCISION, we used Selenium WebDriver to automatically visit the Alexa Top 1 K with both original and modified Chromium browsers. In order to measure our prototype performance with a realistic set of extensions, we installed five of the most popular extensions in the Chrome Web Store: Adblock Plus, Google Translate, Google Dictionary, Evernote Web Clipper, and Tampermonkey.

For each browser, we visited the home pages of the entire list of websites and recorded the total elapsed time. Due to the dynamic nature of ads and their influence on page load time, we repeated the experiment 10 times and measured the average elapsed time. On average, the elapsed times were 3,065 and 3,438 s for the original and modified browsers respectively. Therefore, EXCISION incurred a 12.2% overhead on browsing time on average, which corresponds to a noticeable overhead that is nevertheless acceptable for many users (see Sect. 6.6). To measure the overhead incurred by EXCISION on browser startup time, we launched the modified browser 10 times and measured the average browser launch time. EXCISION caused a 3.2 s delay on browser startup time, which is ameliorated by the fact that this is a one-time performance hit.

## 6.6    Usability

We conducted an experiment to evaluate the impact of EXCISION on the user's browsing experience. We conducted the study on 10 students that self-reported as expert Internet users. We provided each participant with a list of 50 websites that were selected randomly from the Alexa Top 500 and then asked them to visit at least three levels down in each website. Participants were asked to report the number of visited pages and the list of domains reported as malicious by our system. In addition, participants were asked to record the number of errors they encountered while they browsed the websites. Errors were considered to occur when the browser crashed, the appearance of a web page was corrupted, or page load times were abnormally long. Furthermore, in order to ensure that benign extensions were not prevented from executing as expected in the presence of our system, the browser was configured to load the five popular extensions listed in Sect. 6.5 and participants were asked to report any problem while using the extensions.

The results of the study show that out of 5,129 web pages visited by the participants, only 83 errors were encountered and the majority of web pages loaded correctly. Most of these errors happened due to relatively high load times. In addition, none of the participants reported any broken extensions. Furthermore, 31 malicious inclusions were reported by our tool that were automatically processed (without manual examination, for privacy reasons) using VirusTotal. Based on the results, we believe that our proof-of-concept prototype is compatible with frequently used websites and extensions, and can be improved through further engineering to work completely free of errors.

**Ethics.** In designing the usability experiment, we made a conscious effort to avoid collecting personal or sensitive information. In particular, we restricted the kinds of information we asked users to report to incidence counts for each of the categories of information, except for malicious URLs that were reported by our tool. Malicious URLs were automatically submitted to VirusTotal to obtain a malice classification before being discarded, and were not viewed by us or manually inspected. In addition, the participants were asked to avoid browsing websites requiring a login or involving sensitive subject matter.

# 7   Related Work

**Third-party Content Isolation.** Several recent research projects [14,37,39] attempted to improve the security of browsers by isolating browser components in order to minimize data sharing among software components. The main issue with these approaches is that they do not perform any isolation between JavaScript loaded from different domains and web applications, letting untrusted scripts access the main web application's code and data. Efforts such as AdJail [23] attempt to protect privacy by isolating ads into an iframe-based sandbox. However, this approach restricts contextual targeting advertisement in which ad scripts need to have access to host page content.

**Detecting Malicious Domains.** There are multiple approaches to automatically detecting malicious web domains. Madtracer [22] has been proposed to automatically capture malvertising cases. But, this system is not as precise as our approach in identifying the causal relationships among different domains. EXPOSURE [8] employs passive DNS analysis techniques to detect malicious domains. SpiderWeb [36] is also a system that is able to detect malicious web pages by crowd-sourcing redirection chains. Segugio [32] tracks new malware-control domain names in very large ISP networks. WebWitness [27] automatically traces back malware download paths to understand attack trends. While these techniques can be used to automatically detect malicious websites and update blacklists, they are not online systems and may not be effectively used to detect malicious third-party inclusions since users expect a certain level of performance while browsing the Web.

Another effective detection approach is to produce blacklists of malicious sites by scanning the Internet that can be efficiently checked by the browser (e.g., Google Safe Browsing [13]). Blacklist construction requires extensive infrastructure to continuously scan the Internet and bypass cloaking and general malware evasion attempts in order to reliably identify malware distribution sites, phishing pages, and other Web malice. As our evaluation in Sect. 6 demonstrates, these blacklists sometimes lag the introduction of malicious sites on the Internet, or fail to find these malicious sites. However, they are nevertheless effective, and we view the approach we propose as a complementary technique to established blacklist generation and enforcement techniques.

**Policy Enforcement.** Another approach is to search and restrict third-party code included in web applications [12,15,24]. For example, ADsafe [1] removes dangerous JavaScript features (e.g., `eval`), enforcing a whitelist of allowed JavaScript functionality considered safe. It is also possible to protect against malicious JavaScript ads by enforcing policies at runtime [30,33]. For example, Meyerovich et al. [26] introduce a client-side framework that allows web applications to enforce fine-grained security policies for DOM elements. AdSentry [11] provides a shadow JavaScript engine that runs untrusted ad scripts in a sandboxed environment.

## 8    Conclusion

In this paper, we presented EXCISION, an in-browser system to automatically detect and block malicious third-party content inclusions before they can attack the user's browser. Our system is complementary to other defensive approaches such as CSP and Google Safe Browsing, and is implemented as a set of modifications to the Chromium browser. EXCISION does not perform any blacklisting to detect malicious third-party inclusions. Rather, it incrementally constructs an inclusion tree for a given web page and automatically prevents loading malicious resources by classifying their inclusion sequences using a set of pre-built models.

Our evaluation over an 11 month crawl of the Alexa Top 200 K demonstrates that the prototype implementation of EXCISION detects a significant number of malicious third-party content in the wild. In particular, the system achieved a 93.39% detection rate with a false positive rate of 0.59%. EXCISION was also able to detect previously unknown malicious inclusions. We also evaluated the performance and usability of EXCISION when browsing popular websites, and show that the approach is capable of improving the security of users on the Web by detecting 31 malicious inclusions during a user study without significantly degrading the user experience.

**Acknowledgement.** This material is based upon work supported by the National Science Foundation under Grant No. CNS-1409738.

# References

1. ADsafe. http://www.adsafe.org/
2. CSP in Content Scripts. https://developer.chrome.com/extensions/contentSecurity Policy#interactions
3. PhantomJS. http://phantomjs.org/
4. Selenium: Web Browser Automation. http://www.seleniumhq.org/
5. VirtusTotal. https://www.virustotal.com/
6. Cross-Origin Resource Sharing (CORS) (2014). http://www.w3.org/TR/cors/
7. Content Security Policy 1.1 (2015). https://dvcs.w3.org/hg/content-security-policy/raw-file/tip/csp-specification.dev.html
8. Bilge, L., Kirda, E., Kruegel, C., Marco Balduzzi, E.: Finding malicious domains using passive DNS analysis. In: Network and Distributed System Security Symposium (NDSS) (2011)
9. Coldewey, D.: Marriott puts an end to shady ad injection service (2012). http://techcrunch.com/2012/04/09/marriott-puts-an-end-to-shady-ad-injection-service/
10. Cova, M., Kruegel, C., Vigna, G.: Detection and analysis of drive-by-download attacks and malicious javascript code. In: International World Wide Web Conference (WWW) (2010)
11. Dong, X., Tran, M., Liang, Z., Jiang, X.: AdSentry: Comprehensive and flexible confinement of JavaScript-based advertisements. In: Annual Computer Security Applications Conference (ACSAC) (2011)
12. Finifter, M., Weinberger, J., Barth, A.: Preventing capability leaks in secure JavaScript subsets. In: Network and Distributed System Security Symposium (NDSS) (2010)
13. Google, Inc., Google Safe Browsing API (2015). https://developers.google.com/safe-browsing/
14. Grier, C., Tang, S., King, S.T.: Secure web browsing with the OP web browser. In: IEEE Symposium on Security and Privacy (Oakland) (2008)
15. Guarnieri, S., Benjamin Livshits, G.: Mostly static enforcement of security and reliability policies for JavaScript code. In: USENIX Security Symposium (2009)
16. Huang, L.-S., Weinberg, Z., Evans, C., Jackson, C.: Protecting browsers from cross-origin CSS attacks. In: Proceedings of the ACM Conference on Computer and Communications Security (CCS) (2010)
17. Jagpal, N., Dingle, E., Gravel, J.-P., Mavrommatis, P., Provos, N., Rajab, M.A., Thomas, K.: Trends and lessons from three years fighting malicious extensions. In: USENIX Security Symposium (2015)
18. John, J.P., Yu, F., Xie, Y., Krishnamurthy, A., Abadi, M.: deSEO: Combating search-result poisoning. In: USENIX Security Symposium (2011)
19. Kapravelos, A., Grier, C., Chachra, N., Kruegel, C., Vigna, G., Paxson, V.: Hulk: eliciting malicious behavior in browser extensions. In: USENIX Security Symposium (2014)
20. Lewis, D.D.: Naive (Bayes) at forty: the independence assumption in information retrieval. In: Nédellec, C., Rouveirol, C. (eds.) ECML 1998. LNCS, vol. 1398, pp. 4–15. Springer, Heidelberg (1998). doi:10.1007/BFb0026666
21. Li, Z., Alrwais, S., Xie, Y., Yu, F., Wang, X.: Finding the linchpins of the dark web: a study on topologically dedicated hosts on malicious web infrastructures. In: IEEE Symposium on Security and Privacy (Oakland) (2013)

22. Li, Z., Zhang, K., Xie, Y., Yu, F., Wang, X.: Knowing your enemy: understanding and detecting malicious web advertising. In: ACM Conference on Computer and Communications Security (CCS) (2012)
23. Ter Louw, M., Ganesh, K.T., Venkatakrishnan, V.N.: AdJail: practical enforcement of confidentiality and integrity policies on web advertisements. In: USENIX Security Symposium (2010)
24. Maffeis, S., Taly, A.: Language-based isolation of untrusted JavaScript. In: IEEE Computer Security Foundations Symposium (CSF) (2009)
25. Marvin, G.: Google study exposes "tangled web" of companies profiting from ad injection (2015). http://marketingland.com/ad-injector-study-google-127738
26. Meyerovich, L.A., Livshits, B.: ConScript: specifying and enforcing fine-grained security policies for JavaScript in the browser. In: IEEE Symposium on Security and Privacy (Oakland) (2010)
27. Nelms, T., Perdisci, R., Antonakakis, M., Ahamad, M.: WebWitness: investigating, categorizing, and mitigating malware download paths. In: USENIX Security Symposium (2015)
28. Nikiforakis, N., Invernizzi, L., Kapravelos, A., Van Acker, S., Joosen, W., Kruegel, C., Piessens, F., Vigna, G.: You are what You include: large-scale evaluation of remote JavaScript inclusions. In: ACM Conference on Computer and Communications Security (CCS) (2012)
29. Nikiforakis, N., Maggi, F., Stringhini, G., Rafique, M., Joosen, W., Kruegel, C., Piessens, F., Vigna, G., Zanero, S.: Stranger danger: exploring the ecosystem of ad-based URL shortening services. In: International World Wide Web Conference (WWW) (2014)
30. Phung, P.H., Sands, D., Chudnov, A.: Lightweight self-protecting JavaScript. In: ACM Symposium on Information, Computer, and Communications Security (ASIACCS) (2009)
31. Rabiner, L.R.: A tutorial on Hidden Markov Models and selected applications in speech recognition. Proc. IEEE $77(2)$, 257–285 (1989)
32. Rahbarinia, B., Perdisci, R., Antonakakis, M.: Segugio: efficient behavior-based tracking of new malware-control domains in large ISP networks. In: IEEE/IFIP International Conference on Dependable Systems and Networks (DSN) (2015)
33. Reis, C., Dunagan, J., Wang, H.J., Dubrovsky, O., Esmeir, S.: BrowserShield: vulnerability-driven filtering of dynamic HTML. In: USENIX Symposium on Operating Systems Design and Implementation (OSDI) (2006)
34. Son, S., Shmatikov, V.: The postman always rings twice: attacking and defending postMessage in HTML5 websites. In: Network and Distributed System Security Symposium (NDSS) (2013)
35. Stone-Gross, B., Stevens, R., Kemmerer, R., Kruegel, C., Vigna, G., Zarras, A.: Understanding fraudulent activities in online ad exchanges. In: Internet Measurement Conference (IMC) (2011)
36. Stringhini, G., Kruegel, C., Vigna, G.: Shady paths: leveraging surfing crowds to detect malicious web pages. In: ACM Conference on Computer and Communications Security (CCS) (2013)
37. Tang, S., Mai, H., King, S.T.: Trust and protection in the Illinois browser operating system. In: USENIX Symposium on Operating Systems Design and Implementation (OSDI) (2010)
38. Thomas, K., Bursztein, E., Grier, C., Ho, G., Jagpal, N., Kapravelos, A., McCoy, D., Nappa, A., Paxson, V., Pearce, P., Provos, N., Rajab, M.A.: Ad injection at scale: assessing deceptive advertisement modifications. In: IEEE Symposium on Security and Privacy (Oakland) (2015)

39. Wang, H.J., Grier, C., Moshchuk, A., King, S.T., Choudhury, P., Venter, H.: The multi-principal OS construction of the Gazelle web browser. In: USENIX Security Symposium (2009)
40. Weissbacher, M., Lauinger, T., Robertson, W.: Why is CSP failing? Trends and challenges in CSP adoption. In: Stavrou, A., Bos, H., Portokalidis, G. (eds.) RAID 2014. LNCS, vol. 8688, pp. 212–233. Springer, Cham (2014). doi:10.1007/978-3-319-11379-1_11
41. World Wide Web Consortium (W3C). What is the document object model? http://www.w3.org/TR/DOM-Level-2-Core/introduction.html
42. Xing, X., Meng, W., Weinsberg, U., Sheth, A., Lee, B., Perdisci, R., Lee, W.: Unraveling the relationship between ad-injecting browser extensions and malvertising. In: International World Wide Web Conference (WWW) (2015)
43. Zarras, A., Kapravelos, A., Stringhini, G., Holz, T., Kruegel, C., Vigna, G.: The dark alleys of madison avenue: understanding malicious advertisements. In: Proceedings of the Internet Measurement Conference (IMC) (2014)

# A Sensitivity-Adaptive $\rho$-Uncertainty Model for Set-Valued Data

Liuhua Chen, Shenghai Zhong, Li-e Wang, and Xianxian Li$^{(\boxtimes)}$

Guangxi Key Lab of Multi-source Information Mining and Security,
Guangxi Normal University, Guilin 541004, China
liuhuachengxnu@sina.com, wuhanzsh@gmail.com, {wanglie,lixx}@gxnu.edu.cn

**Abstract.** Set-valued data brings enormous opportunities to data mining tasks for various purposes. Many anonymous methods for set-valued data have been proposed to effectively protect an individual's privacy against identify linkable attacks and item linkage attacks. In these methods, sensitive items are protected by a privacy threshold to limit the re-identification probability of sensitive items. However, lots of set-valued data have diverse sensitivity on data items. This leads to the over-protection problem when these existing privacy-preserving methods are applied to process the data items with diverse sensitivity, and it reduces the utility of data. In this paper, we propose a sensitivity-adaptive $\rho$-uncertainty model to prevent over-generalization and over-suppression by using adaptive privacy thresholds. Thresholds, which accurately capture the hidden privacy features of the set-valued dataset, are defined by uneven distribution of different sensitive items. Under the model, we develop a fine-grained privacy preserving technique through Local Generalization and Partial Suppression, which optimizes a balance between privacy protection and data utility. Experiments show that our method effectively improves the utility of anonymous data.

**Keywords:** Set-valued data · Anonymization · Privacy preserving · Generalization · Suppression

## 1 Introduction

With the rapid development of information technology, the Internet produced a sea of data, such as web search query logs [1], electronic health records [2] and set-valued data [3–5], which can service for behavior prediction, commodity recommendation and information retrieval.

Set-valued data, where a set of sensitive and non-sensitive items are relevant to an individual, contains detailed individual information. For example, a transaction dataset is shown in Table 1, where items $a$, $b$, $c$ and $d$ are non-sensitive and $\alpha$, $\beta$ are sensitive. Adversary *Hebe* knows his neighbor *Alice* bought item $b$ and $c$, so that it is easy for him to infer that *Alice* has purchased sensitive items $\alpha$ and $\beta$. In a word, publishing a non-masked dataset will reveal private data of

© International Financial Cryptography Association 2017
J. Grossklags and B. Preneel (Eds.): FC 2016, LNCS 9603, pp. 460–473, 2017.
DOI: 10.1007/978-3-662-54970-4_27

individuals. Thus, we have to sanitize the data before publishing it in order to guarantee privacy.

In order to resist item linkage attack, the $\rho$-uncertainty model has been proposed in [6]. When an adversary knows any non-sensitive or sensitive item, this model protects private information by ensuring that the probability of sensitive items inferred by a known item set $q$ is less than $\rho$.

The traditional approaches [6,7] of $\rho$-uncertainty have a few drawbacks as follows:

1. The "one size fits all" approach ignores the reality that different items have different data distributions.
2. Global suppression completely removes some items directly and incurs the loss of sensitive rules. Therefore, those removed items cannot be used by researchers.
3. Global generalization [8] brings a huge number of pseudo-association rules, so that the utility for data mining has severe distortion.

In this work, we propose a sensitivity-adaptive $\rho$-uncertainty model to address an important limitation of original $\rho$-uncertainty—that it provides only a uniform level of privacy protection for all items in a dataset. We propose a solution, LGPS, integrating local generation and partial suppression, to mask items varying in frequency and sensitivity.

In our LGPS solution, if the frequency of occurrence of a sensitive item is low, the sensitivity of the item is high and vice versa. LGPS divides records into separate groups and guarantees that each sub-group satisfies the proposed model.

**Table 1.** Original Data

| Name | Id | Items |
|------|-----|-------|
| Chris | t1 | $a,d,\alpha,\beta$ |
| Bob | t2 | $a,b,d$ |
| Alice | t3 | $b,c,\alpha,\beta$ |
| Mary | t4 | $a,c,\alpha$ |
| Dan | t5 | $a,b,\alpha$ |
| Lucy | t6 | $a,\alpha$ |

**Example 1.** *Anonymization on set-valued datasets*

For original data as in Table 1, anonymous datasets, shown in Table 2(a), (b) and (c), are masked by using original approach of TDControl ($\rho=0.5$) and our solution. In Table 2(b), the uniform threshold is 0.5. And in Table 2(c), according to the data distribution of the original dataset and formula (2) and (3) the thresholds $\rho_\alpha$ and $\rho_\beta$ for privacy preservation are 0.7 and 0.3 when $\rho$, defined by users, is 0.3. In uneven datasets, flexible thresholds provide personal protection and retain more data utility. Comparing Table 2(a) with (b), the information loss of Table 2(b) is less than that of Table 2(a).

**Table 2.** Anonymization dataset

(a) TDC($\rho$=0.5)

| Id | Items |
|----|-------|
| t1 | $a,d$ |
| t2 | $a,b,d$ |
| t3 | $b,c$ |
| t4 | $a,c$ |
| t5 | $a,b$ |
| t6 | $a$ |

(b) LGPS($\rho = 0.5$)

| Id | Items |
|-----|-------|
| Gr1 | $a,b$ |
|     | $a,\alpha$ |
| Gr2 | $a,d,\beta$ |
|     | $a,b,d$ |
|     | $b,\beta$ |
|     | $a,\alpha$ |

(c) LGPS($\rho_\alpha$=0.7,$\rho_\beta$=0.3)

| Id | Items |
|-----|-------|
| Gr1 | $a,b$ |
|     | $a,\alpha$ |
| Gr2 | $a,B,\beta$ |
|     | $a,b,B$ |
|     | $b,B,\alpha$ |
|     | $a,B,\alpha$ |

For each sensitive rule, such as $a{\rightarrow}\alpha$ or $\beta{\rightarrow}\alpha$, TDControl uses global suppression and global generalization to hide sensitive rules. In the suppression process, the chosen item, which information loss of being suppressed is minimal, is removed in all records. Finally, all sensitive items $\alpha$ and $\beta$ are suppressed in Table 2(a). Anonymous dataset masked by TDControl loses a lot of information and does not preserve enough utility for secondary analysis.

Differing from prior works [6,7,9,10], our contributions can be summarized as follows:

1. We focus on diverse sensitivity on items and propose a sensitivity-adaptive $\rho$-uncertainty model for improving data utility.
2. Under the proposed model, we use the frequency of sensitive items to define flexible privacy thresholds and propose a sensitivity-adaptive $\rho$-uncertainty approach decreasing information loss. A flexible privacy threshold is non-trivial because it is adaptive to the distribution of data and it addresses the over-protection problem incurred by the unified threshold in the TDControl model.
3. Furthermore, we devise an effective algorithm called LGPS by using local generation and partial suppression to achieve anonymization. Not only does LGPS reserve some useful characteristics of those sensitive items, but it also introduces fewer pseudo-rules. Experiments running on real datasets show that our approach is effective and information loss is lower than for the previous methods.

The rest of this paper is organized as follows. Section 2 describes related work on anonymization of set-valued dataset. The privacy model is introduced in Sect. 3. The algorithm is shown in Sect. 4. The result of experiments is demonstrated in Sect. 5. Section 6 concludes this paper.

## 2   Related Work

Sweeney [11] raised the $k$-anonymous model in 2002, which aims to make each QID (quasi-identifier) including at least $k$ matched records in a sanitized dataset, so this model can effectively prevent identity linkage attacks. Yet, $k$-anonymity is insufficient to protect the privacy of set-valued data which is high-dimensional and sparse. So $k^m$-anonymity model, which makes an adversary at most know $m$ items, was proposed in [12]. Unfortunately, $k$-anonymity and $k^m$-anonymity are not able to prevent item linkage attacks. In 2007, Machanavajjhala [13] et al. proposed the $l$-diversity model based on $k$-anonymity, which makes every sensitive attributes in each equivalence having at least $l$ different attribute values, to prevent attribute linkage attacks.

Based on the $k$-anonymous model, Sinhong [14] et al. proposed a new solution to anonymize set-valued data. This anonymous solution constructs a pseudo taxonomy tree based on utility metrics to replace the presetting taxonomy tree, so it can upgrade the data utility and protect an individual's information. Yet, this solution is inadequate to prevent item linkage attacks.

Wang [15] et al. described high-dimensional sparse data using bipartite graphs with the individual's attributes, where the original graph is turned into an anonymous graph by clustering attributes in each node. Chen et al. [16] and Xiao et al. [17] propose two approaches, each of which satisfies differential privacy model, to protect high-dimensional datasets. The aim of the two approaches is mainly protecting the individual's privacy information by adding noise. But these approaches will disclose privacy under item linkage attacks, if a small amount of noise is added.

$(h, k, p)$-coherence ensures that any combination, in which at most $h$ percent of records contain some sensitive items, has at least $k$ records including $p$ items. The work in [18] shows that the optimal solution of $(h, k, p)$-coherence is an NP-hard problem and gives a local optimization algorithm. However, the $(h, k, p)$-coherence criterion is insufficient to protect against an attacker who knows sensitive items of individuals.

The $PS$-rule model proposed in [19], where $P$ is a set of non-sensitive items and $S$ is a set of sensitive items in dataset $D$, can simultaneously prevent identify linkable attacks and item linkage attacks. Given two item sets $I \in P$ and $J \in S$, the rule $I \rightarrow J$ is a $PS$-rule when $\sup(I)$ is $k$ or more and $\mathrm{conf}(I \rightarrow J)$ is no more than $c$.

The $\rho$-uncertainty, a more sophisticated model to preserve sensitive information in set-valued data, was demonstrated in [6]. This criterion ensures that the probability of sensitive items inferred by an attacker is less than $\rho$ and does not restrict background knowledge of attackers.

The $\rho$-uncertainty approach based on partial suppression, presented in [7], can be adapted to either statistical analysis or association rules mining. However, this method does not take into account the difference of the sensitivity between sensitive items, in that overprotection of some low sensitivity items increases information loss. The first research result, published in [20], concerns the difference of sensitivity and proposes a solution to rank sensitive items by the difference of the item's sensitivity.

## 3    Privacy Model

### 3.1    Privacy Concept

In a successful item linkage attack an adversary can infer with high probability which sensitive item is associated to an individual. For example, an adversary knows an individual in Table 1 has bought non-sensitive commodities, $b$ and $c$ $(b, c \in q)$, and he/she can also infer that sensitive items $\alpha$ and $\beta$ were purchased by the person. Therefore, user's privacy would b undermined if the data would be released without masking (Table 3).

**Table 3.** Definition of symbols

| Symbol | Definition |
|---|---|
| $D$ | The original dataset |
| $D'$ | Anonymous dataset |
| $q$ | QID, a sub-group of items |
| $\sup(q)$ | Support of set $q$ |
| $e$ | A sensitive item |
| $F(e)$ | Frequency of $e$ |
| $\rho_e$ | Privacy threshold of sensitive item $e$ |
| $\mathrm{conf}(q \rightarrow e)$ | Confidence of the rule $q \rightarrow e$ |

**Definition 1 (Sensitive association rule).** *Given a sensitive item $e$, the association rule $q \rightarrow e$ is a sensitive association rule.*

**Definition 2 (Confidence of a rule [21]).** *If a rule $q \rightarrow e$, where $e$ is sensitive and $q$ is non sensitive, the confidence of this rule is a conditional probability:*

$$\mathrm{conf}(q \rightarrow e) = \frac{\sup(q \cup e)}{\sup(q)}, \tag{1}$$

*where $\sup(q \cup e)$ is the number of records including $q$ and $e$ and $\sup(q)$ is the number of records including item set $q$.*

**Definition 3 ($\rho$-uncertainty).** *If the confidence of any sensitive association rule in a released dataset is less than $\rho$, the dataset achieves $\rho$-uncertainty $(\rho > 0)$.*

A unique threshold, for preventing item linkage attacks, is inappropriate since the distribution of different sensitive items is uneven. Furthermore, it is natural to assume that a sensitive item involved in most of the records has a low sensitivity. On the other hand, an item has a high sensitivity when it only appears in a handful of records. So we use diverse thresholds correlated with the item's sensitivity to mask data.

**Definition 4 (Adaptive parameter $\delta_e$).** *$\delta_e$ is an adaptive parameter to adjust the threshold $\rho$ and is defined as follows:*

$$F(e) = \sup(e)/|N| \tag{2}$$
$$\delta_e = \varepsilon_e \cdot F(e), \tag{3}$$

*where $e$ denotes a sensitive item, $\sup(e)$ is the number of records including item $e$, and $|N|$ is the number of all records in dataset. $\varepsilon_e (\varepsilon_e > 0)$ is called a sensitive factor of $e$; it is used to tune the value of $\delta_e$ combining with $F(e)$. If $F(e)$ is higher, a larger $\varepsilon_e$ is chosen to prevent privacy disclosure. $\varepsilon_e$ is adjusted by the sensitivity of item $e$ and the user's requirement of the protection strength.*

**Definition 5 (sensitivity-adaptive $\rho$-uncertainty).** *Let $\delta_e$ be an adaptive parameter as defined above and $\rho_e = \rho + \delta_e(1 > \rho_e > 0)$. If the confidence of any sensitive association rule in an anonymous dataset is less than $\rho_e$, then the dataset achieves sensitivity-adaptive $\rho$-uncertainty. Here $\rho$ is the minimum privacy threshold, and $\rho_e$ is the flexible threshold depended on the sensitivity of $e$ and the distribution of $e$ in the dataset.*

**Example 2.** *Definition of flexible privacy thresholds*

Assuming that a dataset has 10 records, $\rho = 0.3$, where 8 records contain item $\alpha$, 6 records contain item $\beta$, and 2 records contain item $\Omega$, the flexible threshold of $\rho_\alpha$, $\rho_\beta$, $\rho_\Omega$ was defined as 0.7, 0.5, 0.3 by the frequency of occurrence as defined in (2) and (3).

## 3.2   Information Loss Metric

Evaluation of the effectiveness is important for any anonymous algorithm. In this paper, the Normalized Certainty Penalty [13,22], an information loss metric for items in a generalization hierarchy, is used to evaluate the effectiveness of our algorithm. As shown in Fig. 1, $a$ and $b$ can be masked by $A$ while $c$ and $d$ can be replaced with $B$. The root node, $ALL$, can represent each item in the dataset.

$NCP$, a popular measurement of information loss for item generalization, is defined in [22]. In our sensitivity-adaptive $\rho$-uncertainty model, $NCP$ is redefined as below:

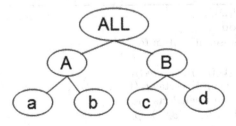

Fig. 1. Item generalization hierarchy $H$

$$NCP_{(a)} = \begin{cases} 1 & \textit{if } a \textit{ is suppressed} \\ \frac{|u_m|}{|I|} & \textit{if } a \textit{ is generalized to node } m \in H, \end{cases} \tag{4}$$

where $a$ represents a child node of $m$, $|u_m|$ is the total number of leaf nodes connected with $m$, and $|I|$ is the total number of non-sensitive items.

**Example 3.** *Information loss of items generalization*
When item $a$ is generalized to $A$ and $c$ is replaced with $B$, the information loss is described as $IL_{(a)} = \frac{|u_A|}{|I|} = \frac{2}{4} = \frac{1}{2}, IL_{(c)} = \frac{|u_B|}{|I|} = \frac{2}{4} = \frac{1}{2}$.

If an item is suppressed such as in [6,7], then the information loss is 1.

For a record $t$ in dataset $D$ and an item $m$ in $t$, let $C_t$ be the number of records in dataset. Then the information loss for the dataset is defined as

$$NCP_{(D)} = \frac{\sum_{t \in D} \sum_{m \in t} NCP_{(m)}}{\sum_{t \in D} C_t}. \tag{5}$$

## 4    Anonymous Algorithm

Usually, there are many anonymous methods applied to mask datasets, such as kd-trees, SRT and AT [6], R-tree [23,24]. In each top-down recursion, items are specialized in the hierarchy tree and records are assigned to different sub-groups. If the sub-group does not meet the sensitivity-adaptive $\rho$-uncertainty model, partial suppression was used to mask the group. Our anonymous method applies two algorithms in the whole anonymization process, so that information loss of the anonymous data set is minimized.

**LGPS:** The LGPS first define the privacy constraints of sensitive items by calculating the frequency of sensitive items. Then, all non-sensitive items are initialized to $ALL$ and information loss of the generalized item is 1. In next step, the algorithm checks the validity of the generalized dataset. While the generalized dataset does not achieve sensitivity-adaptive $\rho$-uncertainty, partial suppression is used to mask this dataset. The algorithm terminates until every sub-group of records has been processed.

---

**Algorithm 1.** *LGPS(D)*

---

1: PrivacyThreshold(D);
2: **for** each $t \in D$ **do**
3:     Initialized all no-sensitive item to ALL;
4: **end for**
5: PartialSuppressor(D,$(\rho_1, \rho_2, \ldots, \rho_h)$);
6: resultParts←Flexible_$\rho$_Uncertainty(D,H,$(\rho_1, \rho_2, \ldots, \rho_h)$);
7: **for**  each subParts in resultParts **do**
8:     specialData(subparts,$(\rho_1, \rho_2, \ldots, \rho_h)$);
9: **end for**

---

---

**Algorithm 2.** *PrivacyThreshold(D)*

---

1: initialize the sup of all sensitive item to 0;
2: **for** each $t \in D$ **do**
3:    update the sup of sensitive item;
4:    $n = n + 1$;
5: **end for**
6: let $F(e)$ be a set of sensitive item frequency;
7: **for** each sensitive item e **do**
8:    $F(e) = \frac{\sup(e)}{n}$;
9:    according $\rho_e = \rho + \varepsilon_e \cdot F(e)$ define compute value $\rho_e$;
10: **end for**

---

The Privacy Constraints define privacy thresholds of various sensitive items. In this part, the algorithm first calculates the support of sensitive items by traversing the entire dataset. In the traversing process, the support of the item is constantly updated while an item occurs again. Finally, the different $\rho$s are defined according to (2) and (3).

**Flexible_$\rho$_Uncertainty Anonymity:** The FUA, which masks, in every top-down recursion, set-valued data by local generalization and partial suppression, is described as follows:

Line(1): The generalized item is added to the set $G$.
Line(2–3): If $G$ is empty and $D$ is impossible to split down further, then $D$ is released.
Line(5–8): As in [22], the splitNode is replaced by its child node in the generalized hierarchy tree. Then, according to different values of the splitNode's child node, $D$ is divided and various records are registered to disjoint subsets.
Line(9–12): For each subset, some items are partially suppressed to hide sensitive rules by a flexible threshold $\rho_e$, and some generalized items are replaced in top-down recursion until $G$ is empty or itself is impossible to further split down.

**Partial Suppressor method** [7]: In each subset, any rule whose confidence is more than its threshold $\rho_Y$, such as conf$(X \to Y) > \rho_Y$, is added to $SR$. Getting $SR$ by flexible threshold is more suitable and effective for hiding sensitive rules. Until $SR$ is empty, some item is masked by partial suppression. For selecting sensitive rule $X \to Y$, if any item appears in $X \cup Y$, until the confidence of this rule is less than the threshold, each of them will be suppressed in records that have this rule. After hiding the selected sensitive rules, $SR$ has to be updated for the next suppression processing.

**Example 4.** *A top-down partitioning using LGPS*
First, the uniform privacy threshold $\rho$ is set to 0.3. In Table 1, items $\alpha$ and $\beta$ are sensitive, while all others are non-sensitive. In the process of finding the flexible thresholds, $\rho_\alpha$ and $\rho_\beta$ are defined as 0.7 respectively 0.3, while the generalization hierarchy tree for non-sensitive items is constructed as in Fig. 1. According to

**Algorithm 3.** $Flexible\_\rho\_Uncertainty(D, H, (\rho_1, \rho_2, \ldots, \rho_h))$

```
1: add generalized item in D to a set G;
2: if no further split down possible for D then
3:    Return and push D;
4: else
5:    splitNode←PickNode(D,G);
6:    for each data in D do
7:       add subParts in D′ ← divideData(D,splitNode);
8:    end for
9:    for each subParts in D′ do
10:      PartialSuppressor(subParts,(ρ₁,ρ₂,…,ρₕ));
11:      Flexible_ρ_Uncertainty(subParts,H,(ρ₁,ρ₂,…,ρₕ));
12:   end for
13: end if
```

**Table 4.** A transaction dataset

(a) $(a, b, c, d) \rightarrow ALL$

| Id | Items |
|----|-------|
| t1 | ALL, $\alpha$, $\beta$ |
| t2 | ALL |
| t3 | ALL, $\alpha$, $\beta$ |
| t4 | ALL, $\alpha$ |
| t5 | ALL, $\alpha$ |
| t6 | ALL, $\alpha$ |

(b) $ALL \rightarrow (A, B)$

| Id | Items |
|----|-------|
| Group1 | A |
|  | A,$\alpha$ |
| Group2 | A,B,$\beta$ |
|  | A,B |
|  | A,B,$\alpha$ |
|  | A,B,$\alpha$ |

(c) In group21 $A \rightarrow (a, b)$

| Id | Items |
|----|-------|
| Group1′ | a,b |
|  | a,$\alpha$ |
| Group21 | a,B,$\beta$ |
|  | a,b,B |
|  | b,B,$\alpha$ |
|  | a,B,$\alpha$ |

the generalization hierarchy tree, all non-sensitive items are initialized to the top value $ALL$. And the dataset is masked as in Table 4(a). Based on the flexible thresholds and the confidence of the sensitive rules, the $SR$ is set as $\{ALL \rightarrow \alpha, ALL \rightarrow \beta, (ALL, \alpha) \rightarrow \beta, (ALL, \beta) \rightarrow \alpha\}$. While the rules in $SR$ disclose information to adversaries, the $\alpha$ in t1 and the $\beta$ in t3 are removed to achieve sensitivity-adaptive $\rho$-uncertainty model. After this suppression, the anonymous data set is described as $\{(ALL, \beta), ALL, (ALL, \alpha), (ALL, \alpha), (ALL, \alpha), (ALL, \alpha)\}$ and the $NCP(D)$ is 14.

Anonymous data, in this example, is an over-generalization, and the data utility is insufficient for some users. In addition, the candidate set of splitNode such as $A$ and $B$ is not empty. Therefore, item ALL is substituted with $\{A\}$, $\{B\}$, $\{A, B\}$ and all records are divided into different subgroups. While each subgroup is valid for the procession of dividing groups, partial suppression is used to mask each subgroup. As a result subgroup $\{A\}$ does not meet sensitivity-adaptive $\rho$-uncertainty, hence item $\alpha$ in t5 is removed. In contrast, any item in group $\{A, B\}$ does not have to be removed. The $NCP(D')$ in Table 4(b), the sum of each subgroups' $NCP$, is equal to 9. Because $NCP(D)$ is larger than $NCP(D')$, this step satisfies the dividing condition.

For *Group1*, the item $A$ in every record is instead by $\{a\}$, $\{b\}$, $\{a,b\}$. Record $t5$ is assigned to $group\{a,b\}$, and another is added into the $group\{a\}$. The number of records is less than $1/\rho_\alpha$, so group $\{A\}$ is not valid. As a result the information loss $NCP(Group1')$ is less than $NCP(Group1)$. This specialization process is valid. In addition, records in $Group1'$ have no generalized item and achieve sensitivity-adaptive $\rho$-uncertainty, so $Group1'$ is released as $\{(a,b),(a,\alpha)\}$.

In *Group2*, generalized items, $A$ and $B$, appear. According to $A$ or $B$, the divided subgroups for all records is not valid. So item $A$ and $B$ are specialized by their child, and the record in this subgroup is described as *Group21* and *Group22*. Because $NCP(Group21)$ is less than $NCP(Group22)$, the best specialization $A \rightarrow (a,b)$ is chosen to specialize records in *Group2*. Then records in this subgroup are released for users.

When this specialization is legal and $NCP(Group21)$ is less than $NCP$ $(Group2)$, this subgroup is described as $\{(a,B,\alpha),(a,b,B),(a,B,\alpha),(a,B,\alpha)\}$. But a generalized item $B$ exists in $G$, hence the specialization $B \rightarrow (c,d)$ is executed. Then four sensitive rules, $\{d \rightarrow \beta, (a,d) \rightarrow \beta, c \rightarrow \alpha$ and $(a,c) \rightarrow \alpha\}$, are added to $SR$. For anonymizing this group, items $d$ in $t1$ and $\alpha$ in $t3$ are suppressed. But $NCP(Group211)$ is greater than $NCP(Group21)$. Therefore, the specialization for item $B$ is illegal and this group is released as $\{(a,B,\alpha),(a,b,B),(a,B,\alpha),(a,B,\alpha)\}$. All records in the original dataset are published as Table 4(c).

## 5 Experimental Study

### 5.1 Dataset and Parameters

Our experiments run on three real-world datasets introduced in [6,7], *BMS-POS*, *BMS-WebView-1* and *BMS-WebView-2*. *BMS-POS* is a transaction log from several years of sales at an electronics retailer. And *BMS-WebView-1* and *BMS-WebView-2* are click-stream data from two e-commerce web sites. All of those are widely used as benchmark datasets in the knowledge discovery community. Information about the three datasets is listed in Table 5.

**Table 5.** Characteristics of the three datasets

| Datasets | #Trans | #Distinct items | # Max. trans. size | # Avg. trans. size |
|----------|--------|-----------------|--------------------|--------------------|
| BMS-WV1  | 59,602  | 497  | 267 | 2.5 |
| BMS-WV2  | 77,512  | 3340 | 161 | 5.0 |
| BMS-POS  | 551,597 | 1657 | 164 | 6.5 |

Specifically, we measure execution time and data utility to compare our LGPS algorithms, with TDControl [6] and Dist [7]. All algorithms were implemented in $C++$ and ran on an *Intel(R) Core(TM) i3-2100 cpu* machine with 4 GB RAM running the Linux operating system.

## 5.2    Data Utility

We evaluate our algorithms with three performance factors: (a) information loss ($KL$-divergence [7]), (b) the difference of the number of mined rules, (c) the size of datasets.

Kullback-Leibler divergence measures the distance between two probability distributions and determines the similarity between the original data and the anonymous data. When $D$ is original data and $D'$ is anonymous data, the $KL$-divergence is defined as follows:

$$KL(D' \parallel D) = \sum_i D(i) \log \frac{D(i)}{D'(i)}, \tag{6}$$

where $D(i)$ and $D'(i)$ are the occurrence probability of item $i$ in the original dataset $D$ and in the anonymized dataset $D'$.

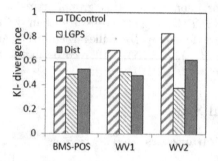

**Fig. 2.** Varying datasets

Due to the limitation of hardware, we have to make length less than or equal to 5 when we find sensitive association rules. In Fig. 2, TDControl and Dist are basic approaches to mask data by the $\rho$-uncertainty model while $\rho$ is the mean of all flexible $\rho_e$ in our approach. Although for the dataset $WV1$, the information loss of LGPS is larger than the information loss of the prior approaches, LGPS provides a stronger protection and gets an anonymous dataset whose data distribution is more similar to the original dataset.

The smaller the difference of the number of mined rules between the anonymous dataset and the original dataset is, the higher the data utility is. So the number of the hidden rules and the pseudo-rules is used to evaluate data utility. In Fig. 3(a) and (b), LGPS hides fewer rules and introduces fewer pseudo-rules than TDControl when the proportion of sensitive items in the original dataset is increasing.

Figure 4(a) shows the experimental results of $KL$-divergence and execution time. LGPS is less efficient than TDControl and Dist when the size of dataset is small. With the increased size of the dataset, LGPS becomes more effective.

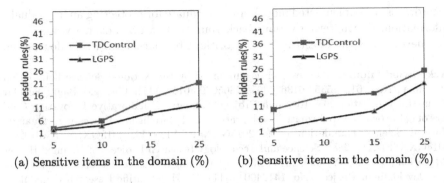

**Fig. 3.** The difference of the number of mined rules

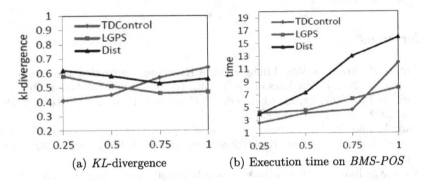

**Fig. 4.** Varying the size of dataset

When we do experiments on the whole *BMS-POS*, as shown in Fig. 4(b), our approach may take more time than TDControl. However, mostly anonymous processes applied in data publication are offline, so it is reasonable that we spend more time and get more utility of anonymous data.

## 6   Conclusion

We proposed a sensitivity-adaptive $\rho$-uncertainty model to mask dataset when the distribution of sensitive items varies widely.r A flexible threshold for different sensitive items is defined by their frequency of occurrence. In order to reduce the information loss and increase the utility of anonymous data, partial suppression and local generalization are used in a top-down recursion. Compared to previous methods [6,7], this approach deletes or generalizes fewer items to satisfy the advanced privacy model.

In future work, we will focus on impact on privacy when the adversary infers information on an individual by the semantic of a combination of different items. We will also pay more attention to the influence of background known by adversary. For example, when the adversary knows an item is not contained in the record, most of implemented models are inadequate for protecting an individual's information. Encountering various backgrounds known by adversary, we should find new models and construct new algorithms to conceal sensitive information.

**Acknowledgments.** The research is supported by the National Science Foundation of China (Nos. 61272535, 61363009, 61365009, 61502111), Guangxi Bagui Scholar Teams for Innovation and Research Project, Guangxi Collaborative Innovation Center of Multi-source Information Integration and Intelligent Processing, Guangxi Natural Science Foundation (Nos. 2015GXNSFBA139246, 2013GXNSFBA019263, 2014GXNSFBA118288), Science and Technology Research Projects of Guangxi Higher Education (Nos. 2013YB029, 2015YB032), the Guangxi Science Research and Technology Development Project (No. 14124004-4-11) ,Youth Scientific Research Foundation of Guangxi Normal University and Innovation Project of Guangxi Graduate Education (No. YCSZ2015104).

# References

1. Saygin, Y., Verykios, V.S., Elmagarmid, A.K.: Privacy preserving association rule mining. In: 2002 Proceedings of the Twelfth International Workshop on Research Issues in Data Engineering: Engineering E-Commerce/E-Business Systems, RIDE-2EC 2002, pp. 151–158. IEEE (2002)
2. Han, J., Luo, F., Lu, J., Peng, H.: Sloms: A privacy preserving data publishing method for multiple sensitive attributes microdata. J. Softw. **8**(12), 3096–3104 (2013)
3. Xiao, X., Tao, Y.: M-invariance: Towards privacy preserving re-publication of dynamic datasets. In: Proceedings of the 2007 ACM SIGMOD International Conference on Management of Data, pp. 689–700. ACM (2007)
4. Ghinita, G., Tao, Y., Kalnis, P.: On the anonymization of sparse high-dimensional data. In: 2008 IEEE 24th International Conference on Data Engineering, ICDE 2008, pp. 715–724. IEEE (2008)
5. Liu, J.Q.: Publishing set-valued data against realistic adversaries. J. Comput. Sci. Technol. **27**(1), 24–36 (2012)
6. Cao, J., Karras, P., Raïssi, C., Tan, K.L.: $\rho$-uncertainty: Inference-proof transaction anonymization. Proc. VLDB Endow. **3**(1–2), 1033–1044 (2010)
7. Jia, X., Pan, C., Xu, X., Zhu, K.Q., Lo, E.: $\rho$-uncertainty anonymization by partial suppression. In: Bhowmick, S.S., Dyreson, C.E., Jensen, C.S., Lee, M.L., Muliantara, A., Thalheim, B. (eds.) DASFAA 2014. LNCS, vol. 8422, pp. 188–202. Springer, Cham (2014). doi:10.1007/978-3-319-05813-9_13
8. Tripathy, B., Reddy, A.J., Manusha, G., Mohisin, G.: Improved algorithms for anonymization of set-valued data. In: Meghanathan, N., Nagamalai, D., Chaki, N. (eds.) Advances in Computing and Information Technology. Advances in Intelligent Systems and Computing, vol. 177, pp. 581–594. Springer, Heidelberg (2013)
9. Vaidya, J., Clifton, C.: Privacy preserving association rule mining in vertically partitioned data. In: Proceedings of the Eighth ACM SIGKDD International Conference on Knowledge Discovery and Data Mining, pp. 639–644. ACM (2002)
10. Fung, B., Wang, K., Yu, P.S.: Top-down specialization for information and privacy preservation. In: 2005 Proceedings. 21st International Conference on Data Engineering, ICDE 2005, pp. 205–216. IEEE (2005)

11. Sweeney, L.: k-anonymity: A model for protecting privacy. Int. J. Uncertainty Fuzziness Knowl. Based Syst. **10**(05), 557–570 (2002)
12. Terrovitis, M., Mamoulis, N., Kalnis, P.: Privacy-preserving anonymization of set-valued data. Proc. VLDB Endow. **1**(1), 115–125 (2008)
13. Machanavajjhala, A., Kifer, D., Gehrke, J., Venkitasubramaniam, M.: L-diversity: Privacy beyond k-anonymity. ACM Trans. Knowl. Discovery Data (TKDD) **1**(1), 3 (2007)
14. Lin, S., Liao, M.: Towards publishing set-valued data with high utility (2014)
15. Wang, L., Li, X.: A clustering-based bipartite graph privacy-preserving approach for sharing high-dimensional data. Int. J. Softw. Eng. Knowl. Eng. **24**(07), 1091–1111 (2014)
16. Chen, R., Mohammed, N., Fung, B.C., Desai, B.C., Xiong, L.: Publishing set-valued data via differential privacy. Proc. VLDB Endow. **4**(11), 1087–1098 (2011)
17. Xiao, X.: Differentially private data release: Improving utility with wavelets and bayesian networks. In: Chen, L., Jia, Y., Sellis, T., Liu, G. (eds.) APWeb 2014. LNCS, vol. 8709, pp. 25–35. Springer, Cham (2014). doi:10.1007/978-3-319-11116-2_3
18. Xu, Y., Wang, K., Fu, A.W.C., Yu, P.S.: Anonymizing transaction databases for publication. In: Proceedings of the 14th ACM SIGKDD International Conference on Knowledge Discovery and Data Mining, pp. 767–775. ACM (2008)
19. Loukides, G., Gkoulalas-Divanis, A., Shao, J.: Anonymizing transaction data to eliminate sensitive inferences. In: Bringas, P.G., Hameurlain, A., Quirchmayr, G. (eds.) DEXA 2010. LNCS, vol. 6261, pp. 400–415. Springer, Heidelberg (2010). doi:10.1007/978-3-642-15364-8_34
20. Ye, Y., Liu, Y., Wang, C., Lv, D., Feng, J.: Decomposition: Privacy preservation for multiple sensitive attributes. In: Zhou, X., Yokota, H., Deng, K., Liu, Q. (eds.) DASFAA 2009. LNCS, vol. 5463, pp. 486–490. Springer, Heidelberg (2009). doi:10.1007/978-3-642-00887-0_42
21. Verykios, V.S., Elmagarmid, A.K., Bertino, E., Saygin, Y., Dasseni, E.: Association rule hiding. IEEE Trans. Knowl. Data Eng. **16**(4), 434–447 (2004)
22. He, Y., Naughton, J.F.: Anonymization of set-valued data via top-down, local generalization. Proc. VLDB Endow. **2**(1), 934–945 (2009)
23. Wang, S.L., Tsai, Y.C., Kao, H.Y., Hong, T.P.: On anonymizing transactions with sensitive items. Appl. Intell. **41**(4), 1043–1058 (2014)
24. Gkoulalas-Divanis, A., Loukides, G.: PCTA: Privacy-constrained clustering-based transaction data anonymization. In: Proceedings of the 4th International Workshop on Privacy and Anonymity in the Information Society, vol. 5. ACM (2011)

# Bitcoin Mining

# Incentive Compatibility of Bitcoin Mining Pool Reward Functions

Okke Schrijvers[✉], Joseph Bonneau, Dan Boneh, and Tim Roughgarden

Stanford University, Stanford, USA
okkes@cs.stanford.edu

**Abstract.** In this paper we introduce a game-theoretic model for reward functions in Bitcoin mining pools. Our model consists only of an unordered history of reported shares and gives participating miners the strategy choices of either reporting or delaying when they discover a share or full solution. We defined a precise condition for incentive compatibility to ensure miners strategy choices optimize the welfare of the pool as a whole. With this definition we show that proportional mining rewards are not incentive compatible in this model. We introduce and analyze a novel reward function which is incentive compatible in this model. Finally we show that the popular reward function pay-per-last-N-shares is also incentive compatible in a more general model.

## 1 Introduction

By almost any measure, Bitcoin [1] has become the most successful cryptocurrency in history. While Bitcoin has evolved into a very complex sociotechnical system which we will not describe in detail here,[1] at its core lies a decentralized consensus protocol allowing all participants to agree on a common global ledger of transactions to prevent double-spends and other disallowed behavior. The key to Bitcoin's consensus protocol (sometimes more broadly called *Nakamoto consensus* after its founder) is a group of entities called *miners* who race to solve a challenging cryptographic puzzle for the right to append a new block of transactions to Bitcoin's ledger, the *blockchain*. A system of incentives encourages these miners to follow the protocol faithfully in exchange for the ability to earn newly-minted coins and transaction fees in proportion to the amount of computational effort they have expended (also called hashing power or mining power).

Finding a single Bitcoin block is very rewarding (today worth at least ₿25, over US$6,000), yet it is also very difficult for smaller miners who might find a block on expectation only every few months or even every few years. As a result, the majority of mining power now consists of miners participate in *mining pools* in which they agree to divide rewards from blocks found by any member of the pool and thus receive a steadier stream of income. Choosing the exact algorithm used to divide up mining pool rewards (the *reward function*) however, turns out to be a challenging incentive design problem.

---

[1] For an academic overview of Bitcoin we refer the reader to [2].

© International Financial Cryptography Association 2017
J. Grossklags and B. Preneel (Eds.): FC 2016, LNCS 9603, pp. 477–498, 2017.
DOI: 10.1007/978-3-662-54970-4_28

Pools are sometimes controversial in the Bitcoin community as they represent a form of centralization. Miller et al. proposed a future cryptocurrency which attempts to prevent their formation [3]. As of today though they are an indispensable part of Bitcoin as well as many related cryptocurrencies (to which our work will also apply). Despite this, relatively little work has focused on the reward functions underlying pools since Rosenfeld's initial overview of the space [4]. Several papers have studied the interaction *between* pools and found that in some plausible circumstances pools will be incentivized to attack each other [5–7]. Yet the incentives underlying reward functions have not been rigorously studied.

In this paper we introduce a formal game-theoretical framework to study these reward functions. We are motivated by a very natural question: if individual miners are interested in maximizing their expected utility, is their behavior optimal for the pool as a group? For example, if miners are incentivized to delay reporting full solutions to the pool, this may lower the pool's overall rewards and even make it more vulnerable to external sabotage [5]. We introduce a simplified model with only a single mining pool and define basic properties that a good reward function should exhibit. Although our model is deliberately simplified, we still show somewhat surprisingly that some reward functions used in practice such as simple proportional payments are not incentive compatible.

We introduce a novel reward function which is incentive compatible within our model while still maintaining other desirable properties. Our reward function will remain incentive compatible even in a more complex informational model (although it may need to be extended if the definition of incentive compatibility is extended to include more complicated attacks).

While our model cannot capture all reward functions used in practice, we consider it an important milestone in analyzing mining pools in Bitcoin and related systems. We further take the first step to analyzing reward functions in more general informational models by carefully examining the popular pay-per-last-N-shares reward function, and show that it is incentive compatible. This indicates that our approach is not limited to the informational assumptions, but can be more generally applied.

## 2 Preliminaries

In this paper we look at a simple model in which miners are bound to working for a particular pool and where their strategic choice is the following: if a miner finds a solution to the cryptographic puzzle, *when* does it report this to the pool. The pool is run by a *pool operator* and contains a fixed number $n$ of miners. Each miner $i$ has a fraction $\alpha_i$ of the total mining power. For most of this paper we will assume that $\sum_{i=1}^n \alpha_i = 1$, meaning that the pool has all the available mining power; there are no other pools or solo miners. In Appendix C we look at the case where the pools total hashing power $\alpha_P = \sum_{i=1}^n \alpha_i < 1$ and show that while this makes a quantitative difference, qualitatively our results carry over.

The time it takes for a miner to find a share is an exponentially distributed random variable with parameter $\alpha_i$; hence in expectation it takes time $1/\alpha_i$ to find a share. Each share is also a full solution with probability $1/D$.

## 2.1 Reward Functions and History Transcripts

Miners report their shares and solutions to the pool operator. When a solution is reported, the operator who collects the block reward from the Bitcoin network and subsequently divides the reward among the $n$ miners according to a *reward function* $R$. The game then restarts. For the mathematical model we assume no variability in the block reward or the transaction fees, although the work can be extended to include this.

The reward function is the only way in which the miners receive any payout and therefore the reward function completely drives the behavior of miners. A perfectly equitable reward function would simply give each miner $i$ a fraction $\frac{\alpha_i}{\alpha_P}$ of the reward in proportion to the fraction of the pool's total mining power to which that miner contributed.

However, the pool operator does not know the actual $\alpha_i$ of each miner. The challenge in designing a reward function $R$ stems from the necessity of estimating this based on reported shares and solutions. The operator's ability to estimate $\alpha_i$ depends on the precise information it has access to. We model this as a *history transcript* $\mathcal{H}$. A reward function $R : \mathcal{H} \to [0,1]^n$ is a function from a history transcript to an allocation $\{a_i\}_{i=1}^n$ with $\sum_i a_i = 1$. We use $R_i : \mathcal{H} \to [0,1]$ to denote the function that yields the $i^{\text{th}}$ component of $R$.

In most of this paper we analyze the case of an unordered history transcript:[2] $\mathcal{H}$ contains for each miner $i$ the total number of shares $b_i \in \mathbb{N}$ that have been reported in that round.[3] Thus, the history transcript is given by a vector $\mathbf{b} \in \mathbb{N}^n$ that contains for each of the $n$ players the total number of shares that she found during the round (where the full solution is also counted as a share). We use vector notation for $\mathbf{b}$, so $\mathbf{b}_1 + \mathbf{b}_2$ means the component-wise addition of $\mathbf{b}_1$ and $\mathbf{b}_2$, and $\|\mathbf{b}\|_1 = \sum_{i=1}^n b_i$ is the sum of the components of $\mathbf{b}$.

This model is perhaps the simplest possible[4] which enables a mining pool to function, yet it captures several basic reward function schemes used in practice. There are also reward functions which require additional information, such as the order in which shares were reported or reports from previous rounds of the game. In Sect. 8 we briefly discuss how to generalize this model and the challenges with characterizing incentive compatibility for them. However, we stress that positive results demonstrated incentive compatibility in our simple model extend to any more complicated model, as the pool operator can always decline to use additional information in its reward function.

---

[2] In Sect. 6 we consider a strictly more general informational model, which will be described there.

[3] We adopt the convention that $\mathbb{N}$ includes the number 0.

[4] A simpler format such as only receiving information about which miner reported a full solution would only allow a replication of solo mining.

## 2.2  Miner Strategy

Now that we defined a model and the reward function $R$, let's look at how the choice of $R$ impacts the behavior of miners. The goal of any mining pool is to earn as many rewards as possible for its members.[5] If miners delay in reporting blocks to the pool, this imposes a risk that an external pool may find the block first, undermining the pool's potential rewards.[6] Note that while we are only modeling a single pool, we build in the assumption that this pool wants to report solutions as fast as possible to the wider network to avoid getting scooped by the competition. Thus we will want our reward function to ensure solutions to be reported and processed as soon as they are found.[7]

In response to a reward rule $R$, miners choose a strategy $\sigma(R)$ which dictates what a miner does when it finds a share or full solution. Ideally the strategy $\sigma(R)$ is to report any share or solution immediately. However, the pool operator cannot directly tell miners what to do; rather they should choose an $R$ such that the miners corresponding strategy $\sigma(R)$ is to immediately report. Formally, let $t$ be the time since miner $i$ started mining, let $T$ be the number of rounds that have been completed at time $t$, and let $\mathbf{b}_j$ be the number of shares per player in round $j$. Miner $i$ is interested in maximizing their throughput:

$$\sigma(R) := \max_{\sigma} \lim_{t \to \infty} \frac{\sum_{j=1}^{T} R_i(\mathbf{b}_j)}{t}. \tag{1}$$

Here $\sigma$ impacts the number $T$ of rounds that were completed, as well as the number of reported shares $\mathbf{b}_j$ in each round.

## 2.3  Reward Function Desiderata

We define three properties which are important for a reward function. The first is a formalization of the intuition above:

*Property 1 (Incentive Compatibility).*  A reward function $R$ is *incentive compatible* when every miner's best response strategy $\sigma(R)$ reports full solutions immediately.

In Sect. 3 we give a mathematical condition that characterizes Property 1, and that can easily be verified for reward functions.

Next, we require that the pool pays miners in proportion to the amount of work they have performed. Miners form pools to reduce the variance in revenue.

---

[5] In this work we are only considering a pool which follows the default mining strategy and does not attempt to implement an deviant strategies to earn disproportionately more rewards than competing pools, such as temporary block withholding [8].

[6] Another way of saying this is that a reward function which does not compel participants to report solutions immediately is *not* welfare maximizing, since the selfish behavior of individuals can hurt the total reward of the group.

[7] While we do not consider fees in this paper, note that a pool operator would also want to optimize throughput if collects a fraction of the reward.

In practice they might accept losing a small fraction $f$ of their expected value in fees, but we would like miner performing an $\alpha_i$ fraction of the work to receive an $\alpha_i$ fraction of the reward.

*Property 2 (Proportional Payments).* A reward function $R$ provides *proportional payments* whenever for each miner $i$

$$\mathbb{E}_{\mathbf{b}}[R_i(\mathbf{b})] = \alpha_i.$$

Finally, we would like the pool operator to never incur a deficit. That is, the reward function $R$ should precisely divide the reward among the $n$ miners at the end of a round. If this is not the case, then either miners may leave some value on the table, or the pool operator may be liable for more then she received herself. This latter condition is particularly dangerous, as it leaves the pool exposed to sabotage attacks [5] in which competing miners purposely withhold full solutions to damage the pool.

*Property 3 (Budget Balanced).* A reward function $R$ is $(\gamma, \delta)$-budget balanced when for all $\mathbf{b}$:

$$\gamma \le \sum_{i=1}^{n} R_i(\mathbf{b}) \le \delta.$$

In particular, an $(\gamma, 1)$-budget balanced reward function will never pay more to the miners than the pool operator received. Our goal will be $(1, 1)$-budget balanced reward functions which share the reward exactly among the $n$ miners.

## 2.4   Common Examples

Perhaps the most obvious reward function is the *proportional* reward function: $R_i(\mathbf{b}) = \mathbf{b}_i/K$, where $K = ||\mathbf{b}||_1 = \sum_{i=1}^{n} b_i$. That is, the reward is shared proportional to the number of shares each miner reported. We show that the proportional rule is not incentive compatible in Sect. 4.1.

Another reward function is the *pay-per-share* reward function: $R_i(\mathbf{b}, s) = b_i/D$, where participants are rewarded a fixed amount per share. In Sect. 4.2 we show that while this method is incentive compatible, it is not budget balanced (defined in Sect. 2.3), which means that the pool operator may be liable to pay out more to miners than she collects from the Bitcoin protocol.

## 2.5   Ensuring Steady Rewards

Miners are interested in maximizing the total reward they receive per time unit, but they join pools primarily to achieve a more consistent stream of revenue. Our goal will be to build a reward function which is as consistent as possible which satisfies the three properties above. It is tempting to isolate one metric, such as the variance or standard deviation of the distribution of rewards, but we will discuss in Sect. 7 why these metrics are probably not the best measures of consistency in practice and provide different simulation results to compare reward functions.

## 3   Incentive Compatibility

We stated that for a reward function $R$ to be incentive compatible, it needs to incentivize miners to report full solutions immediately. In this section we express that as a condition that can easily be checked for any given reward function.

We do this by looking at the strategic choice that a miner faces when she finds a full solution. Either she reports the full solution immediately, or she decides to delay reporting the solution until $d$ more shares have been found. In this section we do not take into account the possibility of another miner finding and reporting a solution during this delay. In Appendix B we show that this is virtually without loss of generality.

Consider the situation when at time $t$, miner $i$ finds a full solution. At this point $\mathbf{b}_t$ shares have been reported to the pool operator (for notational simplicity we assume that the full solution is already included in $\mathbf{b}_t$). The action space of miner $i$ is $d \in \mathbb{N}$ (including 0) where the miner waits for $d$ additional shares to be reported before reporting the full solution. If miner $i$ decides to wait for $d$ shares before reporting, her expected reward at the end of the delay is:

$$\mathbb{E}_{(\mathbf{b} \text{ s.t. } ||\mathbf{b}||_1 = d)}[R_i(\mathbf{b}_t + \mathbf{b})] = \sum_{\mathbf{b} \text{ s.t. } ||\mathbf{b}||_1 = d} \Pr(\text{seeing } \mathbf{b}) \cdot R_i(\mathbf{b}_t + \mathbf{b}).$$

On the other hand, if she decides to report the full solution immediately, she will receive the reward she was entitled to at that moment and a new round will start. So she will additionally get $d$ times the expected reward per share. That is, delaying her report imposes an opportunity cost by not beginning the next round. So her expected reward in this situation after $d$ more shares is:

$$R_i(\mathbf{b}_t) + d \cdot \frac{\mathbb{E}_{\mathbf{b}}[R_i(\mathbf{b})]}{\mathbb{E}_{\mathbf{b}}[||\mathbf{b}||_1]} = R_i(\mathbf{b}) + d \cdot \frac{\mathbb{E}_{\mathbf{b}}[R_i(\mathbf{b})]}{\sum_{k=1}^{\infty} k\left(1 - \frac{1}{D}\right)^{k-1}\frac{1}{D}}$$

$$= R_i(\mathbf{b}_t) + \frac{d}{D} \cdot \mathbb{E}_{\mathbf{b}}[R_i(\mathbf{b})].$$

Reporting the solution immediately will be more profitable than delaying for $d$ shares if and only if:

$$\sum_{\mathbf{b} \text{ s.t. } ||\mathbf{b}||_1 = d} \Pr(\text{seeing } \mathbf{b}) \cdot (R_i(\mathbf{b}_t + \mathbf{b}) - R_i(\mathbf{b}_t)) \leq \frac{d}{D} \cdot \mathbb{E}_{\mathbf{b}}[R_i(\mathbf{b})]. \qquad (2)$$

The miner's best strategy is to report immediately if this condition holds for all $d \in \mathbb{N}\backslash\{0\}$. The following lemma states that there exists a $d \in \mathbb{N}\backslash\{0\}$ for which this condition holds if and only if it holds for $d = 1$. This is a very powerful statement: to determine the incentive compatibility of a reward function, we only need to see if it is profitable to delay reporting for a single additional share. In the following, let $\mathbf{e}_j$ be the $j^{\text{th}}$ standard basis vector that is 0 everywhere except for the $j^{\text{th}}$ component which is 1. Due to space limitations the proofs for all lemmas appear in Appendix A.

**Lemma 1.** *For a reward function $R$, a player $i$ has an incentive to report full solutions immediately, iff the following condition holds for all $\{\alpha_i\}_{i=1}^n, \mathbf{b}_t, D, i$:*

$$\sum_{j=1}^{n} \alpha_j \cdot (R_i(\mathbf{b}_t + \mathbf{e}_j) - R_i(\mathbf{b}_t)) \leq \frac{\mathbb{E}_\mathbf{b}\left[R_i(\mathbf{b})\right]}{D}. \tag{3}$$

So to show that a reward function is incentive compatible, we need to show that condition (3) holds, and conversely when we show that for a reward function condition (3) is not guaranteed to hold, it cannot be incentive compatible.[8]

While for incentive compatibility we do not care about miners reporting shares immediately, this is important in ensuring proportional payments.

**Lemma 2.** *Miners report shares immediately if and only if the reward function $R$ is monotonically increasing each component. That is: for all $i$, and $\mathbf{b}$:*

$$R_i(\mathbf{b} + \mathbf{e}_i) > R_i(\mathbf{b}).$$

## 4   Incentive Compatibility of Existing Methods

Now we will apply our characterization of incentive compatibility to reward functions which are in use today. In this section we restrict ourselves to reward functions that can be modeled by our definition of history transcript as described in Sect. 2.

### 4.1   Proportional Reward Function $R^{(\mathrm{prop})}$

One of the earliest reward functions that is still in use is the proportional reward function. The idea is to divide the reward according to the proportion of shares of a miner compared to all shares that were reported to the pool:

$$R_i^{(\mathrm{prop})}(\mathbf{b}) = \frac{b_i}{||\mathbf{b}||_1}.$$

In expectation, the reward per share for each player is $\alpha_i/D$. This approach is clearly proportional and budget-balanced. Previous work [4] has shown that in the presence of multiple pools, miners can be incentivized to change pools after a certain number of shares has been found. In this section we present a new problem that exists even in the absence of other mining pools and means that the proportional reward function is not incentive compatible.

**Lemma 3.** *The proportional rule $R_i^{(prop)}(\mathbf{b}) = \frac{b_i}{||\mathbf{b}||_1}$ is not incentive compatible.*

---

[8] In Appendix B we show that the possibility of another miner reporting a solution does not materially change the characterization here and in Appendix C we extend this to include the possibility of another pool reporting a full solution.

This result shows that the proportional reward function is *not* incentive compatible for a fundamental reason distinct from previous criticism. Even in the absence of other pools, it does not always compel miners to report solutions immediately. The intuition behind Lemma 3 is that if a player discovers a full solution early but has been unlucky and reported a lower number of shares than they would expect based on their mining power, it is in their incentive to delay reporting their solution since on expectation their fraction of all reported shares will go up. We can draw a number of corollaries immediately from Lemma 3:

- If the current ratio of blocks exceeds the expected ratio, then a player $i$ would report any full solution immediately.
- If the current ratio of blocks is *lower* than a player's expected ratio, then she might hold off to make up for this discrepancy.
- With fewer shares found, it's easier for a player to catch up, hence she is more willing to hold off reporting.
- After $D$ shares have been found, any player will always report a full solution immediately, even if she has not found a single share herself.

## 4.2   Per-Per-Share Reward Function $R^{(\mathrm{pps})}$

The pay-per-share reward function pays a fixed amount for every share that is reported. Recall that each share is a full solution with probability $1/D$, in expectation the pool operator sees $D$ shares for every full solution. Therefore the payout per share is $1/D$ leading to the following reward function:

$$R^{(\mathrm{pps})}(\mathbf{b}) = \frac{b_i}{D}.$$

It's easy to see that pay-per-share *is* incentive compatible.

**Lemma 4.** *The pay-per-share rule $R_i^{(pps)}(\mathbf{b}) = \frac{b_i}{D}$ is incentive compatible.*

*Proof.* The left hand side of (3) evaluates to

$$\sum_{j=1}^{n} \alpha_j \cdot \left( R_i^{(\mathrm{pps})}(\mathbf{b}_t + \mathbf{e}_j) - R_i^{(\mathrm{pps})}(\mathbf{b}_t) \right)$$

$$= \alpha_i \cdot \left( \frac{b_i + 1 - b_i}{D} \right) + (1 - \alpha_i) \cdot \left( \frac{b_i - b_i}{D} \right)$$

$$= \frac{\alpha_i}{D}$$

and the right hand side evaluates to

$$\frac{\mathbb{E}_{\mathbf{b}}\left[ R_i^{(\mathrm{pps})}(\mathbf{b}) \right]}{D} = \frac{\alpha_i}{D}.$$

□

This result comes at no surprise: with pay-per-share there is no benefit to delay reporting a full solution as you receive a constant payment for every reported share (or full solution). As discussed before though, it is not budget balanced.

**Proposition 1.** *The pay-per-share rule* $R_i^{(pps)}(\mathbf{b}) = \frac{b_i}{D}$ *is no better than* $(1/D, \infty)$*-budget balanced.*

*Proof.* On one extreme, if a full solution is reported before any other shares have been reported, then $R^{(\mathrm{pps})}$ pays out $\sum_{i=1}^n R_i^{(\mathrm{pps})}(\mathbf{b}) = 1/D$. On the other extreme there is no bound on how many shares can be found before a full solution must be obtained. Hence $R^{(\mathrm{pps})}$ cannot be $(1/D, C)$-budget balanced for any finite $C$. Therefore it is $(1/D, \infty)$-budget balanced. $\qquad\Box$

In the absence of sabotage attacks, with the pay-per-share rule the pool operator pays out no more than it takes on *on expectation*, but keeping the probability of bankruptcy low requires large reserves for the pool operator [4]. There are several variations that ameliorate the budget balance problem [4, Sect. 4], none of them quite satisfactorily.

# 5    A New Incentive Compatible Reward Function

In the last section we saw that two common existing methods which are possible in our model both lack one of the desiderata for reward functions. The proportional reward function may incentivize miners to delay reporting of solutions, whereas the pay-per-share function may make the pool operator liable for more than she receives from the protocol. In this section we demonstrate a reward function that satisfies all three desiderata of reward functions, while still guaranteeing a steady stream of rewards for all participants.

To satisfy the proportional payments property, it is necessary to estimate the proportion of work that each miner has done. The only information the pool operator receives within our informational model is the total number of shares per miner in the round. When only a few shares have been found in the round, every additional share may change this estimation quite significantly. When satisfying the budget-balanced property, this must translate into a large change in the payout. When there is the possibility of a large payout for an extra share, this may lead to incentive compatibility issues. Note that in practice pay-per-share reward schemes usually avoid this problem by lowering the payment amount in these cases. So to give a scheme that meets all three desiderata, we need to take an additional estimator for $\alpha_i$ into account. In the next subsection we show that we can use the identity of the discoverer of the full solution as this estimator.

## 5.1    The IC Reward Function

We propose the reward function $R_i^{(\mathrm{ic})} : \mathbb{N}^n \times \{1, ..., n\} \to [0, 1]$, that in addition to a count of the shares per miner also includes the identity of the discoverer of the full solution. In the following let $\mathbb{1}\{c\}$ be the indicator function that is 1 if $c$ is true, and 0 otherwise.

$$R_i^{(ic)}(\mathbf{b}, s) = \frac{b_i}{\max\{||\mathbf{b}||_1, D\}} + \mathbb{1}\{i = s\} \cdot \left(1 - \frac{||\mathbf{b}||_1}{\max\{||\mathbf{b}||_1, D\}}\right).$$

There are two cases to consider for the reward function. The easiest is when the total number of reported shares $||\mathbf{b}||_1 \geq D$. In that case $\left(1 - \frac{||\mathbf{b}||_1}{\max\{||\mathbf{b}||_1, D\}}\right) = 0$, hence the reward function is identical to the proportional function. When $||\mathbf{b}||_1 < D$ each share receives a fixed reward of $1/D$, like in the pay-per-share function. However, this would leave some money on the table as the total payout would be $||\mathbf{b}||_1/D$ and $||\mathbf{b}||_1 < D$. So the remainder of the reward is given to the discoverer of the full solution.

**Lemma 5.** *The reward function $R^{(ic)}$ provides proportional payments.*

*Proof.* We first split the expression into the two relevant cases.

$$\mathbb{E}_{\mathbf{b}}\left[R_i^{(ic)}(\mathbf{b}, s)\right] = \Pr(||\mathbf{b}||_1 < D) \cdot \mathbb{E}_{\mathbf{b}}\left[R_i^{(ic)}(\mathbf{b}, s) \mid ||\mathbf{b}||_1 < D\right]$$
$$+ \Pr(||\mathbf{b}||_1 \geq D) \cdot \mathbb{E}_{\mathbf{b}}\left[R_i^{(ic)}(\mathbf{b}, s) \mid ||\mathbf{b}||_1 \geq D\right].$$

We now show that in both cases the expected reward for miner $i$ is $\alpha_i$. When $||\mathbf{b}||_1 \geq D$ the IC rule is no different than the proportional rule, hence

$$\mathbb{E}_{\mathbf{b}}\left[R_i^{(ic)}(\mathbf{b}, s) \mid ||\mathbf{b}||_1 \geq D\right] = \alpha_i.$$

Now for the case where $||\mathbf{b}||_1 < D$:

$$\mathbb{E}_{\mathbf{b}}\left[R_i^{(ic)}(\mathbf{b}, s) \mid ||\mathbf{b}||_1 < D\right]$$
$$= \sum_{k=1}^{D-1} \Pr(||\mathbf{b}||_1 = k \mid ||\mathbf{b}||_1 < D) \cdot \left(\frac{\mathbb{E}[b_i \mid ||\mathbf{b}||_1 = k]}{D} + \Pr(i = s) \cdot \left(1 - \frac{k}{D}\right)\right)$$
$$= \sum_{k=1}^{D-1} \Pr(||\mathbf{b}||_1 = k \mid ||\mathbf{b}||_1 < D) \cdot \left(\frac{\alpha_i \cdot k}{D} + \alpha_i \cdot \left(1 - \frac{k}{D}\right)\right)$$
$$= \sum_{k=1}^{D-1} \Pr(||\mathbf{b}||_1 = k \mid ||\mathbf{b}||_1 < D) \cdot \alpha_i$$
$$= \alpha_i.$$

Here we used the fact that when a full solution is found, the probability that it was discovered by miner $j$ is exactly its power $\alpha_j$.     □

**Theorem 1.** *The reward function $R^{(ic)}$ is incentive compatible.*

*Proof.* By Lemma 5, the right-hand side of condition (3) is $\alpha_i/D$. Now for the left-hand side; if $||\mathbf{b}||_1 \geq D$ the rule is identical to $R^{(\text{prop})}$, so the left-hand side is at most $\alpha_i/D$, hence condition (3) holds in this case. So the only case left to prove is when $||\mathbf{b}||_1 < D$.

$$\sum_{j=1}^{n} \alpha_j \cdot \left( R_i^{(\text{ic})}(\mathbf{b}_t + \mathbf{e}_j, i) - R_i^{(\text{ic})}(\mathbf{b}_t, i) \right)$$

$$= \alpha_i \cdot \left( \frac{b_i + 1 - b_i}{D} \right) + (1 - \alpha_i) \cdot \left( \frac{b_i - b_i}{D} \right) + \left( 1 - \frac{||\mathbf{b}||_1 + 1}{D} \right) - \left( 1 - \frac{||\mathbf{b}||_1}{D} \right)$$

$$= \frac{\alpha_i}{D} - \left( \frac{||\mathbf{b}||_1 + 1}{D} - \frac{||\mathbf{b}||_1}{D} \right)$$

$$= \frac{\alpha_i - 1}{D}$$

$$\leq 0.$$

So when $||\mathbf{b}||_1 < D$ the miner is expected to *lose* utility by delaying, and certainly condition (3) holds. So in all cases condition (3) holds, hence by Lemma 1 $R^{(\text{ic})}$ is incentive compatible. ☐

So $R^{(\text{ic})}$ satisfies proportional payments and incentive compatibility. Finally, it is also a $(1, 1)$-budget balance reward function.

**Proposition 2.** $R^{(ic)}$ *is a* $(1, 1)$-*budget balanced reward function.*

*Proof.* When $||\mathbf{b}||_1 < D$ the total payout is $\sum_{i=1} \frac{b_i}{D} + \sum_{i=1} \frac{b_i}{D} + \frac{D - ||\mathbf{b}||_1}{D} = \frac{||\mathbf{b}||_1}{D} + \frac{D - ||\mathbf{b}||_1}{D} = 1$. When $||\mathbf{b}||_1 \geq D$ the total payout is $\sum_{i=1} \frac{b_i}{||\mathbf{b}||_1} = \frac{||\mathbf{b}||_1}{||\mathbf{b}||_1} = 1$. ☐

### 5.2  Providing a Steady Payment Stream

While $R^{(\text{ic})}$ satisfies all three desiderata for reward functions, it might be a concern that the reward function pays out a potentially large fraction of the reward to a single miner. Miners join a pool because they prefer a steady stream of small payments over periodic large payments. We show here that the majority of the reward is paid out for shares and not full solutions, and hence that the majority of the pool's rewards are redistributed in a steady stream. This ameliorates a large part of the problem of mining alone, while guaranteeing incentive compatibility. In Sect. 7 we give simulation results suggesting that this payment stream is sufficiently steady in practice.

**Lemma 6.** *In expectation, a fraction* $1 - e^{-1} \approx 0.63$ *of the rewards are given based on shares under* $R^{(ic)}$.

*Proof.* The fraction of the reward given to the discoverer of the full solution is

$$\sum_{k=1}^{D-1} \Pr(||\mathbf{b}||_1 = k) \cdot \left(1 - \frac{k}{D}\right) = \sum_{k=1}^{D-1} \frac{1}{D} \cdot \left(1 - \frac{1}{D}\right)^{k-1} \cdot \left(1 - \frac{k}{D}\right)$$

$$= \left(1 - \frac{1}{D}\right)^{D}$$

$$\leq e^{-1}.$$

The remainder of the reward is split among the reported shares, hence the payout to shares in expectation is $1 - e^{-1} \approx 0.63$. □

## 6  Incentive Compatibility of Pay-Per-Last-N-Shares

In previous sections we have given an overview of incentive compatibility for any reward function based on access to a history transcript $\mathcal{H}$ consisting of a count of all reported shares. By deriving incentive compatibility at this high level of abstraction allowed us to easily prove incentive compatibility for any function within this informational model.

In this section we look at incentive compatibility of a *particular* reward function that require a *more general* informational model: the Pay-Per-Last-$N$-Shares (PPLNS) reward function, that is widely used in practice. We first discuss the required changes in the informational model, and how the PPLNS function works, and then we show that the function is incentive compatible.

### 6.1  The PPLNS Reward Function

The PPLNS reward function $R^{(pplns)}$ differs from the reward functions seen so far in two important ways. Firstly, it maintains a history of reported shares that spans *multiple* rounds. So what happens in round $T$ is no longer isolated from what happens in round $T + 1$. Secondly, the method takes the order of reported shares into account in a specific way: it maintains a sliding window of length $N$ and divides the reward proportionally over these $N$ shares. So the history transcript $\mathcal{H}$ that $R^{(pplns)}$ uses is $\mathbf{s} = [s_{t-N}, s_{t+1-N}, ..., s_t]$ (an ordered list of $N$ elements) and the reward function is:

$$R^{(pplns)}(\mathbf{s}) = \frac{\#\{s_j : s_j \in \mathbf{s} \wedge s_j = i\}}{N}.$$

Since the order of reports matter, we say that shares fall into *slots*. Each slot states if the report contains either a full solution or a share, and who the miner was that reported it.

## 6.2    Incentive Compatibility of PPLNS

We do not have a general condition under which reward functions in this informational model are incentive compatible, so we argue incentive compatibility directly. In this section we consider both reporting of shares as well as full solutions. For each, we consider a binary strategy space: either report the share/solution immediately, or delay reporting until one more share is found.[9]

**Lemma 7.** *For the reward function $R^{(pplns)}$; a miner i reports shares immediately when her mining power $\alpha_i < 1 - \frac{D}{N}$.*

In the previous section there were potential benefits, and harms to delaying the report of a share, but there was no opportunity cost. Since miner $i$ did not have a full solution, her delay did not cause unnecessary work for all miners in the pool. For full solutions we have to take the opportunity cost of letting all miners work on a block for which a full solution is already found into account. This will guarantee incentive compatibility whenever $N > D$.

**Lemma 8.** *For the reward function $R^{(pplns)}$; a miner i reports full solutions immediately when $N \geq D$.*

## 7    Simulations

The typical way to compare different reward function is to look at the variance of payout for a single share [4], with a lower variance considered better. However, the raw variance can be quite misleading for a reward function like $R^{(ic)}$ which allocates some revenue in a steady stream and some in a lumpy stream, assigning a variance almost as high as solo mining.

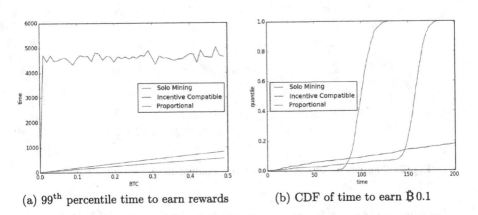

(a) 99th percentile time to earn rewards          (b) CDF of time to earn ฿0.1

**Fig. 1.** Simulation results for our new incentive-compatible reward function.

---

[9] This makes our results slightly less general in this setting than for the reduced information setting, where the miner could delay for any delay $d$.

In Fig. 1a we plot the time it takes for a miner to gain a given number of bitcoins with 99% certainty. We run a simulation for a miner $i$ with $\alpha_i = 0.001$, $D = 1,000,000$. A unit of time corresponds to the expected time it takes for all miners combined to find a full solution (in reality this is about 10 minutes) and we normalize the reward for finding a full solution to be ฿1 (in reality this currently about ฿25, although it changes over time). The lines indicate for each of three reward functions how long one has to wait to gain a given amount of ฿ with 99% probability. First of all, observe that for solo mining the time is about 4500 rounds and it does not increase with time. This is because whether a miner wants to obtain ฿0.001, or ฿0.9, they have to find a full solution to reach this target. So the blue line really indicates the time it takes to find a full solution. Even though in expectation this takes 1000 rounds (for $\alpha_i = 0.001$), in 1% of cases a miner has to wait in excess of 4500 rounds.

It can be seen that the incentive compatible scheme requires somewhat longer to reach the same target than the proportional scheme. This is because not all reward is shared according to the reported shares, but is partly distributed over the discoverers of full solutions. However, no matter what the target is, the difference in time required differs no more than a small multiplicative factor. Finally, note that since it takes longer to reach targets with high probability, the expected payouts between all three functions is the same.

In Fig. 1b we plot the CDF of the time needed to earn ฿0.1. With overwhelming probability $R^{(\mathrm{prop})}$ pays out at least ฿0.1 within 150 rounds, and $R^{(\mathrm{ic})}$ pays out at least ฿0.1 within 200 rounds. Solo mining does not fit on this scale and it wouldn't be until around round 7,000 before a miner makes at least ฿0.1 with overwhelming probability.

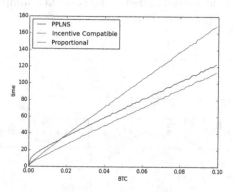

**Fig. 2.** Comparison of the new incentive compatible scheme to PPLNS.

We compare the new incentive compatible scheme to the PPLNS scheme in Fig. 2. Here we can see that the new incentive compatible scheme performs worse by a small multiplicative factor, the PPLNS scheme performs worse by a small additive factor. This means that for small Bitcoin targets it would be faster to use the IC reward function, whereas for larger target the PPLNS reward function performs better.

From these simulations we can conclude that the trade-off for using the incentive compatible or PPLNS reward function compared to the proportional reward function is a modest delay in the time it would take miners to reach a minimal amount of bitcoin with high probability. In return we get a scheme in which it is obvious for miners what the most profitable strategy for them is.

# 8    Conclusions and Open Problems

We set out with a simple question: as a mining pool operator, in the absence of other mining pools or outside options, which reward functions will incentivize miners to report full solutions immediately? In this simple model it would be reasonable to assume that miners always have an incentive to report immediately. However, we show that for proportional rewards, there are situations in which miners prefer to hold on to a full solution temporarily in order to improve their payout, harming the entire pool in the process. We also defined a novel reward function that is incentive compatible in this model (and remains so even in more powerful models). While this new scheme is not quite as efficient as proportional rewards in terms of smoothing the miners' revenue streams, it comes reasonably close in practice. We have also showed that the PPLNS reward function is incentive compatible. For a pool operator there are some tradeoffs in deciding to use our new incentive compatible scheme versus the PPLNS scheme. The latter requires a certain lead-up time, where the rewards to miners are below their fraction of the mining power. It also requires pool operators to maintain a more complex state and the payouts are arguably somewhat less transparent. On the other hand, our new incentive compatible method sometimes pays out a rather large amount to the discoverer of the full solution.

We have given a first informational model for which we can characterize incentive compatibility for all reward functions that fall in the model. We've also looked at a particular reward function that falls outside this model, and proved incentive compatibility from first principles. The next enticing question is to see if we can characterize incentive compatibility in this larger informational model at a high level, so that we can quickly identify which other reward functions would be incentive compatible. There are many reward functions in use today [4] that are not covered by any of our results. For example, the Geometric Method weights shares differently according to the order of shares in a round and Slush's Method takes the time of reported shares in a round into account. Defining a common informational model, characterizing incentive compatibility in this model, and classifying these methods remains an interesting open problem.

We stress that our incentive-compatible reward function will remain so even in a model with more extensive history transcripts. Our goal was to introduce the first rigorous, although simplified by omitting notions of time or order of share reporting, model of Bitcoin mining pools and demonstrate that even this simple model can lead to non-intuitive results.

# A    Proofs

## A.1    Proof of Lemma 1

For a reward function $R$, a player $i$ has an incentive to report full solutions immediately, iff the following condition holds for all $\{\alpha_i\}_{i=1}^n, \mathbf{b}_t, D, i$:

$$\sum_{j=1}^n \alpha_j \cdot (R_i(\mathbf{b}_t + \mathbf{e}_j) - R_i(\mathbf{b}_t)) \leq \frac{\mathbb{E}_\mathbf{b}\left[R_i(\mathbf{b})\right]}{D}. \tag{4}$$

*Proof.* ($\Rightarrow$) This direction is straightforward: when it is beneficial to delay until 1 more share is reported, then there exists a profitable delay (namely $d = 1$).

($\Leftarrow$) We need to prove that for all $d$, the following inequality holds:

$$\sum_{\mathbf{b}\ s.t.\ ||\mathbf{b}||_1 = d} \Pr(\text{seeing } \mathbf{b}) \cdot (R_i(\mathbf{b}_t + \mathbf{b}) - R_i(\mathbf{b}_t)) \leq \frac{d}{D} \mathbb{E}_\mathbf{b}\left[R_i(\mathbf{b})\right].$$

We prove this by induction on $d$, where the induction hypothesis is Eq. (2). For the base case $d = 1$ the statement follows directly from condition (3). So consider the case $d > 1$:

$$\sum_{\mathbf{b}\ s.t.\ ||\mathbf{b}||_1 = d} \Pr(\text{seeing } \mathbf{b}) \cdot (R_i(\mathbf{b}_t + \mathbf{b}) - R_i(\mathbf{b}_t))$$

$$= \sum_{\mathbf{e}_j} \Pr(\text{seeing } \mathbf{e}_j) \left( R_i(\mathbf{b}_t + \mathbf{e}_j) - R_i(\mathbf{b}_t) \right.$$

$$\left. + \sum_{\mathbf{b}\ s.t.\ ||\mathbf{b}||_1 = d-1} \Pr(\text{seeing } \mathbf{b}) \cdot (R_i(\mathbf{b}_t + \mathbf{e}_j + \mathbf{b}) - R_i(\mathbf{b}_t + \mathbf{e}_j)) \right)$$

$$\leq \frac{1}{D} \mathbb{E}_\mathbf{b}\left[R_i(\mathbf{b})\right]$$

$$+ \sum_{\mathbf{e}_j} \Pr(\text{seeing } \mathbf{e}_j) \sum_{\mathbf{b}\ s.t.\ ||\mathbf{b}||_1 = d-1} \Pr(\text{seeing } \mathbf{b}) \cdot (R_i(\mathbf{b}_t + \mathbf{e}_j + \mathbf{b}) - R_i(\mathbf{b}_t + \mathbf{e}_j))$$

$$\leq \frac{1}{D} \mathbb{E}_\mathbf{b}\left[R_i(\mathbf{b})\right] + \sum_{\mathbf{e}_j} \Pr(\text{seeing } \mathbf{e}_j) \frac{d-1}{D} \mathbb{E}_\mathbf{b}\left[R_i(\mathbf{b})\right]$$

$$= \frac{d}{D} \mathbb{E}_\mathbf{b}\left[R_i(\mathbf{b})\right].$$

where the first inequality follows from condition (3), and the second from the induction hypothesis.    □

## A.2    Proof of Lemma 2

Miners report shares immediately if and only if the reward function $R$ is monotonically increasing each component. That is: for all $i$, and $\mathbf{b}$:

$$R_i(\mathbf{b} + \mathbf{e}_i) > R_i(\mathbf{b}).$$

*Proof.* Since the order or timing of shares does not matter, for analysis purposes we can assume the following scheme: as soon as a full solution is reported the pool operator asks all miners for the shares that they found. If the reward function $R$ is monotonically increasing then each additional share that $i$ reports increases her share, hence she will report all shares. Conversely, if $R$ is not monotonically increasing at some $\mathbf{b}$, then if miner $i$ has $b_i + 1$ shares, and all other miners have reported shares according to $\mathbf{b}$, then she will not report her last share.

Now consider the original problem: when a miner finds a share, will she report it immediately? If she finds a share and the reward function is monotonically increasing, then reporting it immediately can only increase her reward, whereas delaying it may mean that someone else reports the full solution before she reports her share, in which case she loses the opportunity to report. Thus she will report immediately. □

## A.3   Proof of Lemma 3

The proportional rule $R_i^{(\mathrm{prop})}(\mathbf{b}) = \frac{b_i}{||\mathbf{b}||_1}$ is not incentive compatible.

*Proof.* Instantiate (3) for the proportional rule. For the right hand side we have:

$$\mathbb{E}_\mathbf{b}\left[R_i^{(\mathrm{prop})}(\mathbf{b}, s)\right]/D = \frac{1}{D}\sum_{k=1}^{\infty}\Pr[\text{full solution is found at } k^{\text{th}} \text{ block}]\frac{\mathbb{E}[b_i|k]}{k}$$

$$= \frac{1}{D}\sum_{k=1}^{\infty}\left(1 - \frac{1}{D}\right)^{k-1}\frac{1}{D}\frac{k\cdot\alpha_i}{k}$$

$$= \frac{\alpha_i}{D}\sum_{k=1}^{\infty}\left(1 - \frac{1}{D}\right)^{k-1}\frac{1}{D}$$

$$= \frac{\alpha_i}{D}.$$

Now for the left hand side. In the following let $k = ||\mathbf{b}_t||_1$:

$$\sum_{j=1}^{n}\alpha_j\cdot\left(R_i^{(\mathrm{prop})}(\mathbf{b}_t + \mathbf{e}_j) - R_i^{(\mathrm{prop})}(\mathbf{b}_t)\right)$$

$$= \alpha_i\cdot\left(\frac{b_i + 1}{k + 1}\right) + (1 - \alpha_i)\cdot\left(\frac{b_i}{k + 1}\right) - \frac{b_i}{k}$$

$$= \frac{\alpha_i b_i + \alpha_i + b_i - \alpha_i b_i}{k + 1} - \frac{b_i}{k}$$

$$= \frac{\alpha_i + b_i}{k + 1} - \frac{b_i}{k}$$

$$= \frac{\alpha_i}{k+1} + b_i \left( \frac{1}{k+1} - \frac{1}{k} \right)$$

$$= \frac{\alpha_i}{k+1} - \frac{b_i}{k(k+1)}$$

$$= \frac{\alpha_i - \frac{b_i}{k}}{k+1}.$$

Recall that for an incentive compatible scheme we need:

$$\frac{\alpha_i - \frac{b_i}{k}}{k+1} \le \frac{\alpha_i}{D}$$

$$\alpha_i - \frac{b_i}{k} \le \alpha_i \frac{k+1}{D}$$

$$\frac{b_i}{k} \ge \alpha_i \left( 1 - \frac{k+1}{D} \right).$$

This condition is not guaranteed to be satisfied. In particular, for every $\alpha_i > 0$ there exist positive values $b_i, k, D$ such that the condition is violated.    □

## A.4   Proof of Lemma 7

For the reward function $R^{(\text{pplns})}$; a miner $i$ reports shares immediately when her mining power $\alpha_i < 1 - \frac{D}{N}$.

*Proof.* We directly calculate the expected revenue for delay versus reporting. When the miner decides to delay reporting a share until one more share/solution is found, she aims to move the sliding window of slots for which the share is eligible to receive reward one further into the future. This means that –as long as no other miner finds a full solution and reports it– the share is active for $N-1$ of the same slots, so any reward she receives from full solutions in those slots she will get regardless of her choice to report immediately versus delaying. On the upshot, it could be the case that the one additional slot she's eligible for in the future yields a full solution. This will happen with probability $1/D$ (since a share constitutes a full solution with probability $1/D$) and in that case the share gets an extra payout of $1/N$ for the delayed share, yielding an expected benefit for delaying of $1/ND$.

However, there is also a risk associated with delaying. With probability $1-\alpha_i$ a share will be found by a different miner, and with probability $1/D$ it will constitute a full solution. When this happens, miner $i$ will no longer be able to report the share as it was discovered for a previous round. The expected value per share is $1/D$ (as it's active for $N$ rounds, in which in expectation $N/D$ full solutions will be reported for a value of $1/N$ each) hence the expected harm for delaying the report is $(1 - \alpha_i)\frac{1}{D^2}$.

So the miner will report the share immediately iff $\frac{1}{ND} < (1-\alpha_i)\cdot\frac{1}{D^2}$. Plugging in $\alpha_i < \frac{D}{N}$ leads to $(1 - \alpha_i) \cdot \frac{1}{D^2} \ge \frac{D}{N} \cdot \frac{1}{D^2} = \frac{1}{ND}$ so the condition holds, and miners report shares immediately.    □

## A.5   Proof of Lemma 8

For the reward function $R^{(\text{pplns})}$; a miner $i$ reports full solutions immediately when $N \geq D$.

*Proof.* In delaying a full solution, the hope is to get another share to report before the miner reports the full solution. This happens with probability $\alpha_1 \cdot \frac{D-1}{D}$ (we need the share to *not* be a full solution) and the additional value to this share would be $\frac{1}{N}$ compared to it being reported after the full solution. However, while waiting for a share, with probability $\frac{1}{D}$ the next share will be a full solution, either found by miner $i$, or one of the other miners. Regardless of who finds the solution, the previous full solution that miner $i$ was sitting on has become worthless: either a different miner reported the full solution ending the round and thus making the delayed full solution worthless, or miner $i$ now has 2 full solutions of which she can report only one. When this happens, she loses the solution whose expected value is $1/D$ (as this is counted as a share for future). So the expected upshot for delaying the solution is $\alpha_1 \frac{D-1}{D} \frac{1}{N}$ and the expected harm is $\frac{1}{D^2}$.

In addition to this, when the miner chooses to delay until one more share is found, she lets all miners in the pool work on a block for which she already has a solution. If everyone were to spend that effort on a new block, that work would in expectation constitute $1/D$ of the work for a new block, of which in expectation miner $i$ would receive $\alpha_i$ of the reward. Thus, the opportunity cost is $\frac{\alpha_i}{D}$. Therefore, a miner will report a full solution immediately iff $\alpha_i \frac{D-1}{D} \frac{1}{N} - \frac{1}{D^2} \leq \frac{\alpha_i}{D}$ which holds whenever $N \geq D$.

## B   Incentive Compatibility When Other Miners Can Find a Block Before You Report

In Sect. 3 we showed that there is a simple condition that precisely characterizes when a reward function $R$ is incentive compatible, under the assumption that no other miner finds and reports a full solution during this delay. In reality a miner does have to take this possibility into account, so in this section we show exactly how the IC condition changes when we drop this assumption.

If we decide to delay reporting the full solution until one additional share is found, then with probability $1/D$ that share will actually be a full solution itself. Without loss of generality we may assume that this solution will be reported immediately (otherwise we could simply ignore its effect). Recall that $\mathbf{b}_t$ is the number of reported shares per miner *including* the unreported full solution that miner $i$ has, and that $\mathbf{e}_j$ is the vector that has zeros everywhere except its $j^{\text{th}}$ component, where it is 1. So the expected payout for delaying for one round becomes:

$$\frac{1}{D} \sum_j \alpha_j R_i(\mathbf{b}_t - \mathbf{e}_i + \mathbf{e}_j) + \frac{D-1}{D} \sum_j \alpha_j R_i(\mathbf{b}_t + \mathbf{e}_j).$$

Thus the condition of incentive compatibility is:

$$\frac{1}{D} \sum_j \alpha_j \left( R_i(\mathbf{b}_t - \mathbf{e}_i + \mathbf{e}_j) - R_i(\mathbf{b}_t) \right)$$

$$+ \frac{D-1}{D} \sum_j \alpha_j \left( R_i(\mathbf{b}_t + \mathbf{e}_j) - R_i(\mathbf{b}_t) \right) \leq \frac{\mathbb{E}_\mathbf{b}[R_i(\mathbf{b})]}{D}.$$

For the reward functions that are monotonic increasing in each component (which by Lemma 2 are precisely the reward functions where miners always report all shares) this additional term is negative. Therefore, the IC condition is only easier to satisfy. This means that reward functions that are proven to be incentive compatible using Lemma 1 are still incentive compatible. However, one might worry that our proof that the proportional reward function is not incentive compatible might break. We show next that the thread of being scooped actually does not impact the result qualitatively.

### B.1 Proportional

For the proportional reward function we can instantiate the left-hand side as (taking $\|\mathbf{b}_t\|_1 = k$):

$$\frac{1}{D} \left( \alpha_i \left( \frac{b_i}{k} - \frac{b_i}{k} \right) + (1 - \alpha_i) \left( \frac{b_i - 1}{k} - \frac{b_i}{k} \right) \right)$$

$$+ \frac{D-1}{D} \left( \alpha_i \left( \frac{b_i + 1}{k+1} - \frac{b_i}{k} \right) + (1 - \alpha_i) \left( \frac{b_i}{k+1} - \frac{b_i}{k} \right) \right)$$

$$= \frac{1}{D} \frac{1 - \alpha_i}{k} + \frac{D-1}{D} \frac{\alpha_i - \frac{b_i}{k}}{k+1}.$$

So the proportional reward function is IC if and only if

$$\frac{1}{D} \frac{1 - \alpha_i}{k} + \frac{D-1}{D} \frac{\alpha_i - \frac{b_i}{k}}{k+1} \leq \frac{\alpha_i}{D}.$$

Again this is not guaranteed to be satisfied, in fact the same parameters as last time, i.e. $b_i = 2$, $k = 10$, $\alpha_i = 1/2$ and $D = 20$. So including the possibility of another miner finding a full solution does not qualitatively change the incentive compatibility results, although quantitatively there may be situations where a miner would choose to delay if she does not fear being scooped, but choose to report if she does include this possibility.

## C   Multiple Pools

In the main text we've assumed that there are no other pools that compete for finding solutions to the cryptographic puzzle. This is reasonable from the perspective of proving positive results: any incentive compatible scheme should be incentive compatible regardless of how much mining power other pools have.

However, to convincingly reject the proportional rule as not incentive compatible, we should take the effect of other pools into account. In the following let $\sum_{i=1}^{n} \alpha_i = \alpha_P < 1$ be the total mining power of the pool, so all other mining power —of both other pools and solo miners— is $1 - \alpha_P$. For notational simplicity we do not consider being scooped by a different miner in our own pool; it's obvious how this can be included by comparing the results to the one in Appendix B. When we consider to delay reporting a full solution until one more share is found —either inside or outside the pool— then our expected utility for doing so is

$$\sum_j \alpha_j R_i(\mathbf{b}_t + \mathbf{e}_j) + (1 - \alpha_P) \left( \frac{1}{D} \cdot 0 + \frac{D-1}{D} R_i(\mathbf{b}_t) \right).$$

We don't really care if some other pool finds another share. This does not affect us. But if another pool finds a full solution and reports it, then our mining pool misses out on a complete payment that it could have received. So the condition for incentive compatibility becomes

$$\sum_{j=1}^{n} \alpha_j \cdot (R_i(\mathbf{b}_t + \mathbf{e}_j) - R_i(\mathbf{b}_t)) - (1 - \alpha_P) \frac{R_i(\mathbf{b})}{D} \leq \alpha_P \frac{\mathbb{E}_\mathbf{b}\left[R_i(\mathbf{b}_t)\right]}{D}.$$

Under the assumption that the pool in expectation will collect $\alpha_P$ of the total reward among pools, and that miner $i$ collects $\frac{\alpha_i}{\alpha_P}$ of the pool she is in, the right-hand side will remain $\frac{\alpha_i}{D}$. The new term on the left-hand side is simply $(1 - \alpha_P)\frac{b_i}{kD}$. The other term on the left-hand side changes slightly:

$$\sum_{j=1}^{n} \alpha_j \cdot \left( R_i^{(\text{prop})}(\mathbf{b}_t + \mathbf{e}_j) - R_i^{(\text{prop})}(\mathbf{b}_t) \right)$$

$$= \alpha_i \cdot \left( \frac{b_i + 1}{k + 1} \right) + (\alpha_P - \alpha_i) \cdot \left( \frac{b_i}{k + 1} \right) - \frac{b_i}{k}$$

$$= \frac{\alpha_i b_i + \alpha_i + \alpha_P b_i - \alpha_i b_i}{k + 1} - \frac{b_i}{k}$$

$$= \frac{\alpha_i + \alpha_P b_i}{k + 1} - \frac{b_i}{k}.$$

This cannot be simplified to the same convenient expression we had in Sect. 3. Combining these terms the condition for incentive compatibility of the proportional reward function becomes:

$$\frac{\alpha_i + \alpha_P b_i}{k + 1} - \frac{b_i}{k} - (1 - \alpha_P)\frac{b_i}{kD} \leq \frac{\alpha_i}{D}$$

and after rewriting this:

$$\frac{\alpha_i}{k+1} + \alpha_P b_i \left( \frac{1}{kD} + \frac{1}{k+1} \right) - \frac{b_i}{k} \left( 1 + \frac{1}{D} \right) \leq \frac{\alpha_i}{D}.$$

# References

1. Nakamoto, S.: Bitcoin: A peer-to-peer electronic cash system. Consulted **1**(2012), 28 (2008)
2. Bonneau, J., Miller, A., Clark, J., Narayanan, A., Kroll, J.A., Felten, E.W.: Research perspectives and challenges for bitcoin and cryptocurrencies. In: 2015 IEEE Symposium on Security and Privacy, May 2015
3. Miller, A., Shi, E., Kosba, A., Katz, J.: Nonoutsourceable Scratch-Off Puzzles to Discourage Bitcoin Mining Coalitions (2014). (preprint)
4. Rosenfeld, M.: Analysis of Bitcoin pooled mining reward systems (2011). arXiv preprint arXiv:1112.4980
5. Eyal, I.: The miner's dilemma. In: IEEE Symposium on Security and Privacy (2015)
6. Laszka, A., Johnson, B., Grossklags, J.: When bitcoin mining pools run dry. In: Brenner, M., Christin, N., Johnson, B., Rohloff, K. (eds.) FC 2015. LNCS, vol. 8976, pp. 63–77. Springer, Heidelberg (2015). doi:10.1007/978-3-662-48051-9_5
7. Johnson, B., Laszka, A., Grossklags, J., Vasek, M., Moore, T.: Game-theoretic analysis of DDoS attacks against bitcoin mining pools. In: Böhme, R., Brenner, M., Moore, T., Smith, M. (eds.) FC 2014. LNCS, vol. 8438, pp. 72–86. Springer, Heidelberg (2014). doi:10.1007/978-3-662-44774-1_6
8. Eyal, I., Sirer, E.G.: Majority is not enough: Bitcoin mining is vulnerable. In: Financial Cryptography (2014)

# When Cryptocurrencies Mine Their Own Business

Jason Teutsch[✉], Sanjay Jain, and Prateek Saxena

School of Computing, National University of Singapore, Singapore 117543, Singapore
{teutsch,sanjay,prateeks}@comp.nus.edu.sg

**Abstract.** Bitcoin and hundreds of other cryptocurrencies employ a consensus protocol called Nakamoto consensus which rewards miners for maintaining a public blockchain. In this paper, we study the security of this protocol with respect to rational miners and show how a minority of the computation power can incentivize the rest of the network to accept a blockchain of the minority's choice. By deviating from the mining protocol, a mining pool which controls at least 38.2% of the network's total computational power can, with modest financial capacity, gain mining advantage over honest mining. Such an attack creates a longer valid blockchain by forking the honest blockchain, and the attacker's blockchain need not disrupt any "legitimate" non-mining transactions present on the honest blockchain. By subverting the consensus protocol, the attacking pool can double-spend money or simply create a blockchain that pays mining rewards to the attacker's pool. We show that our attacks are easy to encode in any Nakamoto-consensus-based cryptocurrency which supports a scripting language that is sufficiently expressive to encode its own mining puzzles.

## 1 Introduction

Hundreds of cryptocurrencies are in use today, and investments in cryptocurrencies continue to increase steadily [1]. Some cryptocurrencies, such as Bitcoin and Ethereum, aim to serve as underlying substrates for financial applications beyond simple distributed ledgers and payment services. Nearly all cryptocurrencies share a protocol known as the Nakamoto consensus protocol as their backbone. The security of the Nakamoto consensus protocol has recently been rigorously analyzed, under the assumption that a majority of the miners follow the protocol honestly [10]. Does this backbone remain secure when miners purely try to maximize their financial payoffs? In this paper, we study this question from the lens of cryptocurrencies which permit expressive transaction semantics.

Cryptocurrencies often allow applications and users to encode semantic operations in blockchain transactions. For example, Bitcoin and Ethereum both permit transaction scripts which allow users to specify conditions, or contracts,

---

J. Teutsch and P. Saxena's research is supported by Singapore Ministry of Education Grant No. R-252-000-560-112. S. Jain is supported in part by NUS grant Nos. R252-000-534-112, R146-000-181-112 and C252-000-087-001.

J. Grossklags and B. Preneel (Eds.): FC 2016, LNCS 9603, pp. 499–514, 2017.
DOI: 10.1007/978-3-662-54970-4_29

which corresponding transactions must satisfy prior to acceptance. Transaction scripts can encode many useful functions, such as validating that a payer owns a coin he is spending or enforcing rules for multi-party transactions.

Scriptable cryptocurrencies allow clients to outsource computational tasks or puzzles [12]. For instance, assuming a sufficiently expressive scripting language, a client might post a computational puzzle and a transaction that together contractually commit him to pay prize money to the first party that conveys a correct solution. Let us call a computational puzzle encoded via a cryptocurrency transaction script a *script puzzle*. Script puzzles are one way for clients to trade computation power directly with coins. We now ask: what are the security implications of allowing script puzzles in a cryptocurrency? When analyzing this question, we will assume that miners in such cryptocurrencies always try to optimize their expected financial gains. This assumption differs from the folklore assumption that the majority of miners always honestly follow the mining protocol, irrespective of whether it gives them a financial advantage. If we assume that miners are rational instead, then is Nakamoto-consesus based crytocurrency secure against a minority of miners deviating from the protocol for financial gain? Given the financial investments in cryptocurrencies today, it is reasonable to ask whether the core protocol is open to manipulation by rational minorities.

In particular, this paper investigates the consequences of casting proof-of-work mining problems as script puzzles. Miners often have dedicated hardware for solving proof-of-work problems, and so they can easily reuse their hardware for solving such script puzzles. In short, miners engage in a game which incentivizes them to split their computation resources between solving script puzzles and mining. We analyze this game and find that, even when the language does not support script puzzles, an attacker with 38.2% of the computation capacity can not only subvert the consensus protocol — effectively reducing the classic 51% attack to a 38.2% attack — but can also increase his share of mining reward per block without double-spending. The expected minimum financial capacity for such an attacker, beyond its cost invested in mining power, is less than a dozen times the reward for mining a new block when the attacker's power exceeds 39.1% of the network. Several mining pools have enjoyed such large share of computation power in the Bitcoin network recently.

## 2    Background

Bitcoin and several other cryptocurrencies use similar mechanism for maintaining consensus about a distributed ledger of transactions. The distributed ledger is maintained as a hash-chain of transaction blocks known as the *blockchain* ledger. The consensus protocol used in nearly all blockchain-based cryptocurrencies, known as *Nakamoto consensus*, achieves eventual consistency assuming an honest majority[1]. *Miners* in a cryptocurrency network solve "mining puzzles" — a cryptographic proof-of-work puzzle (e.g. "inverting" a SHA2 hash [9]) — in

---

[1] It further assumes a favorable broadcast network between miners.

exchange for cryptocurrency mining rewards. When a miner successfully broadcasts the solution of a proof-of-work puzzle, he proves that he has spent the necessary computation power to merit appending his new set of transactions to the distributed ledger. This step awards the miner a set of newly minted coins. Miners solve the next proof-of-work puzzle using the longest blockchain, which implicitly embodies the majority of the network's computational effort with overwhelming probability.

In a blockchain-based cryptocurrency, the cryptographic hash-chain guarantees integrity of accepted transactions. Thus anyone can query the blockchain for the presence of a transaction. Miners on the network race to extend the blockchain in each time epoch (e.g. 10 min in the Bitcoin protocol), and this race effectively generates randomized lottery to elect a leader in each epoch.

## 2.1 The 51% Attack

In principle, the blockchain mechanism only ensures consensus with overwhelming probability. A transaction that appears in the longest, current blockchain can be omitted in a future blockchain which is longer — however, creating such a "forked" blockchain that omits a transaction requires an adversary with computation power larger than half the computation power of the entire network. The backtracking mechanism which permits this kind of double-spending is known as a *51% attack* [15]. Satoshi Nakamoto [2] was aware of this attack when he introduced Bitcoin in 2009. His proof-of-work mechanism ensures correct blockchain consensus under the assumption that the majority of miners are honest. If, for example, the powerful miner spent some money in another fork of the blockchain at the time when that fork appeared to be longest, he would not necessarily have to carry that transaction over to his own fork and could thereby double-spend the money.

## 2.2 Smart Contracts

Bitcoin and several cryptocurrencies allow transactions to specify conditions as scripts. A transaction is deemed valid only if the linked condition holds. Bitcoin's scripts have limited expressiveness, however emerging cryptocurrencies support expressive scripts that enable development of a variety of powerful decentralized applications. The Ethereum cryptocurrency [8] introduced *smart contracts* in which versatile scripts specify whether or not the network should accept given transactions. Ethereum is *Turing-complete* in the sense that one can encode any algorithm in its scripting language.

One can encode a smart contract which pays a reward for solution to a hash inversion puzzle in many different ways. Figure 1 provides an example of how one might realize such a contract in Ethereum. The protocol in this figure permits a puzzle giver to post a blockchain transaction containing a public puzzle such that any prover who notices the puzzle can post a solution on the blockchain. If the miners on the network deem the prover's solution to be correct, the prover may receive the puzzle giver's advertised reward in exchange for the solution.

```
1 init:
2      #Record the initiator, reward and data
3      contract.storage[0]=msg.sender
4      contract.storage[1]=0
5      contract.storage[2]=msg.value
6      #record the difficulty of the puzzle
7      contract.storage[3]=msg.data[0]
8 code:
9      #if the puzzle is solved
10     if contract.storage[4] == 0:
11         return (1)
12     if msg.datasize == 1:
13         #if everything is fine, send the reward
14         if sha256(sha256(msg.data[0])) < contract.storage[3]:
15             send(1000,msg.sender,contract.storage[2])
16             contract.storage[4]=0 #update status
17             contract.storage[5]=msg.data[0] #store result
18             return (2)
19         else:
20             return (1)
```

**Fig. 1.** Code snippet of a contract which asks users to solve a hashing puzzle. The contract will verify the correctness of the result before sending out the reward.

Luu, Teutsch, Kulkarni, and Saxena [12, Sect. 5.2] showed how one can modify a puzzle script, such as the one in Fig. 1, so as to achieve fairness via a commitment scheme. Their protocol rewards the first solution posted and resolves ties as follows. Every potential prover posts a hash of his solution to the puzzle so as both to notify the network that his solution is ready and to prevent him from later changing his answer. The first solutions to appear effectively enter a lottery. Once the network has confirmed the winner of this lottery, the prover publicly reveals his solution. If the network finds that his solution is correct, then he receives the puzzle's reward for his solution. If the solution is incorrect, another prover's solution may be considered.

Any transaction puzzle with suitable computational complexity and monetary reward which incentivizes miners to repurpose their hardware suffices for the attacks in this paper. Ethereum miners use GPU hardware, so in practice one would need to fine tune the puzzle in Fig. 1 into a GPU-friendly form in order to achieve the desired effect.

## 2.3   Assumptions

Our theoretical attack will suppose the following specific conditions about miners' behavior, the attacker's capability, and the underlying cryptocurrency.

1. *Miners always mine on the longest chain.* This is a fundamental and standard assumption for Nakamoto consensus.

2. *Expected time between new blocks is constant.* The network calibrates the difficulty of mining blocks so as to maintain a fixed expected time between new blocks. Both the Ethereum and Bitcoin protocols include periodic adjustments based on the cumulative computational power of active miners.

3. *Miners are rational.* Non-attacking miners on the network distribute their computational resources between mining and puzzle solving in order to maximize expected profits. They do not withhold blocks.

4. *Attacker has limited resources.* The attacker has a fixed amount of capital and computational power at his disposal with which to execute his attack. Section 5 discusses the sufficient capital and computational power needed as well as the tradeoffs between these two parameters for the attack to succeed.

We will elaborate on and further discuss the details of these assumptions in subsequent sections. Empirical testing may shed light on the practical validity of the above assumptions and remains as valuable future work. Finally, for ease of presentation, our analysis will focus on expected values rather than probabilities for various possible outcomes.

## Capital required for double-spending

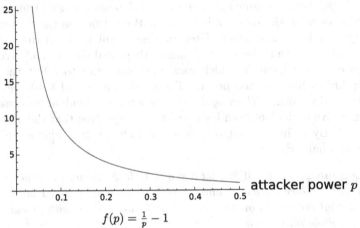

$$f(p) = \tfrac{1}{p} - 1$$

**Fig. 2.** Expected initial capital required to execute a double-spend attack with $p$ fraction of the network power (for $k = 1$ block advantage).

## 3   The Double-Spend Attack

An attacker with sufficient capital, regardless of computational power can double-spend in any cryptocurrency with sufficiently expressive scripting language via a modification of the backtracking 51% attack discussed in Sect. 2. We expect that block-sized hash inversion script puzzles can distribute rewards fairly because the time required to verify the correctness of a solution is small [12].[2]

---

[2] Since the time required to solve these script puzzles is modest, Ethereum's `gaslimit` function does not hinder their execution.

**Attack 1.** Let $M$ be a miner with $p$ fraction of the network's computation power[3]. Let $b$ be the fixed reward for mining a new block. Starting from the current block, $M$ begins, using his full power $p$, privately mining new blocks on a fork which is unknown to other miners. Meanwhile the following is repeated until $M$'s private blockchain is longer than the public one:

> Once per (public) block, $M$ posts a transaction with a hash-inversion puzzle[4] whose solution requires exactly the same amount of work as mining a new block[5]. $M$ offers a prize for its solution exceeding
>
> $$\frac{1 - 2p + \epsilon}{p - \epsilon} \cdot b \qquad (3.1)$$
>
> for some fixed value $0 < \epsilon < p$.

Since $M$ is free to add or not add transactions from the public blockchain into his private blockchain, he may double-spend when the loop finally terminates by revealing his private blockchain.

Each time the miner $M$ from Attack 1 posts a puzzle transaction, the other processors on the network have two options: work on the transaction puzzle or try to mine a new block. Each processor will work on the puzzle with some probability $a$ and hence will mine with probability $1 - a$.[6] We can view this process as a game in which each processor tries to select the value $a$ which optimizes his expected profits. The processors' set of strategies for choosing $a$ are said to form a *Nash equilibrium* when no individual processor has financial incentive to deviate from his current strategy given that the other strategies are fixed. By definition, *rational* processors choose the value $a$ which satisfies the Nash equilibrium.

**Lemma 2.** *Let $t > 0$ and let $0 < a < 1$. If the miner in Attack 1 offers a reward of $a \cdot t$ to solve his puzzle and the reward for mining a new block is $(1 - a)t$, then rational processors on the network will puzzle-solve with probability $a$ and mine with probability $1 - a$.*

*Proof.* Suppose a given processor $R$ has $0 < q < 1$ fraction of the total computational power of the network. When every processor on the network works on the

---

[3] In the following discussions, we assume that the total number of processors on the network is fixed.

[4] The puzzle $M$ chooses may be identical to the nonce he needs to solve in order to extend his private blockchain, and this choice may help $M$ to mine faster on his private chain. We do not attempt to quantify the advantage of implementing this strategy, however, as latency from network broadcasts and puzzle reward commitment schemes make the benefit difficult to estimate.

[5] For simplicity of calculation, we assume that the hardness of the puzzle that $M$ posts in a given block is equally hard compared to the mining problem in the current block.

[6] For the purposes of our calculations, it is equivalent to assume that the miner devotes $a$ fraction of his computational resources to puzzle solving and $1 - a$ fraction to mining.

## Capital required for 38.2% attack

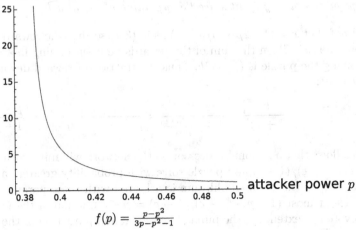

initial captial (in block rewards)

attacker power $p$

$$f(p) = \frac{p - p^2}{3p - p^2 - 1}$$

**Fig. 3.** Expected initial capital required to break even on a 38.2% attack relative to honest mining without double-spending and with $p$ fraction of the network power.

puzzle with probability $a$ and mines with probability $1 - a$, $R$'s expected gain is the sum of his expected fraction of total work on the puzzle times the puzzle prize plus his expected fraction of total work on mining times the mining prize:

$$\frac{aq}{aq + a(1 - q)} \cdot at + \frac{(1 - a)q}{(1 - a)q + (1 - a)(1 - q)} \cdot (1 - a)t = qt.$$

By symmetry, no processor can expect to obtain more than his share of the reward, so an expected reward of $qt$ is optimal on a purely rational network. Suppose that $R$ were to deviate from this strategy by puzzle-solving with probability $a + \delta$ where $0 < \delta < 1 - a$. Then his expected reward would be

$$\frac{(a + \delta)q}{(a + \delta)q + a(1 - q)} \cdot at + \frac{(1 - a - \delta)q}{(1 - a - \delta)q + (1 - a)(1 - q)} \cdot (1 - a)t$$

$$= \frac{aq + \delta q}{a + \delta q} \cdot at + \frac{q - aq - \delta q}{1 - a - \delta q} \cdot (1 - a)t = \frac{a - a^2 - 2\delta aq + \delta q - \delta^2 q}{(a + \delta q)(1 - a - \delta q)} \cdot qt, \quad (3.2)$$

which is less than $qt$ whenever $0 < \delta q < 1 - a$, and in particular this inequality holds for our choice of $\delta < 1 - a$. Indeed for such $\delta$, the denominator of the rightmost fraction of (3.2) is positive and exceeds its numerator by $\delta^2 q - \delta^2 q^2$. By symmetry, $R$ gains no advantage by biasing himself towards mining, either. Hence the given strategy yields a Nash equilibrium. □

We now show that Attack 1 succeeds when the other processors on the network are rational.

**Theorem 3.** *If a miner $M$ has sufficient initial capital, possesses $p$ fraction of the network's computing power and the other processors on the network are rational, then the loop in Attack 1 eventually terminates. Hence $M$ can double-spend any money spent since the beginning of the attack.*

*Proof.* Let $x = (1 - 2p + \epsilon)/(p - \epsilon)$ as in (3.1) so that the reward for solving $M$'s puzzle is $xb$. Then the sum of the rewards between mining in a given block and solving the puzzle is $(1 + x)b$. Thus the fraction of reward devoted to mining is at most:

$$\frac{b}{(1+x)b} = \frac{1}{1 + \frac{1-2p+\epsilon}{p-\epsilon}} = \frac{p - \epsilon}{p - \epsilon + 1 - 2p + \epsilon} = \frac{p - \epsilon}{1 - p}.$$

It follows that a rational processor on the network will mine with probability less than $(p - \epsilon)/(1 - p)$ and puzzle-solve with probability greater than $1 - [(p - \epsilon)/(1 - p)]$ as the Nash equilibrium is achieved with these parameters (Lemma 2). Since at most $(1 - p) \cdot (p - \epsilon)/(1 - p) = p - \epsilon$ fraction of the network power is devoted to extending the public blockchain and $p$ fraction of the network power is devoted to extending $M$'s private chain, $M$'s private chain will eventually become longer than the public one. ☐

## 4 Mining Advantage Without Double-Spending

We now observe that if a miner controls more than $(3 - \sqrt{5})/2 \approx 38.2\%$ of the network's computational power, then he can execute Attack 1 without double-spending and still achieve an overall mining advantage. In the short run, such a miner obtains a per-block advantage over honest mining which, as we discuss at the end of Sect. 5, translates into a gain per unit time after consecutive repetitions of the attack. Unlike our double-spend attack, in this scenario the attacker can offer his puzzle rewards on an external website or system known to the cryptocurrency miners; the puzzles need not be posted as transactions within the cryptocurrency itself. Thus our analysis establishes the insecurity of Nakamoto consensus against a rational-but-dishonest minority of miners without assuming any scriptability properties for transactions.

**Theorem 4.** *A miner $M$ with $p$ fraction of the network's power where $(3 - \sqrt{5})/2 < p \le 1/2$ who executes Attack 1 with appropriately chosen $\epsilon > 0$ so that the reward for each of his puzzles, $xb$, satisfies the additional constraint*

$$x < 1 - p \tag{4.1}$$

*expects to gain a mining reward advantage of at least $[1 - (x + p)]b$ per block when other processors on the network are rational. Thus $M$ can benefit from the Attack 1 without double-spending or otherwise manipulating public transactions in his private blockchain.*

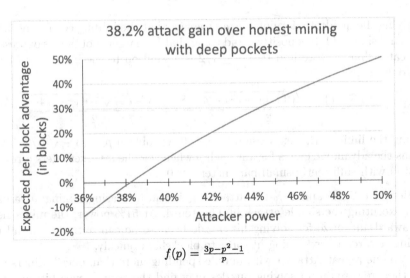

$$f(p) = \frac{3p - p^2 - 1}{p}$$

**Fig. 4.** Expected net gain over honest mining for a 38.2% attack without double-spending with infinite budget for puzzle prizes. In general, the puzzle prize investment may be small compared to the attacker's financial investment in mining hardware.

*Proof.* Since $M$'s reward satisfies the lower bound from Attack 1, the argument in Theorem 3 shows that the length of $M$'s private blockchain will eventually exceed the length of the public one. In particular, we can assume that by the end of the attack $M$'s private blockchain has at least as many blocks in it as the public blockchain. Note that the reward that $M$ would have expected to receive from mining a block without posting the puzzle transaction is $pb$, and the reward he receives per block on his private blockchain is $b$, so the attack is only profitable if the cost of each puzzle is less than $b - pb$, that is, when $x < 1 - p$. Since $M$ can win all the mining rewards from the network when $p > 1/2$ using the 51% attack, the miner receives no additional advantage in posting puzzle transactions when $p > 1/2$.

Finally, let us consider when an $x$ satisfying both (3.1) and (4.1) actually exists. For $\epsilon < p$, this happens when:[7]

$$\frac{1 - 2p + \epsilon}{p - \epsilon} < 1 - p,$$

or equivalently $1 - 2p + \epsilon < p - \epsilon - p^2 + \epsilon p$, which simplifies to

$$p^2 - (3 - \epsilon)p + (1 + 2\epsilon) < 0. \tag{4.2}$$

---

[7] A slightly weaker inequality holds here. At the end of Attack 1, the attacker's private chain is a block longer than the public chain, and so the attacker's expected net gain per block actually exceeds $(1 - p) \cdot b$ by some positive quantity, namely $[(1 - p)\epsilon/(p - \epsilon)] \cdot b$, which tends to zero as $\epsilon \to 0$. In this argument we ultimately care only about what happens as $\epsilon$ approaches 0, and so for now we ignore this quantity. We revisit the present calculation in more detail in Lemma 7.

Applying the quadratic formula, using the fact that the leading coefficient in the left-hand side of (4.2) is positive, and using that the larger root of this expression is greater that $1/2$, we find that $p \leq 1/2$ is a solution to the inequality (4.2) if and only if

$$p > \frac{(3-\epsilon) - \sqrt{(9-6\epsilon+\epsilon^2) - 4 - 8\epsilon}}{2} = \frac{3-\epsilon - \sqrt{5+\epsilon^2 - 14\epsilon}}{2}.$$

Taking the limit of this expression as $\epsilon \to 0$, we obtain $p > (3 - \sqrt{5})/2$, which means the advantage exists for any such $p$ whenever the attacker offers a reward in (3.1) with sufficiently small parameter $\epsilon > 0$.                                  □

Between 38.2% and 50% the attacker gains an increasing mining advantage from executing the simple attack in Theorem 4. At 51% power, the miner need not award any prize for solving his puzzle because he can outright win all the mining rewards by extending his private blockchain quickly.

Can one repeat Attack 1 with double-spending more than once? Miners who lose their rewards from solving puzzles may find themselves once bitten, twice shy. Unlike the double-spend attack described in Theorem 3, the *38.2% attack* in Theorem 4 permits miners to keep their rewards for solving puzzles. Thus the deterrent of "once bitten, twice shy" disappears in the latter form of this attack.

Theorem 4 highlights a tragedy of the commons for rational miners. By working on the puzzle posed in Attack 1, miners place the integrity of the network at risk, yet none of them are individually motivated to switch back to mining. The assumption that miners optimize their personal profit ensures that they work on puzzles even while "honest" miners lose all of their mining rewards.

## 5    How Much Does It Cost?

Both Theorems 3 and 4 assume that the perpetrator $M$ has "sufficient initial capital" to successfully generate the long private fork described in Attack 1. We now estimate how much initial capital is "sufficient." Following the notation of Attack 1, let $p$ denote the fraction of the network's computational power that belongs to the attacker, let $\epsilon$ represent the difference in mining effort during the attack between the attacker and the rest of the network, and let $b$ be the prize offered by the cryptocurrency for mining a new block.

**Lemma 5.** *A miner who executes Attack 1 using*

- *$p$ fraction of the network's computing power,*
- *with $0 < \epsilon < p$ difference in mining effort between the attacker and the rest of the network, and*
- *with prize $b$ for mining a new block*

*expects to spend*

$$\frac{1 - 2p + \epsilon}{\epsilon} \cdot bk \tag{5.1}$$

*on mining puzzles before his private blockchain becomes $k$ blocks longer than the public one when other processors on the network are rational.*

*Proof.* Let $t(p, \epsilon, k)$ denote the expected number of public blocks which are mined before the length of $M$'s private blockchain exceeds the public blockchain's length by at least $k$ blocks, and let $c(p, \epsilon, b)$ denote the cost per block of the puzzle reward given in (3.1). The expected initial capital required to execute Attack 1 for given parameters $p$, $\epsilon$, $k$, and $b$ is then $t(p, \epsilon, k) \cdot c(p, \epsilon, b)$.

Let us assume that the network generates on average one new block per unit time. Then after $s$ units of time, the attacker expects to have generated $ps$ blocks on his private chain, and the rest of the network expects to have generated $(p - \epsilon)s$ blocks on the public chain (see the proof of Theorem 3 for calculation of these estimates). We are interested in the time $s$ at which the difference between these blockchain lengths reaches $k$, that is $k = ps - (p-\epsilon)s$, or equivalently when $s = k/\epsilon$. Thus

$$t(p, \epsilon, k) = s \cdot (p - \epsilon) = \frac{p - \epsilon}{\epsilon} \cdot k \,.$$

For a fixed $\epsilon$, we may now estimate the total expected cost of the attack as

$$t(p, \epsilon, k) \cdot c(p, \epsilon, b) = \frac{p - \epsilon}{\epsilon} \cdot \frac{1 - 2p + \epsilon}{p - \epsilon} \cdot bk$$

when $0 < \epsilon < p$, as required in Attack 1 in order to ensure the puzzle prize value is positive. The above quantity simplifies to (5.1).                                    $\square$

We now compute the $\epsilon$ which minimizes the cost of a successful double-spending attack.

**Theorem 6.** *A miner with $p$ fraction of the network can double-spend using Attack 1 with approximately $b/p - b$ initial capital, where $b$ is the reward for mining a new block, when other processors on the network are rational.*

*Proof.* The attack cost in (5.1) is minimized when $\epsilon$ is as large as possible, that is, as $\epsilon$ approaches $p$. Thus the expected cost of the double-spend attack in Theorem 3 can be made arbitrarily close to $(1/p - 1) \cdot bk$. In the notation of Lemma 5, we may assume $k = 1$ because the attacker's private chain need only be longer than the public chain momentarily in order for the double-spend attack to succeed.[8]                                    $\square$

If an attacker were to double-spend *only* the puzzle prize money, then he would gain approximately $(1 - p)b$ more capital per block from executing the double-spend attack compared to honest mining.

**Lemma 7.** *A miner $M$ with $p$ fraction of the network's power where $(3 - \sqrt{5})/2 < p < 1/2$ who successfully executes a 38.2% attack (that is, Attack 1*

---

[8] Since many Bitcoin users do not consider a transaction confirmed until the transaction is at least 6 places deep in the blockchain, one might wish to wait until the private chain extension is at least 6 blocks long before revealing it. This can be done be choosing an $\epsilon$ satisfying, in the notation of Lemma 5, $t(p, \epsilon, 1) \geq 6 \cdot (p - \epsilon)/p$, or equivalently $\epsilon \leq p/6$.

*without double-spending), using $0 < \epsilon < p$ difference in mining effort from the rest of the network, expects to gain per (private blockchain) block of the attack*

$$\frac{3p - p^2 - 1 - \epsilon}{p} \cdot b \qquad (5.2)$$

*more than he would from honest mining, where $b$ is the reward for mining a new block, when other processors on the network are rational.*

*Proof.* Applying Lemma 5 with $k = 1$, we obtain that $M$'s total expected expenditures on puzzle prizes during the attack is $[(1 - 2p + \epsilon)/\epsilon] \cdot b$, and he earns $(p/\epsilon) \cdot b$ from his length $p/\epsilon$ extension of the private blockchain when it becomes public. His expected reward for mining honestly over these $p/\epsilon$ blocks would have been $p \cdot (p/\epsilon) \cdot b$, and therefore his expected net gain over honest mining throughout the course of the attack is

$$\left[ (1 - p) \cdot \frac{p}{\epsilon} - \frac{1 - 2p + \epsilon}{\epsilon} \right] \cdot b = \frac{3p - p^2 - 1 - \epsilon}{\epsilon} \cdot b.$$

It follows that $M$'s per block expected gain over honest mining is

$$\frac{3p - p^2 - 1 - \epsilon}{\epsilon} \cdot b \div \frac{p}{\epsilon},$$

or equivalently, the quantity in (5.2).    □

   The per block net gain over mining that one can expect to achieve with a 38.2% attack depends on how much initial capital one has available. In order to make the expected gain per block in (5.2) positive, $\epsilon$ must be less than $3p - p^2 - 1$, and substituting this value for $\epsilon$ into the estimated puzzle prize total puzzle (5.1), we obtain the expected break-even cost given in (5.3) below.

**Theorem 8.** *Let $b$ be the block mining reward. A miner with $p$ fraction of the network's power where $(3 - \sqrt{5})/2 < p < 1/2$ expects to spend in total*

$$\frac{p - p^2}{3p - p^2 - 1} \cdot b \qquad (5.3)$$

*on puzzle prizes during a 38.2% attack (without double-spending) in order to break even on the rewards he would have earned from honest mining over the same number of blocks. Moreover, if the miner*

- *chooses a target puzzle prize budget for Attack 1 of $xb$ (by setting $\epsilon = (1 - 2p)/(x - 1)$), and*
- *$xb$ exceeds the quantity in (5.3),*

*then his expected net gain per block (of private mining[9]) over honestly mining will be:*

$$\frac{3p - p^2 - 1 - \frac{1 - 2p}{x - 1}}{p} \cdot b \qquad (5.4)$$

*when other processors on the network are rational.*

---

[9] In the long run, the private blockchain becomes the main chain.

*Proof.* Suppose $(3 - \sqrt{5})/2 < p < 1/2$, $x > (p - p^2)/(3p - p^2 - 1)$ and let $\epsilon = (1 - 2p)/(x - 1)$. We wish to show $0 < \epsilon < p$ so that we may apply Lemma 7. Now

$$\epsilon < \frac{1 - 2p}{\frac{p - p^2}{3p - p^2 - 1} - 1} = \frac{(1 - 2p)(3p - p^2 - 1)}{1 - 2p} = 3p - p^2 - 1 \le p$$

as $p < 1/2$.

Since $p < 1/2$, we have $1 - 2p > 0$, which implies $p - p^2 > 3p - p^2 - 1$, and therefore $x > (p - p^2)/(3p - p^2 - 1) > 1$ as both the numerator and denominator of this fraction are positive whenever $(3 - \sqrt{5})/2 < p \le 1/2$. Since $\epsilon$ is the quotient of two positive reals, we have $\epsilon > 0$.

By Lemma 7, the attacker gains per block $[(3p - p^2 - 1 - \epsilon)/p] \cdot b$, which immediately establishes (5.4) as his total net gain over honest mining through the entire course of the attack. Note that by setting (5.4) equal to 0 and solving for $x$, we obtain the break-even point (5.3) modulo a factor of $b$.  □

Since most cryptocurrencies periodically adjust the hardness of their mining problems so that the expected number of blocks mined per unit time remains constant, we can expect that if one repeats the 38.2% attack several times in row, then the expected gain per block eventually becomes equal to the expected gain per unit clock time for mining one block. Thus, in the long run, one can use the same figures to estimate the profit of performing a 38.2% attack relative to honest mining over clock time as well. Since the attacker's private blockchain becomes the main blockchain in the long run, clock time per block eventually corresponds to per block time on the private chain.

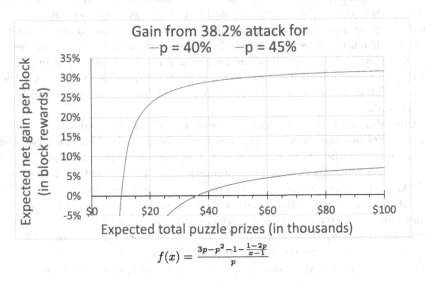

$$f(x) = \frac{3p - p^2 - 1 - \frac{1 - 2p}{x - 1}}{p}$$

**Fig. 5.** Expected net gain over honest mining for a 38.2% attack without double-spending and with $p = 40\%$ and $p = 45\%$ of the network power. The dollar estimates assume 1 block reward = 25 BTC = \$6000 (Sept. 2015).

At the market rate in September 2015 of approximately $b = \$6000$ reward per block in Bitcoin, Theorems 6 and 8 show that a miner with 40% of the network power can execute a 38.2% attack for \$36,000. This cost is significantly lower than the amount one would have to spend to purchase the hardware needed to execute a 51% attack, and moreover the attacker gets his initial capital back after a successful attack. Figures 2 and 3 give the the initial capital required based on the power $p$ for the double spend and 38.2% attacks. Figure 4 gives the gain per block for the 38.2% attack for different power $p$ of the attacker with deep pockets, and Fig. 5 gives the gain per block for the 38.2% attack based on the total capital for the power $p = 40\%$ and $p = 45\%$.

## 6   Rationality and Nakamoto Consensus

When analyzing the ultimate success of Attack 1, we tacitly assumed that miners always mine on the longest available blockchain. Will rational miners actually choose this strategy? We cannot answer this question decisively since many distinct sets of mining strategies achieve Nash equilibrium. The collective strategy which says "everyone mine on the longest chain" is a Nash equilibrium, but so is the collective strategy which says "everyone mine on the same chain as Fred Flintstone." Under the usual convention that the majority of computing power selects valid transactions and blocks, the optimal strategy for an individual miner is always to mine on the chain where most processors are mining.

While one can imagine individuals deciding to mine on chains which are adversarial against Attack 1 or chains which maximize personal capital, miners do have compelling reasons to choose the canonical honest strategy of mining on the longest chain. As an official default strategy, we may view the situation where everyone mines on the longest chain as a *de facto* initial condition. As this initial condition happens to both be a Nash equilibrium and satisfies the desired objective that individuals follow the majority, miners will persist in mining on the longest chain unless some particular influence drives them to change their behavior. Thus, under reasonable assumptions, rational miners will mine on the longest chain.

As established in Sect. 4, puzzle prizes in a 38.2% attack need not be encoded into transactions but rather may appear anywhere in the network ecosystem. This means that the 38.2% attack is not strike against expressiveness of scripting languages but rather Nakamoto consensus itself. Every cryptocurrency based on Nakamoto consensus, including Bitcoin, is vulnerable to a 38.2% attack. Consequently if miners are rational rather than majority-honest, then Bitcoin may be not only insecure when an adversary controls more than half of the network's computation power, as Nakamoto pointed out in his original paper [13], but even when the adversary controls merely 38.2% of the network's power. Can we achieve secure consensus beyond 38.2% under the assumption of rational miners?

# 7  Related Work

Cryptocurrency incentive structure flaws, such as the ones we pointed out in Ethereum and Bitcoin, can be difficult to detect. Other Bitcoin attacks which also rely on misplaced incentives include selfish mining [7] and mining pool block withholding [6,11]. We outline these attacks below. Although all three of these types of attack appeal to parties' rational behavior, the execution mechanisms vary considerably.

Unlike the 38.2% attack, neither selfish mining nor mining pool block withholding attacks use puzzle transactions. The 38.2% attack creates a distraction whereas the other two attacks focus purely on withholding blocks. Consequently, the 38.2% attack motivates other miners to deviate from protocol, while only the attacker deviates in the other two attacks. In other words, the victims miners in a 38.2% attack are rational rather than honest. In contrast to selfish mining, in which the attacker obtains in the short run only a relative per block advantage, the successful attacker in a 38.2% attack achieves an absolute per block advantage. Here "relative" advantage means that selfish mining hurts the mining rewards of all miners, but the attacker's actions penalize himself less than they penalize other victim miners.

Finally, unlike a mining pool block withholding attack, the 38.2% attack has no inherent need for mining pools. If the attacker does happen to have a mining pool, however, rational miners in a 38.2% attack might have incentive to join the attacker's pool. Cortois, Bahack, and Rosenfeld analyzed Bitcoin block withholding attacks [4,5,14]. Bonneau, Felten, Goldfeder, Kroll, and Narayanan [3] investigated a variation of our double-spend attack in which one offers monetary bribes, rather than puzzle rewards, to gain control of the network. We remark that the relative profit margins for a 38.2% attack or double-spend attack exceed those of selfish mining and mining pool block withholding.

*Selfish mining.* Due to sheer luck, a miner who controls a significant portion of the network's computing power will occasionally find himself successfully mining two or three blocks in rapid succession. When this happens, the miner might not immediately announce his blocks but rather continue to mine privately on a private blockchain. At this point, the miner's private blockchain is longer than the public one. Right before the public chain catches up to the private one, the miner reveals his longer chain which the consensus protocol dictates is, in fact, the valid chain. Thus the miner may double-spend any money spent on the public blockchain during the fork. Eyal and Sirer introduced this attack in [7].

*Mining pool block withholding.* In order to obtain a nontrivial chance of winning the race to mine the next block, miners arrange themselves into "pools" which split both the mining work and rewards among members. According to the pool protocol, a miner who solves the nonce should announce it, and then everyone in the pool shares the reward for mining a new block. However, Luu, Saha, Parameshwaran, Saxena, and Hobor [11] and Eyal [6] demonstrated that miners have financial incentive *not* to reveal their solution. A miner can join multiple pools simultaneously, and by not reporting a block in one he increases his chances of obtaining a reward in the other.

**Acknowledgements.** We thank Frank Stephan, Loi Luu, and Gregory J. Duck for useful discussions and helpful feedback.

# References

1. http://coinmarketcap.com/
2. http://www.mail-archive.com/cryptography@metzdowd.com/msg09959.html
3. Bonneau, J.: Why buy when you can rent? bribery attacks on Bitcoin. In: Clark, J., Meiklejohn, S., Ryan, P.Y.A., Wallach, D., Brenner, M., Rohloff, K. (eds.) FC 2016. LNCS, vol. 9604, pp. 19–26. Springer, Heidelberg (2016). doi:10.1007/978-3-662-53357-4_2
4. Courtois, N.T.: On the longest chain rule and programmed self-destruction of crypto currencies. CoRR, abs/1405.0534 (2014)
5. Courtois, N.T., Bahack, L.: On subversive miner strategies and block withholding attack in Bitcoin digital currency. CoRR, abs/1402.1718 (2014)
6. Eyal, I.: The miner's dilemma. In: IEEE Symposium on Security and Privacy (SP 2015), pp. 89–103, May 2015
7. Eyal, I., Sirer, E.G.: Majority is not enough: Bitcoin mining is vulnerable. In: Christin, N., Safavi-Naini, R. (eds.) FC 2014. LNCS, vol. 8437, pp. 436–454. Springer, Heidelberg (2014). doi:10.1007/978-3-662-45472-5_28
8. Ethereum Foundation. Ethereum's white paper (2014). https://github.com/ethereum/wiki/wiki/White-Paper
9. Franco, P.: Understanding Bitcoin: Cryptography, Engineering and Economics. Wiley, New York (2014)
10. Garay, J., Kiayias, A., Leonardos, N.: The Bitcoin backbone protocol: analysis and applications. In: Oswald, E., Fischlin, M. (eds.) EUROCRYPT 2015. LNCS, vol. 9057, pp. 281–310. Springer, Heidelberg (2015). doi:10.1007/978-3-662-46803-6_10
11. Luu, L., Saha, R., Parameshwaran,I., Saxena, P., Hobor, A.: On power splitting games in distributed computation: the case of Bitcoin pooled mining. http://eprint.iacr.org/2015/155
12. Luu, L., Teutsch, J., Kulkarni, R., Saxena, P.: Demystifying incentives in the consensus computer. In: Proceedings of the 22nd ACM SIGSAC Conference on Computer and Communications Security (CCS 2015), pp. 706–719. ACM, New York (2015)
13. Nakamoto, S.: Bitcoin: a peer-to-peer electronic cash system. http://bitcoin.org/bitcoin.pdf
14. Rosenfeld, M.: Analysis of Bitcoin pooled mining reward systems. CoRR, abs/1112.4980 (2011)
15. Tschorsch, F., Scheuermann, B.: Bitcoin and beyond: a technical survey on decentralized digital currencies. http://eprint.iacr.org/2015/464

# Optimal Selfish Mining Strategies in Bitcoin

Ayelet Sapirshtein[1], Yonatan Sompolinsky[1(✉)], and Aviv Zohar[1,2]

[1] School of Engineering and Computer Science,
The Hebrew University of Jerusalem, Jerusalem, Israel
{ayeletsa,yoni_sompo,avivz}@cs.huji.ac.il
[2] Microsoft Research, Herzliya, Israel

**Abstract.** The Bitcoin protocol requires nodes to quickly distribute newly created blocks. Strong nodes can, however, gain higher payoffs by withholding blocks they create and selectively postponing their publication. The existence of such *selfish mining* attacks was first reported by Eyal and Sirer, who have demonstrated a specific deviation from the standard protocol (a strategy that we name SM1).

In this paper we investigate the *profit threshold* – the minimal fraction of resources required for a profitable attack. Our analysis provides a bound under which the system can be considered secure against such attacks. Our techniques can be adapted to protocol modifications to assess their susceptibility to selfish mining, by computing the optimal attack under different variants. We find that the profit threshold is strictly lower than the one induced by the SM1 scheme. The policies given by our algorithm dominate SM1 by better regulating attack-withdrawals. We further evaluate the impact of some previously suggested countermeasures, and show that they are less effective than previously conjectured.

We then gain insight into selfish mining in the presence of communication delays, and show that, under a model that accounts for delays, the profit threshold vanishes, and even small attackers have incentive to occasionally deviate from the protocol. We conclude with observations regarding the combined power of selfish mining and double spending attacks.

## 1 Introduction

In a seminal paper, Eyal and Sirer [9] have highlighted a flaw in the incentive scheme in Bitcoin. Given that most of the network follows the "standard" Bitcoin protocol, a single node (or a pool) which possesses enough computational resources or is extremely well connected to the rest of the network can increase its expected rewards by deviating from the protocol. While the standard Bitcoin protocol requires nodes to immediately publish any block that they find to the rest of the network, Eyal and Sirer have shown that participants can selfishly increase their revenue by selectively withholding blocks. Their strategy, which we denote SM1, thus shows that Bitcoin as currently formulated is not incentive compatible. On the positive side, SM1 (under the model of Eyal and Sirer) becomes profitable only when employed by nodes that possess a large

© International Financial Cryptography Association 2017
J. Grossklags and B. Preneel (Eds.): FC 2016, LNCS 9603, pp. 515–532, 2017.
DOI: 10.1007/978-3-662-54970-4_30

enough share of the computational resources, and are sufficiently well connected to the rest of the network. It is important to note, however, that SM1 *is not* the optimal best-response to honest behaviour, and situations in which SM1 is not profitable may yet have other strategies that are better than strict adherence to the protocol.

Our goal in this paper is to better understand the conditions under which Bitcoin is resilient to selfish mining attacks. We begin with performing this analysis with respect to the standard Bitcoin protocol. Additionally, several protocol modifications have been put forth, some with the explicit goal of alleviating selfish mining, and we suggest our techniques as a tool to provably analyze their resilience to such attacks. To this end, we consider other possible deviations from the classic Bitcoin protocol, and establish bounds on their profitability. We later demonstrate how to apply the same techniques to some of its variants.

The role of incentives in Bitcoin should not be underestimated: Bitcoin transactions are confirmed in batches, called *blocks* whose creation requires generating the solution to computationally expensive proof-of-work "puzzles". The security of Bitcoin against the reversal of payments (so-called double spending attacks) relies on having more computational power held by honest nodes than by misbehaving nodes. Block creation (which is also known as *mining*), is rewarded in bitcoins that are given to the block's creator. These rewards incentivize more honest participants to invest additional computational resources in mining, and thus support the security of Bitcoin.

When all miners follow the Bitcoin protocol, a single miner's share of the payoffs is equal to the fraction of computational power that it controls (out of the computational resources of the entire network). However, Selfish mining schemes allow a strong attacker to increase its revenue at the expense of other nodes. This is done by exploiting the conflict-resolution rule of the protocol, according to which only one chain of blocks can be considered valid, and only blocks on the valid chain receive rewards; the attacker creates a deliberate fork, and (sometimes) manages to force the honest network to abandon and discard some of its blocks.

The consequences of selfish mining attacks are potentially destructive to the Bitcoin system. A successful attacker becomes more profitable than honest nodes, and is able to grow steadily.[1] It may thus eventually drive other nodes out of the system. Profits from selfish mining increase as more computational power is held by the attacker, making its attack increasingly more effective. Eventually, the attacker is able to collect all block rewards, to mount successful double spending attacks at will, and to prevent any transaction from being processed (this is known as the 50% attack, which requires 50% of the computational resources).

We summarize the contributions of this paper as follows:

1. We provide an efficient algorithm that computes an optimal selfish mining policy, for any parametrization of the model in [9] (i.e., one that maximizes the

---

[1] Growth is achieved either by buying more hardware, in the case of a single attacker, or by attracting more miners, in the case of a pool.

revenue of the attacker, given that all other nodes are following the standard Bitcoin protocol). We prove the correctness of our algorithm, and verify our results using simulations.

2. Using our algorithm we show that, indeed, there are selfish mining strategies that earn more money and are profitable for smaller miners compared to SM1. The gains are relatively small (see Fig. 1 below). This can be seen as a positive result, lower bounding the amount of resources needed for a profitable attacker.

3. We evaluate different protocol modifications that were suggested as countermeasures for selfish mining. For the solution suggested by Eyal and Sirer (in which miners randomly break ties between equal chains), we show that attackers with strictly less than 25% of the computational resources can still gain from selfish mining, unlike previously conjectured.

4. We show that in a model that accounts for the delay of block propagation in the network, attackers of *any* size can profit from selfish mining.

5. We discuss the interaction between selfish mining attacks and double spending attacks. We demonstrate how any attacker for which selfish mining is profitable can execute double spending attacks bearing no costs. This sheds light on the security analysis of Satoshi Nakamoto [15], and specifically, on the reason that it cannot be used to show high attack costs, and must instead only bound the probability of a successful attack.

Below we provide a preview of some of our final results, namely, the revenue achieved by optimal policies compared to that of SM1 as well as the profit threshold of the protocol. In the following, $\alpha$ stands for the attacker's relative hashrate, and $\gamma$ is a parameter representing the communication capabilities of the attacker—the fraction of nodes to which it manages to send blocks first in case of a block race (see Sect. 2 for more details). Figure 1 depicts the revenue of an attacker under three strategies: Honest mining, which adheres to the Bitcoin protocol, SM1, and the optimal policies obtained by our algorithm. The three graphs correspond to $\gamma = 0, 0.5, 1$. We additionally illustrate the curve of $\alpha/(1 - \alpha)$, which is an upper bound on the attacker's revenue, achievable only when $\gamma = 1$ (see Sect. 3). Figure 2 depicts the profit threshold for each $\gamma$: If the attacker's hashrate $\alpha$ is below the threshold then honest mining is the most profitable strategy. For comparison, we depict the thresholds induced by SM1 as well.

## 2   Model

We follow and extend the model of [9], to explicitly consider all actions available to the attacker at any given point in time. We assume that the attacker controls a fraction $\alpha$ of the computational power in the network, and that the honest network thus has a $(1 - \alpha)$ fraction. Communication of newly created blocks is

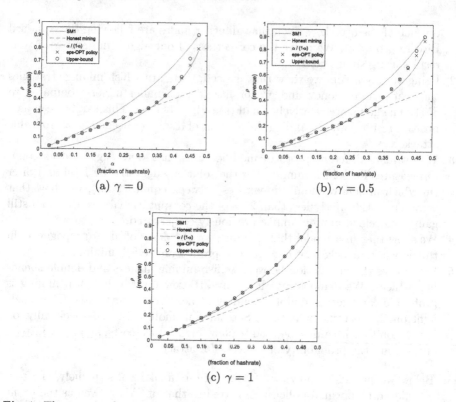

**Fig. 1.** The $\epsilon$-optimal revenue and the computed upper bound, as a function of the attacker's hashrate $\alpha$, compared to SM1, honest mining, and to the hypothetical bound provided in Sect. 3. The graphs differ in the attacker's communication capability, $\gamma$, valued 0, 0.5, and 1. The gains of the $\epsilon$-optimal policies are very close to the computed upper bound, except when $\alpha$ is close to 0.5, in case which the truncation-imposed loss is apparent. See also Table 2.

modeled to be much faster than block creation, so no blocks are generated while others are being transmitted.[2]

Blocks are created in the network according to a Poisson process with rate $\lambda$. A new block belongs to the attacker w.p. $\alpha$ or to the honest network w.p. $(1 - \alpha)$. The honest network follows the Bitcoin protocol, and always builds its newest block on top of the longest known chain. Once an honest node adopts a block, it will discard it only if a strictly longer competing chain exists. Ties are thus handled by each node according to the order of arrival of blocks. Honest nodes immediately broadcast blocks that they create.

Blocks generally form a tree structure, as each block references a single predecessor (save the genesis block). Since honest nodes adopt the longest chain,

---

[2] This is justified by Bitcoin's 10 min block creation interval which is far greater than the propagation time of blocks in the network. This assumption is later removed when we consider networks with delay.

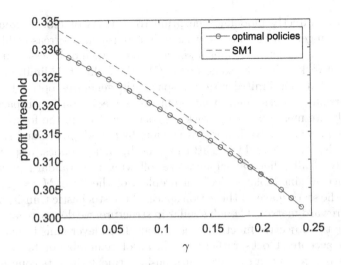

**Fig. 2.** The profit thresholds induced by optimal policies, and by SM1, as a function of $\gamma$. Thresholds at higher $\gamma$ values match those of SM1 (but still, optimal strategies for these values earn more than SM1, once above the threshold).

blocks generate rewards for their creator only if they are eventually part of the longest chain in the block tree (all blocks can be considered revealed eventually).

Following the communication model of Eyal and Sirer, we assume that whenever the attacker learns that a block has been released by the network it is able to transmit an alternative block (which it created beforehand) that will arrive *first* at nodes that possess a fraction $\gamma$ of the computational power of the honest network. Thus, if the network is currently propagating a block of height $h$, and the attacker has a competing block of the same height, it is able to get $\gamma \cdot (1 - \alpha)$ of the computational power (owned by honest nodes) to adopt this block.

The attacker does not necessarily follow the Bitcoin protocol. Rather, at any given time $t$, it may choose to invest computational power in creating blocks that extend any existing block in history, and may withhold blocks it has created for any amount of time. A general selfish mining strategy dictates, therefore, two key behaviours: which block the attacker attempts to extend at any time $t$, and which blocks are released at any given time. However, given that all block creation events are driven by memoryless processes and that broadcast is modeled as instantaneous, any rational decision made by the attacker may only change upon the creation of a new block. The mere passage of time without block creation does not otherwise alter the expected gains from future outcomes.[3] Accordingly, we model the entire decision problem faced by an attacker using a discrete-time process in which each time step corresponds to the creation of a block. The attacker is thus asked to decide on a course of action right after the creation of each block, and this action is pursued until the next event occurs.

---

[3] See Sect. 6 for the implication of delayed broadcasting.

Instead of directly modeling the primitive actions of block extension and publication on general block trees, we can limit our focus to "reasonable" strategies where the attacker maintains a *single* secret branch of blocks that diverged from the network's chain at some point. (We show that this limitation is warranted and that this limited strategy space still generates optimal attacks in the full version). Blocks before that point are agreed upon by all participants. Accordingly, we must only keep track of blocks involved in the fork, and of the accumulated reward up to the fork. We denote by $l_a$ and $l_h$ the number of blocks built after the latest fork, by the attacker and by honest nodes, respectively.

Formally, if all other participants are following the standard protocol, the attacker faces a single-player decision problem of the form $M := \langle S, A, P, R \rangle$, where $S$ is the state space, $A$ the action space, $P$ the stochastic transition matrix, and $R$ the reward matrix. Though similar in structure, we do not regard $M$ as an MDP, since the objective function is nonlinear: The player aims to maximize its share of the accepted blocks, rather than the absolute number of its own accepted ones; its goal is to have a greater return-on-investment than its counterparts.[4]

**Actions.** We begin with the description of the action space $A$, which will motivate the nontrivial construction of the state space.

- **Adopt.** This action represents the attacker's acceptance of the honest network's chain. This action is always feasible, and following it the $l_a$ blocks in the attacker's current chain are discarded.
- **Override.** This action represents the publication of $l_h + 1$ of the attacker's blocks. It is feasible whenever $l_a > l_h$.
- **Match.** Here the attacker responds to a freshly mined block of the honest network with the publication of its block of the same height. The attacker must have a block prepared in advance to execute such a race. The state-space explicitly encodes the feasibility status of this action (see below).
- **Wait.** This is the null action, under which the attacker does not publish new blocks, but keeps working on its branch until a new block is built.

**State Space.** The state space, denoted $S$, is defined by 3-tuples of the form $(l_a, l_h, fork)$. The first two entries represent the lengths of the attacker's chain and the honest network's chain, built after the latest fork (that is, above the most recent block accepted by all). The field $fork$ obtains three possible values, dubbed *irrelevant*, *relevant* and *active*. State of the form $(l_a, l_h, relevant)$ means that the previous state was of the form $(l_a, l_h - 1, \cdot)$; this implies that if $l_a \geq l_h$, the *match* action is feasible. Conversely, $(l_a, l_h, irrelevant)$ denotes the case where the previous state was $(l_a - 1, l_h, \cdot)$, and the attacker has built the most recent block; in this situation, the attacker is unable to match the $h$th block of the honest network, which already propagated through the network. The third label, *active*, represents the case where the honest network is already

---

[4] Another possible motivation for this is the re-targeting mechanism in Bitcoin. When the block creation rate in the network is constant, the adaptive re-targeting implies that the attacker will also increase its absolute payoff, in the long run.

split, due to a previous *match* action; this information affects the transition to the next state, as described below. *We will refer to states as $(l_a, l_h)$ or $(l_a, l_h, \cdot)$, in contexts where the fork label plays no effective role.*

**Transition and Reward Matrices.** In order to keep the time averaging of rewards in scale, every state transition corresponds to the creation of a new block. The initial state $X_0$ is $(1, 0, irrelevant)$ w.p. $\alpha$ or $(0, 1, irrelevant)$ w.p. $(1 - \alpha)$. Rewards are given as elements in $\mathbb{N}^2$, where the first entry represents blocks of the attacker that have been accepted by all parties, and the second one, similarly, for those of the honest network.

The transition matrix $P$ and reward matrix $R$ are succinctly described in Table 1. Largely, an *adopt* action "resets" the game, hence the state following it has the same distribution as $X_0$; its immediate reward is $l_h$ in the coordinate corresponding to the honest network. An *override* reduces the attacker's secret chain by $l_h + 1$ blocks, which it publishes, and which the honest network accepts. This bestows a reward of $l_h + 1$ blocks to the attacker. The state following a *match* action depends on whether the next block is created by the attacker ($\alpha$), by honest nodes working on their branch of the chain ($(1 - \gamma) \cdot (1 - \alpha)$), or by an honest node which accepted the sub-chain that the attacker published ($\gamma \cdot (1 - \alpha)$). In the latter case, the attacker has effectively overridden the honest network's previous chain, and is awarded $l_h$ accordingly.

**Table 1.** A description of the transition and reward matrices $P$ and $R$ in the decision problem $M$. The third column contains the probability of transiting from the state specified in the left-most column, under the action specified therein, to the state on the second one. The corresponding two-dimensional reward (that of the attacker and that of the honest nodes) is specified on the right-most column.

| State × Action | State | Probability | Reward |
|---|---|---|---|
| $(l_a, l_h, \cdot), adopt$ | $(1, 0, irrelevant)$ | $\alpha$ | $(0, l_h)$ |
| | $(0, 1, irrelevant)$ | $1 - \alpha$ | |
| $(l_a, l_h, \cdot), override^{a}$ | $(l_a - l_h, 0, irrelevant)$ | $\alpha$ | $(l_h + 1, 0)$ |
| | $(l_a - l_h - 1, 1, relevant)$ | $1 - \alpha$ | |
| $(l_a, l_h, irrelevant), wait(l_a, l_h, relevant), wait$ | $(l_a + 1, l_h, irrelevant)$ | $\alpha$ | $(0,0)$ |
| | $(l_a, l_h + 1, relevant)$ | $1 - \alpha$ | $(0,0)$ |
| $(l_a, l_h, active), wait(l_a, l_h, relevant), match^{b}$ | $(l_a + 1, l_h, active)$ | $\alpha$ | $(0,0)$ |
| | $(l_a - l_h, 1, relevant)$ | $\gamma \cdot (1 - \alpha)$ | $(l_h, 0)$ |
| | $(l_a, l_h + 1, relevant)$ | $(1 - \gamma) \cdot (1 - \alpha)$ | $(0,0)$ |

[a] feasible only when $l_a > l_h$
[b] feasible only when $l_a \geq l_h$

**Objective Function.** As explained in the introduction, the attacker aims to maximize its relative revenue, rather than its absolute one as usual in MDPs.

Let $\pi$ be a policy of the player; we will write $\pi(l_a, l_h, fork)$ for the action that $\pi$ dictates be taken at state $(l_a, l_h, fork)$. The immediate reward from transiting from state $x$ to state $y$, under the action dictated by $\pi$, is denoted $r(x, y, \pi) = (r^1(x, y, \pi(x)), r^2(x, y, \pi(x)))$. $X_t^\pi$ will denote the $t$'th state that was visited. We will abbreviate $r_t(X_t^\pi, X_{t+1}^\pi, \pi)$ and write simply $r_t(\pi)$ or even $r_t$, when context is clear. The objective function of the player is its *relative* payoff, defined by

$$REV := \mathbb{E}\left[\liminf_{T \to \infty} \frac{\sum_{t=1}^T r_t^1(\pi)}{\sum_{t=1}^T (r_t^1(\pi) + r_t^2(\pi))}\right]. \tag{1}$$

We will specify the parameters of $REV$ depending on the context (e.g., $REV(\pi, \alpha, \gamma)$, $REV(\pi)$, $REV(\alpha)$), and will occasionally denote the value of $REV$ by $\rho$. In addition, for full definiteness of $REV$, we rule out pathological behaviours in which the attacker waits forever—formally, the expected time for the next non-null action of the attacker must be finite.

**Honest Mining and SM1.** We now define two policies of prime interest that will serve as a baseline for future comparisons. Honest mining is the unique policy which adheres to the protocol at every state. It is defined by

$$\text{honest mining} (l_a, l_h, \cdot) = \left\{ \begin{array}{ll} adopt & l_h > l_a \\ override & l_a > l_h \end{array} \right\}, \tag{2}$$

and *wait* otherwise. Notice that under our model, $REV(\text{honest mining}, \alpha, \gamma) = \alpha$ for all $\gamma$.[5] Eyal and Sirer's selfish mining strategy, SM1, can be defined as

$$SM1 (l_a, l_h, \cdot) := \left\{ \begin{array}{ll} adopt & l_h > l_a \\ match & l_h = l_a = 1 \\ override & l_h = l_a - 1 \geq 1 \\ wait & \text{otherwise} \end{array} \right\}. \tag{3}$$

**Profit threshold.** Keeping the attacker's connectivity capabilities ($\gamma$) fixed, we are interested in the minimal $\alpha$ for which employing dishonest mining strategies becomes profitable. We define the profit threshold by:

$$\hat{\alpha}(\gamma) := \inf_\alpha \{\exists \pi \in A : REV(\pi, \alpha, \gamma) > REV(\text{honest mining}, \alpha, \gamma)\}. \tag{4}$$

## 3   A Simple Upper Bound

The mechanism implied by the longest-chain rule leads to an immediate bound on the attacker's relative revenue. Intuitively, we observe that the attacker cannot do better than utilizing every block it creates to override one block of the honest network. The implied bound is provided here merely for general insight—it is usually far from the actual maximal revenue.

---

[5] Indeed, in networks without delays, honest mining is equivalent to the policy $\{ adopt$ if $(l_a, l_h) = (0, 1)$ ; $override$ if $(l_a, l_h) = (1, 0) \}$, as these are the only reachable states.

**Proposition 1.** *For any $\pi$, $REV(\pi, \alpha, \gamma) \leq \frac{\alpha}{1-\alpha}$. Moreover, this bound is tight, and achieved when $\gamma = 1$.*

*Proof.* We can map every block of the honest network which was overridden, to a block of the attacker; this is because *override* requires the attacker to publish a chain longer than that of the honest network's.

Let $k_T$ be the number of blocks that the attacker has built up to time $T$. The honest network thus built $l_T := T - k_T$ by this time. The argument above shows that $l_T - \sum_{t=1}^{T} r_t^2 \leq k_T$. Also, $\Pr(l_T > k_T) \to 1$, when $T \to \infty$. Therefore, the relative revenue satisfies:

$$REV(\pi) = \lim_{T \to \infty} \frac{\sum_{t=1}^{T} r_t^1}{\sum_{t=1}^{T} r_t^1 + \sum_{t=1}^{T} r_t^2} \leq \lim_{T \to \infty} \frac{\sum_{t=1}^{T} r_t^1}{\sum_{t=1}^{T} r_t^1 + l_T - k_T} = \qquad (5)$$

$$\lim_{T \to \infty} \frac{1}{1 + (l_T - k_T) / \left( \sum_{t=1}^{T} r_t^1 \right)} \leq \lim_{T \to \infty} \frac{1}{1 + (l_T - k_T) / k_T} = \lim_{T \to \infty} \frac{k_T}{l_T}. \quad (6)$$

The SLLN applies naturally to $k_T$ and $l_T$, implying that the above equals $\frac{\alpha \cdot T}{(1-\alpha) \cdot T} = \frac{\alpha}{1-\alpha}$ (a.s.).

We claim that when $\gamma = 1$ the bound is achieved by the following policy:

$$\pi(l_a, l_h, \cdot) := \left\{ \begin{array}{ll} adopt & l_h = 1, l_a = 0 \\ match & l_h = l_a \\ wait & otherwise \end{array} \right\}. \qquad (7)$$

Indeed, under $\pi$ the attacker only publishes its current number of blocks $l_a$ when the honest network has the same amount, hence every block of the attacker overrides one block of the honest network. In addition, none of the attacker's blocks are overridden, since the policy never reaches a state where it needs to *adopt* except when $l_a = 0$. This turns both inequalities in (5)–(6) into equalities.    □

## 4    Computing the Optimal Policy

Finding an optimal policy is not a trivial task, as the objective function (1) is nonlinear, and depends on the entire history of the game. To overcome this we introduce the following method. Suppose we are given some value $\rho$ as a candidate for the optimal value of the objective function. We show that one can construct a related MDP, $M_\rho$, which has one important characteristic: If the average reward of its optimal policy is negative, then $\rho$ is above the optimal value, and if it is positive, then $\rho$ is below it. When the optimal average reward is exactly 0, $\rho$ is optimal in the original problem, and the policy that obtains this value in $M_\rho$, obtains a value of $\rho$ in the original problem.

Formally, for any $\rho \in [0, 1]$, define the transformation $w_\rho : \mathbb{N}^2 \to \mathbb{Z}$ by $w_\rho(x, y) := (1 - \rho) \cdot x - \rho \cdot y$. Define the MDP $M_\rho := \langle S, A, P, w_\rho(R) \rangle$; it shares the same state space, actions, and transition matrix as $M$, while $M$'s immediate rewards matrix is transformed according to $w_\rho$. The value of a policy

$\pi$ is defined by $v_\rho^\pi = \mathbb{E}\left[\liminf\limits_{T\to\infty} \frac{1}{T}\sum_{t=1}^{T} w_\rho(r_t(\pi))\right]$, and the optimal value by $v_\rho^* = \max_{\pi\in A}\{v_\rho^\pi\}$.[6] Our solution method is based on the following proposition:

**Proposition 2.** *If for some $\rho \in [0,1]$, $v_\rho^* = 0$, then any policy $\pi^*$ obtaining this value (thus maximizing $v_\rho^\pi$) also maximizes REV, and $\rho = REV(\pi_\rho^*)$. Additionally, $v_\rho^*$ is monotonically decreasing in $\rho$.*

Following these observations we can utilize the family $M_\rho$ to obtain an optimal policy: We simply perform a **search for $\rho \in [0,1]$ such that the optimal solution of $M_\rho$ has a value $v_\rho^* = 0$.** Since $v_\rho^*$ is monotonically decreasing, this can be done efficiently, using binary search.

In practice, this method needs some refinement before it is applied, due to several limitations: First, the search domain $[0,1]$ is continuous, and we must account for some precision error. Second, standard MDP solvers can only deal with finite-state spaces, and even then, only to a limited degree of accuracy. The need to deal with finite state-spaces forces us to work with truncated versions of $M_\rho$ whose optimal values serve as lower bounds to the real optimal one. To circumvent this we have constructed another family of (finite) MDPs which serve as upper bounds. Both bounds are tight, that is, they converge to the optimal value as the truncation increases. A full description of this construction, an algorithm to obtain these tight bounds, and a proof of the algorithm's correctness appear in the full version available online. Proposition 2 follows from the analysis therein.

## 5   Results

### 5.1   Optimal Values

We ran our algorithm for $\gamma$ in $\{0, 0.5, 1\}$, with various values of $\alpha$, using an MDP solver for MATLAB (an implementation of the relative value iteration algorithm developed by Chadès et al. [5]).[7] The values of $\rho$ returned by the algorithm are depicted in Fig. 1 above; additionally, the values for $\gamma = 0$ appear in Table 2. The graphs demonstrate a rather mild gap between the attacker's optimal revenue and the revenue of SM1. In addition, the graphs depict the upper bound on the revenue provided in Sect. 3; as we stated there, the bound is obtained when $\gamma = 1$, which is observed clearly in the corresponding graph.

### 5.2   Optimal Policies

We now present the $\epsilon$-optimal policies returned by our algorithm, in two particular setups. Table 3 above describes the policy for an attacker with $\alpha = 1/3, \gamma = 0$

---

[6] The equivalence of this formalization of the value function and alternatives in which the order of expectation and limit is reversed is discussed in [3].

[7] The error parameter $\epsilon$ was set to be $10^{-5}$ and the truncation was set to $T = 75$. See full version.

**Table 2.** The revenue of the attacker under SM1 and under $\epsilon$-OPT policies, compared to the computed upper bound, for various $\alpha$ and $\gamma = 0$.

| $\alpha$ | SM1 | $\epsilon$-OPT | Upper-bound |
|---|---|---|---|
| 1/3 | 1/3 | 0.33705 | 0.33707 |
| 0.35 | 0.36650 | 0.37077 | 0.37080 |
| 0.375 | 0.42118 | 0.42600 | 0.42614 |
| 0.4 | 0.48372 | 0.48863 | 0.48976 |
| 0.425 | 0.55801 | 0.56788 | 0.57672 |
| 0.45 | 0.65177 | 0.66809 | 0.72203 |
| 0.475 | 0.78254 | 0.7987 | 0.90476 |

**Table 3.** Optimal actions for an attacker with $\alpha = 0.35, \gamma = 0$, in states $(l_a, l_h)$ with $l_a, l_h \leq 7$. See legend in the text (Sect. 5.2).

| $l_a$ \ $l_h$ | 0 | 1 | 2 | 3 | 4 | 5 | 6 | 7 |
|---|---|---|---|---|---|---|---|---|
| 0 | * | a | * | * | * | * | * | * |
| 1 | w | w | w | a | * | * | * | * |
| 2 | w | o | w | w | a | * | * | * |
| 3 | w | w | o | w | w | a | * | * |
| 4 | w | w | w | o | w | w | w | a |
| 5 | w | w | w | w | o | w | w | w |
| 6 | w | w | w | w | w | o | w | w |
| 7 | w | w | w | w | w | w | o | w |

(here *match* is of no consequence, and no forks form). The row indices correspond to $l_a$ and the columns to $l_h$. Table 4 corresponds to $\alpha = 0.45, \gamma = 0.5$. Each entry in it contains a string of three characters, corresponding to the possible status of $fork$: $irrelevant, relevant, active$. Actions are abbreviated to their initials: *adopt*, *override*, *match*, *wait*, while '*' represents an unreachable state.

Looking into these optimal policies we see they differ from SM1 in two ways: First, they defer using *adopt* in the upper triangle of the table, if the gap between

**Table 4.** Optimal actions (abbreviated to their initials) for an attacker with $\alpha = 0.45, \gamma = 0.5$, for states $(l_a, l_h, \cdot)$ with $l_a, l_h \leq 7$. See legend in Sect. 5.2.

| $l_a$ \ $l_h$ | 0 | 1 | 2 | 3 | 4 | 5 | 6 | 7 |
|---|---|---|---|---|---|---|---|---|
| 0 | *** | *a* | *** | *** | *** | *** | *** | *** |
| 1 | w** | *m* | a** | *** | *** | *** | *** | *** |
| 2 | w** | *mw | *m* | w** | a** | *** | *** | *** |
| 3 | w** | *mw | *mw | wm* | w** | a** | *** | *** |
| 4 | w** | *mw | *mw | omw | wm* | w** | w** | a** |
| 5 | w** | *mw | *mw | *mw | omw | wm* | w** | w** |
| 6 | w** | *mw | *mw | *mw | *mw | omw | wm* | w** |
| 7 | w** | *mw | *mw | *mw | *mw | *mw | ooo | w** |

For instance, the string "wm*" in entry $(l_a, l_h) = (3,3)$ reads: "in case a fork is *irrelevant* (i.e., the previous state was $(2,3)$), *wait*; in case it is *relevant* (the previous state was $(3,2)$), *match*; the case where a fork is already *active* is not reachable".

$l_h$ and $l_a$ is not too large, allowing the attacker to "catch up from behind". Thus, apart from block withholding, an optimal attack may also contain another feature: attempting to catch up with the longer public chain from a disadvantage. This implies that the attacker violates the longest-chain rule, a result which counters the claim that the longest-chain rule forms a Nash equilibrium (see [12], and discussion in Sect. 8). Secondly, they utilize *match* more extensively, effectively overriding the honest network's chain (w.p. $\gamma$) using one block less.

## 5.3   Thresholds

Using the bounds provided by our algorithm, we are able to introduce lower bounds on the profit thresholds, i.e., on the minimal fraction of computational resources needed for a profitable attack. The exact methodology is described in the full version. Fig. 2 depicts the thresholds induced by optimal policies, compared to that induced by SM1. The results demonstrate some cutback of the thresholds when considering policies other than SM1.

## 5.4   Evaluation of Protocol Modifications

Several modifications to the Bitcoin protocol have been suggested. It is important to provably verify the resilience of such protocols to selfish mining, especially if their explicit goal is to counter this attack. This can be done by adapting our algorithm to the MDPs induced by these modifications. We demonstrate this below for three protocols.

**GHOST.** First, we make a short note regarding the GHOST protocol, an alternative to the longest-chain rule [18]. We point out that our entire analysis in this paper applies to the GHOST protocol as well, since GHOST coincides with the longest-chain rule when the network suffers no delays.

**Freshness Preferred.** The tie breaking rule in Bitcoin instructs a node to adopt the chain whose tip was received by it first, in case of ties. Freshness Preferred is an alternative suggested in [11]. It uses unforgeable timestamps, and dictates that if less than $w$ seconds passed between the receiving of the two tips, the node adopts the chain which contains the most recent time-stamp. Freshness Preferred disincentivizes block withholding, and in particular counters the SM1 scheme. Unfortunately, when also considering deviations from the longest-chain rule, it can be seen that an attacker of any size can benefit from this protocol by waiting in state $(l_a, l_h) = (0, 1)$, rather than adopting, for a certain period. Such a consideration is also the basis for our following analysis of Eyal and Sirer's suggested tie breaking rule.

**Uniform Tie Breaking.** In case of ties, Eyal and Sirer suggest to instruct nodes to choose between the chains uniformly at random. The immediate effect of this modification is that it restricts the efficiency of the *match* action to $1/2$, even when the attacker's communication capabilities correspond to $\gamma > 1/2$. Admittedly, this limits the power of strongly communicating attackers, and thus guarantees a positive lower bound on the threshold for profitability of SM1.

On the other hand, it has the apparent downside of enhancing the power of poorly communicating attackers—it allows an attacker to *match* with a success-probability $1/2$ even if its "real" $\gamma$ is smaller than $1/2$.

Unfortunately, there is an additional drawback. An attacker is able to *match* even if it did not have a block prepared in advance, thereby granting it additional chances to catch up from behind. Deviation from the longest-chain rule thus becomes even more tempting. Indeed, by applying our algorithm to the setup induced by uniform tie breaking, we found that the profit threshold $\hat{\alpha}(0.5)$ deteriorates from 0.25 to 0.2321.

Figure 3 demonstrates this by comparing the attacker's optimal revenue under the uniform tie breaking protocol with the optimal revenue under the original protocol. The optimal policy is described in the online full version of this paper.

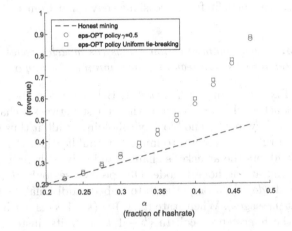

**Fig. 3.** The attacker's optimal revenue under uniform tie breaking, compared to that under the original protocol (with $\gamma = 1/2$) and to honest mining.

## 5.5 Simulations

In order to verify the results above we built a selfish mining simulator which we implemented in Java. We ran the simulator for various values of $\alpha$ and $\gamma$ (as in the figures above), with the attacker following the policies generated by the algorithm. Each run was performed for $10^7$ rounds (block creation events). The relative revenue of the attacker matched the revenues returned by the algorithm, up to an error of at most $\pm 10^{-6}$.

## 6    A Model that Considers Delays

So far our model assumed that no new block is created during the propagation of blocks released earlier. In reality, there are communication delays between nodes in the network, including between the attacker and others. Thus, instead of modeling the attacker's communication capabilities via the parameter $\gamma$, it is better to consider the effect of network latency directly. Delays are especially noticeable when the system's throughput is increased by allowing larger blocks to form or by increasing block creation rates.

We now adjust our model to incorporate communication delays. For simplicity, and to demonstrate how the profit threshold breaks down even when a delay on a single link is introduced, we assume that only messages from the attacker to the honest network suffer delays. We denote this delay by $d_{a,h}$. Messages between honest nodes and from them to the attacker are assumed to be delivered instantaneously, as in the original model. Apart from $l_a$ and $l_h$, the process now encodes also information about the timings of recent messages that are currently propagating on the link from the attacker's node to the honest network's node. Our following result states that under delays the profit threshold is 0. A node of *any* size can benefit from occasional deviation from the longest-chain rule:

**Proposition 3.** *Under communication delays (as modeled above), the attacker has a strict better-response strategy to honest mining, for any $\alpha > 0$.*

*Proof. Part I:* Fix $k \in \mathbb{N}$ and let $T > k + 1$. Below we describe a policy which instructs the attacker whether to adopt the honest network's chain (*adopt*) or not (*wait*). Our policy involves no block withholding at all; it thus deviates from the longest-chain rule, but adheres to immediate-publication. Consequently, the honest network adopts the attacker's chain if and only if the latter is longer by the time it arrived at the honest node. Our policy uses only $(l_a, l_h)$ to decide between *wait* and *adopt* (although the state embeds additional information, e.g., timing of recent messages). When state $(l_a, l_h) = (k - 1, k)$ is reached, our policy deviates from the honest protocol: In $(k - 1, k)$ it waits, instead of adopting, until the $(k+1)$ block of the attacker or of the honest network is created; it then terminates the attack, and continues mining on the honest network's updated chain. Upon termination, the honest network's chain contains the $(k + 1)$ blocks of the attacker only if they have propagated to the honest node in time. This possibility will be incorporated into the immediate reward function below.

Policies as the one described are technically not considered stationary, and a common circumvent is applied in such cases. We add a third bit to our representation of states, which denotes whether $(k - 1, k)$ has been reached during this epoch. Thus, for any state with $(l_a, l_h)$ we write $(l_a, l_h, 0)$, corresponding to the original states. Then, we add four new states that are only reachable from $(k-1, k, 0)$ under the *wait* action: $(k, k, 1), (k+1, k, 1), (k, k+1, 1), (k-1, k+1, 1)$. The original copies of these four states, with the third bit set to 0, are still reachable via $(k, k - 1, 0)$. The states with the bit set to 1 are unreachable under honest mining, hence honest mining can still be seen as living inside this modified state-space.

When the process arrives at either of the states $(\cdot, k + 1, 1)$ or $(k + 1, k, 1)$ it renews (i.e., it transits to $(1, 0, 0)$ or $(0, 1, 0)$). Importantly, the immediate reward in $M_\rho^T$ gained by arriving at $(\cdot, k+1, 1)$ is $(-\rho \cdot (k+1))$, and by arriving at $(k+1, k, 1)$ is $q \cdot (1-\rho) \cdot (k+1) - (1-q) \cdot \rho \cdot (k+1)$, where $q = e^{-(1-\alpha) \cdot 2 \cdot d_{a,h} \cdot \lambda}$. This will be justified shortly. Our policy acts as follows:

$$\pi_k(l_a, l_h, m) := \left\{ \begin{array}{ccc} wait & k-1 \leq l_a \leq k, l_h = k, m = 1 \\ adopt & l_h = k+1, m = 1 \\ honest\ mining(l_a, l_h) & m = 0 \end{array} \right\}.$$

Since $(\cdot, k+1, 1)$ and $(k+1, k, 1)$ are terminating states, there are two possibilities: (a) The attacker managed to create the next two blocks in the network (corresponding to $(k+1, k, 1)$) *and* to propagate them in time to the honest network. Thence the honest network adopts the attacker's longer chain, and it gains an immediate reward of $(1-\rho) \cdot (k+1)$. In reality this happens w.p. $\geq q$, since $q$ is the probability that the honest network created no conflicting blocks during $2 \cdot d_{a,h}$ seconds.[8] (b) State $(\cdot, k+1, 1)$ was reached, or $(k+1, k, 1)$ was reached but the attacker's blocks didn't make it in time to the honest node before the latter created its next one. The immediate reward described above assumes the worst case for the attacker, i.e., that it suffers a loss of $(-\rho \cdot (k+1))$ (in (b)).

*Part II:* Let $\rho = \rho_h := REV$ (honest mining) represent the revenue of the attacker under honest mining. In the full version it is shown that it is sufficient to prove that the expected sum of all immediate rewards accumulated in $M_{\rho_h}^T$, in a single epoch, is greater with $\pi_k$ than with honest mining. Now, the two policies differ only after reaching state $(k-1, k, 0)$, and this state is reached under both policies with positive probability (as will be shown later). It thus suffices to prove this assertion w.r.t the rewards that result from reaching this state. The attacker's expected immediate reward, under $\pi_k$, upon reaching $(k-1, k, 0)$, is $\alpha^2 \cdot q \cdot (1-\rho_h) \cdot (k+1) - (1-\alpha^2 \cdot q) \cdot \rho_h \cdot (k+1)$; this stems from combining the rewards in scenarios (a) and (b). In contrast, under honest mining it gains $(-\rho_h \cdot k)$, since it adopts immediately. In conclusion, it suffices to show that $q \cdot \alpha^2 (1-\rho_h) \cdot (k+1) - (1-q \cdot \alpha^2) \cdot \rho_h \cdot (k+1) - (-\rho_h \cdot k) > 0$. It is easy to see that this is satisfied by any $k > \frac{\rho_h}{q \cdot \alpha^2} - 1$. In particular, there exists a policy under which the expected immediate rewards of an attacker exceed those it would have gained mining honestly. As this holds for any $\alpha > 0$, we conclude that an attacker of any size can benefit from deviating from honest mining.

*Part III:* To complete the proof we show that after each renewal of the process, state $(k-1, k, 0)$ is reached with positive probability, under both policies. Indeed, there is a probability of $\alpha^{k-1}$ to arrive at $(k-1, 0, 0)$, with the attacker creating the first $(k-1)$ blocks. There is then a probability of $(1-\alpha)^k \cdot \left(1 - e^{-(1-\alpha) \cdot \lambda \cdot d_{a,h}}\right)^{k-1}$ to transit to $(k-1, k, 0)$, with the honest network creating the next $k$ blocks before learning of any of the attacker's blocks. $\square$

To gain further understanding of selfish mining under delays it would be important to quantify the optimal gains from such deviations. We leave this as an

---

[8] After $2 \cdot d_{a,h}$ we are guaranteed that the link from the attacker to the honest network is empty.

open question for future research. Still, it is clear that Bitcoin will be more vulnerable to selfish mining if delays become more prominent, e.g., in the case of larger blocks (block-size increases are currently being debated within the Bitcoin developers community).

# 7    Effect on Double Spending Attacks

In this section we discuss the qualitative effect selfish mining has on the security of payments. The regular operation of bitcoin transactions is as follows: A payment maker signs a transaction and pushes it to the Bitcoin network, then nodes add it to the blocks they are attempting to create. Once a node succeeds it publishes the block with its content. Although the payee can now see this update to the public chain of blocks, it still waits for it to be further extended before releasing the good or service paid for. This deferment of acceptance guarantees that a conflicting secret chain of blocks (if one exists) will not be able to bypass and override the public one observed by the payee, thereby discard the transaction. Building a secret chain in an attempt to reverse payments is called a *double spending* attack.

**Success-probability.** Satoshi Nakamoto, in his original white paper, provides an analysis regarding double spending in probabilistic terms: *Given that the block containing the transaction is followed by n subsequent blocks, what is the probability that an attacker with computational power $\alpha$ will be able to override this chain, now or in the future?* Nakamoto showed that the success-probability of double spending attacks decays exponentially with $n$. Alternative and perhaps more accurate analyses, e.g., [17,18], reach similar conclusions.

**Cost.** While a single double spending attack succeeds with negligible probability (as long as the payee waits long enough), regrettably, an attacker which *continuously* executes double spending attempts will eventually succeed (*a.s.*). We should therefore be more interested in the cost of an attack than in its success-probability. Indeed, every failed double spending attack costs the attacker the potential award it could have gotten had it avoided the fork and published its blocks right away.

Observe, however, that a smart strategy for an attacker would be to continuously employ selfish mining attacks, and upon success combine them with a double spending attack. Technically, this can be done by regularly engaging in public transactions, while always hiding a conflicting one in the attacker's secret blocks.[9] There is always some probability that by the time a successful selfish mining attack has ended, the payment receiver has already accepted the payment, which additionally results in a successful double spending.

To summarize, the existence of a miner for which selfish mining is at least as profitable as honest mining fundamentally undermines the security of payments, as this attacker bears no cost for continuously attempting to double spend, and

---

[9] In the worst case, the attacker is frequently engaged in "real" transactions anyways, hence suffers no loss from them being occasionally confirmed, when attacks fail.

it eventually must succeed. Similarly, an attacker that cannot profit from selfish mining alone, might be profitable in the long run if it combines it with double spending, which potentially has grave implications on the profit threshold.

## 8    Related Work

The Bitcoin protocol was introduced in a white paper published in 2008 by Satoshi Nakamoto [15]. In the paper, Nakamoto shows that the blockchain is secure as long as a majority of the nodes in the Bitcoin network follow the protocol. Kroll et al. [12] show that, indeed, always extending the latest block in the blockchain forms a (weak, non-unique) Nash equilibrium, albeit under a simpler model that does not account for block withholding.

On the other hand, it has been suggested by various people in the Bitcoin forum that strong nodes might be incentivized to violate the protocol by withholding their blocks [1]. Eyal and Sirer proved this by formalizing a block withholding strategy SM1 and analyzing its performance [9]. Their strategy thus violates the protocol's instruction to immediately publish one's blocks, but still sticks to the longest-chain rule (save a selective tie breaking). SM1 still abandons its chain if the honest nodes create a longer chain. One result of our paper is that even adhering to the longest-chain rule is not a best response. We also prove what the optimal policies are, and compute the threshold under which honest mining is a (strict, unique) Nash equilibrium.

A recent paper by Göbel et al. has evaluated SM1 in the presence of delays [10]. They show that SM1 is not profitable under a model of delays that greatly differs from our own (in particular, they assume that block transmission occurs as a memoryless process). While SM1 may indeed be unprofitable when delay is modeled, we show that other profitable selfish mining attacks exist. Additional analysis of block creation in the presence of delays and its effects on throughput and double spending appears in [7,14,18].

A recent work by Nayak et al. [16], which was independently conducted in parallel to our own, discusses specific selfish mining strategies which outperform SM1 (that are not necessarily optimal), and analyzes the combination of selfish mining and a network-level attack. Our own work provides provably optimal strategies, which allows us to compute the profit thresholds, and to evaluate the worst attack given various protocol modifications (which can only be done with optimal strategies).

Additional work on selfish mining via block withholding appears in [6]. Another approach to mitigate selfish mining appears in [11]. Transaction propagation in Bitcoin has also been analyzed from the perspective of incentives. Results in [2] show that nodes have an incentive not to propagate transactions, and suggests a mechanism to correct this. Additional analysis from a game theoretic perspective has also been conducted with regards to interactions pools, either from a cooperative game theory perspective [13]; or when considering attacks between pools [8]. Further discussion on Bitcoin's stability can be found in a recent survey by Bonneau et al. [4].

# References

1. https://bitcointalk.org/index.php?topic=2227 (2008). Accessed 07 July 2015
2. Babaioff, M., Dobzinski, S., Oren, S., Zohar, A.: On Bitcoin and red balloons. In: Proceedings of the 13th ACM Conference on Electronic Commerce, pp. 56–73. ACM (2012)
3. Bierth, K.-J.: An expected average reward criterion. Stochas. Processes Their Appl. **26**, 123–140 (1987)
4. Bonneau, J., Miller, A., Clark, J., Narayanan, A., Kroll, J.A., Felten, E.W.: Research perspectives and challenges for Bitcoin and cryptocurrencies, SoK (2015)
5. Chadès, I., Chapron, G., Cros, M.-J., Garcia, F., Sabbadin, R.: MDPtoolbox: a multi-platform toolbox to solve stochastic dynamic programming problems. Ecography **37**(9), 916–920 (2014)
6. Courtois, N.T., Bahack, L.: On subversive miner strategies and block withholding attack in Bitcoin digital currency. arXiv preprint: arXiv:1402.1718 (2014)
7. Decker, C., Wattenhofer, R.: Information propagation in the Bitcoin network. In: 2013 IEEE Thirteenth International Conference on Peer-to-Peer Computing (P2P), pp. 1–10. IEEE (2013)
8. Eyal, I.: The miner's dilemma. arXiv preprint: arXiv:1411.7099 (2014)
9. Eyal, I., Sirer, E.G.: Majority is not enough: bitcoin mining is vulnerable. In: Christin, N., Safavi-Naini, R. (eds.) FC 2014. LNCS, vol. 8437, pp. 436–454. Springer, Heidelberg (2014). doi:10.1007/978-3-662-45472-5_28
10. Göbel, J., Keeler, P., Krzesinski, A.E., Taylor, P.G.: Bitcoin blockchain dynamics: the selfish-mine strategy in the presence of propagation delay. arXiv preprint: arXiv:1505.05343 (2015)
11. Heilman, E.: One weird trick to stop selfish miners: fresh bitcoins, a solution for the honest miner (poster abstract). In: Böhme, R., Brenner, M., Moore, T., Smith, M. (eds.) FC 2014. LNCS, vol. 8438, pp. 161–162. Springer, Heidelberg (2014). doi:10.1007/978-3-662-44774-1_12
12. Kroll, J.A., Davey, I.C., Felten, E.W.: The economics of Bitcoin mining, or Bitcoin in the presence of adversaries. In: Proceedings of WEIS, vol. 2013 (2013)
13. Lewenberg, Y., Bachrach, Y., Sompolinsky, Y., Zohar, A., Rosenschein, J.S.: Bitcoin mining pools: a cooperative game theoretic analysis. In: Proceedings of the 2015 International Conference on Autonomous Agents and Multiagent Systems, pp. 919–927. International Foundation for Autonomous Agents and Multiagent Systems (2015)
14. Lewenberg, Y., Sompolinsky, Y., Zohar, A.: Inclusive block chain protocols. In: Böhme, R., Okamoto, T. (eds.) FC 2015. LNCS, vol. 8975, pp. 528–547. Springer, Heidelberg (2015). doi:10.1007/978-3-662-47854-7_33
15. Nakamoto, S.: Bitcoin: a peer-to-peer electronic cash system. Consulted **1**(2012), 28 (2008)
16. Nayak, K., Kumar, S., Miller, A., Shi, E.: Stubborn mining: generalizing selfish mining and combining with an eclipse attack
17. Rosenfeld, M.: Analysis of hashrate-based double spending. arXiv preprint: arXiv:1402.2009 (2014)
18. Sompolinsky, Y., Zohar, A.: Secure high-rate transaction processing in Bitcoin. In: Böhme, R., Okamoto, T. (eds.) FC 2015. LNCS, vol. 8975, pp. 507–527. Springer, Heidelberg (2015). doi:10.1007/978-3-662-47854-7_32

# Cryptographic Protocols

# A Short Paper on Blind Signatures from Knowledge Assumptions

Lucjan Hanzlik$^{(\boxtimes)}$ and Kamil Kluczniak

Faculty of Fundamental Problems of Technology,
Wrocław University of Technology, Wrocław, Poland
{lucjan.hanzlik,kamil.kluczniak}@pwr.edu.pl

**Abstract.** This paper concerns blind signature schemes. We focus on two moves constructions, which imply concurrent security. There are known efficient blind signature schemes based on the random oracle model and on the common reference string model. However, constructing two move blind signatures in the standard model is a challenging task, as shown by the impossibility results of Fischlin et al. The recent construction by Garg et al. (Eurocrypt'14) bypasses this result by using complexity leveraging, but it is impractical due to the signature size ($\approx 100\,\text{kB}$). Fuchsbauer et al. (Crypto'15) presented a more practical construction, but with a security argument based on interactive assumptions. We present a blind signature scheme that is two-move, setup-free and comparable in terms of efficiency with the results of Fuchsbauer et al. Its security is based on a knowledge assumption.

**Keywords:** Blind signature · Okamoto-Uchiyama cryptosystem · Knowledge assumption

## 1  Introduction

A blind signature scheme is a cryptographic primitive that allows a user to receive a signature under a message in such a way, that the signer does not learn anything about the signed message (*blindness*). In addition, if the user receives a number of signatures, he should not be able to create a signature under a different message (*unforgeability*).

The idea of blind signatures was first introduced by David Chaum in the paper [6]. He used blind signatures for protecting privacy of users in his e-cash system. Thanks to blind signatures the bank cannot trace the usage of a signed e-cash as the structure of a note is not known. From this point on, blind signatures have been used as building blocks in numerous cryptographic schemes, e.g. in e-voting and anonymous credential systems.

Solutions that are *provably secure* in the random oracle model are frequently accepted by researchers and the industry, and are of great value due to their efficiency. However, the random oracle model does not always yield a secure real world instantiation. In order to bypass the random oracle model, authors in [7,11,12]

© International Financial Cryptography Association 2017
J. Grossklags and B. Preneel (Eds.): FC 2016, LNCS 9603, pp. 535–543, 2017.
DOI: 10.1007/978-3-662-54970-4_31

used the common reference string model in their constructions of blind signatures. This model requires that the users perform a setup phase in which they receive the common reference string (CRS) that must be computed by a trusted third party in order to be useful and to ensure the security of the scheme.

Fischlin et al. have shown in [8] a negative result on the existence of three-move blind signature schemes with a black-box reduction in the standard model. Surprisingly, recent results [10,11] present constructions which circumvent the limitation from [8]. To be more specific, the authors present two-move blind signature schemes which are provably secure without ROM or CRS, however use a non-block-box technique called complexity leveraging. Both solutions are not really practical with signature size of hundreds of kB. A more practical solution was proposed by Fuchsbauer et al. in [9] at CRYPTO'15. The signature size of their construction is not greater than 1 kB. The security of the scheme is based on interactive assumptions. However, the interactive assumption is required so that blindness holds in the stronger *malicious-signer* model (where the signer's public key can be chosen in a malicious way). Blindness in the weaker *honest-signer* model (where the signer's public key is honestly generated), holds under the standard Decisional Diffie-Hellman assumption.

*Our Contribution.* We propose a different approach to bypass the impossibility results from [8]. We combine the partially homomorphic Okamoto-Uchiyama cryptosystem, Pedersen commitments and BB signatures in order to get an efficient two-move, setup-free blind signature scheme.

Blindness of our solution is based on the semantic security of the encryption scheme and unforgeability follows from the knowledge of factor assumption [1]. Under this assumption the Okamoto-Uchiyama cryptosystem is secret key aware. Note that this strong extraction assumption implies non-black-box reductions. Blindness of our scheme holds in the weaker *honest-signer* model. The proposed construction is comparable, in terms of signature size and communication size, with the one from [9]. However, since the security of our scheme is based on a different type of assumption, we feel that it is an interesting alternative.

## 2   Preliminaries

**Definition 1 (Bilinear Groups).** *Let us consider cyclic groups* $(\mathbb{G}_1, +)$, $(\mathbb{G}_2, +)$, $(\mathbb{G}_T, \cdot)$ *of prime order* $q$. *Let* $P_1, P_2$ *be generators of respectively* $\mathbb{G}_1$ *and* $\mathbb{G}_2$. *A mapping* $e : \mathbb{G}_1 \times \mathbb{G}_2 \to \mathbb{G}_T$ *is called a* bilinear map *(pairing), if it is efficiently computable and the following conditions hold:*

**bilinearity:** $\forall (S, T) \in \mathbb{G}_1 \times \mathbb{G}_2, \forall a, b \in \mathbb{Z}_q$, *we have* $e(aS, bT) = e(S, T)^{a \cdot b}$,
**non-degeneracy:** $e(P_1, P_2) \neq 1$ *is a generator of group* $\mathbb{G}_T$.

**Definition 2 (Bilinear-group generator).** *A bilinear-group generator is a polynomial-time algorithm* BGGen *that on input a security parameter* $\lambda$ *returns a bilinear group* BG $= (q, \mathbb{G}_1, \mathbb{G}_2, \mathbb{G}_T, e, P_1, P_2)$ *such that* $\mathbb{G}_1 = \langle P_1 \rangle$, $\mathbb{G}_2 = \langle P_2 \rangle$

*and $\mathbb{G}_T$ are groups of order $q$ with $\log_2 q = \lambda$ and $e : \mathbb{G}_1 \times \mathbb{G}_2 \to \mathbb{G}_T$ is a bilinear map. Similar to the authors of [9], we assume that BGGen is deterministic (which is the case for BN-curves [2]).*

## 2.1 Okamoto-Uchiyama Cryptosystem

In our construction we use the Okamoto-Uchiyama cryptosystem [13].

**Key Generation:** Choose two large primes $p, q$ ($|p| = |q| = k$), and let $n = p^2 q$. Choose $g \in \mathbb{Z}_n^*$ randomly such that the order of $g_p = g^{p-1} \mod p^2$ is $p$. Let $h = g^n \mod n$. The public key is the tuple $\mathsf{pk_{Enc}} = (n, g, h)$. The secret key is the tuple $\mathsf{sk_{Enc}} = (p, q)$.

**Encryption:** Let $m \in \mathbb{Z}_p$ be a plaintext. Select $r \xleftarrow{\$} \mathbb{Z}_n$ and output $C = g^m h^r \mod n$. We will simply use $\mathsf{Enc}(m)$ to denote a ciphertext of message $m$, and $\mathsf{Enc}(m, r)$ to additionally identify the randomness $r$ used.

**Decryption:** Compute $C_p = C^{p-1} \mod p^2$, output message $m = \frac{L(C_p)}{L(g_p)} \mod p$, where $L(x) = \frac{x-1}{p}$.

The Okamoto-Uchiyama cryptosystem is semantically secure. In other words, indistinguishability under chosen plaintext attack (IND-CPA) holds for this scheme. It is partially homomorphic:

$$\mathsf{Enc}(m_1, r_1) \cdot \mathsf{Enc}(m_2, r_2)^{m_3} \mod n = \mathsf{Enc}(m_1 + m_2 \cdot m_3, r_1 + r_2 \cdot m_3).$$

Barbosa and Farshim [1] introduced a so-called *knowledge of factor assumption*. It is similar to the well-known knowledge of exponent assumptions [3]. However, it states that one can output an integer of the form $n = p^2 \cdot q$ only if one knows the primes $p$ and $q$. It was shown by Barbosa and Farshim that under the knowledge of factor assumption the Okamoto-Uchiyama cryptosystem is secret-key-aware, i.e. it is possible to extract the secret key from an adversary that has generated the public key for such a cryptosystem.

## 2.2 BB Signatures

We now recall the short signature scheme proposed by Boneh and Boyen [4]. Their signature scheme consists of the following PPT algorithms:

$\mathsf{KeyGen_{BB}}(1^\lambda)$: Select random generators $P_1 \in \mathbb{G}_1$ and $P_2 \in \mathbb{G}_2$, random integers $x, y \in \mathbb{Z}_p^*$. Compute $u = [x]P_2$ and $v = [y]P_2$. The public key is the tuple $\mathsf{pk_{BB}} = (P_1, P_2, u, v)$. The secret key is the triple $\mathsf{sk_{BB}} = (P_1, x, y)$.

$\mathsf{Sign_{BB}}(m, \mathsf{sk_{BB}})$: given the secret key $\mathsf{sk_{BB}} = (P_1, x, y)$ and a message $m \in \mathbb{Z}_p$, pick $r \in \mathbb{Z}_p \backslash \{-\frac{x+m}{y}\}$ at random and compute $s = [\frac{1}{m+x+yr}]P_1$. Then $\sigma = (s, r)$ is a signature of $m$.

$\mathsf{Verify_{BB}}(m, \sigma, \mathsf{pk_{BB}})$: given the public key $\mathsf{pk_{BB}} = (P_1, P_2, u, v)$, a message $m$, and a signature $\sigma = (s, r)$, check whether $e(s, u \cdot [m]P_2 \cdot [r]v) = e(P_1, P_2)$. If the equality holds, then output 1 and 0 otherwise.

Under the $q$-SDH assumption the above signature scheme is secure against strong existential forgery and an adaptive chosen message attack.

## 2.3 Pedersen Commitments

In contrary to the standard approach, where commitments are elements of groups, we require that the commitments are elements of a subset of $\mathbb{Z}_q$. In particular, one can easily transform Pedersen commitments defined over elliptic curves to have this property. Below we give a formal definition of this commitment scheme.

**Definition 3 (Pedersen Commitment with Commitments in $\mathbb{Z}_q$).** *Pedersen commitments consist of the following algorithms:*

Setup$_\mathsf{P}(1^\lambda, q)$:

    *Compute, using the security parameter $1^\lambda$, an ordinary elliptic curve $\mathbb{G} = E(\mathbb{F}_p)$ (where $p < q$) of a prime order $q_\mathsf{P}$. Let $P$ be the generator of $\mathbb{G}$. Choose $z \xleftarrow{\$} \mathbb{Z}_q$, compute $Q = [z]P$ and output the commitment key $\mathsf{cpp} = (\mathbb{G}, P, Q, q_\mathsf{P})$ (which is an implicit parameter to the below algorithms).*

Commit$_\mathsf{P}(m, r)$:

    *On input a message $m \in \mathbb{Z}_{q_\mathsf{P}}$ and randomness $r \in \mathbb{Z}_{q_\mathsf{P}}$, compute $Co = (Co_x, Co_y) = [m]P + [r]Q$, output commitment $Co_x$ and opening $O = r$.*

Open$_\mathsf{P}(Co_x, m, O)$:

    *On input a commitment $Co_x \in \mathbb{F}_p$, message $m$ and opening $O$, compute $(Co_x^*, Co_y^*) = [m]P + [r]Q$ and if $Co_x = Co_x^*$ output $m$, else output $\perp$.*

This modified Pedersen commitment scheme is still perfectly hiding and computationally binding under the DLP assumption in $\mathbb{G}$. Note that it may happen that an adversary breaks the binding property by returning $(m_0, r_0)$ and $(m_1, r_1)$ such that $(Co_x, Co_y) = [m_0]P + [r_0]Q$ and $(Co_x, -Co_y) = [m_1]P + [r_1]Q$. However, in such a case we can still compute the DLP of $Q$ to base $P$ because $m_0 + z \cdot r_0 = -(m_1 + z \cdot r_1)$, which yields $z = -(m_0 + m_1)/(r_0 + r_1)$.

## 3 Blind Signatures

In this section we recall the syntax and security of blind signature schemes.

**Definition 4.** *A blind signature scheme consists of the following PPT algorithms* $\mathsf{BS} = (\mathsf{KeyGen}_\mathsf{BS}, \mathcal{U}_\mathsf{BS}, \mathcal{S}_\mathsf{BS}, \mathsf{Verify}_\mathsf{BS})$ *defined as follows:*

KeyGen$_\mathsf{BS}(1^\lambda)$: *on input a security parameter, this algorithm outputs a pair of public/secret key $(\mathsf{pk}_\mathsf{BS}, \mathsf{sk}_\mathsf{BS})$ of the signer.*

$\langle \mathcal{U}_\mathsf{BS}(m, \mathsf{pk}_\mathsf{BS}), \mathcal{S}_\mathsf{BS}(\mathsf{sk}_\mathsf{BS}) \rangle$: *are executed by a user and a signer. On input the signer's secret key $\mathsf{sk}_\mathsf{BS}$ algorithm $\mathcal{S}_\mathsf{BS}$ interacts with algorithm $\mathcal{U}_\mathsf{BS}$. On input a message $m$, from message space $\mathcal{M}$, and the signer public key $\mathsf{pk}_\mathsf{BS}$, algorithm $\mathcal{U}_\mathsf{BS}$ outputs a signature $\sigma$ on $m$, or $\perp$, if the interaction was not successful.*

Verify$_\mathsf{BS}(m, \sigma, \mathsf{pk}_\mathsf{BS})$: *on input a message $m$, signature $\sigma$ and the signer's public key $\mathsf{pk}_\mathsf{BS}$, this algorithm outputs 1, if $\sigma$ is a valid signature and 0 otherwise.*

*Correctness.* A blind signature scheme BS is *correct*, if for all $\lambda \in \mathbb{N}$, all $(\mathsf{pk}_{\mathsf{BS}}, \mathsf{sk}_{\mathsf{BS}}) \leftarrow \mathsf{KeyGen}_{\mathsf{BS}}(1^\lambda)$, all messages $m \in \mathcal{M}$ and $\sigma \leftarrow \langle \mathcal{U}_{\mathsf{BS}}(m, \mathsf{pk}_{\mathsf{BS}}), \mathcal{S}_{\mathsf{BS}}(\mathsf{sk}_{\mathsf{BS}}) \rangle$ it holds that $\mathsf{Verify}_{\mathsf{BS}}(m, \sigma, \mathsf{pk}_{\mathsf{BS}}) = 1$.

*Unforgeability.* A blind signature scheme BS is *strongly unforgeable*, if for all PPT algorithms $\mathcal{A}$ having access to a signer oracle, we have:

$$\Pr\Big[(\mathsf{pk}_{\mathsf{BS}}, \mathsf{sk}_{\mathsf{BS}}) \leftarrow \mathsf{KeyGen}_{\mathsf{BS}}(1^\lambda), (m_i^*, \sigma_i^*)_{i=1}^{k+1} \leftarrow \mathcal{A}(\mathsf{pk}_{\mathsf{BS}})^{\langle \cdot, \mathcal{S}_{\mathsf{BS}}(\mathsf{sk}_{\mathsf{BS}}) \rangle} :$$

$$(m_i^*, \sigma_i^*) \neq (m_j^*, \sigma_j^*) \quad \text{for } i, j \in \{1, \ldots, k+1\}, i \neq j \quad \text{and}$$

$$\mathsf{Verify}_{\mathsf{BS}}(m_i^*, \sigma_i^*, \mathsf{pk}_{\mathsf{BS}}) = 1 \quad \text{for } i \in \{1, \ldots, k+1\}\Big] \leq \epsilon(\lambda),$$

where $k$ is the number of oracle queries.

*Blindness.* A blind signature scheme BS is *blind* in the *honest-signer* model, if for all PPT algorithms $\mathcal{A}$ with one-time access to two user oracles, we have:

$$\Pr\Big[b \xleftarrow{\$} \{0,1\}, (\mathsf{pk}_{\mathsf{BS}}, \mathsf{sk}_{\mathsf{BS}}) \leftarrow \mathsf{KeyGen}_{\mathsf{BS}}(1^\lambda), (\mathsf{St}_1, m_0, m_1) \leftarrow \mathcal{A}(\mathsf{pk}_{\mathsf{BS}}, \mathsf{sk}_{\mathsf{BS}}),$$

$$(\mathsf{St}_2) \leftarrow \mathcal{A}(\mathsf{St}_1)^{\langle \mathcal{U}_{\mathsf{BS}}(m_b, \mathsf{pk}_{\mathsf{BS}}), \cdot \rangle^{(1)}, \langle \mathcal{U}_{\mathsf{BS}}(m_{1-b}, \mathsf{pk}_{\mathsf{BS}}), \cdot \rangle^{(1)}},$$

Let $\sigma_b$ and $\sigma_{1-b}$ be the resp. outputs of $\mathcal{U}_{\mathsf{BS}}$,

If $\sigma_0 = \bot$ or $\sigma_1 = \bot$ then $(\sigma_0, \sigma_1) = (\bot, \bot)$,

$$b^* \leftarrow \mathcal{A}(\mathsf{St}_2, \sigma_0, \sigma_1) : b = b^*\Big] - \tfrac{1}{2} \leq \epsilon(\lambda).$$

## 4 Construction

The core idea of our construction is to use the partially homomorphic properties of the Okamoto-Uchiyama cryptosystem to perform certain parts of the signing algorithm of BB signatures. However, for correctness the message space of the encryption scheme must be large, so that the computations are performed in $\mathbb{Z}$. To ensure blindness the signed value is not the actual message $m$, but a perfectly-hiding commitment (Definition 3) to $m$. Thus, the message space of the scheme is the same as for the commitment scheme, i.e. $\mathcal{M} = \mathbb{Z}_{qp}$. Finally, the signed commitment and the opening information are given as part of the blind signature. The details of our construction are given in Scheme 1.

**Theorem 1 (Correctness).** *Scheme 1 is correct.*

*Proof.* Let $m$ be the message requested by the user, $Co$ the commitment to it and $\mathsf{pk}_{\mathsf{Enc}} = (n, g_n, h_n)$ the public key of the Okamoto-Uchiyama cryptosystem. In order to answer the request of the user, the signer chooses random $b, r_S \xleftarrow{\$} \mathbb{Z}_q$ and uses the homomorphic property of the cryptosystem to compute the ciphertext $c_\sigma = (c_m \cdot c_r^y \cdot \mathsf{Enc}((x + (r_S \cdot y)) \mod q))^b \mod n$. The ciphertext $c_\sigma$, $r_S$ and $[b]P_1$ are send to the user. The user deciphers $c_\sigma$ and receives: $t = b \cdot (Co + r_S \cdot y + ((x + (r_S \cdot y)) \mod q)) \mod p_n$. However, since the Okamoto-Uchiyama

---

$\mathsf{KeyGen_{BS}}(1^\lambda)$: Generate bilinear group parameters $\mathsf{BG} = (q, \mathbb{G}_1, \mathbb{G}_2, \mathbb{G}_T, e, Q_1, Q_2) \leftarrow \mathsf{BGGen}(1^\lambda)$ and the commitment key $\mathsf{cpp} = (\mathbb{G}, P, Q, q_P) \leftarrow \mathsf{Setup_P}(1^\lambda, q)$. Use parameters $\mathsf{BG}$ to compute random elements $P_1 \xleftarrow{\$} \mathbb{G}_1$, $P_2 \xleftarrow{\$} \mathbb{G}_2$, $x \xleftarrow{\$} \mathbb{Z}_q$ $y \xleftarrow{\$} \mathbb{Z}_q$, the secret key $\mathsf{sk_{BB}} = (P_1, x, y)$ and the public key $\mathsf{pk_{BB}} = (P_1, P_2, u = [x]P_2, v = [y]P_2)$ for the BB signature scheme. Return $\mathsf{pk_{BS}} = (1^\lambda, \mathsf{cpp}, \mathsf{pk_{BB}})$ and $\mathsf{sk_{BS}} = (\mathsf{sk_{BB}})$.

$\mathcal{U}_{BS}^{(1)}(m, \mathsf{pk_{BS}})$: generate the parameters $\mathsf{BG} \leftarrow \mathsf{BGGen}(1^\lambda)$. Compute the commitment $(Co, o_{Co}) = \mathsf{Commit_P}(m, r_{Co})$ for a random $r_{Co} \in \mathbb{Z}_{q_P}$. Generate the Okamoto-Uchiyama cryptosystem with public key $\mathsf{pk_{Enc}} = (n, g_n, h_n)$ and secret key $\mathsf{sk_{Enc}} = (p_n, q_n)$ (where $p_n > 3 \cdot q^2$). Compute $c_m = \mathsf{Enc}(Co)$, choose random $r_U \xleftarrow{\$} \mathbb{Z}_q$ and compute $c_r = \mathsf{Enc}(r_U)$. Set $\rho = (\mathsf{pk_{Enc}}, c_m, c_r)$ and $\mathsf{St_{BS}} = (\rho, (Co, o_{Co}, r_U), \mathsf{sk_{Enc}})$. Send $\rho$ to the signer.

$\mathcal{S}_{BS}(\rho, \mathsf{sk_{BS}})$: Compute $b \xleftarrow{\$} \mathbb{Z}_q$, $c_\sigma = (c_m \cdot c_r^y \cdot \mathsf{Enc}((x + (r_S \cdot y)) \bmod q))^b$ $\bmod n$, for random $r_S \xleftarrow{\$} \mathbb{Z}_q$ and send $\beta = (c_\sigma, r_S, [b]P_1)$ to the user.

$\mathcal{U}_{BS}^{(2)}(\beta, \mathsf{St_{BS}}, \mathsf{pk_{BS}})$: Decrypt ciphertext $c_\sigma$ receiving integer $t = b \cdot (Co + r_S \cdot y + ((x + (r_S \cdot y)) \bmod q))$, compute $s = ([t^{-1}]([b]P_1)$ (so $s = [\frac{1}{Co+x+(r_S+r_U)\cdot y}]P_1)$, $r = r_S + r_U$ and set $\sigma_{BB} = (s, r)$. Return $\perp$ if $\mathsf{Verify_{BB}}(Co, \sigma_{BB}, \mathsf{pk_{BB}}) = 0$; otherwise return $\sigma = (Co, o_{Co}, \sigma_{BB})$.

$\mathsf{Verify_{BS}}(m, \sigma, \mathsf{pk_{BS}})$: return 1 iff $\mathsf{Verify_{BB}}(Co, \sigma_{BB}, \mathsf{pk_{BB}}) = 1$ and $m = \mathsf{Open_P}(Co, m, o_{Co})$.

---

**Scheme 1:** Our Blind Signature Scheme

cryptosystem was generated in such a way that $p_n > 3 \cdot q^2$, we have that $t = b \cdot (Co + r_S \cdot y + ((x + (r_S \cdot y)) \bmod q))$ over $\mathbb{Z}$ and $t = b \cdot (Co + r_S \cdot y + ((x + (r_S \cdot y))$ in $\mathbb{Z}_q$. Thus, by computing $([t^{-1}]([b]P_1)$, the user receives $s = [\frac{1}{Co+x+(r_S+r_U)\cdot y}]P_1)$. It follows, that $\sigma_{BB} = (s, r)$ (where $r = r_S + r_U$) is a valid BB signature on $Co$ and $\mathsf{Verify_{BB}}(Co, \sigma_{BB}, \mathsf{pk_{BB}}) = 1$. It remains to show that $m = \mathsf{Open_P}(Co, m, o_{Co})$ but this follows from the correctness of Pedersen commitments.

**Theorem 2 (Unforgeability).** *If BB signatures are secure against strong existential forgery under an adaptive chosen message attack, Pedersen commitments from Definition 3 are computationally binding and the knowledge of factor assumption holds, then Scheme 1 is strongly unforgeable.*

*Proof (Sketch).* Let $\mathcal{A}$ be a PPT adversary that breaks the strong unforgeability of Scheme 1. We now show that we can construct a reduction $\mathcal{R}$ that, using $\mathcal{A}$ as a procedure, either breaks the strong existential unforgeability of the BB signature scheme or computational binding of the Pedersen commitment scheme. To break strong unforgeability the adversary $\mathcal{A}$ will return $k + 1$ pairs $(m_i^*, \sigma_i^*)_{i=1}^{k+1} = (m_i^*, (Co_i^*, o_{Co_i}^*, \sigma_{BB,i}^*))_{i=1}^{k+1}$, where $k$ is the number of queries made to the signing oracle. We now distinguish two cases leading to two different strategies followed by $\mathcal{R}$ and a different target of the attack:

**Case 1:** all commitments $Co_1^*, \ldots, Co_{k+1}^*$ are distinct,
**Case 2:** there exist $i, j \in \{1, \ldots, k+1\}$, $i \neq j$ for which $Co_i^* = Co_j^*$.

In the first option $\mathcal{R}$ aims to break the unforgeability of the BB signature scheme hoping that all commitments created by $\mathcal{A}$ will be different (if it turns to be false, then the attack fails). $\mathcal{R}$ interacts with $\mathcal{A}$ simulating the environment for the blind signature scheme; at the same time $\mathcal{R}$ uses a BB signing oracle. First, $\mathcal{R}$ computes the commitment key $\mathsf{cpp} \leftarrow \mathsf{Setup}_\mathsf{P}(1^\lambda, q)$ but uses the public key $\mathsf{pk}_\mathsf{BB} = (P_1, P_2, u = [x]P_2, v = [y]P_2)$ from the unforgeability game. It outputs $\mathsf{pk}_\mathsf{BS} = (1^\lambda, \mathsf{cpp}, \mathsf{pk}_\mathsf{BB})$ as its public key for the blind signature scheme. To perfectly simulate the signing queries for this public key, $\mathcal{R}$ extracts $Co$ and $r_U$ from the queries of $\mathcal{A}$. Note that under the knowledge of factor assumption $\mathcal{R}$ can extract the secret key and decrypt those values from $c_m$ and $c_r$, respectively. Then $\mathcal{R}$ queries $Co$ to its signing oracle, receiving a BB signature $(s, r)$ on $Co$, where $s = [\frac{1}{Co+x+r\cdot y}]P_1$. The reduction computes $r_S = r - r_U$, chooses $t \xleftarrow{\$} \mathbb{Z}_{3 \cdot q^2}$, computes $s' = [t]s$ and $c_\sigma = \mathsf{Enc}(t)$. $\mathcal{R}$ answers the query by returning $(c_\sigma, r_S, s')$. Note that $\mathcal{A}$ will receive a valid signature under $Co$. Finally, $\mathcal{R}$ returns $(Co_i^*, \sigma_{\mathsf{BB},i}^*)_{i=1}^{k+1}$ and breaks the strong existential unforgeability of BB signatures.

On the other hand, in order to perform an attack in Case 2, $\mathcal{R}$ breaks the binding property of the Pedersen commitment scheme. The reduction uses the commitment key $\mathsf{cpp} = (\mathbb{G}, P, Q, q_\mathsf{P})$ from the binding game but computes the BB signature public key $\mathsf{pk}_\mathsf{BB}$ according to the protocol. Note that this time the signing key is known to $\mathcal{R}$ and all signing queries of $\mathcal{A}$ can be answered according to the protocol. However, at the end $\mathcal{A}$ outputs the above $k+1$ pairs. If Case 2 occurs, then there exist $i, j \in \{1, \ldots, k+1\}$, $i \neq j$ for which $Co_i^* = Co_j^*$. It follows, that by returning $(m_i^*, o_{Co_i}^*), (m_j^*, o_{Co_j}^*)$ the reduction $\mathcal{R}$ breaks the computational binding of the Pedersen commitment scheme.

**Theorem 3 (Blindness).** *If the Okamoto-Uchiyama cryptosystem is indistinguishable under chosen plaintext attack and the Pedersen commitment is perfectly-hiding, then Scheme 1 is blind in the honest-signer model.*

*Proof (Sketch).* We commence with the observation that if the adversary receives $(\bot, \bot)$, then due to perfect hiding property of Pedersen commitments the adversaries advantage in the blindness experiment is 0. To have a non-negligible advantage, the adversary must receive valid signatures $(\sigma_0, \sigma_1)$. Thus, we assume that the adversary always receives valid signatures in the blindness experiment. We will show that advantage of adversary $\mathcal{A}$ in winning the blindness experiment cannot be greater than the advantage of any adversary against CPA security of the Okamoto-Uchiyama cryptosystem. The idea is that we construct a reduction $\mathcal{R}$ that plays the semantic security experiment and wins it with the same probability as $\mathcal{A}$ wins the blindness experiment. The steps of $\mathcal{R}$ are the following. First, it returns the bits 0 and 1 as the messages to be encrypted in the CPA experiment. As a result, $\mathcal{R}$ receives the public key $\mathsf{pk}_\mathsf{Enc} = (n, g_n, h_n)$ and a ciphertext $C_b = \mathsf{Enc}(b)$, for an unknown bit $b$. The adversary $\mathcal{A}$ returns $m_0, m_1$. Using those values, the reduction computes two commitments $(Co_0, o_{Co_0}) = \mathsf{Commit_P}(m_0, r_{Co_0})$, $(Co_1, o_{Co_1}) = \mathsf{Commit_P}(m_1, r_{Co_1})$ and two ciphertexts: $C_0 = \mathsf{Enc}(Co_0 \cdot (1-b) + Co_1 \cdot b)$ and $C_1 = \mathsf{Enc}(Co_0 \cdot b + Co_1 \cdot (1-b))$. Note that using the partially homomorphic property of the cryptosystem, $\mathcal{R}$ can compute both values. Now depending on the bit $b$ we have $C_0 = \mathsf{Enc}(Co_0), C_1 = \mathsf{Enc}(Co_1)$ if $b = 0$ and $C_0 = \mathsf{Enc}(Co_1), C_1 = \mathsf{Enc}(Co_0)$ if $b = 1$. The reduction then uses $C_0$ as a ciphertext of the message $c_m$ in the first and $C_1$ in the second interaction. However, instead of using the values $\rho_0$ and $\rho_1$ returned by $\mathcal{A}$, the reduction computes the signatures (on $Co_0$ and $Co_1$) itself as it knows the signing key. Finally, $\mathcal{R}$ returns the bit outputted by $\mathcal{A}$.

*Remark 1.* Note that if we would sign the actual message $m$, instead of a commitment to it, then there exists an adversary that can win the blindness game with non-negligible advantage. The adversary guesses the correct bit $b$ and computes $(\beta_0, \beta_1)$ in such a way that procedure $\mathcal{U}_{\mathsf{BS}}^{(2)}$ aborts (with the adversary receiving $(\perp, \perp)$) if the $b$ is guessed wrong and returns a valid signature if bit $b$ was correct. Due to space reasons we omit the details of this oracle attack and describe it in more detail in the full version of this article.

On the other hand, Scheme 1 prevents such an attack using perfectly-hiding commitments. In particular, if the adversary does not receive the openings to the commitments, then its advantage cannot be greater then 0 (as both events are equally probable). This idea is used in the first paragraph of the sketch of the proof. Note that this idea also applies in case of blindness with selective-failure attacks [5], where the adversary is given $(\epsilon, \perp)$ (or $(\perp, \epsilon)$) in case one of the execution succeeded and the second one failed.

## 5   Conclusions

We have proposed a fairly practical two-move blind signature without random oracles and a common reference string. It is efficient in terms of signature size and communication complexity. For a future work we plan to extend blindness to the malicious-signer model, where the adversary generates the signing key. One promising approach is to use the knowledge of exponent assumption to extract the signer's secret key as it only consists of one public value $P_1$ and two discrete logarithms of the public values $X$ and $Y$ to the base $P_2$. Moreover, we plan to extend our construction to partially blind signatures, where the signer and the user share some information (e.g. expiration date of the document) and this information is included in the signature.

**Acknowledgments.** We would like to thank prof. Mirosław Kutyłowski and the anonymous reviewers of FC for their valuable comments on this short paper. This research was supported by the National Science Centre (Poland) based on decision no. 2014/15/N/ST6/04577.

# References

1. Barbosa, M., Farshim, P.: Strong knowledge extractors for public-key encryption schemes. In: Steinfeld, R., Hawkes, P. (eds.) ACISP 2010. LNCS, vol. 6168, pp. 164–181. Springer, Heidelberg (2010). doi:10.1007/978-3-642-14081-5_11. http://dblp.uni-trier.de/db/conf/acisp/acisp2010.html#BarbosaF10a
2. Barreto, P.S.L.M., Naehrig, M.: Pairing-friendly elliptic curves of prime order. In: Preneel, B., Tavares, S. (eds.) SAC 2005. LNCS, vol. 3897, pp. 319–331. Springer, Heidelberg (2006). doi:10.1007/11693383_22. http://dblp.uni-trier.de/db/conf/sacrypt/sacrypt2005.html#BarretoN05
3. Bellare, M., Palacio, A.: The knowledge-of-exponent assumptions and 3-round zero-knowledge protocols. In: Franklin, M. (ed.) CRYPTO 2004. LNCS, vol. 3152, pp. 273–289. Springer, Heidelberg (2004). doi:10.1007/978-3-540-28628-8_17. http://www.iacr.org/cryptodb/archive/2004/CRYPTO/961/961.pdf
4. Boneh, D., Boyen, X.: Short signatures without random oracles and the SDH assumption in bilinear groups. J. Cryptol. 21(2), 149–177 (2008). http://dblp.uni-trier.de/db/journals/joc/joc21.html#BonehB08
5. Camenisch, J., Neven, G., Shelat, A.: Simulatable adaptive oblivious transfer. In: Naor, M. (ed.) EUROCRYPT 2007. LNCS, vol. 4515, pp. 573–590. Springer, Heidelberg (2007). doi:10.1007/978-3-540-72540-4_33
6. Chaum, D.: Blind signatures for untraceable payments. In: Chaum, D., Rivest, R.L., Sherman, A.T. (eds.) CRYPTO 1982, pp. 199–203. Springer, Heidelberg (1982)
7. Fischlin, M.: Round-optimal composable blind signatures in the common reference string model. In: Dwork, C. (ed.) CRYPTO 2006. LNCS, vol. 4117, pp. 60–77. Springer, Heidelberg (2006). doi:10.1007/11818175_4
8. Fischlin, M., Schröder, D.: On the impossibility of three-move blind signature schemes. In: Gilbert, H. (ed.) EUROCRYPT 2010. LNCS, vol. 6110, pp. 197–215. Springer, Heidelberg (2010). doi:10.1007/978-3-642-13190-5_10
9. Fuchsbauer, G., Hanser, C., Slamanig, D.: Practical round-optimal blind signatures in the standard model. Cryptology ePrint Archive, Report 2015/626 (2015). http://eprint.iacr.org/
10. Garg, S., Gupta, D.: Efficient round optimal blind signatures. In: Nguyen, P.Q., Oswald, E. (eds.) EUROCRYPT 2014. LNCS, vol. 8441, pp. 477–495. Springer, Heidelberg (2014). doi:10.1007/978-3-642-55220-5_27
11. Garg, S., Rao, V., Sahai, A., Schröder, D., Unruh, D.: Round optimal blind signatures. In: Rogaway, P. (ed.) CRYPTO 2011. LNCS, vol. 6841, pp. 630–648. Springer, Heidelberg (2011). doi:10.1007/978-3-642-22792-9_36
12. Meiklejohn, S., Shacham, H., Freeman, D.M.: Limitations on transformations from composite-order to prime-order groups: the case of round-optimal blind signatures. In: Abe, M. (ed.) ASIACRYPT 2010. LNCS, vol. 6477, pp. 519–538. Springer, Heidelberg (2010). doi:10.1007/978-3-642-17373-8_30
13. Okamoto, T., Uchiyama, S.: A new public-key cryptosystem as secure as factoring. In: Nyberg, K. (ed.) EUROCRYPT 1998. LNCS, vol. 1403, pp. 308–318. Springer, Heidelberg (1998). doi:10.1007/BFb0054135

# KBID: Kerberos Bracelet Identification
# (Short Paper)

Joseph Carrigan[✉], Paul Martin, and Michael Rushanan

Johns Hopkins University, Baltimore, USA
{joseph.carrigan,pmartin,mrushan1}@jhu.edu

**Abstract.** The most common method for a user to gain access to a system, service, or resource is to provide a secret, often a password, that verifies her identity and thus authenticates her. Password-based authentication is considered strong only when the password meets certain length and complexity requirements, or when it is combined with other methods in multi-factor authentication. Unfortunately, many authentication systems do not enforce strong passwords due to a number of limitations; for example, the time taken to enter complex passwords. We present an authentication system that addresses these limitations by prompting a user for credentials once and then storing an authentication ticket in a wearable device that we call *Kerberos Bracelet Identification* (KBID).

**Keywords:** Authentication · Kerberos · Wearables · Passwords

## 1 Introduction

The use of modern computer systems almost always requires that a user prove their identity through some process of authentication. Specifically, a user can authenticate using methods such as public key authentication, biometrics, and passwords; something you have, are, or know, respectively. Password-based authentication remains the most widely used option for authentication because of its ease of use and simple design.

However, passwords have a human factor weakness as users often choose passwords that are too simplistic and easily guessed [9]. Administrators and systems require users to select more complex passwords as a consequence; thus, decreasing user satisfaction as password selection becomes seemingly difficult. Worst yet, complex passwords interfere in critical workflow such as clinical care where a patient's need is most urgent.

In this paper we describe an authentication system that requires the user to enter a password as infrequently as once a day. Specifically, authentication information is stored on a wearable device, a bracelet in our case, and is transmitted to devices to which the user wishes to authenticate. The transmission between the bracelet and device is achieved via using the user's body as a communication medium [1,2]. Our goal is to reduce the impact on user satisfaction and workflow by removing most of the difficulty of using a complex password.

© International Financial Cryptography Association 2017
J. Grossklags and B. Preneel (Eds.): FC 2016, LNCS 9603, pp. 544–551, 2017.
DOI: 10.1007/978-3-662-54970-4_32

While we focus on authentication in the medical community use case, we anticipate that other areas such as the financial sector may benefit from our system. In addition, it is important to note that this system is not a two-factor authentication solution. The bracelet is not a biometric component and does not provide any additional information outside of what it stores. It is meant to enhance the user experience and encourage the use of complex passwords. Finally, KBID is a work in progress.

## 2   Background

KBID originates from the idea of integrating a wearable device to achieve some additional property in an authentication system (e.g., de-authentication). In particular, we are inspired by the design of zero-effort bilateral recurring authentication (ZEBRA) by Mare et al. [7]. In ZEBRA, a user wears a bracelet that encapsulates a wireless radio, accelerometer, and gyroscope; these components record and transmit wrist movements to a computer system that is currently being used. The computer system continually compares received movement measurements to input it receives from it's keyboard and mouse. If these two measurements are not correlated, the current session is de-authenticated.

At the time, ZEBRA was only envisioned as a method to de-authenticate a user from a computer system and did not include a way to initially authenticate the user to the system. Assuming that the user has already accepted wearing a device that will effectively de-authenticate them, adding functionality to rapidly authenticate them only increases the usefulness of the system.

We avoided using radio frequency (RF) emissions for two reasons. First, RF by it's nature emits information into the environment. That information, once emitted, can be received by various means. Second, RF relies on the underlying communication being secure. If a security flaw is discovered in an RF communication framework, e.g. Bluetooth low energy (BLE) [8], then the systems as it exists could be vulnerable to the flaw. Specifically, there is no need to alter or even monitor the information that is exchanged between the computer system and a wearable device. An attacker would only need to extend the range of the wireless communication in order to gain access to the computer system.

We instead use body-coupled communication (BCC), or transmission of information over the human body as a medium. We are not the first to use BCC to transmit a secret. For example, Chang et al. introduce a system for key exchange over a body area network [2]. By applying a very small voltage to the tissue of a dead mouse, they were able to communicate at a rate of 5 Hz or 5 bits per second. However, this data rate is not acceptable for our work as we would need to communicate authentication data of at least 256 bits, and this would take nearly a minute to transmit.

We designed our authenticated bracelet to be non-transferrable (i.e., authenticating and then giving the bracelet to someone else). To support this feature, we zero all authentication information upon bracelet removal.

## 3    Related Work

In addition to the ZEBRA, which we have described previously, there have been several previous attempts at developing wearable-authentication technology. Two of note include the Bionym Nymi [5] and the Intel Authentication Bracelet [6]. The Bionym Nymi is an authentication wristband that broadcasts a digitally signed authentication signal derived from a user's heartbeat to nearby devices using BLE [4]. The Intel Authentication Bracelet requires a user to log in to a system with a standard password. A credential is then transmitted to the bracelet using BLE. This credential is then broadcast to nearby bracelet-enabled devices in order to allow password-less login.

**Limitations of Existing Work.** Existing authentication wearables use wireless communication technology (typically BLE) to broadcast their authentication credentials. Thus the devices are likely vulnerable to ghost-and-leech attacks [3]. Ghost-and-leech attacks occur when an attacker uses a more powerful radio transmitter than the transmitter found on a wireless device in order to capture and rebroadcast the wireless signal in order to fool a target into believing that the wireless device is in closer proximity to the target than it actually is.

## 4    Threat Model

As a hardware and software solution, the threat model for KBID includes many subjects that apply to any such system. These include attack types (denial of service, message forging or tampering, hardware tampering, and others) as well as a study of potential adversaries and other topics. Here we focus on two threats that are unique to KBID. These threats require an active adversary that has the ability to get close to where KBID is used. It is possible to impersonate an authentication module. An attacker could use a counterfeit authentication module that issues *Get Status* commands when a user touches something connected to it, e.g. a door knob. We discuss mitigating this vector below. Second, while we are using body coupled communication to transmit data without emitting RF, it could be the case that the user's body acts as a broadcast antenna and emits the data into the environment where it could conceivably be intercepted. We plan on assessing the reality of this treat during the development of the next prototype.

## 5    Design

Here we describe in detail the design and implementation of the KBID system. First we discuss the high level design where we explain the four major components of the system. Next, we discuss the interface designs and the communication protocols between the major components. Finally, we discuss the system workflow.

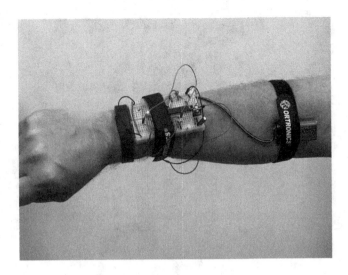

**Fig. 1.** KBID prototype bracelet

## 5.1  High Level Design

The system is composed of four main parts: a bracelet (Fig. 1), an authentication module (Fig. 2) an authentication client, and a Kerberos authentication server. The bracelet is a wearable device that fastened to the user's wrist. The bracelet makes contact with the user's skin and applies a signal directly to the user's skin. The authentication module has a sensor with a button under it. When the user touches the sensor and depresses the button, the authentication module initiates communication with the bracelet. The authentication module is attached via RS-232 serial to the computer system to which the user wants to authenticate. A workstation hosts the authentication client. The client monitors the serial connection for data and when necessary, opens a connection to the Kerberos server for authentication. Finally, the Kerberos server is a default installation and uses the default implementation of the authentication protocol.

## 5.2  Interfaces and Communication

The KBID system includes three interfaces. The interface between the bracelet and the authentication module takes place over the user's skin. The interface between the authentication module and the authentication client takes place over RS-232 serial. Finally, the interface between the authentication client and the Kerberos server uses the network. Since the communication between a client and a Kerberos server is well documented, we will not discuss it in this paper.

**Bracelet to Authentication Module.** The communication protocol between the bracelet and the authentication module is a very lightweight protocol. The messages that the bracelet sends to the authentication modules are called *statuses*. The messages that the authentication module sends to the

**Fig. 2.** KBID prototype authentication module

bracelet are called *commands*. Each message sent over this interface is a length delimited series of bytes. A status message had the following structure: [Status ID] [Device ID] [Data Size (in bytes)] [Data]. The bracelet will send one of two statuses, *authenticated* or *un-authenticated*. If the status is authenticated, the authentication data will be transmitted in the data field.

A command message has the following structure: [Command ID] [Device ID] [Payload Size (in bytes)] [Payload]. The authentication module will send three commands: *Get Status*, *Set Token*, and *De-authenticate*. A Get Status command causes the bracelet to respond with a status message. A Set Token command causes the bracelet to store the payload in memory as authentication data and set its status to authenticated. A De-authenticate command causes the bracelet to clear any token it has and set its status to un-authenticated.

**Authentication Module to Authentication Client.** The authentication module and the authentication client communicate status and command messages as well. The authentication module can send three statuses to the authentication client. First is the *Un-authenticated Bracelet* message. This message is sent to the authentication client when the authentication module receives an un-authenticated status from a bracelet.

Next the authentication module can send an *Authenticated Bracelet* status to the authentication client. It will send this status when the bracelet sends a status of authenticated. The Authenticated Bracelet status will contain the ticket information that was in the token section of the bracelet's message.

Finally, the authentication module can send a *Ticket Written* status to the authentication client. This is a message that lets the client know that the ticket information has been successfully written to the bracelet.

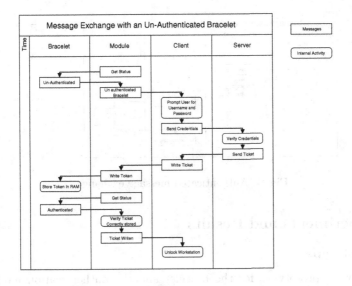

**Fig. 3.** Un-authenticated message exchange

The authentication client sends two commands to the authentication module. First the *Write Ticket* command. This instructs the authentication module to pass the ticket included in the command to the bracelet with a Set Token command. The authentication client can also send a *De-authenticate Bracelet* command. This instructs the authentication module to issue a De-Authenticate command to the bracelet.

## 5.3   System Workflow

The system workflow can be described in two use cases. For the sake of brevity we do not include any error handling. In the first use case (Fig. 3) the user is wearing a bracelet but the bracelet is not yet authenticated. The users touches the sensor on the authentication module, the authentication module sees that the user's bracelet is not authenticated and relays this information to the authentication client. The client prompts the user for their username and password. The client verifies this information with the Kerberos server, then instructs the user to touch the sensor on the authentication module again. The client then instructs the authentication module to write the ticket to the bracelet. Once the ticket has been written, the client unlocks the workstation.

In the second use case (Fig. 4) the user has an authenticated bracelet. The user touches the sensor on the authentication module. The module asks for a status, and the bracelet provides it with the token it has stored. The module passes this information along to the client which interprets the token as a Kerberos ticket. The client verifies the ticket with the Kerberos server and unlocks the workstation. Our goal is to perform this use case in less than one second.

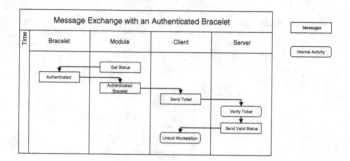

**Fig. 4.** Authenticated message exchange

# 6 Experiments and Results

## 6.1 Prototype

The hardware prototypes for the bracelet and the authentication module are based on the Atmel ATMega328 microcontroller operating at 20 MHz and an LM358AN Amplifier. Both the bracelet and the authentication module have copper pads that make contact with the user's skin. The signal from the skin is fed into the amplifier and the signal to the skin is driven by setting a pin on the microcontroller. We also built a resistive analogue to represent the resistance from a user's wrist to their finger tip. The prototype for the authentication client has been written in Python.

## 6.2 Results

Initial results are encouraging. We are able to send commands from the authentication module to the bracelet. The bracelet can correctly interpret those commands and it responds when issued a Get Status command. The time elapsed for a Get Status command and a status message with a 256 byte token is approximately 500 milliseconds. We also implemented the functionality that clears the authentication information when the bracelet is removed. This was accomplished by using one of the hardware interrupts on the microcontroller.

## 6.3 Hurdles

We encountered two major hurdles during the development of the first prototype. First, in order to successfully send a signal the bracelet and the authentication module must have a common reference for voltage. Second, while we have been able to get the signal to transmit from the authentication module to the bracelet, we have not been able to get the signal to travel in the opposite direction and arrive in a way that the signal can be interpreted by the authentication module. To solve these issues, we plan to either improve the performance of the amplifier or change the method by which the signal is transmitted over the user's skin to capacitive coupling.

# 7   Future Work

Future work will focus on improving the system. We plan to implement the system using a microcontroller that can store larger keys. The Atmel ATMega328 only has 2 kilobytes of RAM. Since the systems needs some RAM to perform operations, the key that is stored in RAM is limited in size to about 1 kilobyte. This is not sufficient space to store authentication information in real world environments. We also plan on hardening the system by adding pre-shared message authentication codes (MACs) to protect against replay and device impersonation attacks.

# References

1. Barth, A.T., Hanson, M.A., Powell, H.C., Unluer, D., Wilson, S.G., Lach, J.: Body-coupled communication for body sensor networks. In: Proceedings of the ICST 3rd International Conference on Body Area Networks (2008). http://dl.acm.org/citation.cfm?id=1460257.1460273
2. Chang, S., Hu, Y., Anderson, H., Fu, T., Huang, E.Y.L.: Body area network security: robust key establishment using human body channel. In: Proceedings of 3rd USENIX Workshop on Health Security and Privacy (HealthSec), August 2013. https://www.usenix.org/conference/healthsec12/workshop-program/presentation/Chang
3. Czeskis, A., Koscher, K., Smith, J.R., Kohno, T.: RFIDS and secret handshakes: defending against ghost-and-leech attacks and unauthorized reads with context-aware communications. In: Proceedings of the 15th ACM conference on Computer and communications security, pp. 479–490. ACM (2008)
4. Gomez, C., Oller, J., Paradells, J.: Overview and evaluation of bluetooth low energy: an emerging low-power wireless technology. Sensors 12(9), 11734 (2012). http://www.mdpi.com/1424-8220/12/9/11734
5. Goode, A.: Bring your own finger-how mobile is bringing biometrics to consumers. Biom. Technol. Today 2014(5), 5–9 (2014)
6. Krzanich, B.: Intel developer forum san francisco opening keynote. Intel Corporation, Technical report (2015)
7. Mare, S., Markham, A., Cornelius, C., Peterson, R., Kotz, D.: Zebra: zero-effort bilateral recurring authentication. In: 2014 IEEE Symposium on Security and Privacy (SP), May 2014
8. Ryan, M.: Bluetooth: with low energy comes low security. In: Proceedings of the 7th USENIX Conference on Offensive Technologies. USENIX Association (2013). http://dl.acm.org/citation.cfm?id=2534748.2534754
9. Yan, J., Blackwell, A., Anderson, R., Grant, A.: Password memorability and security: empirical results. IEEE Secur. Priv. (2004). http://dx.doi.org/10.1109/MSP.2004.81

# Payment Use and Abuse

# The Other Side of the Coin: User Experiences with Bitcoin Security and Privacy

Katharina Krombholz[(✉)], Aljosha Judmayer,
Matthias Gusenbauer, and Edgar Weippl

SBA Research, Vienna, Austria
{kkrombholz,ajudmayer,mgusenbauer,eweippl}@sba-research.org

**Abstract.** We present the first large-scale survey to investigate how users experience the Bitcoin ecosystem in terms of security, privacy and anonymity. We surveyed 990 Bitcoin users to determine Bitcoin management strategies and identified how users deploy security measures to protect their keys and bitcoins. We found that about 46% of our participants use web-hosted solutions to manage at least some of their bitcoins, and about half of them use exclusively such solutions. We also found that many users do not use all security capabilities of their selected Bitcoin management tool and have significant misconceptions on how to remain anonymous and protect their privacy in the Bitcoin network. Also, 22% of our participants have already lost money due to security breaches or self-induced errors. To get a deeper understanding, we conducted qualitative interviews to explain some of the observed phenomena.

## 1 Introduction

With a current market capitalization of more than 3.5 billion USD, Bitcoin is the most successful cryptographic currency at this time. Bitcoin is utilized for roughly 130.000 transactions per day [6] and has gained significant news coverage. With the success of Bitcoin, several other cryptographic currencies were developed either based on Bitcoin or from scratch.

Although the popularity of cryptographic currencies is increasing, they are not yet a mass phenomenon. One of the reasons is that Bitcoin forces its users to deal with public key cryptography. Furthermore, Bitcoin shifts the responsibilities for most security measures to the end user compared to centralized monetary systems. Even though there is a great variety of software available for managing bitcoins, user-experience is still not obviating the need to deal with the technical fundamentals and to perform backups to recover their virtual monetary assets in case of a loss. Hence, these systems are not resilient to human errors. Reports from online forums and mailing-lists show that many Bitcoin users already lost money due to poor usability of key management and security breaches such as malicious exchanges and wallets. This motivates our research on human interactions with the Bitcoin ecosystem.

Bitcoin users have a huge variety of tools available to manage their virtual assets. These tools are commonly referred to as *wallets*. A wallet was originally

J. Grossklags and B. Preneel (Eds.): FC 2016, LNCS 9603, pp. 555–580, 2017.
DOI: 10.1007/978-3-662-54970-4_33

defined as a collection of private keys [8]. Hence, a piece of paper with a private key on it or even a mental representation can be considered a wallet. However, most of these tools provide functionality beyond storing keys, such as performing transactions. In contrary to other public key crypto-systems, e.g. PGP/GPG, Bitcoin is not fully communication channel agnostic. In case of Bitcoin the interaction with the Bitcoin network is an integral part to operate in the distributed system. In contrast to other signing systems, Bitcoin tools need to keep state information on performed transactions and account balances respectively.

As a first step to accommodate these misconceptions on Bitcoin wallets, we introduce the term *Coin Management Tool (CMT)* as an extension to the current narrow definition of a wallet. We define a CMT as a tool or a collection of tools which allows users to manage one or more core tasks of cryptocurrencies. Throughout this paper we are therefore referring to *Bitcoin management*, as it better describes user activities when interacting with the Bitcoin ecosystem. Bitcoin security and privacy aspects have already been studied in the research literature [7,10,14–16]. A first look on the usability of Bitcoin key management has been presented in [8]. However, we are the first to conduct a comprehensive user study to collect evidence on user experiences with Bitcoin security and privacy.

In this paper, we present a comprehensive user study ($n = 990$) to cover human-computer interaction aspects of the Bitcoin ecosystem. The goal was to understand how users interact with Bitcoin and how they manage their virtual assets. We furthermore studied experiences and perceptions related to security, privacy and anonymity in the Bitcoin network. To collect user-reported data, we conducted a comprehensive online survey with 990 participants and qualitative interviews with a subset of 10 participants. Additionally, we extended the evaluation criteria from [8] and provide a method to categorize CMTs depending on the level of control and verifiability a user can exercise with the respective client.

We gathered interesting insights on how users interact with the Bitcoin network and what privacy and security measures they deploy to protect their keys and coins. We found that the first- and third-most used CMTs (Coinbase, Xapo) are web-hosted tools where users shift security responsibilities to a third party. We also found that about a third of their users are not aware whether their CMT data is encrypted or backed-up. Among the participants who use a web-hosted solution, 50% indicated to use it exclusively while the other half used additional local clients to manage their coins. Regarding risk scenarios and their likelihood to occur, the second-highest risk was attributed to vulnerabilities in web-hosted CMTs (after value fluctuation and followed by theft via malware).

We also found that many users have misconceptions about how to remain anonymous. About 25% of our participants reported to use Bitcoin over Tor which has already shown to be disadvantageous in certain cases [1,3]. 22.5% of the participants reported to have lost their bitcoins due to security breaches. About half of them consider this loss as their own fault and the majority of them was not able to recover their bitcoins and lost money permanently. Our work contributes research on user-centric concerns of Bitcoin management, as according to Bonneau [7] Bitcoin is one of the cases where practice is ahead of theory.

The main contributions of this paper are **(1)** **a user study consisting of an online survey and qualitative interviews,** and **(2)** **a method for categorizing Bitcoin CMTs.**

## 2    Bitcoin Background

The Bitcoin currency is based on a distributed P2P system which synchronizes a public ledger of all transactions among all Bitcoin clients. As a consequence, every full client in the Bitcoin network is able to see the entire history containing all prior transactions. Thereby it is possible to determine the current balance of every account. The account information in Bitcoin basically consists of a hash over a public key which can be compared to an account number, the so-called *Bitcoin address*. The protocol does not require a link between account information and personal data. An individual can have more than one account, hence Bitcoin provides a certain degree of pseudonymity [1,9].

To transfer $n$ bitcoins from account $A$, which is under control of Alice, to another account $B$, which is under control of Bob, a new transaction is created by Alice. Thereby, Alice creates a transaction message with the amount of bitcoins she wants to send to Bob and includes the hash of the public key of Bobs account $B$ as a destination before signing it with her secret key $sk_A$. Alice publishes this transaction in the Bitcoin network so that every participant knows that Alice now has $n$ bitcoins less on her account $A$ and Bob has received the difference on his account $B$. When this transaction is successfully propagated in the network, Bob can create new transactions from his account $B$ to another account and spend the previously received bitcoins. This chaining mechanism works fine for passing over arbitrary amounts of bitcoins from one account to another, except in the special case of the first transaction in a chain, because this is where new bitcoins come into existence [20].

Bitcoins are created during the so-called *mining process*. In this procedure every miner collects transactions which have recently been propagated in the P2P network. Then they try to successfully create a new block out of all unconfirmed transactions that have not yet been included in a block of the block chain. A block essentially consists of a collection of valid transactions[1], a nonce value, and a proof of work. The proof of work is a partial pre-image attack on SHA-256 over the whole block as input. For the attack to succeed, the hash has to be a value smaller than the current difficulty in the Bitcoin network. In other words, the SHA-256 hash has to start with a certain number of zero bits. The number of zero bits is referred to as difficulty. Since SHA-256 is categorized as a cryptographic hash function [21], it is easy to verify a previously calculated SHA-256 sum of a block, but it is considered infeasible to generate a specific block that produces a given hash value. To achieve this, the nonce field is constantly incremented to search for a hash value that fulfils the described property. This brute-force process of searching is called *mining*. If one client in the Bitcoin network finds

---

[1] More precisely a Merkle-Tree Hash over those transactions, for details see the specifications [4,5,17].

such a combination of valid transactions and nonce that yields a desired result, he/she publishes this new block in the Bitcoin network and gets rewarded with newly created bitcoins.

The reward comes in form of a new transaction of (currently) 25 bitcoins that has no predecessor and is included as a special so-called *coinbase transaction* by the creator of the respective block. This coinbase transaction also includes the public key/bitcoin address of the creator and marks the first transaction of a new chain of Bitcoin transactions [4,5,17,20].

## 3   Related Work

We build upon already existing work by contributing the first user study with Bitcoin users. Eskandari et al. [8] presented a first look at the key management of Bitcoin by providing a set of evaluation criteria for Bitcoin wallets and a cognitive walkthrough [23] of selected wallets. The work by Eskandari et al. [8] can be considered a first look at the usability of Bitcoin.

Moore and Christin [19] conducted an empirical analysis of Bitcoin exchange risks. They examined the track record of 40 Bitcoin exchanges and found that 18 had been closed, with customer account balances often wiped out. They also found that popularity is a strong indicator to predict the lifetime of an exchange, i.e. popular exchanges have a longer lifespan.

Baur et al. [2] conducted exploratory interviews with individuals of distinct groups and found that most stakeholders perceived the ease of use still as rather low. They also found that the experienced usefulness varies according to the user group.

However, no empirical study has been performed to examine user perceptions of Bitcoin security, privacy and anonymity. For a cryptographic currency like Bitcoin, public key cryptography is required. Regarding the usability of key management and encryption in the context of e-mail various studies have shown that there are numerous usability issues regarding the successful usage of public key cryptography [11,12,22,24]. At this time, for neither domain a fully usable concept has been successful. Human aspects of key management have already been studied in other domains [11–13,22,24]. For the Bitcoin ecosystem however, secure key management alone is not sufficient, as communication is not channel-independent but an integral part of the security concept.

## 4   User Study Methodology

The goal of this study is to empirically investigate end user perceptions and behavior in the Bitcoin ecosystem with an emphasis on security practices as well as coin and key management with the involved security risks. We designed an online questionnaire and additionally conducted qualitative interviews. We derived specific research questions from already existing literature on Bitcoin (as discussed in Sect. 3) as well as from a qualitative content analysis of threads from online forums and mailing lists. Furthermore, we revised the available Bitcoin wallets[2] and their capabilities and used them as inspiration for our questions and the design of the security and privacy risk scenarios. We focus on Bitcoin as it was by far the most popular cryptographic currency at the time we conducted this study (July 2015). While the online survey was intended to broadly measure self-reported Bitcoin management behavior and risk perception, the interviews were conducted to get a deeper understanding on key usability issues, causes of common security incidents and if and how they managed to recover their keys.

### 4.1 Research Questions

We sought answers to the following questions regarding users' perceptions of Bitcoin management and Bitcoin-associated security risks:

- *Q1: What are the main usage scenarios of Bitcoin?*
- *Q2: How do participants manage their Bitcoins? What are participants' current practices and how do they deal with security, privacy and anonymity?*
- *Q3: How do participants perceive Bitcoin-associated security risks?*
- *Q4: What security breaches have affected users and how did they recover their Bitcoin keys and bitcoins?*
- *Q5: What are the main usability challenges that users have to deal with when using Bitcoin?*

We were also interested in categorizing CMTs in a way that users can quickly make an informed decision based on the level of security, privacy and control they prefer? Our categorization can be found in Appendix A.

## 5 Online Survey

We conducted our online survey over July 8–15, 2015. Our survey consisted of both closed- and open-ended questions and covered the following topics: (1) Bitcoin usage and management, (2) CMT choice and usage, (3) security, privacy, anonymity and backup behavior, (4) risk perception, and (5) demographics. The full set of questions is presented in Appendix B. The open-ended questions were coded independently by two researchers independently. After agreeing on a final set of codes, we coded all answer segments for the final analysis. Coding refers to categorizing qualitative data to facilitate analysis [18] and is a common practice in human-computer interaction research.

### 5.1 Recruitment

We hosted our survey at *soscisurvey.de*[3]. To restrict our participants to Bitcoin users only, we deliberately designed our study to exclude all non-Bitcoin users. As it is difficult to construct such a restricted sample on platforms like

---

[2] bitcoin.org.
[3] https://www.soscisurvey.de/.

Amazon Mechanical Turk, we decided to use Bitcoin mailing lists and forums for recruiting. Furthermore, we compensated participants in Bitcoin. The reward for a completed questionnaire was 4.2 m฿(= 0.0042  ฿ ≈ 1.22 USD at that time) After completing the survey, the participants were instructed to enter a valid Bitcoin address to receive the payment. This ensured that everyone who wanted to receive bitcoins as a reward is a Bitcoin user and hence exactly our target audience. Even participants who had not used Bitcoin before had to create a Bitcoin address to receive the compensation.

To motivate participants to spread the word and thus recruit further participants, we displayed a link for re-distribution at the end of the survey. All participants that recruited others received an additional 1 m฿ (≈ 0.29 USD). Table 1 shows that this additional incentive scheme was successful since we received a high number of participants this way. As Table 1 shows, the top 5 re-distributors of the link recruited about one quarter of the overall sample. Initially we distributed the link to our survey over the following channels: *bitcointalk.org* forum[4], *bitcoin-list* mailing list[5], *twitter.com*[6] and an Austrian bitcoin mailing list[7]. We aimed for maximum transparency to avoid that our call for participation would be misinterpreted as scam. Therefore, we proved on the initial page of our survey that we indeed hold a respectable amount of bitcoins[8], by providing our Bitcoin address[9] together with a signature with the according private key (see Appendix C for the signature).

We recruited 1,265 participants over July 8–15, 2015 via these channels. The total sample size after filtering out 275 participants due to incomplete or duplicated submission, or invalid entries, was 990. Of these, 85.2% claimed to be male (m), 10.5% claimed to be female (f). 4.3% of our participants preferred not to provide their gender. Ages ranged from 15 to 72 (median = 28.56). About half of our participants reported to have an IT-related background. According to the collected IP addresses, most of our participants filled out the survey in the US, followed by the UK and Germany. 7.6% accessed the survey site over Tor (Fig. 1). These numbers can of course be biased by VPN usage.

## 5.2   Validity of Our Dataset

Since the survey was designed to be anonymous and we only required a valid Bitcoin address, we had to take special care to avoid abuse. We semi-automatically verified the authenticity of our dataset and were able to exclude 116 submissions we suspected to be fraudulent, and 160 incomplete submissions. Nevertheless, there is still a chance that we missed some manual double submissions. However, due to our deployed countermeasures and the high quality of submitted data (e.g., the open-text questions) we suspect that the overall number

---

[4] https://bitcointalk.org/index.php?topic=1114149.0.

[5] http://sourceforge.net/p/bitcoin/mailman/bitcoin-list/?viewmonth=201507.

[6] https://twitter.com/bit_use.

[7] http://bitcoin-austria.at/.

[8] We purchased our 6.3965 BTC at https://coinfinity.co/.

[9] https://blockchain.info/address/12yeU5ymM67SL5UWVSwErAgwVwwaTd1Nma.

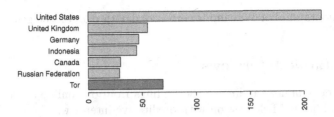

**Fig. 1.** Countries from which our participants accessed the survey site.

**Table 1.** Most refereed links.

| Reference | Occurrences | Reward in BTC/EUR/USD |
|-----------|-------------|-----------------------|
| 455975 | 91 | 0.0952/24.78/27.18 |
| 1295 | 58 | 0.0622/16.19/17.76 |
| 699324 | 51 | 0.0552/14.37/15.76 |
| 932181 | 28 | 0.0322/8.38/9.19 |
| 637623 | 21 | 0.0252/6.56/7.19 |

is negligible. Among other, we deployed the following countermeasure to make automation harder: *reCAPTCHA:* The last page of our survey contained a text box to enter a Bitcoin address for receiving the compensation and a Google reCAPTCHA. This together with the relatively low overall amount of compensations helped to mitigate fully automated submissions. Since reCAPTCHA adapts the difficulty depending on the source IP address, some Tor users complained about hard-to-solve CAPTCHAs. *Meta data:* The meta data like source IP address and information on the user's browser was used to pinpoint simple double submission attempts. *Time:* We considered submissions below a certain threshold fraudulent since it is impossible to provide reasonable answers under a certain lower bound. *Open-text questions:* In suspicious and borderline cases we manually checked the open-text questions to see if the user had meaningful contributions to the survey. *Reference links:* The reference links also provided a good insight when users attempted to submit multiple surveys and always referenced their initial survey. *Bitcoin address:* The uniqueness of a Bitcoin address was also an indicator for double submissions.

In case we detected double submissions, we accepted only the first submission for our dataset as well as for our compensation scheme. All subsequent submissions were excluded. In conclusion, we did not encounter fully automated submissions and that most fraudulent attempts can be attributed to simple manual double submissions. Moreover, the Bitcoin community has proven to be very forthcoming. There have been cases in which participants deliberately did not include Bitcoin addresses, and commenting that they would like to help by saving the reward in order to recruit more participants.

The demographics of our sample correspond with data on the general Bitcoin population[10].

## 6   Qualitative Interviews

To get a deeper understanding of the findings from our online survey, we conducted an additional field session with qualitative interviews.

### 6.1   Design and Recruitment

We recruited participants via a local Bitcoin mailing list and conducted a two-hour field session at a local bar that accepts bitcoins. All interviewees are regularly using Bitcoin and had previously completed our online questionnaire. Two researchers were present during the field session, one conducted the interview and the other one took notes. As all participants were very particular about preserving their privacy, we chose not to audio-record the interviews.

For the evaluation of our qualitative data, we focused on the exploration of ideas and insights of the participants. Some of the numbers gathered from the interviews will be used as rough indicators to discuss and complement the results from our quantitative survey. We interviewed 10 participants in total. All participants were male and frequent users of Bitcoin and other crypto-currencies. All of them reported to have an IT-related background. The purpose of the qualitative interviews was mainly to complement our quantitative results and to explain phenomena and trends from our online survey. After 10 participants, we reached saturation and little to no further insights were gained, so we concluded the study.

### 6.2   Coding

After the interviews, we went through the collected data and produced an initial set of codes. We traversed the data segments collected from each participant for each question and also included statements that did not directly evolve from a question. Two researchers performed the initial coding independently of each other to minimize the susceptibility of biased interpretation. After the initial coding process, we revised the retrieved codes and discussed recurring themes, patterns and interconnections. After agreeing on a final set of codes, we coded the entire interview data. We coded all data segments, regardless if they emerged directly from a question or a continuative discussion.

## 7   Results

In this section, we present an analysis of the participants' responses addressing our research questions defined in Sect. 4.1. At the beginning of each section we analyse the results from our online survey, whereas at the end we compare these results with our qualitative interviews and try to correlate and explain our findings.

---

[10] http://www.coindesk.com/new-coindesk-report-reveals-who-really-uses-bitcoin/.

## 7.1   General Bitcoin Usage (Q1)

Most participants reported to use Bitcoins for tips and donations (38.0%), followed by virtual goods, such as web hosting, online newspapers (33.3%), online shopping (27.5%), altcoins (26.5%), gambling (26.5%) and Bitcoin gift cards (19.9%). About 5% self-reported to buy or have bought drugs with bitcoins. 30.2% of our sample reported to use Bitcoin at least once a week, 25% stated that they use Bitcoin at least once a month and 19% at least once a day. The remainder of the participants indicated to use Bitcoin at least once a year or even less. These results suggest that the majority within our survey frequently uses Bitcoin.

We also asked our participants about the amount of bitcoins they are currently holding. About half of the participants did not want to specify. According to their reports, our sample holds approximately 8000 ฿ in total. The majority of users (70%) started to use Bitcoin between 2013 and 2015. 17% started between 2011 and 2012. 58.0% reported to use other crypto currencies in addition to Bitcoin, most frequently Dogecoin and Litecoin. The most popular Bitcoin exchanges in our sample are BTCE (20.9%), Bittrex (14.0%) and Bitstamp (13.0%). 11.4% of our participants are currently mining bitcoins. Most of them started mining after 2014. Many of those who started earlier have stopped mining as they currently consider it infeasible. 195 (19.7%) participants claimed to be running a full Bitcoin server that is reachable from the Internet. The top-mentioned reason for running a Bitcoin server was to support the Bitcoin network (60.5%), followed by fast transaction propagation (46.6%), network analysis (30.3%) and double-spending detection (26.1%).

All participants from our qualitative interviews are frequent Bitcoin users, and some of them are active in the local Bitcoin association. Most interviewees mentioned that the decentralized nature of Bitcoin was among the main reasons to start using Bitcoin. The second-most mentioned reason was simply curiosity. One participant who used to live in Crimea at the time the Ukrainian-Russian conflict started mentioned socio-political reasons. He used to work for a US company at that time and needed a safe and cheap option to receive his salary in Crimea. He furthermore wanted to make sure to not lose any money due to the annexation to the Russian Federation. In his opinion, Bitcoin was the best option and according to him, many people started using Bitcoin at that time in Crimea. Some participants also mined Bitcoins some years ago when it was still profitable to mine at small scale.

## 7.2   Practices of Bitcoin Management (Q2)

**Bitcoin Wallets and Backup Behavior.** Table 3 shows the most widely used Bitcoin wallets. The participants could mention multiple wallets as it is a common scenario that users use more than one wallet. The table also shows the number of participants from our sample who use a certain wallet as well as the percentage. Furthermore, Table 4 shows whether the users protect their wallets with a password and if these wallets are encrypted. Our findings show that the majority of users protect their wallets with a password. In case of web clients, we observed a lack of background knowledge. For example, 47.7% of Coinbase users in our sample say that their wallet is encrypted and 34% claim that they do not know if it is encrypted. We observed a similar trend for Xapo which is the third-most used wallet in our sample. Just like Coinbase, it is also a web-hosted tool and, similarly to Coinbase, only about half of the users say it is encrypted and about a third does not know if it is encrypted. Regarding backups, only a third of Coinbase users and 43% of Xapo users backup their wallets. 33.9% of Coinbase and 28.5% of Xapo users do not know whether their wallet is backed up. We also found that Bitcoin users with more than 0.42₿ (100 USD) do not backup their CMT more often than users with less bitcoins. This effect is statistically significant in our sample ($\chi^2(1) = 5.1, p = 0.02$).

We also asked our participants whether they create additional backups in case their primary backup gets lost or stolen. In our sample, Bitcoin Core users have the highest rate of additional backups. 64% of them indicated to make a secondary backup of their wallet. Table 2 shows self-reported properties of wallet backups. According to our data, none of our participants stores a backup on an air-gapped computer. The most reported backup properties were encryption and password protection. According to our sample, 197 backups are stored in a cloud.

59.7% of our participants only use one wallet to manage their bitcoins. 22.7% use two, and 10.6% use three wallets. The remaining 7% use four or more wallets. The maximum number of wallets a participant reported to use was 14. This participant justified this high number by reporting that he wanted to try out the wallets before choosing those that met his requirements best. About half of our participants who used a web client did this exclusively to manage their bitcoins. The other half used a web client in addition to a local client. To our surprise our results show that most coins of our participants are stored in Armory[11]. The Armory users in our sample have about 3818 ₿ in their Armorys, where the top five users reported to have 2,000 ₿, 885 ₿, 300 ₿, 230 ₿ and 150 ₿. The highest reported number of bitcoins stored in a participant's web client was 100 ₿. The reported sum of all coins stored in Coinbase is 238 ₿, in Xapo it is 157 ₿. Figure 2 illustrates the accumulated bitcoins per wallet as reported by our participants.

**Anonymity.** We found that 32.3% of our participants think that Bitcoin is per-se anonymous while it is in fact only pseudonymous. 47% thinks that Bitcoin is not per-se anonymous but can be used anonymously. However, about 80% think that it is possible to follow their transactions. 25% reported to have used Bitcoin over Tor to preserve their anonymity.

We also asked participants if they take any additional steps to stay anonymous. 18% reported to frequently apply methods to stay anonymous on the Bitcoin network. Most of them reported to use Bitcoin over Tor followed by multiple addresses, mixing services, multiple wallets and VPN services. As shown

---

[11] https://bitcoinarmory.com/.

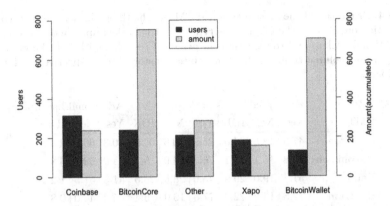

**Fig. 2.** Self-reported wallet usage and accumulated hosted bitcoins per wallet.

**Table 2.** Backup properties in absolute mentions in descending order; a user can have multiple wallets and multiple backups.

| Backup properties | Mentions |
|---|---|
| My backup is encrypted | 662 |
| My backup is password protected | 629 |
| My backup is stored on external storage (e.g. USB drive) | 430 |
| My backup is stored on paper | 334 |
| My backup is stored in the cloud (e.g. Dropbox) | 197 |
| My backup is stored on an air-gapped device | 0 |

**Table 3.** Properties of the most frequently used wallets mentioned by our participants.

| CMT | Number | Percent | Ƀ |
|---|---|---|---|
| Coinbase | 314 | 31.7 | 238 |
| Bitcoin core | 236 | 23.8 | 752 |
| Xapo | 179 | 18.1 | 157 |
| Electrum | 125 | 12.6 | 226 |
| MyCelium | 97 | 9.8 | 62 |

by Biryukov et al. [1,3] using Bitcoin over Tor creates an attack vector for deterministic and stealthy man-in-the-middle attacks and fingerprinting.

## 7.3   Risk Perception (Q3)

We were also interested in user perceptions of risks associated with Bitcoin. We provided the participants with 11 risk scenarios. We selected the risk scenarios based on findings from scientific literature and evidence from online resources.

**Table 4.** Properties of the most mentioned CMTs. The three blocked columns contain information on whether the CMT is encrypted, if it is backed up, whether there exists an additional backup and the mentions in percent (Yes, No and I don't know (IDK)). The rightmost column contains the sum of bitcoins stored in a respective CMT by our participants.

| CMT | Encrypted? | | | Backup? | | | Additional backup? | | |
|---|---|---|---|---|---|---|---|---|---|
| | Yes | No | IDK | Yes | No | IDK | Yes | No | IDK |
| Coinbase | 47.5 | 18.5 | 34.0 | 35.5 | 30.6 | 33.9 | 30.3 | 66.9 | 2.8 |
| Bitcoin core | 72.8 | 16.1 | 11.1 | 76.3 | 14.0 | 9.7 | 64.0 | 32.2 | 3.8 |
| Xapo | 51.4 | 19.0 | 29.9 | 43.0 | 28.5 | 28.5 | 41.3 | 57.5 | 1.2 |
| Electrum | 72.8 | 15.2 | 22.0 | 77.6 | 16.0 | 6.4 | 55.2 | 44.0 | 0.8 |
| MyCelium | 61.9 | 21.6 | 16.5 | 83.5 | 12.4 | 4.1 | 52.6 | 47.2 | 0.2 |

For each risk scenario, we provided an easy-to-understand description and asked the participants whether they think the risk is likely or unlikely to occur. Figure 3 shows the participants' risk estimation. Our results show that the participants consider value fluctuation as the highest risk, followed by vulnerabilities in hosted wallets and Bitcoin theft via malware. Our participants estimated the risk for cryptographic flaws as the lowest, followed by double-spending attacks and DoS attacks on the Bitcoin network.

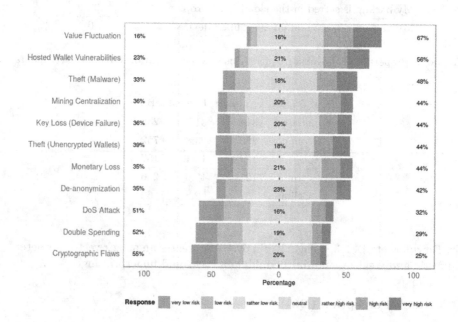

**Fig. 3.** User perceptions of risk scenarios in percentage of participants ($N = 990$).

## 7.4   Security Breaches (Q4)

About 22.5% indicated to have lost bitcoins or Bitcoin keys at least once. Of those, 43.2% mentioned that it was their own fault (e.g., formatted hard drive or lost a physical device with Bitcoin keys). 26.5% reported that their loss stemmed from a hardware failure (e.g., a broken hard drive), followed by software failure (24.4%; e.g. keyfile corruption) and security breaches (18% e.g., malware, hacker).

The majority (77.6%) among those who lost bitcoins did not want to indicate whether they were able to recover their keys. Of those who provided an answer, 65% were not able to recover their keys. Overall, our participants reported to have lost about 660.6873 bitcoins. However, it must be taken into account that we did not ask when the coins were lost. Hence, interpreting this result we must take into consideration that the Bitcoin exchange rate is highly volatile and it is therefore hard to provide an overall estimation in USD. About 40% of our participants reported to have lost money due to a self-classified major security breach. 13.1% of our overall sample reported to have lost bitcoins in HYIPS (high-yield investment programs) and pyramid schemes. 7.9% lost money at Mt. Gox.

We also gave our participants the opportunity to describe how they dealt with the incident. Most participants stated that they did not do anything to recover their keys and simply accepted the loss. Some argued that the financial loss was not worth the effort to take further steps or that they felt helpless as they didn't know what to do. Those who actually took action most frequently mentioned that they filed claims and contacted the exchange or online wallet provider. Those who lost money to a malicious online wallet reported to have moved to other types of wallets instead of hosted/online wallets. The participants who lost money in HYIPS mostly stated that they started to use less risky investments and learned from their previous mistakes. Irrespective of the security breach, many participants reported to have spread the word over forums on the Internet and shared their experiences with other affected users.

*Participant Statements*

- *"I follow the 'do not invest more than you're ready to lose' rule."* (P3848)
- *"I just had to accept that my money was stolen ... and that I learned my lesson to never use exchanges as wallets. Keep everything in your own hand."* (P3763)
- *"Just learned from it. It was exceedingly stupid on my part."* (P853)

Eight participants from our qualitative interviews reported that they have already experienced an intentional or accidental key and/or Bitcoin loss. Three participants were affected from the Mt. Gox security breach and two of them reported to have filed a claim on Kraken[12]. One participant reported to have lost a *physical* Casascius[13] Bitcoin but then stopped searching for it as it was

---

[12]  https://www.kraken.com/.
[13]  https://www.casascius.com/.

only worth about 9 USD at that time. Others also mentioned to have lost their keys due to device failure, corrupted HDDs, or software failure.

## 7.5  Perceptions of Usability (Q5)

Even though most participants of our qualitative interviews were very much concerned about security and privacy aspects of Bitcoin management, eight of them said that they would recommend web wallets and deterministic wallets to non-tech-savvy Bitcoin users. Convenience and easiness of use were highlighted as the main benefits. One participant said that he would definitely recommend a wallet where the private key is stored on a central server to make key recovery easier and to obviate the need for comprehensive backups as well as that mnemonics would help. Six participants also said that they would recommend MyCelium[14] as the most usable wallet. Those who had already used MyCelium consider the paper backup procedure as the most usable and secure way. To create a paper backup with MyCelium, the user has to print out a template that contains some parts of the key and then lets the user fill out the empty spots manually. Some participants expressed initial discomfort when they used paper wallets.

Most interviewees also highlighted the need for fundamental education in early years of childhood. P2 said that Bitcoin is inherently complex, that the fundamental idea of public key cryptography should be taught in school and monetary systems are a matter of culture.

Two participants also highlighted that user interfaces should be simplified and minimalized. Many participants stated that for a fast proliferation of Bitcoin, simple and intuitive UIs are more important than security. They argued that computers proliferated even though most people do not know how computers work and that security is not necessarily an argument for large-scale adoption. They provided examples such as cars in the 1940s, computers, credit cards and WhatsApp. They also said that the amount of money that is circulating in the Bitcoin network is low enough to take the risk of loosing it and compared this scenario to the risk of loosing cash. Some participants also proposed a dedicated device with an intuitive UI for key management and think that such an artifact would be the most secure and usable option.

*Participant Statements*

– *"It somehow didn't feel right for me to go out of the digital realm."* (P6 on paper wallets)
– *"Children learn about our monetary system in their very early days in primary school. This is why society knows how to use cash and credit cards. I'm sure it could be the same thing with a decentralized crypto-currency."* (P7)

---

[14] https://mycelium.com/.

# 8   Discussion

The goal of this paper was to answer the research questions provided in Sect. 4.1 in order to understand how users interact with the Bitcoin ecosystem. As this is the first-ever user study focused on user experiences with Bitcoin security and privacy, we gathered useful insights. In the following we discuss our results in the context of already existing works in the field.

Regarding Bitcoin management tools and practices (Q2), we found that two of the most widely used CMTs were web-hosted solutions that obviate the need for users to deal with key management and backups. Our results show that our participants had clear preferences regarding their choice of CMT. In contrary, this is not the case for Bitcoin exchanges. Our data shows that the Bitcoin exchanges chosen by our participants were almost evenly distributed. Even though our data reveals a clear tendency towards web-hosted solutions, these CMTs do not host the majority of our participants' bitcoins. According to our participants' self-reported data, the highest amount of accumulated bitcoins is hosted in Armory. At the time of writing, if used correctly, Armory is one of the most secure solutions.

For the two most widely used web-hosted CMTs, about a third of our participants are unaware of whether their wallet is encrypted or backed up. In such a scenario, users shift responsibilities to a third party. Even though this seems to be a convenient and usable solution for non-expert users, it implies that the user trusts these third parties to take care of their security. About 50% of web client users indicated to use an additional local client to store their virtual assets. According to our results, users that have a higher number of bitcoins do not necessarily back up their wallets more often. Also, MyCelium users back up their wallets more often than others. Hence we conclude that backup motivation and respectively fatigue depend highly on usability and not on the number of coins.

As the answer to Q4 indicates, participants have already lost money to malicious hosted-wallet providers. Also, our participants perceived vulnerabilities in hosted wallets as the second highest among our risk scenarios (Q5). Some participants from our qualitative interviews said that they would recommend inexperienced users to start with a hosted wallet due to the usability benefits as for most other solutions users are required to have at least a basic understanding of the underlying basics of Bitcoin and the blockchain.

Bitcoin is a pseudonymous system, whereas a wide-spread myth says that it is per-se anonymous. More than a third of our participants still believe in this myth and reported that they think that Bitcoin is fully anonymous. About half of our participants are aware that Bitcoin is not per-se anonymous, but that it can be used anonymously. Regarding anonymity measures, many users reported to use Bitcoin over Tor, which in fact creates an attack vector for deterministic and stealthy MITM attacks, as shown in [3].

Our results also suggest that our participants trust the cryptography behind Bitcoin and are aware of risks according to value fluctuation and software vulnerabilities. Poor usability and the lack of knowledge are major contributors to security failures. Almost a fourth of our participants indicated that they had already lost bitcoins or Bitcoin keys at least once (Q5). To our surprise, almost half of those who lost bitcoins due to a self-induced error which indicates that state of the art CMTs are sometimes still difficult to use or require users to manually take care of security tasks, such as backups and encryption. Our results also indicate that the Bitcoin ecosystem is mostly utilized for tipping and donations as well as acquiring digital goods, but to some extend also for criminal activity and adventurous gambling.

# 9   Conclusion

In this work we presented the first user study to examine how users interact with the Bitcoin ecosystem in terms of security and privacy. We conducted an online survey with 990 Bitcoin users and qualitative interviews with a subset of 10 participants. Furthermore, we introduced the term *Coin Management Tools (CMTs)* to describe tools that let users manage their virtual assets (keys) and interact with the Bitcoin network. Additionally, we proposed a method for categorizing CMTs according to the degree of control and verifiability a user can exercise with this client.

We found that managing bitcoins is still a major challenge for many users, as many of them do not apply sufficient security measures such as encryption and backups. We found that many participants were not even aware of security features provided by their used CMT. Two of the most widely used CMTs among our participants were web-hosted solutions. About half of their users reported to use such solutions exclusively, while the other half also used local clients. Even though web clients ought to be a usable and convenient solution, they require a certain level of trust and shift the responsibilities of encryption and managing backups to a third party. We also found that 22.5% of our participants have already experienced security breaches and lost bitcoins. About half of them mentioned a self-induced error as the reason, which highlights that users find it still difficult to manage their bitcoins in a secure way.

We believe that our insights and suggestions are an important first step towards improving the usability of Bitcoin security. In order to guarantee secure interactions with the Bitcoin ecosystem to both expert and non-expert users, we must re-think the concept of Bitcoin management, since it is more than just the secure handling of secret keys. Bitcoin is a decentralized system where the interactions between peers and the propagation and verification of messages and data is important. If this aspect is ignored, Bitcoin would just consist of signed numbers without value.

**Acknowledgements.** This research was funded by COMET K1, FFG – Austrian Research Promotion Agency and by FFG Bridge Early Stage 846573 A2Bit. We would also like to thank Martin Mulazzani, Artemios G. Voyiatzis and Matthew Smith for their useful comments and feedback. Furthermore, we would like to thank Elizabeth Stobert for her valuable feedback and for her help in recruiting participants.

# A     CMT Categorization

In this section we discuss the term *Coin Management Tool* and provide a methodology to categorize CMTs according to the degree of control and verifiability a user can exercise with his respective client. The proposed scheme is tailored to Bitcoin-like cryptocurrencies, but explicitly designed in an utmost generic way so that it can be applied to other derived cryptocurrencies as long as they are not fundamentally different in their design. Our approach used the evaluation framework from [8] as a starting point. A categorization according to our scheme allows users to quickly distinguish clients according to their underlying security model and hence allows users to make an informed decision on the level of confidence and trust they can put into an individual client.

## A.1     Definitions

When Bitcoin was in its infancy *bitcoind* was the only available Bitcoin client which performed all required tasks: *mining management, P2P network communication and blockchain management, key management* and *virtual asset management*. With the increased popularity of Bitcoin and cryptocurrencies in general, more and more software was developed which focused on a subset of individual tasks of the original implementation. Moreover, the design of Bitcoin allows users to use it even if they do not run mining software or a full P2P client (full node). As a result there exists software with varying feature sets where the handling of public-private key pairs is the most sensitive and hence the most common core feature. A Bitcoin wallet was originally defined as a collection of private keys[15]. Since this definition is very narrow, we introduced the broader definition of a *Coin Management Tool* (CMT) to account for the other areas without whom most cryptocurrencies would not work. Especially the network and blockchain layer of Bitcoin and other cryptocurrencies is not only important for the integrity of the system as a whole, but has a significant impact on the security and privacy of each and every end user.

## A.2     Categorization

To categorize CMTs, we first identified critical CMT tasks which are directly related to security and privacy issues. This covers aspects regarding key management like generating keys/addresses and signing transactions, as well as P2P network communication and blockchain management like handling connections as well as verifying and storing the blockchain. These core tasks can be used to divide CMTs into five different categories. A client can be in more than one category depending on its configuration.

- **cat. 0:** A client which runs on a user-controlled device and is able to perform key management operations, but cannot perform any P2P network

---

[15] https://en.bitcoin.it/wiki/Wallet.

communication. Therefore, it is not a stand-alone solution. This includes some dedicated *hardware clients/wallets* and *cold-storage* clients which require a second online device for transaction processing.

- **cat. I:** A client which runs on a user-controlled device and performs all P2P network communication and blockchain verification related tasks, keeps a copy of the full blockchain, is able to perform all key management related operations and executes the mining algorithm. In other words, this is a client which can perform all required tasks to operate a cryptographic currency (e.g., the Bitcoin core implementation *bitcoind* when the option *setgenerate true* is set).
- **cat. II:** A client which runs on a user-controlled device and performs all P2P tasks related to network communication and blockchain verification, keeps a copy of the full blockchain and is able to perform all key management related operations. This type of client is sometimes referred to as *thick-client* or *full-node*.
- **cat. III:** A client which runs on a user-controlled device and performs certain P2P tasks related to network communication and blockchain verification but does not keep a copy of the full blockchain, although, it is able to perform all key- management-related operations. This type of client is sometimes referred to as *thin-client* or *mobile-client/wallet* and includes so-called SPV-clients/wallets (Simplified Payment Verification) e.g., Electrum.
- **cat. IV:** A client which does not run on a user-controlled device and where all tasks are performed by a trusted third party on behalf of the user. This type of client is sometimes referred to as *hosted-* or *web-client/wallet*. Thereby it is not relevant if the key management is handled in the browser (e.g., via JavaScript) since this would require the user to download (and verify) the script code from the website of the third party every time he/she wants to use it.

# B     Interview Questions

Questions with answer options as "( )" are multiple choice checkboxes whereas answer possibilities marked alphabetical e.g. "a)" are single selections.

## B.1     BTC Demographics

**Q1** Please input which year you started using Bitcoin:
a) 2009 b) 2010 c) 2011 d) 2012 e) 2013 f) 2014 g) 2015

**Q2** Select which main features are responsible for you using Bitcoin (multiple selections possible):
( ) The opportunity of financial gain
( ) Curiosity
( ) Anonymous nature
( ) Decentralized nature
( ) A friend/colleague suggested to me to start using Bitcoin

( ) The possibility to internationally transfer money with relatively low fee
( ) The possibility to accept bitcoins for my services or for my products
( ) Other:

**Q3** What is the estimated sum of bitcoins you are holding?
   *a*) I hold approximately *b*) I do not want to specify

**Q4** Please provide what services or products you pay for with bitcoins (multiple selections possible):
( ) Bars, restaurants
( ) Bitcoin gift cards
( ) Donations, tipping
( ) Drugs
( ) Gambling sites
( ) Hotels, travel
( ) Online marketplaces and auctions
( ) Online shopping (Newegg, ...)
( ) Altcoin (e.g. Litecoin, ...)
( ) Physical stores that accept bitcoins
( ) Underground marketplaces
( ) Virtual goods (webhosting, online newspapers, ...)
( ) Medium for currency exchange
( ) Other:

**Q5** What do you think are the most likely risks associated with Bitcoin?

**Q6** Please select the crypto currencies you are holding or using besides Bitcoin (multiple selections possible):
( ) I do not use other crypto currencies
( ) BanxShares
( ) BitShares
( ) BlackCoin
( ) Bytecoin
( ) Counterparty
( ) Dash
( ) Dogecoin
( ) Litecoin
( ) MaidSafeCoin
( ) MonaCoin
( ) Monero
( ) Namecoin
( ) Nxt
( ) Peercoin
( ) Primecoin
( ) Ripple
( ) Startcoin
( ) Stellar
( ) SuperNET

( ) Vertcoin
( ) YbCoin
( ) Other

**Q7** Select the Bitcoin exchanges you have used in the past or you are using on regularly (multiple selections possible):
( ) None
( ) BanxIO
( ) Bitcoin Exchange Thailand
( ) Bittrex
( ) Bitcoin Indonesia
( ) bitcoin.de
( ) Bitfinex
( ) Bitstamp
( ) BitX South Africa
( ) BTC-e
( ) BTC38
( ) BTCChina
( ) CCEDK
( ) Cryptsy
( ) Gatecoin
( ) hibtc
( ) Kraken
( ) Mt. Gox
( ) OKCoin
( ) Poloniex
( ) QuadrigaCX
( ) The Rock Trading
( ) VirWox
( ) Other:

**Q8** What do you think are the greatest benefits of Bitcoin?
**Q9** How often do you perform Bitcoin transactions?
   a) At least once a day b) At least once a week c) At least once a month
   d) At least once every six months e) At least once a year f) Less than once a year

## B.2    BTC Wallets

**Q10** Please tick which wallets you are currently using (multiple selections possible):
( ) Airbitz
( ) Armory
( ) Bitcoin Core
( ) Bitcoin Wallet (Schildbach Wallet)
( ) BitGo

( ) Bither
( ) breadwallet
( ) Circle
( ) Coinapult
( ) Coinbase
( ) Coinkite
( ) Coinomi
( ) Electrum
( ) Green Address
( ) Hive
( ) Ledger Nano
( ) mSIGNA
( ) MultiBit
( ) Mycelium
( ) Ninki
( ) TREZOR
( ) Xapo
( ) Not in list

**Q11** Why did you choose to use multiple wallets to manage your bitcoins?

## B.3   Wallet Usage

For every selected wallet in Q10 we asked the following questions.

**Q12** Why did you choose ⟨wallet-name⟩ to manage your Bitcoins?
**Q13** How many bitcoins do you have approximately in this wallet?
   *a)* I hold approximately ⟨textfield⟩ bitcoins. *b)* I do not want to specify
**Q14** Is this wallet password protected?
   *a)* Yes *b)* No *c)* I do not care *d)* I do not know
**Q15** Is this wallet encrypted?
   *a)* Yes *b)* No *c)* I do not care *d)* I do not know
**Q16** Is this wallet backed up?
   *a)* Yes *b)* No *c)* I do not know

## B.4   BTC Mining

**Q17** Are you currently mining bitcoins?
   *a)* Yes, since *b)* No, but I have mined from-to *c)* No, I have never mined bitcoins
**Q18** How many bitcoins have you mined in total?
   *a)* I mined approximately *b)* I do not want to specify
**Q19** Do you or have you participated in mining pools?
   *a)* Yes *b)* No

**Q20** Please tick the names of the mining pools you have or are participating in (multiple mentions possible):
( ) 21 Inc.
( ) AntPool
( ) Bitcoin Affiliate Network
( ) BitFury
( ) BitMinter
( ) Bitsolo
( ) BTCChina Pool
( ) BTC Guild
( ) BTC Nuggets
( ) BW.COM
( ) EclipseMC
( ) Eligius
( ) F2Pool
( ) GHash.IO
( ) Kano CKPool
( ) KnCMiner
( ) MegaBigPower
( ) P2Pool
( ) Slush
( ) Telco 214
( ) Other:

## B.5    BTC Server

**Q21** Do you run a full Bitcoin server that is reachable for others from the Internet?
  *a)* Yes *b)* No

**Q22** Please provide some reasons on why you operate a full Bitcoin server (multiple selections possible):
( ) Fast transaction propagation
( ) Double-spending detection
( ) Network analysis
( ) Support the Bitcoin network
( ) Other

## B.6    BTC Security Risks

**Q23** How would you estimate the risk of monetary loss for Bitcoin compared to credit cards?
  (7 Point Likert-Scale from "High" to "Low")

**Q24** How high do you think is the risk of becoming a victim of a successful double spending attack?
  (7 Point Likert-Scale from "High" to "Low")

**Q25** How high or low would you estimate the risk for malware that steals your Bitcoins?
(7 Point Likert-Scale from "High" to "Low")

**Q26** How would you estimate the risk of monetary theft in case the device with your wallet gets lost or stolen?
(7 Point Likert-Scale from "High" to "Low")

**Q27** How would you estimate the risk of de-anonymization?
(7 Point Likert-Scale from "High" to "Low")

**Q28** How high do you think the risk of cryptographic flaws is?
(7 Point Likert-Scale from "High" to "Low")

**Q29** How high do you think is the risk of security vulnerabilities in hosted/web wallets or Exchange services?
(7 Point Likert-Scale from "High" to "Low")

**Q30** How high do you think is the risk of key loss due to a device failure?
(7 Point Likert-Scale from "High" to "Low")

**Q31** How high do you think is the risk that the Bitcoin network is temporarily not available?
(7 Point Likert-Scale from "High" to "Low")

**Q32** How high do you think is the risk of a centralization of mining?
(7 Point Likert-Scale from "High" to "Low")

**Q33** How high do you think is the risk of a strong fluctuation in the Bitcoin exchange rate (e.g. BTC to USD and vice versa)?
(7 Point Likert-Scale from "High" to "Low")

## B.7    BTC Anonymity

**Q34** Do you think that Bitcoin usage is anonymous?
*a)* Yes, Bitcoin is fully anonymous *b)* No, Bitcoin is not anonymous *c)* Not per se, but it can be used in an anonymous manner

**Q35** Do you think it is possible to follow your transactions?
*a)* Yes *b)* No

**Q36** Have you ever used Bitcoin over Tor<b title = "Tor is free software and an open network that helps you defend against traffic analysis, a form of network surveillance that threatens personal freedom and privacy, confidential business activities and relationships, and state security. More info at www. torproject.org"?
*a)* Yes *b)* No

**Q37** Do you take additional steps to ensure your privacy using Bitcoin?
*a)* Yes *b)* No

## B.8    BTC Security Breaches

**Q38** Have you ever lost your bitcoins or Bitcoin keys?
   *a*) Yes *b*) No
**Q39** Please select the reason for your key/Bitcoin loss (multiple selections possible):
   ( ) Hardware failure (e.g. hard drive broke, etc.)
   ( ) Software failure (e.g. keyfile corruption, etc.)
   ( ) Self induced event (e.g. hard drive formatted, physical device lost, etc.)
   ( ) Malicious event (e.g. malware, hacker, etc.)
   ( ) Other

**Q40** Have you been able to recover your keys?
   *a*) Yes, *b*) No,
**Q41** How many bitcoins did you loose due to this incident?
   *a*) bitcoins *b*) I do not want to specify
**Q42** Please select the security incidents you have been affected by (multiple selections possible):
   ( ) None
   ( ) Mt. Gox incident
   ( ) Silk Road bust
   ( ) inputs.io hack
   ( ) Pony botnet malware
   ( ) Pyramid schemes/HYIPS (High yield investment programs)
   ( ) Mining hardware scams (Labcoin, Active Mining Corporation, Ice Drill, AsicMiningEquipment.com Dragon-Miner.com, ...)
   ( ) Mining pool scams
   ( ) Scam wallets
   ( ) Bitcoin exchange scam
   ( ) Other:

**Q43** How did you deal with the incident?
**Q44** What was the approximate value of your lost bitcoins in USD?
   *a*) USD *b*) I do not want to specify *c*) I do not know

## B.9    Demographics

**Q45** Please provide your age:
**Q45** Please provide your gender:
   *a*) Female *b*) Male *c*) Do not want to specify
**Q46** Please select your highest completed level of education:
   *a*) Did Not Complete High School *b*) High School/GED *c*) Some College *d*) Bachelor's Degree *e*) Master's Degree *f*) Advanced Graduate work or Ph.D. *g*) Not Sure
**Q47** Do you work or study in a computer science related field?
   *a*) Yes *b*) No

**Q48** How would you describe yourself in terms of privacy behaviour?
A continouos slider between "I am not concerned about my privacy" and "I would describe myself as a privacy fundamentalist"

## B.10   End

**Q49** You can enter your Bitcoin address in the textfield below. Please make sure that your address is correct in order to receive your incentive.

**Q49** This is the place where you can provide suggestions, complaints or any other information we may have forgotten to ask in the questionnaire.

## C   Address Signature

```
./bitcoin-cli signmessage 12yeU5ymM67SL5UWVSwErAgwVwwaTd1Nma\
''https://www.soscisurvey.de/BTC_study/"
HzzNxFmeRhbhAwVZ4DsraBkXkW7JYjOOtAlIPAnHB2z5P12eddFilWXJmwGm\
PkgS/v8W0DNr0Z1qLwroPbWWMoE=
```

## D   Reference link issue

We had a problem in our implementation of this last page of the survey which also showed the link to the survey containing a random reference which should identify this particular participant in our rewarding scheme. If the CAPTCHA was not solved successfully the side reloads itself and would also calculate and show a different reference link. The references link will only be stored and linked to this particular participant if the CAPTCHA is entered correctly. Therefore, all users which just copied the first link and then entered a wrong CAPTCHA distributed a link we where not able to attribute correctly at the end of the survey.

## References

1. Biryukov, A., Khovratovich, D., Pustogarov, I.: Deanonymisation of clients in Bitcoin P2P network. CoRR, abs/1405.7418 (2014)
2. Baur, A.W., Bühler, J., Bick, M., Bonorden, C.S.: Cryptocurrencies as a disruption? Empirical findings on user adoption and future potential of bitcoin and co. In: Janssen, M., Mäntymäki, M., Hidders, J., Klievink, B., Lamersdorf, W., Loenen, B., Zuiderwijk, A. (eds.) I3E 2015. LNCS, vol. 9373, pp. 63–80. Springer, Cham (2015). doi:10.1007/978-3-319-25013-7_6
3. Biryukov, A., Pustogarov, I.: Bitcoin over Tor isn't a good idea. arXiv preprint arXiv:1410.6079 (2014)
4. Bitcoin Community: Bitcoin developer guide, October 2014. Accessed 14 Oct 2014
5. Bitcoin Community: Bitcoin protocol specification, October 2014. Accessed 14 Oct 2014
6. Blockchain.info: Bitcoin currency statistics, April 2014. Accessed 05 Apr 2014

7. Bonneau, J., Miller, A., Clark, J., Narayanan, A., Kroll, J.A., Felten, E.W.: SoK: research perspectives and challenges for Bitcoin and cryptocurrencies (2015)
8. Eskandari, S., Barrera, D., Stobert, E., Clark, J.: A first look at the usability of Bitcoin key management. In: Workshop on Usable Security (USEC) (2015)
9. Reid, F., Harrigan, M.: An analysis of anonymity in the Bitcoin system. In: 2011 IEEE International Conference on Privacy, Security, Risk, and Trust, and IEEE International Conference on Social Computing (2011)
10. Garay, J., Kiayias, A., Leonardos, N.: The Bitcoin backbone protocol: analysis and applications. In: Oswald, E., Fischlin, M. (eds.) EUROCRYPT 2015. LNCS, vol. 9057, pp. 281–310. Springer, Heidelberg (2015). doi:10.1007/978-3-662-46803-6_10
11. Garfinkel, S.L., Margrave, D., Schiller, J.I., Nordlander, E., Miller, R.C.: How to make secure email easier to use. In: Proceedings of the SIGCHI Conference on Human Factors in Computing Systems, pp. 701–710. ACM (2005)
12. Garfinkel, S.L., Miller, R.C.: Johnny 2: a user test of key continuity management with S/MIME and outlook express. In: Proceedings of the 2005 Symposium on Usable Privacy and Security, pp. 13–24. ACM (2005)
13. Gaw, S., Felten, E.W., Fernandez-Kelly, P.: Secrecy, flagging, and paranoia: adoption criteria in encrypted email. In: Proceedings of the SIGCHI Conference on Human Factors in Computing Systems, pp. 591–600. ACM (2006)
14. Gervais, A., Ritzdorf, H., Karame, G.O., Capkun, S.: Tampering with the delivery of blocks and transactions in Bitcoin. Technical report, Cryptology ePrint Archive, Report 2015/578 (2015). http://eprint.iacr.org
15. Goldfeder, S., Gennaro, R., Kalodner, H., Bonneau, J., Kroll, J., Felten, E.W., Narayanan, A.: Securing Bitcoin wallets via a new DSA/ECDSA threshold signature scheme. Accessed 09 June 2015
16. Heilman, E., Kendler, A., Zohar, A., Goldberg, S.: Eclipse attacks on Bitcoin's peer-to-peer network. In: 24th USENIX Security Symposium (USENIX Security 15), Washington, D.C., pp. 129–144. USENIX Association, August 2015
17. Okupski, K.: Bitcoin protocol specification, October 2014. Accessed 14 Oct 2014
18. Lazar, J., Feng, J.H., Hochheiser, H.: Research Methods in Human-Computer Interaction. Wiley, Hoboken (2010)
19. Moore, T., Christin, N.: Beware the middleman: empirical analysis of Bitcoin-exchange risk. In: Sadeghi, A.-R. (ed.) FC 2013. LNCS, vol. 7859, pp. 25–33. Springer, Heidelberg (2013). doi:10.1007/978-3-642-39884-1_3
20. Nakamoto, S.: Bitcoin: a peer-to-peer electronic cash system, December 2008
21. NIST: FIPS 180–4: Secure Hash Standard (SHS), March 2012
22. Sheng, S., Broderick, L., Koranda, C.A., Hyland, J.J.: Why Johnny still can't encrypt: evaluating the usability of email encryption software. In: Symposium on Usable Privacy and Security (2006)
23. Wharton, C., Rieman, J., Lewis, C., Polson, P.: The cognitive walkthrough method: a practitioner's guide. In: Usability Inspection Methods, pp. 105–140. Wiley (1994)
24. Whitten, A., Tygar, J.D.: Why Johnny can't encrypt: a usability evaluation of PGP 5.0. In: Usenix Security, vol. 1999 (1999)

# Refund Attacks on Bitcoin's Payment Protocol

Patrick McCorry[✉], Siamak F. Shahandashti, and Feng Hao

School of Computing Science, Newcastle University, Newcastle upon Tyne, UK
{patrick.mccorry,siamak.shahandashti,feng.hao}@ncl.ac.uk

**Abstract.** BIP70 is a community-accepted Payment Protocol standard that governs how merchants and customers perform payments in Bitcoin. This standard is supported by most major wallets and the two dominant Payment Processors: Coinbase and BitPay, who collectively provide the infrastructure for accepting Bitcoin as a form of payment to more than 100,000 merchants. In this paper, we present new attacks on the Payment Protocol, which affect all BIP70 merchants. The *Silkroad Trader* attack highlights an authentication vulnerability in the Payment Protocol while the *Marketplace Trader* attack exploits the refund policies of existing Payment Processors. Both attacks have been experimentally verified on real-life merchants using a modified Bitcoin wallet. The attacks have been acknowledged by both Coinbase and Bitpay with temporary mitigation measures put in place. However, to fully address the identified issues will require revising the BIP70 standard. We present a concrete proposal to revise BIP70 by providing the merchant with publicly verifiable evidence to prevent both attacks.

## 1 Introduction

Bitcoin [20], the world's first successful crypto-currency, is increasingly becoming a popular method of payment for e-commerce due to low transaction fees and the ease of use supplied by third party Payment Processors. BitPay and Coinbase are currently the two dominant Payment Processors that handle Bitcoin payments for more than 100,000 merchants. Their customers include Dell, Microsoft, Overstock, Shopify, Paypal and CeX. This demonstrates that large organisations are placing trust in Bitcoin as a viable form of payment. In fact, Overstock claimed to have made $3 million worth of Bitcoin sales in 2014 [12]. These Payment Processors are attractive due to their ability to convert bitcoins into fiat currency instantly which removes the risk involved in Bitcoin's price volatility on behalf of the merchant.

Both Payment Processors and all merchants are recommended to follow the community accepted BIP70: Payment Protocol standard that was proposed by Andresen and Hearn [5] to be used with Bitcoin. The motivation for this protocol is to reduce the complexity of Bitcoin payments as customers are no longer required to handle Bitcoin addresses[1]. Instead, the customer can verify the merchant's identity using a human-readable name before authorising a payment.

---

[1] A form of identity (26–35 alphanumeric characters) that is related to a public-private key pair and is used to send/receive bitcoins.

© International Financial Cryptography Association 2017
J. Grossklags and B. Preneel (Eds.): FC 2016, LNCS 9603, pp. 581–599, 2017.
DOI: 10.1007/978-3-662-54970-4_34

At the time of a payment authorisation, the customer's wallet will also send a refund Bitcoin address to the merchant that should be used in the event of a future refund.

The Payment Protocol provides two pieces of evidence that can be used in case of a dispute with an arbitrator. The customer has evidence that they were requested to authorise a payment if they keep a copy of the signed *Payment Request* message. This can be considered evidence as the customer could not have produced the signature without the co-operation of the merchant. The second piece of evidence for both the customer and the merchant is the payment transaction as the payment is signed by the customer and time-stamped on Bitcoin's Blockchain, that is stored by most users of the network. In this paper, we argue that a third piece of evidence is required to authenticate the refund address sent from the customer as the protocol recommends the customer's payment and refund addresses not be the same. This flexibility leads to the following attacks:

- The *Silkroad Trader* attack relies on a vulnerability in the Payment Protocol as the customer can authenticate that messages originate from the merchant, but not vice-versa. This allows a customer to route payments to an illicit trader via a merchant and then plausibly deny their own involvement.
- The *Marketplace Trader* attack focuses on the current refund policies of Coinbase and BitPay who both accept the refund address over e-mail [9, 26]. This allows a rogue trader to use the reputation of a trusted merchant to entice customers to fall victim to a phishing-style attack.

Without the knowledge of our attacks, Schildbach asked the Bitcoin-Development mailing list why the refund address in the Payment Protocol was currently unprotected [24] and one of the original authors responded:

*We talked about signing it with one of the keys that's signing the Bitcoin transaction as well. But it seems like a bit overkill. Usually it'll be submitted over HTTPS or a (secured!) Bluetooth channel though so tampering with it should not be possible. - Mike Hearn [13]*

As seen above, a solution may involve the customer endorsing a refund address using one of the public keys that authorised the transaction. However, the author stated this solution was an overkill as the refund address is currently protected in an HTTPS communication channel. We demonstrate that the HTTPS communication channel cannot protect the refund address as it only provides one-way authentication, the customer can authenticate messages originated from the merchant, but not vice-versa. At first glance, the 'overkill' solution suggested by Hearn could provide the evidence required for the merchant. Unfortunately, this solution opens the door to another attack which allows a malicious co-signer the sole authority to endorse the refund address used by the merchant and thus steal the bitcoins of other co-signers. We will discuss this in detail in Sect. 5.

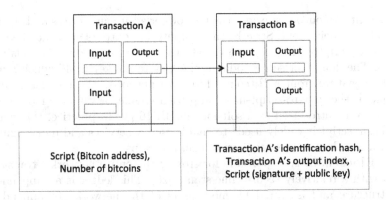

**Fig. 1.** Information stored in the inputs and outputs of Bitcoin transactions

**Contributions.** Our contributions in this paper are summarised below:

- We present new attacks on Bitcoin's Payment Protocol and the current practice of both the Payment Processors,
- We present real-world experiments that demonstrate how merchants today are vulnerable to both attacks using a modified Bitcoin wallet.
- We propose a solution that removes the incentive to perform both attacks as the merchant is provided with publicly verifiable evidence whose origin can be verified by an arbitrator.

## 2    Background

We discuss background information about Bitcoin before presenting the community accepted Payment Protocol standard.

### 2.1    Bitcoin

We discuss three concepts that are needed to understand Bitcoin's Payment Protocol. These include Bitcoin addresses that act as a form of identification, Transactions that are used to send/receive bitcoins and the Blockchain that stores all transactions on the network.

A **Bitcoin address** is a form of identification in the Bitcoin community that is used to receive bitcoins and authorise payments. An address can be described as the hash of an EC (Elliptic Curve) public key and the accompanying private key is used to produce ECDSA (Elliptic Curve Digital Signature Algorithm) signatures to authorise payments.

A **Transaction** consists of one or more inputs and one or more outputs as seen in Fig. 1. Briefly, an input specifies the source of bitcoins being spent (the previous transaction's identification hash and an index to one of its output) and is accompanied with signature(s) and public key(s) of the sender to authorise the payment. An output specifies the new owner's Bitcoin address and the number of bitcoins being sent. Strictly, these inputs and outputs are controlled using a Forth-like scripting language to dictate the conditions required to claim the bitcoins. The dominant script today is the 'pay-to-pubkey-hash' which requires a single signature from a Bitcoin address to authorise the payment. On the other hand, the 'pay-to-script-hash' approach enables a variety of transaction types and was introduced as a soft-fork in BIP16 [4]. In practice, this 'pay-to-script-hash' script is widely used[2] to enable escrow services and multi-signature authorisation ($k$ of $n$ keys required to claim bitcoins).

The **Blockchain** is responsible for storing the entire network's transaction history with a relatively secure time-stamp [20]. This ledger is an append-only data structure and is stored by most users of the network. To append new transactions to this ledger requires a computationally difficult proof of work puzzle to be solved. 'Miners' are responsible for computing this proof of work and are rewarded in bitcoins for appending a new 'block' of transactions to the ledger.

## 2.2  Payment Protocol

Andresen and Hearn proposed the Payment Protocol which has been accepted as a standard in BIP70 [5] and is supported by several prominent wallets. The goal of this protocol is described in the standard as the following:

> *"This BIP describes a protocol for communication between a merchant and their customer, enabling both a better customer experience and better security against man-in-the-middle attacks on the payment process."*

Communication between the customer and merchant is sent over HTTPS[3] and importantly, the customer is also responsible for broadcasting the payment transaction to the Bitcoin network. In this HTTPS setting, the merchant must have an X.509 certificate issued by a trusted Certificate Authority. This is necessary to let the customer authenticate messages from the merchant.

Figure 2 outlines the messages exchanged and actions performed for the protocol. To initiate, the customer clicks the 'Pay Now' button on the merchant's website to generate a Bitcoin URI. This URI opens the customer's Bitcoin wallet and downloads the *Payment Request* message from the merchant's website. The wallet verifies the digital signature for the message using the public key found in the merchant's X.509 certificate (and checks the merchant's certificate for authenticity using the operating system's list of root certificate authorities). A human-readable name for the merchant[4] and the number of requested bitcoins is displayed on-screen and the customer must check this information before clicking 'Send'. Upon authorisation, the wallet performs two actions:

---

[2] Currently 8.9% of all bitcoins are stored using the 'pay-to-script-hash' approach [1].

[3] The protocol specification allows messages to be sent over HTTP and for the merchant not to have an X.509 certificate, but this is not considered secure.

[4] URL from the X.509 certificate's 'common name' field.

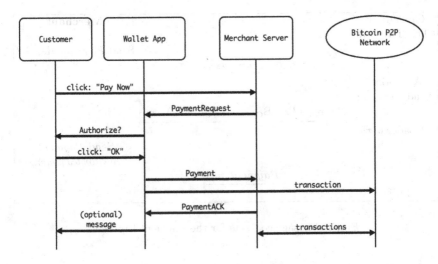

**Fig. 2.** Overview of the Payment Protocol [5]

1. The customer's wallet sends one or more payment transactions to the Bitcoin network.
2. The *Payment* message which includes the payment transactions and refund addresses is sent to the merchant's website.

The merchant responds to the customer's *Payment* message with a *Payment Acknowledgement* message which notifies the customer's wallet to display a confirmatory 'Thank you' message. Furthermore, once the merchant has detected the payment transaction on the Bitcoin network, the customer's web browser is refreshed to display a confirmation page. For the rest of this paper, we focus on messages sent over the HTTPS communication channel as seen in Fig. 2 and for simplicity we assume the customer only sends a single payment transaction. The content for each message is the following:

- The **Payment Request** message contains a unique payment address M, requested number of bitcoins ฿, creation time for request $t_1$, expiry time for request $t_2$, a memo message $m_M$, a payment URL $u_M$ and some merchant-specific data to link any future payments $z_M$. The contents of this message is signed using the private key $xsk_M$ that corresponds to the merchant's X.509 certificate public key such that $\sigma_M = S_{xsk_M}(M, ฿, t_1, t_2, m_M, u_M, z_M)$ where $S$ is the signature algorithm.
- The **Payment** message contains a repeat of the merchant-specific data $z_M$, a payment transactions $\tau_C{}^5$, a list of refund addresses $(R_{C_1}, ..., R_{C_n})$ and the number of bitcoins ฿ that should be refunded to each address such that $((R_{C_1}, ฿_1), ..., (R_{C_n}, ฿_n))$ and a memo from the customer $m_C$. There is no

---

[5] A single payment transaction $\tau_C$ is considered for simplicity. The protocol supports one or more payment transactions, and our results still apply in this case.

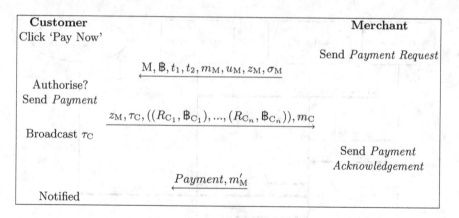

**Fig. 3.** Message contents for the Payment Protocol

restriction to the number of refund addresses sent to the merchant and the customer is responsible for deciding how the bitcoins are refunded amongst the refund addresses provided. Merchants expect one or more *Payment* messages until all requested bitcoins have been received (Fig. 3).

- The **Payment Acknowledgement** message is a repeat of the customer's *Payment* message and includes an optional memo $m'_M$ from the merchant.

The refund address sent in the *Payment* message is not digitally signed by the customer and its integrity relies on the HTTPS communication channel established between the customer and the merchant to prevent man-in-the-middle attacks. This lack of mutual authentication in the Payment Protocol and the refund policy of both Payment Processors to accept refund addresses over e-mail enables the attacks outlined in the next section.

# 3  Attacking the Payment Protocol

In this section, we outline attacks which are feasible due to an authentication vulnerability in the Payment Protocol and the refund policy of both Payment Processors. Fundamentally, our attacks rely on the merchant's inability to distinguish if the refund address originated from the same pseudonymous customer that authorised the payment. As well, these attacks are successful even when all messages are sent over an HTTPS communication channel.

## 3.1  Silkroad Trader Attack

This attack allows a customer to route payments to an illicit trader via an honest merchant and then plausibly deny their own involvement in the refund transaction. The main idea behind this attack relies on the customer's ability to swap the refund address in their *Payment* message with a Bitcoin address under

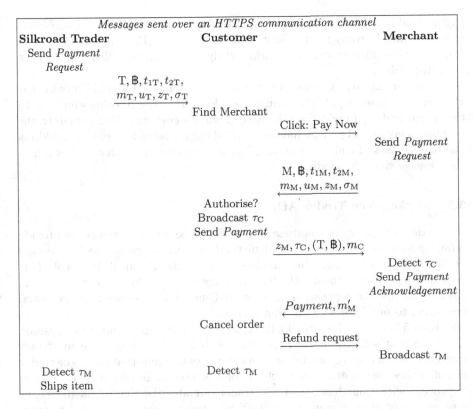

**Fig. 4.** *Silkroad Trader* attack allows a customer to route bitcoins to an illicit trader via an honest merchant and then plausibly deny their involvement.

the control of an illicit trader. Most importantly, the customer is not required to endorse the illicit trader's Bitcoin address with a digital signature.

Figure 4 is an outline of the Silkroad Trader attack. It begins with the customer visiting the website of an illicit trader. The customer downloads a *Payment Request* message for the desired 'illicit goods' they wish to purchase before searching for a merchant who supports the Payment Protocol and is selling an item approximately equal (or greater) in price. Once a merchant and item has been found, the customer clicks 'Pay now' to start the payment process and downloads a *Payment Request* message from the merchant's website. To commence the attack, the customer's wallet authorises the payment transaction $\tau_C$ and inserts the illicit trader's payment address T in the *Payment* message as the refund address (instead of their own refund address) and then sends the message to the merchant.

The customer must request a refund to finish the attack once their Bitcoin wallet has received the *Payment Acknowledgement* message alongside a confirmation e-mail from the merchant. Assuming the merchant follows the Payment Protocol faithfully, the refunded bitcoins in $\tau_M$ are sent to the illicit trader's payment address T. Also, the customer can detect the refund transaction (merchant sending bitcoins to the illicit trader) $\tau_M$ on the Bitcoin network before contacting the illicit trader for an acknowledgement that the 'illicit goods' have been dispatched.

Ideally, if this attack happened in practice, the merchant could provide the *Payment* message as publicly verifiable evidence that the bitcoins were sent to the refund address provided by the pseudonymous customer. Unfortunately, the customer may plausibly deny having supplied the illicit trader's payment address due to their lack of endorsement, and hence claim that the merchant has forged the message single-handedly.

## 3.2  Marketplace Trader Attack

In practice, the policy of Coinbase and BitPay encourages customers to provide refund addresses using an external method of communication such as e-mail [9,26] which ignores the refund address sent in the Payment Protocol. This deviation from the protocol is the basis of a new phishing style attack as a 'rogue trader' can use the reputation of a 'trusted' merchant to encourage potential customers to purchase an item from their website.

Figure 5 outlines this attack. It begins with the rogue trader establishing a website that sells the latest products well below the market rate to attract customers to their store. Most customers may be suspicious that the rogue trader can offer these prices and may wisely think it is a scam. To encourage customers to proceed with a purchase, the rogue trader can advertise that all payments are sent to a trusted merchant such as CeX and there is little reason not to trust them. When a customer proceeds to checkout on the rogue trader's website and clicks 'Pay now', the rogue trader's website can automatically fetch a *Payment Request* message from the trusted merchant's website and forward this to the customer. The customer's wallet opens the genuine *Payment Request* message and displays a human-readable name for the trusted merchant alongside the number of requested bitcoins. This can boost the customer's confidence that the rogue trader is legitimate as the payment is sent to the 'trusted' merchant.

Unfortunately, the customer falls victim to the attack upon authorising the payment as they are unwittingly paying for a purchase on behalf of the rogue trader to the trusted merchant. The rogue trader detects the payment[6] transaction on the Bitcoin network and refreshes the victim's web browser to display a fake confirmation page (remember, the customer's web browser is connected to the rogue trader's website). The rogue trader can proceed to cancel the order and send a new refund address over e-mail to the trusted merchant. As the merchant's policy is to use an external method of communication to authenticate customers and deviate from the Payment Protocol standard - then the refund address sent by the rogue trader over e-mail should receive the bitcoins.

Furthermore, the customer cannot be aware this attack has occurred as they lack enough information to identify the refund transaction on the Bitcoin network.

---

[6] Currently 50% of nodes on the network receive a new transaction within 5 s [2].

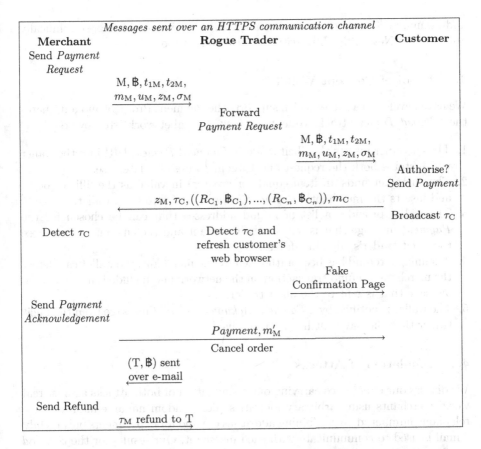

**Fig. 5.** *Marketplace Trader* attack involves a rogue trader using the reputation of a 'trusted' merchant to encourage customers to fall victim to a phishing-style attack.

More importantly, this attack is deployable single-handedly by a rogue trader and does not require the co-operation of a 'trusted' merchant. In fact, the trusted merchant may only become aware of this scam if contacted in the future by the customer.

## 4    Real-World Experiments

Our experiments aim to verify the current practice of processing refunds by merchants, and assess the feasibility of the attacks. We purchased items from real-life merchants using a modified Bitcoin wallet before requesting for the order to be cancelled and a refund processed. The attack is considered successful if the refunded bitcoins are received by the adversary's wallet. The merchants used during these experiments are based in the UK and are supported by BitPay or Coinbase. The bitcoins used for the experiments are owned by the authors and no money is sent to any illicit trader. All experiments have been ethnically approved by Newcastle University's ethical committee.

### 4.1 Proof of Concept Wallet

We have developed a wallet which supports the Payment Protocol and automates the *Silkroad Trader* attack. We explain how our wallet works step-by-step:

1. The customer inserts the illicit trader's *Payment Request* URI into the wallet which stores both the request and Bitcoin address for later use.
2. The customer finds an item equal (or greater) in value as the 'illicit goods' and inserts the merchant's *Payment Request* URI into their wallet.
3. The wallet provides a list of refund addresses that can be chosen for the *Payment* message that is sent to the merchant and the customer can choose the illicit trader's Bitcoin address.
4. Assuming a refund has been authorised by the merchant, the wallet can detect the merchant's refund transaction on the network and include it in a *Payment* message that is sent to the illicit trader.
5. The wallet is notified by a *Payment Acknowledgement* message from the illicit trader that the payment has been received.

### 4.2 Simulation of Attacks

We discuss our experience carrying out a simulation of both attacks against real world merchants using arbitrary identities (i.e., random name, e-mail address, telephone number, delivery/billing addresses created for experiments only). Only e-mail is used to communicate with each merchant. Our results for the *Silkroad Trader* attack are as follows:

**Cex** refunded the bitcoins within 3 h of cancelling the order and used the refund address from the Payment Protocol.

**Pimoroni Ltd** refunded the bitcoins within a single business day and used the refund address from the Payment Protocol.

**Scan** refunded the bitcoins after 26 days and used the refund address from the Payment Protocol. The delay was due to Scan initially requesting us to provide a refund address over e-mail, but we insisted using the one specified in the original payment message.

**Dell** were unable to process the refund due to 'technical difficulties' and requested our bank details. We informed them that we did not own a bank account and Dell suggested sending the refund as a cheque. While not the experiment's aim, this potentially opens Dell as an exchange for laundering tainted bitcoins.

To simulate the *Marketplace Trader* attacks we sent the refund address in an e-mail to the merchants. Assuming the merchants accepted e-mail as a good form of authentication and ignored the refund address sent in the Payment Protocol, then the phishing-style attack we described earlier could happen in practice. Our results were the following:

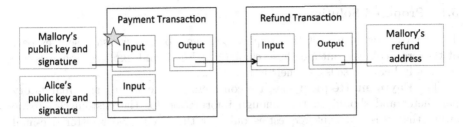

**Fig. 6.** The malicious co-signer attack allows a co-signer the sole authority to endorse the refund address used by the merchant and thus steal the bitcoins of other co-signers

**Something Geeky** refunded the bitcoins within a single business day to a refund address sent over e-mail.

**Girl meets dress** refunded the bitcoins within 11 business days to a refund address sent over e-mail. The delay was due to the merchant initially thinking we paid using a bank transfer.

**BitRoad** refunded the bitcoins within a single business day to a refund address sent over e-mail. In this experiment, we registered using a non-existing e-mail address and requested for the order to be cancelled using a variant of the e-mail address. This demonstrates that even the registered e-mail address to initiate the purchase is not being used to authenticate the customer.

## 5   Solution

We propose providing the merchant with publicly verifiable evidence that can cryptographically prove the refund address received during the protocol was endorsed by the same pseudonymous customer who authorised the payment.

A solution proposed by Hearn [13] assumes the payment transaction is authorised by a single customer and recommends endorsing the refund address using any key which authorised the transaction. However, it is not valid to assume that a transaction has been authorised by a single customer due to the nature of a Bitcoin transaction. If the adversary is responsible for sending the *Payment* message to the merchant, then they have the sole authority to endorse the refund address used by the merchant as seen in Fig. 6.

Our proposed solution prevents this attack by requiring each key that authorised the transaction to also endorse its own refund address. In the event of a refund the merchant sends the same (or less) number of bitcoins received[7] from each transaction input to an associated refund address.

---

[7] A transaction input does not record the number of bitcoins 'sent' and instead references an output from a previous transaction which specifies the bitcoins.

## 5.1   Proposed Solution

To achieve a signature solution requires changes to each message sent as part of the protocol. We outline these changes in Fig. 7 and explain each message separately before discussing their implications.

The **Payment Request** message considers the memo $m_M$ as a mandatory parameter and should contain enough information for the customer(s) to be aware that this payment request is only for them, e.g. the registered e-mail address, delivery address, product information, etc. This memo field should also include customer-specified instructions to provide evidence that the merchant followed any instructions provided by the customer. The payment address M should be unique for each *Payment Request* and like before, there should be no restriction on the number of times a customer can download the same *Payment Request* to support paying from multiple devices or sharing with others.

The **Payment** message aims to associate each transaction input $\pi_{C_i}$ with a refund address $R_{C_i}$ by endorsing the refund address using the same keys that authorised the transaction input. We assume the customer is no longer responsible for broadcasting the payment transaction $\tau_C$ to the Bitcoin network; instead, the responsibility of broadcasting the payment transaction should fall on the merchant (as recommended by one of the original authors of the Payment Protocol[8]). For simplicity, we describe our solution using a single *Payment* message and payment transaction $\tau_C$[9].

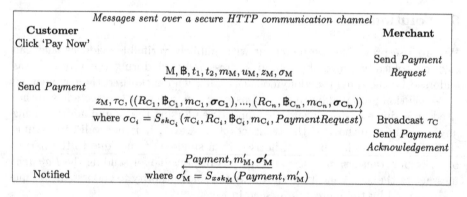

**Fig. 7.** A single customer sends a payment to the merchant

Each refund address endorsement signature is $\sigma_{C_i} = S_{sk_{C_i}}(\pi_{C_i}, R_{C_i}, \mathbb{B}_{C_i}, m_{C_i}$ *Payment Request*), where $S$ is the signature algorithm, $sk_{C_i}$ is the private key

---

[8] https://groups.google.com/forum/#!msg/bitcoinj/ymFRupTSRJQ/zANj2RpslCcJ.

[9] Our solution continues to allow customers to send one or more *Payment* messages to the merchant until all requested bitcoins have been received. Furthermore, these messages can contain a list payment transactions.

which corresponds to the key that authorised the transaction input, $\pi_{C_i}$ is a concatenation of the elements that constitute the signed transaction input, $R_{C_i}$ is the refund address, $\text{\Bitcoin}_{C_i}$ is the number of bitcoins to refund, $m_{C_i}$ is an additional memo from the customer and *Payment Request* is the signed message from the merchant. These parameters were chosen to clarify which transaction input is associated with the endorsed refund address and to ensure this endorsement is only valid for this *Payment Request* message. The concatenated information $\pi_{C_i}$ is the data stored inside the transaction input and includes: the previous transaction identification hash, an index for the output in the referenced transaction and the script which contains a signature to authorise the payment and its corresponding public key.

A new refund policy for the merchant is required as each transaction input is responsible for endorsing a refund address. We propose the bitcoins associated with each refund address must be equal to (or less than) the number of bitcoins sent in the respective transaction input. The merchant must also check that the total number of bitcoins associated with all refund addresses in this message is equal to (or less than) the number of bitcoins he received in the payment transaction. These checks are necessary as the payment transaction can have additional outputs for change and the merchant needs to ensure he does not refund more bitcoins than he received from each transaction input. For example, if the transaction has a single input of ₿5 (from the customer) and two outputs: ₿4 (to the merchant) and ₿1 (to the customer as change), then the merchant must ensure the customer is only refunded ₿4 (and not ₿5).

The message content sent to the merchant is outlined in Fig. 7 and includes: the merchant-specific data $z_M$, the complete transaction $\tau_C$ and a list of refund addresses alongside their associated endorsement signatures and the number of bitcoins to refund $((R_{C_1}, \text{\Bitcoin}_{C_1}, m_{C_1}, \sigma_{C_1}), ..., (R_{C_n}, \text{\Bitcoin}_{C_n}, m_{C_n}, \sigma_{C_n}))$.

The **Payment Acknowledgement** message is signed using the merchant's X.509 private key and repeats the customer's *Payment* message alongside an additional memo $m'_M$. The signature is $\sigma'_M = S_{xsk_M}(Payment, m'_M)$ where $S$ is the signature algorithm and $xsk_M$ is the private key that corresponds to the merchant's public key in their X.509 certificate.

We simplified the notation for $\sigma_{C_i}$ to only show the case when the customer endorses the $i$th refund address using a *single* signing key. However, if the multi-signature approach is used to authorise the transaction input, then a threshold of $k$ signing keys should be used to endorse the respective refund address. Each customer with control of 1 of $k$ keys can independently authorise the transaction input and the corresponding refund address. Both signatures which endorse the refund address and authorise transaction input are sent to the other co-signers to be included in the *Payment* message.

## 5.2  Discussion

Our solution provides a **proof of endorsement** as the refund address received by the merchant is signed using the same set of keys used to authorise the transaction. This evidence removes the customer's plausible deniability for their involvement in the *Silkroad Trader* attack and provides an incentive for the merchant to use the refund address sent during the Payment Protocol which prevents the *Marketplace Trader* attack. The merchant does not need to distinguish whether or not the payment has been split which preserves the customers privacy and prevents the malicious co-signer attack as co-signers cannot endorse the refund addresses of others. These additional signatures are handled by the wallet on behalf of the user. Also, **no connection to the peer to peer network** is required for the customer as the merchant is responsible for broadcasting the payment transaction $\tau_C$ and this prepares the Payment Protocol to **support off-chain transactions** such as the Lightning Network [21].

Furthermore, we explored other potential solutions such as requesting the customer to provide a signature from the refund address at the time of payment (instead of using the same keys that authorised the transaction) or including secret data inside the merchant-specific data field $z_M$. The former is not satisfactory as proving ownership of the refund address does not necessarily link the refund address to the same keys that authorised the transaction and the latter remains vulnerable to the *Marketplace Trader* attack as the rogue trader has access to the *Payment Request* message. As well, the attacks introduced in this paper also stem from the fact that merchants have no community-accepted refund protocol today. While researchers have proposed secure post-payment communication protocols [15] in the past which could conceivably be used to support arranging refund in a private and authenticated manner, this remains a subject for further investigation in future work.

Payment Processors are expected to perform anti-money-laundering policies on behalf of their merchants [10]. The state of New York recently released Bitlicense [25] to outline regulation for Bitcoin businesses. Our solution enhances the book-keeping required for this license as the signed *Payment* message is cryptographic evidence that the pseudonymous customer has endorsed the transaction-related information required for auditing by investigators. We improve the mandatory customer receipt which is currently a static web-page or an e-mail by using the *Payment Acknowledgement* message as a cryptographic receipt as it is signed by the merchant's X.509 private key. Similar cryptographic evidence has been explored in the Bitcoin research community and two examples include: providing a warrant to hold a mixer accountable in the event of any wrongdoing with Mixcoin/Blindcoin [8,27], and to compute a proof of solvency [11] that demonstrates the business is financially in good standing to customers.

Clustering techniques have been demonstrated to link a group of Bitcoin addresses to a single pseudonymous user [6]. Meiklejohn et al. [17] identified that 374.49 BTC stolen from Betcoin in April 2012 and 4,588 BTC from the Bitcoinica theft in May 2012 were sold at Bitcoin-24, Mt Gox, BTC-e, CampBX and Bitstamp. Also, Reid et al. [22] tracked 25k stolen bitcoins and deduced LulSec's involvement in the theft. These analysis techniques using the Blockchain are currently supporting criminal charges in the Silkroad Trial [3]. However, privacy-enhancing protocols [14,16,23] and altcoins [18,19] are actively reducing the effectiveness of these analysis techniques. Nevertheless, these techniques provide a platform for the *Silkroad Trader* attack as independent observers may discover merchants sending bitcoins to an illicit trader and then publicly release the 'evidence'. Our solution provides the merchant with publicly verifiable evidence to demonstrate a customer's deception.

### 5.3   Inherent Issues Due to Bitcoin

We outline four issues that are inherent due to Bitcoin that need to be considered for our solution:

**First**, the *proof of endorsement* evidence can only authenticate pseudonymous customers as the Payment Protocol lacks the type of *real-life identity endorsement* that comes with banks. While protecting an honest merchant, our solution cannot prevent a malicious merchant simulating both attacks and insisting they were tricked.

**Second**, in a similar way to the original protocol, an observer of the Blockchain may be able to link the payment and refund transactions using the denominations of bitcoins sent and received.

**Third**, customers can re-sign the transaction to change the identification hash and broadcast it to the network. We recommend the merchant keeps a copy of the payment transaction received in the *Payment* message as a re-signed transaction cannot be used to verify the endorsement in the future.

**Fourth**, we assume merchants maintain the UTXO (Unspent Transaction Output) set to participate in the Payment Protocol. Without this list of spendable outputs, the merchant cannot independently verify transactions or calculate the number of bitcoins to refund for each transaction input. On the other hand, customers do not require the UTXO set and can continue to use SPV (Simplified Payment Verification) wallets for the Payment Protocol.

### 5.4   Solution Performance

All tests are carried out on a MacBook Pro mid-2012 running OS X 10.9.1 with 2.3 GHz Intel Core i7 and 16 GB DDR3 RAM. Time performance in Table 1 represents both the current Payment Protocol implementation and our proposed modifications for the Bitcoin Core Client while utilising 1 core. Furthermore, both signing operations in steps 3 and 8, and the verification operation in step 9, are performed using the Secp256k1 implementation which has recently replaced OpenSSL in Bitcoin Core [28]. Each step was executed 100 times and the reported times represent the average.

Steps 1–5 represent the customer's perspective in the current Payment Protocol's implementation. The wallet verifies the merchant's certificate authenticity using the chain of certificates that lead to a trusted root authority and verifies the merchant's signature on the *Payment Request* message before authorising at least one transaction input to authorise the payment. Then, the wallet fetches a list of pre-generated refund addresses and Step 4b only occurs if this list is empty as a new refund address must be generated. This refund address is associated

**Table 1.** Time performance for proposed changes to the Payment Protocol

| Step | Description | Time |
|------|-------------|------|
| | *Customer in the current protocol* | |
| 1 | Verify merchant's certificate and chain of certificates authenticity | 0.83 ms |
| 2 | Verify merchant's signature on the Payment Request message | 0.08 ms |
| 3 | Sign a single transaction input | 0.08 ms |
| 4a | Fetch a list of previously generated refund addresses $R_{C_1}, ..., R_{C_k}$ | 0.72 ms |
| 4b | Generate a new refund address $R_C$ from the wallet's key pool | 110.55 ms |
| 5 | Update wallet's address book with the refund address $R_C$ | 72.68 ms |
| | *Total without 4b:* | *74.39 ms* |
| | *Total with 4b:* | *184.94 ms* |
| | *Merchant in the current protocol* | |
| 6 | Verify the customer's payment transaction | 0.29 ms |
| | *Total:* | *0.29 ms* |
| | *Additional changes proposed for the customer* | |
| 7 | Produce endorsement signature $\sigma_C$ using the private key $sk_C$ | 0.11 ms |
| | *New total without 4b:* | *74.49 ms* |
| | *New total with 4b:* | *185.04 ms* |
| | *Additional changes proposed for the merchant* | |
| 8 | Fetch the transaction input's referenced transaction output | 0.01 ms |
| 9 | Verify the transaction input's endorsement signature $\sigma_C$ | 0.13 ms |
| | *New total:* | *0.43 ms* |

with the payment for future reference. These steps require 74.39 ms if the list of pre-generated refund addresses is not empty, otherwise 184.94 ms is required. Our proposed change in Step 7 takes 0.11 ms and requires the customer's wallet to sign an endorsement message for the refund address, obtaining the signature $\sigma_C$. In total, the time required for the customer is 185.04 ms with Step 4b, and 74.49 ms without Step 4b.

Step 6 represents the merchant's perspective in the current Payment Protocol's implementation and requires 0.29 ms to check if the payment transaction with a single input is valid. We propose in Steps 8–9 that the merchant fetches the transaction output referenced in the payment transaction's input to let the merchant check the number of bitcoins associated with each refund address. Then, the transaction input's public key $C$ is used to verify the endorsement signature. These proposed changes require 0.14 ms, and in total the time required for the merchant is 0.43 ms.

# 6    Payment Processors Response

We privately disclosed our attacks to the Payment Processors and received the following response:

**BitPay** acknowledged "the researchers have done their homework" and that "refunds are definitely a significant money laundering attack vector". They are now actively monitoring for refund activity on behalf of their merchants. Furthermore, after we disclosed our results, BitPay released a new refund flow [7] that recommends using the refund address provided in the Payment Protocol rather than the one supplied by email.

**Coinbase** acknowledged the 'Silkroad Trader' attack as a good example of an authentication vulnerability in the Payment Protocol. To prevent the *Marketplace Trader* attack, Coinbase no longer provides merchants the API to change the refund address if it has been supplied by the Payment Protocol. Also, they have updated their user documentation to discourage merchants sending the refund using their own bitcoins to bypass the API changes.

**Bitt** is preparing to launch merchant services for the Caribbean and acknowledged both attacks. They believe the endorsement evidence may support Payment Processors become more 'airtight' for future regulation.

These temporary mitigation measures help to address the *Marketplace Trader* attack, but not the *Silkroad Trader* attack. To fully address the latter, the BIP70 standard would need to be revised, as we have discussed in Sect. 5.

# 7    Conclusion

This paper presented two attacks that leverage an authentication vulnerability in Bitcoin's Payment Protocol and the refund policies of the two largest Payment Processors: Coinbase and BitPay. We experimentally demonstrated both attacks on real-life merchants using a proof of concept wallet before proposing a solution that provides the merchant with cryptographic evidence that the refund address received during the Payment Protocol has been endorsed from the same pseudonymous customer who authorised the transaction. Both Payment Processors have acknowledged our attacks and have implemented mitigation measures.

**Acknowledgements.** The second and third authors are supported by the European Research Council (ERC) Starting Grant (No. 306994). We would like to thank the original authors of the Payment Protocol; Mike Hearn for his constructive feedback on our proposed solution and recommendation to include customer-specified instructions and Gavin Andresen for reviewing this paper and giving feedback. Also, we thank the anonymous reviewers for their very good feedback.

# References

1. Alcio: Monitor pay to script hash adoption, May 2015. http://p2sh.info/. Accessed 21 May 2015
2. Ali, S.T., McCorry, P., Lee, P.H.-J., Hao, F.: ZombieCoin: powering next-generation botnets with Bitcoin. In: Brenner, M., Christin, N., Johnson, B., Rohloff, K. (eds.) FC 2015. LNCS, vol. 8976, pp. 34–48. Springer, Heidelberg (2015). doi:10.1007/978-3-662-48051-9_3
3. Allison, I.: Silk road prosecutors talk about Bitcoin, ripple and money laundering. International Business Times, August 2015. http://www.ibtimes.co.uk/silk-road-prosecutors-talk-about-bitcoin-ripple-money-laundering-1517414
4. Andresen, G.: Pay to script hash. Bitcoin Improvement Process (2012). https://github.com/bitcoin/bips/blob/master/bip-0016.mediawiki. Accessed 07 Dec 2015
5. Andresen, G., Hearn, M.: BIP 70: payment protocol. Bitcoin Improvement Process, July 2013. https://github.com/bitcoin/bips/blob/master/bip-0070.mediawiki. Accessed 15 Jan 2015
6. Androulaki, E., Karame, G.O., Roeschlin, M., Scherer, T., Capkun, S.: Evaluating user privacy in Bitcoin. In: Sadeghi, A.-R. (ed.) FC 2013. LNCS, vol. 7859, pp. 34–51. Springer, Heidelberg (2013). doi:10.1007/978-3-642-39884-1_4
7. BitPay: New invoice adjustment and refund flow, August 2015. https://blog.bitpay.com/new-refund-flow/. Accessed 20 Sept 2015
8. Bonneau, J., Narayanan, A., Miller, A., Clark, J., Kroll, J.A., Felten, E.W.: Mixcoin: anonymity for Bitcoin with accountable mixes. In: Christin, N., Safavi-Naini, R. (eds.) FC 2014. LNCS, vol. 8437, pp. 486–504. Springer, Heidelberg (2014). doi:10.1007/978-3-662-45472-5_31
9. Coinbase: How do i do a customer refund with the API? May 2015. https://support.coinbase.com/customer/portal/articles/1521752-how-do-i-do-a-customer-refund-with-the-api-. Accessed 15 May 2015
10. Fincen: Request for administrative ruling on the application of FinCENs regulations to a virtual currency payment system (2015). http://www.fincen.gov/news_room/rp/rulings/pdf/FIN-2014-R012.pdf. Accessed 07 Sept 2015
11. Dagher, G., Bunz, B., Bonneau, J., Clarke, J., Boneah, D.: Provisions: privacy-preserving proofs of solvency for Bitcoin exchanges. In: The 22nd ACM Conference on Computer and Communications Security (2015)
12. Geiger, B.: Overstock.com offers its staff the option of being paid in Bitcoin (2015). http://fortune.com/2015/01/09/overstock-com-offers-its-staff-the-option-of-being-paid-in-bitcoin/. Accessed 26 Feb 2015
13. Hearn, M.: Re: [Bitcoin-development] BIP 70 refund field. Bitcoin-Development, March 2014. http://sourceforge.net/p/bitcoin/mailman/message/32157661/. Accessed 01 Feb 2015
14. Maxwell, G.: CoinJoin: Bitcoin privacy for the real world (2013). https://bitcointalk.org/index.php?topic=279249. Accessed 20 May 2015
15. McCorry, P., Shahandashti, S.F., Clarke, D., Hao, F.: Authenticated key exchange over Bitcoin. In: Chen, L., Matsuo, S. (eds.) SSR 2015. LNCS, vol. 9497, pp. 3–20. Springer, Cham (2015). doi:10.1007/978-3-319-27152-1_1
16. Meiklejohn, S., Orlandi, C.: Privacy-enhancing overlays in Bitcoin. In: Brenner, M., Christin, N., Johnson, B., Rohloff, K. (eds.) FC 2015. LNCS, vol. 8976, pp. 127–141. Springer, Heidelberg (2015). doi:10.1007/978-3-662-48051-9_10

17. Meiklejohn, S., Pomarole, M., Jordan, G., Levchenko, K., McCoy, D., Voelker, G.M., Savage, S.: A fistful of Bitcoins: characterizing payments among men with no names. In: Proceedings of the 2013 Conference on Internet Measurement Conference, pp. 127–140. ACM (2013)
18. Miers, I., Garman, C., Green, M., Rubin, A.: Zerocoin: anonymous distributed e-cash from Bitcoin. In: 2013 IEEE Symposium on Security and Privacy (SP), pp. 397–411. IEEE (2013)
19. Monero: Monero is a secure, private, untraceable currency. It is open-source and freely available to all (2015). https://getmonero.org/home. Accessed 08 Dec 2015
20. Nakamoto, S.: Bitcoin: a peer-to-peer electronic cash system, November 2008. https://bitcoin.org/bitcoin.pdf. Accessed 01 Jan 2015
21. Perez, Y.: Could the Bitcoin lightning network solve blockchain scalability? (2015). http://www.coindesk.com/could-the-bitcoin-lightning-network-solve-blockchain-scalability/. Accessed 15 May 2015
22. Reid, F., Harrigan, M.: An analysis of anonymity in the Bitcoin system. In: Privacy, Security, Risk and Trust (PASSAT), 2011 IEEE Third International Conference on and 2011 IEEE Third International Conference on Social Computing, pp. 1318–1326, October 2011
23. Ruffing, T., Moreno-Sanchez, P., Kate, A.: CoinShuffle: practical decentralized coin mixing for Bitcoin. In: Kutyłowski, M., Vaidya, J. (eds.) ESORICS 2014. LNCS, vol. 8713, pp. 345–364. Springer, Cham (2014). doi:10.1007/978-3-319-11212-1_20
24. Schildbach, A.: Re: [Bitcoin-development] BIP 70 refund field. Bitcoin-Development, March 2014. http://sourceforge.net/p/bitcoin/mailman/message/32157651/. Accessed 1 Feb 2015
25. State, N.Y.: Chapter i regulations of the superintendent of financial services, part 200. Virtual currencies. Department of Finance Services, February 2015
26. Tur, M.: Can BitPay refund my order? (2015). https://support.bitpay.com/hc/en-us/articles/203411523-Can-BitPay-refund-my-order-. Accessed 07 Apr 2015
27. Valenta, L., Rowan, B.: Blindcoin: blinded, accountable mixes for Bitcoin. In: Brenner, M., Christin, N., Johnson, B., Rohloff, K. (eds.) FC 2015. LNCS, vol. 8976, pp. 112–126. Springer, Heidelberg (2015). doi:10.1007/978-3-662-48051-9_9
28. Wuille, P.: Switch to libsecp256k1-based ECDSA validation. Bitcoin Github Repository, November 2015. https://github.com/bitcoin/bitcoin/pull/6954. Accessed 31 Dec 2015

# Are Payment Card Contracts Unfair?
## (Short Paper)

Steven J. Murdoch[1]([✉]), Ingolf Becker[1], Ruba Abu-Salma[1], Ross Anderson[2],
Nicholas Bohm[3], Alice Hutchings[2], M. Angela Sasse[1], and Gianluca Stringhini[1]

[1] University College London (UCL), London, UK
s.murdoch@ucl.ac.uk
[2] Computer Laboratory, University of Cambridge, Cambridge, UK
[3] Foundation for Information Policy Research, Takeley, UK

**Abstract.** Fraud victims are often refused a refund by their bank on the
grounds that they failed to comply with their bank's terms and conditions
about PIN safety. We, therefore, conducted a survey of how many PINs
people have, and how they manage them. We found that while only a
third of PINs are ever changed, almost half of bank customers write at
least one PIN down. We also found bank conditions that are too vague
to test, or even contradictory on whether PINs could be shared across
cards. Yet, some hazardous practices are not forbidden by many banks: of
the 22.9% who re-use PINs across devices, half also use their bank PINs
on their mobile phones. We conclude that many bank contracts fail a
simple test of reasonableness, and 'strong authentication', as required by
the Payment Services Directive II, should include usability testing.

## 1   Introduction

Many research papers on payment security focus on the technical mechanisms
used to prevent fraud. Yet, these often fail, and consumer confidence in payment
systems depends on whether fraudulent transactions can be reversed, or the
victim reimbursed. If a customer disputes a transaction, and there is no evidence
that the merchant colluded, the question may be simply whether the bank gives
the customer a refund. Will the bank be able to hide behind its contract terms
in theory, and will it do so in practice?

Fifteen years ago, Bohm, Brown and Gladman surveyed the terms and conditions that banks were imposing on customers in the rush to put banking services
on-line [2]. They found some bank contracts said that a customer who accepted
a password for on-line banking would be liable for any transaction the bank
claimed was made with that password, regardless of whether she had actually
made it. This was a huge change from the law on cheques, where a forged signature is null and void, so banks cannot make customers liable for forged cheques by
their terms and conditions. The new electronic banking contracts subtly shifted
the burden of proof to the customer.

So, where are we fifteen years later? In the US, regulations require that
disputed consumer transactions be refunded, unless the bank can show that the

© International Financial Cryptography Association 2017
J. Grossklags and B. Preneel (Eds.): FC 2016, LNCS 9603, pp. 600–608, 2017.
DOI: 10.1007/978-3-662-54970-4_35

customer actually performed the transaction, or authorised someone else to do so. In the EU, the 2007 Payment Services Directive ruled that customers are entitled to a refund unless they have been "grossly negligent" in complying with the security procedures set out in the contract with their bank. Thus, banks may be permitted to refuse a refund if the customer fails to follow security guidelines correctly; and even in the USA, a bank might claim that a customer who had let a thief get hold of their card and PIN had authorised them to debit the account.

This might be a reasonable line to take, but only if the bank's contract terms are fair. So, have banks been able to cheat by setting unreasonable rules (e.g., 'choose a password you can't remember and don't write it down')? Or, are their security rules so vague that in the case of dispute, they can always claim that the customer is in breach? In this project, we try to find out.

We examine UK banking terms and conditions in the context of national and EU legislation. We focus on card-present payments and ATM withdrawals because the fraud risk of these transactions falls on the banks, maximising the incentive for customers to be refused a refund. The most reported cases involve a card being stolen (resulting in £59.7 m fraud in the UK in 2014 [11]), counterfeited (£47.8m), or intercepted in the post (£10.1m). We exclude card-not-present (e.g., Internet) transactions (£331.5m), as their fraud risk falls on the merchant.

The vast majority of card-present transactions in the EU now require a PIN. In these cases, the bank may claim that the customer must have been grossly negligent in protecting it. Hence, we study how people actually use cards and PINs. We are interested in whether customers can practicably comply with typical bank contract terms, and whether they actually do in reality.

## 2 Legal and Regulatory Context

Banking contract terms are regulated everywhere. In the US, Federal Reserve regulations E and Z limit consumer liability for fraudulent debit and credit transactions at $50 (unless for debit transactions the customer did not promptly notify the bank of a lost or stolen card, in which case the limit is $500). Liability does not depend on whether the customer was negligent, and the only way to refuse a refund is to argue that the customer actually authorised the transaction or authorised someone else to perform it. In practice, fraud victims are generally refunded unless the bank suspects they are in cahoots with the merchant.

Practice in the EU was harmonised in 2007 by the Payment Services Directive (PSD), which states that customers are not liable for unauthorised transactions when their card is not stolen, and liability would be capped at €150 if it was. However, these limitations do not apply if the customers "failed with intent or gross negligence to fulfil one or more of his obligations under Article 56", which requires that customers comply with banking terms and conditions and, in particular, to "take all reasonable steps to keep its personalised security features safe". So, what counts as 'reasonable'?

European banks typically use the "gross negligence" exception when they choose to deny a refund, but its definition is left to national rules and practices.

As an example, banks commonly state that it is gross negligence to write down a PIN and keep it with the card. However, in practice, for a customer to be held liable, it is only necessary for the adjudicator to believe that gross negligence is, on the balance of probabilities, the most likely explanation.

The PSD requires that there be a means of adjudicating disputes without going to court. This was considered necessary because many European countries practice 'costs shifting', whereby the loser of a civil case pays the winner's costs, which could far exceed the sums in dispute.

The UK adjudicator is the Financial Ombudsman Service, from whose decisions we can see what they consider to be gross negligence. For example, in one case [5], a stolen debit card was used, and while the customer denied writing down the PIN, the bank records showed that the correct card and PIN had been used. The adjudicator observed that the customer had not used the card on the day (reducing the likelihood of shoulder-surfing), and concluded that the most likely explanation for the transactions was that the PIN was kept with the card. The customer was, therefore, held liable.

In one of the few UK cases to get to court [7], the judge also found that the most likely explanation for disputed ATM transactions was that either the customer had made the transactions, or the customer allowed them through intent or negligence. This decision was based on expert witness testimony from the bank, stating that there had never been a breach of the Chip and PIN system at an ATM, the disputed transactions were near the customer's home, and the total disputed amount did not exceed the available balance of the account. The customer was refused a refund and ordered to pay £15,000 of the bank's costs.

Of course, there are other explanations for how the PIN could have been obtained in both of these cases; the same PIN could have been used on another card or on the customer's mobile phone, or the PIN check could have been bypassed technically [8]. The outcome may turn on whether the adjudicator believes the bank or the complainant, which in turn may depend on their access to independent expertise.

The facts that people tend to choose PINs that are easy to guess, and that they tend to set the same PIN on multiple cards, mean that guessing a PIN is possible for about 1 in 11 stolen wallets [3], but a bank could argue that this is only a result of poor PIN choice and still amounts to gross negligence. Therefore, we examine guidance given to customers, to see if customers are set sufficiently clear and consistent rules with which they can reasonably be expected to comply.

## 3   Review of Banking Terms and Conditions

We surveyed the terms and conditions of a number of banks. We looked for instructions or advice on how users should handle the PINs associated with their cards. As an example, we consider HSBC [6], one of the big British banks.

**PIN Memo Clauses.** Banks' terms of service often provide guidance on writing down and recording PINs. HSBC forbids its users from writing PINs down anywhere, except in an "obfuscated" fashion that others cannot easily reconstruct. It stipulates: *"Never writing down or otherwise recording your PINs and other security details in a way that can be understood by someone else"*. It is not specified whether it is the PIN that should not be understood, or the connection between the PIN and the card.

**PIN Change Clauses.** Some banks tell customers whether they can change their PINs, and how to choose a PIN. HSBC's rules are concise, but general: *"These precautions include ... not choose security details that may be easy to guess"*.

**PIN Re-use Clauses.** Many banks have rules on whether a customer can re-use a PIN for multiple cards. HSBC states that customer precautions include *"keeping your security details unique to your accounts with us ..."*. This is actually in conflict with the advice given earlier by the UK banks' trade association, which recommends customers to change all their PINs to the PIN issued for one of their cards. The UK banks have also taken the necessary technical measures to ensure that cardholders from any bank can change their PIN at any ATM.

**PIN Advice Clauses.** Common conditions include not telling the PIN to any third party. HSBC stipulates that the PIN advice letter must be destroyed immediately after receipt: *"Safely destroying any Card PIN advice we send you immediately after receipt, e. g., by shredding it ..."*.

## 4   Survey of Payment Card PIN Usage

We conducted an on-line questionnaire study of how people use payment cards, and, in particular, how many PINs they have, and how they are remembered. We also investigated their behaviour towards storing, resetting and sharing PINs.

### 4.1   Questionnaire Setup

The questionnaire was set up using LimeSurvey[1], and the participants were recruited using Prolific Academic[2]. We restricted submissions to British residents aged 18 or over. Participants were paid £1.50 for successfully completing the questionnaire. The questionnaire took five minutes on average to complete. We received 241 (out of 250) valid responses, and verified that the IP address used was from the UK in all but 5 cases[3].

Questions that required categorical responses by the participants had a set of predefined choices as well as a free text response field. The predefined choices were sourced from a small qualitative preliminary study. In nearly all cases the participants did not make use of the free text response field.

---

[1] www.limesurvey.org.

[2] www.prolific.ac.

[3] IP address geo-location has a non-trivial error rate, but this still confirms that our sample is predominantly from the UK, as intended.

## 4.2  Results

Of the participants, 61% are female and 39% are male. The age of the participants spans 18 to 71 years, with a mean of 31.2. Our participants are better
educated than average bank customers: 38% have at least an undergraduate
degree (BSc, BA or similar), while a further 17% have postgraduate education.
30% did not attend higher education, and a third of these (10%) have a General Certificate of Secondary Education (GCSE) as their highest qualification.
49% of the participants are employed; a further 13% are self-employed; 24% of
participants are students; only 13% are unemployed.

**Table 1.** Distribution of participants' PINs

|          | 0   | 1  | 2  | 3  | 4  | 5 | 6 | 7 | 8 | 9 | Mean |
|----------|-----|----|----|----|----|---|---|---|---|---|------|
| 4 digits | 1   | 88 | 65 | 41 | 31 | 8 | 5 | 1 | 1 | 0 | 2.28 |
| 5 digits | 233 | 5  | 3  | 0  | 0  | 0 | 0 | 0 | 0 | 0 | 0.05 |
| 6 digits | 228 | 8  | 4  | 1  | 0  | 0 | 0 | 0 | 0 | 0 | 0.08 |

The participants report having 1 to 9 payment cards (mean = 2.53). This
contrasts with the number of 4-digit, 5-digit, and 6-digit PINs each participant
has in Table 1. The vast majority of customers have only 4-digit PINs, but the
mean number of PINs is 2.28 – statistically significantly lower than the mean
number of cards per customer (dependent t-test, $t = -4.38$, $p < 0.0001$).

Table 2 analyzes how often participants use their PINs. No participant had
more than eight 4-digit PINs, or more than two 5-digit ones or three 6-digit
ones. We see at once that as the number of PINs increases, their usage drops.
Only one participant uses more than one unique PIN on a daily basis. About
half (48%) of the PINs are used at most once a month, and PIN #4 is used on
average around twice a year. This supports the bank industry 'folk wisdom' that
if you want customers to use cards other than their main card you must let them
change their PINs.

**Table 2.** Frequency of usage of participants' PINs

|                      | 4-digit PINs | | | | | | | | | 5-digit PINs | | | 6-digit PINs | | | |
|----------------------|----|----|----|----|----|----|----|----|-----|----|----|-----|----|----|----|-----|
|                      | #1 | #2 | #3 | #4 | #5 | #6 | #7 | #8 | Sum | #1 | #2 | Sum | #1 | #2 | #3 | Sum |
| Every day            | 34 | 0  | 0  | 1  | 0  | 0  | 0  | 0  | 35  | 0  | 0  | 0   | 1  | 1  | 0  | 2   |
| Several times a week | 117| 30 | 3  | 3  | 0  | 0  | 0  | 1  | 154 | 1  | 0  | 1   | 5  | 2  | 1  | 8   |
| Once per week        | 59 | 35 | 12 | 3  | 0  | 0  | 0  | 0  | 109 | 2  | 1  | 3   | 0  | 0  | 0  | 0   |
| Once per month       | 21 | 37 | 24 | 8  | 3  | 0  | 0  | 0  | 93  | 4  | 2  | 6   | 3  | 2  | 0  | 5   |
| Several times a year | 6  | 24 | 24 | 12 | 2  | 2  | 1  | 0  | 71  | 1  | 0  | 1   | 3  | 0  | 0  | 3   |
| Once a year or less  | 1  | 14 | 10 | 10 | 4  | 1  | 0  | 0  | 40  | 0  | 0  | 0   | 1  | 0  | 0  | 1   |
| Never                | 2  | 12 | 14 | 9  | 6  | 4  | 1  | 0  | 48  | 0  | 0  | 0   | 0  | 0  | 0  | 0   |

**Table 3.** Source of 4-digit participants' PINs

|  | #1 | #2 | #3 | #4 | #5 | #6 | #7 | #8 | Sum |
|---|---|---|---|---|---|---|---|---|---|
| I chose it myself | 75 | 56 | 28 | 15 | 3 | 3 | 1 | 0 | 181 |
| Assigned to me, I decided not to change it | 161 | 94 | 56 | 31 | 11 | 3 | 1 | 0 | 357 |
| Assigned it to me, I am not allowed to change it | 4 | 2 | 3 | 0 | 1 | 1 | 0 | 1 | 12 |

Table 3 documents PIN change, and we see that two-thirds of PINs are left as their default. Interestingly, there is no correlation between frequency of PIN use (Table 2) and PIN origin (Table 3). Virtually all participants are allowed to change their PINs in the UK. The details for 5- and 6-digit PINs have been omitted here for brevity. We also investigated the reasons for PIN change. Of the participants that set their own PIN, 61% reported changing their PIN on first receipt, a further 23% stated they changed their PIN because they felt it was compromised, but only 6% claimed to change their PIN on a regular basis.

Our participants keep their PINs for a long time: Only 13% of PINs were changed in the last year, with over 39% having been in use for over 5 years.

**Remembering PINs.** A quarter of the participants reported forgetting a 4-digit PIN at least once. Of these, 48% remembered or retrieved their PIN themselves, 24% were issued with a new PIN, and 15% used the bank's services to retrieve their PIN. Finally, 10% did not bother retrieving the forgotten PIN; half of these said they transferred their money to a different account.

**Table 4.** Location of written down PINs by participants. 79 (32.9%), 4 (50.0%), and 0 (0.0%) wrote down their 4-, 5-, and 6-digit PINs, respectively.

|  | 4-digit | 5-digit | 6-digit | Sum |
|---|---|---|---|---|
| On the card | 1% | 0% | 0% | 1% |
| I kept the original PIN slip | 0% | 0% | 0% | 0% |
| On paper – kept in desk | 16% | 25% | 0% | 17% |
| On paper – kept in wallet | 10% | 0% | 0% | 10% |
| In a notebook/diary/planner, etc. | 41% | 25% | 0% | 40% |
| File on computer | 10% | 25% | 0% | 11% |
| File on phone | 42% | 25% | 0% | 41% |

As many banks insist that PINs must not be written down, we decided to investigate this in reality. Table 4 describes our participants' strategies towards writing down PINs. Not a single participant kept the original PIN mailer. The prevailing method of PIN storage is on mobile phones – typically disguised as a phone number. 13% of the participants use a mnemonic for 4-digit PINs, the most common technique being the derivation of the PIN from a specific date. (This was also reported by Bonneau et al. [3].)

**Table 5.** A variety of locations where participants' PINs are re-used. 55 (22.9%), 0 (0.0%), and 1 (7.7%) re-used their 4-, 5-, and 6-digit PINs, respectively.

|  | 4-digit | 5-digit | 6-digit | Sum |
|---|---|---|---|---|
| Unlocking mobile phone | 49% | 0% | 0% | 48% |
| Burglar alarm | 2% | 0% | 0% | 2% |
| Voicemail | 15% | 0% | 0% | 14% |
| SIM card unlock | 7% | 0% | 0% | 7% |
| Unlocking computer | 5% | 0% | 100% | 7% |
| On-line Banking | 25% | 0% | 0% | 24% |

**PIN Re-use.** 16% of our participants stated they use the same PIN on many payment cards; when a PIN was re-used, it was used on 2.8 payment cards on average, with the maximum being 9 cards! PINs were also used in a variety of other locations (Table 5): 22.9% of participants are re-using their 4-digit payment card PINs, half of whom use a payment card PIN to unlock their mobile phone.

**Table 6.** Sharing of PINs by participants. 102 (42.5%), 2 (25.0%), and 1 (7.7%) shared their 4-, 5-, and 6-digit PINs, respectively.

|  | 4-digit | 5-digit | 6-digit | Sum |
|---|---|---|---|---|
| Stranger | 0% | 0% | 0% | 0% |
| Family member | 37% | 0% | 100% | 37% |
| Flatmate (if accommodation shared) | 3% | 0% | 0% | 3% |
| Spouse/partner | 75% | 100% | 0% | 74% |
| Casual acquaintance | 1% | 0% | 0% | 1% |
| Close friend | 14% | 0% | 0% | 13% |

**PIN Sharing.** Finally, an impressive 42.5% of our participants share their PINs, in many cases with more than one person (Table 6). Sharing predominantly occurs with a spouse or partner (32% of participants) or other family members (16%), but also, in some cases, close friends (6%).

## 5    Conclusion

In general, it is difficult for customers to be certain whether they are complying with bank rules, as these rules lack detail and can even be contradicted. For example, HSBC prohibits PIN re-use, whereas the UK bank trade body recommends this [4]. Vague and contradictory guidance puts customers in a weak position should a bank claim that a disputed transaction must have been caused by a failure to comply with its rules.

Our survey of PIN use confirms the practical difficulty of remembering PINs. Customers are commonly asked to remember four or more PINs, some of which they only use every month at most. The combined effect of forgetting over time [10], as well as interference between the different PINs remembered [1], makes unaided recall of these PINs a difficult task. In one study after 3 weeks, the majority of participants were unable to remember a PIN, and even after 1 week 45% had forgotten it [9]. In current usage scenarios, customers can only cope by re-using PINs or writing them down.

The 4-digit PIN system worked adequately in the environment for which it was originally designed: a single regularly-used ATM card. Today's usage scenarios are different, but the mechanism, and terms and conditions, remain unchanged. Not considering the usability implications pushes customers towards insecure PIN practices banned by the banks' contracts. Each PIN re-use allows a thief another 6 guesses, and mobile phone touchscreens can give away PIN digits directly. Not all customers can be expected to disguise PINs securely, but remembering an infrequently-used PIN is impractical without some kind of assistance. Customers who do not comply with their banking contract are then blamed for security failures that are actually caused by a system that is not fit for purpose.

The successor to the PSD – PSD II – adds a requirement that banks must use strong authentication for payments. This is defined as "authentication based on the use of two or more elements categorised as knowledge (something only the user knows), possession (something only the user possesses) and inherence (something the user is) that are independent". The European Banking Authority is responsible for evaluating proposed solutions. Our study shows that an authentication technique must be evaluated in the context of normal use (e. g., multiple payment instruments, some used infrequently) and only considered strong if real people can use it in the course of their normal life. Otherwise, it risks becoming just another excuse for some banks to shift fraud liability to their customers.

Banks want customers to use multiple cards, so they can earn more fees. Regulators want people to use multiple cards to enhance competition. Secure methods for using a single PIN (or two-factor authentication technique) over all devices would remove the need for the ad-hoc coping mechanisms we see in the survey. Alternatively, to take the US approach, enshrine strong consumer protection in law; expect banks to use fraud detection to manage risks and absorb the residual fraud; and by increasing trust, increase transaction volumes and, thus, increase revenues and profits overall.

**Data Availability.** The survey data used in this paper can be downloaded from http://dx.doi.org/10.14324/000.ds.1473489.

**Acknowledgements.** We are grateful to Adam Beautement, Brian Glass, Boris Hemkemeier and Kat Krol for helpful discussions. Steven J. Murdoch is supported by The Royal Society [grant number UF110392]; Ingolf Becker is supported by the Engineering and Physical Sciences Research Council [grant number EP/G037264/1].

# References

1. Anderson, M.C., Neely, J.H.: Interference and inhibition in memory retrieval. In: Memory. Handbook of Perception and Cognition, 2 edn., pp. 237–313. Academic Press (1996)
2. Bohm, N., Brown, I., Gladman, B.: Electronic commerce: who carries the risk of fraud. J. Inf. Law Technol. **2003**(3) (2000)
3. Bonneau, J., Preibusch, S., Anderson, R.: A birthday present every eleven wallets? The security of customer-chosen banking PINs. In: Keromytis, A.D. (ed.) FC 2012. LNCS, vol. 7397, pp. 25–40. Springer, Heidelberg (2012). doi:10.1007/978-3-642-32946-3_3
4. Bowerman, M.: Radio interview with APACS spokesperson. BBC Radio Merseyside, 19 February 2007
5. Financial Ombudsman Service: Ombudsman news (March/April 2014), case 116/2. http://www.financial-ombudsman.org.uk/publications/ombudsman-news/116/116-disputed-transactions.html
6. HSBC, UK: General, current accounts and savings accounts terms and conditions. Accessed 1 Sept 2015
7. Kelman, A.: Job v Halifax PLC (not reported) case number 7BQ00307. In: Digital Evidence and Electronic Signature Law Review, vol. 6 (2009)
8. Murdoch, S.J., Drimer, S., Anderson, R., Bond, M.: Chip and PIN is broken. In: IEEE Symposium on Security and Privacy, pp. 433–446, May 2010
9. Renaud, K., Ramsay, J.: How helpful is colour-cueing of PIN entry? July 2014. arXiv:1407.8007 [cs]
10. Squire, L.R.: On the course of forgetting in very long-term memory. J. Exp. Psychol. Learn. Mem. Cogn. **15**(2), 241–245 (1989)
11. UK Cards Association: Plastic fraud figures (2015). http://www.theukcardsassociation.org.uk/plastic_fraud_figures/index.asp

# The Bitcoin Brain Drain: Examining the Use and Abuse of Bitcoin Brain Wallets

Marie Vasek[1]([✉]), Joseph Bonneau[2], Ryan Castellucci[3], Cameron Keith[4],
and Tyler Moore[1]

[1] Tandy School of Computer Science, The University of Tulsa, Tulsa, USA
{marie-vasek,tyler-moore}@utulsa.edu
[2] Applied Crypto Group, Stanford University, Stanford, USA
jbonneau@cs.stanford.edu
[3] White Ops, New York, USA
pubs@ryanc.org.
[4] Computer Science and Engineering Department,
Southern Methodist University, Dallas, USA
ckeith@smu.edu

**Abstract.** In the cryptocurrency Bitcoin, users can deterministically derive the private keys used for transmitting money from a password. Such "brain wallets" are appealing because they free users from storing their private keys on untrusted computers. Unfortunately, they also enable attackers to conduct unlimited offline password guessing. In this paper, we report on the first large-scale measurement of the use of brain wallets in Bitcoin. Using a wide range of word lists, we evaluated around 300 billion passwords. Surprisingly, after excluding activities by researchers, we identified just 884 brain wallets worth around $100K in use from September 2011 to August 2015. We find that all but 21 wallets were drained, usually within 24 h but often within minutes. We find that around a dozen "drainers" are competing to liquidate brain wallets as soon as they are funded. We find no evidence that users of brain wallets loaded with more bitcoin select stronger passwords, but we do find that brain wallets with weaker passwords are cracked more quickly.

**Keywords:** Bitcoin · Brain wallets · Passwords · Cybercrime measurement

## 1 Introduction

Bitcoin, launched in 2009, is the most successful cryptographic currency to date and has recently attracted considerable research [2,5]. Similar to many other designs for cryptographic currencies, transactions which transfer control of bitcoins are authorized by ECDSA digital signatures. The popularity of Bitcoin, particularly with populations who had not previously used cryptographic software [7], has resulted in a large number of users attempting to manage private keys for the first time.

© International Financial Cryptography Association 2017
J. Grossklags and B. Preneel (Eds.): FC 2016, LNCS 9603, pp. 609–618, 2017.
DOI: 10.1007/978-3-662-54970-4_36

In this paper we study the use of *brain wallets*, or private keys which are deterministically derived from passwords. Compared to other paradigms for managing Bitcoin keys, such as storing them on a personal computer or a dedicated hardware device, this approach is convenient as the user can spend their bitcoins simply by typing their password. Because their private keys are not permanently stored on devices, brain wallets cannot be exfiltrated by malware [1].

However, there is a big downside: anyone who guesses a user's password can immediately steal their funds. Worse, attackers can perform unthrottled (offline) guessing to test candidate passwords. Attackers guessing a password can quickly test whether it matches *any* user's brain wallet by scanning for use of the derived public key on the Bitcoin block chain, a public ledger of all transactions. We replicate this password-guessing attack in a research setting by non-invasively testing candidate passwords for historical use as a Bitcoin brain wallet address.

Others have investigated brain wallets. Eskandari et al. studied bitcoin wallet software and found that while brain wallets are supported across platforms and require little trust in devices, the threat of weak passwords eclipses those benefits [10]. BIP 38 [6] specifies a format for password-protected private key encryption as a second factor. Our work also builds upon work on passwords for financial systems. While there is little evidence that users choose significantly stronger passwords to protect financial online accounts [4], Herley argues that users rationally choose weak passwords for online accounts [13] as they are protected by anti-fraud systems.

In this work we report on the first large-scale attempt to measure brain wallet use and abuse in the wild. Surprisingly, we identified a relatively small number of brain wallets in use: fewer than 1 000 total. This is despite a significant amount of interest in the concept and the existence of several software tools for creating and using brain wallets.

Our results are necessarily incomplete in that password-derived public keys are indistinguishable from pseudorandomly-generated public keys without knowledge of the password. Put another way, we do not know how many brain wallets are in use for which we were not able to guess the password. Nonetheless, given that we tried over 300 billion passwords from over twenty customized word lists, we are confident that the use of brain wallets remains quite rare.

Our results reveal the existence of an active attacker community that rapidly steals funds from vulnerable brain wallets in nearly all cases we identify. In total, approximately $100K worth of bitcoin has been loaded into brain wallets, with the ten most valuable wallets accounting for over three quarters of the total value. Many brain wallets are drained within minutes, and while those storing larger values are emptied faster, nearly all wallets are drained within 24 h.

## 2    Data Collection Methodology

We first review how the candidate passwords[1] were constructed and then explain how we checked for their usage in brain wallets.

---

[1] Technically these are passwords and passphrases. We use password for simplicity of presentation.

*Password Corpora.* We have constructed an extensive set of passwords derived from publicly available sources. This includes prior password leaks (e.g., Rockyou, Yahoo!, LinkedIn) word and derived phrase lists (e.g., English Wikipedia, Wikiquote), and information gleaned from Bitcoin discussion forums. In total, we tested approximately 300 billion passwords for usage in brain wallets. Testing was carried out using the open-source project Brainflayer[2].

Word lists were tried directly unless otherwise specified. The following word lists were used:

1. **English:** English word list packaged with Ubuntu 12.04.
2. **Urban Dictionary:** Terms and phrases from the crowd-sourced slang dictionary[3]. The "combinator" tool was used to check all pairs of terms [12].
3. **Two Words:** English pairs of words using the combinator tool.
4. **English/Slang Urban Dictionary:** Single word entries from Urban Dictionary are combined with English words. Additionally, the results are run through the combinator tool for all phrases up to 20 characters long.
5. **English Wikipedia.**
6. **WikiQuotes:** English, Spanish, Russian and German quotes from 3/2013.
7. **Phrases:** Permutations of WikiQuote, wikipedia and Naxxatoe phrases.
8. **xkcd:** Lists obtained on July $10^{th}$, 2014 from three sources[4]. Combinations up to three words with and without spaces. All words used for 2 word combinations; words common to all three lists used for 3 word combinations.
9. **Lyrics:** lyrics and song titles purchased from https://andymoore.info/mysql-lyrics-database/.
10. **Blockchain.info tags:** All public bitcoin address tags obtained from https://blockchain.info/tags.
11. **Password dumps** LinkedIn, MySpace, RockYou, Rootkit.com
12. **Leet MRL:** De-duplicated merge of MySpace, Rockyou and LinkedIn (hence MRL) dumps, with leet-speak substitutions.
13. **Prince MRL:** MRL list applying the Prince attack [14].
14. **Security industry lists:** CrackStation, Naxxatoe, Uniqpass (combination of 2012-01-01 and 2012-04-01 lists), Skull Security[5] (RockYou list excluded).

In addition to the aforementioned word lists, we tested the following:

1. **Reddit User Challenge:** Post about a brain wallet password on Reddit[6].
2. **Brute Force:** All numbers up to 9 digits and printable ASCII up to 5 characters.
3. **Modified BW Passwords:** Appended and prepended one and two ASCII characters to passwords of previously cracked brain wallets using combinator.

Table 1 in Sect. 3 details the number of brain wallet passwords obtained from each source, along with the total amount drained.

---

[2] https://github.com/ryancdotorg/brainflayer.

[3] List was sourced from https://github.com/inieves/urban-dictionary-scraper/blob/4a86fd9ef4c2f8812dc78f5862c327912213436a/dict/UrbanDictionary.txt.

[4] https://xkpasswd.net/s/, http://correcthorsebatterystaple.net/, and http://preshing.com/20110811/xkcd-password-generator/.

[5] https://wiki.skullsecurity.org/Passwords.

[6] https://www.reddit.com/r/Bitcoin/comments/3gycp1/-/cu3316a.

*Observing Bitcoin Brain Wallet Usage.* We use the SHA256 hash of the password as the private key. We then generate the corresponding public key using a few speedups to the secp256k1 curve library[7] [8]. We download the Bitcoin blockchain using Bitcoin core software[8] and extract all the unique Bitcoin addresses using znort987's block parser[9]. We then add all the addresses to a bloom filter for quick lookup and a sorted list for false positive detection. We compare all the addresses generated from candidate passwords against the bloom filter and confirm positive results against the sorted list. After we find all of the used brain wallet addresses, we supplement this information by querying all our brain wallet addresses against the blockchain.info API to obtain precise timestamps for all transactions. Transactions with brain wallets as recipients are incoming payments and transactions with brain wallets as sources are outgoing payments.

## 3   Results

We investigate brain wallet usage by examining all block chain transactions through 8/2015.[10] We report on their prevalence, draining, and password strength.

*How Prevalent are Brain Wallets?* We have found 884 distinct brain wallets using 845 different passwords. The slight difference is from to the small number of instances where compressed and uncompressed wallets were used for the same password. In total, these brain wallets received 1 806 BTC (approx. $103K[11]).

Table 1 reports the brain wallets identified, broken down according to the password sources. The single most popular source is the security word list Crack-Station, which included 640 of the 884 brain wallet passwords identified. Notably, 37 of these passwords were only found by CrackStation, also the highest figure for any list. By contrast, the list with the second highest number of matches, Uniq-pass, only reported passwords that were also found by at least one other source. Notably, the second-largest source of unique brain wallets, the combinations of English and slang words, only identified 63 wallet passwords.

The password sources used for our study can of course also be used by attackers. One way to estimate the popularity of password sources among attackers is to compare how often repeated drains occur. The fifth column shows the $90^{th}$ percentile for number of drains observed on passwords identified by each source.

---

[7] https://github.com/bitcoin-core/secp256k1.

[8] https://github.com/bitcoin/bitcoin.

[9] https://github.com/znort987/blockparser.

[10] We excluded 17 784 brain wallets that were suddenly assigned a tiny amount of bitcoin from 36 linked input addresses within a few hours on August 31, 2013. We strongly suspect these brain wallets were set up by a researcher. We also excluded 15 brain wallets used in over 20 000 transactions between June and August 2015 as part of a network "stress test".

[11] All USD calculations presented here are normalized by the corresponding day's exchange rate on Bitstamp, as reported by bitcoincharts.com.

**Table 1.** Brain wallets and values associated with different password sources.

| Source | # Wallets | (Non-empty) | Unique | 90% # drains | Total BTC | Total USD |
|---|---|---|---|---|---|---|
| *Word lists* | | | | | | |
| Urban dictionary | 296 | 3 | 2 | 3.00 | 561.95 | 43 120.77 |
| Two words | 13 | 3 | 0 | 4.00 | 0.79 | 92.65 |
| Eng/slang urban dict. | 63 | 14 | 28 | 2.00 | 0.90 | 124.96 |
| Eng. Wikipedia | 250 | 0 | 0 | 2.00 | 505.77 | 38 833.16 |
| WikiQuotes | 35 | 0 | 0 | 12.00 | 60.96 | 17 620.50 |
| Phrases | 283 | 0 | 0 | 3.00 | 578.69 | 57 376.80 |
| xkcd | 90 | 3 | 3 | 13.00 | 97.66 | 29 140.44 |
| Lyrics | 329 | 4 | 16 | 3.00 | 230.45 | 26 788.97 |
| Blockchain.info tags | 112 | 0 | 10 | 7.00 | 577.93 | 31 683.29 |
| Rootkit | 123 | 2 | 0 | 6.00 | 4.50 | 570.78 |
| MySpace | 59 | 0 | 0 | 3.00 | 1.14 | 210.44 |
| RockYou | 415 | 3 | 2 | 3.00 | 113.82 | 33 807.17 |
| LinkedIn | 213 | 0 | 0 | 2.00 | 10.11 | 738.52 |
| LEET MRL | 3 | 0 | 0 | 1.00 | 0.01 | 1.49 |
| Prince MRL | 295 | 4 | 7 | 3.00 | 88.93 | 21 028.02 |
| CrackStation | 640 | 3 | 37 | 2.00 | 396.09 | 41 326.80 |
| Naxxatoe | 388 | 0 | 2 | 2.00 | 41.56 | 3 389.31 |
| Skull security | 414 | 3 | 3 | 2.00 | 71.73 | 20 756.32 |
| Uniqpass | 490 | 3 | 0 | 2.00 | 134.95 | 35 266.27 |
| *Non-word lists* | | | | | | |
| Reddit user challenge | 1 | 0 | 1 | 1.00 | 0.01 | 2.62 |
| Brute force | 200 | 3 | 3 | 3.00 | 22.47 | 3 895.99 |
| Modified BW passwords | 74 | 1 | 9 | 2.00 | 2.25 | 209.98 |
| Overall | 884 | 21 | 139 | 2.00 | 1 806.22 | 103 472.13 |

Larger numbers indicate that more attackers are using the source. Perhaps unsurprisingly, passwords derived from xkcd are drained repeatedly the most.

The last two columns provide an alternative way to value the passwords obtained from different sources. Each represents the total value put into brain wallets whose passwords are identified by these sources (in BTC and USD, respectively). By this measure, the Phrases word list is the most valuable at $57K, followed by English Wikipedia, CrackStation, and Urban Dictionary. By contrast, the relatively unique English and slang combination passwords are not worth much – all 63 collectively stored just 0.90 BTC.

Figure 1 plots when wallets were first used over time, beginning with the first brain wallet established in September 2011. Monthly totals of new wallets are reported, and the bar chart breaks down the use of compressed and uncompressed brain wallets. We can see that the number of new brain wallets has increased since Bitcoin's early days, though the total remains small.

Relatively speaking, uncompressed wallets are more prevalent. We found 798 uncompressed wallets compared to 71 compressed. Note that the brain wallet service bitaddress.org offers only uncompressed brain wallets whereas the

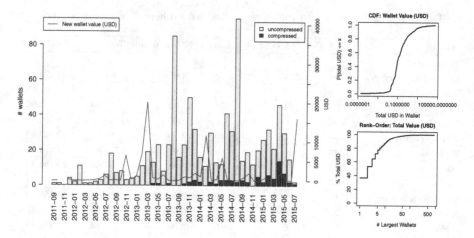

**Fig. 1.** New brain wallet usage per month (compressed and uncompressed, left); CDF and rank-order plot of total value stored in brain wallets (right).

(defunct) brainwallet.org defaulted to uncompressed brain wallets (though it supported both). Compressed keys are only supported in versions of Bitcoin clients released after March 30, 2012; we observed 20 brain wallets before then, the first being "one two three four five six seven" seen in September 2011.

Also plotted in Fig. 1 is the USD value of the brain wallets each month. We can see that this is quite volatile. Most months, the total value hovers around a few thousand dollars, but frequently the amount stored spikes greatly, including to a peak of over \$40K in March 2013. Notably, there is no discernible relationship between the number of new wallets created and the value stored.

The top plot in Fig. 1 (right) gives the CDF of brain wallet value in USD. While most brain wallets store little money (just 6% of the brain wallets received the equivalent of \$100 or more), the bulk of the total value in brain wallets is associated with a small number of addresses. The bottom plot of Fig. 1 (right) presents a rank-order plot, which reveals that just 10 wallets account for approximately 85% of the total dollar value placed into all brain wallets.

*Draining Brain Wallets.* As explained in Sect. 1, because the addresses used by brain wallets are deterministically computed from passwords, there is a risk that attackers might guess the password and drain the wallet's value. Many users select brain wallets with the intention of keeping their bitcoin there for a long time, analogous to hiding cash under a mattress. Therefore, when bitcoins are drained from these addresses (i.e., the account balance falls to zero), it strongly suggests that an attack may have taken place.

Perhaps the best way to quantify brain wallet insecurity is to examine the time required to drain wallets. Figure 2 (left) plots a CDF of the observed time-to-drain. The solid black line shows the distribution for all wallets. Half of the wallets are drained in 21 min or less. Subsequently, the rate of draining slows,

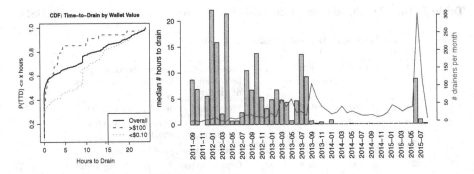

**Fig. 2.** CDF of the # of hours to drain brain wallets for wallets by value stored (left); how time-to-drain changes over time (median time-to-drain reported per month, right).

but nearly all brain wallets are drained within 24 h. While some of these drains are initiated by the brain wallet owners, it is likely that most are not.

We can also see the difference in draining speed when wallets are loaded with large or small amounts of money. The red dashed line plots the cumulative distribution for wallets loaded with at least $100. These wallets are consistently drained faster than other wallets, while those loaded with 10 cents or less (indicated by the dotted blue line) are drained more slowly. From this, we can conclude that time-to-drain is influenced by the stored value, but that in any case the wallet will almost certainly be drained within one day of funding.

How often are brain wallets drained? 98% of the brain wallets have been drained at least once. We observed 1 895 distinct draining events on 884 brain wallets. 69% of wallets are drained exactly once, while 19% are drained twice, and 1.9% are drained more than ten times. Figure 2 (right) plots the median time-to-drain by month. While this is always brief (less than one day), by September 2013 it becomes measured in minutes and seconds rather than hours.

How can these drains occur so fast? Many bots monitor for new transactions depositing into known brain wallets. These *drainers* quickly send the money to their own addresses, often with a sizable fee to encourage miners to pick up the transaction quickly. In contrast to many criminals who take steps to cover their tracks (e.g., by funneling transactions through many addresses), drainers are proud of their achievements. Consequently, they make it easy for all to see that they have done the draining, such as by using the same address for all drains. This makes it easier for researchers to document their activities.

How many drainers did we find? The graph in Fig. 2 (right) also plots in red the number of drainers actively receiving money from brain wallets. Overall, their numbers are increasing – unsurprising given the reduction in time-to-drain.

Digging deeper, we manually inspected all 48 addresses that received at least 100 USD from brain wallets, as well as the 13 addresses receiving payment from at least 20 distinct brain wallets. The top results are presented in Table 2, sorted by the total amount drained in USD. The table indicates how many distinct brain

**Table 2.** Top 10 drain addresses from brain wallets, sorted by amount drained in USD.

| Rank | Drained # pwd | Drained (USD) | Drained (BTC) | Drains | Description |
|------|------|------|------|------|------|
| 1 | 1 | 22 466 | 250.01 | 1 | Woodchuck drain (unintentionally done by researcher Castellucci, https://rya.nc/dc23) |
| 2 | 1 | 15 267 | 250.00 | 1 | Woodchuck drain (done by owner) |
| 3 | 10 | 14 554 | 50.02 | 19 | Drainer https://bitcointalk.org/index.php?topic=878639.460 |
| 4 | 2 | 11 528 | 18.25 | 2 | Drainer https://redd.it/2c5jot |
| 5 | 29 | 6 784 | 12.15 | 49 | Drainer https://bitcointalk.org/index.php?topic=347828.0 |
| 6 | 1 | 5 800 | 500.00 | 1 | "bitcoin is awesome" drain |
| 7 | 100 | 3 219 | 9.96 | 155 | Drainer https://bitcointalk.org/index.php?topic=817294.10 |
| 8 | 1 | 1 863 | 38.69 | 1 | Owner of 1N8gLjZEhRxLRRjg8ymS6Zez8KVegEKtb1 |
| 9 | 1 | 1 429 | 14.29 | 1 | "deadsheep" drain |
| 10 | 1 | 1 322 | 97.66 | 59 | "thequickbrownfoxjumpedoverthelazydog" drain |

wallets were drained, the associated value in BTC and USD, and the number of drain events that occurred. 34 addresses were associated with a single password drain, suggesting these could be the owner. In a few cases, this is explicitly confirmed by online postings. Nonetheless, we confirmed at least 14 drainers targeting multiple brain wallets, corroborated by reports on discussion forums.

A few drainers are very successful while the rest do not make very much. The top 4 drainers have netted the equivalent of $35 000 between them. The drainer who has emptied the most brain wallets – 100 in all – has earned $3 219 for the effort. But other drainers have stolen very little money. For example, one drainer stole from 78 different brain wallets but netted only $62 worth of bitcoin. Why is this? Looking back at Fig. 2 at the money flowing into brain wallets indicates this amount has diminished as Bitcoin's overall popularity has risen.

We also investigated the behavior of successful drainers. Some have claimed that drainers purposely avoid emptying brain wallets with small stores of value [11]:

> Another example is brainwallets, we have clear evidence that people who crack brainwallets intentionally avoid sweeping small amounts (And even coordinate among each other) in order to avoid alerting users prematurely.

We did not find any evidence for this practice among the most successful drainers. The median value of a drained brain wallet among each of the most successful drainers was under $1 (typically a few cents).

*Impact of Password Strength.* Measuring the "strength" (or resistance to guessing) of an individual password is a hard problem. Many standard metrics, such as the NIST "entropy" formula, have been shown to be poor predictors of actual cracking time [16]. In practice, many websites use inconsistent and poorly specified methods for giving users feedback on password strength [9]. The gold-standard of non-parametric statistics requires very large sample sizes and is hence impractical in our setting [3]. Instead, we use the `wheelerzxcvbn` formula as a rough measure of password strength. While it produces an integer value for the estimated cracking time of any string, we conservatively use the value only to induce an ordinal ranking on the strength of our cracked passwords.

Using this metric, we are able to test several hypotheses about the impact of factors such as the time a brain wallet was created or the total amount stored on the strength of the passwords chosen. For each hypothesis we computed the (non-parametric) Spearman's rank-correlation coefficient ($\rho$) against a null hypothesis of no correlation. We did not observe statistically significant correlations ($p > 0.1$ in all cases) between the estimated password strength and the date the brain wallet address was initially used or the total amount ever sent to the address. We did observe a positive correlation of $\rho = 0.54$ ($p = 0.013$) between the estimated strength and the time it took for the wallet to initially be drained of funds. This result suggests we can reject the null hypothesis with over 95% confidence (applying a Holm-Bonferonni correction for $m = 3$ hypotheses tested).

This suggests that, consistent with previous password research, we find no evidence that users are able to pick stronger passwords when protecting a larger quantity of money. But we do see that addresses protected by weaker passwords are generally attacked quicker than stronger passwords. The cause of this correlation is that attacks have improved over time, so stronger passwords may have survived earlier cracking efforts but fall to later cracking efforts, giving a longer overall survival time. This could partially be due to the rise of ASIC mining [15], leaving Bitcoin enthusiasts with idle GPUs ripe for brain wallet cracking.

## 4    Conclusion

The idea behind brain wallets is elegant and alluring: remembering a password is surely easier than a private key. Unfortunately, as this paper makes clear, it is also an extremely insecure way to store bitcoin. Drainers lurk over the blockchain, ready to pounce as soon as new brain wallets are established.

By examining 300 billion candidate passwords, we found 884 brain wallets that were active at some point in time. Unfortunately, we also found that nearly all were drained – usually quickly. While our findings are necessarily incomplete, they certainly suggest that brain wallets are not a secure method for using bitcoin. Perhaps the most surprising result of our analysis is the relative scarcity of brain wallets in use today. This is actually quite encouraging, because it means that fewer users are at risk to these attacks than has previously been supposed.

**Acknowledgements.** We thank the anonymous reviewers and paper shepherd Sarah Meiklejohn for their helpful feedback. Some authors are funded by the Department of Homeland Security (DHS) Science and Technology Directorate, Cyber Security

Division (DHSS&T/CSD) Broad Agency Announcement 11.02, the Government of
Australia and SPAWAR Systems Center Pacific via contract number N66001-13-C-
0131. Support from the Oak Ridge Associated Universities Ralph Powe Junior Faculty
Enhancement Award is also gratefully acknowledged. This paper represents the position of the authors and not that of the aforementioned agencies.

# References

1. Barber, S., Boyen, X., Shi, E., Uzun, E.: Bitter to better — how to make bitcoin a
better currency. In: Keromytis, A.D. (ed.) FC 2012. LNCS, vol. 7397, pp. 399–414.
Springer, Heidelberg (2012). doi:10.1007/978-3-642-32946-3_29
2. Böhme, R., Christin, N., Edelman, B., Moore, T.: Bitcoin: economics, technology,
and governance. J. Econ. Perspect. **29**(2), 213–238 (2015)
3. Bonneau, J.: Statistical metrics for individual password strength (transcript of
discussion). In: Christianson, B., Malcolm, J., Stajano, F., Anderson, J. (eds.)
Security Protocols 2012. LNCS, vol. 7622, pp. 87–95. Springer, Heidelberg (2012).
doi:10.1007/978-3-642-35694-0_11
4. Bonneau, J.: The science of guessing: analyzing an anonymized corpus of 70 million
passwords. In: 2012 IEEE Symposium on Security and Privacy, May 2012
5. Bonneau, J., Miller, A., Clark, J., Narayanan, A., Kroll, J.A., Felten, E.W.:
Research perspectives and challenges for Bitcoin and cryptocurrencies. In: IEEE
Symposium on Security and Privacy, May 2015
6. Caldwell, M., Voisine, A.: BIP 38: passphrase-protected private key, November
2012
7. Christin, N.: Traveling the silk road: a measurement analysis of a large anonymous
online marketplace. In: Proceedings of the 22nd International World Wide Web
Conference, pp. 213–224 (2013)
8. Courtois, N., Song, G., Castellucci, R.: Speed optimizations in Bitcoin key recovery
attacks. http://eprint.iacr.org/2016/103.pdf
9. de Carnavalet, X.C., Mannan, M.: From very weak to very strong: analyzing
password-strength meters. In: Network and Distributed System Security Symposium (NDSS 2014). Internet Society (2014)
10. Eskandari, S., Barrera, D., Stobert, E., Clark, J.: A first look at the usability
of Bitcoin key management. In: Proceedings of the NDSS Workshop on Usable
Security (USEC) (2015)
11. gmaxwell: #bitcoin-wizards (2015). https://botbot.me/freenode/bitcoin-wizards/
2015-09-22/
12. hashcat: Combinator attack (2015). https://hashcat.net/wiki/doku.php?
id=combinator_attack
13. Herley, C.: So long, and no thanks for the externalities: the rational rejection of
security advice by users. In: Proceedings of the 2009 Workshop on New Security
Paradigms, pp. 133–144. ACM (2009)
14. Steube, J.: PRINCE: modern password guessing algorithm. https://hashcat.net/
events/p14-trondheim/prince-attack.pdf
15. Taylor, M.B.: Bitcoin and the age of bespoke silicon. In: Proceedings of the 2013
International Conference on Compilers, Architectures and Synthesis for Embedded
Systems, p. 16. IEEE (2013)
16. Weir, M., Aggarwal, S., Collins, M., Stern, H.: Testing metrics for password creation policies by attacking large sets of revealed passwords. In: Proceedings of the
17th ACM Conference on Computer and Communications Security, pp. 162–175.
ACM (2010)

# Author Index

Printed in the United States
By Bookmasters